THE WORKS OF
CHARLES AND MARY LAMB

ΕΛΙΑ
ηδια

Charles Lamb
from the first sketch by Daniel Maclise.
for 'FRASER'S MAGAZINE'.

THE WORKS OF
CHARLES AND MARY LAMB

EDITED BY

E. V. LUCAS

VOLUME II.

ELIA AND THE LAST ESSAYS OF ELIA

METHUEN & CO.
36 ESSEX STREET W.C.
LONDON

1903

AMS PRESS
NEW YORK

Reprinted with the permission of Methuen & Co. Ltd.
From the edition of 1903, London
First AMS EDITION published 1968
Manufactured in the United States of America

Reprinted from a copy in the collections of the
Harvard College Library.

Library of Congress Catalogue Card Number: 68-59332

AMS PRESS, INC.
New York, N.Y. 10003

INTRODUCTION

THIS volume contains the work by which Charles Lamb is best known and upon which his fame will rest—*Elia* and *The Last Essays of Elia*. Although one essay is as early as 1811, and one is perhaps as late as 1832, the book represents the period between 1820 and 1826, when Lamb was between forty-five and fifty-one. This was the richest period of his literary life.

The text of the present volume is that of the first edition of each book—*Elia*, 1823, and *The Last Essays of Elia*, 1833. The principal differences between the essays as they were printed in the *London Magazine* and elsewhere, and as they were revised for book form by their author, are shown in the Notes. The three-part essay on "The Old Actors" (*London Magazine*, February, April, and October, 1822), from which Lamb prepared the three essays "On Some of the Old Actors," "The Artificial Comedy of the Last Century," and "The Acting of Munden," is printed in the Appendix as it first appeared. The absence of the "Confessions of a Drunkard" from this volume is due to the fact that Lamb did not include it in the first edition of *The Last Essays of Elia*. It was inserted later, in place of "A Death-Bed," on account of objections that were raised to that essay by the family of Randal Norris. The story is told in the notes to "A Death-Bed," on page 452. The "Confessions of a Drunkard" will be found in Vol. I.

With regard to the Notes, I should like to repeat what I said in the General Introduction to this edition, in Vol. I.—that their fulness is due to the circumstance that, in addition to an attempt to show the place of each essay in Lamb's life and to relate his writings to each other, I have endeavoured to account for every allusion in the text not likely to be fully understood by the ordinary reader. This necessarily means that the more literary reader will find much in the Notes that he knew before; which is, I think, a less evil than that other readers should have to turn away baffled of information. In tracing the phrases borrowed by Lamb from older authors I have confined myself almost exclusively to those which he places between quotation marks. To comment upon the others would be, although a very interesting task, an endless and possibly a pedantic one, certainly beyond the capacity of the present editor. No author's style is so charged, as was Lamb's, with felicitous recollections of the Elizabethans.

Two or three quotations still baffle research; and, without the assistance of better-stored memories than my own, I should not have been able to give many of the references which will be found. Chief among those to whom I am indebted is Mr. W. J. Craig. Where I have borrowed from previous editors of Lamb I have acknowledged the obligation.

The portrait which serves as frontispiece to this volume is from a drawing by Daniel Maclise, preserved in the South Kensington Museum.

E. V. L.

May, 1903

CONTENTS

ELIA

CONTENTS

APPENDIX

ILLUSTRATIONS

ILLUSTRATIONS IN THE NOTES

ELIA

(From the 1st Edition, 1823.)

THE SOUTH-SEA HOUSE

READER, in thy passage from the Bank—where thou hast been receiving thy half-yearly dividends (supposing thou art a lean annuitant like myself)—to the Flower Pot, to secure a place for Dalston, or Shacklewell, or some other thy suburban retreat northerly,—didst thou never observe a melancholy looking, handsome, brick and stone edifice, to the left—where Threadneedle-street abuts upon Bishopsgate? I dare say thou hast often admired its magnificent portals ever gaping wide, and disclosing to view a grave court, with cloisters and pillars, with few or no traces of goers-in or comers-out—a desolation something like Balclutha's.[1]

This was once a house of trade,—a centre of busy interests. The throng of merchants was here—the quick pulse of gain—and here some forms of business are still kept up, though the soul be long since fled. Here are still to be seen stately porticos; imposing staircases; offices roomy as the state apartments in palaces—deserted, or thinly peopled with a few straggling clerks; the still more sacred interiors of court and committee rooms, with venerable faces of beadles, door-keepers—directors seated in form on solemn days (to proclaim a dead dividend,) at long worm-eaten tables, that have been mahogany, with tarnished gilt-leather coverings, supporting massy silver inkstands long since dry;—the oaken wainscots hung with pictures of deceased governors and sub-governors, of queen Anne, and the two first monarchs of the Brunswick dynasty;—huge charts, which subsequent discoveries have antiquated;—dusty maps of Mexico, dim as dreams,—and soundings of the Bay of Panama!—The long passages hung with buckets, appended, in idle row, to walls, whose substance might defy any, short of the last, conflagration:—with vast ranges of cellarage under all, where dollars and pieces of eight once lay, an "unsunned heap," for Mammon to have solaced his solitary heart

[1] I passed by the walls of Balclutha, and they were desolate.—OSSIAN.

withal,—long since dissipated, or scattered into air at the blast of
the breaking of that famous BUBBLE.——

Such is the SOUTH SEA-HOUSE. At least, such it was forty years
ago, when I knew it,—a magnificent relic! What alterations may
have been made in it since, I have had no opportunities of verifying.
Time, I take for granted, has not freshened it. No wind has resuscitated the face of the sleeping waters. A thicker crust by this
time stagnates upon it. The moths, that were then battening
upon its obsolete ledgers and day-books, have rested from their
depredations, but other light generations have succeeded, making
fine fretwork among their single and double entries. Layers of
dust have accumulated (a superfœtation of dirt!) upon the old
layers, that seldom used to be disturbed, save by some curious
finger, now and then, inquisitive to explore the mode of book-
keeping in Queen Anne's reign; or, with less hallowed curiosity,
seeking to unveil some of the mysteries of that tremendous HOAX,
whose extent the petty peculators of our day look back upon with
the same expression of incredulous admiration, and hopeless ambition of rivalry, as would become the puny face of modern conspiracy
contemplating the Titan size of Vaux's superhuman plot.

Peace to the manes of the BUBBLE! Silence and destitution are
upon thy walls, proud house, for a memorial!

Situated as thou art, in the very heart of stirring and living
commerce,—amid the fret and fever of speculation—with the
Bank, and the 'Change, and the India-house about thee, in the
hey-day of present prosperity, with their important faces, as it
were, insulting thee, their *poor neighbour out of business*—to
the idle and merely contemplative,—to such as me, old house!
there is a charm in thy quiet:—a cessation—a coolness from
business — an indolence almost cloistral — which is delightful!
With what reverence have I paced thy great bare rooms and
courts at eventide! They spoke of the past:—the shade of some
dead accountant, with visionary pen in ear, would flit by me, stiff
as in life. Living accounts and accountants puzzle me. I have
no skill in figuring. But thy great dead tomes, which scarce three
degenerate clerks of the present day could lift from their enshrining
shelves—with their old fantastic flourishes, and decorative rubric
interlacings—their sums in triple columniations, set down with
formal superfluity of cyphers—with pious sentences at the beginning, without which our religious ancestors never ventured to open
a book of business, or bill of lading—the costly vellum covers of
some of them almost persuading us that we are got into some
better library,—are very agreeable and edifying spectacles. I
can look upon these defunct dragons with complacency. Thy
heavy odd-shaped ivory-handled penknives (our ancestors had

every thing on a larger scale than we have hearts for) are as good as any thing from Herculaneum. The pounce-boxes of our days have gone retrograde.

The very clerks which I remember in the South Sea-House—I speak of forty years back—had an air very different from those in the public offices that I have had to do with since. They partook of the genius of the place !

They were mostly (for the establishment did not admit of super-fluous salaries) bachelors. Generally (for they had not much to do) persons of a curious and speculative turn of mind. Old-fashioned, for a reason mentioned before. Humorists, for they were of all descriptions ; and, not having been brought together in early life (which has a tendency to assimilate the members of corporate bodies to each other), but, for the most part, placed in this house in ripe or middle age, they necessarily carried into it their separate habits and oddities, unqualified, if I may so speak, as into a common stock. Hence they formed a sort of Noah's ark. Odd fishes. A lay-monastery. Domestic retainers in a great house, kept more for show than use. Yet pleasant fellows, full of chat— and not a few among them had arrived at considerable proficiency on the German flute.

The cashier at that time was one Evans, a Cambro-Briton. He had something of the choleric complexion of his countrymen stamped on his visage, but was a worthy sensible man at bottom. He wore his hair, to the last, powdered and frizzed out, in the fashion which I remember to have seen in caricatures of what were termed, in my young days, *Maccaronies*. He was the last of that race of beaux. Melancholy as a gib-cat over his counter all the forenoon, I think I see him, making up his cash (as they call it) with tremulous fingers, as if he feared every one about him was a defaulter ; in his hypochondry ready to imagine himself one ; haunted, at least, with the idea of the possibility of his becoming one : his tristful visage clearing up a little over his roast neck of veal at Anderton's at two (where his picture still hangs, taken a little before his death by desire of the master of the coffee-house, which he had frequented for the last five-and-twenty years), but not attaining the meridian of its animation till evening brought on the hour of tea and visiting. The simultaneous sound of his well-known rap at the door with the stroke of the clock announcing six, was a topic of never-failing mirth in the families which this dear old bachelor gladdened with his presence. Then was his *forte*, his glorified hour ! How would he chirp, and expand, over a muffin ! How would he dilate into secret history ! His country-man, Pennant himself, in particular, could not be more eloquent than he in relation to old and new London—the site of old theatres, churches, streets gone to decay—where Rosomond's pond stood—the Mulberry-gardens—and the Conduit in Cheap—with many a pleasant anecdote, derived from paternal tradition, of those grotesque figures which Hogarth has immortalized in his picture of *Noon*,—the worthy descendants of those heroic confessors, who, flying to this country, from the wrath of Louis the Fourteenth and his dragoons, kept alive the flame of pure religion in the sheltering obscurities of Hog-lane, and the vicinity of the Seven Dials!

Deputy, under Evans, was Thomas Tame. He had the air and stoop of a nobleman. You would have taken him for one, had you met him in one of the passages leading to Westminster-hall. By stoop, I mean that gentle bending of the body forwards, which, in great men, must be supposed to be the effect of an habitual condescending attention to the applications of their inferiors. While he held you in converse, you felt strained to the height in the colloquy. The conference over, you were at leisure to smile at the comparative insignificance of the pretensions which had just awed you. His intellect was of the shallowest order. It did not reach to a saw or a proverb. His mind was in its original state of white paper. A sucking babe might have posed him. What was it then? Was he rich? Alas, no! Thomas Tame was very poor. Both he and his wife looked outwardly gentlefolks, when I fear all was not well at all times within. She had a neat meagre person, which it was evident she had not sinned in over-pampering; but in its veins was noble blood. She traced her descent, by some labyrinth of relationship, which I never thoroughly understood,— much less can explain with any heraldic certainty at this time of day,—to the illustrious, but unfortunate house of Derwentwater. This was the secret of Thomas's stoop. This was the thought— the sentiment—the bright solitary star of your lives,—ye mild and happy pair,—which cheered you in the night of intellect, and in the obscurity of your station! This was to you instead of riches, instead of rank, instead of glittering attainments: and it was worth them all together. You insulted none with it; but, while you wore it as a piece of defensive armour only, no insult likewise could reach you through it. *Decus et solamen*.

Of quite another stamp was the then accountant, John Tipp. He neither pretended to high blood, nor in good truth cared one fig about the matter. He " thought an accountant the greatest character in the world, and himself the greatest accountant in it." Yet John was not without his hobby. The fiddle relieved his vacant hours. He sang, certainly, with other notes than to the Orphean lyre. He did, indeed, scream and scrape most abominably. His fine suite of official rooms in Threadneedle-street, which, without any thing very substantial appended to them, were enough to enlarge a man's notions of himself that lived in them, (I know not who is the occupier of them now) resounded fortnightly to the notes of a concert of " sweet breasts," as our ancestors would have called them, culled from club-rooms and orchestras—chorus singers—first and second violoncellos—double basses—and clari-onets—who ate his cold mutton, and drank his punch, and praised his ear. He sate like Lord Midas among them. But at the desk Tipp was quite another sort of creature. Thence all ideas, that were purely ornamental, were banished. You could not speak of any thing romantic without rebuke. Politics were excluded. A newspaper was thought too refined and abstracted. The whole duty of man consisted in writing off dividend warrants. The striking of the annual balance in the company's books (which, perhaps, differed from the balance of last year in the sum of 25l. 1s. 6d.) occupied his days and nights for a month previous. Not that Tipp was blind to the deadness of *things* (as they call them in the city) in his beloved house, or did not sigh for a return of the old stirring days when South Sea hopes were young—(he was indeed equal to the wielding of any the most intricate accounts of the most flourishing company in these or those days) :—but to a genuine accountant the difference of proceeds is as nothing. The fractional farthing is as dear to his heart as the thousands which stand before it. He is the true actor, who, whether his part be a prince or a peasant, must act it with like intensity. With Tipp form was every thing. His life was formal. His actions seemed ruled with a ruler. His pen was not less erring than his heart. He made the best executor in the world : he was plagued with incessant executorships accordingly, which excited his spleen and soothed his vanity in equal ratios. He would swear (for Tipp swore) at the little orphans, whose rights he would guard with a tenacity like the grasp of the dying hand, that commended their interests to his protection. With all this there was about him a sort of timidity— (his few enemies used to give it a worse name)—a something which, in reverence to the dead, we will place, if you please, a little on this side of the heroic. Nature certainly had been pleased to endow John Tipp with a sufficient measure of the principle of self-preservation. There is a cowardice which we do not despise, because it has nothing base or treacherous in its elements ; it betrays itself, not you : it is mere temperament ; the absence of the romantic and the enterprising ; it sees a lion in the way, and will not, with Fortinbras, " greatly find quarrel in a straw," when some supposed honour is at stake. Tipp never mounted the box of a stage-coach in his life ; or leaned against the rails of a balcony ; or walked upon the ridge of a parapet ; or looked down a precipice ; or let off a gun ; or went upon a water-party ; or would willingly let you go if he could have helped it : neither was it recorded of him, that for lucre, or for intimidation, he ever forsook friend or principle.

Whom next shall we summon from the dusty dead, in whom common qualities become uncommon ? Can I forget thee, Henry Man, the wit, the polished man of letters, the *author*, of the South Sea House ? who never enteredst thy office in a morning, or quittedst it in mid-day—(what didst *thou* in an office ?)—without some quirk that left a sting ! Thy gibes and thy jokes are now extinct, or survive but in two forgotten volumes, which I had the good fortune to rescue from a stall in Barbican, not three days ago, and found thee terse, fresh, epigrammatic, as alive. Thy wit is a little gone by in these fastidious days—thy topics are staled by the " new-born gauds " of the time :—but great thou used to be in Public Ledgers, and in Chronicles, upon Chatham, and Shelburne, and Rockingham, and Howe, and Burgoyne, and Clinton, and the war which ended in the tearing from Great Britain her rebellious colonies,—and Keppel, and Wilkes, and Sawbridge, and Bull, and Dunning, and Pratt, and Richmond,—and such small politics.—

A little less facetious, and a great deal more obstreperous, was fine rattling, rattleheaded Plumer. He was descended,—not in a right line, reader, (for his lineal pretensions, like his personal, favoured a little of the sinister bend) from the Plumers of Hertfordshire. So tradition gave him out ; and certain family features not a little sanctioned the opinion. Certainly old Walter Plumer (his reputed author) had been a rake in his days, and visited much in Italy, and had seen the world. He was uncle, bachelor-uncle, to the fine old whig still living, who has represented the county in so many successive parliaments, and has a fine old mansion near Ware. Walter flourished in George the Second's days, and was the same who was summoned before the House of Commons about a business of franks, with the old Duchess of Marlborough. You may read of it in Johnson's Life of Cave. Cave came off cleverly in that business. It is certain our Plumer did nothing to discountenance the rumour. He rather seemed pleased whenever it was, with all gentleness, insinuated. But, besides his family pretensions, Plumer was an engaging fellow, and sang gloriously.—

Not so sweetly sang Plumer as thou sangest, mild, child-like, pastoral M— ; a flute's breathing less divinely whispering than thy Arcadian melodies, when, in tones worthy of Arden, thou didst chant that song sung by Amiens to the banished Duke, which proclaims the winter wind more lenient than for a man to be ungrateful. Thy sire was old surly M—, the unapproachable churchwarden of Bishopsgate. He knew not what he did, when he begat thee, like spring, gentle offspring of blustering winter :—only unfortunate in thy ending, which should have been mild, conciliatory, swan-like.—

Much remains to sing. Many fantastic shapes rise up, but they must be mine in private :—already I have fooled the reader to the top of his bent ;—else could I omit that strange creature Woollett, who existed in trying the question, and *bought litigations* ?—and still stranger, inimitable, solemn Hepworth, from whose gravity Newton might have deduced the law of gravitation. How profoundly would he nib a pen—with what deliberation would he wet a wafer !—

But it is time to close—night's wheels are rattling fast over me— it is proper to have done with this solemn mockery.

Reader, what if I have been playing with thee all this while— peradventure the very *names*, which I have summoned up before thee, are fantastic—insubstantial—like Henry Pimpernel, and old John Naps of Greece :—

Be satisfied that something answering to them has had a being. Their importance is from the past.

OXFORD IN THE VACATION

CASTING a preparatory glance at the bottom of this article— as the wary connoisseur in prints, with cursory eye (which, while it reads, seems as though it read not,) never fails to consult the *quis sculpsit* in the corner, before he pronounces some rare piece to be a Vivares, or a Woollet—methinks I hear you exclaim, Reader, *Who is Elia* ?

Because in my last I tried to divert thee with some half-forgotten humours of some old clerks defunct, in an old house of business, long since gone to decay, doubtless you have already set me down in your mind as one of the self-same college—a votary of the desk— a notched and cropt scrivener—one that sucks his sustenance, as certain sick people are said to do, through a quill.

Well, I do agnize something of the sort. I confess that it is my humour, my fancy—in the forepart of the day, when the mind of your man of letters requires some relaxation—(and none better than such as at first sight seems most abhorrent from his beloved studies) —to while away some good hours of my time in the contemplation of indigos, cottons, raw silks, piece-goods, flowered or otherwise. In the

first place * * * * * * and then it sends you home with such
increased appetite to your books * * * * not to say, that your
outside sheets, and waste wrappers of foolscap, do receive into them,
most kindly and naturally, the impression of· sonnets, epigrams,
essays—so that the very parings of a counting-house are, in some
sort, the settings up of an author.   The enfranchised quill, that has
plodded all the morning among the cart-rucks of figures and
cyphers, frisks and curvets so at its ease over the flowery carpet-
ground of a midnight dissertation.—It feels its promotion. * * *
* * So that you see, upon the whole, the literary dignity of *Elia*
is very little, if at all, compromised in the condescension.

Not that, in my anxious detail of the many commodities in-
cidental to the life of a public office, I would be thought blind to
certain flaws, which a cunning carper might be able to pick in this
Joseph's vest.   And here I must have leave, in the fulness of my
soul, to regret the abolition, and doing-away-with altogether, of
those consolatory interstices, and sprinklings of freedom, through
the four seasons,—the *red-letter days*, now become, to all intents
and purposes, *dead-letter days*.   There was Paul, and Stephen,
and Barnabas—

Andrew and John, men famous in old times

—we were used to keep all their days holy, as long back as I was at
school at Christ's.   I remember their effigies, by the same token, in
the old *Baskett* Prayer Book.   There hung Peter in his uneasy
posture—holy Bartlemy in the troublesome act of flaying, after the
famous Marsyas by Spagnoletti.—I honoured them all, and could
almost have wept the defalcation of Iscariot—so much did we love
to keep holy memories sacred :—only methought I a little grudged
at the coalition of the *better Jude* with Simon—clubbing (as it
were) their sanctities together, to make up one poor gaudy-day
between them—as an economy unworthy of the dispensation.

These were bright visitations in a scholar's and a clerk's life—" far
off their coming shone."—I was as good as an almanac in those days.
I could have told you such a saint's-day falls out next week, or the
week after.   Peradventure the Epiphany, by some periodical infelicity, would, once in six years, merge in a Sabbath.   Now am I
little better than one of the profane.   Let me not be thought to
arraign the wisdom of my civil superiors, who have judged the
further observation of these holy tides to be papistical, superstitious.
Only in a custom of such long standing, methinks, if their Holi-
nesses the Bishops had, in decency, been first sounded——but I am
wading out of my depths.   I am not the man to decide the limits
of civil and ecclesiastical authority——I am plain Elia—no Selden,
nor Archbishop Usher—though at present in the thick of their

books, here in the heart of learning, under the shadow of the mighty Bodley.

I can here play the gentleman, enact the student. To such a one as myself, who has been defrauded in his young years of the sweet food of academic institution, nowhere is so pleasant, to while away a few idle weeks at, as one or other of the Universities. Their vacation, too, at this time of the year, falls in so pat with *ours*. Here I can take my walks unmolested, and fancy myself of what degree or standing I please. I seem admitted *ad eundem*. I fetch up past opportunities. I can rise at the chapel-bell, and dream that it rings for *me*. In moods of humility I can be a Sizar, or a Servitor. When the peacock vein rises, I strut a Gentleman Commoner. In graver moments, I proceed Master of Arts. Indeed I do not think I am much unlike that respectable character. I have seen your dim-eyed vergers, and bed-makers in spectacles, drop a bow or curtsy, as I pass, wisely mistaking me for something of the sort. I go about in black, which favours the notion. Only in Christ Church reverend quadrangle, I can be content to pass for nothing short of a Seraphic Doctor.

The walks at these times are so much one's own,—the tall trees of Christ's, the groves of Magdalen! The halls deserted, and with open doors, inviting one to slip in unperceived, and pay a devoir to some Founder, or noble or royal Benefactress (that should have been ours) whose portrait seems to smile upon their over-looked beadsman, and to adopt me for their own. Then, to take a peep in by the way at the butteries, and sculleries, redolent of antique hospitality : the immense caves of kitchens, kitchen fire-places, cordial recesses ; ovens whose first pies were baked four centuries ago ; and spits which have cooked for Chaucer! Not the meanest minister among the dishes but is hallowed to me through his imagination, and the Cook goes forth a Manciple.

Antiquity! thou wondrous charm, what art thou? that, being nothing, art every thing! When thou *wert*, thou wert not antiquity—then thou wert nothing, but hadst a remoter *antiquity*, as thou called'st it, to look back to with blind veneration ; thou thyself being to thyself flat, jejune, *modern*! What mystery lurks in this retroversion? or what half Januses [1] are we, that cannot look forward with the same idolatry with which we for ever revert! The mighty future is as nothing, being every thing! the past is every thing, being nothing!

What were thy *dark ages*? Surely the sun rose as brightly then as now, and man got him to his work in the morning. Why is it that we can never hear mention of them without an accom-

---

[1] Januses of one face.—SIR THOMAS BROWNE.

panying feeling, as though a palpable obscure had dimmed the face
of things, and that our ancestors wandered to and fro groping!

Above all thy rarities, old Oxenford, what do most arride
and solace me, are thy repositories of mouldering learning, thy
shelves——

What a place to be in is an old library! It seems as though
all the souls of all the writers, that have bequeathed their labours
to these Bodleians, were reposing here, as in some dormitory, or
middle state. I do not want to handle, to profane the leaves, their
winding-sheets. I could as soon dislodge a shade. I seem to in-
hale learning, walking amid their foliage; and the odour of their
old moth-scented coverings is fragrant as the first bloom of those
sciential apples which grew amid the happy orchard.

Still less have I curiosity to disturb the elder repose of MSS.
Those *variæ lectiones,* so tempting to the more erudite palates,
do but disturb and unsettle my faith. I am no Herculanean
raker. The credit of the three witnesses might have slept un-
impeached for me. I leave these curiosities to Porson, and to
G. D.—whom, by the way, I found busy as a moth over some
rotten archive, rummaged out of some seldom-explored press, in a
nook at Oriel. With long poring, he is grown almost into a
book. He stood as passive as one by the side of the old shelves.
I longed to new-coat him in Russia, and assign him his place. He
might have mustered for a tall Scapula.

D. is assiduous in his visits to these seats of learning. No inconsiderable portion of his moderate fortune, I apprehend, is
consumed in journeys between them and Clifford's-inn——where,
like a dove on the asp's nest, he has long taken up his unconscious
abode, amid an incongruous assembly of attorneys, attorneys'
clerks, apparitors, promoters, vermin of the law, among whom he
sits, "in calm and sinless peace." The fangs of the law pierce him
not—the winds of litigation blow over his humble chambers—the
hard sheriff's officer moves his hat as he passes—legal nor illegal
discourtesy touches him—none thinks of offering violence or injustice to him—you would as soon "strike an abstract idea."

D. has been engaged, he tells me, through a course of laborious
years, in an investigation into all curious matter connected with
the two Universities; and has lately lit upon a MS. collection of
charters, relative to C——, by which he hopes to settle some disputed points—particularly that long controversy between them as
to priority of foundation. The ardor with which he engages in
these liberal pursuits, I am afraid, has not met with all the
encouragement it deserved, either here, or at C——. Your caputs,
and heads of colleges, care less than any body else about these
questions.—Contented to suck the milky fountains of their Alma

Maters, without inquiring into the venerable gentlewomen's years, they rather hold such curiosities to be impertinent—unreverend. They have their good glebe lands *in manu,* and care not much to rake into the title-deeds. I gather at least so much from other sources, for D. is not a man to complain.

D. started like an unbroke heifer, when I interrupted him. *A priori* it was not very probable that we should have met in Oriel. But D. would have done the same, had I accosted him on the sudden in his own walks in Clifford's-inn, or in the Temple. In addition to a provoking short-sightedness (the effect of late studies and watchings at the midnight oil) D. is the most absent of men. He made a call the other morning at our friend *M.*'s in Bedford-square ; and, finding nobody at home, was ushered into the hall, where, asking for pen and ink, with great exactitude of purpose he enters me his name in the book—which ordinarily lies about in such places, to record the failures of the untimely or unfortunate visitor—and takes his leave with many ceremonies, and professions of regret. Some two or three hours after, his walking destinies returned him into the same neighbourhood again, and again the quiet image of the fire-side circle at *M.*'s—Mrs. *M.* presiding at it like a Queen Lar, with pretty *A. S.* at her side—striking irresistibly on his fancy, he makes another call (forgetting that they were " certainly not to return from the country before that day week ") and disappointed a second time, inquires for pen and paper as before : again the book is brought, and in the line just above that in which he is about to print his second name (his re-script)—his first name (scarce dry) looks out upon him like another Sosia, or as if a man should suddenly encounter his own duplicate !—The effect may be conceived. D. made many a good resolution against any such lapses in future. I hope he will not keep them too rigorously.

For with G. D.—to be absent from the body, is sometimes (not to speak it profanely) to be present with the Lord. At the very time when, personally encountering thee, he passes on with no recognition——or, being stopped, starts like a thing surprised—at that moment, reader, he is on Mount Tabor—or Parnassus—or co-sphered with Plato—or, with Harrington, framing " immortal commonwealths "—devising some plan of amelioration to thy country, or thy species——peradventure meditating some individual kindness or courtesy, to be done to *thee thyself,* the returning consciousness of which made him to start so guiltily at thy obtruded personal presence.

D. is delightful any where, but he is at the best in such places as these. He cares not much for Bath. He is out of his element at Buxton, at Scarborough, or Harrowgate. The Cam and the Isis are to him " better than all the waters of Damascus." On the Muses'

hill he is happy, and good, as one of the Shepherds on the Delectable Mountains ; and when he goes about with you to show you
the halls and colleges, you think you have with you the Interpreter
at the House Beautiful.

CHRIST'S HOSPITAL FIVE AND THIRTY YEARS AGO

IN Mr. Lamb's " Works," published a year or two since, I find a
magnificent eulogy on my old school,[1] such as it was, or now
appears to him to have been, between the years 1782 and 1789. It
happens, very oddly, that my own standing at Christ's was nearly
corresponding with his ; and, with all gratitude to him for his
enthusiasm for the cloisters, I think he has contrived to bring together whatever can be said in praise of them, dropping all the other
side of the argument most ingeniously.

I remember L. at school ; and can well recollect that he had some
peculiar advantages, which I and others of his schoolfellows had not.
His friends lived in town, and were near at hand ; and he had the
privilege of going to see them, almost as often as he wished, through
some invidious distinction, which was denied to us. The present
worthy sub-treasurer to the Inner Temple can explain how that
happened. He had his tea and hot rolls in a morning, while we
were battening upon our quarter of a penny loaf—our *crug*—
moistened with attenuated small beer, in wooden piggins, smacking
of the pitched leathern jack it was poured from. Our Monday's
milk porritch, blue and tasteless, and the pease soup of Saturday,
coarse and choking, were enriched for him with a slice of " extraordinary bread and butter," from the hot-loaf of the Temple. The
Wednesday's mess of millet, somewhat less repugnant—(we had
three banyan to four meat days in the week)—was endeared to his
palate with a lump of double-refined, and a smack of ginger (to
make it go down the more glibly) or the fragrant cinnamon. In lieu
of our *half-pickled* Sundays, or *quite fresh* boiled beef on Thurs-
days (strong as *caro equina*), with detestable marigolds floating in
the pail to poison the broth—our scanty mutton crags on Fridays
—and rather more savoury, but grudging, portions of the same flesh,
rotten-roasted or rare, on the Tuesdays (the only dish which excited
our appetites, and disappointed our stomachs, in almost equal

---

[1] Recollections of Christ's Hospital.

proportion)—he had his hot plate of roast veal, or the more tempting griskin (exotics unknown to our palates), cooked in the paternal kitchen (a great thing), and brought him daily by his maid or aunt! I remember the good old relative (in whom love forbade pride) squatting down upon some odd stone in a by-nook of the cloisters, disclosing the viands (of higher regale than those cates which the ravens ministered to the Tishbite); and the contending passions of L. at the unfolding. There was love for the bringer; shame for the thing brought, and the manner of its bringing; sympathy for those who were too many to share in it; and, at top of all, hunger (eldest, strongest of the passions!) predominant, breaking down the stony fences of shame, and awkwardness, and a troubling over-consciousness.

I was a poor friendless boy. My parents, and those who should care for me, were far away. Those few acquaintances of theirs, which they could reckon upon being kind to me in the great city, after a little forced notice, which they had the grace to take of me on my first arrival in town, soon grew tired of my holiday visits. They seemed to them to recur too often, though I thought them few enough; and, one after another, they all failed me, and I felt myself alone among six hundred playmates.

O the cruelty of separating a poor lad from his early homestead! The yearnings which I used to have towards it in those unfledged years! How, in my dreams, would my native town (far in the west) come back, with its church, and trees, and faces! How I would wake weeping, and in the anguish of my heart exclaim upon sweet Calne in Wiltshire!

To this late hour of my life, I trace impressions left by the recollection of those friendless holidays. The long warm days of summer never return but they bring with them a gloom from the haunting memory of those *whole-day-leaves*, when, by some strange arrangement, we were turned out, for the live-long day, upon our own hands, whether we had friends to go to, or none. I remember those bathing-excursions to the New-River, which L. recalls with such relish, better, I think, than he can—for he was a home-seeking lad, and did not much care for such water-pastimes:—How merrily we would sally forth into the fields; and strip under the first warmth of the sun; and wanton like young dace in the streams; getting us appetites for noon, which those of us that were pennyless (our scanty morning crust long since exhausted) had not the means of allaying—while the cattle, and the birds, and the fishes, were at feed about us, and we had nothing to satisfy our cravings—the very beauty of the day, and the exercise of the pastime, and the sense of liberty, setting a keener edge upon them!—How faint and languid, finally, we would return, towards nightfall, to our desired morsel,

half-rejoicing, half-reluctant, that the hours of our uneasy liberty
had expired!

It was worse in the days of winter, to go prowling about the streets
objectless—shivering at cold windows of print-shops, to extract a
little amusement; or haply, as a last resort, in the hope of a little
novelty, to pay a fifty-times repeated visit (where our individual
faces should be as well known to the warden as those of his own
charges) to the Lions in the Tower—to whose levée, by courtesy
immemorial, we had a prescriptive title to admission.

L.'s governor (so we called the patron who presented us to the
foundation) lived in a manner under his paternal roof. Any complaint which he had to make was sure of being attended to. This
was understood at Christ's, and was an effectual screen to him
against the severity of masters, or worse tyranny of the monitors.
The oppressions of these young brutes are heart-sickening to call to
recollection. I have been called out of my bed, and *waked for the
purpose*, in the coldest winter nights—and this not once, but
night after night—in my shirt, to receive the discipline of a
leathern thong, with eleven other sufferers, because it pleased my
callow overseer, when there has been any talking heard after we
were gone to bed, to make the six last beds in the dormitory, where
the youngest children of us slept, answerable for an offence they
neither dared to commit, nor had the power to hinder.—The same
execrable tyranny drove the younger part of us from the fires, when
our feet were perishing with snow; and, under the cruelest
penalties, forbad the indulgence of a drink of water, when we lay
in sleepless summer nights, fevered with the season, and the day's
sports.

There was one H——, who, I learned, in after days, was seen
expiating some maturer offence in the hulks. (Do I flatter myself
in fancying that this might be the planter of that name, who
suffered—at Nevis, I think, or St. Kits,—some few years since?
My friend Tobin was the benevolent instrument of bringing him to
the gallows.) This petty Nero actually branded a boy, who had
offended him, with a red hot iron; and nearly starved forty of us,
with exacting contributions, to the one half of our bread, to
pamper a young ass, which, incredible as it may seem, with the
connivance of the nurse's daughter (a young flame of his) he had contrived to smuggle in, and keep upon the leads of the *ward*, as they
called our dormitories. This game went on for better than a week,
till the foolish beast, not able to fare well but he must cry roast
meat—happier than Caligula's minion, could he have kept his own
counsel—but, foolisher, alas! than any of his species in the fables
—waxing fat, and kicking, in the fulness of bread, one unlucky
minute would needs proclaim his good fortune to the world below;

and, laying out his simple throat, blew such a ram's horn blast, as (toppling down the walls of his own Jericho) set concealment any longer at defiance. The client was dismissed, with certain attentions, to Smithfield; but I never understood that the patron underwent any censure on the occasion. This was in the stewardship of L.'s admired Perry.

Under the same *facile* administration, can L. have forgotten the cool impunity with which the nurses used to carry away openly, in open platters, for their own tables, one out of two of every hot joint, which the careful matron had been seeing scrupulously weighed out for our dinners? These things were daily practised in that magnificent apartment, which L. (grown connoisseur since, we presume) praises so highly for the grand paintings "by Verrio, and others," with which it is "hung round and adorned." But the sight of sleek well-fed blue-coat boys in pictures was, at that time, I believe, little consolatory to him, or us, the living ones, who saw the better part of our provisions carried away before our faces by harpies; and ourselves reduced (with the Trojan in the hall of Dido)

> To feed our mind with idle portraiture.

L. has recorded the repugnance of the school to *gags*, or the fat of fresh beef boiled; and sets it down to some superstition. But these unctuous morsels are never grateful to young palates (children are universally fat-haters) and in strong, coarse, boiled meats, *unsalted*, are detestable. A *gag-eater* in our time was equivalent to a *goul*, and held in equal detestation. —— suffered under the imputation.

> —— 'Twas said
> He ate strange flesh.

He was observed, after dinner, carefully to gather up the remnants left at his table (not many, nor very choice fragments, you may credit me)—and, in an especial manner, these disreputable morsels, which he would convey away, and secretly stow in the settle that stood at his bed-side. None saw when he ate them. It was rumoured that he privately devoured them in the night. He was watched, but no traces of such midnight practices were discoverable. Some reported, that, on leave-days, he had been seen to carry out of the bounds a large blue check handkerchief, full of something. This then must be the accursed thing. Conjecture next was at work to imagine how he could dispose of it. Some said he sold it to the beggars. This belief generally prevailed. He went about moping. None spake to him. No one would play with him. He was excommunicated; put out of the pale of the school. He was too powerful a boy to be beaten, but he underwent every mode of that negative punishment, which is more grievous than many stripes. Still he persevered. At length he was observed by two of his school-fellows, who were determined to get at the secret, and had traced him one leave-day for that purpose, to enter a large worn-out building, such as there exist specimens of in Chancery-lane, which are let out to various scales of pauperism with open door, and a common staircase. After him they silently slunk in, and followed by stealth up four flights, and saw him tap at a poor wicket, which was opened by an aged woman, meanly clad. Suspicion was now ripened into certainty. The informers had secured their victim. They had him in their toils. Accusation was formally preferred, and retribution most signal was looked for. Mr. Hathaway, the then steward (for this happened a little after my time), with that patient sagacity which tempered all his conduct, determined to investigate the matter, before he proceeded to sentence. The result was, that the supposed mendicants, the receivers or purchasers of the mysterious scraps, turned out to be the parents of ——, an honest couple come to decay,—whom this seasonable supply had, in all probability, saved from mendicancy; and that this young stork, at the expense of his own good name, had all this while been only feeding the old birds!— The governors on this occasion, much to their honour, voted a present relief to the family of ——, and presented him with a silver medal. The lesson which the steward read upon RASH JUDG-MENT, on the occasion of publicly delivering the medal to ——, I believe, would not be lost upon his auditory.—I had left school then, but I well remember ——. He was a tall, shambling youth, with a cast in his eye, not at all calculated to conciliate hostile prejudices. I have since seen him carrying a baker's basket. I think I heard he did not do quite so well by himself, as he had done by the old folks.

I was a hypochondriac lad; and the sight of a boy in fetters, upon the day of my first putting on the blue clothes, was not exactly fitted to assuage the natural terrors of initiation. I was of tender years, barely turned of seven; and had only read of such things in books, or seen them but in dreams. I was told he had *run away*. This was the punishment for the first offence.—As a novice I was soon after taken to see the dungeons. These were little, square, Bedlam cells, where a boy could just lie at his length upon straw and a blanket—a mattress, I think, was after-wards substituted—with a peep of light, let in askance, from a prison-orifice at top, barely enough to read by. Here the poor boy was locked in by himself all day, without sight of any but the porter who brought him his bread and water—who *might not speak to him*;—or of the beadle, who came twice a week to call him out to receive his periodical chastisement, which was almost welcome, because it separated him for a brief interval from solitude: —and here he was shut up by himself *of nights*, out of the reach of any sound, to suffer whatever horrors the weak nerves, and superstition incident to his time of life, might subject him to.[1] This was the penalty for the second offence.—Wouldst thou like, reader, to see what became of him in the next degree?

The culprit, who had been a third time an offender, and whose expulsion was at this time deemed irreversible, was brought forth, as at some solemn *auto da fe*, arrayed in uncouth and most appalling attire—all trace of his late " watchet weeds " carefully effaced, he was exposed in a jacket, resembling those which London lamplighters formerly delighted in, with a cap of the same. The effect of this divestiture was such as the ingenious devisers of it could have anticipated. With his pale and frighted features, it was as if some of those disfigurements in Dante had seized upon him. In this disguisement he was brought into the hall (*L.'s favourite state-room*), where awaited him the whole number of his school-fellows, whose joint lessons and sports he was thenceforth to share no more ; the awful presence of the steward, to be seen for the last time ; of the executioner beadle, clad in his state robe for the occasion ; and of two faces more, of direr import, because never but in these extremities visible. These were governors; two of whom, by choice, or charter, were always accustomed to officiate at these *Ultima Supplicia ;* not to mitigate (so at least we understood it), but to enforce the uttermost stripe. Old Bamber Gascoigne, and Peter Aubert, I remember, were colleagues on one occasion, when the beadle turning rather pale, a glass of brandy was ordered to prepare him for the mysteries. The scourging was, after the old Roman fashion, long and stately. The lictor accompanied the criminal quite round the hall. We were generally too faint with attending to the previous disgusting circumstances, to make accurate report with our eyes of the degree of corporal suffering inflicted. Report, of course, gave out the back knotty and livid. After scourging, he was made over, in his *San Benito*, to his friends, if he had any (but commonly such poor runagates were friendless), or to his parish officer, who, to enhance the effect of the scene, had his station allotted to him on the outside of the hall gate.

These solemn pageantries were not played off so often as to

---

[1] One or two instances of lunacy, or attempted suicide, accordingly, at length convinced the governors of the impolicy of this part of the sentence, and the midnight torture to the spirits was dispensed with.—This fancy of dungeons for children was a sprout of Howard's brain ; for which (saving the reverence due to Holy Paul) methinks, I could willingly spit upon his statue.

spoil the general mirth of the community. We had plenty of exercise and recreation *after* school hours ; and, for myself, I must confess, that I was never happier, than *in* them. The Upper and the Lower Grammar Schools were held in the same room ; and an imaginary line only divided their bounds. Their character was as different as that of the inhabitants on the two sides of the Pyrennees. The Rev. James Boyer was the Upper Master ; but the Rev. Matthew Field presided over that portion of the apartment, of which I had the good fortune to be a member. We lived a life as careless as birds. We talked and did just what we pleased, and nobody molested us. We carried an accidence, or a grammar, for form ; but, for any trouble it gave us, we might take two years in getting through the verbs deponent, and another two in forgetting all that we had learned about them. There was now and then the formality of saying a lesson, but if you had not learned it, a brush across the shoulders (just enough to disturb a fly) was the sole remonstrance. Field never used the rod ; and in truth he wielded the cane with no great good will—holding it " like a dancer." It looked in his hands rather like an emblem than an instrument of authority; and an emblem, too, he was ashamed of. He was a good easy man, that did not care to ruffle his own peace, nor perhaps set any great consideration upon the value of juvenile time. He came among us, now and then, but often staid away whole days from us; and when he came, it made no difference to us—he had his private room to retire to, the short time he staid, to be out of the sound of our noise. Our mirth and uproar went on. We had classics of our own, without being beholden to " insolent Greece or haughty Rome," that passed current among us—Peter Wilkins—the Adventures of the Hon. Capt. Robert Boyle—the Fortunate Blue Coat Boy—and the like. Or we cultivated a turn for mechanic or scientific operations ; making little sun-dials of paper ; or weaving those ingenious parentheses, called *cat-cradles ;* or making dry peas to dance upon the end of a tin pipe ; or studying the art military over that laudable game " French and English," and a hundred other such devices to pass away the time—mixing the useful with the agreeable—as would have made the souls of Rousseau and John Locke chuckle to have seen us.

Matthew Field belonged to that class of modest divines who affect to mix in equal proportion the *gentleman,* the *scholar,* and the *Christian ;* but, I know not how, the first ingredient is generally found to be the predominating dose in the composition. He was engaged in gay parties, or with his courtly bow at some episcopal levée, when he should have been attending upon us. He had for many years the classical charge of a hundred children, during the four or five first years of their education ; and his very

highest form seldom proceeded further than two or three of the
introductory fables of Phædrus. How things were suffered to go
on thus, I cannot guess. Boyer, who was the proper person to
have remedied these abuses, always affected, perhaps felt, a delicacy
in interfering in a province not strictly his own. I have not been
without my suspicions, that he was not altogether displeased at the
contrast we presented to his end of the school. We were a sort of
Helots to his young Spartans. He would sometimes, with ironic
deference, send to borrow a rod of the Under Master, and then,
with Sardonic grin, observe to one of his upper boys, "how neat
and fresh the twigs looked." While his pale students were batter-
ing their brains over Xenophon and Plato, with a silence as deep
as that enjoined by the Samite, we were enjoying ourselves at our
ease in our little Goshen. We saw a little into the secrets of his
discipline, and the prospect did but the more reconcile us to our
lot. His thunders rolled innocuous for us ; his storms came near,
but never touched us ; contrary to Gideon's miracle, while all
around were drenched, our fleece was dry.[1] His boys turned out
the better scholars ; we, I suspect, have the advantage in temper.
His pupils cannot speak of him without something of terror allaying their gratitude ; the remembrance of Field comes back with all
the soothing images of indolence, and summer slumbers, and work
like play, and innocent idleness, and Elysian exemptions, and life
itself a "playing holiday."

Though sufficiently removed from the jurisdiction of Boyer, we
were near enough (as I have said) to understand a little of his
system. We occasionally heard sounds of the *Ululantes*, and caught
glances of Tartarus. B. was a rabid pedant. His English style
was crampt to barbarism. His Easter anthems (for his duty obliged
him to those periodical flights) were grating as scrannel pipes.[2]—
He would laugh, ay, and heartily, but then it must be at Flaccus's
quibble about *Rex*——or at the *tristis severitas in vultu*, or
inspicere in patinas, of Terence—thin jests, which at their first
broaching could hardly have had *vis* enough to move a Roman
muscle.—He had two wigs, both pedantic, but of differing omen.
The one serene, smiling, fresh powdered, betokening a mild day.
The other, an old discoloured, unkempt, angry caxon, denoting
frequent and bloody execution. Woe to the school, when he made

---

[1] Cowley.

[2] In this and every thing B. was the antipodes of his co-adjutor. While the former
was digging his brains for crude anthems, worth a pig-nut, F. would be recreating
his gentlemanly fancy in the more flowery walks of the Muses. A little dramatic
effusion of his, under the name of Vertumnus and Pomona, is not yet forgotten by
the chroniclers of that sort of literature. It was accepted by Garrick, but the town
did not give it their sanction.—B. used to say of it, in a way of half-compliment,
half-irony, that it was *too classical for representation*.

his morning appearance in his *passy,* or *passionate wig.* No comet expounded surer.—J. B. had a heavy hand. I have known him double his knotty fist at a poor trembling child-(the maternal milk hardly dry upon its lips) with a "Sirrah, do you presume to set your wits at me?"—Nothing was more common than to see him make a head-long entry into the school-room, from his inner recess, or library, and, with turbulent eye, singling out a lad, roar out, "Od's my life, Sirrah," (his favourite adjuration) "I have a great mind to whip you,"—then, with as sudden a retracting impulse, fling back into his lair—and, after a cooling lapse of some minutes (during which all but the culprit had totally forgotten the context) drive headlong out again, piecing out his imperfect sense, as if it had been some Devil's Litany, with the expletory yell—"*and I* WILL, *too.*"—In his gentler moods, when the *rabidus furor* was assuaged, he had resort to an ingenious method, peculiar, for what I have heard, to himself, of whipping the boy, and reading the Debates, at the same time; a paragraph, and a lash between; which in those times, when parliamentary oratory was most at a height and flourishing in these realms, was not calculated to impress the patient with a veneration for the diffuser graces of rhetoric.

Once, and but once, the uplifted rod was known to fall ineffectual from his hand—when droll squinting W—— having been caught putting the inside of the master's desk to a use for which the architect had clearly not designed it, to justify himself, with great simplicity averred, that *he did not know that the thing had been forewarned.* This exquisite irrecognition of any law antecedent to the *oral* or *declaratory*, struck so irresistibly upon the fancy of all who heard it (the pedagogue himself not excepted) that remission was unavoidable.

L. has given credit to B.'s great merits as an instructor. Coleridge, in his literary life, has pronounced a more intelligible and ample encomium on them. The author of the Country Spectator doubts not to compare him with the ablest teachers of antiquity. Perhaps we cannot dismiss him better than with the pious ejaculation of C.—when he heard that his old master was on his death-bed—"Poor J.B.!—may all his faults be forgiven; and may he be wafted to bliss by little cherub boys, all head and wings, with no *bottoms* to reproach his sublunary infirmities."

Under him were many good and sound scholars bred.—First Grecian of my time was Lancelot Pepys Stevens, kindest of boys and men, since Co-grammar-master (and inseparable companion) with Dr. T——e. What an edifying spectacle did this brace of friends present to those who remembered the anti-socialities of their predecessors!—You never met the one by chance in the street without a wonder, which was quickly dissipated by the almost immediate sub-appearance of the other.   Generally arm in arm, these kindly coadjutors lightened for each other the toilsome duties of their profession, and when, in advanced age, one found it convenient to retire, the other was not long in discovering that it suited him to lay down the fasces also.   Oh, it is pleasant, as it is rare, to find the same arm linked in yours at forty, which at thirteen helped it to turn over the *Cicero De Amicitia*, or some tale of Antique Friendship, which the young heart even then was burning to anticipate !—Co-Grecian with S. was Th—, who has since executed with ability various diplomatic functions at the Northern courts.   Th— was a tall, dark, saturnine youth, sparing of speech, with raven locks.— Thomas Fanshaw Middleton followed him (now Bishop of Calcutta) a scholar and a gentleman in his teens.   He has the reputation of an excellent critic ; and is author (besides the Country Spectator) of a Treatise on the Greek Article, against Sharpe.—M. is said to bear his mitre high in India, where the *regni novitas* (I dare say) sufficiently justifies the bearing.   A humility quite as primitive as that of Jewel or Hooker might not be exactly fitted to impress the minds of those Anglo-Asiatic diocesans with a reverence for home institutions, and the church which those fathers watered. The manners of M. at school, though firm, were mild, and unassuming.—Next to M. (if not senior to him) was Richards, author of the Aboriginal Britons, the most spirited of the Oxford Prize Poems ; a pale, studious Grecian.—Then followed poor S——, ill-fated M—— ! of these the Muse is silent.

> Finding some of Edward's race
> Unhappy, pass their annals by.

Come back into memory, like as thou wert in the day-spring of thy fancies, with hope like a fiery column before thee—the dark pillar not yet turned—Samuel Taylor Coleridge—Logician, Metaphysician, Bard !—How have I seen the casual passer through the Cloisters stand still, intranced with admiration (while he weighed the disproportion between the *speech* and the *garb* of the young Mirandula), to hear thee unfold, in thy deep and sweet intonations, the mysteries of Jamblichus, or Plotinus (for even in those years thou waxedst not pale at such philosophic draughts), or reciting Homer in his Greek, or Pindar——while the walls of the old Grey Friars re-echoed to the accents of the *inspired charity-boy !*— Many were the " wit-combats," (to dally awhile with the words of old Fuller,) between him and C. V. Le G——, " which two I behold like a Spanish great gallion, and an English man of war ; Master Coleridge, like the former, was built far higher in learning, solid, but slow in his performances.   C. V. L., with the English man of war, lesser in bulk, but lighter in sailing, could turn with all tides, tack about, and take advantage of all winds, by the quickness of his wit and invention."

Nor shalt thou, their compeer, be quickly forgotten, Allen, with the cordial smile, and still more cordial laugh, with which thou wert wont to make the old Cloisters shake, in thy cognition of some poignant jest of theirs ; or the anticipation of some more material, and, peradventure, practical one, of thine own. Extinct are those smiles, with that beautiful countenance, with which (for thou wert the *Nireus formosus* of the school), in the days of thy maturer waggery, thou didst disarm the wrath of infuriated town-damsel, who, incensed by provoking pinch, turning tigress-like round, suddenly converted by thy angel-look, exchanged the half-formed terrible " *bl*——," for a gentler greeting—" *bless thy handsome face !* "

Next follow two, who ought to be now alive, and the friends of Elia—the junior Le G—— and F—— ; who impelled, the former by a roving temper, the latter by too quick a sense of neglect—ill capable of enduring the slights poor Sizars are sometimes subject to in our seats of learning—exchanged their Alma Mater for the camp; perishing, one by climate, and one on the plains of Salamanca :— Le G——, sanguine, volatile, sweet-natured ; F—— dogged, faithful, anticipative of insult, warm-hearted, with something of the old Roman height about him.

Fine, frank-hearted Fr——, the present master of Hertford, with Marmaduke T——, mildest of Missionaries—and both my good friends still—close the catalogue of Grecians in my time.

THE TWO RACES OF MEN

THE human species, according to the best theory I can form of it, is composed of two distinct races, *the men who borrow*, and *the men who lend*. To these two original diversities may be reduced all those impertinent classifications of Gothic and Celtic tribes, white men, black men, red men. All the dwellers upon earth, " Parthians, and Medes, and Elamites," flock hither, and do naturally fall in with one or other of these primary distinctions. The infinite superiority of the former, which I choose to designate as the *great race*, is discernible in their figure, port, and a certain instinctive sovereignty. The latter are born degraded. " He shall serve his brethren." There is something in the air of one of this cast, lean and suspicious; contrasting with the open, trusting, generous manners of the other.

Observe who have been the greatest borrowers of all ages—Alcibiades—Falstaff—Sir Richard Steele—our late incomparable Brinsley—what a family likeness in all four!

What a careless, even deportment hath your borrower! what rosy gills! what a beautiful reliance on Providence doth he manifest,—taking no more thought than lilies! What contempt for money,—accounting it (yours and mine especially) no better than dross What a liberal confounding of those pedantic distinctions of *meum* and *tuum!* or rather, what a noble simplification of language (beyond Tooke), resolving these supposed opposites into one clear, intelligible pronoun adjective!—What near approaches doth he make to the primitive *community*,—to the extent of one half of the principle at least!—

He is the true taxer who " calleth all the world up to be taxed;" and the distance is as vast between him and *one of us*, as subsisted betwixt the Augustan Majesty and the poorest obolary Jew that paid it tribute-pittance at Jerusalem!—His exactions, too, have such a cheerful, voluntary air! So far removed from your sour parochial or state-gatherers,—those ink-horn varlets, who carry their want of welcome in their faces! He cometh to you with a smile, and troubleth you with no receipt; confining himself to no set season. Every day is his Candlemas, or his Feast of Holy Michael. He applieth the *lene tormentum* of a pleasant look to your purse,—which to that gentle warmth expands her silken leaves, as naturally as the cloak of the traveller, for which sun and wind contended! He is the true Propontic which never ebbeth! The sea which taketh handsomely at each man's hand. In vain the victim, whom he delighteth to honour, struggles with destiny; he is in the net. Lend therefore cheerfully, O man ordained to lend—that thou lose not in the end, with thy worldly penny, the reversion promised. Combine not preposterously in thine own person the penalties of Lazarus and of Dives!—but, when thou seest the proper authority coming, meet it smilingly, as it were half-way. Come, a handsome sacrifice! See how light *he* makes of it! Strain not courtesies with a noble enemy.

Reflections like the foregoing were forced upon my mind by the death of my old friend, Ralph Bigod, Esq., who departed this life on Wednesday evening; dying, as he had lived, without much trouble. He boasted himself a descendant from mighty ancestors of that name, who heretofore held ducal dignities in this realm. In his actions and sentiments he belied not the stock to which he pretended. Early in life he found himself invested with ample revenues; which, with that noble disinterestedness which I have noticed as inherent in men of the *great race*, he took almost immediate measures entirely to dissipate and bring to nothing: for there is something revolting in the idea of a king holding a private purse; and the thoughts of Bigod were all regal. Thus furnished, by the very act of disfurnishment; getting rid of the cumbersome luggage of riches, more apt (as one sings)

> To slacken virtue, and abate her edge,
> Than prompt her to do aught may merit praise,

he set forth, like some Alexander, upon his great enterprise, "borrowing and to borrow!"

In his periegesis, or triumphant progress throughout this island, it has been calculated that he laid a tythe part of the inhabitants under contribution. I reject this estimate as greatly exaggerated: —but having had the honour of accompanying my friend, divers times, in his perambulations about this vast city, I own I was greatly struck at first with the prodigious number of faces we met, who claimed a sort of respectful acquaintance with us. He was one day so obliging as to explain the phenomenon. It seems, these were his tributaries; feeders of his exchequer; gentlemen, his good friends (as he was pleased to express himself), to whom he had occasionally been beholden for a loan. Their multitudes did no way disconcert him. He rather took a pride in numbering them; and, with Comus, seemed pleased to be "stocked with so fair a herd."

With such sources, it was a wonder how he contrived to keep his treasury always empty. He did it by force of an aphorism, which he had often in his mouth, that "money kept longer than three days stinks." So he made use of it while it was fresh. A good part he drank away (for he was an excellent toss-pot), some he gave away, the rest he threw away, literally tossing and hurling it violently from him—as boys do burrs, or as if it had been infectious,—into ponds, or ditches, or deep holes,—inscrutable cavities of the earth;—or he would bury it (where he would never seek it again) by a river's side under some bank, which (he would facetiously observe) paid no interest—but out away from him it must go peremptorily, as Hagar's offspring into the wilderness, while it was sweet. He never missed it. The streams were perennial which fed his fisc. When new supplies became necessary, the first person that had the felicity to fall in with him, friend or stranger, was sure to contribute to the deficiency. For Bigod had an *undeniable* way with him. He had a cheerful, open exterior, a quick jovial eye, a bald forehead, just touched with grey (*cana fides*). He anticipated no excuse, and found none. And, waiving for a while my theory as to the *great race*, I would put it to the most untheorising reader, who may at times have disposable coin in his pocket, whether it is not more repugnant to the kindliness of his nature to refuse such a one as I am describing, than to say *no* to a poor petitionary rogue (your bastard borrower), who, by his mumping visnomy, tells you, that he expects nothing better; and, therefore, whose preconceived notions and expectations you do in reality so much less shock in the refusal.

When I think of this man; his fiery glow of heart; his swell of feeling; how magnificent, how *ideal* he was; how great at the midnight hour; and when I compare with him the companions with whom I have associated since, I grudge the saving of a few idle ducats, and think that I am fallen into the society of *lenders*, and *little men*.

To one like Elia, whose treasures are rather cased in leather covers than closed in iron coffers, there is a class of alienators more formidable than that which I have touched upon; I mean your *borrowers of books*—those mutilators of collections, spoilers of the symmetry of shelves, and creators of odd volumes. There is Comberbatch, matchless in his depredations!

That foul gap in the bottom shelf facing you, like a great eye-tooth knocked out—(you are now with me in my little back study in Bloomsbury, reader!)——with the huge Switzer-like tomes on each side (like the Guildhall giants, in their reformed posture, guardant of nothing) once held the tallest of my folios, *Opera Bonaventuræ*, choice and massy divinity, to which its two supporters (school divinity also, but of a lesser calibre,—Bellarmine, and Holy Thomas), showed but as dwarfs,—itself an Ascapart!—*that* Comberbatch abstracted upon the faith of a theory he holds, which is more easy, I confess, for me to suffer by than to refute, namely, that "the title to property in a book (my Bonaventure, for instance), is in exact ratio to the claimant's powers of understanding and appreciating the same." Should he go on acting upon this theory, which of our shelves is safe?

The slight vacuum in the left-hand case—two shelves from the ceiling—scarcely distinguishable but by the quick eye of a loser—was whilom the commodious resting-place of Brown on Urn Burial. C. will hardly allege that he knows more about that treatise than I do, who introduced it to him, and was indeed the first (of the moderns) to discover its beauties—but so have I known a foolish lover to praise his mistress in the presence of a rival more qualified to carry her off than himself.—Just below, Dodsley's dramas want their fourth volume, where Vittoria Corombona is! The remainder nine are as distasteful as Priam's refuse sons, when the Fates *borrowed* Hector. Here stood the Anatomy of Melancholy, in sober state.—There loitered the Complete Angler; quiet as in life, by some stream side.—In yonder nook, John Buncle, a widower-volume, with " eyes closed," mourns his ravished mate.

One justice I must do my friend, that if he sometimes, like the sea, sweeps away a treasure, at another time, sea-like, he throws up as rich an equivalent to match it. I have a small under-collection of this nature (my friend's gatherings in his various calls), picked up, he has forgotten at what odd places, and deposited with as little memory as mine. I take in these orphans, the twice-deserted. These proselytes of the gate are welcome as the true Hebrews. There they stand in conjunction; natives, and naturalised. The latter seem as little disposed to inquire out their true lineage as I am.—I charge no warehouse-room for these deodands, nor shall ever put myself to the ungentlemanly trouble of advertising a sale of them to pay expenses.

To lose a volume to C. carries some sense and meaning in it. You are sure that he will make one hearty meal on your viands, if he can give no account of the platter after it. But what moved thee, wayward, spiteful K., to be so importunate to carry off with thee, in spite of tears and adjurations to thee to forbear, the Letters of that princely woman, the thrice noble Margaret New-castle?—knowing at the time, and knowing that I knew also, thou most assuredly wouldst never turn over one leaf of the illustrious folio:—what but the mere spirit of contradiction, and childish love of getting the better of thy friend?—Then, worst cut of all! to transport it with thee to the Gallican land—

> Unworthy land to harbour such a sweetness,
> A virtue in which all ennobling thoughts dwelt,
> Pure thoughts, kind thoughts, high thoughts, her sex's wonder!

——hadst thou not thy play-books, and books of jests and fancies, about thee, to keep thee merry, even as thou keepest all companies with thy quips and mirthful tales?—Child of the Green-room, it was unkindly done of thee. Thy wife, too, that part-French, better-part Englishwoman!—that *she* could fix upon no other treatise to bear away, in kindly token of remembering us, than the works of Fulke Greville, Lord Brook—of which no Frenchman, nor woman of France, Italy, or England, was ever by nature constituted to comprehend a tittle! *Was there not Zimmerman on Solitude?*

Reader, if haply thou art blessed with a moderate collection, be shy of showing it; or if thy heart overfloweth to lend them, lend thy books; but let it be to such a one as S. T. C.—he will return them (generally anticipating the time appointed) with usury; enriched with annotations, tripling their value. I have had ex-perience. Many are these precious MSS. of his — (in *matter* oftentimes, and almost in *quantity* not unfrequently, vying with the originals)—in no very clerkly hand—legible in my Daniel; in old Burton; in Sir Thomas Browne; and those abstruser cogitations of the Greville, now, alas! wandering in Pagan lands.—I counsel thee, shut not thy heart, nor thy library, against S. T. C.

NEW YEAR'S EVE

E VERY man hath two birth-days: two days, at least, in every year, which set him upon revolving the lapse of time, as it affects his mortal duration. The one is that which in an especial manner he termeth *his*. In the gradual desuetude of old observances, this custom of solemnizing our proper birth-day hath nearly passed away, or is left to children, who reflect nothing at all about the matter, nor understand any thing in it beyond cake and orange. But the birth of a New Year is of an interest too wide to be pretermitted by king or cobbler. No one ever regarded the First of January with indifference. It is that from which all date their time, and count upon what is left. It is the nativity of our common Adam.

Of all sounds of all bells—(bells, the music nighest bordering upon heaven)—most solemn and touching is the peal which rings out the Old Year. I never hear it without a gathering-up of my mind to a concentration of all the images that have been diffused over the past twelvemonth; all I have done or suffered, performed or neglected—in that regretted time. I begin to know its worth, as when a person dies. It takes a personal colour; nor was it a poetical flight in a contemporary, when he exclaimed

> I saw the skirts of the departing Year.

It is no more than what in sober sadness every one of us seems to be conscious of, in that awful leave-taking. I am sure I felt it, and all felt it with me, last night; though some of my companions affected rather to ᴧmanifest an exhilaration at the birth of the coming year, than any very tender regrets for the decease of its predecessor. But I am none of those who—

> Welcome the coming, speed the parting guest.

I am naturally, beforehand, shy of novelties; new books, new faces, new years,—from some mental twist which makes it difficult in me to face the prospective. I have almost ceased to hope; and am sanguine only in the prospects of other (former) years. I plunge into foregone visions and conclusions. I encounter pell-mell with past disappointments. I am armour-proof against old discouragements. I forgive, or overcome in fancy, old adversaries. I play over again *for love*, as the gamesters phrase it, games, for which I once paid so dear. I would scarce now have any of those untoward accidents and events of my life reversed. I would no more alter them than the incidents of some well-contrived novel. Methinks, it is better that I should have pined away seven of my goldenest years, when I was thrall to the fair hair, and fairer eyes, of Alice W——n, than that so passionate a love-adventure should be lost. It was better that our family should have missed that legacy, which old Dorrell cheated us of, than that I should have at this moment two thousand pounds *in banco*, and be without the idea of that specious old rogue.

In a degree beneath manhood, it is my infirmity to look back upon those early days. Do I advance a paradox, when I say, that, skipping over the intervention of forty years, a man may have leave to love *himself*, without the imputation of self-love?

If I know aught of myself, no one whose mind is introspective—and mine is painfully so—can have a less respect for his present identity, than I have for the man Elia. I know him to be light, and vain, and humorsome; a notorious * * *; addicted to * * * *: averse from counsel, neither taking it, nor offering it; —* * * besides; a stammering buffoon; what you will; lay it on, and spare not; I subscribe to it all, and much more, than thou canst be willing to lay at his door — — — but for the child Elia—that " other me," there, in the back-ground—I must take leave to cherish the remembrance of that young master—with as little reference, I protest, to this stupid changeling of five-and-forty, as if it had been a child of some other house, and not of my parents. I can cry over its patient small-pox at five, and rougher medicaments. I can lay its poor fevered head upon the sick pillow at Christ's, and wake with it in surprise at the gentle posture of maternal tenderness hanging over it, that unknown had watched its sleep. I know how it shrank from any the least colour of falsehood.—God help thee, Elia, how art thou changed! Thou art sophisticated.—I know how honest, how courageous (for a weakling) it was—how religious, how imaginative, how hopeful! From what have I not fallen, if the child I remember was indeed myself,—and not some dissembling guardian, presenting a false identity, to give the rule to my unpractised steps, and regulate the tone of my moral being!

That I am fond of indulging, beyond a hope of sympathy, in such retrospection, may be the symptom of some sickly idiosyncrasy. Or is it owing to another cause; simply, that being without wife or family, I have not learned to project myself enough out of myself; and having no offspring of my own to dally with, I turn back upon memory, and adopt my own early idea, as my heir and favourite? If these speculations seem fantastical to thee, reader—(a busy man, perchance), if I tread out of the way of thy sympathy, and am singularly-conceited only, I retire, impenetrable to ridicule, under the phantom cloud of Elia.

The elders, with whom I was brought up, were of a character not likely to let slip the sacred observance of any old institution; and the ringing out of the Old Year was kept by them with circumstances of peculiar ceremony.—In those days the sound of those midnight chimes, though it seemed to raise hilarity in all around me, never failed to bring a train of pensive imagery into my fancy. Yet I then scarce conceived what it meant, or thought of it as a reckoning that concerned me. Not childhood alone, but the young man till thirty, never feels practically that he is mortal. He knows it indeed, and, if need were, he could preach a homily on the fragility of life; but he brings it not home to himself, any more than in a hot June we can appropriate to our imagination the freezing days of December. But now, shall I confess a truth?—I feel these audits but too powerfully. I begin to count the probabilities of my duration, and to grudge at the expenditure of moments and shortest periods, like miser's farthings. In proportion as the years both lessen and shorten, I set more count upon their periods, and would fain lay my ineffectual finger upon the spoke of the great wheel. I am not content to pass away "like a weaver's shuttle." Those metaphors solace me not, nor sweeten the unpalatable draught of mortality. I care not to be carried with the tide, that smoothly bears human life to eternity; and reluct at the inevitable course of destiny. I am in love with this green earth; the face of town and country; the unspeakable rural solitudes, and the sweet security of streets. I would set up my tabernacle here. I am content to stand still at the age to which I am arrived; I, and my friends: to be no younger, no richer, no handsomer. I do not want to be weaned by age; or drop, like mellow fruit, as they say, into the grave.—Any alteration, on this earth of mine, in diet or in lodging, puzzles and discomposes me. My household-gods plant a terrible fixed foot, and are not rooted up without blood. They do not willingly seek Lavinian shores. A new state of being staggers me.

Sun, and sky, and breeze, and solitary walks, and summer holidays, and the greenness of fields, and the delicious juices of meats and fishes, and society, and the cheerful glass, and candle-light, and fire-side conversations, and innocent vanities, and jests, and *irony itself*—do these things go out with life?

Can a ghost laugh, or shake his gaunt sides, when you are pleasant with him ?

And you, my midnight darlings, my Folios ! must I part with the intense delight of having you (huge armfuls) in my embraces ? Must knowledge come to me, if it come at all, by some awkward experiment of intuition, and no longer by this familiar process of reading ?

Shall I enjoy friendships there, wanting the smiling indications which point me to them here,—the recognisable face—the " sweet assurance of a look "— ?

In winter this intolerable disinclination to dying—to give it its mildest name—does more especially haunt and beset me. In a genial August noon, beneath a sweltering sky, death is almost problematic. At those times do such poor snakes as myself enjoy an immortality. Then we expand and burgeon. Then are we as strong again, as valiant again, as wise again, and a great deal taller. The blast that nips and shrinks me, puts me in thoughts of death. All things allied to the insubstantial, wait upon that master feeling ; cold, numbness, dreams, perplexity ; moonlight itself, with its shadowy and spectral appearances,—that cold ghost of the sun, or Phœbus' sickly sister, like that innutritious one denounced in the Canticles :—I am none of her minions—I hold with the Persian.

Whatsoever thwarts, or puts me out of my way, brings death into my mind. All partial evils, like humours, run into that capital plague-sore.—I have heard some profess an indifference to life. Such hail the end of their existence as a port of refuge ; and speak of the grave as of some soft arms, in which they may slumber as on a pillow. Some have wooed death — — — but out upon thee, I say, thou foul, ugly phantom ! I detest, abhor, execrate, and (with Friar John) give thee to six-score thousand devils, as in no instance to be excused or tolerated, but shunned as a universal viper ; to be branded, proscribed, and spoken evil of ! In no way can I be brought to digest thee, thou thin, melancholy *Privation*, or more frightful and confounding *Positive !*

Those antidotes, prescribed against the fear of thee, are altogether frigid and insulting, like thyself. For what satisfaction hath a man, that he shall " lie down with kings and emperors in death," who in his life-time never greatly coveted the society of such bed-fellows ?—or, forsooth, that " so shall the fairest face appear ? "—why, to comfort me, must Alice W——n be a goblin ? More than all, I conceive disgust at those impertinent and misbecoming familiarities, inscribed upon your ordinary tombstones. Every dead man must take upon himself to be lecturing me with his odious truism, that " such as he now is, I must shortly be."

Not so shortly, friend, perhaps, as thou imaginest. In the meantime I am alive. I move about. I am worth twenty of thee. Know thy betters! Thy New Years' Days are past. I survive, a jolly candidate for 1821. Another cup of wine—and while that turn-coat bell, that just now mournfully chanted the obsequies of 1820 departed, with changed notes lustily rings in a successor, let us attune to its peal the song made on a like occasion, by hearty, cheerful Mr. Cotton.—

THE NEW YEAR.

HARK, the cock crows, and yon bright star
Tells us, the day himself's not far;
And see where, breaking from the night,
He gilds the western hills with light.
With him old Janus doth appear,
Peeping into the future year,
With such a look as seems to say,
The prospect is not good that way.
Thus do we rise ill sights to see,
And 'gainst ourselves to prophesy;
When the prophetic fear of things
A more tormenting mischief brings,
More full of soul-tormenting gall,
Than direst mischiefs can befall.
But stay! but stay! methinks my sight,
Better inform'd by clearer light,
Discerns sereneness in that brow,
That all contracted seem'd but now.
His revers'd face may show distaste,
And frown upon the ills are past;
But that which this way looks is clear,
And smiles upon the New-born Year.
He looks too from a place so high,
The Year lies open to his eye;
And all the moments open are
To the exact discoverer.
Yet more and more he smiles upon
The happy revolution.
Why should we then suspect or fear
The influences of a year,
So smiles upon us the first morn,
And speaks us good so soon as born?
Plague on't! the last was ill enough,
This cannot but make better proof;
Or, at the worst, as we brush'd through
The last, why so we may this too;
And then the next in reason shou'd
Be superexcellently good:
For the worst ills (we daily see)
Have no more perpetuity,
Than the best fortunes that do fall;
Which also bring us wherewithal
Longer their being to support,
Than those do of the other sort:
And who has one good year in three,
And yet repines at destiny,

Appears ungrateful in the case,
And merits not the good he has.
Then let us welcome the New Guest
With lusty brimmers of the best;
Mirth always should Good Fortune meet,
And renders e'en Disaster sweet:
And though the Princess turn her back,
Let us but line ourselves with sack,
We better shall by far hold out,
Till the next Year she face about.

How say you, reader—do not these verses smack of the rough
magnanimity of the old English vein? Do they not fortify like a
cordial; enlarging the heart, and productive of sweet blood, and
generous spirits, in the concoction? Where be those puling fears
of death, just now expressed or affected?—Passed like a cloud—
absorbed in the purging sunlight of clear poetry—clean washed
away by a wave of genuine Helicon, your only Spa for these
hypochondries—And now another cup of the generous! and a
merry New Year, and many of them, to you all, my masters!

MRS. BATTLE'S OPINIONS ON WHIST.

" A CLEAR fire, a clean hearth, and the rigour of the game."
This was the celebrated *wish* of old Sarah Battle (now
with God) who, next to her devotions, loved a good game at whist.
She was none of your lukewarm gamesters, your half and half
players, who have no objection to take a hand, if you want one to
make up a rubber; who affirm that they have no pleasure in winning; that they like to win one game, and lose another; that they
can while away an hour very agreeably at a card-table, but are
indifferent whether they play or no; and will desire an adversary,
who has slipt a wrong card, to take it up and play another. These
insufferable triflers are the curse of a table. One of these flies will
spoil a whole pot. Of such it may be said, that they do not play
at cards, but only play at playing at them.

Sarah Battle was none of that breed. She detested them, as I
do, from her heart and soul; and would not, save upon a striking
emergency, willingly seat herself at the same table with them. She
loved a thorough-paced partner, a determined enemy. She took,
and gave, no concessions. She hated favours. She never made a
revoke, nor ever passed it over in her adversary without exacting
the utmost forfeiture. She fought a good fight: cut and thrust.

She held not her good sword (her cards) "like a dancer." She sate bolt upright; and neither showed you her cards, nor desired to see yours. All people have their blind side—their superstitions; and I have heard her declare, under the rose, that Hearts was her favourite suit.

I never in my life—and I knew Sarah Battle many of the best years of it—saw her take out her snuff-box when it was her turn to play; or snuff a candle in the middle of a game; or ring for a servant, till it was fairly over. She never introduced, or connived at, miscellaneous conversation during its process. As she emphatic-ally observed, cards were cards: and if I ever saw unmingled distaste in her fine last-century countenance, it was at the airs of a young gentleman of a literary turn, who had been with difficulty persuaded to take a hand; and who, in his excess of candour, declared, that he thought there was no harm in unbending the mind now and then, after serious studies, in recreations of that kind! She could not bear to have her noble occupation, to which she wound up her faculties, considered in that light. It was her business, her duty, the thing she came into the world to do,—and she did it. She unbent her mind afterwards—over a book.

Pope was her favourite author: his Rape of the Lock her favour-ite work. She once did me the favour to play over with me (with the cards) his celebrated game of Ombre in that poem; and to explain to me how far it agreed with, and in what points it would be found to differ from, tradrille. Her illustrations were apposite and poignant; and I had the pleasure of sending the substance of them to Mr. Bowles: but I suppose they came too late to be in-serted among his ingenious notes upon that author.

Quadrille, she has often told me, was her first love; but whist had engaged her maturer esteem. The former, she said, was showy and specious, and likely to allure young persons. The uncertainty and quick shifting of partners—a thing which the constancy of whist abhors;—the dazzling supremacy and regal investiture of Spadille—absurd, as she justly observed, in the pure aristocrasy of whist, where his crown and garter give him no proper power above his brother-nobility of the Aces;—the giddy vanity, so taking to the inexperienced, of playing alone:—above all, the overpowering attractions of a *Sans Prendre Vole*,—to the triumph of which there is certainly nothing parallel or approaching, in the contin-gencies of whist;—all these, she would say, make quadrille a game of captivation to the young and enthusiastic. But whist was the *solider* game: that was her word. It was a long meal; not, like quadrille, a feast of snatches. One or two rubbers might co-extend in duration with an evening. They gave time to form rooted friendships, to cultivate steady enmities. She despised the chance-

started, capricious, and ever fluctuating alliances of the other. The
skirmishes of quadrille, she would say, reminded her of the petty
ephemeral embroilments of the little Italian states, depicted by
Machiavel; perpetually changing postures and connexions; bitter
foes to-day, sugared darlings to-morrow; kissing and scratching in
a breath;—but the wars of whist were comparable to the long,
steady, deep-rooted, rational, antipathies of the great French and
English nations.

A grave simplicity was what she chiefly admired in her favourite
game. There was nothing silly in it, like the nob in cribbage—
nothing superfluous. No *flushes*—that most irrational of all pleas
that a reasonable being can set up:—that any one should claim
four by virtue of holding cards of the same mark and colour, without reference to the playing of the game, or the individual worth
or pretensions of the cards themselves! She held this to be a
solecism; as pitiful an ambition at cards as alliteration is in authorship. She despised superficiality, and looked deeper than the
colours of things.—Suits were soldiers, she would say, and must
have a uniformity of array to distinguish them: but what should
we say to a foolish squire, who should claim a merit from dressing
up his tenantry in red jackets, that never were to be marshalled—
never to take the field?—She even wished that whist were more
simple than it is; and, in my mind, would have stript it of some
appendages, which, in the state of human frailty, may be venially,
and even commendably allowed of. She saw no reason for the
deciding of the trump by the turn of the card. Why not one suit
always trumps?—Why two colours, when the mark of the suits
would have sufficiently distinguished them without it?—

"But the eye, my dear Madam, is agreeably refreshed with the
variety. Man is not a creature of pure reason—he must have his
senses delightfully appealed to. We see it in Roman Catholic
countries, where the music and the paintings draw in many to worship, whom your quaker spirit of unsensualizing would have kept
out.—You, yourself, have a pretty collection of paintings—but
confess to me, whether, walking in your gallery at Sandham,
among those clear Vandykes, or among the Paul Potters in the
ante-room, you ever felt your bosom glow with an elegant delight,
at all comparable to *that* you have it in your power to experience
most evenings over a well-arranged assortment of the court cards?
—the pretty antic habits, like heralds in a procession—the gay
triumph-assuring scarlets—the contrasting deadly-killing sables—
the 'hoary majesty of spades'—Pam in all his glory!—

"All these might be dispensed with; and, with their naked
names upon the drab pasteboard, the game might go on very well,
picture-less. But the *beauty* of cards would be extinguished for

ever. Stripped of all that is imaginative in them, they must degenerate into mere gambling.—Imagine a dull deal board, or drum head, to spread them on, instead of that nice verdant carpet (next to nature's), fittest arena for those courtly combatants to play their gallant jousts and turneys in!—Exchange those delicately-turned ivory markers—(work of Chinese artist, unconscious of their symbol,—or as profanely slighting their true application as the arrantest Ephesian journeyman that turned out those little shrines for the goddess)—exchange them for little bits of leather (our ancestors' money) or chalk and a slate!"—

The old lady, with a smile, confessed the soundness of my logic; and to her approbation of my arguments on her favourite topic that evening, I have always fancied myself indebted for the legacy of a curious cribbage board, made of the finest Sienna marble, which her maternal uncle (old Walter Plumer, whom I have elsewhere celebrated) brought with him from Florence:—this, and a trifle of five hundred pounds, came to me at her death.

The former bequest (which I do not least value) I have kept with religious care; though she herself, to confess a truth, was never greatly taken with cribbage. It was an essentially vulgar game, I have heard her say,—disputing with her uncle, who was very partial to it. She could never heartily bring her mouth to pronounce "go"—or "that's a go." She called it an ungrammatical game. The pegging teased her. I once knew her to forfeit a rubber (a five dollar stake), because she would not take advantage of the turn-up knave, which would have given it her, but which she must have claimed by the disgraceful tenure of declaring "two for his heels." There is something extremely genteel in this sort of self-denial. Sarah Battle was a gentlewoman born.

Piquet she held the best game at the cards for two persons, though she would ridicule the pedantry of the terms—such as pique—repique—the capot—they savoured (she thought) of affectation. But games for two, or even three, she never greatly cared for. She loved the quadrate, or square. She would argue thus:—Cards are warfare: the ends are gain, with glory. But cards are war, in disguise of a sport: when single adversaries encounter, the ends proposed are too palpable. By themselves, it is too close a fight; with spectators, it is not much bettered. No looker on can be interested, except for a bet, and then it is a mere affair of money; he cares not for your luck *sympathetically*, or for your play.— Three are still worse; a mere naked war of every man against every man, as in cribbage, without league or alliance; or a rotation of petty and contradictory interests, a succession of heartless leagues, and not much more hearty infractions of them, as in tradrille.—But in square games (*she meant whist*) all that is possible to be attained in card-playing is accomplished. There are the incentives of profit with honour, common to every species—though the *latter* can be but very imperfectly enjoyed in those other games, where the spectator is only feebly a participator. But the parties in whist are spectators and principals too. They are a theatre to themselves, and a looker-on is not wanted. He is rather worse than nothing, and an impertinence. Whist abhors neutrality, or interests beyond its sphere. You glory in some surprising stroke of skill or fortune, not because a cold—or even an interested—by-stander witnesses it, but because your *partner* sympathises in the contingency. You win for two. You triumph for two. Two are exalted. Two again are mortified; which divides their disgrace, as the conjunction doubles (by taking off the invidiousness) your glories. Two losing to two are better reconciled, than one to one in that close butchery. The hostile feeling is weakened by multiplying the channels. War becomes a civil game.—By such reasonings as these the old lady was accustomed to defend her favourite pastime.

No inducement could ever prevail upon her to play at any game, where chance entered into the composition, *for nothing.* Chance, she would argue—and here again, admire the subtlety of her conclusion!—chance is nothing, but where something else depends upon it. It is obvious, that cannot be *glory.* What rational cause of exultation could it give to a man to turn up size acea hundred times together by himself? or before spectators, where no stake was depending?—Make a lottery of a hundred thousand tickets with but one fortunate number—and what possible principle of our nature, except stupid wonderment, could it gratify to gain that number as many times successively, without a prize?—Therefore she disliked the mixture of chance in backgammon, where it was not played for money. She called it foolish, and those people idiots, who were taken with a lucky hit under such circumstances. Games of pure skill were as little to her fancy. Played for a stake, they were a mere system of over-reaching. Played for glory, they were a mere setting of one man's wit,—his memory, or combination-faculty rather—against another's; like a mock-engagement at a review, bloodless and profitless.—She could not conceive a *game* wanting the spritely infusion of chance,—the handsome excuses of good fortune. Two people playing at chess in a corner of a room, whilst whist was stirring in the centre, would inspire her with insufferable horror and ennui. Those well-cut similitudes of Castles, and Knights, the *imagery* of the board, she would argue, (and I think in this case justly) were entirely misplaced and senseless. Those hard head-contests can in no instance ally with the fancy. They reject form and colour. A pencil and dry slate (she used to say) were the proper arena for such combatants.

To those puny objectors against cards, as nurturing the bad passions, she would retort, that man is a gaming animal. He must be always trying to get the better in something or other :—that this passion can scarcely be more safely expended than upon a game at cards : that cards are a temporary illusion ; in truth, a mere drama ; for we do but *play* at being mightily concerned, where a few idle shillings are at stake, yet, during the illusion, we *are* as mightily concerned as those whose stake is crowns and kingdoms. They are a sort of dream-fighting ; much ado ; great battling, and little bloodshed ; mighty means for disproportioned ends ; quite as diverting, and a great deal more innoxious, than many of those more serious *games* of life, which men play, without esteeming them to be such.——

With great deference to the old lady's judgment on these matters, I think I have experienced some moments in my life, when playing at cards *for nothing* has even been agreeable. When I am in sickness, or not in the best spirits, I sometimes call for the cards, and play a game at piquet *for love* with my cousin Bridget—Bridget Elia.

I grant there is something sneaking in it ; but with a tooth-ache, or a sprained ancle,—when you are subdued and humble,—you are glad to put up with an inferior spring of action.

There is such a thing in nature, I am convinced, as *sick whist*.—

I grant it is not the highest style of man—I deprecate the manes of Sarah Battle—she lives not, alas ! to whom I should apologise.—

At such times, those *terms* which my old friend objected to, come in as something admissible.—I love to get a tierce or a quatorze, though they mean nothing. I am subdued to an inferior interest. Those shadows of winning amuse me.

That last game I had with my sweet cousin (I capotted her)— (dare I tell thee, how foolish I am ?)—I wished it might have lasted for ever, though we gained nothing, and lost nothing, though it was a mere shade of play : I would be content to go on in that idle folly for ever. The pipkin should be ever boiling, that was to prepare the gentle lenitive to my foot, which Bridget was doomed to apply after the game was over : and, as I do not much relish appliances, there it should ever bubble. Bridget and I should be ever playing.

A CHAPTER ON EARS.

I HAVE no ear.—

Mistake me not, reader,—nor imagine that I am by nature destitute of those exterior twin appendages, hanging ornaments, and (architecturally speaking) handsome volutes to the human capital. Better my mother had never borne me.—I am, I think, rather delicately than copiously provided with those conduits ; and I feel no disposition to envy the mule for his plenty, or the mole for her exactness, in those ingenious labyrinthine inlets—those indispensable side-intelligencers.

Neither have I incurred, or done any thing to incur, with Defoe, that hideous disfigurement, which constrained him to draw upon assurance—to feel "quite unabashed," and at ease upon that article. I was never, I thank my stars, in the pillory; nor, if I read them aright, is it within the compass of my destiny, that I ever should be.

When therefore I say that I have no ear, you will understand me to mean—*for music.*—To say that this heart never melted at the concourse of sweet sounds, would be a foul self-libel.—" *Water parted from the sea* " never fails to move it strangely. So does " *In Infancy.*" But they were used to be sung at her harpsichord (the old-fashioned instrument in vogue in those days) by a gentlewoman—the gentlest, sure, that ever merited the appellation—the sweetest—why should I hesitate to name Mrs. S——, once the blooming Fanny Weatheral of the Temple—who had power to thrill the soul of Elia, small imp as he was, even in his long coats ; and to make him glow, tremble, and blush with a passion, that not faintly indicated the day-spring of that absorbing sentiment, which was afterwards destined to overwhelm and subdue his nature quite, for Alice W——n.

I even think that *sentimentally* I am disposed to harmony. But *organically* I am incapable of a tune. I have been practising " *God save the King* " all my life ; whistling and humming of it over to myself in solitary corners ; and am not yet arrived, they tell me, within many quavers of it. Yet hath the loyalty of Elia never been impeached.

I am not without suspicion, that I have an undeveloped faculty of music within me. For, thrumming, in my wild way, on my friend A.'s piano, the other morning, while he was engaged in an adjoining parlour,—on his return he was pleased to say, " *he thought it could not be the maid !* " On his first surprise at hearing the keys touched in somewhat an airy and masterful way, not dreaming of me, his suspicions had lighted on *Jenny.* But a grace, snatched from a superior refinement, soon convinced him that some being,—technically perhaps deficient, but higher informed from a principle common to all the fine arts,—had swayed the keys to a mood which Jenny, with all her (less-cultivated) enthusiasm, could never have elicited from them. I mention this as a proof of my friend's penetration, and not with any view of disparaging Jenny.

Scientifically I could never be made to understand (yet have I taken some pains) what a note in music is ; or how one note should differ from another. Much less in voices can I distinguish a soprano from a tenor. Only sometimes the thorough bass I contrive to guess at, from its being supereminently harsh and disagreeable. I tremble, however, for my misapplication of the simplest terms of *that* which I disclaim. While I profess my ignorance, I scarce know what to *say* I am ignorant of. I hate, perhaps, by misnomers. *Sostenuto* and *adagio* stand in the like relation of obscurity to me ; and *Sol, Fa, Mi, Re,* is as conjuring as *Baralipton.*

It is hard to stand alone—in an age like this,—(constituted to the quick and critical perception of all harmonious combinations, I verily believe, beyond all preceding ages, since Jubal stumbled upon the gamut)—to remain, as it were, singly unimpressible to the magic influences of an art, which is said to have such an especial stroke at soothing, elevating, and refining the passions.—Yet rather than break the candid current of my confessions, I must avow to you, that I have received a great deal more pain than pleasure from this so cried-up faculty.

I am constitutionally susceptible of noises. A carpenter's hammer, in a warm summer noon, will fret me into more than midsummer madness. But those unconnected, unset sounds are nothing to the measured malice of music. The ear is passive to those single strokes ; willingly enduring stripes, while it hath no task to con. To music it cannot be passive. It will strive—mine at least will—'spite of its inaptitude, to thrid the maze ; like an unskilled eye painfully poring upon hieroglyphics. I have sat through an Italian Opera, till, for sheer pain, and inexplicable anguish, I have rushed out into the noisiest places of the crowded streets, to solace myself with sounds, which I was not obliged to follow, and get rid of the distracting torment of endless, fruitless, barren attention ! I take refuge in the unpretending assemblage of honest common-life sounds ;—and the purgatory of the Enraged Musician becomes my paradise.

I have sat at an Oratorio (that profanation of the purposes of the cheerful playhouse) watching the faces of the auditory in the pit (what a contrast to Hogarth's Laughing Audience !) immoveable, or affecting some faint emotion,—till (as some have said, that our occupations in the next world will be but a shadow of what delighted us in this) I have imagined myself in some cold Theatre in Hades, where some of the *forms* of the earthly one should be kept up, with none of the *enjoyment ;* or like that—

————Party in a parlour,
All silent, and all DAMNED !

Above all, those insufferable concertos, and pieces of music, as they are called, do plague and embitter my apprehension.—Words are something ; but to be exposed to an endless battery of mere sounds ; to be long a dying, to lie stretched upon a rack of roses ; to keep up languor by unintermitted effort ; to pile honey upon sugar, and sugar upon honey, to an interminable tedious sweetness ; to fill up sound with feeling, and strain ideas to keep pace with it ; to gaze on empty frames, and be forced to make the pictures for yourself ; to read a book, *all stops*, and be obliged to supply the verbal matter ; to invent extempore tragedies to answer to the vague gestures of an inexplicable rambling mime—these are faint shadows of what I have undergone from a series of the ablest-executed pieces of this empty *instrumental music*.

I deny not, that in the opening of a concert, I have experienced something vastly lulling and agreeable :—afterwards followeth the languor, and the oppression. Like that disappointing book in Patmos ; or, like the comings on of melancholy, described by Burton, doth music make her first insinuating approaches :—" Most pleasant it is to such as are melancholy given, to walk alone in some solitary grove, betwixt wood and water, by some brook side, and to meditate upon some delightsome and pleasant subject, which shall affect him most, *amabilis insania,* and *mentis gratissimus error.* A most incomparable delight to build castles in the air, to go smiling to themselves, acting an infinite variety of parts, which they suppose, and strongly imagine, they act, or that they see done.—So delightsome these toys at first, they could spend whole days and nights without sleep, even whole years in such contemplations, and fantastical meditations, which are like so many dreams, and will hardly be drawn from them—winding and unwinding themselves as so many clocks, and still pleasing their humours, until at last the SCENE TURNS UPON A SUDDEN, and they being now habitated to such meditations and solitary places, can endure no company, can think of nothing but harsh and distasteful subjects. Fear, sorrow, suspicion, *subrusticus pudor,* discontent, cares, and weariness of life, surprise them on a sudden, and they can think of nothing else : continually suspecting, no sooner are their eyes open, but this infernal plague of melancholy seizeth on them, and terrifies their souls, representing some dismal object to their minds ; which now, by no means, no labour, no persuasions they can avoid, they cannot be rid of it, they cannot resist."

Something like this "SCENE-TURNING" I have experienced at the evening parties, at the house of my good Catholic friend *Nov*——; who, by the aid of a capital organ, himself the most finished of players, converts his drawing-room into a chapel, his week days into Sundays, and these latter into minor heavens.[1]

When my friend commences upon one of those solemn anthems, which peradventure struck upon my heedless ear, rambling in the side aisles of the dim abbey, some five and thirty years since, waking a new sense, and putting a soul of old religion into my young apprehension—(whether it be *that*, in which the psalmist, weary of the persecutions of bad men, wisheth to himself dove's wings—or *that other*, which, with a like measure of sobriety and pathos, inquireth by what means the young man shall best cleanse his mind) —a holy calm pervadeth me.—I am for the time

——rapt above earth,
And possess joys not promised at my birth.

But when this master of the spell, not content to have laid a soul prostrate, goes on, in his power, to inflict more bliss than lies in her capacity to receive,—impatient to overcome her " earthly " with his " heavenly,"—still pouring in, for protracted hours, fresh waves and fresh from the sea of sound, or from that inexhausted *German* ocean, above which, in triumphant progress, dolphin-seated, ride those Arions *Haydn* and *Mozart*, with their attendant tritons, *Bach*, *Beethoven*, and a countless tribe, whom to attempt to reckon up would but plunge me again in the deeps,—I stagger under the weight of harmony, reeling to and fro at my wit's end ;—clouds, as of frankincense, oppress me—priests, altars, censers, dazzle before me—the genius of *his* religion hath me in her toils—a shadowy triple tiara invests the brow of my friend, late so naked, so in-genuous—he is Pope,—and by him sits, like as in the anomaly of dreams, a she-Pope too,—tri-coroneted like himself !—I am con-verted, and yet a Protestant ;—at once *malleus hereticorum*, and myself grand heresiarch : or three heresies centre in my person :—I am Marcion, Ebion, and Cerinthus—Gog and Magog—what not ? —till the coming in of the friendly supper-tray dissipates the fig-ment, and a draught of true Lutheran beer (in which chiefly my friend shows himself no bigot) at once reconciles me to the rational-ities of a purer faith ; and restores to me the genuine unterrifying aspects of my pleasant-countenanced host and hostess.

[1] I have been there, and still would go ;
'Tis like a little heaven below.—*Dr. Watts.*

ALL FOOLS' DAY.

THE compliments of the season to my worthy masters, and a merry first of April to us all!

Many happy returns of this day to you—and you—and *you*, Sir —nay, never frown, man, nor put a long face upon the matter. Do not we know one another? what need of ceremony among friends? we have all a touch of *that same*—you understand me —a speck of the motley. Beshrew the man who on such a day as this, the *general festival*, should affect to stand aloof. I am none of those sneakers. I am free of the corporation, and care not who knows it. He that meets me in the forest to-day, shall meet with no wise-acre, I can tell him. *Stultus sum.* Translate me that, and take the meaning of it to yourself for your pains. What, man, we have four quarters of the globe on our side, at the least computation.

Fill us a cup of that sparkling gooseberry—we will drink no wise, melancholy, politic port on this day—and let us troll the catch of Amiens—*duc ad me—duc ad me*—how goes it?

> Here shall he see
> Gross fools as he.

Now would I give a trifle to know historically and authentically, who was the greatest fool that ever lived. I would certainly give him in a bumper. Marry, of the present breed, I think I could without much difficulty name you the party.

Remove your cap a little further, if you please; it hides my bauble. And now each man bestride his hobby, and dust away his bells to what tune he pleases. I will give you, for my part,

> ———The crazy old church clock,
> And the bewildered chimes.

Good master Empedocles, you are welcome. It is long since you went a salamander-gathering down Ætna. Worse than samphire-picking by some odds. 'Tis a mercy your worship did not singe your mustachios.

Ha! Cleombrotus! and what salads in faith did you light upon at the bottom of the Mediterranean? You were founder, I take it, of the disinterested sect of the Calenturists.

Gebir, my old free-mason, and prince of plasterers at Babel, bring in your trowel, most Ancient Grand! You have claim to a seat here at my right hand, as patron of the stammerers. You left your work, if I remember Herodotus correctly, at eight hundred million toises, or thereabout, above the level of the sea. Bless us, what a

long bell you must have pulled, to call your top workmen to their
nuncheon on the low grounds of Sennaar. Or did you send up
your garlick and onions by a rocket? I am a rogue if I am not
ashamed to show you our Monument on Fish-street Hill, after your
altitudes. Yet we think it somewhat.

What, the magnanimous Alexander in tears?—cry, baby, put its
finger in its eye, it shall have another globe, round as an orange,
pretty moppet!

Mister Adams——'odso, I honour your coat—pray do us the
favour to read to us that sermon, which you lent to Mistress
Slipslop—the twenty and second in your portmanteau there—on
Female Incontinence—the same—it will come in most irrelevantly
and impertinently seasonable to the time of the day.

Good Master Raymund Lully, you look wise. Pray correct that
error.——

Duns, spare your definitions. I must fine you a bumper, or a
paradox. We will have nothing said or done syllogistically this
day. Remove those logical forms, waiter, that no gentleman break
the tender shins of his apprehension stumbling across them.

Master Stephen, you are late.—Ha! Cokes, is it you?—Aguecheek, my dear knight, let me pay my devoir to you.—Master
Shallow, your worship's poor servant to command.—Master Silence,
I will use few words with you.—Slender, it shall go hard if I edge
not you in somewhere.—You six will engross all the poor wit of
the company to-day.—I know it, I know it.

Ha! honest R——, my fine old Librarian of Ludgate, time out
of mind, art thou here again? Bless thy doublet, it is not over-
new, threadbare as thy stories:—what dost thou flitting about the
world at this rate?—Thy customers are extinct, defunct, bed-rid,
have ceased to read long ago.—Thou goest still among them, seeing
if, peradventure, thou canst hawk a volume or two.—Good Granville S——, thy last patron, is flown.

> King Pandion, he is dead,
> All thy friends are lapt in lead.—

Nevertheless, noble R——, come in, and take your seat here,
between Armado and Quisada: for in true courtesy, in gravity, in
fantastic smiling to thyself, in courteous smiling upon others, in
the goodly ornature of well-apparelled speech, and the commendation of wise sentences, thou art nothing inferior to those accomplished Dons of Spain. The spirit of chivalry forsake me for ever,
when I forget thy singing the song of Macheath, which declares
that he might be *happy with either*, situated between those two
ancient spinsters—when I forget the inimitable formal love which
thou didst make, turning now to the one, and now to the other,

with that Malvolian smile—as if Cervantes, not Gay, had written it for his hero ; and as if thousands of periods must revolve, before the mirror of courtesy could have given his invidious preference between a pair of so goodly-propertied and meritorious-equal damsels.   *   *   *   *   *

To descend from these altitudes, and not to protract our Fools' Banquet beyond its appropriate day,—for I fear the second of April is not many hours distant—in sober verity I will confess a truth to thee, reader.   I love a *Fool*—as naturally, as if I were of kith and kin to him.   When a child, with child-like apprehensions, that dived not below the surface of the matter, I read those *Parables*—not guessing at their involved wisdom—I had more yearnings towards that simple architect, that built his house upon the sand, than I entertained for his more cautious neighbour ; I grudged at the hard censure pronounced upon the quiet soul that kept his talent ; and—prizing their simplicity beyond the more provident, and, to my apprehension, somewhat *unfeminine* wariness of their competitors—I felt a kindliness, that almost amounted to a *tendre*, for those five thoughtless virgins.—I have never made an acquaintance since, that lasted ; or a friendship, that answered ; with any that had not some tincture of the absurd in their characters.   I venerate an honest obliquity of understanding.   The more laughable blunders a man shall commit in your company, the more tests he giveth you, that he will not betray or overreach you.   I love the safety, which a palpable hallucination warrants ; the security, which a word out of season ratifies.   And take my word for this, reader, and say a fool told it you, if you please, that he who hath not a dram of folly in his mixture, hath pounds of much worse matter in his composition.   It is observed, that " the foolisher the fowl or fish,—woodcocks,—dotterels,—cod's-heads, &c. the finer the flesh thereof," and what are commonly the world's received fools, but such whereof the world is not worthy ? and what have been some of the kindliest patterns of our species, but so many darlings of absurdity, minions of the goddess, and her white boys ? —Reader, if you wrest my words beyond their fair construction, it is you, and not I, that are the *April Fool*.

A QUAKER'S MEETING.

Still-born Silence! thou that art
Flood-gate of the deeper heart!
Offspring of a heavenly kind!
Frost o' the mouth, and thaw o' the mind!
Secrecy's confident, and he
Who makes religion mystery!
Admiration's speaking'st tongue!
Leave, thy desert shades among,
Reverend hermits' hallowed cells,
Where retired devotion dwells!
With thy enthusiasms come,
Seize our tongues, and strike us dumb! [1]

READER, would'st thou know what true peace and quiet mean; would'st thou find a refuge from the noises and clamours of the multitude; would'st thou enjoy at once solitude and society; would'st thou possess the depth of thy own spirit in stillness, without being shut out from the consolatory faces of thy species; would'st thou be alone, and yet accompanied; solitary, yet not desolate; singular, yet not without some to keep thee in countenance; a unit in aggregate; a simple in composite :—come with me into a Quaker's Meeting.

Dost thou love silence deep as that "before the winds were made?" go not out into the wilderness, descend not into the profundities of the earth; shut not up thy casements; nor pour wax into the little cells of thy ears, with little-faith'd self-mistrusting Ulysses.—Retire with me into a Quaker's Meeting.

For a man to refrain even from good words, and to hold his peace, it is commendable; but for a multitude, it is great mastery.

What is the stillness of the desert, compared with this place? what the uncommunicating muteness of fishes?—here the goddess reigns and revels.—"Boreas, and Cesias, and Argestes loud," do not with their inter-confounding uproars more augment the brawl —nor the waves of the blown Baltic with their clubbed sounds— than their opposite (Silence her sacred self) is multiplied and rendered more intense by numbers, and by sympathy. She too hath her deeps, that call unto deeps. Negation itself hath a positive more and less; and closed eyes would seem to obscure the great obscurity of midnight.

There are wounds, which an imperfect solitude cannot heal. By imperfect I mean that which a man enjoyeth by himself. The perfect is that which he can sometimes attain in crowds, but nowhere so absolutely as in a Quaker's Meeting.—Those first hermits

[1] From "Poems of all sorts," by Richard Fleckno, 1653.

did certainly understand this principle, when they retired into Egyptian solitudes, not singly, but in shoals, to enjoy one another's want of conversation. The Carthusian is bound to his brethren by this agreeing spirit of incommunicativeness. In secular occasions, what so pleasant as to be reading a book through a long winter evening, with a friend sitting by—say, a wife—he, or she, too, (if that be probable), reading another, without interruption, or oral communication ?—can there be no sympathy without the gabble of words ?—away with this inhuman, shy, single, shade-and-cavern-haunting solitariness. Give me, Master Zimmerman, a sympathetic solitude.

To pace alone in the cloisters, or side aisles of some cathedral, time-stricken ;

> Or under hanging mountains,
> Or by the fall of fountains ;

is but a vulgar luxury, compared with that which those enjoy, who come together for the purposes of more complete, abstracted solitude. This is the loneliness " to be felt."—The Abbey Church of Westminster hath nothing so solemn, so spirit-soothing, as the naked walls and benches of a Quaker's Meeting. Here are no tombs, no inscriptions,

> ————sands, ignoble things,
> Dropt from the ruined sides of kings—

but here is something, which throws Antiquity herself into the fore-ground—SILENCE—eldest of things—language of old Night—primitive Discourser—to which the insolent decays of mouldering grandeur have but arrived by a violent, and, as we may say, un-natural progression.

> How reverend is the view of these hushed heads,
> Looking tranquillity !

Nothing-plotting, nought-caballing, unmischievous synod ! convocation without intrigue ! parliament without debate ! what a lesson dost thou read to council, and to consistory !—if my pen treat of you lightly—as haply it will wander—yet my spirit hath gravely felt the wisdom of your custom, when sitting among you in deepest peace, which some out-welling tears would rather confirm than disturb, I have reverted to the times of your beginnings, and the sowings of the seed by Fox and Dewesbury.—I have witnessed that, which brought before my eyes your heroic tranquillity, inflexible to the rude jests and serious violences of the insolent soldiery, republican or royalist, sent to molest you—for ye sate betwixt the fires of two persecutions, the out-cast and off-scowering of church and presbytery.—I have seen the reeling sea-ruffian, who had wandered into your receptacle, with the avowed intention of disturbing your quiet, from the very spirit of the place receive in a moment a new heart, and presently sit among ye as a lamb amidst lambs. And I remembered Penn before his accusers, and Fox in the bail-dock, where he was lifted up in spirit, as he tells us, and "the Judge and the Jury became as dead men under his feet."

Reader, if you are not acquainted with it, I would recommend to you, above all church-narratives, to read Sewel's History of the Quakers. It is in folio, and is the abstract of the journals of Fox, and the primitive Friends. It is far more edifying and affecting than any thing you will read of Wesley and his colleagues. Here is nothing to stagger you, nothing to make you mistrust, no suspicion of alloy, no drop or dreg of the worldly or ambitious spirit. You will here read the true story of that much-injured, ridiculed man (who perhaps hath been a by-word in your mouth,)—James Naylor: what dreadful sufferings, with what patience, he endured even to the boring through of his tongue with red-hot irons without a murmur; and with what strength of mind, when the delusion he had fallen into, which they stigmatised for blasphemy, had given way to clearer thoughts, he could renounce his error, in a strain of the beautifullest humility, yet keep his first grounds, and be a Quaker still!—so different from the practice of your common converts from enthusiasm, who, when they apostatize, *apostatize all*, and think they can never get far enough from the society of their former errors, even to the renunciation of some saving truths, with which they had been mingled, not implicated.

Get the Writings of John Woolman by heart; and love the early Quakers.

How far the followers of these good men in our days have kept to the primitive spirit, or in what proportion they have substituted formality for it, the Judge of Spirits can alone determine. I have seen faces in their assemblies, upon which the dove sate visibly brooding. Others again I have watched, when my thoughts should have been better engaged, in which I could possibly detect nothing but a blank inanity. But quiet was in all, and the disposition to unanimity, and the absence of the fierce controversial workings.— If the spiritual pretensions of the Quakers have abated, at least they make few pretences. Hypocrites they certainly are not, in their preaching. It is seldom indeed that you shall see one get up amongst them to hold forth. Only now and then a trembling, female, generally *ancient*, voice is heard—you cannot guess from what part of the meeting it proceeds—with a low, buzzing, musical sound, laying out a few words which "she thought might suit the condition of some present," with a quaking diffidence, which leaves no possibility of supposing that any thing of female vanity was mixed up, where the tones were so full of tenderness, and a restraining modesty.—The men, for what I observed, speak seldomer.

Once only, and it was some years ago, I witnessed a sample of the old Foxian orgasm. It was a man of giant stature, who, as Wordsworth phrases it, might have danced "from head to foot equipt in iron mail." His frame was of iron too. But *he* was malleable. I saw him shake all over with the spirit—I dare not say, of delusion. The strivings of the outer man were unutterable —he seemed not to speak, but to be spoken from. I saw the strong man bowed down, and his knees to fail—his joints all seemed loosening—it was a figure to set off against Paul Preaching—the words he uttered were few, and sound—he was evidently resisting his will—keeping down his own word-wisdom with more mighty effort, than the world's orators strain for theirs. "He had been a WIT in his youth," he told us, with expressions of a sober remorse. And it was not till long after the impression had begun to wear away, that I was enabled, with something like a smile, to recall the striking incongruity of the confession—understanding the term in its worldly acceptation—with the frame and physiognomy of the person before me. His brow would have scared away the Levities —the Jocos Risus-que—faster than the Loves fled the face of Dis at Enna.—By *wit*, even in his youth, I will be sworn he understood something far within the limits of an allowable liberty.

More frequently the Meeting is broken up without a word having been spoken. But the mind has been fed. You go away with a sermon, not made with hands. You have been in the milder caverns of Trophonius; or as in some den, where that fiercest and savagest of all wild creatures, the TONGUE, that unruly member, has strangely lain tied up and captive. You have bathed with stillness. —O when the spirit is sore fretted, even tired to sickness of the janglings, and nonsense-noises of the world, what a balm and a solace it is, to go and seat yourself, for a quiet half hour, upon some undisputed corner of a bench, among the gentle Quakers!

Their garb and stillness conjoined, present an uniformity, tranquil and herd-like—as in the pasture—"forty feeding like one."—

The very garments of a Quaker seem incapable of receiving a soil; and cleanliness in them to be something more than the absence of its contrary. Every Quakeress is a lily; and when they come up in bands to their Whitsun-conferences, whitening the easterly streets of the metropolis, from all parts of the United Kingdom, they show like troops of the Shining Ones.

THE OLD AND THE NEW SCHOOLMASTER

M Y reading has been lamentably desultory and immethodical. Odd, out of the way, old English plays, and treatises, have supplied me with most of my notions, and ways of feeling. In every thing that relates to *science*, I am a whole Encyclopædia behind the rest of the world. I should have scarcely cut a figure among the franklins, or country gentlemen, in king John's days. I know less geography than a school-boy of six weeks' standing. To me a map of old Ortelius is as authentic as Arrowsmith. I do not know whereabout Africa merges into Asia; whether Ethiopia lie in one or other of those great divisions; nor can form the remotest conjecture of the position of New South Wales, or Van Diemen's Land. Yet do I hold a correspondence with a very dear friend in the first-named of these two Terræ Incognitæ. I have no astronomy. I do not know where to look for the Bear, or Charles's Wain; the place of any star; or the name of any of them at sight. I guess at Venus only by her brightness—and if the sun on some portentous morn were to make his first appearance in the West, I verily believe, that, while all the world were gasping in apprehension about me, I alone should stand unterrified, from sheer incuriosity and want of observation. Of history and chronology I possess some vague points, such as one cannot help picking up in the course of miscellaneous study; but I never deliberately sat down to a chronicle, even of my own country. I have most dim apprehensions of the four great monarchies; and sometimes the Assyrian, sometimes the Persian, floats as *first* in my fancy. I make the widest conjectures concerning Egypt, and her shepherd kings. My friend *M.*, with great pains-taking, got me to think I understood the first proposition in Euclid, but gave me over in despair at the second. I am entirely un-acquainted with the modern languages; and, like a better man than myself, have " small Latin and less Greek." I am a stranger to the shapes and texture of the commonest trees, herbs, flowers—not from the circumstance of my being town-born—for I should have brought the same inobservant spirit into the world with me, had I first seen it in " on Devon's leafy shores,"—and am no less at a loss among purely town-objects, tools, engines, mechanic processes.— Not that I affect ignorance—but my head has not many mansions, nor spacious; and I have been obliged to fill it with such cabinet curiosities as it can hold without aching. I sometimes wonder, how I have passed my probation with so little discredit in the world, as I have done, upon so meagre a stock. But the fact is, a man may do very well with a very little knowledge, and scarce be found out, in mixed company; every body is so much more ready to produce

his own, than to call for a display of your acquisitions. But in a
tête-à-tête there is no shuffling. The truth will out. There is
nothing which I dread so much, as the being left alone for a quarter
of an hour with a sensible, well-informed man, that does not know
me. I lately got into a dilemma of this sort.—

In one of my daily jaunts between Bishopsgate and Shacklewell,
the coach stopped to take up a staid-looking gentleman, about the
wrong side of thirty, who was giving his parting directions (while
the steps were adjusting), in a tone of mild authority, to a tall
youth, who seemed to be neither his clerk, his son, nor his servant,
but something partaking of all three. The youth was dismissed,
and we drove on. As we were the sole passengers, he naturally
enough addressed his conversation to me ; and we discussed the
merits of the fare, the civility and punctuality of the driver ; the
circumstance of an opposition coach having been lately set up, with
the probabilities of its success—to all which I was enabled to return
pretty satisfactory answers, having been drilled into this kind of
etiquette by some years' daily practice of riding to and fro in the
stage aforesaid—when he suddenly alarmed me by a startling
question, whether I had seen the show of prize cattle that morning
in Smithfield ? Now as I had not seen it, and do not greatly care
for such sort of exhibitions, I was obliged to return a cold negative.
He seemed a little mortified, as well as astonished, at my declara-
tion, as (it appeared) he was just come fresh from the sight, and
doubtless had hoped to compare notes on the subject. However he
assured me that I had lost a fine treat, as it far exceeded the show
of last year. We were now approaching Norton Falgate, when the
sight of some shop-goods *ticketed* freshened him up into a dissertation upon the cheapness of cottons this spring. I was now a little
in heart, as the nature of my morning avocations had brought me
into some sort of familiarity with the raw material ; and I was
surprised to find how eloquent I was becoming on the state of the
India market—when, presently, he dashed my incipient vanity to the
earth at once, by inquiring whether I had ever made any calculation
as to the value of the rental of all the retail shops in London. Had
he asked of me, what song the Sirens sang, or what name Achilles
assumed when he hid himself among women, I might, with Sir
Thomas Browne, have hazarded a " wide solution." [1] My companion saw my embarrassment, and, the almshouses beyond Shore-
ditch just coming in view, with great good-nature and dexterity
shifted his conversation to the subject of public charities ; which led
to the comparative merits of provision for the poor in past and
present times, with observations on the old monastic institutions,

[1] Urn Burial.

and charitable orders ;—but, finding me rather dimly impressed with some glimmering notions from old poetic associations, than strongly fortified with any speculations reducible to calculation on the subject, he gave the matter up ; and, the country beginning to open more and more upon us, as we approached the turnpike at Kingsland (the destined termination of his journey), he put a home thrust upon me, in the most unfortunate position he could have chosen, by advancing some queries relative to the North Pole Expedition. While I was muttering out something about the Panorama of those strange regions (which I had actually seen), by way of parrying the question, the coach stopping relieved me from any further apprehensions. My companion getting out, left me in the comfortable possession of my ignorance ; and I heard him, as he went off, putting questions to an outside passenger, who had alighted with him, regarding an epidemic disorder, that had been rife about Dalston ; and which, my friend assured him, had gone through five or six schools in that neighbourhood. The truth now flashed upon me, that my companion was a schoolmaster ; and that the youth, whom he had parted from at our first acquaintance, must have been one of the bigger boys, or the usher.—He was evidently a kind-hearted man, who did not seem so much desirous of provoking discussion by the questions which he put, as of obtaining information at any rate. It did not appear that he took any interest, either, in such kind of inquiries, for their own sake ; but that he was in some way bound to seek for knowledge. A greenish-coloured coat, which he had on, forbade me to surmise that he was a clergyman. The adventure gave birth to some reflections on the difference between persons of his profession in past and present times.

Rest to the souls of those fine old Pedagogues ; the breed, long since extinct, of the Lilys, and the Linacres : who believing that all learning was contained in the languages which they taught, and despising every other acquirement as superficial and useless, came to their task as to a sport ! Passing from infancy to age, they dreamed away all their days as in a grammar-school. Revolving in a perpetual cycle of declensions, conjugations, syntaxes, and prosodies ; renewing constantly the occupations which had charmed their studious childhood ; rehearsing continually the part of the past ; life must have slipped from them at last like one day. They were always in their first garden, reaping harvests of their golden time, among their *Flori* and their *Spici-legia ;* in Arcadia still, but kings ; the ferule of their sway not much harsher, but of like dignity with that mild sceptre attributed to king Basileus ; the Greek and Latin, their stately Pamela and their Philoclea ; with the occasional duncery of some untoward Tyro, serving for a refreshing interlude of a Mopsa, or a clown Damætas !

With what a savour doth the Preface to Colet's, or (as it is sometimes called) Paul's Accidence, set forth ! " To exhort every man to the learning of grammar, that intendeth to attain the understanding of the tongues, wherein is contained a great treasury of wisdom and knowledge, it would seem but vain and lost labour; for so much as it is known, that nothing can surely be ended, whose beginning is either feeble or faulty ; and no building be perfect, whereas the foundation and ground-work is ready to fall, and unable to uphold the burden of the frame." How well doth this stately preamble (comparable to those which Milton commendeth as " having been the usage to prefix to some solemn law, then first promulgated by Solon, or Lycurgus ") correspond with and illustrate that pious zeal for conformity, expressed in a succeeding clause, which would fence about grammar-rules with the severity of faith-articles !—" as for the diversity of grammars, it is well profitably taken away by the king majesties wisdom, who foreseeing the inconvenience, and favourably providing the remedie, caused one kind of grammar by sundry learned men to be diligently drawn, and so to be set out, only everywhere to be taught for the use of learners, and for the hurt in changing of schoolmaisters." What a *gusto* in that which follows : " wherein it is profitable that he can orderly decline his noun, and his verb." *His* noun!

The fine dream is fading away fast ; and the least concern of a teacher in the present day is to inculcate grammar-rules.

The modern schoolmaster is expected to know a little of every thing, because his pupil is required not to be entirely ignorant of any thing. He must be superficially, if I may so say, omniscient. He is to know something of pneumatics ; of chemistry ; of whatever is curious, or proper to excite the attention of the youthful mind ; an insight into mechanics is desirable, with a touch of statistics; the quality of soils, &c. botany, the constitution of his country, *cum multis aliis.* You may get a notion of some part of his expected duties by consulting the famous Tractate on Education addressed to Mr. Hartlib.

All these things—these, or the desire of them—he is expected to instil, not by set lessons from professors, which he may charge in the bill, but at school-intervals, as he walks the streets, or saunters through green fields (those natural instructors), with his pupils. The least part of what is expected from him, is to be done in school-hours. He must insinuate knowledge at the *mollia tempora fandi.* He must seize every occasion—the season of the year—the time of the day—a passing cloud—a rainbow—a waggon of hay—a regiment of soldiers going by—to inculcate something useful. He can receive no pleasure from a casual glimpse of Nature, but must catch at it as an object of instruction. He must interpret beauty into the picturesque. He cannot relish a beggar-man, or a gipsy, for thinking of the suitable improvement. Nothing comes to him, not spoiled by the sophisticating medium of moral uses. The Universe—that Great Book, as it has been called—is to him indeed, to all intents and purposes, a book, out of which he is doomed to read tedious homilies to distasting schoolboys.—Vacations themselves are none to him, he is only rather worse off than before; for commonly he has some intrusive upper-boy fastened upon him at such times; some cadet of a great family; some neglected lump of nobility, or gentry; that he must drag after him to the play, to the Panorama, to Mr. Bartley's Orrery, to the Panopticon, or into the country, to a friend's house, or to his favourite watering-place. Wherever he goes, this uneasy shadow attends him. A boy is at his board, and in his path, and in all his movements. He is boy-rid, sick of perpetual boy.

Boys are capital fellows in their own way, among their mates; but they are unwholesome companions for grown people. The restraint is felt no less on the one side, than on the other.—Even a child, that "plaything for an hour," tires *always*. The noises of children, playing their own fancies—as I now hearken to them by fits, sporting on the green before my window, while I am engaged in these grave speculations at my neat suburban retreat at Shackle-well—by distance made more sweet—inexpressibly take from the labour of my task. It is like writing to music. They seem to modulate my periods. They ought at least to do so—for in the voice of that tender age there is a kind of poetry, far unlike the harsh prose-accents of man's conversation.—I should but spoil their sport, and diminish my own sympathy for them, by mingling in their pastime.

I would not be domesticated all my days with a person of very superior capacity to my own—not, if I know myself at all, from any considerations of jealousy or self-comparison, for the occasional communion with such minds has constituted the fortune and felicity of my life—but the habit of too constant intercourse with spirits above you, instead of raising you, keeps you down. Too frequent doses of original thinking from others, restrain what lesser portion of that faculty you may possess of your own. You get entangled in another man's mind, even as you lose yourself in another man's grounds. You are walking with a tall varlet, whose strides out-pace yours to lassitude. The constant operation of such potent agency would reduce me, I am convinced, to imbecility. You may derive thoughts from others; your way of thinking, the mould in which your thoughts are cast, must be your own. Intellect may be imparted, but not each man's intellectual frame.—

As little as I should wish to be always thus dragged upwards, as little (or rather still less) is it desirable to be stunted downwards by your associates. The trumpet does not more stun you by its loudness, than a whisper teases you by its provoking inaudibility.

Why are we never quite at our ease in the presence of a school-master?—because we are conscious that he is not quite at his ease in ours. He is awkward, and out of place, in the society of his equals. He comes like Gulliver from among his little people, and he cannot fit the stature of his understanding to yours. He cannot meet you on the square. He wants a point given him, like an indifferent whist-player. He is so used to teaching, that he wants to be teaching *you*. One of these professors, upon my complaining that these little sketches of mine were any thing but methodical, and that I was unable to make them otherwise, kindly offered to instruct me in the method by which young gentlemen in *his* semi-nary were taught to compose English themes.—The jests of a schoolmaster are coarse, or thin. They do not *tell* out of school. He is under the restraint of a formal and didactive hypocrisy in company, as a clergyman is under a moral one. He can no more let his intellect loose in society, than the other can his inclinations. —He is forlorn among his co-evals; his juniors cannot be his friends.

"I take blame to myself," said a sensible man of this profession, writing to a friend respecting a youth who had quitted his school abruptly, "that your nephew was not more attached to me. But persons in my situation are more to be pitied, than can well be imagined. We are surrounded by young, and, consequently, ardently affectionate hearts, but *we* can never hope to share an atom of their affections. The relation of master and scholar forbids this. *How pleasing this must be to you, how I envy your feelings*, my friends will sometimes say to me, when they see young men, whom I have educated, return after some years absence from school, their eyes shining with pleasure, while they shake hands with their old master, bringing a present of game to me, or a toy to my wife, and thanking me in the warmest terms for my care of their educa-tion. A holiday is begged for the boys; the house is a scene of happiness; I, only, am sad at heart—This fine-spirited and warm-hearted youth, who fancies he repays his master with gratitude for the care of his boyish years—this young man—in the eight long years I watched over him with a parent's anxiety, never could re-pay me with one look of genuine feeling. He was proud, when I praised; he was submissive, when I reproved him; but he did never *love* me—and what he now mistakes for gratitude and kind-ness for me, is but the pleasant sensation, which all persons feel at revisiting the scene of their boyish hopes and fears; and the seeing on equal terms the man they were accustomed to look up to with reverence. My wife too," this interesting correspondent goes on

to say, "my once darling Anna, is the wife of a schoolmaster.—
When I married her—knowing that the wife of a schoolmaster
ought to be a busy notable creature, and fearing that my gentle
Anna would ill supply the loss of my dear bustling mother, just
then dead, who never sat still, was in every part of the house in a
moment, and whom I was obliged sometimes to threaten to fasten
down in a chair, to save her from fatiguing herself to death—I expressed my fears, that I was bringing her into a way of life unsuit-
able to her; and she, who loved me tenderly, promised for my sake
to exert herself to perform the duties of her new situation. She
promised, and she has kept her word. What wonders will not
woman's love perform?—My house is managed with a propriety
and decorum, unknown in other schools; my boys are well fed,
look healthy, and have every proper accommodation; and all this
performed with a careful economy, that never descends to meanness.
But I have lost my gentle, *helpless* Anna!—When we sit down to
enjoy an hour of repose after the fatigue of the day, I am compelled to listen to what have been her useful (and they are really
useful) employments through the day, and what she proposes for
her to-morrow's task. Her heart and her features are changed by
the duties of her situation. To the boys, she never appears other
than the *master's wife*, and she looks up to me as the *boys'
master;* to whom all show of love and affection would be highly
improper, and unbecoming the dignity of her situation and mine.
Yet *this* my gratitude forbids me to hint to her. For my sake
she submitted to be this altered creature, and can I reproach her
for it?"—For the communication of this letter, I am indebted to
my cousin Bridget.

VALENTINE'S DAY

HAIL to thy returning festival, old Bishop Valentine! Great
is thy name in the rubric, thou venerable Arch-flamen of
Hymen! Immortal Go-between! who and what manner of person
art thou? Art thou but a *name*, typifying the restless principle
which impels poor humans to seek perfection in union? or wert
thou indeed a mortal prelate, with thy tippet and thy rochet, thy
apron on, and decent lawn sleeves? Mysterious personage! like
unto thee, assuredly, there is no other mitred father in the calendar; not Jerome, nor Ambrose, nor Cyril; nor the consigner of

undipt infants to eternal torments, Austin, whom all mothers hate ; nor he who hated all mothers, Origen ; nor Bishop Bull, nor Archbishop Parker, nor Whitgift. Thou comest attended with thousands and ten thousands of little Loves, and the air is

Brush'd with the hiss of rustling wings.

Singing Cupids are thy choristers and thy precentors ; and instead of the crosier, the mystical arrow is borne before thee.

In other words, this is the day on which those charming little missives, ycleped Valentines, cross and intercross each other at every street and turning. The weary and all for-spent twopenny postman sinks beneath a load of delicate embarrassments, not his own. It is scarcely credible to what an extent this ephemeral courtship is carried on in this loving town, to the great enrichment of porters, and detriment of knockers and bell-wires. In these little visual interpretations, no emblem is so common as the *heart*,—that little three-cornered exponent of all our hopes and fears,—the bestuck and bleeding heart ; it is twisted and tortured into more allegories and affectations than an opera hat. What authority we have in history or mythology for placing the head-quarters and metropolis of God Cupid in this anatomical seat rather than in any other, is not very clear ; but we have got it, and it will serve as well as any other. Else we might easily imagine, upon some other system which might have prevailed for any thing which our pathology knows to the contrary, a lover addressing his mistress, in perfect simplicity of feeling, " Madam, my *liver* and fortune are entirely at your disposal ; " or putting a delicate question, " Amanda, have you a *midriff* to bestow ? " But custom has settled these things, and awarded the seat of sentiment to the aforesaid triangle, while its less fortunate neighbours wait at animal and anatomical distance.

Not many sounds in life, and I include all urban and all rural sounds, exceed in interest a *knock at the door*. It " gives a very echo to the throne where Hope is seated." But its issues seldom answer to this oracle within. It is so seldom that just the person we want to see comes. But of all the clamorous visitations the welcomest in expectation is the sound that ushers in, or seems to usher in, a Valentine. As the raven himself was hoarse that announced the fatal entrance of Duncan, so the knock of the postman on this day is light, airy, confident, and befitting one that bringeth good tidings. It is less mechanical than on other days ; you will say, " That is not the post, I am sure." Visions of Love, of Cupids, of Hymens !—delightful eternal common-places, which " having been will always be ; " which no school-boy nor school-man can write away ; having your irreversible throne in the fancy and affections—what are your transports, when the happy maiden,

opening with careful finger, careful not to break the emblematic
seal, bursts upon the sight of some well-designed allegory, some
type, some youthful fancy, not without verses—

> Lovers all,
> A madrigal,

or some such device, not over abundant in sense—young Love
disclaims it,—and not quite silly—something between wind and
water, a chorus where the sheep might almost join the shepherd,
as they did, or as I apprehend they did, in Arcadia.

All Valentines are not foolish; and I shall not easily forget thine,
my kind friend (if I may have leave to call you so) E. B.—E. B.
lived opposite a young maiden, whom he had often seen, unseen,
from his parlour window in C—e-street. She was all joyousness
and innocence, and just of an age to enjoy receiving a Valentine,
and just of a temper to bear the disappointment of missing one
with good humour. E. B. is an artist of no common powers;
in the fancy parts of designing, perhaps inferior to none; his
name is known at the bottom of many a well executed vignette
in the way of his profession, but no further; for E. B. is modest,
and the world meets nobody half-way. E. B. meditated how he
could repay this young maiden for many a favour which she had
done him unknown; for when a kindly face greets us, though but
passing by, and never knows us again, nor we it, we should feel it
as an obligation; and E. B. did. This good artist set himself at
work to please the damsel. It was just before Valentine's day
three years since. He wrought, unseen and unsuspected, a wondrous
work. We need not say it was on the finest gilt paper with
borders—full, not of common hearts and heartless allegory, but all
the prettiest stories of love from Ovid, and older poets than Ovid
(for E. B. is a scholar.) There was Pyramus and Thisbe, and be
sure Dido was not forgot, nor Hero and Leander, and swans more
than sang in Cayster, with mottos and fanciful devices, such as
beseemed,—a work in short of magic. Iris dipt the woof. This
on Valentine's eve he commended to the all-swallowing indiscriminate orifice—(O ignoble trust!)—of the common post; but the
humble medium did its duty, and from his watchful stand, the
next morning, he saw the cheerful messenger knock, and by and
by the precious charge delivered. He saw, unseen, the happy girl
unfold the Valentine, dance about, clap her hands, as one after one
the pretty emblems unfolded themselves. She danced about, not
with light love, or foolish expectations, for she had no lover; or,
if she had, none she knew that could have created those bright
images which delighted her. It was more like some fairy present;
a God-send, as our familiarly pious ancestors termed a benefit received, where the benefactor was unknown. It would do her no

harm. It would do her good for ever after. It is good to love the unknown. I only give this as a specimen of E. B. and his modest way of doing a concealed kindness.

Good-morrow to my Valentine, sings poor Ophelia; and no better wish, but with better auspices, we wish to all faithful lovers, who are not too wise to despise old legends, but are content to rank themselves humble diocesans of old Bishop Valentine, and his true church.

IMPERFECT SYMPATHIES

I am of a constitution so general, that it consorts and sympathizeth with all things, I have no antipathy, or rather idiosyncracy in any thing. Those national repugnancies do not touch me, nor do I behold with prejudice the French, Italian, Spaniard, or Dutch.—*Religio Medici.*

THAT the author of the Religio Medici, mounted upon the airy stilts of abstraction, conversant about notional and conjectural essences ; in whose categories of Being the possible took the upper hand of the actual ; should have overlooked the impertinent individualities of such poor concretions as mankind, is not much to be admired. It is rather to be wondered at, that in the genus of animals he should have condescended to distinguish that species at all. For myself—earth-bound and fettered to the scene of my activities,—

Standing on earth, not rapt above the sky,

I confess that I do feel the differences of mankind, national or individual, to an unhealthy excess. I can look with no indifferent eye upon things or persons. Whatever is, is to me a matter of taste or distaste ; or when once it becomes indifferent, it begins to be disrelishing. I am, in plainer words, a bundle of prejudices— made up of likings and dislikings—the veriest thrall to sympathies, apathies, antipathies. In a certain sense, I hope it may be said of me that I am a lover of my species. I can feel for all indifferently, but I cannot feel towards all equally. The more purely-English word that expresses sympathy will better explain my meaning. I can be a friend to a worthy man, who upon another account cannot be my mate or *fellow.* I cannot *like* all people alike.[1]

[1] I would be understood as confining myself to the subject of *imperfect sympathies.* To nations or classes of men there can be no direct *antipathy.* There may

I have been trying all my life to like Scotchmen, and am obliged to desist from the experiment in despair. They cannot like me—and in truth, I never knew one of that nation who attempted to do it. There is something more plain and ingenuous in their mode of proceeding. We know one another at first sight. There is an order of imperfect intellects (under which mine must be content to rank) which in its constitution is essentially anti-Caledonian. The owners of the sort of faculties I allude to, have minds rather suggestive than comprehensive. They have no pretences to much clearness or precision in their ideas, or in their manner of expressing them. Their intellectual wardrobe (to confess fairly) has few whole pieces in it. They are content with fragments and scattered pieces of Truth. She presents no full front to them—a feature or side-face at the most. Hints and glimpses, germs and crude essays at a system, is the utmost they pretend to. They beat up a little game peradventure—and leave it to knottier heads, more robust constitutions, to run it down. The light that lights them is not steady and polar, but mutable and shifting : waxing, and again waning. Their conversation is accordingly. They will throw out a random word in or out of season, and be content to let it pass for what it is worth. They cannot speak always as if they were upon their oath—but must be understood, speaking or writing, with some abatement. They seldom wait to mature a proposition, but e'en bring it to market in the green ear. They delight to impart their defective discoveries as they arise, without waiting for their full developement. They are no systematizers, and would but err more by attempting it. Their minds, as I said before, are suggestive merely. The brain of a true Caledonian (if I am not mistaken) is constituted upon quite a different plan. His Minerva is born in panoply. You are never

be individuals born and constellated so opposite to another individual nature, that the same sphere cannot hold them. I have met with my moral antipodes, and can believe the story of two persons meeting (who never saw one another before in their lives) and instantly fighting.

> ——We by proof find there should be
> 'Twixt man and man such an antipathy,
> That though he can show no just reason why
> For any former wrong or injury,
> Can neither find a blemish in his fame,
> Nor aught in face or feature justly blame,
> Can challenge or accuse him of no evil,
> Yet notwithstanding hates him as a devil.

The lines are from old Heywood's " Hierarchie of Angels," and he subjoins a curious story in confirmation, of a Spaniard who attempted to assassinate a King Ferdinand of Spain, and being put to the rack could give no other reason for the deed but an inveterate antipathy which he had taken to the first sight of the King.

> ——The cause which to that act compell'd him
> Was, he ne'er loved him since he first beheld him.

admitted to see his ideas in their growth—if, indeed, they do grow, and are not rather put together upon principles of clock-work. You never catch his mind in an undress. He never hints or suggests any thing, but unlades his stock of ideas in perfect order and completeness. He brings his total wealth into company, and gravely unpacks it. His riches are always about him. He never stoops to catch a glittering something in your presence, to share it with you, before he quite knows whether it be true touch or not. You cannot cry *halves* to any thing that he finds. He does not find, but bring. You never witness his first apprehension of a thing. His understanding is always at its meridian—you never see the first dawn, the early streaks.—He has no falterings of self-suspicion. Surmises, guesses, misgivings, half-intuitions, semi-consciousnesses, partial illuminations, dim instincts, embryo conceptions, have no place in his brain, or vocabulary. The twilight of dubiety never falls upon him. Is he orthodox—he has no doubts. Is he an infidel—he has none either. Between the affirmative and the negative there is no border-land with him. You cannot hover with him upon the confines of truth, or wander in the maze of a probable argument. He always keeps the path. You cannot make excursions with him—for he sets you right. His taste never fluctuates. His morality never abates. He cannot compromise, or understand middle actions. There can be but a right and a wrong. His conversation is as a book. His affirmations have the sanctity of an oath. You must speak upon the square with him. He stops a metaphor like a suspected person in an enemy's country. " A healthy book ! "—said one of his countrymen to me, who had ventured to give that appellation to John Buncle,—" did I catch rightly what you said ?   I have heard of a man in health, and of a healthy state of body, but I do not see how that epithet can be properly applied to a book." Above all, you must beware of indirect expressions before a Caledonian. Clap an extinguisher upon your irony, if you are unhappily blest with a vein of it. Remember you are upon your oath. I have a print of a graceful female after Leonardo da Vinci, which I was showing off to Mr. ****. After he had examined it minutely, I ventured to ask him how he liked MY BEAUTY (a foolish name it goes by among my friends)—when he very gravely assured me, that " he had considerable respect for my character and talents " (so he was pleased to say), " but had not given himself much thought about the degree of my personal pretensions." The misconception staggered me, but did not seem much to disconcert him.—Persons of this nation are particularly fond of affirming a truth—which nobody doubts. They do not so properly affirm, as annunciate it. They do indeed appear to have such a love of truth (as if, like virtue, it were valuable for itself) that all truth becomes equally valuable, whether the proposition that contains it be new or old, disputed, or such as is impossible to become a subject of disputation. I was present not long since at a party of North Britons, where a son of Burns was expected ; and happened to drop a silly expression (in my South British way), that I wished it were the father instead of the son—when four of them started up at once to inform me, that " that was impossible, because he was dead." An impracticable wish, it seems, was more than they could conceive. Swift has hit off this part of their character, namely their love of truth, in his biting way, but with an illiberality that necessarily confines the passage to the margin.[1] The tediousness of these people is certainly provoking. I wonder if they ever tire one another !—In my early life I had a passionate fondness for the poetry of Burns. I have sometimes foolishly hoped to ingratiate myself with his countrymen by expressing it. But I have always found that a true Scot resents your admiration of his compatriot, even more than he would your contempt of him. The latter he imputes to your " imperfect acquaintance with many of the words which he uses ; " and the same objection makes it a presumption in you to suppose that you can admire him.—Thomson they seem to have forgotten. Smollett they have neither forgotten nor forgiven for his delineation of Rory and his companion, upon their first introduction to our metropolis.—Speak of Smollett as a great genius, and they will retort upon you Hume's History compared with *his* Continuation of it. What if the historian had continued Humphrey Clinker ?

I have, in the abstract, no disrespect for Jews. They are a piece of stubborn antiquity, compared with which Stonehenge is in its nonage. They date beyond the pyramids. But I should not care to be in habits of familiar intercourse with any of that nation. I confess that I have not the nerves to enter their synagogues. Old prejudices cling about me. I cannot shake off the story of Hugh of Lincoln. Centuries of injury, contempt, and hate, on the one side,—of cloaked revenge, dissimulation, and hate, on the other, between our and their fathers, must, and ought, to affect the blood of the children. I cannot believe it can run clear and kindly yet ; or that a few fine words, such as candour, liberality, the light of a nineteenth century, can close up the breaches of so

---

[1] There are some people who think they sufficiently acquit themselves, and entertain their company, with relating facts of no consequence, not at all out of the road of such common incidents as happen every day; and this I have observed more frequently among the Scots than any other nation, who are very careful not to omit the minutest circumstances of time or place; which kind of discourse, if it were not a little relieved by the uncouth terms and phrases, as well as accent and gesture peculiar to that country, would be hardly tolerable.—*Hints towards an Essay on Conversation.*

deadly a disunion. A Hebrew is nowhere congenial to me. He is least distasteful on 'Change—for the mercantile spirit levels all distinctions, as all are beauties in the dark. I boldly confess that I do not relish the approximation of Jew and Christian, which has become so fashionable. The reciprocal endearments have, to me, something hypocritical and unnatural in them. I do not like to see the Church and Synagogue kissing and congeeing in awkward postures of an affected civility. If *they* are converted, why do they not come over to us altogether ? Why keep up a form of separation, when the life of it is fled ? If they can sit with us at table, why do they keck at our cookery ? I do not understand these half convertites. Jews christianizing—Christians judaizing— puzzle me. I like fish or flesh. A moderate Jew is a more confounding piece of anomaly than a wet Quaker. The spirit of the synagogue is essentially *separative*. B—— would have been more in keeping if he had abided by the faith of his forefathers. There is a fine scorn in his face, which nature meant to be of —— Christians. The Hebrew spirit is strong in him, in spite of his proselytism. He cannot conquer the Shibboleth. How it breaks out, when he sings, " The Children of Israel passed through the Red Sea ! " The auditors, for the moment, are as Egyptians to him, and he rides over our necks in triumph. There is no mistaking him.— B—— has a strong expression of sense in his countenance, and it is confirmed by his singing. The foundation of his vocal excellence is sense. He sings with understanding, as Kemble delivered dialogue. He would sing the Commandments, and give an appropriate character to each prohibition. His nation, in general, have not ever-sensible countenances. How should they ?—but you seldom see a silly expression among them. Gain, and the pursuit of gain, sharpen a man's visage. I never heard of an idiot being born among them.—Some admire the Jewish female-physiognomy. I admire it—but with trembling. Jael had those full dark inscrutable eyes.

In the Negro countenance you will often meet with strong traits of benignity. I have felt yearnings of tenderness towards some of these faces—or rather masks—that have looked out kindly upon one in casual encounters in the streets and highways. I love what Fuller beautifully calls—these " images of God cut in ebony." But I should not like to associate with them, to share my meals and my good-nights with them—because they are black.

I love Quaker ways, and Quaker worship. I venerate the Quaker principles. It does me good for the rest of the day when I meet any of their people in my path. When I am ruffled or disturbed by any occurrence, the sight, or quiet voice of a Quaker, acts upon me as a ventilator, lightening the air, and taking off a load from the bosom. But I cannot like the Quakers (as Desdemona would say) " to live with them." I am all over sophisticated—with humours, fancies, craving hourly sympathy. I must have books, pictures, theatres, chit-chat, scandal, jokes, ambiguities, and a thousand whim-whams, which their simpler taste can do without. I should starve at their primitive banquet. My appetites are too high for the salads which (according to Evelyn) Eve dressed for the angel, my gusto too excited

> To sit a guest with Daniel at his pulse.

The indirect answers which Quakers are often found to return to a question put to them may be explained, I think, without the vulgar assumption, that they are more given to evasion and equivocating than other people. They naturally look to their words more carefully, and are more cautious of committing themselves. They have a peculiar character to keep up on this head. They stand in a manner upon their veracity. A Quaker is by law exempted from taking an oath. The custom of resorting to an oath in extreme cases, sanctified as it is by all religious antiquity, is apt (it must be confessed) to introduce into the laxer sort of minds the notion of two kinds of truth—the one applicable to the solemn affairs of justice, and the other to the common proceedings of daily intercourse. As truth bound upon the conscience by an oath can be but truth, so in the common affirmations of the shop and the market-place a latitude is expected, and conceded upon questions wanting this solemn covenant. Something less than truth satisfies. It is common to hear a person say, " You do not expect me to speak as if I were upon my oath." Hence a great deal of incorrectness and inadvertency, short of falsehood, creeps into ordinary conversation; and a kind of secondary or laic-truth is tolerated, where clergy-truth—oath-truth, by the nature of the circumstances, is not required. A Quaker knows none of this distinction. His simple affirmation being received, upon the most sacred occasions, without any further test, stamps a value upon the words which he is to use upon the most indifferent topics of life. He looks to them, naturally, with more severity. You can have of him no more than his word. He knows, if he is caught tripping in a casual expression, he forfeits, for himself, at least, his claim to the invidious exemption. He knows that his syllables are weighed—and how far a consciousness of this particular watchfulness, exerted against a person, has a tendency to produce indirect answers, and a diverting of the question by honest means, might be illustrated, and the practice justified, by a more sacred example than is proper to be adduced upon this occasion. The admirable presence of mind, which is notorious in Quakers upon all contingencies, might be traced to this imposed self-watchfulness—if it did not seem rather an humble and secular scion of that old stock of religious constancy, which never bent or faltered, in the Primitive Friends, or gave way to the winds of persecution, to the violence of judge or accuser, under trials and racking examinations. "You will never be the wiser, if I sit here answering your questions till midnight," said one of those upright Justicers to Penn, who had been putting law-cases with a puzzling subtlety. "Thereafter as the answers may be," retorted the Quaker. The astonishing composure of this people is sometimes ludicrously displayed in lighter instances.—I was travelling in a stage-coach with three male Quakers, buttoned up in the straitest non-conformity of their sect. We stopped to bait at Andover, where a meal, partly tea apparatus, partly supper, was set before us. My friends confined themselves to the tea-table. I in my way took supper. When the landlady brought in the bill, the eldest of my companions discovered that she had charged for both meals. This was resisted. Mine hostess was very clamorous and positive. Some mild arguments were used on the part of the Quakers, for which the heated mind of the good lady seemed by no means a fit recipient. The guard came in with his usual peremptory notice. The Quakers pulled out their money, and formally tendered it—so much for tea —I, in humble imitation, tendering mine—for the supper which I had taken. She would not relax in her demand. So they all three quietly put up their silver, as did myself, and marched out of the room, the eldest and gravest going first, with myself closing up the rear, who thought I could not do better than follow the example of such grave and warrantable personages. We got in. The steps went up. The coach drove off. The murmurs of mine hostess, not very indistinctly or ambiguously pronounced, became after a time inaudible—and now my conscience, which the whimsical scene had for a while suspended, beginning to give some twitches, I waited, in the hope that some justification would be offered by these serious persons for the seeming injustice of their conduct. To my great surprise, not a syllable was dropped on the subject. They sate as mute as at a meeting. At length the eldest of them broke silence, by inquiring of his next neighbour, "Hast thee heard how indigos go at the India House?" and the question operated as a soporific on my moral feeling as far as Exeter.

WITCHES, AND OTHER NIGHT-FEARS

WE are too hasty when we set down our ancestors in the gross for fools, for the monstrous inconsistencies (as they seem to us) involved in their creed of witchcraft. In the relations of this visible world we find them to have been as rational, and shrewd to detect an historic anomaly, as ourselves. But when once the invisible world was supposed to be opened, and the lawless agency of bad spirits assumed, what measures of probability, of decency, of fitness, or proportion—of that which distinguishes the likely from the palpable absurd—could they have to guide them in the rejection or admission of any particular testimony?—That maidens pined away, wasting inwardly as their waxen images consumed before a fire—that corn was lodged, and cattle lamed—that whirlwinds uptore in diabolic revelry the oaks of the forest—or that spits and kettles only danced a fearful-innocent vagary about some rustic's kitchen when no wind was stirring—were all equally probable where no law of agency was understood. That the prince of the powers of darkness, passing by the flower and pomp of the earth, should lay preposterous siege to the weak fantasy of indigent eld—has neither likelihood nor unlikelihood à *priori* to us, who have no measure to guess at his policy, or standard to estimate what rate those anile souls may fetch in the devil's market. Nor, when the wicked are expressly symbolized by a goat, was it to be wondered at so much, that *he* should come sometimes in that body, and assert his metaphor.—That the intercourse was opened at all between both worlds was perhaps the mistake—but that once assumed, I see no reason for disbelieving one attested story of this nature more than another on the score of absurdity. There is no law to judge of the lawless, or canon by which a dream may be criticised.

I have sometimes thought that I could not have existed in the days of received witchcraft; that I could not have slept in a village where one of those reputed hags dwelt. Our ancestors were bolder or more obtuse. Amidst the universal belief that these wretches were in league with the author of all evil, holding hell tributary to their muttering, no simple Justice of the Peace seems to have scrupled issuing, or silly Headborough serving, a warrant upon them—as if they should subpœna Satan!—Prospero in his boat, with his books and wand about him, suffers himself to be conveyed away at the mercy of his enemies to an unknown island. He might have raised a storm or two, we think, on the passage. His acquiescence is in exact analogy to the non-resistance of witches to the constituted powers.—What stops the Fiend in Spenser from tearing

Guyon to pieces—or who had made it a condition of his prey, that Guyon must take assay of the glorious bait—we have no guess. We do not know the laws of that country.

From my childhood I was extremely inquisitive about witches and witch-stories. My maid, and more legendary aunt, supplied me with good store. But I shall mention the accident which directed my curiosity originally into this channel. In my father's book-closet, the History of the Bible, by Stackhouse, occupied a distinguished station. The pictures with which it abounds—one of the ark, in particular, and another of Solomon's temple, delineated with all the fidelity of ocular admeasurement, as if the artist had been upon the spot—attracted my childish attention. There was a picture, too, of the Witch raising up Samuel, which I wish that I had never seen. We shall come to that hereafter. Stackhouse is in two huge tomes—and there was a pleasure in removing folios of that magnitude, which, with infinite straining, was as much as I could manage, from the situation which they occupied upon an upper shelf. I have not met with the work from that time to this, but I remember it consisted of Old Testament stories, orderly set down, with the *objection* appended to each story, and the *solution* of the objection regularly tacked to that. The *objection* was a summary of whatever difficulties had been opposed to the credibility of the history, by the shrewdness of ancient or modern infidelity, drawn up with an almost complimentary excess of candour. The *solution* was brief, modest, and satisfactory. The bane and antidote were both before you. To doubts so put, and so quashed, there seemed to be an end for ever. The dragon lay dead, for the foot of the veriest babe to trample on. But—like as was rather feared than realised from that slain monster in Spenser—from the womb of those crushed errors young dragonets would creep, exceeding the prowess of so tender a Saint George as myself to vanquish. The habit of expecting objections to every passage, set me upon starting more objections, for the glory of finding a solution of my own for them. I became staggered and perplexed, a sceptic in long coats. The pretty Bible stories which I had read, or heard read in church, lost their purity and sincerity of impression, and were turned into so many historic or chronologic theses to be defended against whatever impugners. I was not to disbelieve them, but—the next thing to that—I was to be quite sure that some one or other would or had disbelieved them. Next to making a child an infidel, is the letting him know that there are infidels at all. Credulity is the man's weakness, but the child's strength. O, how ugly sound scriptural doubts from the mouth of a babe and a suckling!—I should have lost myself in these mazes, and have pined away, I think, with such unfit sustenance as these husks afforded, but for a fortunate piece of ill-fortune, which about this time befel me. Turning over the picture of the ark with too much haste, I unhappily made a breach in its ingenious fabric—driving my inconsiderate fingers right through the two larger quadrupeds—the elephant, and the camel— that stare (as well they might) out of the two last windows next the steerage in that unique piece of naval architecture. Stackhouse was henceforth locked up, and became an interdicted treasure. With the book, the *objections* and *solutions* gradually cleared out of my head, and have seldom returned since in any force to trouble me.—But there was one impression which I had imbibed from Stackhouse, which no lock or bar could shut out, and which was destined to try my childish nerves rather more seriously.—That detestable picture!

I was dreadfully alive to nervous terrors. The night-time solitude, and the dark, were my hell. The sufferings I endured in this nature would justify the expression. I never laid my head on my pillow, I suppose, from the fourth to the seventh or eighth year of my life—so far as memory serves in things so long ago— without an assurance, which realized its own prophecy, of seeing some frightful spectre. Be old Stackhouse then acquitted in part, if I say, that to his picture of the Witch raising up Samuel—(O that old man covered with a mantle!) I owe—not my midnight terrors, the hell of my infancy—but the shape and manner of their visita- tion. It was he who dressed up for me a hag that nightly sate upon my pillow—a sure bed-fellow, when my aunt or my maid was far from me. All day long, while the book was permitted me, I dreamed waking over his delineation, and at night (if I may use so bold an expression) awoke into sleep, and found the vision true. I durst not, even in the day-light, once enter the chamber where I slept, without my face turned to the window, aversely from the bed where my witch-ridden pillow was.—Parents do not know what they do when they leave tender babes alone to go to sleep in the dark. The feeling about for a friendly arm—the hoping for a familiar voice— when they wake screaming—and find none to soothe them—what a terrible shaking it is to their poor nerves! The keeping them up till midnight, through candle-light and the unwholesome hours, as they are called,—would, I am satisfied, in a medical point of view, prove the better caution.—That detestable picture, as I have said, gave the fashion to my dreams—if dreams they were—for the scene of them was invariably the room in which I lay. Had I never met with the picture, the fears would have come self-pictured in some shape or other—

Headless bear, black man, or ape—

but, as it was, my imaginations took that form.—It is not book, or picture, or the stories of foolish servants, which create these terrors in children. They can at most but give them a direction. Dear little T.H. who of all children has been brought up with the most scrupulous exclusion of every taint of superstition—who was never allowed to hear of goblin or apparition, or scarcely to be told of bad men, or to read or hear of any distressing story—finds all this world of fear, from which he has been so rigidly excluded *ab extra*, in his own " thick-coming fancies ; " and from his little midnight pillow, this nurse-child of optimism will start at shapes, unborrowed of tradition, in sweats to which the reveries of the cell-damned murderer are tranquillity.

Gorgons, and Hydras, and Chimæras—dire stories of Celæno and the Harpies—may reproduce themselves in the brain of superstition —but they were there before. They are transcripts, types—the archetypes are in us, and eternal. How else should the recital of that, which we know in a waking sense to be false, come to affect us at all ?—or

> ——Names, whose sense we see not,
> Fray us with things that be not ?

Is it that we naturally conceive terror from such objects, considered in their capacity of being able to inflict upon us bodily injury ?—O, least of all ! These terrors are of older standing. They date beyond body—or, without the body, they would have been the same. All the cruel, tormenting, defined devils in Dante—tearing, mangling, choking, stifling, scorching demons—are they one half so fearful to the spirit of a man, as the simple idea of a spirit unembodied following him—

> Like one that on a lonesome road
> Doth walk in fear and dread,
> And having once turn'd round, walks on,
> And turns no more his head ;
> Because he knows a frightful fiend
> Doth close behind him tread. [1]

That the kind of fear here treated of is purely spiritual—that it is strong in proportion as it is objectless upon earth—that it predominates in the period of sinless infancy—are difficulties, the solution of which might afford some probable insight into our antemundane condition, and a peep at least into the shadow-land of pre-existence.

My night-fancies have long ceased to be afflictive. I confess an occasional night-mare ; but I do not, as in early youth, keep a stud of them. Fiendish faces, with the extinguished taper, will come

[1] Mr. Coleridge's Ancient Mariner.

and look at me ; but I know them for mockeries, even while I cannot elude their presence, and I fight and grapple with them.   For the credit of my imagination, I am almost ashamed to say how tame and prosaic my dreams are grown.   They are never romantic, seldom even rural.   They are of architecture and of buildings—cities abroad, which I have never seen, and hardly have hope to see. I have traversed, for the seeming length of a natural day, Rome, Amsterdam, Paris, Lisbon—their churches, palaces, squares, market-places, shops, suburbs, ruins, with an inexpressible sense of delight—a map-like distinctness of trace—and a day-light vividness of vision, that was all but being awake.—I have formerly travelled among the Westmoreland fells—my highest Alps,—but they are objects too mighty for the grasp of my dreaming recognition ; and I have again and again awoke with ineffectual struggles of the inner eye, to make out a shape in any way whatever, of Helvellyn.   Methought I was in that country, but the mountains were gone.   The poverty of my dreams mortifies me.   There is Coleridge, at his will can conjure up icy domes, and pleasure-houses for Kubla Khan, and Abyssinian maids, and songs of Abara, and caverns,

Where Alph, the sacred river, runs,

to solace his night solitudes—when I cannot muster a fiddle.   Barry Cornwall has his tritons and his nereids gamboling before him in nocturnal visions, and proclaiming sons born to Neptune—when my stretch of imaginative activity can hardly, in the night season, raise up the ghost of a fish-wife.   To set my failures in somewhat a mortifying light—it was after reading the noble Dream of this poet, that my fancy ran strong upon these marine spectra ; and the poor plastic power, such as it is, within me set to work, to humour my folly in a sort of dream that very night.   Methought I was upon the ocean billows at some sea nuptials, riding and mounted high, with the customary train sounding their conchs before me, (I myself, you may be sure, the *leading god*,) and jollily we went careering over the main, till just where Ino Leucothea should have greeted me (I think it was Ino) with a white embrace, the billows gradually subsiding, fell from a sea-roughness to a sea-calm, and thence to a river-motion, and that river (as happens in the familiarization of dreams) was no other than the gentle Thames, which landed me, in the wafture of a placid wave or two, alone, safe and inglorious, somewhere at the foot of Lambeth palace.

The degree of the soul's creativeness in sleep might furnish no whimsical criterion of the quantum of poetical faculty resident in the same soul waking.   An old gentleman, a friend of mine, and a humorist, used to carry this notion so far, that when he saw any stripling of his acquaintance ambitious of becoming a poet, his first

question would be,—"Young man, what sort of dreams have you?"
I have so much faith in my old friend's theory, that when I feel that
idle vein returning upon me, I presently subside into my proper
element of prose, remembering those eluding nereids, and that
inauspicious inland landing.

MY RELATIONS

I AM arrived at that point of life, at which a man may account
it a blessing, as it is a singularity, if he have either of his
parents surviving.   I have not that felicity—and sometimes think
feelingly of a passage in Browne's Christian Morals, where he speaks
of a man that hath lived sixty or seventy years in the world.   "In
such a compass of time," he says, "a man may have a close apprehension what it is to be forgotten, when he hath lived to find none
who could remember his father, or scarcely the friends of his youth,
and may sensibly see with what a face in no long time OBLIVION
will look upon himself."

I had an aunt, a dear and good one.   She was one whom single
blessedness had soured to the world.   She often used to say, that I
was the only thing in it which she loved; and, when she thought
I was quitting it, she grieved over me with mother's tears.   A
partiality quite so exclusive my reason cannot altogether approve.
She was from morning till night poring over good books, and devotional exercises.   Her favourite volumes were Thomas à Kempis, in
Stanhope's Translation; and a Roman Catholic Prayer Book, with
the *matins* and *complines* regularly set down,—terms which I was
at that time too young to understand.   She persisted in reading
them, although admonished daily concerning their Papistical tendency; and went to church every Sabbath, as a good Protestant
should do.   These were the only books she studied; though, I
think, at one period of her life, she told me, she had read with
great satisfaction the Adventures of an Unfortunate Young Nobleman.   Finding the door of the chapel in Essex-street open one day
—it was in the infancy of that heresy—she went in, liked the
sermon, and the manner of worship, and frequented it at intervals
for some time after.   She came not for doctrinal points, and never
missed them.   With some little asperities in her constitution, which
I have above hinted at, she was a steadfast, friendly being, and a
fine *old Christian*.   She was a woman of strong sense, and a

shrewd mind—extraordinary at a *repartee;* one of the few occasions of her breaking silence—else she did not much value wit. The only secular employment I remember to have seen her engaged in, was, the splitting of French beans, and dropping them into a China basin of fair water. The odour of those tender vegetables to this day comes back upon my sense, redolent of soothing recollections. Certainly it is the most delicate of culinary operations.

Male aunts, as somebody calls them, I had none—to remember. By the uncle's side I may be said to have been born an orphan. Brother, or sister, I never had any—to know them. A sister, I think, that should have been Elizabeth, died in both our infancies. What a comfort, or what a care, may I not have missed in her!— But I have cousins, sprinkled about in Hertfordshire—besides *two,* with whom I have been all my life in habits of the closest intimacy, and whom I may term cousins *par excellence.* These are James and Bridget Elia. They are older than myself by twelve, and ten, years; and neither of them seems disposed, in matters of advice and guidance, to waive any of the prerogatives which primogeniture confers. May they continue still in the same mind; and when they shall be seventy-five, and seventy-three, years old (I cannot spare them sooner), persist in treating me in my grand climacteric precisely as a stripling, or younger brother!

James is an inexplicable cousin. Nature hath her unities, which not every critic can penetrate; or, if we feel, we cannot explain them. The pen of Yorick, and of none since his, could have drawn J. E. entire—those fine Shandian lights and shades, which make up his story. I must limp after in my poor antithetical manner, as the fates have given me grace and talent. J. E. then— to the eye of a common observer at least—seemeth made up of contradictory principles.—The genuine child of impulse, the frigid philosopher of prudence—the phlegm of my cousin's doctrine is invariably at war with his temperament, which is high sanguine. With always some fire-new project in his brain, J. E. is the systematic opponent of innovation, and crier down of every thing that has not stood the test of age and experiment. With a hundred fine notions chasing one another hourly in his fancy, he is startled at the least approach to the romantic in others; and, determined by his own sense in every thing, commends *you* to the guidance of common sense on all occasions.—With a touch of the eccentric in all which he does, or says, he is only anxious that *you* should not commit yourself by doing any thing absurd or singular. On my once letting slip at table, that I was not fond of a certain popular dish, he begged me at any rate not to *say* so—for the world would think me mad. He disguises a passionate fondness for works of high art (whereof he hath amassed a choice collection), under the pretext of buying only to sell again—that his enthusiasm may give no encouragement to yours. Yet, if it were so, why does that piece of tender, pastoral Dominichino hang still by his wall ?—is the ball of his sight much more dear to him ?—or what picture-dealer can talk like him ?

Whereas mankind in general are observed to warp their speculative conclusions to the bent of their individual humours, *his* theories are sure to be in diametrical opposition to his constitution. He is courageous as Charles of Sweden, upon instinct ; chary of his person, upon principle, as a travelling Quaker.—He has been preaching up to me, all my life, the doctrine of bowing to the great—the necessity of forms, and manner, to a man's getting on in the world. He himself never aims at either, that I can discover, —and has a spirit, that would stand upright in the presence of the Cham of Tartary. It is pleasant to hear him discourse of patience— extolling it as the truest wisdom—and to see him during the last seven minutes that his dinner is getting ready. Nature never ran up in her haste a more restless piece of workmanship than when she moulded this impetuous cousin—and Art never turned out a more elaborate orator than he can display himself to be, upon his favourite topic of the advantages of quiet, and contentedness in the state, whatever it may be, that we are placed in. He is triumphant on this theme, when he has you safe in one of those short stages that ply for the western road, in a very obstructing manner, at the foot of John Murray's street—where you get in when it is empty, and are expected to wait till the vehicle hath completed her just freight—a trying three quarters of an hour to some people. He wonders at your fidgetiness,—" where could we be better than we are, *thus sitting, thus consulting ?* "—" prefers, for his part, a state of rest to locomotion,"—with an eye all the while upon the coachman—till at length, waxing out of all patience, at *your want of it*, he breaks out into a pathetic remonstrance at the fellow for detaining us so long over the time which he had professed, and declares peremptorily, that " the gentleman in the coach is determined to get out, if he does not drive on that instant."

Very quick at inventing an argument, or detecting a sophistry, he is incapable of attending *you* in any chain of arguing. Indeed he makes wild work with logic ; and seems to jump at most admirable conclusions by some process, not at all akin to it. Consonantly enough to this, he hath been heard to deny, upon certain occasions, that there exists such a faculty at all in man as *reason ;* and wondereth how man came first to have a conceit of it—enforcing his negation with all the might of *reasoning* he is master of. He has some speculative notions against laughter, and will maintain that laughing is not natural to *him*—when peradventure the next

moment his lungs shall crow like Chanticleer. He says some of
the best things in the world—and declareth that wit is his aversion.
It was he who said, upon seeing the Eton boys at play in their
grounds—*What a pity to think, that these fine ingenuous lads
in a few years will all be changed into frivolous Members of
Parliament!*

His youth was fiery, glowing, tempestuous—and in age he
discovereth no symptom of cooling. This is that which I admire
in him. I hate people who meet Time half-way. I am for no
compromise with that inevitable spoiler. While he lives, J. E.
will take his swing.—It does me good, as I walk towards the street
of my daily avocation, on some fine May morning, to meet him
marching in a quite opposite direction, with a jolly handsome
presence, and shining sanguine face, that indicates some purchase
in his eye—a Claude—or a Hobbima—for much of his enviable
leisure is consumed at Christie's, and Phillips's—or where not, to
pick up pictures, and such gauds. On these occasions he mostly
stoppeth me, to read a short lecture on the advantage a person
like me possesses above himself, in having his time occupied with
business which he *must do*—assureth me that he often feels it hang
heavy on his hands—wishes he had fewer holidays—and goes off—
Westward Ho!—chanting a tune, to Pall Mall—perfectly convinced
that he has convinced me—while I proceed in my opposite direction
tuneless.

It is pleasant again to see this Professor of Indifference doing
the honours of his new purchase, when he has fairly housed it.
You must view it in every light, till *he* has found the best—placing
it at this distance, and at that, but always suiting the focus of your
sight to his own. You must spy at it through your fingers, to
catch the aërial perspective—though you assure him that to you
the landscape shows much more agreeable without that artifice.
Wo be to the luckless wight, who does not only not respond to his
rapture, but who should drop an unseasonable intimation of preferring one of his anterior bargains to the present!—The last is
always his best hit—his "Cynthia of the minute."—Alas! how
many a mild Madonna have I known to *come in*—a Raphael!—
keep its ascendancy for a few brief moons—then, after certain
intermedial degradations, from the front drawing-room to the back
gallery, thence to the dark parlour,—adopted in turn by each of
the Carracci, under successive lowering ascriptions of filiation, mildly
breaking its fall—consigned to the oblivious lumber-room, *go out*
at last a Lucca Giordano, or plain Carlo Maratti!—which things
when I beheld—musing upon the chances and mutabilities of fate
below, hath made me to reflect upon the altered condition of great
personages, or that woful Queen of Richard the Second—

—— set forth in pomp,
She came adorned hither like sweet May.
Sent back like Hollowmass or shortest day.

With great love for *you*, J. E. hath but a limited sympathy
with what you feel or do. He lives in a world of his own, and
makes slender guesses at what passes in your mind. He never
pierces the marrow of your habits. He will tell an old established
play-goer, that Mr. Such-a-one, of So-and-so (naming one of the
theatres), is a very lively comedian—as a piece of news! He
advertised me but the other day of some pleasant green lanes which
he had found out for me, *knowing me to be a great walker*, in my
own immediate vicinity—who have haunted the identical spot any
time these twenty years!—He has not much respect for that class
of feelings which goes by the name of sentimental. He applies the
definition of real evil to bodily sufferings exclusively—and rejecteth
all others as imaginary. He is affected by the sight, or the bare
supposition, of a creature in pain, to a degree which I have
never witnessed out of womankind. A constitutional acuteness
to this class of sufferings may in part account for this. The
animal tribe in particular he taketh under his especial protection.
A broken-winded or spur-galled horse is sure to find an
advocate in him. An over-loaded ass is his client for ever. He
is the apostle to the brute kind—the never-failing friend of those
who have none to care for them. The contemplation of a lobster
boiled, or eels skinned *alive*, will wring him so, that " all for pity
he could die." It will take the savour from his palate, and the
rest from his pillow, for days and nights. With the intense feeling
of Thomas Clarkson, he wanted only the steadiness of pursuit, and
unity of purpose, of that " true yoke-fellow with Time," to have
effected as much for the *Animal*, as *he* hath done for the *Negro
Creation*. But my uncontrollable cousin is but imperfectly formed
for purposes which demand co-operation. He cannot wait. His
amelioration-plans must be ripened in a day. For this reason he
has cut but an equivocal figure in benevolent societies, and combinations for the alleviation of human sufferings. His zeal constantly
makes him to outrun, and put out, his coadjutors. He thinks of
relieving,—while they think of debating. He was black-balled out
of a society for the Relief of   *   *   *   *   *   *
     *   *   *   *   , because the fervor of his humanity
toiled beyond the formal apprehension, and creeping processes, of
his associates. I shall always consider this distinction as a patent
of nobility in the Elia family!
Do I mention these seeming inconsistencies to smile at, or upbraid, my unique cousin? Marry, heaven, and all good manners, and
the understanding that should be between kinsfolk, forbid!—With

all the strangenesses of this *strangest of the Elias*—I would not have him in one jot or tittle other than he is; neither would I barter or exchange my wild kinsman for the most exact, regular, and every-way consistent kinsman breathing.

In my next, reader, I may perhaps give you some account of my cousin Bridget—if you are not already surfeited with cousins—and take you by the hand, if you are willing to go with us, on an excursion which we made a summer or two since, in search of *more cousins*—

Through the green plains of pleasant Hertfordshire.

MACKERY END, IN HERTFORDSHIRE

BRIDGET ELIA has been my housekeeper for many a long year. I have obligations to Bridget, extending beyond the period of memory. We house together, old bachelor and maid, in a sort of double singleness; with such tolerable comfort, upon the whole, that I, for one, find in myself no sort of disposition to go out upon the mountains, with the rash king's offspring, to bewail my celibacy. We agree pretty well in our tastes and habits—yet so, as " with a difference." We are generally in harmony, with occasional bickerings—as it should be among near relations. Our sympathies are rather understood, than expressed ; and once, upon my dissembling a tone in my voice more kind than ordinary, my cousin burst into tears, and complained that I was altered. We are both great readers in different directions. While I am hanging over (for the thousandth time) some passage in old Burton, or one of his strange contemporaries, she is abstracted in some modern tale, or adventure, whereof our common reading-table is daily fed with assiduously fresh supplies. Narrative teazes me. I have little concern in the progress of events. She must have a story—well, ill, or indifferently told—so there be life stirring in it, and plenty of good or evil accidents. The fluctuations of fortune in fiction—and almost in real life—have ceased to interest, or operate but dully upon me. Out-of-the-way humours and opinions—heads with some diverting twist in them—the oddities of authorship please me most. My cousin has a native disrelish of any thing that sounds odd or bizarre. Nothing goes down with her, that is quaint, irregular, or out of the road of common sympathy. She " holds Nature more clever." I can pardon her blindness to the beautiful obliquities of the Religio Medici; but she must apologise to me for certain disrespectful insinuations, which she has been pleased to throw out latterly, touching the intellectuals of a dear favourite of mine, of the last century but one—the thrice noble, chaste, and virtuous,—but again somewhat fantastical, and original-brain'd, generous Margaret Newcastle.

It has been the lot of my cousin, oftener perhaps than I could have wished, to have had for her associates and mine, free-thinkers—leaders, and disciples, of novel philosophies and systems; but she neither wrangles with, nor accepts, their opinions. That which was good and venerable to her, when a child, retains its authority over her mind still. She never juggles or plays tricks with her understanding.

We are both of us inclined to be a little too positive; and I have observed the result of our disputes to be almost uniformly this—that in matters of fact, dates, and circumstances, it turns out, that I was in the right, and my cousin in the wrong. But where we have differed upon moral points; upon something proper to be done, or let alone; whatever heat of opposition, or steadiness of conviction, I set out with, I am sure always, in the long run, to be brought over to her way of thinking.

I must touch upon the foibles of my kinswoman with a gentle hand, for Bridget does not like to be told of her faults. She hath an awkward trick (to say no worse of it) of reading in company: at which times she will answer *yes* or *no* to a question, without fully understanding its purport—which is provoking, and derogatory in the highest degree to the dignity of the putter of the said question. Her presence of mind is equal to the most pressing trials of life, but will sometimes desert her upon trifling occasions. When the purpose requires it, and is a thing of moment, she can speak to it greatly; but in matters which are not stuff of the conscience, she hath been known sometimes to let slip a word less seasonably.

Her education in youth was not much attended to; and she happily missed all that train of female garniture, which passeth by the name of accomplishments. She was tumbled early, by accident or design, into a spacious closet of good old English reading, without much selection or prohibition, and browsed at will upon that fair and wholesome pasturage. Had I twenty girls, they should be brought up exactly in this fashion. I know not whether their chance in wedlock might not be diminished by it; but I can answer for it, that it makes (if the worst come to the worst) most incomparable old maids.

In a season of distress, she is the truest comforter; but in the teazing accidents, and minor perplexities, which do not call out the *will* to meet them, she sometimes maketh matters worse by an excess of participation. If she does not always divide your trouble, upon the pleasanter occasions of life she is sure always to treble your satisfaction. She is excellent to be at a play with, or upon a visit; but best, when she goes a journey with you.

We made an excursion together a few summers since, into Hertfordshire, to beat up the quarters of some of our less-known relations in that fine corn country.

The oldest thing I remember is Mackery End; or Mackarel End, as it is spelt, perhaps more properly, in some old maps of Hertfordshire; a farm-house,—delightfully situated within a gentle walk from Wheathampstead. I can just remember having been there, on a visit to a great-aunt, when I was a child, under the care of Bridget; who, as I have said, is older than myself by some ten years. I wish that I could throw into a heap the remainder of our joint existences, that we might share them in equal division. But that is impossible. The house was at that time in the occupation of a substantial yeoman, who had married my grandmother's sister. His name was Gladman. My grandmother was a Bruton, married to a Field. The Gladmans and the Brutons are still flourishing in that part of the county, but the Fields are almost extinct. More than forty years had elapsed since the visit I speak of; and, for the greater portion of that period, we had lost sight of the other two branches also. Who or what sort of persons inherited Mackery End—kindred or strange folk—we were afraid almost to conjecture, but determined some day to explore.

By somewhat a circuitous route, taking the noble park at Luton in our way from Saint Alban's, we arrived at the spot of our anxious curiosity about noon. The sight of the old farm-house, though every trace of it was effaced from my recollection, affected me with a pleasure which I had not experienced for many a year. For though *I* had forgotten it, *we* had never forgotten being there together, and we had been talking about Mackery End all our lives, till memory on my part became mocked with a phantom of itself, and I thought I knew the aspect of a place, which, when present, O how unlike it was to *that*, which I had conjured up so many times instead of it!

Still the air breathed balmily about it; the season was in the "heart of June," and I could say with the poet,

> But thou, that didst appear so fair
> To fond imagination,
> Dost rival in the light of day
> Her delicate creation!

Bridget's was more a waking bliss than mine, for she easily remembered her old acquaintance again—some altered features, of

course, a little grudged at. At first, indeed, she was ready to
disbelieve for joy ; but the scene soon re-confirmed itself in her
affections—and she traversed every out-post of the old mansion, to
the wood-house, the orchard, the place where the pigeon-house had
stood (house and birds were alike flown)—with a breathless impatience of recognition, which was more pardonable perhaps than
decorous at the age of fifty odd. But Bridget in some things is
behind her years.

The only thing left was to get into the house—and that was a
difficulty which to me singly would have been insurmountable ; for
I am terribly shy in making myself known to strangers and out-of-
date kinsfolk. Love, stronger than scruple, winged my cousin in
without me ; but she soon returned with a creature that might
have sat to a sculptor for the image of Welcome. It was the
youngest of the Gladmans ; who, by marriage with a Bruton, had
become mistress of the old mansion. A comely brood are the
Brutons. Six of them, females, were noted as the handsomest
young women in the county. But this adopted Bruton, in my
mind, was better than they all—more comely. She was born too
late to have remembered me. She just recollected in early life to
have had her cousin Bridget once pointed out to her, climbing a
style. But the name of kindred, and of cousinship, was enough.
Those slender ties, that prove slight as gossamer in the rending
atmosphere of a metropolis, bind faster, as we found it, in hearty,
homely, loving Hertfordshire. In five minutes we were as
thoroughly acquainted as if we had been born and bred up together ; were familiar, even to the calling each other by our
Christian names. So Christians should call one another. To
have seen Bridget, and her—it was like the meeting of the two
scriptural cousins ! There was a grace and dignity, an amplitude
of form and stature, answering to her mind, in this farmer's wife,
which would have shined in a palace—or so we thought it. We
were made welcome by husband and wife equally—we, and our
friend that was with us—I had almost forgotten him—but B. F.
will not so soon forget that meeting, if peradventure he shall read
this on the far distant shores where the Kangaroo haunts. The
fatted calf was made ready, or rather was already so, as if in
anticipation of our coming ; and, after an appropriate glass of
native wine, never let me forget with what honest pride this
hospitable cousin made us proceed to Wheathampstead, to introduce us (as some new-found rarity) to her mother and sister
Gladmans, who did indeed know something more of us, at a time
when she almost knew nothing.—With what corresponding kindness we were received by them also—how Bridget's memory,
exalted by the occasion, warmed into a thousand half-obliterated

recollections of things and persons, to my utter astonishment, and her own—and to the astoundment of B. F. who sat by, almost the only thing that was not a cousin there,—old effaced images of more than half-forgotten names and circumstances still crowding back upon her, as words written in lemon come out upon exposure to a friendly warmth,—when I forget all this, then may my country cousins forget me; and Bridget no more remember, that in the days of weakling infancy I was her tender charge—as I have been her care in foolish manhood since—in those pretty pastoral walks, long ago, about Mackery End, in Hertfordshire.

MODERN GALLANTRY

IN comparing modern with ancient manners, we are pleased to compliment ourselves upon the point of gallantry; a certain obsequiousness, or deferential respect, which we are supposed to pay to females, as females.

I shall believe that this principle actuates our conduct, when I can forget, that in the nineteenth century of the era from which we date our civility, we are but just beginning to leave off the very frequent practice of whipping females in public, in common with the coarsest male offenders.

I shall believe it to be influential, when I can shut my eyes to the fact, that in England women are still occasionally—hanged.

I shall believe in it, when actresses are no longer subject to be hissed off a stage by gentlemen.

I shall believe in it, when Dorimant hands a fish-wife across the kennel; or assists the apple-woman to pick up her wandering fruit, which some unlucky dray has just dissipated.

I shall believe in it, when the Dorimants in humbler life, who would be thought in their way notable adepts in this refinement, shall act upon it in places where they are not known, or think themselves not observed—when I shall see the traveller for some rich tradesman part with his admired box-coat, to spread it over the defenceless shoulders of the poor woman, who is passing to her parish on the roof of the same stage-coach with him, drenched in the rain—when I shall no longer see a woman standing up in the pit of a London theatre, till she is sick and faint with the exertion, with men about her, seated at their ease, and jeering at her distress; till one, that seems to have more manners or conscience than the rest, significantly declares " she should be welcome to his seat, if she were a little younger and handsomer." Place this dapper warehouseman, or that rider, in a circle of their own female acquaintance, and you shall confess you have not seen a politer-bred man in Lothbury.

Lastly, I shall begin to believe that there is some such principle influencing our conduct, when more than one-half of the drudgery and coarse servitude of the world shall cease to be performed by women.

Until that day comes, I shall never believe this boasted point to be any thing more than a conventional fiction ; a pageant got up between the sexes, in a certain rank, and at a certain time of life, in which both find their account equally.

I shall be even disposed to rank it among the salutary fictions of life, when in polite circles I shall see the same attentions paid to age as to youth, to homely features as to handsome, to coarse complexions as to clear—to the woman, as she is a woman, not as she is a beauty, a fortune, or a title.

I shall believe it to be something more than a name, when a well-dressed gentleman in a well-dressed company can advert to the topic of *female old age* without exciting, and intending to excite, a sneer :—when the phrases " antiquated virginity," and such a one has " overstood her market," pronounced in good company, shall raise immediate offence in man, or woman, that shall hear them spoken.

Joseph Paice, of Bread-street-hill, merchant, and one of the Directors of the South-Sea company—the same to whom Edwards, the Shakspeare commentator, has addressed a fine sonnet—was the only pattern of consistent gallantry I have met with. He took me under his shelter at an early age, and bestowed some pains upon me. I owe to his precepts and example whatever there is of the man of business (and that is not much) in my composition. It was not his fault that I did not profit more. Though bred a Presbyterian, and brought up a merchant, he was the finest gentleman of his time. He had not *one* system of attention to females in the drawing-room, and *another* in the shop, or at the stall. I do not mean that he made no distinction. But he never lost sight of sex, or overlooked it in the casualties of a disadvantageous situation. I have seen him stand bare-headed—smile if you please—to a poor servant girl, while she has been inquiring of him the way to some street—in such a posture of unforced civility, as neither to embarrass her in the acceptance, nor himself in the offer, of it. He was no dangler, in the common acceptation of the word, after women : but he reverenced and upheld, in every form in which it came before him, *womanhood.* I have seen him—nay, smile not—

tenderly escorting a market-woman, whom he had encountered in a shower, exalting his umbrella over her poor basket of fruit, that it might receive no damage, with as much carefulness as if she had been a Countess. To the reverend form of Female Eld he would yield the wall (though it were to an ancient beggar-woman) with more ceremony than we can afford to show our grandams. He was the Preux Chevalier of Age; the Sir Calidore, or Sir Tristan, to those who have no Calidores or Tristans to defend them. The roses, that had long faded thence, still bloomed for him in those withered and yellow cheeks.

He was never married, but in his youth he paid his addresses to the beautiful Susan Winstanley—old Winstanley's daughter of Clapton—who dying in the early days of their courtship, confirmed in him the resolution of perpetual bachelorship. It was during their short courtship, he told me, that he had been one day treating his mistress with a profusion of civil speeches—the common gallantries—to which kind of thing she had hitherto manifested no repugnance—but in this instance with no effect. He could not obtain from her a decent acknowledgment in return. She rather seemed to resent his compliments. He could not set it down to caprice, for the lady had always shown herself above that littleness. When he ventured on the following day, finding her a little better humoured, to expostulate with her on her coldness of yesterday, she confessed, with her usual frankness, that she had no sort of dislike to his attentions; that she could even endure some high-flown compliments; that a young woman placed in her situation had a right to expect all sort of civil things said to her; that she hoped she could digest a dose of adulation, short of insincerity, with as little injury to her humility as most young women: but that—a little before he had commenced his compliments—she had overheard him by accident, in rather rough language, rating a young woman, who had not brought home his cravats quite to the appointed time, and she thought to herself, " As I am Miss Susan Winstanley, and a young lady—a reputed beauty, and known to be a fortune,—I can have my choice of the finest speeches from the mouth of this very fine gentleman who is courting me—but if I had been poor Mary Such-a-one (*naming the milliner*),—and had failed of bringing home the cravats to the appointed hour—though perhaps I had sat up half the night to forward them—what sort of compliments should I have received then?—And my woman's pride came to my assistance; and I thought, that if it were only to do *me* honour, a female, like myself, might have received handsomer usage: and I was determined not to accept any fine speeches, to the compromise of that sex, the belonging to which was after all my strongest claim and title to them."

I think the lady discovered both generosity, and a just way of thinking, in this rebuke which she gave her lover ; and I have sometimes imagined, that the uncommon strain of courtesy, which through life regulated the actions and behaviour of my friend towards all of womankind indiscriminately, owed its happy origin to this seasonable lesson from the lips of his lamented mistress.

I wish the whole female world would entertain the same notion of these things that Miss Winstanley showed. Then we should see something of the spirit of consistent gallantry ; and no longer witness the anomaly of the same man—a pattern of true politeness to a wife—of cold contempt, or rudeness, to a sister—the idolater of his female mistress—the disparager and despiser of his no less female aunt, or unfortunate—still female—maiden cousin. Just so much respect as a woman derogates from her own sex, in whatever condition placed—her handmaid, or dependent—she deserves to have diminished from herself on that score ; and probably will feel the diminution, when youth, and beauty, and advantages, not inseparable from sex, shall lose of their attraction. What a woman should demand of a man in courtship, or after it, is first—respect for her as she is a woman ;—and next to that—to be respected by him above all other women. But let her stand upon her female character as upon a foundation ; and let the attentions, incident to individual preference, be so many pretty additaments and ornaments—as many, and as fanciful, as you please—to that main structure. Let her first lesson be—with sweet Susan Winstanley —to *reverence her sex.*

<hr />

THE OLD BENCHERS OF THE INNER TEMPLE

I WAS born, and passed the first seven years of my life, in the Temple. Its church, its halls, its gardens, its fountain, its river, I had almost said—for in those young years, what was this king of rivers to me but a stream that watered our pleasant places ? —these are of my oldest recollections. I repeat, to this day, no verses to myself more frequently, or with kindlier emotion, than those of Spenser, where he speaks of this spot.

> There when they came, whereas those bricky towers,
> The which on Themmes brode aged back doth ride,
> Where now the studious lawyers have their bowers,
> There whylome wont the Templer knights to bide,
> Till they decayd through pride.

Indeed, it is the most elegant spot in the metropolis.   What a transition for a countryman visiting London for the first time—the passing from the crowded Strand or Fleet-street, by unexpected avenues, into its magnificent ample squares, its classic green recesses !   What a cheerful, liberal look hath that portion of it, which, from three sides, overlooks the greater garden : that goodly pile

> Of building strong, albeit of Paper hight,

confronting, with massy contrast, the lighter, older, more fantastically shrouded one, named of Harcourt, with the cheerful Crown-office Row (place of my kindly engendure), right opposite the stately stream, which washes the garden-foot with her yet scarcely trade-polluted waters, and seems but just weaned from her Twickenham Naiades ! a man would give something to have been born in such places.   What a collegiate aspect has that fine Elizabethan hall, where the fountain plays, which I have made to rise and fall, how many times ! to the astoundment of the young urchins, my contemporaries, who, not being able to guess at its recondite machinery, were almost tempted to hail the wondrous work as magic !   What an antique air had the now almost effaced sun-dials, with their moral inscriptions, seeming coevals with that Time which they measured, and to take their revelations of its flight immediately from heaven, holding correspondence with the fountain of light! How would the dark line steal imperceptibly on, watched by the eye of childhood, eager to detect its movement, never catched, nice as an evanescent cloud, or the first arrests of sleep !

> Ah ! yet doth beauty like a dial-hand
> Steal from his figure, and no pace perceived !

What a dead thing is a clock, with its ponderous embowelments of lead and brass, its pert or solemn dulness of communication, compared with the simple altar-like structure, and silent heart-language of the old dial !   It stood as the garden god of Christian gardens. Why is it almost every where vanished ?   If its business-use be superseded by more elaborate inventions, its moral uses, its beauty, might have pleaded for its continuance.   It spoke of moderate labours, of pleasures not protracted after sun-set, of temperance, and good-hours.   It was the primitive clock, the horologe of the first world.   Adam could scarce have missed it in Paradise.   It was the measure appropriate for sweet plants and flowers to spring by, for the birds to apportion their silver warblings by, for flocks to pasture and be led to fold by.   The shepherd " carved it out quaintly in the sun ; " and, turning philosopher by the very occupation, provided it with mottos more touching than tombstones.   It was a

pretty device of the gardener, recorded by Marvell, who, in the days
of artificial gardening, made a dial out of herbs and flowers. I
must quote his verses a little higher up, for they are full, as all his
serious poetry was, of a witty delicacy. They will not come in
awkwardly, I hope, in a talk of fountains and sun-dials. He is
speaking of sweet garden scenes :

> What wondrous life in this I lead!
> Ripe apples drop about my head.
> The luscious clusters of the vine
> Upon my mouth do crush their wine.
> The nectarine, and curious peach,
> Into my hands themselves do reach.
> Stumbling on melons, as I pass,
> Insnared with flowers, I fall on grass.
> Meanwhile the mind from pleasure less
> Withdraws into its happiness.
> The mind, that ocean, where each kind
> Does straight its own resemblance find;
> Yet it creates, transcending these,
> Far other worlds, and other seas;
> Annihilating all that's made
> To a green thought in a green shade.
> Here at the fountain's sliding foot,
> Or at some fruit-tree's mossy root,
> Casting the body's vest aside,
> My soul into the boughs does glide:
> There, like a bird, it sits and sings,
> Then whets and claps its silver wings;
> And, till prepared for longer flight,
> Waves in its plumes the various light.
> How well the skilful gardner drew,
> Of flowers and herbs, this dial new!
> Where, from above, the milder sun
> Does through a fragrant zodiac run:
> And, as it works, the industrious bee
> Computes its time as well as we.
> How could such sweet and wholesome hours
> Be reckon'd, but with herbs and flowers? [1]

The artificial fountains of the metropolis are, in like manner, fast
vanishing. Most of them are dried up, or bricked over. Yet,
where one is left, as in that little green nook behind the South Sea
House, what a freshness it gives to the dreary pile! Four little
winged marble boys used to play their virgin fancies, spouting out
ever fresh streams from their innocent-wanton lips, in the square of
Lincoln's-inn, when I was no bigger than they were figured. They
are gone, and the spring choked up. The fashion, they tell me, is
gone by, and these things are esteemed childish. Why not then
gratify children, by letting them stand? Lawyers, I suppose, were
children once. They are awakening images to them at least. \Why
must every thing smack of man, and mannish? Is the world all

---

[1] From a copy of verses entitled The Garden.

grown up? Is childhood dead? Or is there not in the bosoms of the wisest and the best some of the child's heart left, to respond to its earliest enchantments? The figures were grotesque. Are the stiff-wigged living figures, that still flitter and chatter about that area, less gothic in appearance? or is the splutter of their hot rhetoric one half so refreshing and innocent as the little cool playful streams those exploded cherubs uttered?

They have lately gothicised the entrance to the Inner Temple-hall, and the library front, to assimilate them, I suppose, to the body of the hall, which they do not at all resemble. What is become of the winged horse that stood over the former? a stately arms! and who has removed those frescoes of the Virtues, which Italianized the end of the Paper-buildings?—my first hint of allegory! They must account to me for these things, which I miss so greatly.

The terrace is, indeed, left, which we used to call the parade; but the traces are passed away of the footsteps which made its pavement awful! It is become common and profane. The old benchers had it almost sacred to themselves, in the forepart of the day at least. They might not be sided or jostled. Their air and dress asserted the parade. You left wide spaces betwixt you, when you passed them. We walk on even terms with their successors. The roguish eye of J——ll, ever ready to be delivered of a jest, almost invites a stranger to vie a repartee with it. But what insolent familiar durst have mated Thomas Coventry?—whose person was a quadrate, his step massy and elephantine, his face square as the lion's, his gait peremptory and path-keeping, indivertible from his way as a moving column, the scarecrow of his inferiors, the brow-beater of equals and superiors, who made a solitude of children wherever he came, for they fled his insufferable presence, as they would have shunned an Elisha bear. His growl was as thunder in their ears, whether he spake to them in mirth or in rebuke, his invitatory notes being, indeed, of all, the most repulsive and horrid. Clouds of snuff, aggravating the natural terrors of his speech, broke from each majestic nostril, darkening the air. He took it, not by pinches, but a palmful at once, diving for it under the mighty flaps of his old-fashioned waistcoat pocket; his waistcoat red and angry, his coat dark rappee, tinctured by dye original, and by adjuncts, with buttons of obsolete gold. And so he paced the terrace.

By his side a milder form was sometimes to be seen; the pensive gentility of Samuel Salt. They were coevals, and had nothing but that and their benchership in common. In politics Salt was a whig, and Coventry a staunch tory. Many a sarcastic growl did the latter cast out—for Coventry had a rough spinous humour—at the political confederates of his associate, which rebounded from the gentle bosom of the latter like cannon-balls from wool. You could not ruffle Samuel Salt.

S. had the reputation of being a very clever man, and of excellent discernment in the chamber practice of the law. I suspect his knowledge did not amount to much. When a case of difficult disposition of money, testamentary or otherwise, came before him, he ordinarily handed it over with a few instructions to his man Lovel, who was a quick little fellow, and would despatch it out of hand by the light of natural understanding, of which he had an uncommon share. It was incredible what repute for talents S. enjoyed by the mere trick of gravity. He was a shy man; a child might pose him in a minute—indolent and procrastinating to the last degree. Yet men would give him credit for vast application in spite of himself. He was not to be trusted with himself with impunity. He never dressed for a dinner party but he forgot his sword—they wore swords then—or some other necessary part of his equipage. Lovel had his eye upon him on all these occasions, and ordinarily gave him his cue. If there was any thing which he could speak unseasonably, he was sure to do it.—He was to dine at a relative's of the unfortunate Miss Blandy on the day of her execution;—and L. who had a wary foresight of his probable hallucinations, before he set out, schooled him with great anxiety not in any possible manner to allude to her story that day. S. promised faithfully to observe the injunction. He had not been seated in the parlour, where the company was expecting the dinner summons, four minutes, when, a pause in the conversation ensuing, he got up, looked out of window, and pulling down his ruffles— an ordinary motion with him—observed, "it was a gloomy day," and added, "Miss Blandy must be hanged by this time, I suppose." Instances of this sort were perpetual. Yet S. was thought by some of the greatest men of his time a fit person to be consulted, not alone in matters pertaining to the law, but in the ordinary niceties and embarrassments of conduct—from force of manner entirely. He never laughed. He had the same good fortune among the female world,—was a known toast with the ladies, and one or two are said to have died for love of him—I suppose, because he never trifled or talked gallantry with them, or paid them, indeed, hardly common attentions. He had a fine face and person, but wanted, methought, the spirit that should have shown them off with advantage to the women. His eye lacked lustre.—Not so, thought Susan P——; who, at the advanced age of sixty, was seen, in the cold evening time, unaccompanied, wetting the pavement of B——d Row, with tears that fell in drops which might be heard, because her friend had died that day—he, whom she had pursued with a hopeless passion for the last forty years—a passion, which years could not extinguish or abate ; nor the long resolved, yet gently enforced, puttings off of unrelenting bachelorhood dissuade from its cherished purpose. Mild Susan P——, thou hast now thy friend in heaven !

Thomas Coventry was a cadet of the noble family of that name. He passed his youth in contracted circumstances, which gave him early those parsimonious habits which in after-life never forsook him ; so that, with one windfall or another, about the time I knew him he was master of four or five hundred thousand pounds ; nor did he look, or walk, worth a moidore less. He lived in a gloomy house opposite the pump in Serjeant's-inn, Fleet-street. J., the counsel, is doing self-imposed penance in it, for what reason I divine not, at this day. C. had an agreeable seat at North Cray, where he seldom spent above a day or two at a time in the summer; but preferred, during the hot months, standing at his window in this damp, close, well-like mansion, to watch, as he said, "the maids drawing water all day long." I suspect he had his within-door reasons for the preference. *Hic currus et arma fuére.* He might think his treasures more safe. His house had the aspect of a strong box. C. was a close hunks—a hoarder rather than a miser—or, if a miser, none of the mad Elwes breed, who have brought discredit upon a character, which cannot exist without certain admirable points of steadiness and unity of purpose. One may hate a true miser, but cannot, I suspect, so easily despise him. By taking care of the pence, he is often enabled to part with the pounds, upon a scale that leaves us careless generous fellows halting at an immeasurable distance behind. C. gave away 30,000*l.* at once in his life-time to a blind charity. His house-keeping was severely looked after, but he kept the table of a gentleman. He would know who came in and who went out of his house, but his kitchen chimney was never suffered to freeze.

Salt was his opposite in this, as in all—never knew what he was worth in the world ; and having but a competency for his rank, which his indolent habits were little calculated to improve, might have suffered severely if he had not had honest people about him. Lovel took care of every thing. He was at once his clerk, his good servant, his dresser, his friend, his "flapper," his guide, stop-watch, auditor, treasurer. He did nothing without consulting Lovel, or failed in any thing without expecting and fearing his admonishing. He put himself almost too much in his hands, had they not been the purest in the world. He resigned his title almost to respect as a master, if L. could ever have forgotten for a moment that he was a servant.

I knew this Lovel. He was a man of an incorrigible and losing honesty. A good fellow withal, and "would strike." In the cause of the oppressed he never considered inequalities, or calculated the number of his opponents. He once wrested a sword out of the hand of a man of quality that had drawn upon him ; and pommelled him severely with the hilt of it. The swordsman had offered insult to a female—an occasion upon which no odds against him could have prevented the interference of Lovel. He would stand next day bare-headed to the same person, modestly to excuse his interference—for L. never forgot rank, where something better was not concerned. L. was the liveliest little fellow breathing, had a face as gay as Garrick's, whom he was said greatly to resemble (I have a portrait of him which confirms it), possessed a fine turn for humorous poetry—next to Swift and Prior—moulded heads in clay or plaster of Paris to admiration, by the dint of natural genius merely ; turned cribbage boards, and such small cabinet toys, to perfection ; took a hand at quadrille or bowls with equal facility ; made punch better than any man of his degree in England ; had the merriest quips and conceits, and was altogether as brimful of rogueries and inventions as you could desire. He was a brother of the angle, moreover, and just such a free, hearty, honest companion as Mr. Isaac Walton would have chosen to go a fishing with. I saw him in his old age and the decay of his faculties, palsy-smitten, in the last sad stage of human weakness—" a remnant most forlorn of what he was,"—yet even then his eye would light up upon the mention of his favourite Garrick. He was greatest, he would say, in Bayes—" was upon the stage nearly throughout the whole performance, and as busy as a bee." At intervals, too, he would speak of his former life, and how he came up a little boy from Lincoln to go to service, and how his mother cried at parting with him, and how he returned, after some few years' absence, in his smart new livery to see her, and she blessed herself at the change, and could hardly be brought to believe that it was " her own bairn." And then, the excitement subsiding, he would weep, till I have wished that sad second-childhood might have a mother still to lay its head upon her lap. But the common mother of us all in no long time after received him gently into hers.

With Coventry, and with Salt, in their walks upon the terrace, most commonly Peter Pierson would join, to make up a third. They did not walk linked arm in arm in those days—" as now our stout triumvirs sweep the streets,"—but generally with both hands folded behind them for state, or with one at least behind, the other carrying a cane. P. was a benevolent, but not a prepossessing man. He had that in his face which you could not term unhappiness ; it rather implied an incapacity of being happy. His cheeks were colourless, even to whiteness. His look was uninviting, resembling (but without his sourness) that of our great philanthropist.   I know that he *did* good acts, but I could never make out what he *was*.   Contemporary with these, but subordinate, was Daines Barrington—another oddity—he walked burly and square—in imitation, I think, of Coventry—howbeit he attained not to the dignity of his prototype.   Nevertheless, he did pretty well, upon the strength of being a tolerable antiquarian, and having a brother a bishop.   When the account of his year's treasurership came to be audited, the following singular charge was unanimously disallowed by the bench : " Item, disbursed Mr. Allen, the gardener, twenty shillings, for stuff to poison the sparrows, by my orders." Next to him was old Barton—a jolly negation, who took upon him the ordering of the bills of fare for the parliament chamber, where the benchers dine—answering to the combination rooms at college —much to the easement of his less epicurean brethren.   I know nothing more of him.—Then Read, and Twopenny—Read, good-humoured and personable—Twopenny, good-humoured, but thin, and felicitous in jests upon his own figure.   If T. was thin, Wharry was attenuated and fleeting.   Many must remember him (for he was rather of later date) and his singular gait, which was per-formed by three steps and a jump regularly succeeding.   The steps were little efforts, like that of a child beginning to walk ; the jump comparatively vigorous, as a foot to an inch.   Where he learned this figure, or what occasioned it, I could never discover.   It was neither graceful in itself, nor seemed to answer the purpose any better than common walking.   The extreme tenuity of his frame, I suspect, set him upon it.   It was a trial of poising.   Twopenny would often rally him upon his leanness, and hail him as Brother Lusty ; but W. had no relish of a joke.   His features were spiteful. I have heard that he would pinch his cat's ears extremely, when any thing had offended him.   Jackson—the omniscient Jackson he was called—was of this period.   He had the reputation of possess-ing more multifarious knowledge than any man of his time.   He was the Friar Bacon of the less literate portion of the Temple.   I remember a pleasant passage, of the cook applying to him, with much formality of apology, for instructions how to write down *edge* bone of beef in his bill of commons.   He was supposed to know, if any man in the world did.   He decided the orthography to be— as I have given it—fortifying his authority with such anatomical reasons as dismissed the manciple (for the time) learned and happy. Some do spell it yet perversely, *aitch* bone, from a fanciful re-semblance between its shape, and that of the aspirate so denominated. I had almost forgotten Mingay with the iron hand—but he was somewhat later.   He had lost his right hand by some accident, and supplied it with a grappling hook, which he wielded with a toler-able adroitness.   I detected the substitute, before I was old enough to reason whether it were artificial or not. I remember the astonishment it raised in me. He was a blustering, loud-talking person ; and I reconciled the phenomenon to my ideas as an emblem of power—somewhat like the horns in the forehead of Michael Angelo's Moses. Baron Maseres, who walks (or did till very lately) in the costume of the reign of George the Second, closes my imperfect recollections of the old benchers of the Inner Temple.

Fantastic forms, whither are ye fled ? Or, if the like of you exist, why exist they no more for me ? Ye inexplicable, half-understood appearances, why comes in reason to tear away the preternatural mist, bright or gloomy, that enshrouded you ? Why make ye so sorry a figure in my relation, who made up to me—to my childish eyes—the mythology of the Temple ? In those days I saw Gods, as " old men covered with a mantle," walking upon the earth. Let the dreams of classic idolatry perish,—extinct be the fairies and fairy trumpery of legendary fabling,—in the heart of childhood, there will, for ever, spring up a well of innocent or wholesome superstition—the seeds of exaggeration will be busy there, and vital—from every-day forms educing the unknown and the uncommon. In that little Goshen there will be light, when the grown world flounders about in the darkness of sense and materiality. While childhood, and while dreams, reducing childhood, shall be left, imagination shall not have spread her holy wings totally to fly the earth.

P.S. I have done injustice to the soft shade of Samuel Salt. See what it is to trust to imperfect memory, and the erring notices of childhood ! Yet I protest I always thought that he had been a bachelor ! This gentleman, R. N. informs me, married young, and losing his lady in child-bed, within the first year of their union, fell into a deep melancholy, from the effects of which, probably, he never thoroughly recovered. In what a new light does this place his rejection (O call it by a gentler name !) of mild Susan P——, unravelling into beauty certain peculiarities of this very shy and retiring character !—Henceforth let no one receive the narratives of Elia for true records ! They are, in truth, but shadows of fact—verisimilitudes, not verities—or sitting but upon the remote edges and outskirts of history. He is no such honest chronicler as R. N., and would have done better perhaps to have consulted that gentleman, before he sent these incondite reminiscences to press. But the worthy sub-treasurer—who respects his old and his new masters—would but have been puzzled at the indecorous liberties of Elia. The good man wots not, peradventure, of the license which *Magazines* have arrived at in this plain-

speaking age, or hardly dreams of their existence beyond the
Gentleman's—his furthest monthly excursions in this nature
having been long confined to the holy ground of honest *Urban's*
obituary. May it be long before his own name shall help to
swell those columns of unenvied flattery!—Meantime, O ye New
Benchers of the Inner Temple, cherish him kindly, for he is himself
the kindliest of human creatures. Should infirmities over-take him
—he is yet in green and vigorous senility—make allowances for
them, remembering that "ye yourselves are old." So may the
Winged Horse, your ancient badge and cognisance, still flourish!
so may future Hookers and Seldens illustrate your church and
chambers! so may the sparrows, in default of more melodious
quiristers, unpoisoned hop about your walks! so may the fresh-
coloured and cleanly nursery maid, who, by leave, airs her playful
charge in your stately gardens, drop her prettiest blushing curtsy
as ye pass, reductive of juvenescent emotion! so may the younkers
of this generation eye you, pacing your stately terrace, with the
same superstitious veneration, with which the child Elia gazed on
the Old Worthies that solemnized the parade before ye!

GRACE BEFORE MEAT

THE custom of saying grace at meals had, probably, its origin
in the early times of the world, and the hunter-state of man,
when dinners were precarious things, and a full meal was something
more than a common blessing; when a belly-full was a windfall, and
looked like a special providence. In the shouts and triumphal
songs with which, after a season of sharp abstinence, a lucky booty
of deer's or goat's flesh would naturally be ushered home, existed,
perhaps, the germ of the modern grace. It is not otherwise easy to
be understood, why the blessing of food—the act of eating—should
have had a particular expression of thanksgiving annexed to it,
distinct from that implied and silent gratitude with which we are
expected to enter upon the enjoyment of the many other various
gifts and good things of existence.

I own that I am disposed to say grace upon twenty other
occasions in the course of the day besides my dinner. I want a form
for setting out upon a pleasant walk, for a moonlight ramble, for a
friendly meeting, or a solved problem. Why have we none for
books, those spiritual repasts—a grace before Milton—a grace

before Shakspeare—a devotional exercise proper to be said before reading the Fairy Queen?—but, the received ritual having prescribed these forms to the solitary ceremony of manducation, I shall confine my observations to the experience which I have had of the grace, properly so called ; commending my new scheme for extension to a niche in the grand philosophical, poetical, and perchance in part heretical, liturgy, now compiling by my friend Homo Humanus, for the use of a certain snug congregation of Utopian Rabelæsian Christians, no matter where assembled.

The form then of the benediction before eating has its beauty at a poor man's table, or at the simple and unprovocative repasts of children. It is here that the grace becomes exceedingly graceful. The indigent man, who hardly knows whether he shall have a meal the next day or not, sits down to his fare with a present sense of the blessing, which can be but feebly acted by the rich, into whose minds the conception of wanting a dinner could never, but by some extreme theory, have entered. The proper end of food—the animal sustenance—is barely contemplated by them. The poor man's bread is his daily bread, literally his bread for the day. Their courses are perennial.

Again, the plainest diet seems the fittest to be preceded by the grace. That which is least stimulative to appetite, leaves the mind most free for foreign considerations. A man may feel thankful, heartily thankful, over a dish of plain mutton with turnips, and have leisure to reflect upon the ordinance and institution of eating ; when he shall confess a perturbation of mind, inconsistent with the purposes of the grace, at the presence of venison or turtle. When I have sate (a *rarus hospes*) at rich men's tables, with the savoury soup and messes steaming up the nostrils, and moistening the lips of the guests with desire and a distracted choice, I have felt the introduction of that ceremony to be unseasonable. With the ravenous orgasm upon you, it seems impertinent to interpose a religious sentiment. It is a confusion of purpose to mutter out praises from a mouth that waters. The heats of epicurism put out the gentle flame of devotion. The incense which rises round is pagan, and the belly-god intercepts it for his own. The very excess of the provision beyond the needs, takes away all sense of proportion between the end and means. The giver is veiled by his gifts. You are startled at the injustice of returning thanks—for what ?—for having too much, while so many starve. It is to praise the Gods amiss.

I have observed this awkwardness felt, scarce consciously perhaps, by the good man who says the grace. I have seen it in clergymen and others—a sort of shame—a sense of the co-presence of circumstances which unhallow the blessing. After a devotional tone put on for a few seconds, how rapidly the speaker will fall into his common voice, helping himself or his neighbour, as if to get rid of some uneasy sensation of hypocrisy. Not that the good man was a hypocrite, or was not most conscientious in the discharge of the duty; but he felt in his inmost mind the incompatibility of the scene and the viands before him with the exercise of a calm and rational gratitude.

I hear somebody exclaim,—Would you have Christians sit down at table, like hogs to their troughs, without remembering the Giver? —no—I would have them sit down as Christians, remembering the Giver, and less like hogs. Or if their appetites must run riot, and they must pamper themselves with delicacies for which east and west are ransacked, I would have them postpone their benediction to a fitter season, when appetite is laid; when the still small voice can be heard, and the reason of the grace returns—with temperate diet and restricted dishes. Gluttony and surfeiting are no proper occasions for thanksgiving. When Jeshurun waxed fat, we read that he kicked. Virgil knew the harpy-nature better, when he put into the mouth of Celæno any thing but a blessing. We may be gratefully sensible of the deliciousness of some kinds of food beyond others, though that is a meaner and inferior gratitude: but the proper object of the grace is sustenance, not relishes; daily bread, not delicacies; the means of life, and not the means of pampering the carcass. With what frame or composure, I wonder, can a city chaplain pronounce his benediction at some great Hall feast, when he knows that his last concluding pious word—and that, in all probability, the sacred name which he preaches—is but the signal for so many impatient harpies to commence their foul orgies, with as little sense of true thankfulness (which is temperance) as those Virgilian fowl! It is well if the good man himself does not feel his devotions a little clouded, those foggy sensuous steams mingling with and polluting the pure altar sacrifice.

The severest satire upon full tables and surfeits is the banquet which Satan, in the Paradise Regained, provides for a temptation in the wilderness:

> A table richly spread in regal mode,
> With dishes piled, and meats of noblest sort
> And savour; beasts of chase, or fowl of game,
> In pastry built, or from the spit, or boiled,
> Gris-amber-steamed; all fish from sea or shore,
> Freshet or purling brook, for which was drained
> Pontus, and Lucrine bay, and Afric coast.

The Tempter, I warrant you, thought these cates would go down without the recommendatory preface of a benediction. They are like to be short graces where the devil plays the host.—I am afraid the poet wants his usual decorum in this place. Was he thinking of the old Roman luxury, or of a gaudy day at Cambridge? This was a temptation fitter for a Heliogabalus. The whole banquet is too civic and culinary, and the accompaniments altogether a profanation of that deep, abstracted, holy scene. The mighty artillery of sauces, which the cook-fiend conjures up, is out of proportion to the simple wants and plain hunger of the guest. He that disturbed him in his dreams, from his dreams might have been taught better. To the temperate fantasies of the famished Son of God, what sort of feasts presented themselves?—He dreamed indeed,

> ————As appetite is wont to dream,
> Of meats and drinks, nature's refreshment sweet.

But what meats?—

> Him thought, he by the brook of Cherith stood,
> And saw the ravens with their horny beaks
> Food to Elijah bringing, even and morn;
> Though ravenous, taught to abstain from what they brought:
> He saw the prophet also how he fled
> Into the desert, and how there he slept
> Under a juniper; then how awaked
> He found his supper on the coals prepared,
> And by the angel was bid rise and eat,
> And ate the second time after repose,
> The strength whereof sufficed him forty days:
> Sometimes, that with Elijah he partook,
> Or as a guest with Daniel at his pulse.

Nothing in Milton is finelier fancied than these temperate dreams of the divine Hungerer. To which of these two visionary banquets, think you, would the introduction of what is called the grace have been most fitting and pertinent?

Theoretically I am no enemy to graces; but practically I own that (before meat especially) they seem to involve something awkward and unseasonable. Our appetites, of one or another kind, are excellent spurs to our reason, which might otherwise but feebly set about the great ends of preserving and continuing the species. They are fit blessings to be contemplated at a distance with a becoming gratitude; but the moment of appetite (the judicious reader will apprehend me) is, perhaps, the least fit season for that exercise. The Quakers who go about their business, of every description, with more calmness than we, have more title to the use of these benedictory prefaces. I have always admired their silent grace, and the more because I have observed their applications to the meat and drink following to be less passionate and sensual than ours. They are neither gluttons nor wine-bibbers as a people. They eat, as a horse bolts his chopt hay, with indifference, calmness, and cleanly circumstances. They neither grease nor slop themselves. When I see a citizen in his bib and tucker, I cannot imagine it a surplice.

I am no Quaker at my food.   I confess I am not indifferent to
the kinds of it.   Those unctuous morsels of deer's flesh were not
made to be received with dispassionate services.   I hate a man who
swallows it, affecting not to know what he is eating.   I suspect his
taste in higher matters.   I shrink instinctively from one who
professes to like minced veal.   There is a physiognomical character
in the tastes for food.   C —— holds that a man cannot have a
pure mind who refuses apple-dumplings.   I am not certain but he
is right.   With the decay of my first innocence, I confess a less and
less relish daily for those innocuous cates.   The whole vegetable
tribe have lost their gust with me.   Only I stick to asparagus,
which still seems to inspire gentle thoughts.   I am impatient and
querulous under culinary disappointments, as to come home at the
dinner hour, for instance, expecting some savoury mess, and to
find one quite tasteless and sapidless.   Butter ill melted — that
commonest of kitchen failures—puts me beside my tenour.—The
author of the Rambler used to make inarticulate animal noises
over a favourite food.   Was this the music quite proper to be
preceded by the grace ?   or would the pious man have done better
to postpone his devotions to a season when the blessing might be
contemplated with less perturbation ?   I quarrel with no man's
tastes, nor would set my thin face against those excellent things,
in their way, jollity and feasting.   But as these exercises, however
laudable, have little in them of grace or gracefulness, a man should
be sure, before he ventures so to grace them, that while he is pretending his devotions otherwhere, he is not secretly kissing his hand
to some great fish—his Dagon—with a special consecration of no
ark but the fat tureen before him.   Graces are the sweet preluding
strains to the banquets of angels and children ; to the roots and
severer repasts of the Chartreuse ; to the slender, but not slenderly
acknowledged, refection of the poor and humble man : but at the
heaped-up boards of the pampered and the luxurious they become of
dissonant mood, less timed and tuned to the occasion, methinks,
than the noise of those better befitting organs would be, which
children hear tales of, at Hog's Norton.   We sit too long at our
meals, or are too curious in the study of them, or too disordered in
our application to them, or engross too great a portion of those
good things (which should be common) to our share, to be able
with any grace to say grace.   To be thankful for what we grasp
exceeding our proportion is to add hypocrisy to injustice.   A
lurking sense of this truth is what makes the performance of this
duty so cold and spiritless a service at most tables.   In houses
where the grace is as indispensable as the napkin, who has not seen
that never settled question arise, as to *who shall say it ;* while the
good man of the house and the visitor clergyman, or some other

guest belike of next authority from years or gravity, shall be
bandying about the office between them as a matter of compliment,
each of them not unwilling to shift the awkward burthen of an
equivocal duty from his own shoulders?

I once drank tea in company with two Methodist divines of
different persuasions, whom it was my fortune to introduce to each
other for the first time that evening. Before the first cup was
handed round, one of these reverend gentlemen put it to the other,
with all due solemnity, whether he chose to *say any thing*. It
seems it is the custom with some sectaries to put up a short prayer
before this meal also. His reverend brother did not at first quite
apprehend him, but upon an explanation, with little less importance he made answer, that it was not a custom known in his
church: in which courteous evasion the other acquiescing for good
manner's sake, or in compliance with a weak brother, the supplementary or tea-grace was waived altogether. With what spirit
might not Lucian have painted two priests, of *his* religion, playing
into each other's hands the compliment of performing or omitting
a sacrifice,—the hungry God meantime, doubtful of his incense,
with expectant nostrils hovering over the two flamens, and (as between two stools) going away in the end without his supper.

A short form upon these occasions is felt to want reverence; a
long one, I am afraid, cannot escape the charge of impertinence.
I do not quite approve of the epigrammatic conciseness with which
that equivocal wag (but my pleasant school-fellow) C. V. L., when
importuned for a grace, used to inquire, first slyly leering down
the table, "Is there no clergyman here?"—significantly adding,
"thank G—." Nor do I think our old form at school quite pertinent, where we were used to preface our bald bread and cheese
suppers with a preamble, connecting with that humble blessing a
recognition of benefits the most awful and overwhelming to the
imagination which religion has to offer. *Non tunc illis erat locus.*
I remember we were put to it to reconcile the phrase "good
creatures," upon which the blessing rested, with the fare set before
us, wilfully understanding that expression in a low and animal
sense,—till some one recalled a legend, which told how in the golden
days of Christ's, the young Hospitallers were wont to have smoking
joints of roast meat upon their nightly boards, till some pious
benefactor, commiserating the decencies, rather than the palates,
of the children, commuted our flesh for garments, and gave us—
horresco referens—trowsers instead of mutton.

MY FIRST PLAY

AT the north end of Cross-court there yet stands a portal, of some architectural pretensions, though reduced to humble use, serving at present for an entrance to a printing-office. This old door-way, if you are young, reader, you may not know was the identical pit entrance to Old Drury—Garrick's Drury—all of it that is left. I never pass it without shaking some forty years from off my shoulders, recurring to the evening when I passed through it to see *my first play*. The afternoon had been wet, and the condition of our going (the elder folks and myself) was, that the rain should cease. With what a beating heart did I watch from the window the puddles, from the stillness of which I was taught to prognosticate the desired cessation ! I seem to remember the last spurt, and the glee with which I ran to announce it.

We went with orders, which my godfather F. had sent us. He kept the oil shop (now Davies's) at the corner of Featherstone-building, in Holborn. F. was a tall grave person, lofty in speech, and had pretensions above his rank. He associated in those days with John Palmer, the comedian, whose gait and bearing he seemed to copy ; if John (which is quite as likely) did not rather borrow somewhat of his manner from my godfather. He was also known to, and visited by, Sheridan. It was to his house in Holborn that young Brinsley brought his first wife on her elopement with him from a boarding-school at Bath—the beautiful Maria Linley. My parents were present (over a quadrille table) when he arrived in the evening with his harmonious charge.—From either of these connexions it may be inferred that my godfather could command an order for the then Drury-lane theatre at pleasure—and, indeed, a pretty liberal issue of those cheap billets, in Brinsley's easy autograph, I have heard him say was the sole remuneration which he had received for many years' nightly illumination of the orchestra and various avenues of that theatre—and he was content it should be so. The honour of Sheridan's familiarity—or supposed familiarity—was better to my godfather than money.

F. was the most gentlemanly of oilmen ; grandiloquent, yet courteous. His delivery of the commonest matters of fact was Ciceronian. He had two Latin words almost constantly in his mouth (how odd sounds Latin from an oilman's lips !), which my better knowledge since has enabled me to correct. In strict pronunciation they should have been sounded *vice versâ*—but in those young years they impressed me with more awe than they would now do, read aright from Seneca or Varro—in his own peculiar pronunciation, monosyllabically elaborated, or Anglicized, into some-

thing like *verse verse*.   By an imposing manner, and the help of
these distorted syllables, he climbed (but that was little) to the
highest parochial honours which St. Andrew's has to bestow.

He is dead—and thus much I thought due to his memory, both
for my first orders (little wondrous talismans!—slight keys, and insignificant to outward sight, but opening to me more than Arabian
paradises!) and moreover, that by his testamentary beneficence I
came into possession of the only landed property which I could ever
call my own—situate near the road-way village of pleasant Puckeridge, in Hertfordshire.   When I journeyed down to take possession,
and planted foot on my own ground, the stately habits of the donor
descended upon me, and I strode (shall I confess the vanity?) with
larger paces over my allotment of three quarters of an acre, with its
commodious mansion in the midst, with the feeling of an English
freeholder that all betwixt sky and centre was my own.   The estate
has passed into more prudent hands, and nothing but an agrarian
can restore it.

In those days were pit orders.   Beshrew the uncomfortable
manager who abolished them!—with one of these we went.   I
remember the waiting at the door—not that which is left—but
between that and an inner door in shelter—O when shall I be such
an expectant again!—with the cry of nonpareils, an indispensable
play-house accompaniment in those days.   As near as I can recollect, the fashionable pronunciation of the theatrical fruiteresses
then was, " Chase some oranges, chase some numparels, chase a bill
of the play ; "—chase *pro* chuse.   But when we got in, and I beheld
the green curtain that veiled a heaven to my imagination, which was
soon to be disclosed——the breathless anticipations I endured!   I
had seen something like it in the plate prefixed to Troilus and
Cressida, in Rowe's Shakspeare—the tent scene with Diomede—and
a sight of that plate can always bring back in a measure the feeling
of that evening.—The boxes at that time, full of well-dressed
women of quality, projected over the pit ; and the pilasters reaching
down were adorned with a glistering substance (I know not what)
under glass (as it seemed), resembling—a homely fancy—but I
judged it to be sugar-candy—yet, to my raised imagination, divested
of its homelier qualities, it appeared a glorified candy!—The
orchestra lights at length arose, those " fair Auroras! "   Once .the
bell sounded.   It was to ring out yet once again—and, incapable of
the anticipation, I reposed my shut eyes in a sort of resignation
upon the maternal lap.   It rang the second time.   The curtain
drew up—I was not past six years old—and the play was Artaxerxes!

I had dabbled a little in the Universal History—the ancient
part of it—and here was the court of Persia.   It was being ad-

mitted to a sight of the past. I took no proper interest in the action going on, for I understood not its import—but I heard the word Darius, and I was in the midst of Daniel. All feeling was absorbed in vision. Gorgeous vests, gardens, palaces, princesses, passed before me. I knew not players. I was in Persepolis for the time; and the burning idol of their devotion almost converted me into a worshipper. I was awe-struck, and believed those significations to be something more than elemental fires. It was all enchantment and a dream. No such pleasure has since visited me but in dreams.—Harlequin's Invasion followed; where, I remember, the transformation of the magistrates into reverend beldams seemed to me a piece of grave historic justice, and the tailor carrying his own head to be as sober a verity as the legend of St. Denys.

The next play to which I was taken was the Lady of the Manor, of which, with the exception of some scenery, very faint traces are left in my memory. It was followed by a pantomime, called Lun's Ghost—a satiric touch, I apprehend, upon Rich, not long since dead—but to my apprehension (too sincere for satire), Lun was as remote a piece of antiquity as Lud—the father of a line of Harlequins—transmitting his dagger of lath (the wooden sceptre) through countless ages. I saw the primeval Motley come from his silent tomb in a ghastly vest of white patch-work, like the apparition of a dead rainbow. So Harlequins (thought I) look when they are dead.

My third play followed in quick succession. It was the Way of the World. I think I must have sat at it as grave as a judge; for, I remember, the hysteric affectations of good Lady Wishfort affected me like some solemn tragic passion. Robinson Crusoe followed; in which Crusoe, man Friday, and the parrot, were as good and authentic as in the story.—The clownery and pantaloonery of these pantomimes have clean passed out of my head. I believe, I no more laughed at them, than at the same age I should have been disposed to laugh at the grotesque Gothic heads (seeming to me then replete with devout meaning) that gape, and grin, in stone around the inside of the old Round Church (my church) of the Templars.

I saw these plays in the season 1781-2, when I was from six to seven years old. After the intervention of six or seven other years (for at school all play-going was inhibited) I again entered the doors of a theatre. That old Artaxerxes evening had never done ringing in my fancy. I expected the same feelings to come again with the same occasion. But we differ from ourselves less at sixty and sixteen, than the latter does from six. In that interval what had I not lost! At the first period I knew nothing, understood nothing, discriminated nothing. I felt all, loved all, wondered all—

> Was nourished, I could not tell how—

I had left the temple a devotee, and was returned a rationalist. The same things were there materially; but the emblem, the reference, was gone!—The green curtain was no longer a veil, drawn between two worlds, the unfolding of which was to bring back past ages, to present "a royal ghost,"—but a certain quantity of green baize, which was to separate the audience for a given time from certain of their fellow-men who were to come forward and pretend those parts. The lights—the orchestra lights—came up a clumsy machinery. The first ring, and the second ring, was now but a trick of the prompter's bell—which had been, like the note of the cuckoo, a phantom of a voice, no hand seen or guessed at which ministered to its warning. The actors were men and women painted. I thought the fault was in them; but it was in myself, and the alteration which those many centuries—of six short twelve-months—had wrought in me.—Perhaps it was fortunate for me that the play of the evening was but an indifferent comedy, as it gave me time to crop some unreasonable expectations, which might have interfered with the genuine emotions with which I was soon after enabled to enter upon the first appearance to me of Mrs. Siddons in Isabella. Comparison and retrospection soon yielded to the present attraction of the scene; and the theatre became to me, upon a new stock, the most delightful of recreations.

DREAM-CHILDREN;

A REVERIE

CHILDREN love to listen to stories about their elders, when *they* were children; to stretch their imagination to the conception of a traditionary great-uncle, or grandame, whom they never saw. It was in this spirit that my little ones crept about me the other evening to hear about their great-grandmother Field, who lived in a great house in Norfolk (a hundred times bigger than that in which they and papa lived) which had been the scene—so at least it was generally believed in that part of the country—of the tragic incidents which they had lately become familiar with from the ballad of the Children in the Wood. Certain it is that the whole story of the children and their cruel uncle was to be seen fairly carved out in wood upon the chimney-piece of the great hall, the whole story down to the Robin Redbreasts, till a foolish rich person pulled it down to set up a marble one of modern invention in its stead, with no story upon it. Here Alice put out one of her dear mother's looks, too tender to be called upbraiding. Then I went on to say, how religious and how good their great-grandmother Field was, how beloved and respected by every body, though she was not indeed the mistress of this great house, but had only the charge of it (and yet in some respects she might be said to be the mistress of it too) committed to her by the owner, who preferred living in a newer and more fashionable mansion which he had purchased somewhere in the adjoining county; but still she lived in it in a manner as if it had been her own, and kept up the dignity of the great house in a sort while she lived, which after-wards came to decay, and was nearly pulled down, and all its old ornaments stripped and carried away to the owner's other house, where they were set up, and looked as awkward as if some one were to carry away the old tombs they had seen lately at the Abbey, and stick them up in Lady C.'s tawdry gilt drawing-room. Here John smiled, as much as to say, " that would be foolish indeed." And then I told how, when she came to die, her funeral was attended by a concourse of all the poor, and some of the gentry too, of the neighbourhood for many miles round, to show their respect for her memory, because she had been such a good and religious woman; so good indeed that she knew all the Psaltery by heart, ay, and a great part of the Testament besides. Here little Alice spread her hands. Then I told what a tall, upright, graceful person their great-grandmother Field once was; and how in her youth she was esteemed the best dancer—here Alice's little right foot played an involuntary movement, till, upon my looking grave, it desisted—the best dancer, I was saying, in the county, till a cruel disease, called a cancer, came, and bowed her down with pain; but it could never bend her good spirits, or make them stoop, but they were still upright, because she was so good and religious. Then I told how she was used to sleep by herself in a lone chamber of the great lone house; and how she believed that an apparition of two infants was to be seen at midnight gliding up and down the great staircase near where she slept, but she said " those innocents would do her no harm; " and how frightened I used to be, though in those days I had my maid to sleep with me, because I was never half so good or religious as she —and yet I never saw the infants. Here John expanded all his eye-brows and tried to look courageous. Then I told how good she was to all her grand-children, having us to the great-house in the holydays, where I in particular used to spend many hours by myself, in gazing upon the old busts of the Twelve Cæsars, that had been Emperors of Rome, till the old marble heads would seem to live again, or I to be turned into marble with them; how I never could be tired with roaming about that huge mansion, with its vast empty rooms, with their worn-out hangings, fluttering tapestry, and carved oaken pannels, with the gilding almost rubbed out—sometimes in the spacious old-fashioned gardens, which I had almost to myself, unless when now and then a solitary gardening man would cross me—and how the nectarines and peaches hung upon the walls, without my ever offering to pluck them, because they were forbidden fruit, unless now and then,—and because I had more pleasure in strolling about among the old melancholy-looking yew trees, or the firs, and picking up the red berries, and the fir apples, which were good for nothing but to look at—or in lying about upon the fresh grass, with all the fine garden smells around me—or basking in the orangery, till I could almost fancy myself ripening too along with the oranges and the limes in that grateful warmth—or in watching the dace that darted to and fro in the fish-pond, at the bottom of the garden, with here and there a great sulky pike hanging midway down the water in silent state, as if it mocked at their impertinent friskings,—I had more pleasure in these busy-idle diversions than in all the sweet flavours of peaches, nectarines, oranges, and such like common baits of children. Here John slyly deposited back upon the plate a bunch of grapes, which, not unobserved by Alice, he had meditated dividing with her, and both seemed willing to relinquish them for the present as irrelevant. Then in somewhat a more heightened tone, I told how, though their great-grandmother Field loved all her grand-children, yet in an especial manner she might be said to love their uncle, John L——, because he was so handsome and spirited a youth, and a king to the rest of us; and, instead of moping about in solitary corners, like some of us, he would mount the most mettlesome horse he could get, when but an imp no bigger than themselves, and make it carry him half over the county in a morning, and join the hunters when there were any out—and yet he loved the old great house and gardens too, but had too much spirit to be always pent up within their boundaries—and how their uncle grew up to man's estate as brave as he was handsome, to the admiration of every body, but of their great-grandmother Field most especially; and how he used to carry me upon his back when I was a lame-footed boy—for he was a good bit older than me—many a mile when I could not walk for pain;—and how in after life he became lame-footed too, and I did not always (I fear) make allowances enough for him when he was impatient, and in pain, nor remember sufficiently how considerate he had been to me when I was lame-footed ; and how when he died, though he had not been dead an hour, it seemed as if he had died a great while ago, such a distance there is betwixt life and death ; and how I bore his death as I thought pretty well at first, but afterwards it haunted and haunted me ; and though I did not cry or take it to heart as some do, and as I think he would have done if I had died, yet I missed him all day long, and knew not till then how much I had loved him. I missed his kindness, and I missed his crossness, and wished him to be alive again, to be quarrelling with him (for we quarreled some-times), rather than not have him again, and was as uneasy without him, as he their poor uncle must have been when the doctor took off his limb. Here the children fell a crying, and asked if their little mourning which they had on was not for uncle John, and they looked up, and prayed me not to go on about their uncle, but to tell them some stories about their pretty dead mother. Then I told how for seven long years, in hope sometimes, sometimes in despair, yet persisting ever, I courted the fair Alice W—n ; and, as much as children could understand, I explained to them what coyness, and difficulty, and denial meant in maidens—when suddenly, turning to Alice, the soul of the first Alice looked out at her eyes with such a reality of re-presentment, that I became in doubt which of them stood there before me, or whose that bright hair was ; and while I stood gazing, both the children gradually grew fainter to my view, receding, and still receding till nothing at last but two mournful features were seen in the uttermost distance, which, without speech, strangely impressed upon me the effects of speech ; " We are not of Alice, nor of thee, nor are we children at all. The children of Alice called Bartrum father. We are nothing ; less than nothing, and dreams. We are only what might have been, and must wait upon the tedious shores of Lethe millions of ages before we have existence, and a name"——and immediately awaking, I found myself quietly seated in my bachelor arm-chair, where I had fallen asleep, with the faithful Bridget unchanged by my side—but John L. (or James Elia) was gone for ever.

DISTANT CORRESPONDENTS

In a Letter to B. F. Esq. at Sydney, New South Wales

MY dear F.—When I think how welcome the sight of a letter from the world where you were born must be to you in that strange one to which you have been transplanted, I feel some compunctious visitings at my long silence. But, indeed, it is no easy effort to set about a correspondence at our distance. The weary world of waters between us oppresses the imagination. It is difficult to conceive how a scrawl of mine should ever stretch across it. It is a sort of presumption to expect that one's thoughts should live so far. It is like writing for posterity ; and reminds me of one of Mrs. Rowe's superscriptions, " Alcander to Strephon, in the shades." Cowley's Post-Angel is no more than would be expedient in such an intercourse. One drops a packet at Lombard-street, and in twenty-four hours a friend in Cumberland gets it as fresh as if it came in ice. It is only like whispering through a long trumpet. But suppose a tube let down from the moon, with yourself at one end, and *the man* at the other ; it would be some balk to the spirit of conversation, if you knew that the dialogue exchanged with that interesting theosophist would take two or three revolutions of a higher luminary in its passage. Yet for aught I know, you may be some parasangs nigher that primitive idea— Plato's man—than we in England here have the honour to reckon ourselves.

Epistolary matter usually compriseth three topics ; news, sentiment, and puns. In the latter, I include all non-serious subjects ; or subjects serious in themselves, but treated after my fashion, non-seriously.—And first, for news. In them the most desirable circumstance, I suppose, is that they shall be true. But what security can I have that what I now send you for truth shall not before you get it unaccountably turn into a lie ? For instance, our mutual friend P. is at this present writing—*my Now*—in good health, and enjoys a fair share of worldly reputation. You are glad to hear it. This is natural and friendly. But at this present reading—*your Now*—he may possibly be in the Bench, or going to be hanged, which in reason ought to abate something of your transport (*i.e.* at hearing he was well, &c.), or at least considerably to modify it. I am going to the play this evening, to have a laugh with Munden. You have no theatre, I think you told me, in your land of d——d realities. You naturally lick your lips, and envy me my felicity. Think but a moment, and you will correct the hateful emotion. Why, it is Sunday morning with you, and 1823.

This confusion of tenses, this grand solecism of *two presents*, is in a degree common to all postage.   But if I sent you word to Bath or the Devises, that I was expecting the aforesaid treat this evening, though at the moment you received the intelligence my full feast of fun would be over, yet there would be for a day or two after, as you would well know, a smack, a relish left upon my mental palate, which would give rational encouragement for you to foster a portion at least of the disagreeable passion, which it was in part my intention to produce.   But ten months hence your envy or your sympathy would be as useless as a passion spent upon the dead.   Not only does truth, in these long intervals, un-essence herself, but (what is harder) one cannot venture a crude fiction for the fear that it may ripen into a truth upon the voyage.   What a wild improbable banter I put upon you some three years since—— of Will Weatherall having married a servant-maid !   I remember gravely consulting you how we were to receive her—for Will's wife was in no case to be rejected ; and your no less serious replication in the matter ; how tenderly you advised an abstemious introduction of literary topics before the lady, with a caution not to be too forward in bringing on the carpet matters more within the sphere of her intelligence ; your deliberate judgment, or rather wise suspension of sentence, how far jacks, and spits, and mops, could with propriety be introduced as subjects ; whether the conscious avoiding of all such matters in discourse would not have a worse look than the taking of them casually in our way ; in what manner we should carry ourselves to our maid Becky, Mrs William Weatherall being by ; whether we should show more delicacy, and a truer sense of respect for Will's wife, by treating Becky with our customary chiding before her, or by an unusual deferential civility paid to Becky as to a person of great worth, but thrown by the caprice of fate into a humble station.   There were difficulties, I remember, on both sides, which you did me the favour to state with the precision of a lawyer, united to the tenderness of a friend.   I laughed in my sleeve at your solemn pleadings, when lo ! while I was valuing myself upon this flam put upon you in New South Wales, the devil in England, jealous possibly of any lie-children not his own, or working after my copy, has actually instigated our friend (not three days since) to the commission of a matrimony, which I had only conjured up for your diversion. William Weatherall has married Mrs Cotterel's maid.   But to take it in its truest sense, you will see, my dear F., that news from me must become history to you ; which I neither profess to write, nor indeed care much for reading.   No person, under a diviner, can with any prospect of veracity conduct a correspondence at such an arm's length.   Two prophets, indeed, might thus interchange

intelligence with effect; the epoch of the writer (Habbakuk)
falling in with the true present time of the receiver (Daniel);
but then we are no prophets.

Then as to sentiment. It fares little better with that. This
kind of dish, above all, requires to be served up hot; or sent off in
water-plates, that your friend may have it almost as warm as
yourself. If it have time to cool, it is the most tasteless of all
cold meats. I have often smiled at a conceit of the late Lord C.
It seems that travelling somewhere about Geneva, he came to some
pretty green spot, or nook, where a willow, or something, hung so
fantastically and invitingly over a stream—was it?—or a rock?—
no matter—but the stillness and the repose, after a weary journey
'tis likely, in a languid moment of his lordship's hot restless life, so
took his fancy, that he could imagine no place so proper, in the
event of his death, to lay his bones in. This was all very natural
and excusable as a sentiment, and shows his character in a very
pleasing light. But when from a passing sentiment it came to be
an act; and when, by a positive testamentary disposal, his remains
were actually carried all that way from England; who was there,
some desperate sentimentalists excepted, that did not ask the
question, Why could not his lordship have found a spot as
solitary, a nook as romantic, a tree as green and pendent, with a
stream as emblematic to his purpose, in Surrey, in Dorset, or in
Devon? Conceive the sentiment boarded up, freighted, entered
at the Custom House (startling the tide-waiters with the novelty),
hoisted into a ship. Conceive it pawed about and handled between
the rude jests of tarpaulin ruffians—a thing of its delicate texture
—the salt bilge wetting it till it became as vapid as a damaged
lustring. Suppose it in material danger (mariners have some
superstition about sentiments) of being tossed over in a fresh gale
to some propitiatory shark (spirit of Saint Gothard, save us from a
quietus so foreign to the deviser's purpose!) but it has happily
evaded a fishy consummation. Trace it then to its lucky landing
—at Lyons shall we say?—I have not the map before me—jostled
upon four men's shoulders—baiting at this town—stopping to
refresh at t'other village—waiting a passport here, a license there;
the sanction of the magistracy in this district, the concurrence of
the ecclesiastics in that canton; till at length it arrives at its
destination, tired out and jaded, from a brisk sentiment, into a
feature of silly pride or tawdry senseless affectation. How few
sentiments, my dear F., I am afraid we can set down, in the sailor's
phrase, as quite sea-worthy.

Lastly, as to the agreeable levities, which, though contemptible
in bulk, are the twinkling corpuscula which should irradiate a right
friendly epistle—your puns and small jests are, I apprehend, extremely

circumscribed in their sphere of action. They are so far from a
capacity of being packed up and sent beyond sea, they will scarce
endure to be transported by hand from this room to the next.
Their vigour is as the instant of their birth. Their nutriment for
their brief existence is the intellectual atmosphere of the by-
standers : or this last, is the fine slime of Nilus—the *melior lutus,*
—whose maternal recipiency is as necessary as the *sol pater* to
their equivocal generation. A pun hath a hearty kind of present
ear-kissing smack with it ; you can no more transmit it in its
pristine flavour, than you can send a kiss.—Have you not tried in
some instances to palm off a yesterday's pun upon a gentleman, and has it answered ? Not but it was new to his hearing,
but it did not seem to come new from you. It did not hitch in.
It was like picking up at a village ale-house a two days old newspaper. You have not seen it before, but you resent the stale thing
as an affront. This sort of merchandise above all requires a quick
return. A pun, and its recognitory laugh, must be co-instantaneous.
The one is the brisk lightning, the other the fierce thunder. A
moment's interval, and the link is snapped. A pun is reflected
from a friend's face as from a mirror. Who would consult his
sweet visnomy, if the polished surface were two or three minutes
(not to speak of twelve-months, my dear F.) in giving back its
copy ?

I cannot image to myself whereabout you are. When I try
to fix it, Peter Wilkins's island comes across me. Sometimes you
seem to be in the *Hades* of *Thieves.* I see Diogenes prying among
you with his perpetual fruitless lantern. What must you be
willing by this time to give for the sight of an honest man ! You
must almost have forgotten how *we* look. And tell me, what your
Sydneyites do ? are they th**v*ng all day long ? Merciful heaven !
what property can stand against such a depredation ! The kan-
garoos—your Aborigines—do they keep their primitive simplicity
un-Europe-tainted, with those little short fore-puds, looking like
a lesson framed by nature to the pickpocket ! Marry, for diving
into fobs they are rather lamely provided *a priori ;* but if the hue
and cry were once up, they would show as fair a pair of hind-
shifters as the expertest loco-motor in the colony.—We hear the
most improbable tales at this distance. Pray, is it true that the
young Spartans among you are born with six fingers, which spoils
their scanning ?—It must look very odd ; but use reconciles. For
their scansion, it is less to be regretted, for if they take it into
their heads to be poets, it is odds but they turn out, the greater
part of them, vile plagiarists.—Is there much difference to see to
between the son of a th**f, and the grandson ? or where does the
taint stop ? Do you bleach in three or in four generations ?—I

have many questions to put, but ten Delphic voyages can be made in a shorter time than it will take to satisfy my scruples.—Do you grow your own hemp?—What is your staple trade, exclusive of the national profession, I mean? Your lock-smiths, I take it, are some of your great capitalists.

I am insensibly chatting to you as familiarly as when we used to exchange good-morrows out of our old contiguous windows, in pump-famed Hare-court in the Temple. Why did you ever leave that quiet corner?—Why did I?—with its complement of four poor elms, from whose smoke-dyed barks, the theme of jesting ruralists, I picked my first lady-birds! My heart is as dry as that spring sometimes proves in a thirsty August, when I revert to the space that is between us; a length of passage enough to render obsolete the phrases of our English letters before they can reach you. But while I talk, I think you hear me,—thoughts dallying with vain surmise—

> Aye me! while thee the seas and sounding shores
> Hold far away.

Come back, before I am grown into a very old man, so as you shall hardly know me. Come, before Bridget walks on crutches. Girls whom you left children have become sage matrons, while you are tarrying there. The blooming Miss W—r (you remember Sally W—r) called upon us yesterday, an aged crone. Folks, whom you knew, die off every year. Formerly, I thought that death was wearing out,—I stood ramparted about with so many healthy friends. The departure of J. W., two springs back corrected my delusion. Since then the old divorcer has been busy. If you do not make haste to return, there will be little left to greet you, of me, or mine.

***

THE PRAISE OF CHIMNEY-SWEEPERS

I LIKE to meet a sweep—understand me—not a grown sweeper —old chimney-sweepers are by no means attractive—but one of those tender novices, blooming through their first nigritude, the maternal washings not quite effaced from the cheek—such as come forth with the dawn, or somewhat earlier, with their little professional notes sounding like the *peep peep* of a young sparrow; or liker to the matin lark should I pronounce them, in their aerial ascents not seldom anticipating the sun-rise?

I have a kindly yearning towards these dim specks—poor blots—innocent blacknesses—

I reverence these young Africans of our own growth—these almost clergy imps, who sport their cloth without assumption; and from their little pulpits (the tops of chimneys), in the nipping air of a December morning, preach a lesson of patience to mankind.

When a child, what a mysterious pleasure it was to witness their operation! to see a chit no bigger than one's-self enter, one knew not by what process, into what seemed the *fauces Averni*—to pursue him in imagination, as he went sounding on through so many dark stifling caverns, horrid shades!—to shudder with the idea that "now, surely, he must be lost for ever!"—to revive at hearing his feeble shout of discovered day-light—and then (O fulness of delight) running out of doors, to come just in time to see the sable phenomenon emerge in safety, the brandished weapon of his art victorious like some flag waved over a conquered citadel! I seem to remember having been told, that a bad sweep was once left in a stack with his brush, to indicate which way the wind blew. It was an awful spectacle certainly; not much unlike the old stage direction in Macbeth, where the "Apparition of a child crowned with a tree in his hand rises."

Reader, if thou meetest one of these small gentry in thy early rambles, it is good to give him a penny. It is better to give him two-pence. If it be starving weather, and to the proper troubles of his hard occupation, a pair of kibed heels (no unusual accompaniment) be superadded, the demand on thy humanity will surely rise to a tester.

There is a composition, the ground-work of which I have understood to be the sweet wood 'yclept sassafras. This wood boiled down to a kind of tea, and tempered with an infusion of milk and sugar, hath to some tastes a delicacy beyond the China luxury. 1 know not how thy palate may relish it; for myself, with every deference to the judicious Mr. Read, who hath time out of mind kept open a shop (the only one he avers in London) for the vending of this " wholesome and pleasant beverage, on the south side of Fleet-street, as thou approachest Bridge-street—*the only Salopian house,*—I have never yet adventured to dip my own particular lip in a basin of his commended ingredients—a cautious premonition to the olfactories constantly whispering to me, that my stomach must infallibly, with all due courtesy, decline it. Yet I have seen palates, otherwise not uninstructed in dietetical elegances, sup it up with avidity.

I know not by what particular conformation of the organ it happens, but I have always found that this composition is surprisingly gratifying to the palate of a young chimney-sweeper—

whether the oily particles (sassafras is slightly oleaginous) do
attenuate and soften the fuliginous concretions, which are sometimes
found (in dissections) to adhere to the roof of the mouth in these
unfledged practitioners ; or whether Nature, sensible that she had
mingled too much of bitter wood in the lot of these raw victims,
caused to grow out of the earth her sassafras for a sweet lenitive—
but so it is, that no possible taste or odour to the senses of a young
chimney-sweeper can convey a delicate excitement comparable to
this mixture. Being penniless, they will yet hang their black heads
over the ascending steam, to gratify one sense if possible, seemingly
no less pleased than those domestic animals—cats—when they purr
over a new-found sprig of valerian. There is something more in
these sympathies than philosophy can inculcate.

Now albeit Mr. Read boasteth, not without reason, that his is the
only Salopian house ; yet be it known to thee, reader—if thou art
one who keepest what are called good hours, thou art haply
ignorant of the fact—he hath a race of industrious imitators, who
from stalls, and under open sky, dispense the same savoury mess to
humbler customers, at that dead time of the dawn, when (as extremes
meet) the rake, reeling home from his midnight cups, and the hard-
handed artisan leaving his bed to resume the premature labours of
the day, jostle, not unfrequently to the manifest disconcerting of the
former, for the honours of the pavement. It is the time when, in
summer, between the expired and the not yet relumined kitchen-
fires, the kennels of our fair metropolis give forth their least satisfactory odours. The rake, who wisheth to dissipate his o'er-night
vapours in more grateful coffee, curses the ungenial fume, as he
passeth ; but the artisan stops to taste, and blesses the fragrant
breakfast.

This is *Saloop*—the precocious herb-woman's darling—the delight of the early gardener, who transports his smoking cabbages by
break of day from Hammersmith to Covent-garden's famed piazzas
—the delight, and, oh I fear, too often the envy, of the unpennied
sweep. Him shouldest thou haply encounter, with his dim visage
pendent over the grateful steam, regale him with a sumptuous basin
(it will cost thee but three half-pennies) and a slice of delicate bread
and butter (an added halfpenny)—so may thy culinary fires, eased
of the o'er-charged secretions from thy worse-placed hospitalities,
curl up a lighter volume to the welkin—so may the descending soot
never taint thy costly well-ingredienced soups—nor the odious cry,
quick-reaching from street to street, of the *fired chimney*, invite
the rattling engines from ten adjacent parishes, to disturb for a
casual scintillation thy peace and pocket !

I am by nature extremely susceptible of street affronts ; the jeers
and taunts of the populace ; the low-bred triumph they display over

the casual trip, or splashed stocking, of a gentleman.   Yet can I
endure the jocularity of a young sweep with something more than
forgiveness.—In the last winter but one, pacing along Cheapside with my accustomed precipitation when I walk westward, a
treacherous slide brought me upon my back in an instant.   I
scrambled up with pain and shame enough—yet outwardly trying to
face it down, as if nothing had happened—when the roguish grin of
one of these young wits encountered me.   There he stood, pointing
me out with his dusky finger to the mob, and to a poor woman (I
suppose his mother) in particular, till the tears for the exquisiteness
of the fun (so he thought it) worked themselves out at the corners
of his poor red eyes, red from many a previous weeping, and soot-
inflamed, yet twinkling through all with such a joy, snatched out of
desolation, that Hogarth——but Hogarth has got him already
(how could he miss him?) in the March to Finchley, grinning at the
pye-man——there he stood, as he stands in the picture, irremov-
able, as if the jest was to last for ever—with such a maximum of
glee, and minimum of mischief, in his mirth—for the grin of a
genuine sweep hath absolutely no malice in it—that I could have
been content, if the honour of a gentleman might endure it, to have
remained his butt and his mockery till midnight.

I am by theory obdurate to the seductiveness of what are called
a fine set of teeth.   Every pair of rosy lips (the ladies must pardon
me) is a casket, presumably holding such jewels ; but, methinks,
they should take leave to " air " them as frugally as possible.   The
fine lady, or fine gentleman, who show me their teeth, show me
bones.   Yet must I confess, that from the mouth of a true sweep a
display (even to ostentation) of those white and shining ossifications,
strikes me as an agreeable anomaly in manners, and an allowable
piece of foppery.   It is, as when

> A sable cloud
> Turns forth her silver lining on the night.

It is like some remnant of gentry not quite extinct; a badge of
better days ; a hint of nobility :—and, doubtless, under the ob-
scuring darkness and double night of their forlorn disguisement,
oftentimes lurketh good blood, and gentle conditions, derived from
lost ancestry, and a lapsed pedigree.   The premature apprentice-
ments of these tender victims give but too much encouragement, I
fear, to clandestine, and almost infantile abductions ; the seeds of
civility and true courtesy, so often discernible in these young grafts
(not otherwise to be accounted for) plainly hint at some forced
adoptions ; many noble Rachels mourning for their children, even in
our days, countenance the fact ; the tales of fairy-spiriting may
shadow a lamentable verity, and the recovery of the young Montagu

be but a solitary instance of good fortune, out of many irreparable
and hopeless *defiliations*.

In one of the state-beds at Arundel Castle, a few years since—
under a ducal canopy—(that seat of the Howards is an object of
curiosity to visitors, chiefly for its beds, in which the late duke was
especially a connoisseur) — encircled with curtains of delicatest
crimson, with starry coronets inwoven—folded between a pair of
sheets whiter and softer than the lap where Venus lulled Ascanius—
was discovered by chance, after all methods of search had failed, at
noon-day, fast asleep, a lost chimney-sweeper. The little creature,
having somehow confounded his passage among the intricacies of
those lordly chimneys, by some unknown aperture had alighted
upon this magnificent chamber ; and, tired with his tedious
explorations, was unable to resist the delicious invitement to
repose, which he there saw exhibited ; so, creeping between the
sheets very quietly, laid his black head upon the pillow, and slept
like a young Howard.

Such is the account given to the visitors at the Castle.—But
I cannot help seeming to perceive a confirmation of what I have
just hinted at in this story. A high instinct was at work in the
case, or I am mistaken. Is it probable that a poor child of that
description, with whatever weariness he might be visited, would
have ventured, under such a penalty, as he would be taught
to expect, to uncover the sheets of a Duke's bed, and deliberately
to lay himself down between them, when the rug, or the carpet,
presented an obvious couch, still far above his pretensions—is this
probable, I would ask, if the great power of nature, which I contend for, had not been manifested within him, prompting to
the adventure ? Doubtless this young nobleman (for such my
mind misgives me that he must be) was allured by some memory,
not amounting to full consciousness, of his condition in infancy,
when he was used to be lapt by his mother, or his nurse, in just
such sheets as he there found, into which he was now but creeping
back as into his proper *incunabula*, and resting-place.—By no
other theory, than by this sentiment of a pre-existent state (as I
may call it), can I explain a deed so venturous, and, indeed, upon
any other system, so indecorous, in this tender, but unseasonable,
sleeper.

My pleasant friend JEM WHITE was so impressed with a belief
of metamorphoses like this frequently taking place, that in some
sort to reverse the wrongs of fortune in these poor changelings, he
instituted an annual feast of chimney-sweepers, at which it was his
pleasure to officiate as host and waiter. It was a solemn supper
held in Smithfield, upon the yearly return of the fair of St. Bartholomew. Cards were issued a week before to the master-sweeps

in and about the metropolis, confining the invitation to their younger fry. Now and then an elderly stripling would get in among us, and be good-naturedly winked at ; but our main body were infantry. One unfortunate wight, indeed, who, relying upon his dusky suit, had intruded himself into our party, but by tokens was providentially discovered in time to be no chimney-sweeper (all is not soot which looks so), was quoited out of the presence with universal indignation, as not having on the wedding garment ; but in general the greatest harmony prevailed. The place chosen was a convenient spot among the pens, at the north side of the fair, not so far distant as to be impervious to the agreeable hubbub of that vanity ; but remote enough not to be obvious to the interruption of every gaping spectator in it. The guests assembled about seven. In those little temporary parlours three tables were spread with napery, not so fine as substantial, and at every board a comely hostess presided with her pan of hissing sausages. The nostrils of the young rogues dilated at the savour. JAMES WHITE, as head waiter, had charge of the first table ; and myself, with our trusty companion BIGOD, ordinarily ministered to the other two. There was clambering and jostling, you may be sure, who should get at the first table — for Rochester in his maddest days could not have done the humours of the scene with more spirit than my friend. After some general expression of thanks for the honour the company had done him, his inaugural ceremony was to clasp the greasy waist of old dame Ursula (the fattest of the three), that stood frying and fretting, half-blessing, half-cursing " the gentleman," and imprint upon her chaste lips a tender salute, whereat the universal host would set up a shout that tore the concave, while hundreds of grinning teeth startled the night with their brightness. O it was a pleasure to see the sable younkers lick in the unctuous meat, with *his* more unctuous sayings —how he would fit the tit bits to the puny mouths, reserving the lengthier links for the seniors—how he would intercept a morsel even in the jaws of some young desperado, declaring it " must to the pan again to be browned, for it was not fit for a gentleman's eating "—how he would recommend this slice of white bread, or that piece of kissing-crust, to a tender juvenile, advising them all to have a care of cracking their teeth, which were their best patrimony,—how genteelly he would deal about the small ale, as if it were wine, naming the brewer, and protesting, if it were not good, he should lose their custom ; with a special recommendation to wipe the lip before drinking. Then we had our toasts—" The King,"—the " Cloth,"—which, whether they understood or not, was equally diverting and flattering ;—and for a crowning sentiment, which never failed, " May the Brush supersede the Laurel ! "

All these, and fifty other fancies, which were rather felt than comprehended by his guests, would he utter, standing upon tables, and prefacing every sentiment with a " Gentlemen, give me leave to propose so and so," which was a prodigious comfort to those young orphans ; every now and then stuffing into his mouth (for it did not do to be squeamish on these occasions) indiscriminate pieces of those reeking sausages, which pleased them mightily, and was the savouriest part, you may believe, of the entertainment.

> Golden lads and lasses must,
> As chimney-sweepers, come to dust—

JAMES WHITE is extinct, and with him these suppers have long ceased. He carried away with him half the fun of the world when he died—of my world at least. His old clients look for him among the pens ; and, missing him, reproach the altered feast of St. Bartholomew, and the glory of Smithfield departed for ever.

A COMPLAINT OF THE DECAY OF BEGGARS IN THE METROPOLIS

THE all-sweeping besom of societarian reformation—your only modern Alcides' club to rid the time of its abuses—is uplift with many-handed sway to extirpate the last fluttering tatters of the bugbear MENDICITY from the metropolis. Scrips, wallets, bags —staves, dogs, and crutches—the whole mendicant fraternity with all their baggage are fast posting out of the purlieus of this eleventh persecution. From the crowded crossing, from the corners of streets and turnings of allies, the parting Genius of Beggary is " with sighing sent."

I do not approve of this wholesale going to work, this impertinent crusado, or *bellum ad exterminationem*, proclaimed against a species. Much good might be sucked from these Beggars.

They were the oldest and the honourablest form of pauperism. Their appeals were to our common nature ; less revolting to an ingenuous mind than to be a suppliant to the particular humours or caprice of any fellow-creature, or set of fellow-creatures, parochial or societarian. Theirs were the only rates uninvidious in the levy, ungrudged in the assessment.

There was a dignity springing from the very depth of their

desolation; as to be naked is to be so much nearer to the being a man, than to go in livery.

The greatest spirits have felt this in their reverses; and when Dionysius from king turned schoolmaster, do we feel any thing towards him but contempt? Could Vandyke have made a picture of him, swaying a ferula for a sceptre, which would have affected our minds with the same heroic pity, the same compassionate admiration, with which we regard his Belisarius begging for an *obolum*? Would the moral have been more graceful, more pathetic?

The Blind Beggar in the legend—the father of pretty Bessy—whose story doggrel rhymes and ale-house signs cannot so degrade or attenuate, but that some sparks of a lustrous spirit will shine through the disguisements—this noble Earl of Cornwall (as indeed he was) and memorable sport of fortune, fleeing from the unjust sentence of his liege lord, stript of all, and seated on the flowering green of Bethnal, with his more fresh and springing daughter by his side, illumining his rags and his beggary—would the child and parent have cut a better figure, doing the honours of a counter, or expiating their fallen condition upon the three-foot eminence of some sempstering shop-board?

In tale or history your Beggar is ever the just antipode to your King. The poets and romancical writers (as dear Margaret Newcastle would call them) when they would most sharply and feelingly paint a reverse of fortune, never stop till they have brought down their hero in good earnest to rags and the wallet. The depth of the descent illustrates the height he falls from. There is no medium which can be presented to the imagination without offence. There is no breaking the fall. Lear, thrown from his palace, must divest him of his garments, till he answer "mere nature;" and Cresseid, fallen from a prince's love, must extend her pale arms, pale with other whiteness than of beauty, supplicating lazar alms with bell and clap-dish.

The Lucian wits knew this very well; and, with a converse policy, when they would express scorn of greatness without the pity, they show us an Alexander in the shades cobbling shoes, or a Semiramis getting up foul linen.

How would it sound in song, that a great monarch had declined his affections upon the daughter of a baker! yet do we feel the imagination at all violated when we read the "true ballad," where King Cophetua wooes the beggar maid?

Pauperism, pauper, poor man, are expressions of pity, but pity alloyed with contempt. No one properly contemns a beggar. Poverty is a comparative thing, and each degree of it is mocked by its "neighbour grice." Its poor rents and comings-in are soon

summed up and told.   Its pretences to property are almost ludicrous.
Its pitiful attempts to save excite a smile.   Every scornful companion can weigh his trifle-bigger purse against it.   Poor man
reproaches poor man in the streets with impolitic mention of his
condition, his own being a shade better, while the rich pass by and
jeer at both.   No rascally comparative insults a Beggar, or thinks
of weighing purses with him.   He is not in the scale of comparison.
He is not under the measure of property.   He confessedly hath
none, any more than a dog or a sheep.   No one twitteth him with
ostentation above his means.   No one accuses him of pride, or
upbraideth him with mock humility.   None jostle with him for
the wall, or pick quarrels for precedency.   No wealthy neighbour
seeketh to eject him from his tenement.   No man sues him.   No
man goes to law with him.   If I were not the independent gentleman that I am, rather than I would be a retainer to the great, a
led captain, or a poor relation, I would choose, out of the delicacy
and true greatness of my mind, to be a Beggar.

Rags, which are the reproach of poverty, are the Beggar's robes,
and graceful *insignia* of his profession, his tenure, his full dress,
the suit in which he is expected to show himself in public.   He is
never out of the fashion, or limpeth awkwardly behind it.   He is
not required to put on court mourning.   He weareth all colours,
fearing none.   His costume hath undergone less change than the
Quaker's.   He is the only man in the universe who is not obliged
to study appearances.   The ups and downs of the world concern
him no longer.   He alone continueth in one stay.   The price of
stock or land affecteth him not.   The fluctuations of agricultural
or commercial prosperity touch him not, or at worst but change
his customers.   He is not expected to become bail or surety for
any one.   No man troubleth him with questioning his religion or
politics.   He is the only free man in the universe.

The Mendicants of this great city were so many of her sights, her
lions.   I can no more spare them than I could the Cries of London.
No corner of a street is complete without them.   They are as indispensable as the Ballad Singer ; and in their picturesque attire as
ornamental as the Signs of old London.   They were the standing
morals, emblems, mementos, dial-mottos, the spital sermons, the
books for children, the salutary checks and pauses to the high and
rushing tide of greasy citizenry—

————Look
Upon that poor and broken bankrupt there.

Above all, those old blind Tobits that used to line the wall of
Lincoln's Inn Garden, before modern fastidiousness had expelled
them, casting up their ruined orbs to catch a ray of pity, and (if

possible) of light, with their faithful Dog Guide at their feet,—
whither are they fled? or into what corners, blind as themselves,
have they been driven, out of the wholesome air and sun-warmth?
immersed between four walls, in what withering poor-house do they
endure the penalty of double darkness, where the chink of the dropt
half-penny no more consoles their forlorn bereavement, far from the
sound of the cheerful and hope-stirring tread of the passenger?
Where hang their useless staves? and who will farm their dogs?—
Have the overseers of St. L—— caused them to be shot? or were
they tied up in sacks, and dropt into the Thames, at the suggestion
of B——, the mild rector of ——?

Well fare the soul of unfastidious Vincent Bourne, most classical,
and at the same time, most English, of the Latinists!—who has
treated of this human and quadrupedal alliance, this dog and man
friendship, in the sweetest of his poems, the *Epitaphium in
Canem*, or, *Dog's Epitaph*. Reader, peruse it; and say, if customary sights, which could call up such gentle poetry as this, were
of a nature to do more harm or good to the moral sense of the
passengers through the daily thoroughfares of a vast and busy
metropolis.

> Pauperis hic Iri requiesco Lyciscus, herilis,
> Dum vixi, tutela vigil columenque senectæ,
> Dux cæco fidus : nec, me ducente, solebat,
> Prætenso hinc atque hinc baculo, per iniqua locorum
> Incertam explorare viam ; sed fila secutus,
> Quæ dubios regerent passûs, vestigia tuta
> Fixit inoffenso gressu ; gelidumque sedile
> In nudo nactus saxo, quà prætereuntium
> Unda frequens confluxit, ibi miserisque tenebras
> Lamentis, noctemque oculis ploravit obortam.
> Ploravit nec frustra ; obolum dedit alter et alter,
> Queis corda et mentem indiderat natura benignam.
> Ad latus interea jacui sopitus herile,
> Vel mediis vigil in somnis ; ad herilia jussa
> Auresque atque animum arrectus, seu frustula amicè
> Porrexit sociasque dapes, seu longa diei
> Tædia perpessus, reditum sub nocte parabat.
>   Hi mores, hæc vita fuit, dum fata sinebant,
> Dum neque languebam morbis, nec inerte senectâ ;
> Quæ tandem obrepsit, veterique satellite cæcum
> Orbavit dominum : prisci sed gratia facti
> Ne tota intereat, longos deleta per annos,
> Exiguum hunc Irus tumulum de cespite fecit,
> Etsi inopis, non ingratæ, munuscula dextræ ;
> Carmine signavitque brevi, dominumque canemque
> Quod memoret, fidumque canem dominumque benignum.

> Poor Irus' faithful wolf-dog here I lie,
> That wont to tend my old blind master's steps,
> His guide and guard: nor, while my service lasted,
> Had he occasion for that staff, with which
> He now goes picking out his path in fear
> Over the highways and crossings ; but would plant,

Safe in the conduct of my friendly string,
A firm foot forward still, till he had reach'd
His poor seat on some stone, nigh where the tide
Of passers by in thickest confluence flow'd :
To whom with loud and passionate laments
From morn to eve his dark estate he wail'd.
Nor wail'd to all in vain : some here and there,
The well-disposed and good, their pennies gave.
I meantime at his feet obsequious slept;
Not all-asleep in sleep, but heart and ear
Prick'd up at his least motion; to receive
At his kind hand my customary crums,
And common portion in his feast of scraps ;
Or when night warn'd us homeward, tired and spent
With our long day and tedious beggary.
   These were my manners, this my way of life,
Till age and slow disease me overtook,
And sever'd from my sightless master's side.
But lest the grace of so good deeds should die,
Through tract of years in mute oblivion lost,
This slender tomb of turf hath Irus reared,
Cheap monument of no ungrudging hand,
And with short verse inscribed it, to attest,
In long and lasting union to attest,
The virtues of the Beggar and his Dog.

These dim eyes have in vain explored for some months past a well-known figure, or part of the figure, of a man, who used to glide his comely upper half over the pavements of London, wheeling along with most ingenious celerity upon a machine of wood ; a spectacle to natives, to foreigners, and to children. He was of a robust make, with a florid sailor-like complexion, and his head was bare to the storm and sunshine. He was a natural curiosity, a speculation to the scientific, a prodigy to the simple. The infant would stare at the mighty man brought down to his own level. The common cripple would despise his own pusillanimity, viewing the hale stoutness, and hearty heart, of this half-limbed giant. Few but must have noticed him ; for the accident, which brought him low, took place during the riots of 1780, and he has been a groundling so long. He seemed earth-born, an Antæus, and to suck in fresh vigour from the soil which he neighboured. He was a grand fragment; as good as an Elgin marble. The nature, which should have recruited his reft legs and thighs, was not lost, but only retired into his upper parts, and he was half a Hercules. I heard a tremendous voice thundering and growling, as before an earthquake, and casting down my eyes, it was this mandrake reviling a steed that had started at his portentous appearance. He seemed to want but his just stature to have rent the offending quadruped in shivers. He was as the man-part of a Centaur, from which the horse-half had been cloven in some dire Lapithan controversy. He moved on, as if he could have made shift with yet half of the body-portion which was left him. The *os sublime* was not wanting ;

and he threw out yet a jolly countenance upon the heavens.
Forty-and-two years had he driven this out of door trade, and now
that his hair is grizzled in the service, but his good spirits no way
impaired, because he is not content to exchange his free air and
exercise for the restraints of a poor-house, he is expiating his contumacy in one of those houses (ironically christened) of Correction.

Was a daily spectacle like this to be deemed a nuisance, which
called for legal interference to remove? or not rather a salutary and
a touching object, to the passers-by in a great city? Among her
shows, her museums, and supplies for ever-gaping curiosity (and
what else but an accumulation of sights—endless sights—*is* a great
city; or for what else is it desirable?) was there not room for one
Lusus (not *Naturæ*, indeed, but) *Accidentium?* What if in
forty-and-two years' going about, the man had scraped together
enough to give a portion to his child (as the rumour ran) of a few
hundreds—whom had he injured?—whom had he imposed upon?
The contributors had enjoyed their *sight* for their pennies. What
if after being exposed all day to the heats, the rains, and the frosts
of heaven—shuffling his ungainly trunk along in an elaborate and
painful motion—he was enabled to retire at night to enjoy himself
at a club of his fellow cripples over a dish of hot meat and
vegetables, as the charge was gravely brought against him by a
clergyman deposing before a House of Commons' Committee—was
this, or was his truly paternal consideration, which (if a fact)
deserved a statue rather than a whipping-post, and is inconsistent at
least with the exaggeration of nocturnal orgies which he has been
slandered with—a reason that he should be deprived of his chosen,
harmless, nay edifying, way of life, and be committed in hoary age
for a sturdy vagabond?—

There was a Yorick once, whom it would not have shamed to
have sate down at the cripples' feast, and to have thrown in his
benediction, ay, and his mite too, for a companionable symbol.
" Age, thou hast lost thy breed."—

Half of these stories about the prodigious fortunes made by
begging are (I verily believe) misers' calumnies. One was much
talked of in the public papers some time since, and the usual
charitable inferences deduced. A clerk in the Bank was surprised
with the announcement of a five hundred pound legacy left him by
a person whose name he was a stranger to. It seems that in his
daily morning walks from Peckham (or some village thereabouts)
where he lived, to his office, it had been his practice for the last
twenty years to drop his halfpenny duly into the hat of some blind
Bartimeus, that sate begging alms by the way-side in the Borough.
The good old beggar recognised his daily benefactor by the voice
only; and, when he died, left all the amassings of his alms (that

had been half a century perhaps in the accumulating) to his old Bank friend. Was this a story to purse up people's hearts, and pennies, against giving an alms to the blind?—or not rather a beautiful moral of well-directed charity on the one part, and noble gratitude upon the other?

I sometimes wish I had been that Bank clerk.

I seem to remember a poor old grateful kind of creature, blinking, and looking up with his no eyes in the sun—

Is it possible I could have steeled my purse against him?

Perhaps I had no small change.

Reader, do not be frightened at the hard words, imposition, imposture—*give, and ask no questions*. Cast thy bread upon the waters. Some have unawares (like this Bank clerk) entertained angels.

Shut not thy purse-strings always against painted distress. Act a charity sometimes. When a poor creature (outwardly and visibly such) comes before thee, do not stay to inquire whether the "seven small children," in whose name he implores thy assistance, have a veritable existence. Rake not into the bowels of unwelcome truth, to save a halfpenny. It is good to believe him. If he be not all that he pretendeth, *give*, and under a personate father of a family, think (if thou pleasest) that thou hast relieved an indigent bachelor. When they come with their counterfeit looks, and mumping tones, think them players. You pay your money to see a comedian feign these things, which, concerning these poor people, thou canst not certainly tell whether they are feigned or not.

A DISSERTATION UPON ROAST PIG

MANKIND, says a Chinese manuscript, which my friend M. was obliging enough to read and explain to me, for the first seventy thousand ages ate their meat raw, clawing or biting it from the living animal, just as they do in Abyssinia to this day. This period is not obscurely hinted at by their great Confucius in the second chapter of his Mundane Mutations, where he designates a kind of golden age by the term Cho-fang, literally the Cooks' holiday. The manuscript goes on to say, that the art of roasting, or rather broiling (which I take to be the elder brother) was accidentally discovered in the manner following. The swine-herd, Ho-ti, having gone out into the woods one morning, as his manner was, to collect mast for his hogs, left his cottage in the care of his eldest son Bo-bo, a great lubberly boy, who being fond of playing with fire, as younkers of his age commonly are, let some sparks escape into a bundle of straw, which kindling quickly, spread the conflagration over every part of their poor mansion, till it was reduced to ashes. Together with the cottage (a sorry antediluvian make-shift of a building, you may think it), what was of much more importance, a fine litter of new-farrowed pigs, no less than nine in number, perished. China pigs have been esteemed a luxury all over the East from the remotest periods that we read of. Bo-bo was in the utmost consternation, as you may think, not so much for the sake of the tenement, which his father and he could easily build up again with a few dry branches, and the labour of an hour or two, at any time, as for the loss of the pigs. While he was thinking what he should say to his father, and wringing his hands over the smoking remnants of one of those untimely sufferers, an odour assailed his nostrils, unlike any scent which he had before experienced. What could it proceed from?—not from the burnt cottage—he had smelt that smell before—indeed this was by no means the first accident of the kind which had occurred through the negligence of this unlucky young fire-brand. Much less did it resemble that of any known herb, weed, or flower. A premonitory moistening at the same time overflowed his nether lip. He knew not what to think. He next stooped down to feel the pig, if there were any signs of life in it. He burnt his fingers, and to cool them he applied them in his booby fashion to his mouth. Some of the crums of the scorched skin had come away with his fingers, and for the first time in his life (in the world's life indeed, for before him no man had known it) he tasted—*crackling!* Again he felt and fumbled at the pig. It did not burn him so much now, still he licked his fingers from a sort of habit. The truth at length broke into his slow understanding, that it was the pig that smelt so, and the pig that tasted so delicious; and, surrendering himself up to the new-born pleasure, he fell to tearing up whole handfuls of the scorched skin with the flesh next it, and was cramming it down his throat in his beastly fashion, when his sire entered amid the smoking rafters, armed with retributory cudgel, and finding how affairs stood, began to rain blows upon the young rogue's shoulders, as thick as hail-stones, which Bo-bo heeded not any more than if they had been flies. The tickling pleasure, which he experienced in his lower regions, had rendered him quite callous to any inconveniences he might feel in those remote quarters. His father might lay on, but he could not beat him from his pig, till he had fairly made an end of it, when, becoming a little more sensible of his situation, something like the following dialogue ensued.

"You graceless whelp, what have you got there devouring? Is it not enough that you have burnt me down three houses with your dog's tricks, and be hanged to you, but you must be eating fire, and I know not what—what have you got there, I say?"

"O father, the pig, the pig, do come and taste how nice the burnt pig eats."

The ears of Ho-ti tingled with horror. He cursed his son, and he cursed himself that ever he should beget a son that should eat burnt pig.

Bo-bo, whose scent was wonderfully sharpened since morning, soon raked out another pig, and fairly rending it asunder, thrust the lesser half by main force into the fists of Ho-ti, still shouting out "Eat, eat, eat the burnt pig, father, only taste—O Lord,"— with such-like barbarous ejaculations, cramming all the while as if he would choke.

Ho-ti trembled every joint while he grasped the abominable thing, wavering whether he should not put his son to death for an unnatural young monster, when the crackling scorching his fingers, as it had done his son's, and applying the same remedy to them, he in his turn tasted some of its flavour, which, make what sour mouths he would for a pretence, proved not altogether displeasing to him. In conclusion (for the manuscript here is a little tedious) both father and son fairly sat down to the mess, and never left off till they had despatched all that remained of the litter.

Bo-bo was strictly enjoined not to let the secret escape, for the neighbours would certainly have stoned them for a couple of abominable wretches, who could think of improving upon the good meat which God had sent them. Nevertheless, strange stories got about. It was observed that Ho-ti's cottage was burnt down now more frequently than ever. Nothing but fires from this time forward. Some would break out in broad day, others in the night-time. As often as the sow farrowed, so sure was the house of Ho-ti to be in a blaze; and Ho-ti himself, which was the more remarkable, instead of chastising his son, seemed to grow more indulgent to him than ever. At length they were watched, the terrible mystery discovered, and father and son summoned to take their trial at Pekin, then an inconsiderable assize town. Evidence was given, the obnoxious food itself produced in court, and verdict about to be pronounced, when the foreman of the jury begged that some of the burnt pig, of which the culprits stood accused, might be handed into the box. He handled it, and they all handled it, and burning their fingers, as Bo-bo and his father had done before them, and nature prompting to each of them the same remedy, against the face of all the facts, and the clearest charge which judge had ever given,—to the surprise of the whole court, towns-folk, strangers, reporters, and all present—without leaving the box, or any manner of consultation whatever, they brought in a simul-taneous verdict of Not Guilty.

The judge, who was a shrewd fellow, winked at the manifest iniquity of the decision : and, when the court was dismissed, went privily, and bought up all the pigs that could be had for love or money. In a few days his Lordship's town house was observed to be on fire. The thing took wing, and now there was nothing to be seen but fires in every direction. Fuel and pigs grew enormously dear all over the district. The insurance offices one and all shut up shop. People built slighter and slighter every day, until it was feared that the very science of architecture would in no long time be lost to the world. Thus this custom of firing houses continued, till in process of time, says my manuscript, a sage arose, like our Locke, who made a discovery, that the flesh of swine, or indeed of any other animal, might be cooked (*burnt*, as they called it) with-out the necessity of consuming a whole house to dress it. Then first began the rude form of a gridiron. Roasting by the string, or spit, came in a century or two later, I forget in whose dynasty. By such slow degrees, concludes the manuscript, do the most useful, and seemingly the most obvious arts, make their way among man-kind.——

Without placing too implicit faith in the account above given, it must be agreed, that if a worthy pretext for so dangerous an ex-periment as setting houses on fire (especially in these days) could be assigned in favour of any culinary object, that pretext and excuse might be found in ROAST PIG.

Of all the delicacies in the whole *mundus edibilis*, I will main-tain it to be the most delicate—*princeps obsoniorum*.

I speak not of your grown porkers—things between pig and pork —those hobbydehoys—but a young and tender suckling—under a moon old—guiltless as yet of the sty—with no original speck of the *amor immunditiæ*, the hereditary failing of the first parent, yet manifest—his voice as yet not broken, but something between a childish treble, and a grumble—the mild forerunner, or *præ-ludium*, of a grunt.

He must be roasted. I am not ignorant that our ancestors ate them seethed, or boiled—but what a sacrifice of the exterior tegu-ment !

There is no flavour comparable, I will contend, to that of the crisp, tawny, well-watched, not over-roasted, *crackling*, as it is well called—the very teeth are invited to their share of the pleasure at this banquet in overcoming the coy, brittle resistance—with the adhesive oleaginous—O call it not fat—but an indefinable sweetness growing up to it—the tender blossoming of fat—fat cropped in the bud — taken in the shoot — in the first innocence — the cream and quintessence of the child-pig's yet pure food——the lean, no lean, but a kind of animal manna—or, rather, fat and lean (if it must be so) so blended and running into each other, that both together make but one ambrosian result, or common substance.

Behold him, while he is doing—it seemeth rather a refreshing warmth, than a scorching heat, that he is so passive to. How equably he twirleth round the string!—Now he is just done. To see the extreme sensibility of that tender age, he hath wept out his pretty eyes—radiant jellies—shooting stars—

See him in the dish, his second cradle, how meek he lieth!—wouldst thou have had this innocent grow up to the grossness and indocility which too often accompany maturer swinehood? Ten to one he would have proved a glutton, a sloven, an obstinate, disagreeable animal—wallowing in all manner of filthy conversation—from these sins he is happily snatched away—

> Ere sin could blight, or sorrow fade,
> Death came with timely care—

his memory is odoriferous — no clown curseth, while his stomach half rejecteth, the rank bacon — no coalheaver bolteth him in reeking sausages—he hath a fair sepulchre in the grateful stomach of the judicious epicure—and for such a tomb might be content to die.

He is the best of Sapors. Pine-apple is great. She is indeed almost too transcendent—a delight, if not sinful, yet so like to sinning, that really a tender-conscienced person would do well to pause — too ravishing for mortal taste, she woundeth and excoriateth the lips that approach her—like lovers' kisses, she biteth—she is a pleasure bordering on pain from the fierceness and insanity of her relish—but she stoppeth at the palate—she meddleth not with the appetite—and the coarsest hunger might barter her consistently for a mutton chop.

Pig—let me speak his praise—is no less provocative of the appetite, than he is satisfactory to the criticalness of the censorious palate. The strong man may batten on him, and the weakling refuseth not his mild juices.

Unlike to mankind's mixed characters, a bundle of virtues and vices, inexplicably intertwisted, and not to be unravelled without hazard, he is—good throughout. No part of him is better or worse than another. He helpeth, as far as his little means extend, all around. He is the least envious of banquets. He is all neighbours' fare.

I am one of those, who freely and ungrudgingly impart a share of the good things of this life which fall to their lot (few as mine are in this kind) to a friend.   I protest I take as great an interest in my friend's pleasures, his relishes, and proper satisfactions, as in mine own.   " Presents," I often say, " endear Absents."   Hares, pheasants, partridges, snipes, barn - door chicken (those " tame villatic fowl"), capons, plovers, brawn, barrels of oysters, I dispense as freely as I receive them.   I love to taste them, as it were, upon the tongue of my friend.   But a stop must be put somewhere. One would not, like Lear, " give every thing."   I make my stand upon pig.   Methinks it is an ingratitude to the Giver of all good flavours, to extra-domiciliate, or send out of the house, slightingly, (under pretext of friendship, or I know not what) a blessing so particularly adapted, predestined, I may say, to my individual palate—It argues an insensibility.

I remember a touch of conscience in this kind at school.   My good old aunt, who never parted from me at the end of a holiday without stuffing a sweet-meat, or some nice thing, into my pocket, had dismissed me one evening with a smoking plum-cake, fresh from the oven.   In my way to school (it was over London bridge) a grey-headed old beggar saluted me (I have no doubt at this time of day that he was a counterfeit).   I had no pence to console him with, and in the vanity of self-denial, and the very coxcombry of charity, school-boy-like, I made him a present of—the whole cake !   I walked on a little, buoyed up, as one is on such occasions, with a sweet soothing of self-satisfaction ; but before I had got to the end of the bridge, my better feelings returned, and I burst into tears, thinking how ungrateful I had been to my good aunt, to go and give her good gift away to a stranger, that I had never seen before, and who might be a bad man for aught I knew ; and then I thought of the pleasure my aunt would be taking in thinking that I—I myself, and not another—would eat her nice cake—and what should I say to her the next time I saw her—how naughty I was to part with her pretty present—and the odour of that spicy cake came back upon my recollection, and the pleasure and the curiosity I had taken in seeing her make it, and her joy when she sent it to the oven, and how disappointed she would feel that I had never had a bit of it in my mouth at last—and I blamed my impertinent spirit of alms-giving, and out-of-place hypocrisy of goodness, and above all I wished never to see the face again of that insidious, good-for-nothing, old grey impostor.

Our ancestors were nice in their method of sacrificing these tender victims.   We read of pigs whipt to death with something of a shock, as we hear of any other obsolete custom.   The age of discipline is gone by, or it would be curious to inquire (in a philosophical light merely) what effect this process might have towards intenerating and dulcifying a substance, naturally so mild and dulcet as the flesh of young pigs.   It looks like refining a violet.   Yet we should be cautious, while we condemn the inhumanity, how we censure the wisdom of the practice.   It might impart a gusto—

I remember an hypothesis, argued upon by the young students, when I was at St. Omer's, and maintained with much learning and pleasantry on both sides, " Whether, supposing that the flavour of a pig who obtained his death by whipping (*per flagellationem extremam*) superadded a pleasure upon the palate of a man more intense than any possible suffering we can conceive in the animal, is man justified in using that method of putting the animal to death ? "   I forget the decision.

His sauce should be considered.   Decidedly, a few bread crums, done up with his liver and brains, and a dash of mild sage.   But, banish, dear Mrs. Cook, I beseech you, the whole onion tribe.   Barbecue your whole hogs to your palate, steep them in shalots, stuff them out with plantations of the rank and guilty garlic; you cannot poison them, or make them stronger than they are—but consider, he is a weakling—a flower.

———

A BACHELOR'S COMPLAINT OF THE BEHAVIOUR OF MARRIED PEOPLE

AS a single man, I have spent a good deal of my time in noting down the infirmities of Married People, to console myself for those superior pleasures, which they tell me I have lost by remaining as I am.

I cannot say that the quarrels of men and their wives ever made any great impression upon me, or had much tendency to strengthen me in those anti-social resolutions, which I took up long ago upon more substantial considerations.   What oftenest offends me at the houses of married persons where I visit, is an error of quite a different description ;—it is that they are too loving.

Not too loving neither: that does not explain my meaning. Besides, why should that offend me?   The very act of separating themselves from the rest of the world, to have the fuller enjoyment of each other's society, implies that they prefer one another to all the world.

But what I complain of is, that they carry this preference so undisguisedly, they perk it up in the faces of us single people so shame-lessly, you cannot be in their company a moment without being made to feel, by some indirect hint or open avowal, that *you* are not the object of this preference. Now there are some things which give no offence, while implied or taken for granted merely; but expressed, there is much offence in them. If a man were to accost the first homely-featured or plain-dressed young woman of his acquaintance, and tell her bluntly, that she was not handsome or rich enough for him, and he could not marry her, he would deserve to be kicked for his ill manners; yet no less is implied in the fact, that having access and opportunity of putting the question to her, he has never yet thought fit to do it. The young woman under-stands this as clearly as if it were put into words; but no reasonable young woman would think of making this the ground of a quarrel. Just as little right have a married couple to tell me by speeches, and looks that are scarce less plain than speeches, that I am not the happy man,—the lady's choice. It is enough that I know I am not: I do not want this perpetual reminding.

The display of superior knowledge or riches may be made sufficiently mortifying; but these admit of a palliative. The knowledge which is brought out to insult me, may accidentally improve me; and in the rich man's houses and pictures,—his parks and gardens, I have a temporary usufruct at least. But the display of married happiness has none of these palliatives: it is throughout pure, unrecompensed, unqualified insult.

Marriage by its best title is a monopoly, and not of the least in-vidious sort. It is the cunning of most possessors of any exclusive privilege to keep their advantage as much out of sight as possible, that their less favoured neighbours, seeing little of the benefit, may the less be disposed to question the right. But these married monopolists thrust the most obnoxious part of their patent into our faces.

Nothing is to me more distasteful than that entire complacency and satisfaction which beam in the countenances of a new-married couple,—in that of the lady particularly: it tells you, that her lot is disposed of in this world: that *you* can have no hopes of her. It is true, I have none; nor wishes either, perhaps: but this is one of those truths which ought, as I said before, to be taken for granted, not expressed.

The excessive airs which those people give themselves, founded on the ignorance of us unmarried people, would be more offensive if they were less irrational. We will allow them to understand the mysteries belonging to their own craft better than we who have not had the happiness to be made free of the company: but their arrogance is not content within these limits. If a single person

presume to offer his opinion in their presence, though upon the
most indifferent subject, he is immediately silenced as an incompetent person.   Nay, a young married lady of my acquaintance,
who, the best of the jest was, had not changed her condition above
a fortnight before, in a question on which I had the misfortune to
differ from her, respecting the properest mode of breeding oysters
for the London market, had the assurance to ask with a sneer, how
such an old Bachelor as I could pretend to know any thing about
such matters.

But what I have spoken of hitherto is nothing to the airs which
these creatures give themselves when they come, as they generally
do, to have children.   When I consider how little of a rarity
children are,—that every street and blind alley swarms with them,
—that the poorest people commonly have them in most abundance,
—that there are few marriages that are not blest with at least one
of these bargains,—how often they turn out ill, and defeat the fond
hopes of their parents, taking to vicious courses, which end in
poverty, disgrace, the gallows, &c.—I cannot for my life tell what
cause for pride there can possibly be in having them.   If they were
young phœnixes, indeed, that were born but one in a year, there
might be a pretext.   But when they are so common——

I do not advert to the insolent merit which they assume with
their husbands on these occasions.   Let them look to that.   But
why *we*, who are not their natural-born subjects, should be expected
to bring our spices, myrrh, and incense,—our tribute and homage of
admiration,—I do not see.

"Like as the arrows in the hand of the giant, even so are the
young children:" so says the excellent office in our Prayer-book
appointed for the churching of women.   "Happy is the man that
hath his quiver full of them:"   So say I; but then don't let him
discharge his quiver upon us that are weaponless;—let them be
arrows, but not to gall and stick us.   I have generally observed that
these arrows are double-headed: they have two forks, to be sure to
hit with one or the other.   As for instance, when you come into a
house which is full of children, if you happen to take no notice of
them (you are thinking of something else, perhaps, and turn a deaf
ear to their innocent caresses), you are set down as untractable,
morose, a hater of children.   On the other hand, if you find them
more than usually engaging,—if you are taken with their pretty
manners, and set about in earnest to romp and play with them,
some pretext or other is sure to be found for sending them out of
the room: they are too noisy or boisterous, or Mr. —— does not
like children.   With one or other of these forks the arrow is sure to
hit you.

I could forgive their jealousy, and dispense with toying with their brats, if it gives them any pain ; but I think it unreasonable to be called upon to *love* them, where I see no occasion,—to love a whole family, perhaps, eight, nine, or ten, indiscriminately,—to love all the pretty dears, because children are so engaging.

I know there is a proverb, " Love me, love my dog : " that is not always so very practicable, particularly if the dog be set upon you to tease you or snap at you in sport.   But a dog, or a lesser thing, —any inanimate substance, as a keep-sake, a watch or a ring, a tree, or the place where we last parted when my friend went away upon a long absence, I can make shift to love, because I love him, and any thing that reminds me of him ; provided it be in its nature indifferent, and apt to receive whatever hue fancy can give it.   But children have a real character and an essential being of themselves : they are amiable or unamiable *per se ;* I must love or hate them as I see cause for either in their qualities.   A child's nature is too serious a thing to admit of its being regarded as a mere appendage to another being, and to be loved or hated accordingly : they stand with me upon their own stock, as much as men and women do.   O ! but you will say, sure it is an attractive age,—there is something in the tender years of infancy that of itself charms us.   That is the very reason why I am more nice about them.   I know that a sweet child is the sweetest thing in nature, not even excepting the delicate creatures which bear them ; but the prettier the kind of a thing is, the more desirable it is that it should be pretty of its kind.   One daisy differs not much from another in glory ; but a violet should look and smell the daintiest.—I was always rather squeamish in my women and children.

But this is not the worst: one must be admitted into their familiarity at least, before they can complain of inattention.   It implies visits, and some kind of intercourse.   But if the husband be a man with whom you have lived on a friendly footing before marriage,—if you did not come in on the wife's side,—if you did not sneak into the house in her train, but were an old friend in fast habits of intimacy before their courtship was so much as thought on,—look about you—your tenure is precarious—before a twelve-month shall roll over your head, you shall find your old friend gradually grow cool and altered towards you, and at last seek opportunities of breaking with you.   I have scarce a married friend of my acquaintance, upon whose firm faith I can rely, whose friendship did not commence *after the period of his marriage.* With some limitations they can endure that : but that the good man should have dared to enter into a solemn league of friendship in which they were not consulted, though it happened before they knew him,—before they that are now man and wife ever met,—this is intolerable to them.   Every long friendship, every old authentic intimacy, must be brought into their office to be new stamped with their currency, as a sovereign Prince calls in the good old money that was coined in some reign before he was born or thought of, to be new marked and minted with the stamp of his authority, before he will let it pass current in the world. You may guess what luck generally befalls such a rusty piece of metal as I am in these *new mintings*.

Innumerable are the ways which they take to insult and worm you out of their husband's confidence. Laughing at all you say with a kind of wonder, as if you were a queer kind of fellow that said good things, *but an oddity*, is one of the ways;—they have a particular kind of stare for the purpose;—till at last the husband, who used to defer to your judgment, and would pass over some excrescences of understanding and manner for the sake of a general vein of observation (not quite vulgar) which he perceived in you, begins to suspect whether you are not altogether a humorist,— a fellow well enough to have consorted with in his bachelor days, but not quite so proper to be introduced to ladies. This may be called the staring way; and is that which has oftenest been put in practice against me.

Then there is the exaggerating way, or the way of irony: that is, where they find you an object of especial regard with their husband, who is not so easily to be shaken from the lasting attachment founded on esteem which he has conceived towards you; by never-qualified exaggerations to cry up all that you say or do, till the good man, who understands well enough that it is all done in compliment to him, grows weary of the debt of gratitude which is due to so much candour, and by relaxing a little on his part, and taking down a peg or two in his enthusiasm, sinks at length to that kindly level of moderate esteem,—that "decent affection and complacent kindness" towards you, where she herself can join in sympathy with him without much stretch and violence to her sincerity.

Another way (for the ways they have to accomplish so desirable a purpose are infinite) is, with a kind of innocent simplicity, continually to mistake what it was which first made their husband fond of you. If an esteem for something excellent in your moral character was that which riveted the chain which she is to break, upon any imaginary discovery of a want of poignancy in your conversation, she will cry, "I thought, my dear, you described your friend, Mr. —— as a great wit." If, on the other hand, it was for some supposed charm in your conversation that he first grew to like you, and was content for this to overlook some trifling irregularities in your moral deportment, upon the first notice of any of these she as readily exclaims, "This, my dear, is your good

Mr. ——." One good lady whom I took the liberty of expostula-
ting with for not showing me quite so much respect as I thought
due to her husband's old friend, had the candour to confess to me
that she had often heard Mr. —— speak of me before marriage,
and that she had conceived a great desire to be acquainted with
me, but that the sight of me had very much disappointed her
expectations; for from her husband's representations of me, she
had formed a notion that she was to see a fine, tall, officer-like
looking man (I use her very words); the very reverse of which
proved to be the truth. This was candid; and I had the civility
not to ask her in return, how she came to pitch upon a standard of
personal accomplishments for her husband's friends which differed
so much from his own; for my friend's dimensions as near as
possible approximate to mine; he standing five feet five in his shoes,
in which I have the advantage of him by about half an inch; and
he no more than myself exhibiting any indications of a martial
character in his air or countenance.

These are some of the mortifications which I have encountered in
the absurd attempt to visit at their houses. To enumerate them
all would be a vain endeavour: I shall therefore just glance at the
very common impropriety of which married ladies are guilty,—of
treating us as if we were their husbands, and *vice versâ*. I mean,
when they use us with familiarity, and their husbands with ceremony. *Testacea*, for instance, kept me the other night two or
three hours beyond my usual time of supping, while she was
fretting because Mr. —— did not come home, till the oysters were
all spoiled, rather than she would be guilty of the impoliteness of
touching one in his absence. This was reversing the point of good
manners: for ceremony is an invention to take off the uneasy
feeling which we derive from knowing ourselves to be less the
object of love and esteem with a fellow-creature than some other
person is. It endeavours to make up, by superior attentions in
little points, for that invidious preference which it is forced to
deny in the greater. Had *Testacea* kept the oysters back for me,
and withstood her husband's importunities to go to supper, she
would have acted according to the strict rules of propriety. I
know no ceremony that ladies are bound to observe to their
husbands, beyond the point of a modest behaviour and decorum:
therefore I must protest against the vicarious gluttony of *Cerasia*,
who at her own table sent away a dish of Morellas, which I was
applying to with great good will, to her husband at the other end
of the table, and recommended a plate of less extraordinary goose-
berries to my unwedded palate in their stead. Neither can I
excuse the wanton affront of——.

But I am weary of stringing up all my married acquaintance by

Roman denominations. Let them amend and change their manners, or I promise to record the full-length English of their names, to the terror of all such desperate offenders in future.

ON SOME OF THE OLD ACTORS

THE casual sight of an old Play Bill, which I picked up the other day—I know not by what chance it was preserved so long—tempts me to call to mind a few of the Players, who make the principal figure in it. It presents the cast of parts in the Twelfth Night, at the old Drury-lane Theatre two-and-thirty years ago. There is something very touching in these old remembrances. They make us think how we *once* used to read a Play Bill—not, as now peradventure, singling out a favorite performer, and casting a negligent eye over the rest ; but spelling out every name, down to the very mutes and servants of the scene ;— when it was a matter of no small moment to us whether Whitfield, or Packer, took the part of Fabian ; when Benson, and Burton, and Phillimore—names of small account—had an importance, beyond what we can be content to attribute now to the time's best actors.—" Orsino, by Mr. Barrymore."—What a full Shakspearian sound it carries ! how fresh to memory arise the image, and the manner, of the gentle actor !

Those who have only seen Mrs. Jordan within the last ten or fifteen years, can have no adequate notion of her performance of such parts as Ophelia ; Helena, in All's Well that Ends Well ; and Viola in this play. Her voice had latterly acquired a coarseness, which suited well enough with her Nells and Hoydens, but in those days it sank, with her steady melting eye, into the heart. Her joyous parts—in which her memory now chiefly lives—in her youth were outdone by her plaintive ones. There is no giving an account how she delivered the disguised story of her love for Orsino. It was no set speech, that she had foreseen, so as to weave it into an harmonious period, line necessarily following line, to make up the music—yet I have heard it so spoken, or rather *read*, not without its grace and beauty—but, when she had declared her sister's history to be a " blank," and that she " never told her love," there was a pause, as if the story had ended—and then the image of the " worm in the bud " came up as a new suggestion—and the heightened image of " Patience " still followed after that, as by some growing (and not mechanical) process, thought springing up after thought, I would almost say, as they were watered by her tears.   So in those fine lines—

Write loyal cantos of contemned love—
Hollow your name to the reverberate hills—

there was no preparation made in the foregoing image for that which was to follow.   She used no rhetoric in her passion; or it was nature's own rhetoric, most legitimate then, when it seemed altogether without rule or law.

Mrs. Powel (now Mrs. Renard), then in the pride of her beauty, made an admirable Olivia.   She was particularly excellent in her unbending scenes in conversation with the Clown.   I have seen some Olivias—and those very sensible actresses too—who in these interlocutions have seemed to set their wits at the jester, and to vie conceits with him in downright emulation.   But she used him for her sport, like what he was, to trifle a leisure sentence or two with, and then to be dismissed, and she to be the Great Lady still.   She touched the imperious fantastic humour of the character with nicety.   Her fine spacious person filled the scene.

The part of Malvolio has in my judgment been so often misunderstood, and the *general merits* of the actor, who then played it, so unduly appreciated, that I shall hope for pardon, if I am a little prolix upon these points.

Of all the actors who flourished in my time—a melancholy phrase if taken aright, reader—Bensley had most of the swell of soul, was greatest in the delivery of heroic conceptions, the emotions consequent upon the presentment of a great idea to the fancy. He had the true poetical enthusiasm—the rarest faculty among players.   None that I remember possessed even a portion of that fine madness which he threw out in Hotspur's famous rant about glory, or the transports of the Venetian incendiary at the vision of the fired city.   His voice had the dissonance, and at times the inspiriting effect of the trumpet.   His gait was uncouth and stiff, but no way embarrassed by affectation; and the thorough-bred gentleman was uppermost in every movement.   He seized the moment of passion with the greatest truth; like a faithful clock, never striking before the time; never anticipating or leading you to anticipate.   He was totally destitute of trick and artifice.   He seemed come upon the stage to do the poet's message simply, and he did it with as genuine fidelity as the nuncios in Homer deliver the errands of the gods.   He let the passion or the sentiment do its own work without prop or bolstering.   He would have scorned to mountebank it; and betrayed none of that *cleverness* which is the bane of serious acting.   For this reason, his Iago was the only endurable one which I remember to have seen. No spectator from his action could divine more of his artifice than Othello was supposed to do. His confessions in soliloquy alone put you in possession of the mystery. There were no by-intimations to make the audience fancy their own discernment so much greater than that of the Moor—who commonly stands like a great helpless mark set up for mine Ancient, and a quantity of barren spectators, to shoot their bolts at. The Iago of Bensley did not go to work so grossly. There was a triumphant tone about the character, natural to a general consciousness of power ; but none of that petty vanity which chuckles and cannot contain itself upon any little successful stroke of its knavery—as is common with your small villains, and green probationers in mischief. It did not clap or crow before its time. It was not a man setting his wits at a child, and winking all the while at other children who are mightily pleased at being let into the secret ; but a consummate villain entrapping a noble nature into toils, against which no discernment was available, where the manner was as fathomless as the purpose seemed dark, and without motive. The part of Malvolio, in the Twelfth Night, was performed by Bensley, with a richness and a dignity, of which (to judge from some recent castings of that character) the very tradition must be worn out from the stage. No manager in those days would have dreamed of giving it to Mr. Baddeley, or Mr. Parsons : when Bensley was occasionally absent from the theatre, John Kemble thought it no derogation to succeed to the part. Malvolio is not essentially ludicrous. He becomes comic but by accident. He is cold, austere, repelling ; but dignified, consistent, and, for what appears, rather of an over-stretched morality. Maria describes him as a sort of Puritan ; and he might have worn his gold chain with honour in one of our old round-head families, in the service of a Lambert, or a Lady Fairfax. But his morality and his manners are misplaced in Illyria. He is opposed to the proper *levities* of the piece, and falls in the unequal contest. Still his pride, or his gravity, (call it which you will) is inherent, and native to the man, not mock or affected, which latter only are the fit objects to excite laughter. His quality is at the best unlovely, but neither buffoon nor contemptible. His bearing is lofty, a little above his station, but probably not much above his deserts. We see no reason why he should not have been brave, honourable, accomplished. His careless committal of the ring to the ground (which he was commissioned to restore to Cesario), bespeaks a generosity of birth and feeling. His dialect on all occasions is that of a gentleman, and a man of education. We must not confound him with the eternal old, low steward of comedy. He is master of the household to a great Princess ; a dignity probably conferred upon him for other respects than age or length of service. Olivia, at the first indication of his supposed madness, declares that she " would not have him miscarry for half of her dowry." Does this look as if the character was meant to appear little or insignificant ? Once, indeed, she accuses him to his face—of what ?—of being " sick of self-love,"—but with a gentleness and considerateness which could not have been, if she had not thought that this particular infirmity shaded some virtues. His rebuke to the knight, and his sottish revellers, is sensible and spirited ; and when we take into consideration the unprotected condition of his mistress, and the strict regard with which her state of real or dissembled mourning would draw the eyes of the world upon her house-affairs, Malvolio might feel the honour of the family in some sort in his keeping ; as it appears not that Olivia had any more brothers, or kinsmen, to look to it—for Sir Toby had dropped all such nice respects at the buttery hatch. That Malvolio was meant to be represented as possessing estimable qualities, the expression of the Duke in his anxiety to have him reconciled, almost infers. " Pursue him, and entreat him to a peace." Even in his abused state of chains and darkness, a sort of greatness seems never to desert him. He argues highly and well with the supposed Sir Topas, and philosophises gallantly upon his straw.[1] There must have been some shadow of worth about the man ; he must have been something more than a mere vapour—a thing of straw, or Jack in office —before Fabian and Maria could have ventured sending him upon a courting-errand to Olivia. There was some consonancy (as he would say) in the undertaking, or the jest would have been too bold even for that house of misrule.

Bensley, accordingly, threw over the part an air of Spanish loftiness. He looked, spake, and moved like an old Castilian. He was starch, spruce, opinionated, but his superstructure of pride seemed bottomed upon a sense of worth. There was something in it beyond the coxcomb. It was big and swelling, but you could not be sure that it was hollow. You might wish to see it taken down, but you felt that it was upon an elevation. He was magnificent from the outset ; but when the decent sobrieties of the character began to give way, and the poison of self-love, in his conceit of the Countess's affection, gradually to work, you would have thought that the hero of La Mancha in person stood before you. How he went smiling to himself ! with what ineffable carelessness would he twirl his gold chain ! what a dream it was ! you

---

[1] *Clown.* What is the opinion of Pythagoras concerning wild fowl ?
Mal. That the soul of our grandam might haply inhabit a bird.
Clown. What thinkest thou of his opinion ?
Mal. I think nobly of the soul, and no way approve of his opinion.

were infected with the illusion, and did not wish that it should be removed! you had no room for laughter! if an unseasonable reflection of morality obtruded itself, it was a deep sense of the pitiable infirmity of man's nature, that can lay him open to such frenzies—but in truth you rather admired than pitied the lunacy while it lasted—you felt that an hour of such mistake was worth an age with the eyes open. Who would not wish to live but for a day in the conceit of such a lady's love as Olivia? Why, the Duke would have giv'n his principality but for a quarter of a minute, sleeping or waking, to have been so deluded. The man seemed to tread upon air, to taste manna, to walk with his head in the clouds, to mate Hyperion. O! shake not the castles of his pride—endure yet for a season bright moments of confidence— "stand still ye watches of the element," that Malvolio may be still in fancy fair Olivia's lord—but fate and retribution say no—I hear the mischievous titter of Maria—the witty taunts of Sir Toby— the still more insupportable triumph of the foolish knight—the counterfeit Sir Topas is unmasked—and "thus the whirligig of time," as the true clown hath it, "brings in his revenges." I confess that I never saw the catastrophe of this character, while Bensley played it, without a kind of tragic interest. There was good foolery too. Few now remember Dodd. What an Ague-cheek the stage lost in him! Lovegrove, who came nearest to the old actors, revived the character some few seasons ago, and made it sufficiently grotesque; but Dodd was *it*, as it came out of nature's hands. It might be said to remain *in puris naturalibus*. In expressing slowness of apprehension this actor surpassed all others. You could see the first dawn of an idea stealing slowly over his countenance, climbing up by little and little, with a painful process, till it cleared up at last to the fulness of a twilight conception—its highest meridian. He seemed to keep back his intellect, as some have had the power to retard their pulsation. The balloon takes less time in filling, than it took to cover the expansion of his broad moony face over all its quarters with expression. A glimmer of understanding would appear in a corner of his eye, and for lack of fuel go out again. A part of his forehead would catch a little intelligence, and be a long time in communicating it to the remainder.

I am ill at dates, but I think it is now better than five and twenty years ago that walking in the gardens of Gray's Inn—they were then far finer than they are now—the accursed Verulam Buildings had not encroached upon all the east side of them, cutting out delicate green crankles, and shouldering away one of two of the stately alcoves of the terrace—the survivor stands gaping and relationless as if it remembered its brother—they are still the best gardens of any of the Inns of Court, my beloved Temple not forgotten—have the gravest character, their aspect being altogether reverend and law-breathing—Bacon has left the impress of his foot upon their gravel walks——taking my afternoon solace on a summer day upon the aforesaid terrace, a comely sad personage came towards me, whom, from his grave air and deportment, I judged to be one of the old Benchers of the Inn., He had a serious thoughtful forehead, and seemed to be in meditations of mortality. As I have an instinctive awe of old Benchers, I was passing him with that sort of subindicative token of respect which one is apt to demonstrate towards a venerable stranger, and which rather denotes an inclination to greet him, than any positive motion of the body to that effect—a species of humility and will-worship which I observe, nine times out of ten, rather puzzles than pleases the person it is offered to—when the face turning full upon me strangely identified itself with that of Dodd. Upon close inspection I was not mistaken. But could this sad thoughtful countenance be the same vacant face of folly which I had hailed so often under circumstances of gaiety; which I had never seen without a smile, or recognised but as the usher of mirth; that looked out so formally flat in Foppington, so frothily pert in Tattle, so impotently busy in Backbite; so blankly divested of all meaning, or resolutely expressive of none, in Acres, in Fribble, and a thousand agreeable impertinences? Was this the face—full of thought and carefulness—that had so often divested itself at will of every trace of either to give me diversion, to clear my cloudy face for two or three hours at least of its furrows? Was this the face—manly, sober, intelligent,—which I had so often despised, made mocks at, made merry with? The remembrance of the freedoms which I had taken with it came upon me with a reproach of insult. I could have asked it pardon. I thought it looked upon me with a sense of injury. There is something strange as well as sad in seeing actors—your pleasant fellows particularly—subjected to and suffering the common lot—their fortunes, their casualties, their deaths, seem to belong to the scene, their actions to be amenable to poetic justice only. We can hardly connect them with more awful responsibilities. The death of this fine actor took place shortly after this meeting. He had quitted the stage some months; and, as I learned afterwards, had been in the habit of resorting daily to these gardens almost to the day of his decease. In these serious walks probably he was divesting himself of many scenic and some real vanities—weaning himself from the frivolities of the lesser and the greater theatre—doing gentle penance for a life of no very reprehensible fooleries,—taking off by degrees the buffoon mask which he might feel he had worn too long—and rehearsing for a

more solemn cast of part. Dying he " put on the weeds of
Dominic." [1]

If few can remember Dodd, many yet living will not easily forget
the pleasant creature, who in those days enacted the part of the
Clown to Dodd's Sir Andrew.—Richard, or rather Dicky Suett—
for so in his life-time he delighted to be called, and time hath
ratified the appellation—lieth buried on the north side of the
cemetery of Holy Paul, to whose service his nonage and tender
years were dedicated. There are who do yet remember him at that
period—his pipe clear and harmonious. He would often speak of
his chorister days, when he was " cherub Dicky."

What clipped his wings, or made it expedient that he should
exchange the holy for the profane state ; whether he had lost his
good voice (his best recommendation to that office), like Sir John,
" with hallooing and singing of anthems ; " or whether he was
adjudged to lack something, even in those early years, of the gravity
indispensable to an occupation which professeth to " commerce with
the skies "—I could never rightly learn ; but we find him, after the
probation of a twelvemonth or so, reverting to a secular condition,
and become one of us.

I think he was not altogether of that timber, out of which
cathedral seats and sounding boards are hewed. But if a glad heart
—kind and therefore glad—be any part of sanctity, then might the
robe of Motley, with which he invested himself with so much
humility after his deprivation, and which he wore so long with so
much blameless satisfaction to himself and to the public, be accepted
for a surplice—his white stole, and *albe*.

The first fruits of his secularization was an engagement upon the
boards of Old Drury, at which theatre he commenced, as I have
been told, with adopting the manner of Parsons in old men's
characters. At the period in which most of us knew him, he was no
more an imitator than he was in any true sense himself imitable.

He was the Robin Good-Fellow of the stage. He came in to
trouble all things with a welcome perplexity, himself no whit
troubled for the matter. He was known, like Puck, by his note—
Ha! Ha! Ha!—sometimes deepening to *Ho! Ho! Ho!* with an
irresistible accession, derived perhaps remotely from his ecclesiastical
education, foreign to his prototype of,—*O La!* Thousands of

---

[1] Dodd was a man of reading, and left at his death a choice collection of old
English literature. I should judge him to have been a man of wit. I know one
instance of an impromptu which no length of study could have bettered. My merry
friend, Jem White, had seen him one evening in Aguecheek, and recognising Dodd
the next day in Fleet Street, was irresistibly impelled to take off his hat and salute
him as the identical Knight of the preceding evening with a " Save you, *Sir
Andrew*." Dodd, not at all disconcerted at this unusual address from a stranger,
with a courteous half-rebuking wave of the hand, put him off with an " Away, *Fool*."

hearts yet respond to the chuckling *O La!* of Dicky Suett, brought back to their remembrance by the faithful transcript of his friend Mathews's mimicry.   The "force of nature could no further go." He drolled upon the stock of these two syllables richer than the cuckoo.

Care, that troubles all the world, was forgotten in his composition.   Had he had but two grains (nay, half a grain) of it, he could never have supported himself upon those two spider's strings, which served him (in the latter part of his unmixed existence) as legs.   A doubt or a scruple must have made him totter, a sigh have puffed him down; the weight of a frown had staggered him, a wrinkle made him lose his balance.   But on he went, scrambling upon those airy stilts of his, with Robin Good-Fellow, "thorough brake, thorough briar," reckless of a scratched face or a torn doublet.

Shakspeare foresaw him, when he framed his fools and jesters. They have all the true Suett stamp, a loose and shambling gait, a slippery tongue, this last the ready midwife to a without-pain-delivered jest; in words, light as air, venting truths deep as the centre; with idlest rhymes tagging conceit when busiest, singing with Lear in the tempest, or Sir Toby at the buttery-hatch.

Jack Bannister and he had the fortune to be more of personal favourites with the town than any actors before or after.   The difference, I take it, was this:—Jack was more *beloved* for his sweet, good-natured, moral pretensions.   Dicky was more *liked* for his sweet, good-natured, no pretensions at all.   Your whole conscience stirred with Bannister's performance of Walter in the Children in the Wood—but Dicky seemed like a thing, as Shakspeare says of Love, too young to know what conscience is.   He put us into Vesta's days.   Evil fled before him—not as from Jack, as from an antagonist,—but because it could not touch him, any more than a cannon-ball a fly.   He was delivered from the burthen of that death; and, when Death came himself, not in metaphor, to fetch Dicky, it is recorded of him by Robert Palmer, who kindly watched his exit, that he received the last stroke, neither varying his accustomed tranquillity, nor tune, with the simple exclamation, worthy to have been recorded in his epitaph—*O La! O La! Bobby!*

The elder Palmer (of stage-treading celebrity) commonly played Sir Toby in those days; but there is a solidity of wit in the jests of that half-Falstaff which he did not quite fill out.   He was as much too showy as Moody (who sometimes took the part) was dry and sottish.   In sock or buskin there was an air of swaggering gentility about Jack Palmer.   He was a *gentleman* with a slight infusion of *the footman.*   His brother Bob (of recenter memory) who was his shadow in every thing while he lived, and dwindled into less than a shadow afterwards—was a *gentleman* with a little stronger infusion of the *latter ingredient;* that was all. It is amazing how a little of the more or less makes a difference in these things. When you saw Bobby in the Duke's Servant,[1] you said, what a pity such a pretty fellow was only a servant. When you saw Jack figuring in Captain Absolute, you thought you could trace his promotion to some lady of quality who fancied the handsome fellow in his top-knot, and had bought him a commission. Therefore Jack in Dick Amlet was insuperable.

Jack had two voices,—both plausible, hypocritical, and insinuating; but his secondary or supplemental voice still more decisively histrionic than his common one. It was reserved for the spectator; and the dramatis personæ were supposed to know nothing at all about it. The *lies* of young Wilding, and the *sentiments* in Joseph Surface, were thus marked out in a sort of italics to the audience. This secret correspondence with the company before the curtain (which is the bane and death of tragedy) has an extremely happy effect in some kinds of comedy, in the more highly artificial comedy of Congreve or of Sheridan especially, where the absolute sense of reality (so indispensable to scenes of interest) is not required, or would rather interfere to diminish your pleasure. The fact is, you do not believe in such characters as Surface—the villain of artificial comedy—even while you read or see them. If you did, they would shock and not divert you. When Ben, in Love for Love, returns from sea, the following exquisite dialogue occurs at his first meeting with his father—

> *Sir Sampson.* Thou hast been many a weary league, Ben, since I saw thee.
> *Ben.* Ey, ey, been! Been far enough, an that be all.—Well, father, and how do all at home? how does brother Dick, and brother Val?
> *Sir Sampson.* Dick! body o' me, Dick has been dead these two years. I writ you word when you were at Leghorn.
> *Ben.* Mess, that's true; Marry, I had forgot. Dick's dead, as you say—Well, and how?—I have a many questions to ask you—

Here is an instance of insensibility which in real life would be revolting, or rather in real life could not have co-existed with the warm-hearted temperament of the character. But when you read it in the spirit with which such playful selections and specious combinations rather than strict *metaphrases* of nature should be taken, or when you saw Bannister play it, it neither did, nor does wound the moral sense at all. For what is Ben—the pleasant sailor which Bannister gives us—but a piece of satire—a creation of Congreve's fancy—a dreamy combination of all the accidents of a sailor's character—his contempt of money—his credulity to women—with that necessary estrangement from home which it is just within the

---

[1] High Life Below Stairs.

verge of credibility to suppose *might* produce such an hallucination as is here described.   We never think the worse of Ben for it, or feel it as a stain upon his character.   But when an actor comes, and instead of the delightful phantom—the creature dear to half-belief—which Bannister exhibited—displays before our eyes a downright concretion of a Wapping sailor—a jolly warm-hearted Jack Tar—and nothing else—when instead of investing it with a delicious confusedness of the head, and a veering undirected goodness of purpose—he gives to it a downright daylight understanding, and a full consciousness of its actions; thrusting forward the sensibilities of the character with a pretence as if it stood upon nothing else, and was to be judged by them alone—we feel the discord of the thing ; the scene is disturbed ; a real man has got in among the dramatis personæ, and puts them out.   We want the sailor turned out.   We feel that his true place is not behind the curtain but in the first or second gallery.

ON THE ARTIFICIAL COMEDY OF THE LAST CENTURY

THE artificial Comedy, or Comedy of manners, is quite extinct on our stage.   Congreve and Farquhar show their heads once in seven years only, to be exploded and put down! instantly. The times cannot bear them.   Is it for a few wild speeches, an occasional license of dialogue ?   I think not altogether.   The business of their dramatic characters will not stand the moral test. We screw every thing up to that.   Idle gallantry in a fiction, a dream, the passing pageant of an evening, startles us in the same way as the alarming indications of profligacy in a son or ward in real life should startle a parent or guardian.   We have no such middle emotions as dramatic interests left.   We see a stage libertine playing his loose pranks of two hours' duration, and of no after consequence, with the severe eyes which inspect real vices with their bearings upon two worlds.   We are spectators to a plot or intrigue (not reducible in life to the point of strict morality) and take it all for truth.   We substitute a real for a dramatic person, and judge him accordingly.   We try him in our courts, from which there is no appeal to the *dramatis personæ*, his peers.   We have been spoiled with—not sentimental comedy—but a tyrant far more pernicious to our pleasures which has suc-

ceeded to it, the exclusive and all devouring drama of common
life; where the moral point is every thing; where, instead of the
fictitious half-believed personages of the stage (the phantoms of
old comedy) we recognise ourselves, our brothers, aunts, kinsfolk,
allies, patrons, enemies,—the same as in life,—with an interest in
what is going on so hearty and substantial, that we cannot afford
our moral judgment, in its deepest and most vital results, to
compromise or slumber for a moment.   What is *there* transacting, by no modification is made to affect us in any other
manner than the same events or characters would do in our
relationships of life.   We carry our fire-side concerns to the theatre
with us.   We do not go thither, like our ancestors, to escape from
the pressure of reality, so much as to confirm our experience of it;
to make assurance double, and take a bond of fate.   We must live
our toilsome lives twice over, as it was the mournful privilege
of Ulysses to descend twice to the shades.   All that neutral
ground of character, which stood between vice and virtue; or
which in fact was indifferent to neither, where neither properly
was called in question; that happy breathing-place from the
burthen of a perpetual moral questioning—the sanctuary and
quiet Alsatia of hunted casuistry—is broken up and disfranchised,
as injurious to the interests of society.   The privileges of the
place are taken away by law.   We dare not dally with
images, or names, of wrong.   We bark like foolish dogs at
shadows.   We dread infection from the scenic representation of
disorder; and fear a painted pustule.   In our anxiety that our
morality should not take cold, we wrap it up in a great blanket
surtout of precaution against the breeze and sunshine.

I confess for myself that (with no great delinquencies to answer
for) I am glad for a season to take an airing beyond the diocese
of the strict conscience,—not to live always in the precincts of
the law-courts,—but now and then, for a dream-while or so, to
imagine a world with no meddling restrictions—to get into recesses, whither the hunter cannot follow me—

> ————Secret shades
> Of woody Ida's inmost grove,
> While yet there was no fear of Jove—

I come back to my cage and my restraint the fresher and more
healthy for it.   I wear my shackles more contentedly for having
respired the breath of an imaginary freedom.   I do not know
how it is with others, but I feel the better always for the perusal
of one of Congreve's—nay, why should I not add even of Wycherley's—comedies.   I am the gayer at least for it; and I could never
connect those sports of a witty fancy in any shape with any result
to be drawn from them to imitation in real life.   They are a

world of themselves almost as much as fairy-land. Take one of their characters, male or female (with few exceptions they are alike), and place it in a modern play, and my virtuous indignation shall rise against the profligate wretch as warmly as the Catos of the pit could desire ; because in a modern play I am to judge of the right and the wrong. The standard of *police* is the measure of *political justice.* The atmosphere will blight it, it cannot live here. It has got into a moral world, where it has no business, from which it must needs fall headlong ; as dizzy, and incapable of making a stand, as a Swedenborgian bad spirit that has wandered unawares into the sphere of one of his Good Men, or Angels. But in its own world do we feel the creature is so very bad ?—The Fainalls and the Mirabels, the Dorimants and the Lady Touchwoods, in their own sphere, do not offend my moral sense ; in fact they do not appeal to it at all. They seem engaged in their proper element. They break through no laws, or conscientious restraints. They know of none. They have got out of Christendom into the land—what shall I call it ?—of cuckoldry—the Utopia of gallantry, where pleasure is duty, and the manners perfect freedom. It is altogether a speculative scene of things, which has no reference whatever to the world that is. No good person can be justly offended as a spectator, because no good person suffers on the stage. Judged morally, every character in these plays—the few exceptions only are *mistakes* — is alike essentially vain and worthless. The great art of Congreve is especially shown in this, that he has entirely excluded from his scenes,—some little generosities in the part of Angelica perhaps excepted,—not only any thing like a faultless character, but any pretensions to goodness or good feelings whatsoever. Whether he did this designedly, or instinctively, the effect is as happy, as the design (if design) was bold. I used to wonder at the strange power which his Way of the World in particular possesses of interesting you all along in the pursuits of characters, for whom you absolutely care nothing—for you neither hate nor love his personages—and I think it is owing to this very indifference for any, that you endure the whole. He has spread a privation of moral light, I will call it, rather than by the ugly name of palpable darkness, over his creations ; and his shadows flit before you without distinction or preference. Had he introduced a good character, a single gush of moral feeling, a revulsion of the judgment to actual life and actual duties, the impertinent Goshen would have only lighted to the discovery of deformities, which now are none, because we think them none.

Translated into real life, the characters of his, and his friend

Wycherley's dramas, are profligates and strumpets,—the business of their brief existence, the undivided pursuit of lawless gallantry. No other spring of action, or possible motive of conduct, is recognised; principles which, universally acted upon, must reduce this frame of things to a chaos. But we do them wrong in so translating them. No such effects are produced in *their* world. When we are among them, we are amongst a chaotic people. We are not to judge them by our usages. No reverend institutions are insulted by their proceedings,—for they have none among them. No peace of families is violated,—for no family ties exist among them. No purity of the marriage bed is stained,—for none is supposed to have a being. No deep affections are disquieted,—no holy wedlock bands are snapped asunder, —for affection's depth and wedded faith are not of the growth of that soil. There is neither right nor wrong,—gratitude or its opposite,—claim or duty,—paternity or sonship. Of what consequence is it to virtue, or how is she at all concerned about it, whether Sir Simon, or Dapperwit, steal away Miss Martha; or who is the father of Lord Froth's, or Sir Paul Pliant's children.

The whole is a passing pageant, where we should sit as unconcerned at the issues, for life or death, as at a battle of the frogs and mice. But, like Don Quixote, we take part against the puppets, and quite as impertinently. We dare not contemplate an Atlantis, a scheme, out of which our coxcombical moral sense is for a little transitory ease excluded. We have not the courage to imagine a state of things for which there is neither reward nor punishment. We cling to the painful necessities of shame and blame. We would indict our very dreams.

Amidst the mortifying circumstances attendant upon growing old, it is something to have seen the School for Scandal in its glory. This comedy grew out of Congreve and Wycherley, but gathered some allays of the sentimental comedy which followed theirs. It is impossible that it should be now *acted*, though it continues, at long intervals, to be announced in the bills. Its hero, when Palmer played it at least, was Joseph Surface. When I remember the gay boldness, the graceful solemn plausibility, the measured step, the insinuating voice—to express it in a word—the downright *acted* villany of the part, so different from the pressure of conscious actual wickedness,—the hypocritical assumption of hypocrisy,— which made Jack so deservedly a favourite in that character, I must needs conclude the present generation of play-goers more virtuous than myself, or more dense. I freely confess that he divided the palm with me with his better brother; that, in fact, I liked him quite as well. Not but there are passages,—like that, for instance, where Joseph is made to refuse a pittance to a poor relation,—incongruities which Sheridan was forced upon by the attempt to join the artificial with the sentimental comedy, either of which must destroy the other—but over these obstructions Jack's manner floated him so lightly, that a refusal from him no more shocked you, than the easy compliance of Charles gave you in reality any pleasure; you got over the paltry question as quickly as you could, to get back into the regions of pure comedy, where no cold moral reigns.   The highly artificial manner of Palmer in this character counteracted every disagreeable impression which you might have received from the contrast, supposing them real, between the two brothers.   You did not believe in Joseph with the same faith with which you believed in Charles.   The latter was a pleasant reality, the former a no less pleasant poetical foil to it.   The comedy, I have said, is incongruous; a mixture of Congreve with sentimental incompatibilities: the gaiety upon the whole is buoyant; but it required the consummate art of Palmer to reconcile the discordant elements.

A player with Jack's talents, if we had one now, would not dare to do the part in the same manner.   He would instinctively avoid every turn which might tend to unrealise, and so to make the character fascinating.   He must take his cue from his spectators, who would expect a bad man and a good man as rigidly opposed to each other as the death-beds of those geniuses are contrasted in the prints, which I am sorry to say have disappeared from the windows of my old friend Carrington Bowles, of St. Paul's Church-yard memory—(an exhibition as venerable as the adjacent cathedral, and almost coeval) of the bad and good man at the hour of death; where the ghastly apprehensions of the former,—and truly the grim phantom with his reality of a toasting fork is not to be despised,—so finely contrast with the meek complacent kissing of the rod,—taking it in like honey and butter,—with which the latter submits to the scythe of the gentle bleeder, Time, who wields his lancet with the apprehensive finger of a popular young ladies' surgeon.   What flesh, like loving grass, would not covet to meet half-way the stroke of such a delicate mower?—John Palmer was twice an actor in this exquisite part.   He was playing to you all the while that he was playing upon Sir Peter and his lady. You had the first intimation of a sentiment before it was on his lips.   His altered voice was meant to you, and you were to suppose that his fictitious co-flutterers on the stage perceived nothing at all of it.   What was it to you if that half-reality, the husband, was over-reached by the puppetry—or the thin thing (Lady Teazle's reputation) was persuaded it was dying of a plethory?   The fortunes of Othello and Desdemona were not concerned in it. Poor Jack has past from the stage in good time, that he did

VOL. II.—10

not live to this our age of seriousness. The pleasant old Teazle *King*, too, is gone in good time. His manner would scarce have past current in our day. We must love or hate—acquit or condemn—censure or pity—exert our detestable coxcombry of moral judgment upon every thing. Joseph Surface, to go down now, must be a downright revolting villain—no compromise—his first appearance must shock and give horror—his specious plausibilities, which the pleasurable faculties of our fathers welcomed with such hearty greetings, knowing that no harm (dramatic harm even) could come, or was meant to come of them, must inspire a cold and killing aversion. Charles (the real canting person of the scene—for the hypocrisy of Joseph has its ulterior legitimate ends, but his brother's professions of a good heart centre in downright self-satisfaction) must be *loved*, and Joseph *hated*. To balance one disagreeable reality with another, Sir Peter Teazle must be no longer the comic idea of a fretful old bachelor bridegroom, whose teasings (while King acted it) were evidently as much played off at you, as they were meant to concern any body on the stage,—he must be a real person, capable in law of sustaining an injury—a person towards whom duties are to be acknowledged—the genuine crim-con antagonist of the villanous seducer Joseph. To realise him more, his sufferings under his unfortunate match must have the downright pungency of life—must (or should) make you not mirthful but uncomfortable, just as the same predicament would move you in a neighbour or old friend. The delicious scenes which give the play its name and zest, must affect you in the same serious manner as if you heard the reputation of a dear female friend attacked in your real presence. Crabtree, and Sir Benjamin—those poor snakes that live but in the sunshine of your mirth—must be ripened by this hot-bed process of realization into asps or amphisbænas; and Mrs. Candour—O! frightful! become a hooded serpent. Oh who that remembers Parsons and Dodd—the wasp and butterfly of the School for Scandal—in those two characters; and charming natural Miss Pope, the perfect gentlewoman as distinguished from the fine lady of comedy, in this latter part—would forego the true scenic delight—the escape from life—the oblivion of consequences—the holiday barring out of the pedant Reflection—those Saturnalia of two or three brief hours, well won from the world—to sit instead at one of our modern plays—to have his coward conscience (that forsooth must not be left for a moment) stimulated with perpetual appeals—dulled rather, and blunted, as a faculty without repose must be—and his moral vanity pampered with images of notional justice, notional beneficence, lives saved without the spectators' risk, and fortunes given away that cost the author nothing?

No piece was, perhaps, ever so completely cast in all its parts as this *manager's comedy*.   Miss Farren had succeeded to Mrs. Abingdon in Lady Teazle; and Smith, the original Charles, had retired, when I first saw it.   The rest of the characters, with very slight exceptions, remained.   I remember it was then the fashion to cry down John Kemble, who took the part of Charles after Smith; but, I thought, very unjustly.   Smith, I fancy, was more airy, and took the eye with a certain gaiety of person.   He brought with him no sombre recollections of tragedy.   He had not to expiate the fault of having pleased beforehand in lofty declamation.   He had no sins of Hamlet or of Richard to atone for.   His failure in these parts was a passport to success in one of so opposite a tendency.   But, as far as I could judge, the weighty sense of Kemble made up for more personal incapacity than he had to answer for.   His harshest tones in this part came steeped and dulcified in good humour.   He made his defects a grace.   His exact declamatory manner, as he managed it, only served to convey the points of his dialogue with more precision.   It seemed to head the shafts to carry them deeper.   Not one of his sparkling sentences was lost.   I remember minutely how he delivered each in succession, and cannot by any effort imagine how any of them could be altered for the better.   No man could deliver brilliant dialogue—the dialogue of Congreve or of Wycherley—because none understood it—half so well as John Kemble.   His Valentine, in Love for Love, was, to my recollection, faultless.   He flagged sometimes in the intervals of tragic passion.   He would slumber over the level parts of an heroic character.   His Macbeth has been known to nod.   But he always seemed to me to be particularly alive to pointed and witty dialogue.   The relaxing levities of tragedy have not been touched by any since him—the playful court-bred spirit in which he condescended to the players in Hamlet —the sportive relief which he threw into the darker shades of Richard—disappeared with him.   He had his sluggish moods, his torpors—but they were the halting-stones and resting-places of his tragedy—politic savings, and fetches of the breath—husbandry of the lungs, where nature pointed him to be an economist— rather, I think, than errors of the judgment.   They were, at worst, less painful than the eternal tormenting unappeasable vigilance, the " lidless dragon eyes," of present fashionable tragedy.

ON THE ACTING OF MUNDEN

NOT many nights ago I had come home from seeing this extraordinary performer in Cockletop ; and when I retired to my pillow, his whimsical image still stuck by me, in a manner as to threaten sleep. In vain I tried to divest myself of it, by conjuring up the most opposite associations. I resolved to be serious. I raised up the gravest topics of life ; private misery, public calamity. All would not do.

> ———There the antic sate
> Mocking our state—

his queer visnomy—his bewildering costume—all the strange things which he had raked together—his serpentine rod, swagging about in his pocket—Cleopatra's tear, and the rest of his relics—O'Keefe's wild farce, and *his* wilder commentary—till the passion of laughter, like grief in excess, relieved itself by its own weight, inviting the sleep which in the first instance it had driven away.

But I was not to escape so easily. No sooner did I fall into slumbers, than the same image, only more perplexing, assailed me in the shape of dreams. Not one Munden, but five hundred, were dancing before me, like the faces which, whether you will or no, come when you have been taking opium—all the strange combinations, which this strangest of all strange mortals ever shot his proper countenance into, from the day he came commissioned to dry up the tears of the town for the loss of the now almost forgotten Edwin. O for the power of the pencil to have fixed them when I awoke ! A season or two since there was exhibited a Hogarth gallery. I do not see why there should not be a Munden gallery. In richness and variety the latter would not fall far short of the former.

There is one face of Farley, one face of Knight, one (but what a one it is !) of Liston ; but Munden has none that you can properly pin down, and call *his*. When you think he has exhausted his battery of looks, in unaccountable warfare with your gravity, suddenly he sprouts out an entirely new set of features, like Hydra. He is not one, but legion. Not so much a comedian, as a company. If his name could be multiplied like his countenance, it might fill a play-bill. He, and he alone, literally *makes faces :* applied to any other person, the phrase is a mere figure, denoting certain modifications of the human countenance. Out of some invisible wardrobe he dips for faces, as his friend Suett used for wigs, and fetches them out as easily. I should not be surprised to see him some day put out the head of a river horse ; or come forth a pewitt, or lapwing, some feathered metamorphosis.

I have seen this gifted actor in Sir Christopher Curry—in Old Dornton—diffuse a glow of sentiment which has made the pulse of a crowded theatre beat like that of one man ; when he has come in aid of the pulpit, doing good to the moral heart of a people. I have seen some faint approaches to this sort of excellence in other players. But in the grand grotesque of farce, Munden stands out as single and unaccompanied as Hogarth. Hogarth, strange to tell, had no followers. The school of Munden began, and must end with himself.

Can any man *wonder*, like him? can any man *see ghosts*, like him? or *fight with his own shadow*—" sessa "—as he does in that strangely-neglected thing, the Cobbler of Preston—where his alternations from the Cobbler to the Magnifico, and from the Magnifico to the Cobbler, keep the brain of the spectator in as wild a ferment, as if some Arabian Night were being acted before him. Who like him can throw, or ever attempted to throw, a preternatural interest over the commonest daily-life objects? A table, or a joint stool, in his conception, rises into a dignity equivalent to Cassiopeia's chair. It is invested with constellatory importance. You could not speak of it with more deference, if it were mounted into the firmament. A beggar in the hands of Michael Angelo, says Fuseli, rose the Patriarch of Poverty. So the gusto of Munden antiquates and ennobles what it touches. His pots and his ladles are as grand and primal as the seething-pots and hooks seen in old prophetic vision. A tub of butter, contemplated by him, amounts to a Platonic idea. He understands a leg of mutton in its quiddity. He stands wondering, amid the common-place materials of life, like primæval man with the sun and stars about him.

THE LAST ESSAYS OF ELIA

(From the 1st Edition, 1833)

PREFACE

BY A FRIEND OF THE LATE ELIA

THIS poor gentleman, who for some months past had been in a declining way, hath at length paid his final tribute to nature.

To say truth, it is time he were gone. The humour of the thing, if there was ever much in it, was pretty well exhausted ; and a two years' and a half existence has been a tolerable duration for a phantom.

I am now at liberty to confess, that much which I have heard objected to my late friend's writings was well-founded. Crude they are, I grant you—a sort of unlicked, incondite things—villainously pranked in an affected array of antique modes and phrases. They had not been *his*, if they had been other than such ; and better it is, that a writer should be natural in a self-pleasing quaintness, than to affect a naturalness (so called) that should be strange to him. Egotistical they have been pronounced by some who did not know, that what he tells us, as of himself, was often true only (historically) of another ; as in a former Essay (to save many instances)—where under the *first person* (his favourite figure) he shadows forth the forlorn estate of a country-boy placed at a London school, far from his friends and connections—in direct opposition to his own early history. If it be egotism to imply and twine with his own identity the griefs and affections of another—making himself many, or reducing many unto himself—then is the skilful novelist, who all along brings in his hero, or heroine, speaking of themselves, the greatest egotist of all ; who yet has never, therefore, been accused of that narrowness. And how shall the intenser dramatist escape being faulty, who doubtless, under cover of passion uttered by another, oftentimes gives blameless vent to his most inward feelings, and expresses his own story modestly ?

My late friend was in many respects a singular character. Those who did not like him, hated him ; and some, who once liked him, afterwards became his bitterest haters. The truth is, he gave himself too little concern what he uttered, and in whose presence. He observed neither time nor place, and would e'en out with what came uppermost. With the severe religionist he would pass for a free-thinker ; while the other faction set him down for a bigot, or persuaded themselves that he belied his sentiments. Few understood him ; and I am not certain that at all times he quite understood himself. He too much affected that dangerous figure—irony. He sowed doubtful speeches, and reaped plain, unequivocal hatred. —He would interrupt the gravest discussion with some light jest ; and yet, perhaps, not quite irrelevant in ears that could understand it. Your long and much talkers hated him. The informal habit of his mind, joined to an inveterate impediment of speech, forbade him to be an orator ; and he seemed determined that no one else should play that part when he was present. He was *petit* and ordinary in his person and appearance. I have seen him sometimes in what is called good company, but where he has been a stranger, sit silent, and be suspected for an odd fellow ; till some unlucky occasion provoking it, he would stutter out some senseless pun (not altogether senseless perhaps, if rightly taken), which has stamped his character for the evening. It was hit or miss with him ; but nine times out of ten, he contrived by this device to send away a whole company his enemies. His conceptions rose kindlier than his utterance, and his happiest *impromptus* had the appearance of effort. He has been accused of trying to be witty, when in truth he was but struggling to give his poor thoughts articulation. He chose his companions for some individuality of character which they manifested.—Hence, not many persons of science, and few professed *literati*, were of his councils. They were, for the most part, persons of an uncertain fortune ; and, as to such people commonly nothing is more obnoxious than a gentleman of settled (though moderate) income, he passed with most of them for a great miser. To my knowledge this was a mistake. His *intimados*, to confess a truth, were in the world's eye a ragged regiment. He found them floating on the surface of society ; and the colour, or something else, in the weed pleased him. The burrs stuck to him—but they were good and loving burrs for all that. He never greatly cared for the society of what are called good people. If any of these were scandalised (and offences were sure to arise), he could not help it. When he has been remonstrated with for not making more concessions to the feelings of good people, he would retort by asking, what one point did these good people ever concede to him ? He was temperate in his meals and diversions, but always kept a little

on this side of abstemiousness. Only in the use of the Indian weed
he might be thought a little excessive. He took it, he would say,
as a solvent of speech. Marry—as the friendly vapour ascended,
how his prattle would curl up sometimes with it ! the ligaments,
which tongue-tied him, were loosened, and the stammerer proceeded
a statist !

I do not know whether I ought to bemoan or rejoice that
my old friend is departed. His jests were beginning to grow
obsolete, and his stories to be found out. He felt the approaches
of age ; and while he pretended to cling to life, you saw how
slender were the ties left to bind him. Discoursing with him
latterly on this subject, he expressed himself with a pettishness,
which I thought unworthy of him. In our walks about his
suburban retreat (as he called it) at Shacklewell, some children
belonging to a school of industry had met us, and bowed and
curtseyed, as he thought, in an especial manner to *him*. " They
take me for a visiting governor," he muttered earnestly. He
had a horror, which he carried to a foible, of looking like
anything important and parochial. He thought that he
approached nearer to that stamp daily. He had a general
aversion from being treated like a grave or respectable character,
and kept a wary eye upon the advances of age that should so
entitle him. He herded always, while it was possible, with
people younger than himself. He did not conform to the
march of time, but was dragged along in the procession. His
manners lagged behind his years. He was too much of the boy-
man. The *toga virilis* never sate gracefully on his shoulders.
The impressions of infancy had burnt into him, and he resented
the impertinence of manhood. These were weaknesses ; but such
as they were, they are a key to explicate some of his writings.

BLAKESMOOR IN H——SHIRE

I DO not know a pleasure more affecting than to range at
will over the deserted apartments of some fine old family
mansion. The traces of extinct grandeur admit of a better
passion than envy : and contemplations on the great and good,
whom we fancy in succession to have been its inhabitants, weave
for us illusions, incompatible with the bustle of modern occupancy,
and vanities of foolish present aristocracy. The same difference

of feeling, I think, attends us between entering an empty and a crowded church. In the latter it is chance but some present human frailty—an act of inattention on the part of some of the auditory—or a trait of affectation, or worse, vain-glory, on that of the preacher—puts us by our best thoughts, disharmonising the place and the occasion. But would'st thou know the beauty of holiness ?—go alone on some week-day, borrowing the keys of good Master Sexton, traverse the cool aisles of some country church : think of the piety that has kneeled there—the congregations, old and young, that have found consolation there—the meek pastor — the docile parishioner. With no disturbing emotions, no cross conflicting comparisons, drink in the tranquillity of the place, till thou thyself become as fixed and motionless as the marble effigies that kneel and weep around thee.

Journeying northward lately, I could not resist going some few miles out of my road to look upon the remains of an old great house with which I had been impressed in this way in infancy. I was apprised that the owner of it had lately pulled it down ; still I had a vague notion that it could not all have perished, that so much solidity with magnificence could not have been crushed all at once into the mere dust and rubbish which I found it.

The work of ruin had proceeded with a swift hand indeed, and the demolition of a few weeks had reduced it to—an antiquity.

I was astonished at the indistinction of everything. Where had stood the great gates ?   What bounded the court-yard ? Whereabout did the out-houses commence ? a few bricks only lay as representatives of that which was so stately and so spacious.

Death does not shrink up his human victim at this rate. The burnt ashes of a man weigh more in their proportion.

Had I seen these brick-and-mortar knaves at their process of destruction, at the plucking of every pannel I should have felt the varlets at my heart. I should have cried out to them to spare a plank at least out of the cheerful store-room, in whose hot window-seat I used to sit and read Cowley, with the grass-plat before, and the hum and flappings of that one solitary wasp that ever haunted it about me—it is in mine ears now, as oft as summer returns ; or a pannel of the yellow room.

Why, every plank and pannel of that house for me had magic in it. The tapestried bed-rooms—tapestry so much better than painting—not adorning merely, but peopling the wainscots—at which childhood ever and anon would steal a look, shifting its coverlid (replaced as quickly) to exercise its tender courage in a momentary eye-encounter with those stern bright visages, staring reciprocally—all Ovid on the walls, in colours vivider than his descriptions. Actæon in mid sprout, with the unappeasable prudery of Diana; and the still more provoking, and almost culinary coolness of Dan Phœbus, eel-fashion, deliberately divesting of Marsyas.

Then, that haunted room—in which old Mrs. Battle died—whereinto I have crept, but always in the day-time, with a passion of fear; and a sneaking curiosity, terror-tainted, to hold communication with the past.—*How shall they build it up again?*

It was an old deserted place, yet not so long deserted but that traces of the splendour of past inmates were everywhere apparent. Its furniture was still standing—even to the tarnished gilt leather battledores, and crumbling feathers of shuttlecocks in the nursery, which told that children had once played there. But I was a lonely child, and had the range at will of every apartment, knew every nook and corner, wondered and worshipped everywhere.

The solitude of childhood is not so much the mother of thought, as it is the feeder of love, and silence, and admiration. So strange a passion for the place possessed me in those years, that, though there lay—I shame to say how few roods distant from the mansion —half hid by trees, what I judged some romantic lake, such was the spell which bound me to the house, and such my carefulness not to pass its strict and proper precincts, that the idle waters lay unexplored for me ; and not till late in life, curiosity prevailing over elder devotion, I found, to my astonishment, a pretty brawling brook had been the Lacus Incognitus of my infancy. Variegated views, extensive prospects—and those at no great distance from the house—I was told of such—what were they to me, being out of the boundaries of my Eden ?—So far from a wish to roam, I would have drawn, methought, still closer the fences of my chosen prison; and have been hemmed in by a yet securer cincture of those excluding garden walls. I could have exclaimed with that garden-loving poet—

> Bind me, ye woodbines, in your 'twines,
> Curl me about, ye gadding vines ;
> And oh so close your circles lace,
> That I may never leave this place ;
> But, lest your fetters prove too weak,
> Ere I your silken bondage break,
> Do you, O brambles, chain me too,
> And, courteous briars, nail me through !

I was here as in a lonely temple. Snug firesides—the low-built roof—parlours ten feet by ten—frugal boards, and all the homeliness of home—these were the condition of my birth—the wholesome soil which I was planted in. Yet, without impeachment to their tenderest lessons, I am not sorry to have had glances of something beyond; and to have taken, if but a peep, in childhood, at the contrasting accidents of a great fortune.

To have the feeling of gentility, it is not necessary to have been born gentle. The pride of ancestry may be had on cheaper terms than to be obliged to an importunate race of ancestors; and the coatless antiquary in his unemblazoned cell, revolving the long line of a Mowbray's or De Clifford's pedigree, at those sounding names may warm himself into as gay a vanity as those who do inherit them. The claims of birth are ideal merely, and what herald shall go about to strip me of an idea? Is it trenchant to their swords? can it be hacked off as a spur can? or torn away like a tarnished garter?

What, else, were the families of the great to us? what pleasure should we take in their tedious genealogies, or their capitulatory brass monuments? What to us the uninterrupted current of their bloods, if our own did not answer within us to a cognate and correspondent elevation?

Or wherefore, else, O tattered and diminished 'Scutcheon that hung upon the time-worn walls of thy princely stairs, BLAKESMOOR! have I in childhood so oft stood poring upon thy mystic characters —thy emblematic supporters, with their prophetic " Resurgam "— till, every dreg of peasantry purging off, I received into myself Very Gentility? Thou wert first in my morning eyes; and of nights, hast detained my steps from bedward, till it was but a step from gazing at thee to dreaming on thee.

This is the only true gentry by adoption; the veritable change of blood, and not, as empirics have fabled, by transfusion.

Who it was by dying that had earned the splendid trophy, I know not, I inquired not; but its fading rags, and colours cobweb-stained, told that its subject was of two centuries back.

And what if my ancestor at that date was some Damœtas—feeding flocks, not his own, upon the hills of Lincoln—did I in less earnest vindicate to myself the family trappings of this once proud Ægon?—repaying by a backward triumph the insults he might possibly have heaped in his life-time upon my poor pastoral progenitor.

If it were presumption so to speculate, the present owners of the mansion had least reason to complain. They had long forsaken the old house of their fathers for a newer trifle; and I was left to appropriate to myself what images I could pick up, to raise my fancy, or to soothe my vanity.

I was the true descendant of those old W——s; and not the present family of that name, who had fled the old waste places.

Mine was that gallery of good old family portraits, which as

I have gone over, giving them in fancy my own family name, one
—and then another—would seem to smile, reaching forward from
the canvas, to recognise the new relationship; while the rest looked
grave, as it seemed, at the vacancy in their dwelling, and thoughts
of fled posterity.

That Beauty with the cool blue pastoral drapery, and a lamb—
that hung next the great bay window—with the bright yellow
H——shire hair, and eye of watchet hue—so like my Alice!—I am
persuaded she was a true Elia—Mildred Elia, I take it.

Mine too, BLAKESMOOR, was thy noble Marble Hall, with its
mosaic pavements, and its Twelve Cæsars—stately busts in marble
—ranged round: of whose countenances, young reader of faces as I
was, the frowning beauty of Nero, I remember, had most of my
wonder; but the mild Galba had my love. There they stood in the
coldness of death, yet freshness of immortality.

Mine too, thy lofty Justice Hall, with its one chair of authority,
high-backed and wickered, once the terror of luckless poacher, or
self-forgetful maiden—so common since, that bats have roosted in it.

Mine too—whose else?—thy costly fruit-garden, with its sun-
baked southern wall; the ampler pleasure-garden, rising backwards
from the house in triple terraces, with flower-pots now of palest
lead, save that a speck here and there, saved from the elements, be-
spake their pristine state to have been gilt and glittering; the
verdant quarters backwarder still; and, stretching still beyond, in
old formality, thy firry wilderness, the haunt of the squirrel, and the
day-long murmuring woodpigeon, with that antique image in the
centre, God or Goddess I wist not; but child of Athens or old Rome
paid never a sincerer worship to Pan or to Sylvanus in their native
groves, than I to that fragmental mystery.

Was it for this, that I kissed my childish hands too fervently in
your idol worship, walks and windings of BLAKESMOOR! for this, or
what sin of mine, has the plough passed over your pleasant places?
I sometimes think that as men, when they die, do not die all, so of
their extinguished habitations there may be a hope—a germ to be
revivified.

POOR RELATIONS

A POOR Relation—is the most irrelevant thing in nature,—
a piece of impertinent correspondency,—an odious approximation,—a haunting conscience,—a preposterous shadow, lengthen-

ing in the noontide of your prosperity,—an unwelcome remembrancer,—a perpetually recurring mortification,—a drain on your purse,—a more intolerable dun upon your pride,—a drawback upon success,—a rebuke to your rising,—a stain in your blood,—a blot on your scutcheon,—a rent in your garment,—a death's head at your banquet,—Agathocles' pot,—a Mordecai in your gate,—a Lazarus at your door,—a lion in your path,—a frog in your chamber,—a fly in your ointment,—a mote in your eye,—a triumph to your enemy, an apology to your friends,—the one thing not needful,—the hail in harvest,—the ounce of sour in a pound of sweet.

He is known by his knock. Your heart telleth you "That is Mr. ——." A rap, between familiarity and respect ; that demands, and, at the same time, seems to despair of, entertainment. He entereth smiling, and—embarrassed. He holdeth out his hand to you to shake, and—draweth it back again. He casually looketh in about dinner time—when the table is full. He offereth to go away, seeing you have company—but is induced to stay. He filleth a chair, and your visiter's two children are accommodated at a side table. He never cometh upon open days, when your wife says with some complacency, " My dear, perhaps Mr. —— will drop in to-day." He remembereth birth-days—and professeth he is fortunate to have stumbled upon one. He declareth against fish, the turbot being small—yet suffereth himself to be importuned into a slice against his first resolution. He sticketh by the port—yet will be prevailed upon to empty the remainder glass of claret, if a stranger press it upon him. He is a puzzle to the servants, who are fearful of being too obsequious, or not civil enough, to him. The guests think " they have seen him before." Every one speculateth upon his condition ; and the most part take him to be—a tide-waiter. He calleth you by your Christian name, to imply that his other is the same with your own. He is too familiar by half, yet you wish he had less diffidence. With half the familiarity he might pass for a casual dependent ; with more boldness he would be in no danger of being taken for what he is. He is too humble for a friend, yet taketh on him more state than befits a client. He is a worse guest than a country tenant, inasmuch as he bringeth up no rent—yet 'tis odds, from his garb and demeanour, that your guests take him for one. He is asked to make one at the whist table ; refuseth on the score of poverty, and—resents being left out. When the company break up, he proffereth to go for a coach—and lets the servant go. He recollects your grandfather ; and will thrust in some mean, and quite unimportant anecdote of—the family. He knew it when it was not quite so flourishing as "he is blest in seeing it now." He reviveth past situations, to institute what he calleth—favourable comparisons. With a reflecting sort of congratulation, he will inquire the price of your furniture; and insults you with a special commendation of your window-curtains. He is of opinion that the urn is the more elegant shape, but, after all, there was something more comfortable about the old tea-kettle—which you must remember. He dare say you must find a great convenience in having a carriage of your own, and appealeth to your lady if it is not so. Inquireth if you have had your arms done on vellum yet; and did not know till lately, that such-and-such had been the crest of the family. His memory is unseasonable; his compliments perverse; his talk a trouble; his stay pertinacious; and when he goeth away, you dismiss his chair into a corner, as precipitately as possible, and feel fairly rid of two nuisances.

There is a worse evil under the sun, and that is—a female Poor Relation. You may do something with the other; you may pass him off tolerably well; but your indigent she-relative is hopeless. " He is an old humourist," you may say, " and affects to go threadbare. His circumstances are better than folks would take them to be. You are fond of having a Character at your table, and truly he is one." But in the indications of female poverty there can be no disguise. No woman dresses below herself from caprice. The truth must out without shuffling. " She is plainly related to the L—s; or what does she at their house ? " She is, in all probability, your wife's cousin. Nine times out of ten, at least, this is the case. Her garb is something between a gentlewoman and a beggar, yet the former evidently predominates. She is most provokingly humble, and ostentatiously sensible to her inferiority. He may require to be repressed sometimes—*aliquando sufflaminandus erat*—but there is no raising her. You send her soup at dinner, and she begs to be helped—after the gentlemen. Mr. —— requests the honour of taking wine with her; she hesitates between Port and Madeira, and chooses the former—because he does. She calls the servant *Sir;* and insists on not troubling him to hold her plate. The housekeeper patronizes her. The children's governess takes upon her to correct her, when she has mistaken the piano for a harpsichord.

Richard Amlet, Esq., in the play, is a notable instance of the disadvantages, to which this chimerical notion of *affinity constituting a claim to acquaintance,* may subject the spirit of a gentleman. A little foolish blood is all that is betwixt him and a lady of great estate. His stars are perpetually crossed by the malignant maternity of an old woman, who persists in calling him " her son Dick." But she has wherewithal in the end to recompense his indignities, and float him again upon the brilliant surface, under which it had been her seeming business and pleasure all along to sink him. All

men, besides, are not of Dick's temperament. I knew an Amlet in
real life, who, wanting Dick's buoyancy, sank indeed. Poor W——
was of my own standing at Christ's, a fine classic, and a youth of
promise. If he had a blemish, it was too much pride ; but its
quality was inoffensive ; it was not of that sort which hardens
the heart, and serves to keep inferiors at a distance ; it only
sought to ward off derogation from itself. It was the principle of
self-respect carried as far as it could go, without infringing upon
that respect, which he would have every one else equally maintain
for himself. He would have you to think alike with him on this
topic. Many a quarrel have I had with him, when we were rather
older boys, and our tallness made us more obnoxious to observation
in the blue clothes, because I would not thread the alleys and blind
ways of the town with him to elude notice, when we have been out
together on a holiday in the streets of this sneering and prying
metropolis. W—— went, sore with these notions, to Oxford,
where the dignity and sweetness of a scholar's life, meeting with the
alloy of a humble introduction, wrought in him a passionate
devotion to the place, with a profound aversion from the society.
The servitor's gown (worse than his school array) clung to him with
Nessian venom. He thought himself ridiculous in a garb, under
which Latimer must have walked erect ; and in which Hooker, in
his young days, possibly flaunted in a vein of no discommendable
vanity. In the depth of college shades, or in his lonely chamber,
the poor student shrunk from observation. He found shelter
among books, which insult not ; and studies, that ask no questions
of a youth's finances. He was lord of his library, and seldom cared
for looking out beyond his domains. The healing influence of
studious pursuits was upon him, to soothe and to abstract. He was
almost a healthy man ; when the waywardness of his fate broke out
against him with a second and worse malignity. The father of
W—— had hitherto exercised the humble profession of house-
painter at N——, near Oxford. A supposed interest with some of
the heads of the colleges had now induced him to take up his abode
in that city, with the hope of being employed upon some public
works which were talked of. From that moment I read in the
countenance of the young man, the determination which at length
tore him from academical pursuits for ever. To a person un-
acquainted with our Universities, the distance between the gowns-
men and the townsmen, as they are called—the trading part of the
latter especially—is carried to an excess that would appear harsh and
incredible. The temperament of W——'s father was diametrically
the reverse of his own. Old W—— was a little, busy, cringing
tradesman, who, with his son upon his arm, would stand bowing
and scraping, cap in hand, to any-thing that wore the semblance of

a gown—insensible to the winks and opener remonstrances of the young man, to whose chamber-fellow, or equal in standing, perhaps, he was thus obsequiously and gratuitously ducking. Such a state of things could not last. W—— must change the air of Oxford or be suffocated. He chose the former; and let the sturdy moralist, who strains the point of the filial duties as high as they can bear, censure the dereliction; he cannot estimate the struggle. I stood with W——, the last afternoon I ever saw him, under the eaves of his paternal dwelling. It was in the fine lane leading from the High-street to the back of ***** college, where W—— kept his rooms. He seemed thoughtful, and more reconciled. I ventured to rally him—finding him in a better mood—upon a representation of the Artist Evangelist, which the old man, whose affairs were beginning to flourish, had caused to be set up in a splendid sort of frame over his really handsome shop, either as a token of prosperity, or badge of gratitude to his saint. W—— looked up at the Luke, and, like Satan, "knew his mounted sign—and fled." A letter on his father's table the next morning, announced that he had accepted a commission in a regiment about to embark for Portugal. He was among the first who perished before the walls of St. Sebastian.

I do not know how, upon a subject which I began with treating half seriously, I should have fallen upon a recital so eminently painful; but this theme of poor relationship is replete with so much matter for tragic as well as comic associations, that it is difficult to keep the account distinct without blending. The earliest impressions which I received on this matter, are certainly not attended with anything painful, or very humiliating, in the recalling. At my father's table (no very splendid one) was to be found, every Saturday, the mysterious figure of an aged gentleman, clothed in neat black, of a sad yet comely appearance. His deportment was of the essence of gravity; his words few or none; and I was not to make a noise in his presence. I had little inclination to have done so—for my cue was to admire in silence. A particular elbow chair was appropriated to him, which was in no case to be violated. A peculiar sort of sweet pudding, which appeared on no other occasion, distinguished the days of his coming. I used to think him a prodigiously rich man. All I could make out of him was, that he and my father had been schoolfellows a world ago at Lincoln, and that he came from the Mint. The Mint I knew to be a place where all the money was coined—and I thought he was the owner of all that money. Awful ideas of the Tower twined themselves about his presence. He seemed above human infirmities and passions. A sort of melancholy grandeur invested him. From some inexplicable doom I fancied him obliged to go about in an eternal suit of mourning; a captive—a stately being, let out of the Tower on Saturdays. Often have I wondered at the temerity of my father, who, in spite of an habitual general respect which we all in common manifested towards him, would venture now and then to stand up against him in some argument, touching their youthful days. The houses of the ancient city of Lincoln are divided (as most of my readers know) between the dwellers on the hill, and in the valley. This marked distinction formed an obvious division between the boys who lived above (however brought together in a common school) and the boys whose paternal residence was on the plain; a sufficient cause of hostility in the code of these young Grotiuses. My father had been a leading Mountaineer; and would still maintain the general superiority, in skill and hardihood, of the *Above Boys* (his own faction) over the *Below Boys* (so were they called), of which party his contemporary had been a chieftain. Many and hot were the skirmishes on this topic —the only one upon which the old gentleman was ever brought out—and bad blood bred; even sometimes almost to the recommencement (so I expected) of actual hostilities. But my father, who scorned to insist upon advantages, generally contrived to turn the conversation upon some adroit by-commendation of the old Minster; in the general preference of which, before all other cathedrals in the island, the dweller on the hill, and the plainborn, could meet on a conciliating level, and lay down their less important differences. Once only I saw the old gentleman really ruffled, and I remembered with anguish the thought that came over me: "Perhaps he will never come here again." He had been pressed to take another plate of the viand, which I have already mentioned as the indispensable concomitant of his visits. He had refused, with a resistance amounting to rigour—when my aunt, an old Lincolnian, but who had something of this, in common with my cousin Bridget, that she would sometimes press civility out of season—uttered the following memorable application—"Do take another slice, Mr. Billet, for you do not get pudding every day." The old gentleman said nothing at the time—but he took occasion in the course of the evening, when some argument had intervened between them, to utter with an emphasis which chilled the company, and which chills me now as I write it—"Woman, you are superannuated." John Billet did not survive long, after the digesting of this affront; but he survived long enough to assure me that peace was actually restored! and, if I remember aright, another pudding was discreetly substituted in the place of that which had occasioned the offence. He died at the Mint (Anno 1781) where he had long held, what he accounted, a comfortable independence; and with five pounds, fourteen shillings, and a penny, which were found in his escrutoire after his decease, left the world, blessing God that he had enough to bury him, and that he had never been obliged to any man for a sixpence. This was—a Poor Relation.

———

STAGE ILLUSION

A PLAY is said to be well or ill acted in proportion to the scenical illusion produced. Whether such illusion can in any case be perfect, is not the question. The nearest approach to it, we are told, is, when the actor appears wholly unconscious of the presence of spectators. In tragedy—in all which is to affect the feelings—this undivided attention to his stage business, seems indispensable. Yet it is, in fact, dispensed with every day by our cleverest tragedians; and while these references to an audience, in the shape of rant or sentiment, are not too frequent or palpable, a sufficient quantity of illusion for the purposes of dramatic interest may be said to be produced in spite of them. But, tragedy apart, it may be inquired whether, in certain characters in comedy, especially those which are a little extravagant, or which involve some notion repugnant to the moral sense, it is not a proof of the highest skill in the comedian when, without absolutely appealing to an audience, he keeps up a tacit understanding with them; and makes them, unconsciously to themselves, a party in the scene. The utmost nicety is required in the mode of doing this; but we speak only of the great artists in the profession.

The most mortifying infirmity in human nature, to feel in ourselves, or to contemplate in another, is, perhaps, cowardice. To see a coward *done to the life* upon a stage would produce anything but mirth. Yet we most of us remember Jack Bannister's cowards. Could any thing be more agreeable, more pleasant? We loved the rogues. How was this effected but by the exquisite art of the actor in a perpetual sub-insinuation to us, the spectators, even in the extremity of the shaking fit, that he was not half such a coward as we took him for? We saw all the common symptoms of the malady upon him; the quivering lip, the cowering knees, the teeth chattering; and could have sworn "that man was frightened." But we forgot all the while—or kept it almost a secret to ourselves—that he never once lost his self-possession; that he let out by a thousand droll looks and gestures—meant at *us*, and not at all supposed to be visible to his fellows in the scene, that his confidence in his own resources had never once deserted him. Was this a genuine picture of a coward? or not rather a likeness, which the clever artist contrived to palm upon us instead of an original; while we secretly connived at the delusion for the purpose of greater pleasure, than a more genuine counterfeiting of the imbecility, helplessness, and utter self-desertion, which we know to be concomitants of cowardice in real life, could have given us?

Why are misers so hateful in the world, and so endurable on the stage, but because the skilful actor, by a sort of sub-reference, rather than direct appeal to us, disarms the character of a great deal of its odiousness, by seeming to engage *our* compassion for the insecure tenure by which he holds his money bags and parchments? By this subtle vent half of the hatefulness of the character—the self-closeness with which in real life it coils itself up from the sympathies of men—evaporates. The miser becomes sympathetic; *i.e.* is no genuine miser. Here again a diverting likeness is substituted for a very disagreeable reality.

Spleen, irritability—the pitiable infirmities of old men, which produce only pain to behold in the realities, counterfeited upon a stage, divert not altogether for the comic appendages to them, but in part from an inner conviction that they are *being acted* before us; that a likeness only is going on, and not the thing itself. They please by being done under the life, or beside it; not *to the life*. When Gatty acts an old man, is he angry indeed? or only a pleasant counterfeit, just enough of a likeness to recognise, without pressing upon us the uneasy sense of reality?

Comedians, paradoxical as it may seem, may be too natural. It was the case with a late actor. Nothing could be more earnest or true than the manner of Mr. Emery; this told excellently in his Tyke, and characters of a tragic cast. But when he carried the same rigid exclusiveness of attention to the stage business, and wilful blindness and oblivion of everything before the curtain into his comedy, it produced a harsh and dissonant effect. He was out of keeping with the rest of the *Personæ Dramatis*. There was as little link between him and them as betwixt himself and the audience. He was a third estate, dry, repulsive, and unsocial to all. Individually considered, his execution was masterly. But comedy is not this unbending thing; for this reason, that the same degree of credibility is not required of it as to serious scenes. The degrees of credibility demanded to the two things may be illustrated by the different sort of truth which we expect when a man tells us a mournful or a merry story. If we suspect the former of falsehood in any one tittle, we reject it altogether. Our tears refuse to flow at a suspected imposition. But the teller of a mirthful tale has

latitude allowed him. We are content with less than absolute
truth. 'Tis the same with dramatic illusion. We confess we love
in comedy to see an audience naturalised behind the scenes, taken
in into the interest of the drama, welcomed as by-standers however.
There is something ungracious in a comic actor holding himself
aloof from all participation or concern with those who are come to
be diverted by him. Macbeth must see the dagger, and no ear but
his own be told of it ; but an old fool in farce may think he *sees
something*, and by conscious words and looks express it, as plainly
as he can speak, to pit, box, and gallery. When an impertinent in
tragedy, an Osric, for instance, breaks in upon the serious passions of
the scene, we approve of the contempt with which he is treated. But
when the pleasant impertinent of comedy, in a piece purely meant
to give delight, and raise mirth out of whimsical perplexities, worries
the studious man with taking up his leisure, or making his house
his home, the same sort of contempt expressed (however *natural*)
would destroy the balance of delight in the spectators. To make
the intrusion comic, the actor who plays the annoyed man must a
little desert nature ; he must, in short, be thinking of the audience,
and express only so much dissatisfaction and peevishness as is consistent with the pleasure of comedy. In other words, his perplexity
must seem half put on. If he repel the intruder with the sober set
face of a man in earnest, and more especially if he deliver his expostulations in a tone which in the world must necessarily provoke
a duel ; his real-life manner will destroy the whimsical and purely
dramatic existence of the other character (which to render it comic
demands an antagonist comicality on the part of the character
opposed to it), and convert what was meant for mirth, rather than
belief, into a downright piece of impertinence indeed, which would
raise no diversion in us, but rather stir pain, to see inflicted in
earnest upon any unworthy person. A very judicious actor (in
most of his parts) seems to have fallen into an error of this sort in
his playing with Mr. Wrench in the farce of Free and Easy.

Many instances would be tedious ; these may suffice to show that
comic acting at least does not always demand from the performer
that strict abstraction from all reference to an audience, which is
exacted of it ; but that in some cases a sort of compromise may take
place, and all the purposes of dramatic delight be attained by a
judicious understanding, not too openly announced, between the
ladies and gentlemen—on both sides of the curtain.

———

TO THE SHADE OF ELLISTON

JOYOUSEST of once embodied spirits, whither at length hast thou flown? to what genial region are we permitted to conjecture that thou hast flitted.

Art thou sowing thy WILD OATS yet (the harvest time was still to come with thee) upon casual sands of Avernus? or art thou enacting ROVER (as we would gladlier think) by wandering Elysian streams?

This mortal frame, while thou didst play thy brief antics amongst us, was in truth any thing but a prison to thee, as the vain Platonist dreams of this *body* to be no better than a county gaol, forsooth, or some house of durance vile, whereof the five senses are the fetters. Thou knewest better than to be in a hurry to cast off those gyves; and had notice to quit, I fear, before thou wert quite ready to abandon this fleshly tenement. It was thy Pleasure House, thy Palace of Dainty Devices; thy Louvre, or thy White Hall.

What new mysterious lodgings dost thou tenant now? or when may we expect thy aërial house-warming?

Tartarus we know, and we have read of the Blessed Shades; now cannot I intelligibly fancy thee in either.

Is it too much to hazard a conjecture, that (as the schoolmen admitted a receptacle apart for Patriarchs and un-chrisom Babes) there may exist—not far perchance from that storehouse of all vanities, which Milton saw in visions—a LIMBO somewhere for PLAYERS? and that

Up thither like aërial vapours fly
Both all Stage things, and all that in Stage things
Built their fond hopes of glory, or lasting fame?
All the unaccomplish'd works of Authors' hands,
Abortive, monstrous, or unkindly mix'd,
Damn'd upon earth, fleet thither—
Play, Opera, Farce, with all their trumpery—

There, by the neighbouring moon (by some not improperly supposed thy Regent Planet upon earth) mayst thou not still be acting thy managerial pranks, great disembodied Lessee? but Lessee still, and still a Manager.

In Green Rooms, impervious to mortal eye, the muse beholds thee wielding posthumous empire.

Thin ghosts of Figurantes (never plump on earth) circle thee in endlessly, and still their song is *Fye on sinful Phantasy*.

Magnificent were thy capriccios on this globe of earth, ROBERT WILLIAM ELLISTON! for as yet we know not thy new name in heaven.

It irks me to think, that, stript of thy regalities, thou shouldst ferry over, a poor forked shade, in crazy Stygian wherry. Methinks I hear the old boatman, paddling by the weedy wharf, with raucid voice, bawling "Sculls, Sculls:" to which, with waving hand, and majestic action, thou deignest no reply, other than in two curt monosyllables, "No: Oars."

But the laws of Pluto's kingdom know small difference between king, and cobbler; manager, and call-boy; and, if haply your dates of life were conterminant, you are quietly taking your passage, cheek by cheek (O ignoble levelling of Death) with the shade of some recently departed candle-snuffer.

But mercy! what strippings, what tearing off of histrionic robes, and private vanities! what denudations to the bone, before the surly Ferryman will admit you to set a foot within his battered lighter!

Crowns, sceptres; shield, sword, and truncheon; thy own coronation robes (for thou hast brought the whole property man's wardrobe with thee, enough to sink a navy); the judge's ermine; the coxcomb's wig; the snuff-box *à la Foppington*—all must overboard, he positively swears—and that ancient mariner brooks no denial; for, since the tiresome monodrame of the old Thracian Harper, Charon, it is to be believed, hath shown small taste for theatricals.

Aye, now 'tis done. You are just boat weight; *pura et puta anima.*

But bless me, how *little* you look!

So shall we all look—kings, and keysars—stript for the last voyage.

But the murky rogue pushes off. Adieu, pleasant, and thrice pleasant shade! with my parting thanks for many a heavy hour of life lightened by thy harmless extravaganzas, public or domestic.

Rhadamanthus, who tries the lighter causes below, leaving to his two brethren the heavy calendars—honest Rhadamanth, always partial to players, weighing their parti-coloured existence here upon earth,—making account of the few foibles, that may have shaded thy *real life* as we call it, (though, substantially, scarcely less a vapour than thy idlest vagaries upon the boards of Drury,) as but of so many echoes, natural re-percussions, and results to be expected from the assumed extravagancies of thy *secondary* or *mock life*, nightly upon a stage—after a lenient castigation, with rods lighter than of those Medusean ringlets, but just enough to "whip the offending Adam out of thee"—shall courteously dismiss thee at the right hand gate—the o. p. side of Hades—that conducts to masques, and merry-makings, in the Theatre Royal of Proserpine.

PLAUDITO, ET VALETO.

ELLISTONIANA

MY acquaintance with the pleasant creature, whose loss we all deplore, was but slight.

My first introduction to E., which afterwards ripened into an acquaintance a little on this side of intimacy, was over a counter of the Leamington Spa Library, then newly entered upon by a branch of his family. E., whom nothing misbecame—to auspicate, I suppose, the filial concern, and set it a going with a lustre—was serving in person two damsels fair, who had come into the shop ostensibly to inquire for some new publication, but in reality to have a sight of the illustrious shopman, hoping some conference. With what an air did he reach down the volume, dispassionately giving his opinion upon the worth of the work in question, and launching out into a dissertation on its comparative merits with those of certain publications of a similar stamp, its rivals! his enchanted customers fairly hanging on his lips, subdued to their authoritative sentence. So have I seen a gentleman in comedy *acting* the shopman. So Lovelace sold his gloves in King Street. I admired the histrionic art, by which he contrived to carry clean away every notion of disgrace, from the occupation he had so generously submitted to; and from that hour I judged him, with no after repentance, to be a person, with whom it would be a felicity to be more acquainted.

To descant upon his merits as a Comedian would be superfluous. With his blended private and professional habits alone I have to do; that harmonious fusion of the manners of the player into those of every day life, which brought the stage boards into streets, and dining-parlours, and kept up the play when the play was ended.— " I like Wrench," a friend was saying to him one day, " because he is the same natural, easy creature, *on* the stage, that he is *off*." " My case exactly," retorted Elliston—with a charming forgetfulness, that the converse of a proposition does not always lead to the same conclusion—" I am the same person *off* the stage that I am *on*." The inference, at first sight, seems identical; but examine it a little, and it confesses only, that the one performer was never, and the other always, *acting*.

And in truth this was the charm of Elliston's private deportment. You had a spirited performance always going on before your eyes, with nothing to pay. As where a monarch takes up his casual abode for a night, the poorest hovel which he honours by his sleeping in it, becomes *ipso facto* for that time a palace; so whereever Elliston walked, sate, or stood still, there was the theatre. He carried about with him his pit, boxes, and galleries, and set up his portable playhouse at corners of streets, and in the market-places. Upon flintiest pavements he trod the boards still ; and if his theme chanced to be passionate, the green baize carpet of tragedy spontaneously rose beneath his feet. Now this was hearty, and showed a love for his art. So Apelles *always* painted—in thought. So G. D. *always* poetises. I hate a lukewarm artist. I have known actors—and some of them of Elliston's own stamp—who shall have agreeably been amusing you in the part of a rake or a coxcomb, through the two or three hours of their dramatic existence ; but no sooner does the curtain fall with its leaden clatter, but a spirit of lead seems to seize on all their faculties. They emerge sour, morose persons, intolerable to their families, servants, &c. Another shall have been expanding your heart with generous deeds and sentiments, till it even beats with yearnings of universal sympathy ; you absolutely long to go home, and do some good action. The play seems tedious, till you can get fairly out of the house, and realise your laudable intentions. At length the final bell rings, and this cordial representative of all that is amiable in human breasts steps forth—a miser. Elliston was more of a piece. Did he *play* Ranger ? and did Ranger fill the general bosom of the town with satisfaction ? why should *he* not be Ranger, and diffuse the same cordial satisfaction among his private circles ? with *his* temperament, *his* animal spirits, *his* good-nature, *his* follies perchance, could he do better than identify himself with his impersonation ? Are we to like a pleasant rake, or coxcomb, on the stage, and give ourselves airs of aversion for the identical character presented to us in actual life ? or what would the performer have gained by divesting himself of the impersonation ? Could the man Elliston have been essentially different from his part, even if he had avoided to reflect to us studiously, in private circles, the airy briskness, the forwardness, and 'scape goat trickeries of his prototype ?

" But there is something not natural in this everlasting *acting ;* we want the real man."

Are you quite sure that it is not the man himself, whom you cannot, or will not see, under some adventitious trappings, which, nevertheless, sit not at all inconsistently upon him ? What if it is the nature of some men to be highly artificial ? The fault is least reprehensible in *players.* Cibber was his own Foppington, with almost as much wit as Vanburgh could add to it.

" My conceit of his person,"—it is Ben Jonson speaking of Lord Bacon,—" was never increased towards him by his *place* or *honours.* But I have, and do reverence him for the *greatness,* that was only proper to himself ; in that he seemed to me ever one of the *greatest* men, that had been in many ages. In his adversity I ever prayed that heaven would give him strength ; for *greatness* he could not want."

The quality here commended was scarcely less conspicuous in the subject of these idle reminiscences, than in my Lord Verulam. Those who have imagined that an unexpected elevation to the direction of a great London Theatre, affected the consequence of Elliston, or at all changed his nature, knew not the essential *greatness* of the man whom they disparage. It was my fortune to encounter him near St. Dunstan's Church (which, with its punctual giants, is now no more than dust and a shadow), on the morning of his election to that high office. Grasping my hand with a look of significance, he only uttered,—" Have you heard the news ? "— then with another look following up the blow, he subjoined, " I am the future Manager of Drury Lane Theatre."—Breathless as he saw me, he stayed not for congratulation or reply, but mutely stalked away, leaving me to chew upon his new-blown dignities at leisure. In fact, nothing could be said to it. Expressive silence alone could muse his praise. This was in his *great* style.

But was he less *great*, (be witness, O ye Powers of Equanimity, that supported in the ruins of Carthage the consular exile, and more recently transmuted for a more illustrious exile, the barren constableship of Elba into an image of Imperial France), when, in melancholy after-years, again, much near the same spot, I met him, when that sceptre had been wrested from his hand, and his dominion was curtailed to the petty managership, and part proprietorship, of the small Olympic, *his Elba ?* He still played nightly upon the boards of Drury, but in parts alas ! allotted to him, not magnificently distributed by him. Waiving his great loss as nothing, and magnificently sinking the sense of fallen *material* grandeur in the more liberal resentment of depreciations done to his more lofty *intellectual* pretensions, " Have you heard " (his customary exordium) —" have you heard," said he, " how they treat me ? they put me in *comedy.*" Thought I—but his finger on his lips forbade any verbal interruption—" where! could they have put you better ? " Then, after a pause—" Where I formerly played Romeo, I now play Mercutio,"—and so again he stalked away, neither staying, nor caring for, responses.

O, it was a rich scene,—but Sir A—— C——, the best of story-tellers and surgeons, who mends a lame narrative almost as well as he sets a fracture, alone could do justice to it—that I was witness to, in the tarnished room (that had once been green) of that same little Olympic. There, after his deposition from Imperial Drury, he substituted a throne. That Olympic Hill was his " highest heaven ; " himself " Jove in his chair." There he sat in state, while before him, on complaint of prompter, was brought for judgment—

how shall I describe her?—one of those little tawdry things that flirt at the tails of choruses—a probationer for the town, in either of its senses—the pertest little drab—a dirty fringe and appendage of the lamps' smoke—who, it seems, on some disapprobation expressed by a "highly respectable" audience, had precipitately quitted her station on the boards, and withdrawn her small talents in disgust.

"And how dare you," said her Manager—assuming a censorial severity which would have crushed the confidence of a Vestris, and disarmed that beautiful Rebel herself of her professional caprices— I verily believe, he thought *her* standing before him—"how dare you, Madam, withdraw yourself, without a notice, from your theatrical duties?" "I was hissed, Sir." "And you have the presumption to decide upon the taste of the town?" "I don't know that, Sir, but I will never stand to be hissed," was the subjoinder of young Confidence—when gathering up his features into one significant mass of wonder, pity, and expostulatory indignation—in a lesson never to have been lost upon a creature less forward than she who stood before him—his words were these: "They have hissed *me*."

'Twas the identical argument *a fortiori*, which the son of Peleus uses to Lycaon trembling under his lance, to persuade him to take his destiny with a good grace. "I too am mortal." And it is to be believed that in both cases the rhetoric missed of its application, for want of a proper understanding with the faculties of the respective recipients.

"Quite an Opera pit," he said to me, as he was courteously conducting me over the benches of his Surrey Theatre, the last retreat, and recess, of his every-day waning grandeur.

Those who knew Elliston, will know the *manner* in which he pronounced the latter sentence of the few words I am about to record. One proud day to me he took his roast mutton with us in the Temple, to which I had superadded a preliminary haddock. After a rather plentiful partaking of the meagre banquet, not unrefreshed with the humbler sort of liquors, I made a sort of apology for the humility of the fare, observing that for my own part I never ate but of one dish at dinner. "I too never eat but one thing at dinner"—was his reply—then after a pause—"reckoning fish as nothing." The manner was all. It was as if by one peremptory sentence he had decreed the annihilation of all the savory esculents, which the pleasant and nutritious-food-giving Ocean pours forth upon poor humans from her watery bosom. This was *greatness*, tempered with considerate *tenderness* to the feelings of his scanty but welcoming entertainer.

Great wert thou in thy life, Robert William Elliston! and *not lessened* in thy death, if report speak truly, which says that thou didst direct that thy mortal remains should repose under no inscription but one of pure *Latinity*.   Classical was thy bringing up ! and beautiful was the feeling on thy last bed, which, connecting the man with the boy, took thee back in thy latest exercise of imagination, to the days when, undreaming of Theatres and Managerships, thou wert a scholar, and an early ripe one, under the roofs builded by the munificent and pious Colet.   For thee the Pauline Muses weep.   In elegies, that shall silence this crude prose, they shall celebrate thy praise.

DETACHED THOUGHTS ON BOOKS AND READING

To mind the inside of a book is to entertain one's self with the forced product of another man's brain.   Now I think a man of quality and breeding may be much amused with the natural sprouts of his own.

Lord Foppington in the Relapse.

AN ingenious acquaintance of my own was so much struck with this bright sally of his Lordship, that he has left off reading altogether, to the great improvement of his originality.   At the hazard of losing some credit on this head, I must confess that I dedicate no inconsiderable portion of my time to other people's thoughts.   I dream away my life in others' speculations.   I love to lose myself in other men's minds.   When I am not walking, I am reading ; I cannot sit and think.   Books think for me.

I have no repugnances.   Shaftesbury is not too genteel for me, nor Jonathan Wild too low.   I can read any thing which I call a *book*.   There are things in that shape which I cannot allow for such.

In this catalogue of *books which are no books*—*biblia a-biblia* —I reckon Court Calendars, Directories, Pocket Books, Draught Boards bound and lettered at the back, Scientific Treatises, Almanacks, Statutes at Large ;   the works of Hume, Gibbon, Robertson, Beattie, Soame Jenyns, and, generally, all those volumes which " no gentleman's library should be without : " the Histories of Flavius Josephus (that learned Jew), and Paley's Moral Philosophy.   With these exceptions, I can read almost any thing.   I bless my stars for a taste so catholic, so unexcluding.

I confess that it moves my spleen to see these *things in books' clothing* perched upon shelves, like false saints, usurpers of true shrines, intruders into the sanctuary, thrusting out the legitimate occupants. To reach down a well-bound semblance of a volume, and hope it is some kind-hearted play-book, then, opening what "seem its leaves," to come bolt upon a withering Population Essay. To expect a Steele, or a Farquhar, and find—Adam Smith. To view a well-arranged assortment of blockheaded Encyclopædias (Anglicanas or Metropolitanas) set out in an array of Russia, or Morocco, when a tithe of that good leather would comfortably re-clothe my shivering folios ; would renovate Paracelsus himself, and enable old Raymund Lully to look like himself again in the world. I never see these impostors, but I long to strip them, to warm my ragged veterans in their spoils.

To be strong-backed and neat-bound is the desideratum of a volume. Magnificence comes after. This, when it can be afforded, is not to be lavished upon all kinds of books indiscriminately. I would not dress a set of Magazines, for instance, in full suit. The dishabille, or half-binding (with Russia backs ever) is *our* costume. A Shakespeare, or a Milton (unless the first editions), it were mere foppery to trick out in gay apparel. The possession of them confers no distinction. The exterior of them (the things themselves being so common), strange to say, raises no sweet emotions, no tickling sense of property in the owner. Thomson's Seasons, again, looks best (I maintain it) a little torn, and dog's-eared. How beautiful to a genuine lover of reading are the sullied leaves, and worn out appearance, nay, the very odour (beyond Russia), if we would not forget kind feelings in fastidiousness, of an old "Circulating Library" Tom Jones, or Vicar of Wakefield ! How they speak of the thousand thumbs, that have turned over their pages with delight !—of the lone sempstress, whom they may have cheered (milliner, or harder-working mantua-maker) after her long day's needle-toil, running far into midnight, when she has snatched an hour, ill spared from sleep, to steep her cares, as in some Lethean cup, in spelling out their enchanting contents ! Who would have them a whit less soiled ? What better condition could we desire to see them in ?

In some respects the better a book is, the less it demands from binding. Fielding, Smollet, Sterne, and all that class of perpetually self-reproductive volumes—Great Nature's Stereotypes—we see them individually perish with less regret, because we know the copies of them to be " eterne." But where a book is at once both good and rare—where the individual is almost the species, and when *that* perishes,

> We know not where is that Promethean torch
> That can its light relumine "—

such a book, for instance, as the Life of the Duke of Newcastle, by his Duchess—no casket is rich enough, no casing sufficiently durable, to honour and keep safe such a jewel.

Not only rare volumes of this description, which seem hopeless ever to be reprinted ; but old editions of writers, such as Sir Philip Sydney, Bishop Taylor, Milton in his prose-works, Fuller—of whom we *have* reprints, yet the books themselves, though they go about, and are talked of here and there, we know, have not endenizened themselves (nor possibly ever will) in the national heart, so as to become stock books—it is good to possess these in durable and costly covers. I do not care for a First Folio of Shakspeare. I rather prefer the common editions of Rowe and Tonson, without notes, and with *plates*, which, being so execrably bad, serve as maps, or modest remembrancers, to the text ; and without pretending to any supposable emulation with it, are so much better than the Shakspeare gallery *engravings*, which *did*. I have a community of feeling with my countrymen about his Plays, and I like those editions of him best, which have been oftenest tumbled about and handled.—On the contrary, I cannot read Beaumont and Fletcher but in Folio. The Octavo editions are painful to look at. I have no sympathy with them. If they were as much read as the current editions of the other poet, I should prefer them in that shape to the older one. I do not know a more heartless sight than the reprint of the Anatomy of Melancholy. What need was there of unearthing the bones of that fantastic old great man, to expose them in a winding-sheet of the newest fashion to modern censure ? what hapless stationer could dream of Burton ever becoming popular ?—The wretched Malone could not do worse, when he bribed the sexton of Stratford church to let him white-wash the painted effigy of old Shakspeare, which stood there, in rude but lively fashion depicted, to the very colour of the cheek, the eye, the eye-brow, hair, the very dress he used to wear—the only authentic testimony we had, however imperfect, of these curious parts and parcels of him. They covered him over with a coat of white paint. By ——, if I had been a justice of peace for Warwickshire, I would have clapt both commentator and sexton fast in the stocks, for a pair of meddling sacrilegious varlets.

I think I see them at their work—these sapient trouble-tombs.

Shall I be thought fantastical, if I confess, that the names of some of our poets sound sweeter, and have a finer relish to the ear —to mine, at least—than that of Milton or of Shakspeare ? It may be, that the latter are more staled and rung upon in common discourse. The sweetest names, and which carry a perfume in the mention, are, Kit Marlowe, Drayton, Drummond of Hawthornden, and Cowley.

Much depends upon *when* and *where* you read a book. In the five or six impatient minutes, before the dinner is quite ready, who would think of taking up the Fairy Queen for a stop-gap, or a volume of Bishop Andrewes' sermons ?

Milton almost requires a solemn service of music to be played before you enter upon him. But he brings his music, to which, who listens, had need bring docile thoughts, and purged ears.

Winter evenings—the world shut out—with less of ceremony the gentle Shakspeare enters. At such a season, the Tempest, or his own Winter's Tale—

These two poets you cannot avoid reading aloud—to yourself, or (as it chances) to some single person listening. More than one— and it degenerates into an audience.

Books of quick interest, that hurry on for incidents, are for the eye to glide over only. It will not do to read them out. I could never listen to even the better kind of modern novels without extreme irksomeness.

A newspaper, read out, is intolerable. In some of the Bank offices it is the custom (to save so much individual time) for one of the clerks—who is the best scholar—to commence upon the Times, or the Chronicle, and recite its entire contents aloud *pro bono publico*. With every advantage of lungs and elocution, the effect is singularly vapid. In barbers' shops and public-houses a fellow will get up, and spell out a paragraph, which he communicates as some discovery. Another follows with *his* selection. So the entire journal transpires at length by piece-meal. Seldom-readers are slow readers, and, without this expedient no one in the company would probably ever travel through the contents of a whole paper.

Newspapers always excite curiosity. No one ever lays one down without a feeling of disappointment.

What an eternal time that gentleman in black, at Nando's, keeps the paper ! I am sick of hearing the waiter bawling out incessantly, " the Chronicle is in hand, Sir."

Coming in to an inn at night—having ordered your supper— what can be more delightful than to find lying in the window-seat, left there time out of mind by the carelessness of some former guest —two or three numbers of the old Town and Country Magazine, with its amusing *tête-à-tête* pictures—" The Royal Lover and Lady G——; " " The Melting Platonic and the old Beau,"—and such like antiquated scandal ? Would you exchange it—at that time, and in that place—for a better book ?

Poor Tobin, who latterly fell blind, did not regret it so much for the weightier kinds of reading—the Paradise Lost, or Comus, he could have *read* to him—but he missed the pleasure of skimming over with his own eye a magazine, or a light pamphlet.

I should not care to be caught in the serious avenues of some cathedral alone, and reading *Candide.*

I do not remember a more whimsical surprise than having been once detected—by a familiar damsel—reclined at my ease upon the grass, on Primrose Hill (her Cythera), reading—*Pamela.* There was nothing in the book to make a man seriously ashamed at the exposure; but as she seated herself down by me, and seemed determined to read in company, I could have wished it had been—any other book. We read on very sociably for a few pages; and, not finding the author much to her taste, she got up, and—went away. Gentle casuist, I leave it to thee to conjecture, whether the blush (for there was one between us) was the property of the nymph or the swain in this dilemma. From me you shall never get the secret.

I am not much a friend to out-of-doors reading. I cannot settle my spirits to it. I knew a Unitarian minister, who was generally to be seen upon Snow-hill (as yet Skinner's-street *was not*), between the hours of ten and eleven in the morning, studying a volume of Lardner. I own this to have been a strain of abstraction beyond my reach. I used to admire how he sidled along, keeping clear of secular contacts. An illiterate encounter with a porter's knot, or a bread basket, would have quickly put to flight all the theology I am master of, and have left me worse than indifferent to the five points.

There is a class of street-readers, whom I can never contemplate without affection—the poor gentry, who, not having wherewithal to buy or hire a book, filch a little learning at the open stalls—the owner, with his hard eye, casting envious looks at them all the while, and thinking when they will have done. Venturing tenderly, page after page, expecting every moment when he shall interpose his interdict, and yet unable to deny themselves the gratification, they "snatch a fearful joy." Martin B——, in this way, by daily fragments, got through two volumes of Clarissa, when the stall-keeper damped his laudable ambition, by asking him (it was in his younger days) whether he meant to purchase the work. M. declares, that under no circumstances of his life did he ever peruse a book with half the satisfaction which he took in those uneasy snatches. A quaint poetess of our day has moralised upon this subject in two very touching but homely stanzas.

> I saw a boy with eager eye
> Open a book upon a stall,
> And read, as he'd devour it all;
> Which when the stall-man did espy,
> Soon to the boy I heard him call,
> "You, Sir, you never buy a book,
> Therefore in one you shall not look."

The boy pass'd slowly on, and with a sigh
He wish'd he never had been taught to read,
Then of the old churl's books he should have had no need.

Of sufferings the poor have many,
Which never can the rich annoy :
I soon perceiv'd another boy,
Who look'd as if he'd not had any
Food, for that day at least—enjoy
The sight of cold meat in a tavern larder.
This boy's case, then thought I, is surely harder,
Thus hungry, longing, thus without a penny,
Beholding choice of dainty-dressed meat :
No wonder if he wish he ne'er had learn'd to eat.

THE OLD MARGATE HOY

I AM fond of passing my vacations (I believe I have said so before) at one or other of the Universities. Next to these my choice would fix me at some woody spot, such as the neighbourhood of Henley affords in abundance, upon the banks of my beloved Thames. But somehow or other my cousin contrives to wheedle me once in three or four seasons to a watering place. Old attachments cling to her in spite of experience. We have been dull at Worthing one summer, duller at Brighton another, dullest at Eastbourn a third, and are at this moment doing dreary penance at—Hastings !—and all because we were happy many years ago for a brief week at—Margate. That was our first sea-side experiment, and many circumstances combined to make it the most agreeable holyday of my life. We had neither of us seen the sea, and we had never been from home so long together in company.

Can I forget thee, thou old Margate Hoy, with thy weather-beaten, sun-burnt captain, and his rough accommodations—ill exchanged for the foppery and fresh-water niceness of the modern steam-packet ? To the winds and waves thou committedst thy goodly freightage, and didst ask no aid of magic fumes, and spells, and boiling cauldrons. With the gales of heaven thou wentest swimmingly ; or, when it was their pleasure, stoodest still with sailor-like patience. Thy course was natural, not forced, as in a hot-bed ; nor didst thou go poisoning the breath of ocean with sulphureous smoke—a great sea-chimæra, chimneying and furnacing the deep ; or liker to that fire-god parching up Scamander.

VOL. II.—12

Can I forget thy honest, yet slender crew, with their coy reluctant responses (yet to the suppression of anything like contempt) to the raw questions, which we of the great city would be ever and anon putting to them, as to the uses of this or that strange naval implement? 'Specially can I forget thee, thou happy medium, thou shade of refuge between us and them, conciliating interpreter of their skill to our simplicity, comfortable ambassador between sea and land!—whose sailor-trowsers did not more convincingly assure thee to be an adopted denizen of the former, than thy white cap, and whiter apron over them, with thy neat-fingered practice in thy culinary vocation, bespoke thee to have been of inland nurture heretofore—a master cook of East-cheap? How busily didst thou ply thy multifarious occupation, cook, mariner, attendant, chamberlain; here, there, like another Ariel, flaming at once about all parts of the deck, yet with kindlier ministrations—not to assist the tempest, but, as if touched with a kindred sense of our infirmities, to soothe the qualms which that untried motion might haply raise in our crude land-fancies. And when the o'er-washing billows drove us below deck (for it was far gone in October, and we had stiff and blowing weather) how did thy officious ministerings, still catering for our comfort, with cards, and cordials, and thy more cordial conversation, alleviate the closeness and the confinement of thy else (truth to say) not very savoury, nor very inviting, little cabin!

With these additaments to boot, we had on board a fellow-passenger, whose discourse in verity might have beguiled a longer voyage than we meditated, and have made mirth and wonder abound as far as the Azores. He was a dark, Spanish complexioned young man, remarkably handsome, with an officer-like assurance, and an insuppressible volubility of assertion. He was, in fact, the greatest liar I had met with then, or since. He was none of your hesitating, half story-tellers (a most painful description of mortals) who go on sounding your belief, and only giving you as much as they see you can swallow at a time—the nibbling pickpockets of your patience—but one who committed downright, day-light depredations upon his neighbour's faith. He did not stand shivering upon the brink, but was a hearty thorough-paced liar, and plunged at once into the depths of your credulity. I partly believe, he made pretty sure of his company. Not many rich, not many wise, or learned, composed at that time the common stowage of a Margate packet. We were, I am afraid, a set of as unseasoned Londoners (let our enemies give it a worse name) as Aldermanbury, or Watling-street, at that time of day could have supplied. There might be an exception or two among us, but I scorn to make any invidious distinctions among such a jolly, companionable ship's company, as those were whom I sailed with. Something too must be conceded to the *Genius Loci*. Had the confident fellow told us half the legends on land, which he favoured us with on the other element, I flatter myself the good sense of most of us would have revolted. But we were in a new world, with everything unfamiliar about us, and the time and place disposed us to the reception of any prodigious marvel whatsoever. Time has obliterated from my memory much of his wild fablings; and the rest would appear but dull, as written, and to be read on shore. He had been Aid-de-camp (among other rare accidents and fortunes) to a Persian prince, and at one blow had stricken off the head of the King of Carimania on horseback. He, of course, married the Prince's daughter. I forget what unlucky turn in the politics of that court, combining with the loss of his consort, was the reason of his quitting Persia; but with the rapidity of a magician he transported himself, along with his hearers, back to England, where we still found him in the confidence of great ladies. There was some story of a Princess—Elizabeth, if I remember— having intrusted to his care an extraordinary casket of jewels, upon some extraordinary occasion—but as I am not certain of the name or circumstance at this distance of time, I must leave it to the Royal daughters of England to settle the honour among themselves in private. I cannot call to mind half his pleasant wonders; but I perfectly remember, that in the course of his travels he had seen a phœnix; and he obligingly undeceived us of the vulgar error, that there is but one of that species at a time, assuring us that they were not uncommon in some parts of Upper Egypt. Hitherto he had found the most implicit listeners. His dreaming fancies had transported us beyond the "ignorant present." But when (still hardying more and more in his triumphs over our simplicity) he went on to affirm that he had actually sailed through thᵣ legs of the Colossus at Rhodes, it really became necessary to makᵤ a stand. And here I must do justice to the good sense and intrepidity of one of our party, a youth, that had hitherto been one of his most deferential auditors, who, from his recent reading, made bold to assure the gentleman, that there must be some mistake, as " the Colossus in question had been destroyed long since : " to whose opinion, delivered with all modesty, our hero was obliging enough to concede thus much, that " the figure was indeed a little damaged." This was the only opposition he met with, and it did not at all seem to stagger him, for he proceeded with his fables, which the same youth appeared to swallow with still more complacency than ever,—confirmed, as it were, by the extreme candour of that concession. With these prodigies he wheedled us on till we came in sight of the Reculvers, which one of our own company (having been the voyage before) immediately recognising, and pointing out to us, was considered by us as no ordinary seaman.

All this time sat upon the edge of the deck quite a different character. It was a lad, apparently very poor, very infirm, and very patient. His eye was ever on the sea, with a smile : and, if he caught now and then some snatches of these wild legends, it was by accident, and they seemed not to concern him. The waves to him whispered more pleasant stories. He was as one, being with us, but not of us. He heard the bell of dinner ring without stirring ; and when some of us pulled out our private stores— our cold meat and our salads—he produced none, and seemed to want none. Only a solitary biscuit he had laid in ; provision for the one or two days and nights, to which these vessels then were oftentimes obliged to prolong their voyage. Upon a nearer acquaintance with him, which he seemed neither to court nor decline, we learned that he was going to Margate, with the hope of being admitted into the Infirmary there for sea-bathing. His disease was a scrofula, which appeared to have eaten all over him. He expressed great hopes of a cure ; and when we asked him, whether he had any friends where he was going, he replied, " he *had* no friends."

These pleasant, and some mournful passages, with the first sight of the sea, co-operating with youth, and a sense of holydays, and out-of-door adventure, to me that had been pent up in populous cities for many months before,—have left upon my mind the fragrance as of summer days gone by, bequeathing nothing but their remembrance for cold and wintry hours to chew upon.

Will it be thought a digression (it may spare some unwelcome comparisons), if I endeavour to account for the *dissatisfaction* which I have heard so many persons confess to have felt (as I did myself feel in part on this occasion), *at the sight of the sea for the first time ?* I think the reason usually given—referring to the incapacity of actual objects for satisfying our preconceptions of them—scarcely goes deep enough into the question. Let the same person see a lion, an elephant, a mountain, for the first time in his life, and he shall perhaps feel himself a little mortified. The things do not fill up that space, which the idea of them seemed to take up in his mind. But they have still a correspondency to his first notion, and in time grow up to it, so as to produce a very similar impression : enlarging themselves (if I may say so) upon familiarity. But the sea remains a disappointment.—Is it not, that in *the latter* we had expected to behold (absurdly, I grant, but, I am afraid, by the law of imagination unavoidably) not a definite object, as those wild beasts, or that mountain compassable by the eye, but *all the sea at once*, THE COMMENSURATE ANTAGONIST OF THE EARTH ! I do not say we tell ourselves so much, but the craving of the mind is to be satisfied with nothing less. I will suppose the case of a young person of fifteen (as I then was) knowing nothing of the sea, but from description. He comes to it for the first time—all that he has been reading of it all his life, and *that* the most enthusiastic part of life,—all he has gathered from narratives of wandering seamen; what he has gained from true voyages, and what he cherishes as credulously from romance and poetry; crowding their images, and exacting strange tributes from expectation.—He thinks of the great deep, and of those who go down unto it; of its thousand isles, and of the vast continents it washes; of its receiving the mighty Plata, or Orellana, into its bosom, without disturbance, or sense of augmentation; of Biscay swells, and the mariner

> For many a day, and many a dreadful night,
> Incessant labouring round the stormy Cape;

of fatal rocks, and the " still-vexed Bermoothes ; " of great whirl-pools, and the water-spout ; of sunken ships, and sumless treasures swallowed up in the unrestoring depths : of fishes and quaint monsters, to which all that is terrible on earth—

> Be but as buggs to frighten babes withal,
> Compared with the creatures in the sea's entral;

of naked savages, and Juan Fernandez ; of pearls, and shells ; of coral beds, and of enchanted isles ; of mermaids' grots—

I do not assert that in sober earnest he expects to be shown all these wonders at once, but he is under the tyranny of a mighty faculty, which haunts him with confused hints and shadows of all these ; and when the actual object opens first upon him, seen (in tame weather too most likely) from our unromantic coasts—a speck, a slip of sea-water, as it shows to him—what can it prove but a very unsatisfying and even diminutive entertainment ? Or if he has come to it from the mouth of a river, was it much more than the river widening ? and, even out of sight of land, what had he but a flat watery horizon about him, nothing comparable to the vast o'er-curtaining sky, his familiar object, seen daily without dread or amazement ?—Who, in similar circumstances, has not been tempted to exclaim with Charoba, in the poem of Gebir,—

> Is this the mighty ocean ?—is this *all* ?

I love town, or country ; but this detestable Cinque Port is neither. I hate these scrubbed shoots, thrusting out their starved foliage from between the horrid fissures of dusty innutritious rocks; which the amateur calls " verdure to the edge of the sea." I require woods, and they show me stunted coppices. I cry out for the water-brooks, and pant for fresh streams, and inland murmurs. I cannot stand all day on the naked beach, watching the capricious hues of the sea, shifting like the colours of a dying mullet. I am tired of looking out at the windows of this island-prison. I would fain retire into the interior of my cage. While I gaze upon the sea, I want to be on it, over it, across it. It binds me in with chains, as of iron. My thoughts are abroad. I should not so feel in Staffordshire. There is no home for me here. There is no sense of home at Hastings. It is a place of fugitive resort, an heterogeneous assemblage of sea-mews and stock-brokers, Amphitrites of the town, and misses that coquet with the Ocean. If it were what it was in its primitive shape, and what it ought to have remained, a fair honest fishing town, and no more, it were something—with a few straggling fishermen's huts scattered about, artless as its cliffs, and with their materials filched from them, it were something. I could abide to dwell with Meschek; to assort with fisher-swains, and smugglers. There are, or I dream there are, many of this latter occupation here. Their faces become the place. I like a smuggler. He is the only honest thief. He robs nothing but the revenue,—an abstraction I never greatly cared about. I could go out with them in their mackarel boats, or about their less ostensible business, with some satisfaction. I can even tolerate those poor victims to monotony, who from day to day pace along the beach, in endless progress and recurrence, to watch their illicit countrymen—townsfolk or brethren perchance—whistling to the sheathing and unsheathing of their cutlasses (their only solace), who under the mild name of preventive service, keep up a legitimated civil warfare in the deplorable absence of a foreign one, to show their detestation of run hollands, and zeal for old England. But it is the visitants from town, that come here to *say* that they have been here, with no more relish of the sea than a pond perch, or a dace might be supposed to have, that are my aversion. I feel like a foolish dace in these regions, and have as little toleration for myself here, as for them. What can they want here? if they had a true relish of the ocean, why have they brought all this land luggage with them? or why pitch their civilised tents in the desert? What mean these scanty book-rooms—marine libraries as they entitle them—if the sea were, as they would have us believe, a book " to read strange matter in ? " what are their foolish concert-rooms, if they come, as they would fain be thought to do, to listen to the music of the waves? All is false and hollow pretention. They come, because it is the fashion, and to spoil the nature of the place. They are mostly, as I have said, stock-brokers; but I have watched the better sort of them—now and then, an honest citizen (of the old stamp), in the simplicity of his heart, shall bring down his wife and daughters, to taste the sea breezes. I always know the date of their arrival. It is easy to see it in their countenance. A day or two they go wandering on the shingles, picking up cockle-shells, and thinking them great things; but, in a poor week, imagination slackens: they begin to discover that cockles produce no pearls, and then—O then!—if I could interpret for the pretty creatures (I know they have not the courage to confess it themselves) how gladly would they exchange their sea-side rambles for a Sunday walk on the green-sward of their accustomed Twickenham meadows!

I would ask of one of these sea-charmed emigrants, who think they truly love the sea, with its wild usages, what would their feelings be, if some of the unsophisticated aborigines of this place, encouraged by their courteous questionings here, should venture, on the faith of such assured sympathy between them, to return the visit, and come up to see—London. I must imagine them with their fishing tackle on their back, as we carry our town necessaries. What a sensation would it cause in Lothbury? What vehement laughter would it not excite among

> The daughters of Cheapside, and wives of Lombard-street.

I am sure that no town-bred, or inland-born subjects, can feel their true and natural nourishment at these sea-places. Nature, where she does not mean us for mariners and vagabonds, bids us stay at home. The salt foam seems to nourish a spleen. I am not half so good-natured as by the milder waters of my natural river. I would exchange these sea-gulls for swans, and scud a swallow for ever about the banks of Thamesis.

THE CONVALESCENT

A PRETTY severe fit of indisposition which, under the name of a nervous fever, has made a prisoner of me for some weeks past, and is but slowly leaving me, has reduced me to an incapacity of reflecting upon any topic foreign to itself. Expect no healthy conclusions from me this month, reader; I can offer you only sick men's dreams.

And truly the whole state of sickness is such; for what else is it but a magnificent dream for a man to lie a-bed, and draw day-light curtains about him; and, shutting out the sun, to induce a total oblivion of all the works which are going on under it? To become insensible to all the operations of life, except the beatings of one feeble pulse ?

If there be a regal solitude, it is a sick bed. How the patient lords it there! what caprices he acts without controul! how king-like he sways his pillow—tumbling, and tossing, and shifting, and lowering, and thumping, and flatting, and moulding it, to the ever varying requisitions of his throbbing temples.

He changes *sides* oftener than a politician. Now he lies full length, then half-length, obliquely, transversely, head and feet quite across the bed ; and none accuses him of tergiversation. Within the four curtains he is absolute. They are his Mare Clausum.

How sickness enlarges the dimensions of a man's self to himself! he is his own exclusive object. Supreme selfishness is inculcated upon him as his only duty. 'Tis the Two Tables of the Law to him. He has nothing to think of but how to get well. What passes out of doors, or within them, so he hear not the jarring of them, affects him not.

A little while ago he was greatly concerned in the event of a law-suit, which was to be the making or the marring of his dearest friend. He was to be seen trudging about upon this man's errand to fifty quarters of the town at once, jogging this witness, refreshing that solicitor. The cause was to come on yesterday. He is absolutely as indifferent to the decision, as if it were a question to be tried at Pekin. Peradventure from some whispering, going on about the house, not intended for his hearing, he picks up enough to make him understand, that things went cross-grained in the Court yesterday, and his friend is ruined. But the word "friend," and the word "ruin," disturb him no more than so much jargon. He is not to think of any thing but how to get better.

What a world of foreign cares are merged in that absorbing consideration !

He has put on the strong armour of sickness, he is wrapped in the callous hide of suffering; he keeps his sympathy, like some curious vintage, under trusty lock and key, for his own use only.

He lies pitying himself, honing and moaning to himself; he yearneth over himself; his bowels are even melted within him, to think what he suffers ; he is not ashamed to weep over himself.

He is for ever plotting how to do some good to himself; studying little stratagems and artificial alleviations.

He makes the most of himself; dividing himself, by an allowable fiction, into as many distinct individuals, as he hath sore and sorrowing members. Sometimes he meditates—as of a thing apart from him—upon his poor aching head, and that dull pain which, dozing or waking, lay in it all the past night like a log, or palpable substance of pain, not to be removed without opening the very scull, as it seemed, to take it thence. Or he pities his long, clammy, attenuated fingers. He compassionates himself all over; and his bed is a very discipline of humanity, and tender heart.

He is his own sympathiser; and instinctively feels that none can so well perform that office for him. He cares for few spectators to his tragedy. Only that punctual face of the old nurse pleases him, that announces his broths, and his cordials. He likes it because it is so unmoved, and because he can pour forth his feverish ejaculations before it as unreservedly as to his bed-post.

To the world's business he is dead. He understands not what the callings and occupations of mortals are; only he has a glimmering conceit of some such thing, when the doctor makes his daily call: and even in the lines of that busy face he reads no multiplicity of patients, but solely conceives of himself as *the sick man*. To what other uneasy couch the good man is hastening, when he slips out of his chamber, folding up his thin douceur so carefully for fear of rustling—is no speculation which he can at present entertain. He thinks only of the regular return of the same phenomenon at the same hour to-morrow.

Household rumours touch him not. Some faint murmur, indicative of life going on within the house, soothes him, while he knows not distinctly what it is. He is not to know any thing, not to think of any thing. Servants gliding up or down the distant staircase, treading as upon velvet, gently keep his ear awake, so long as he troubles not himself further than with some feeble guess at their errands. Exacter knowledge would be a burthen to him: he can just endure the pressure of conjecture. He opens his eye faintly at the dull stroke of the muffled knocker, and closes it again without asking " who was it? " He is flattered by a general notion that inquiries are making after him, but he cares not to know the name of the inquirer. In the general stillness, and awful hush of the house, he lies in state, and feels his sovereignty.

To be sick is to enjoy monarchal prerogatives. Compare the silent tread, and quiet ministry, almost by the eye only, with which he is served—with the careless demeanour, the unceremonious goings in and out (slapping of doors, or leaving them open) of the very same attendants, when he is getting a little better—and you will confess, that from the bed of sickness (throne let me rather call it) to the elbow chair of convalescence, is a fall from dignity, amounting to a deposition.

How convalescence shrinks a man back to his pristine stature! where is now the space, which he occupied so lately, in his own, in the family's eye? The scene of his regalities, his sick room, which was his presence chamber, where he lay and acted his despotic fancies—how is it reduced to a common bed-room ! The trimness. of the very bed has something petty and unmeaning about it. It is *made* every day. How unlike to that wavy, many-furrowed, oceanic surface, which it presented so short a time since, when to *make* it was a service not to be thought of at oftener than three or four day revolutions, when the patient was with pain and grief to be lifted for a little while out of it, to submit to the encroachments of unwelcome neatness, and decencies which his shaken frame deprecated ; then to be lifted into it again, for another three or four days' respite, to flounder it out of shape again, while every fresh furrow was a historical record of some shifting posture, some uneasy turning, some seeking for a little ease ; and the shrunken skin scarce told a truer story than the crumpled coverlid.

Hushed are those mysterious sighs—those groans—so much more awful, while we knew not from what caverns of vast hidden suffering they proceeded. The Lernean pangs are quenched. The riddle of sickness is solved ; and Philoctetes is become an ordinary personage.

Perhaps some relic of the sick man's dream of greatness survives in the still lingering visitations of the medical attendant. But how is he too changed with every thing else ! Can this be he— this man of news—of chat—of anecdote—of every thing but physic —can this be he, who so lately came between the patient and his cruel enemy, as on some solemn embassy from Nature, erecting herself into a high mediating party ?—Pshaw! 'tis some old woman.

Farewell with him all that made sickness pompous—the spell that hushed the household—the desart-like stillness, felt throughout its inmost chambers—the mute attendance—the inquiry by looks— the still softer delicacies of self-attention—the sole and single eye of distemper alonely fixed upon itself—world-thoughts excluded— the man a world unto himself—his own theatre—

What a speck is he dwindled into !

In this flat swamp of convalescence, left by the ebb of sickness, yet far enough from the terra firma of established health, your note, dear Editor, reached me, requesting—an article. In Articulo Mortis, thought I ; but it is something hard—and the quibble, wretched as it was, relieved me. The summons, unseasonable as it appeared, seemed to link me on again to the petty businesses of life, which I had lost sight of ; a gentle call to activity, however trivial ; a wholesome weaning from that preposterous dream of self-absorption—the puffy state of sickness—in which I confess to have lain so long, insensible to the magazines and monarchies, of the world alike ; to its laws, and to its literature. The hypochondriac flatus is subsiding ; the acres, which in imagination I had spread over—for the sick man swells in the sole contemplation of his single sufferings, till he becomes a Tityus to himself—are wasting to a span ; and for the giant of self-importance, which I was so lately, you have me once again in my natural pretensions—the lean and meagre figure of your insignificant Essayist.

SANITY OF TRUE GENIUS

SO far from the position holding true, that great wit (or genius, in our modern way of speaking), has a necessary alliance with insanity, the greatest wits, on the contrary, will ever be found to be the sanest writers. It is impossible for the mind to conceive of a mad Shakspeare. The greatness of wit, by which the poetic talent is here chiefly to be understood, manifests itself in the admirable balance of all the faculties. Madness is the disproportionate straining or excess of any one of them. " So strong a wit," says Cowley, speaking of a poetical friend,

> " ——did Nature to him frame,
> As all things but his judgment overcame,
> His judgment like the heavenly moon did show,
> Tempering that mighty sea below."

The ground of the mistake is, that men, finding in the raptures of the higher poetry a condition of exaltation, to which they have no parallel in their own experience, besides the spurious resemblance of it in dreams and fevers, impute a state of dreaminess and fever to the poet. But the true poet dreams being awake. He is not possessed by his subject, but has dominion over it. In the groves of Eden he walks familiar as in his native paths. He ascends the empyrean heaven, and is not intoxicated. He treads the burning marl without dismay ; he wins his flight without self-loss through realms of chaos " and old night." Or if, abandoning himself to that severer chaos of a " human mind untuned," he is content awhile to be mad with Lear, or to hate mankind (a sort of madness) with Timon, neither is that madness, nor this misanthropy, so unchecked, but that,—never letting the reins of reason wholly go, while most he seems to do so,—he has his better genius still whispering at his ear, with the good servant Kent suggesting saner counsels, or with the honest steward Flavius recommending kindlier resolutions. Where he seems most to recede from humanity, he will be found the truest to it. From beyond the scope of Nature if he

summon possible existences, he subjugates them to the law of her
consistency. He is beautifully loyal to that sovereign directress,
even when he appears most to betray and desert her. His ideal
tribes submit to policy ; his very monsters are tamed to his hand,
even as that wild sea-brood, shepherded by Proteus. He tames,
and he clothes them with attributes of flesh and blood, till they
wonder at themselves, like Indian Islanders forced to submit to
European vesture. Caliban, the Witches, are as true to the laws of
their own nature (ours with a difference), as Othello, Hamlet, and
Macbeth. Herein the great and the little wits are differenced ;
that if the latter wander ever so little from nature or actual existence, they lose themselves, and their readers. Their phantoms are
lawless ; their visions nightmares. They do not create, which
implies shaping and consistency. Their imaginations are not
active—for to be active is to call something into act and form—but
passive, as men in sick dreams. For the super-natural, or something super-added to what we know of nature, they give you the
plainly non-natural. And if this were all, and that these mental
hallucinations were discoverable only in the treatment of subjects
out of nature, or transcending it, the judgment might with some
plea be pardoned if it ran riot, and a little wantonized : but even in
the describing of real and every day life, that which is before their
eyes, one of these lesser wits shall more deviate from nature—show
more of that inconsequence, which has a natural alliance with
frenzy,—than a great genius in his "maddest fits," as Withers
somewhere calls them. We appeal to any one that is acquainted
with the common run of Lane's novels,—as they existed some
twenty or thirty years back,—those scanty intellectual viands of
the whole female reading public, till a happier genius arose, and expelled for ever the innutritious phantoms,—whether he has not
found his brain more " betossed," his memory more puzzled, his
sense of when and where more confounded, among the improbable
events, the incoherent incidents, the inconsistent characters, or no-
characters, of some third-rate love intrigue—where the persons
shall be a Lord Glendamour and a Miss Rivers, and the scene only
alternate between Bath and Bond-street—a more bewildering
dreaminess induced upon him, than he has felt wandering over all
the fairy grounds of Spenser. In the productions we refer to,
nothing but names and places is familiar ; the persons are neither of
this world nor of any other conceivable one ; an endless string of
activities without purpose, of purposes destitute of motive :—we
meet phantoms in our known walks ; *fantasques* only christened.
In the poet we have names which announce fiction ; and we have
absolutely no place at all, for the things and persons of the Fairy
Queen prate not of their " whereabout." But in their inner nature,

and the law of their speech and actions, we are at home and upon acquainted ground. The one turns life into a dream ; the other to the wildest dreams gives the sobrieties of every day occurrences. By what subtile art of tracing the mental processes it is effected, we are not philosophers enough to explain, but in that wonderful episode of the cave of Mammon, in which the Money God appears first in the lowest form of a miser, is then a worker of metals, and becomes the god of all the treasures of the world ; and has a daughter, Ambition, before whom all the world kneels for favours – with the Hesperian fruit, the waters of Tantalus, with Pilate washing his hands vainly, but not impertinently, in the same stream—that we should be at one moment in the cave of an old hoarder of treasures, at the next at the forge of the Cyclops, in a palace and yet in hell, all at once, with the shifting mutations of the most rambling dream, and our judgment yet all the time awake, and neither able nor willing to detect the fallacy,—is a proof of that hidden sanity which still guides the poet in his widest seeming-aberrations.

It is not enough to say that the whole episode is a copy of the mind's conceptions in sleep ; it is, in some sort—but what a copy ! Let the most romantic of us, that has been entertained all night with the spectacle of some wild and magnificent vision, recombine it in the morning, and try it by his waking judgment. That which appeared so shifting, and yet so coherent, while that faculty was passive, when it comes under cool examination, shall appear so reasonless and so unlinked, that we are ashamed to have been so deluded ; and to have taken, though but in sleep, a monster for a god. But the transitions in this episode are every whit as violent as in the most extravagant dream, and yet the waking judgment ratifies them.

CAPTAIN JACKSON

A MONG the deaths in our obituary for this month, I observe with concern " At his cottage on the Bath road, Captain Jackson." The name and attribution are common enough ; but a feeling like reproach persuades me, that this could have been no other in fact than my dear old friend, who some five-and-twenty years ago rented a tenement, which he was pleased to dignify with the appellation here used, about a mile from Westbourn Green. Alack, how good men, and the good turns they do us, slide out of memory, and are recalled but by the surprise of some such sad memento as that which now lies before us !

He whom I mean was a retired half-pay officer, with a wife and two grown-up daughters, whom he maintained with the port and notions of gentlewomen upon that slender professional allowance. Comely girls they were too.

And was I in danger of forgetting this man?—his cheerful suppers—the noble tone of hospitality, when first you set your foot in *the cottage*—the anxious ministerings about you, where little or nothing (God knows) was to be ministered.—Althea's horn in a poor platter—the power of self-enchantment, by which, in his magnificent wishes to entertain you, he multiplied his means to bounties.

You saw with your bodily eyes indeed what seemed a bare scrag —cold savings from the foregone meal—remnant hardly sufficient to send a mendicant from the door contented. But in the copious will—the revelling imagination of your host—the " mind, the mind, Master Shallow," whole beeves were spread before you— hecatombs—no end appeared to the profusion.

It was the widow's cruse—the loaves and fishes ; carving could not lessen nor helping diminish it—the stamina were left—the elemental bone still flourished, divested of its accidents.

" Let us live while we can," methinks I hear the open-handed creature exclaim ; " while we have, let us not want," " here is plenty left ; " " want for nothing "—with many more such hospitable sayings, the spurs of appetite, and old concomitants of smoking boards, and feast-oppressed chargers. Then sliding a slender ratio of Single Gloucester upon his wife's plate, or the daughter's, he would convey the remanent rind into his own, with a merry quirk of " the nearer the bone," &c., and declaring that he universally preferred the outside. For we had our table distinctions, you are to know, and some of us in a manner sate above the salt. None but his guest or guests dreamed of tasting flesh luxuries at night, the fragments were *verè hospitibus sacra*. But of one thing or another there was always enough, and leavings : only he would sometimes finish the remainder crust, to show that he wished no savings.

Wine he had none ; nor, except on very rare occasions, spirits ; but the sensation of wine was there. Some thin kind of ale I remember—" British beverage," he would say ! " Push about, my boys ; " " Drink to your sweethearts, girls." At every meagre draught a toast must ensue, or a song. All the forms of good liquor were there, with none of the effects wanting. Shut your eyes, and you would swear a capacious bowl of punch was foaming in the centre, with beams of generous Port or Madeira radiating to

it from each of the table corners. You got flustered, without
knowing whence ; tipsy upon words ; and reeled under the potency
of his unperforming Bacchanalian encouragements.

We had our songs—" Why, Soldiers, Why "—and the " British
Grenadiers "—in which last we were all obliged to bear chorus.
Both the daughters sang. Their proficiency was a nightly theme
—the masters he had given them—the " no-expence " which he
spared to accomplish them in a science " so necessary to young
women." But then—they could not sing "without the instrument."

Sacred, and by me, never-to-be violated, Secrets of Poverty !
Should I disclose your honest aims at grandeur, your makeshift
efforts of magnificence ? Sleep, sleep, with all thy broken keys, if
one of the bunch be extant ; thrummed by a thousand ancestral
thumbs ; dear, cracked spinnet of dearer Louisa ! Without
mention of mine, be dumb, thou thin accompanier of her thinner
warble ! A veil be spread over the dear delighted face of the
well-deluded father, who now haply listening to cherubic notes,
scarce feels sincerer pleasure than when she awakened thy time-
shaken chords responsive to the twitterings of that slender image
of a voice.

We were not without our literary talk either. It did not extend
far, but as far as it went, it was good. It was bottomed well ; had
good grounds to go upon. In *the cottage* was a room, which
tradition authenticated to have been the same in which Glover, in
his occasional retirements, had penned the greater part of his
Leonidas. This circumstance was nightly quoted, though none of
the present inmates, that I could discover, appeared ever to have
met with the poem in question. But that was no matter. Glover
had written there, and the anecdote was pressed into the account
of the family importance. It diffused a learned air through the
apartment, the little side casement of which (the poet's study
window), opening upon a superb view as far as to the pretty spire
of Harrow, over domains and patrimonial acres, not a rood nor
square yard whereof our host could call his own, yet gave occasion
to an immoderate expansion of—vanity shall I call it ?—in his
bosom, as he showed them in a glowing summer evening. It was
all his, he took it all in, and communicated rich portions of it to
his guests. It was a part of his largess, his hospitality ; it was
going over his grounds ; he was lord for the time of showing them,
and you the implicit lookers-up to his magnificence.

He was a juggler, who threw mists before your eyes—you had
no time to detect his fallacies. He would say " hand me the *silver*
sugar tongs ; " and, before you could discover it was a single spoon,
and that *plated*, he would disturb and captivate your imagination
by a misnomer of " the urn " for a tea kettle ; or by calling a

homely bench a sofa. Rich men direct you to their furniture, poor
ones divert you from it; he neither did one nor the other, but by
simply assuming that everything was handsome about him, you
were positively at a demur what you did, or did not see, at *the
cottage.* With nothing to live on, he seemed to live on everything. He had a stock of wealth in his mind; not that which is
properly termed *Content,* for in truth he was not to be *contained*
at all, but overflowed all bounds by the force of a magnificent self-
delusion.

Enthusiasm is catching; and even his wife, a sober native of
North Britain, who generally saw things more as they were, was
not proof against the continual collision of his credulity. Her
daughters were rational and discreet young women; in the main,
perhaps, not insensible to their true circumstances. I have seen
them assume a thoughtful air at times. But such was the pre-
ponderating opulence of his fancy, that I am persuaded, not for
any half hour together, did they ever look their own prospects
fairly in the face. There was no resisting the vortex of his temperament. His riotous imagination conjured up handsome settle-
ments before their eyes, which kept them up in the eye of the
world too, and seem at last to have realised themselves; for they
both have married since, I am told, more than respectably.

It is long since, and my memory waxes dim on some subjects, or
I should wish to convey some notion of the manner in which the
pleasant creature described the circumstances of his own wedding-
day. I faintly remember something of a chaise and four, in which
he made his entry into Glasgow on that morning to fetch the bride
home, or carry her thither, I forget which. It so completely made
out the stanza of the old ballad—

> When we came down through Glasgow town,
>   We were a comely sight to see;
> My love was clad in black velvet,
>   And I myself in cramasie.

I suppose it was the only occasion, upon which his own actual
splendour at all corresponded with the world's notions on that
subject. In homely cart, or travelling caravan, by whatever
humble vehicle they chanced to be transported in less prosperous
days, the ride through Glasgow came back upon his fancy, not as a
humiliating contrast, but as a fair occasion for reverting to that
one day's state. It seemed an " equipage etern " from which no
power of fate or fortune, once mounted, had power thereafter to
dislodge him.

There is some merit in putting a handsome face upon indigent
circumstances. To bully and swagger away the sense of them before
strangers, may be not always discommendable. Tibbs, and Bobadil,

even when detected, have more of our admiration than contempt. But for a man to put the cheat upon himself; to play the Bobadil at home; and, steeped in poverty up to the lips, to fancy himself all the while chin-deep in riches, is a strain of constitutional philosophy, and a mastery over fortune, which was reserved for my old friend Captain Jackson.

———

THE SUPERANNUATED MAN

Sera tamen respexit
Libertas.   VIRGIL.

A Clerk I was in London gay.
                         O'KEEFE.

IF peradventure, Reader, it has been thy lot to waste the golden years of thy life—thy shining youth—in the irksome confinement of an office; to have thy prison days prolonged through middle age down to decrepitude and silver hairs, without hope of release or respite; to have lived to forget that there are such things as holidays, or to remember them but as the prerogatives of childhood; then, and then only, will you be able to appreciate my deliverance.

It is now six and thirty years since I took my seat at the desk in Mincing-lane. Melancholy was the transition at fourteen from the abundant play-time, and the frequently-intervening vacations of school days, to the eight, nine, and sometimes ten hours' a-day attendance at a counting-house. But time partially reconciles us to anything. I gradually became content—doggedly contented, as wild animals in cages.

It is true I had my Sundays to myself; but Sundays, admirable as the institution of them is for purposes of worship, are for that very reason the very worst adapted for days of unbending and recreation. In particular, there is a gloom for me attendant upon a city Sunday, a weight in the air. I miss the cheerful cries of London, the music, and the ballad-singers—the buzz and stirring murmur of the streets. Those eternal bells depress me. The closed shops repel me. Prints, pictures, all the glittering and endless succession of knacks and gewgaws, and ostentatiously displayed wares of tradesmen, which make a week-day saunter through the less busy parts of the metropolis so delightful—are shut out. No book-stalls deliciously to idle over—No busy faces to recreate the idle man who contemplates them ever passing by—the very face of business a charm by contrast to his temporary relaxation from it. Nothing to be seen but unhappy countenances—or half-happy at best—of emancipated 'prentices and little tradesfolks, with here and there a servant maid that has got leave to go out, who, slaving all the week, with the habit has lost almost the capacity of enjoying a free hour ; and livelily expressing the hollowness of a day's pleasuring. The very strollers in the fields on that day look anything but comfortable.

But besides Sundays I had a day at Easter, and a day at Christmas, with a full week in the summer to go and air myself in my native fields of Hertfordshire. This last was a great indulgence ; and the prospect of its recurrence, I believe, alone kept me up through the year, and made my durance tolerable. But when the week came round, did the glittering phantom of the distance keep touch with me ? or rather was it not a series of seven uneasy days, spent in restless pursuit of pleasure, and a wearisome anxiety to find out how to make the most of them ? Where was the quiet, where the promised rest ? Before I had a taste of it, it was vanished. I was at the desk again, counting upon the fifty-one tedious weeks that must intervene before such another snatch would come. Still the prospect of its coming threw something of an illumination upon the darker side of my captivity. Without it, as I have said, I could scarcely have sustained my thraldom.

Independently of the rigours of attendance, I have ever been haunted with a sense (perhaps a mere caprice) of incapacity for business. This, during my latter years, had increased to such a degree, that it was visible in all the lines of my countenance. My health and my good spirits flagged. I had perpetually a dread of some crisis, to which I should be found unequal. Besides my daylight servitude, I served over again all night in my sleep, and would awake with terrors of imaginary false entries, errors in my accounts, and the like. I was fifty years of age, and no prospect of emancipation presented itself. I had grown to my desk, as it were ; and the wood had entered into my soul.

My fellows in the office would sometimes rally me upon the trouble legible in my countenance ; but I did not know that it had raised the suspicions of any of my employers, when, on the 5th of last month, a day ever to be remembered by me, L——, the junior partner in the firm, calling me on one side, directly taxed me with my bad looks, and frankly inquired the cause of them. So taxed, I honestly made confession of my infirmity, and added that I was afraid I should eventually be obliged to resign his service. He spoke some words of course to hearten me, and there the matter

rested.   A whole week I remained labouring under the impression
that I had acted imprudently in my disclosure ; that I had foolishly
given a handle against myself, and had been anticipating my own
dismissal.   A week passed in this manner, the most anxious one, I
verily believe, in my whole life, when on the evening of the 12th of
April, just as I was about quitting my desk to go home (it might
be about eight o'clock) I received an awful summons to attend the
presence of the whole assembled firm in the formidable back parlour.
I thought, now my time is surely come, I have done for myself, I am
going to be told that they have no longer occasion for me.   L——,
I could see, smiled at the terror I was in, which was a little relief to
me,—when to my utter astonishment B——, the eldest partner,
began a formal harangue to me on the length of my services, my
very meritorious conduct during the whole of the time (the deuce,
thought I, how did he find out that ?   I protest I never had the
confidence to think as much).   He went on to descant on the
expediency of retiring at a certain time of life (how my heart
panted !) and asking me a few questions as to the amount of my own
property, of which I have a little, ended with a proposal, to which
his three partners nodded a grave assent, that I should accept from
the house, which I had served so well, a pension for life to the
amount of two-thirds of my accustomed salary—a magnificent offer !
I do not know what I answered between surprise and gratitude, but
it was understood that I accepted their proposal, and I was told
that I was free from that hour to leave their service.   I stammered
out a bow, and at just ten minutes after eight I went home—for
ever.   This noble benefit—gratitude forbids me to conceal their
names—I owe to the kindness of the most munificent firm in the
world—the house of Boldero, Merryweather, Bosanquet, and Lacy.

Esto perpetua !

For the first day or two I felt stunned, overwhelmed.   I could
only apprehend my felicity ; I was too confused to taste it sincerely.
I wandered about, thinking I was happy, and knowing that I was
not.   I was in the condition of a prisoner in the old Bastile,
suddenly let loose after a forty years' confinement.   I could scarce
trust myself with myself.   It was like passing out of Time into
Eternity—for it is a sort of Eternity for a man to have his Time all
to himself.   It seemed to me that I had more time on my hands
than I could ever manage.   From a poor man, poor in Time, I was
suddenly lifted up into a vast revenue ; I could see no end of my
possessions ; I wanted some steward, or judicious bailiff, to manage
my estates in Time for me.   And here let me caution persons grown
old in active business, not lightly, nor without weighing their own

resources, to forego their customary employment all at once, for there may be danger in it.   I feel it by myself, but I know that my resources are sufficient ; and now that those first giddy raptures have subsided, I have a quiet home-feeling of the blessedness of my condition.   I am in no hurry.   Having all holidays, I am as though I had none.   If Time hung heavy upon me, I could walk it away ; but I do *not* walk all day long, as I used to do in those old transient holidays, thirty miles a day, to make the most of them.   If Time were troublesome, I could read it away, but I do *not* read in that violent measure, with which, having no Time my own but candle-light Time, I used to weary out my head and eyesight in by-gone winters.   I walk, read or scribble (as now) just when the fit seizes me.   I no longer hunt after pleasure ; I let it come to me.   I am like the man

————That's born, and has his years come to him,
In some green desert.

" Years," you will say ! " what is this superannuated simpleton calculating upon ?   He has already told us, he is past fifty."

I have indeed lived nominally fifty years, but deduct out of them the hours which I have lived to other people, and not to myself, and you will find me still a young fellow.   For *that* is the only true Time, which a man can properly call his own, that which he has all to himself ; the rest, though in some sense he may be said to live it, is other people's time, not his.   The remnant of my poor days, long or short, is at least multiplied for me three-fold.   My ten next years, if I stretch so far, will be as long as any preceding thirty.   'Tis a fair rule-of-three sum.

Among the strange fantasies which beset me at the commence-ment of my freedom, and of which all traces are not yet gone, one was, that a vast tract of time had intervened since I quitted the Counting House.   I could not conceive of it as an affair of yester-day.   The partners, and the clerks, with whom I had for so many years, and for so many hours in each day of the year, been closely associated—being suddenly removed from them—they seemed as dead to me.   There is a fine passage, which may serve to illustrate this fancy, in a Tragedy by Sir Robert Howard, speaking of a friend's death :

————'Twas but just now he went away ;
I have not since had time to shed a tear ;
And yet the distance does the same appear
As if he had been a thousand years from me.
Time takes no measure in Eternity.

To dissipate this awkward feeling, I have been fain to go among them once or twice since ; to visit my old desk-fellows—my co-brethren of the quill—that I had left below in the state militant.

Not all the kindness with which they received me could quite restore to me that pleasant familiarity, which I had heretofore enjoyed among them. We cracked some of our old jokes, but methought they went off but faintly. My old desk; the peg where I hung my hat, were appropriated to another. I knew it must be, but I could not take it kindly. D——l take me, if I did not feel some remorse—beast, if I had not,—at quitting my old compeers, the faithful partners of my toils for six and thirty years, that smoothed for me with their jokes and conundrums the ruggedness of my professional road. Had it been so rugged then after all? or was I a coward simply? Well, it is too late to repent; and I also know, that these suggestions are a common fallacy of the mind on such occasions. But my heart smote me. I had violently broken the bands betwixt us. It was at least not courteous. I shall be some time before I get quite reconciled to the separation. Farewell, old cronies, yet not for long, for again and again I will come among ye, if I shall have your leave. Farewell Ch——, dry, sarcastic, and friendly! Do——, mild, slow to move, and gentlemanly! Pl——, officious to do, and to volunteer, good services!—and thou, thou dreary pile, fit mansion for a Gresham or a Whittington of old, stately House of Merchants; with thy labyrinthine passages, and light-excluding, pent-up offices, where candles for one half the year supplied the place of the sun's light; unhealthy contributor to my weal, stern fosterer of my living, farewell! In thee remain, and not in the obscure collection of some wandering bookseller, my "works!" There let them rest, as I do from my labours, piled on thy massy shelves, more MSS. in folio than ever Aquinas left, and full as useful! My mantle I bequeath among ye.

A fortnight has passed since the date of my first communication. At that period I was approaching to tranquillity, but had not reached it. I boasted of a calm indeed, but it was comparative only. Something of the first flutter was left; an unsettling sense of novelty; the dazzle to weak eyes of unaccustomed light. I missed my old chains, forsooth, as if they had been some necessary part of my apparel. I was a poor Carthusian, from strict cellular discipline suddenly by some revolution returned upon the world. I am now as if I had never been other than my own master. It is natural to me to go where I please, to do what I please. I find myself at eleven o'clock in the day in Bond-street, and it seems to me that I have been sauntering there at that very hour for years past. I digress into Soho, to explore a book-stall. Methinks I have been thirty years a collector. There is nothing strange nor new in it. I find myself before a fine picture in a morning. Was it ever otherwise? What is become of Fish-street Hill?

Where is Fenchurch-street? Stones of old Mincing-lane, which I have worn with my daily pilgrimage for six and thirty years, to the footsteps of what toil-worn clerk are your everlasting flints now vocal? I indent the gayer flags of Pall Mall. It is Change time, and I am strangely among the Elgin marbles. It was no hyperbole when I ventured to compare the change in my condition to a passing into another world. Time stands still in a manner to me. I have lost all distinction of season. I do not know the day of the week, or of the month. Each day used to be individually felt by me in its reference to the foreign post days; in its distance from, or propinquity to, the next Sunday. I had my Wednesday feelings, my Saturday nights' sensations. The genius of each day was upon me distinctly during the whole of it, affecting my appetite, spirits, &c. The phantom of the next day, with the dreary five to follow, sate as a load upon my poor Sabbath recreations. What charm has washed that Ethiop white? What is gone of Black Monday? All days are the same. Sunday itself —that unfortunate failure of a holyday as it too often proved, what with my sense of its fugitiveness, and over-care to get the greatest quantity of pleasure out of it—is melted down into a week day. I can spare to go to church now, without grudging the huge cantle which it used to seem to cut out of the holyday. I have Time for everything. I can visit a sick friend. I can interrupt the man of much occupation when he is busiest. I can insult over him with an invitation to take a day's pleasure with me to Windsor this fine May-morning. It is Lucretian pleasure to behold the poor drudges, whom I have left behind in the world, carking and caring; like horses in a mill, drudging on in the same eternal round—and what is it all for? A man can never have too much Time to himself, nor too little to do. Had I a little son, I would christen him NOTHING-TO-DO; he should do nothing. Man, I verily believe, is out of his element as long as he is operative. I am altogether for the life contemplative. Will no kindly earthquake come and swallow up those accursed cotton mills? Take me that lumber of a desk there, and bowl it down

> As low as to the fiends.

I am no longer ******, clerk to the Firm of &c. I am Retired Leisure. I am to be met with in trim gardens. I am already come to be known by my vacant face and careless gesture, perambulating at no fixed pace, nor with any settled purpose. I walk about; not to and from. They tell me, a certain *cum dignitate* air, that has been buried so long with my other good parts, has begun to shoot forth in my person. I grow into gentility perceptibly. When I take up a newspaper, it is to read the state of the opera. *Opus operatum est.* I have done all that I came into this world to do. I have worked task work, and have the rest of the day to myself.

THE GENTEEL STYLE IN WRITING

IT is an ordinary criticism, that my Lord Shaftesbury, and Sir William Temple, are models of the genteel style in writing. We should prefer saying—of the lordly, and the gentlemanly. Nothing can be more unlike than the inflated finical rhapsodies of Shaftesbury, and the plain natural chit-chat of Temple. The man of rank is discernible in both writers; but in the one it is only insinuated gracefully, in the other it stands out offensively. The peer seems to have written with his coronet on, and his Earl's mantle before him; the commoner in his elbow chair and undress. —What can be more pleasant than the way in which the retired statesman peeps out in the essays, penned by the latter in his delightful retreat at Shene? They scent of Nimeguen, and the Hague. Scarce an authority is quoted under an ambassador. Don Francisco de Melo, a "Portugal Envoy in England," tells him it was frequent in his country for men, spent with age or other decays, so as they could not hope for above a year or two of life, to ship themselves away in a Brazil fleet, and after their arrival there to go on a great length, sometimes of twenty or thirty years, or more, by the force of that vigour they recovered with that remove. "Whether such an effect (Temple beautifully adds) might grow from the air, or the fruits of that climate, or by approaching nearer the sun, which is the fountain of light and heat, when their natural heat was so far decayed: or whether the piecing out of an old man's life were worth the pains; I cannot tell: perhaps the play is not worth the candle."—Monsieur Pompone, "French Ambassador in his (Sir William's) time at the Hague," certifies him, that in his life he had never heard of any man in France that arrived at a hundred years of age; a limitation of life which the old gentleman imputes to the excellence of their climate, giving them such a liveliness of temper and humour, as disposes them to more pleasures of all kinds than in other countries; and moralises upon the matter very sensibly. The "late Robert Earl of Leicester" furnishes him with a story of a Countess of Desmond, married out of England in Edward the Fourth's time, and who lived far in King

James's reign.   The "same noble person" gives him an account, how such a year, in the same reign, there went about the country a set of morrice-dancers, composed of ten men who danced, a Maid Marian, and a tabor and pipe; and how these twelve, one with another, made up twelve hundred years.   "It was not so much (says Temple) that so many in one small county (Herefordshire) should live to that age, as that they should be in vigour and in humour to travel and to dance."   Monsieur Zulichem, one of his "colleagues at the Hague," informs him of a cure for the gout; which is confirmed by another "Envoy," Monsieur Serinchamps, in that town, who had tried it.—Old Prince Maurice of Nassau recommends to him the use of hammocks in that complaint; having been allured to sleep, while suffering under it himself, by the "constant motion or swinging of those airy beds."   Count Egmont, and the Rhinegrave who "was killed last summer before Maestricht," impart to him their experiences.

But the rank of the writer is never more innocently disclosed, than where he takes for granted the compliments paid by foreigners to his fruit-trees.   For the taste and perfection of what we esteem the best, he can truly say, that the French, who have eaten his peaches and grapes at Shene in no very ill year, have generally concluded that the last are as good as any they have eaten in France on this side Fontainebleau; and the first as good as any they have eat in Gascony.   Italians have agreed his white figs to be as good as any of that sort in Italy, which is the earlier kind of white fig there; for in the later kind and the blue, we cannot come near the warm climates, no more than in the Frontignac or Muscat grape. His orange-trees too, are as large as any he saw when he was young in France, except those of Fontainebleau, or what he has seen since in the Low Countries; except some very old ones of the Prince of Orange's.   Of grapes he had the honour of bringing over four sorts into England, which he enumerates, and supposes that they are all by this time pretty common among some gardeners in his neighbourhood, as well as several persons of quality; for he ever thought all things of this kind "the commoner they are made the better."   The garden pedantry with which he asserts that 'tis to little purpose to plant any of the best fruits, as peaches or grapes, hardly, he doubts, beyond Northamptonshire at the furthest northwards; and praises the "｜Bishop of Munster at Cosevelt," for attempting nothing beyond cherries in that cold climate; is equally pleasant and in character.   "I may perhaps" (he thus ends his sweet Garden Essay with a passage worthy of Cowley) "be allowed to know something of this trade, since I have so long allowed myself to be good for nothing else, which few men will do, or enjoy their gardens, without often looking abroad to see how other matters play, what motions in the state, and what invitations they may hope for into other scenes.   For my own part, as the country life, and this part of it more particularly, were the inclination of my youth itself, so they are the pleasure of my age ; and I can truly say that, among many great employments that have fallen to my share, I have never asked or sought for any of them, but have often endeavoured to escape from them, into the ease and freedom of a private scene, where a man may go his own way and his own pace, in the common paths and circles of life.   The measure of choosing well is whether a man likes what he has chosen, which I thank God has befallen me ; and though among the follies of my life, building and planting have not been the least, and have cost me more than I have the confidence to own ; yet they have been fully recompensed by the sweetness and satisfaction of this retreat, where, since my resolution taken of never entering again into any public employments, I have passed five years without ever once going to town, though I am almost in sight of it, and have a house there always ready to receive me.   Nor has this been any sort of affectation, as some have thought it, but a mere want of desire or humour to make so small a remove ; for when I am in this corner, I can truly say with Horace, *Me quoties reficit, &c.*

> " Me, when the cold Digentian stream revives,
> What does my friend believe I think or ask ?
> Let me yet less possess, so I may live,
> Whate'er of life remains, unto myself.
> May I have books enough ; and one year's store,
> Not to depend upon each doubtful hour :
> This is enough of mighty Jove to pray,
> Who, as he pleases, gives and takes away."

The writings of Temple are, in general, after this easy copy. On one occasion, indeed, his wit, which was mostly subordinate to nature and tenderness, has seduced him into a string of felicitous antitheses ; which, it is obvious to remark, have been a model to Addison and succeeding essayists.   " Who would not be covetous, and with reason," he says, " if health could be purchased with gold? who not ambitious, if it were at the command of power, or restored by honour ? but, alas ! a white staff will not help gouty feet to walk better than a common cane ; nor a blue riband bind up a wound so well as a fillet.   The glitter of gold, or of diamonds, will but hurt sore eyes instead of curing them ; and an aching head will be no more eased by wearing a crown, than a common night-cap." In a far better style, and more accordant with his own humour of plainness, are the concluding sentences of his " Discourse upon Poetry."   Temple took a part in the controversy about the ancient and the modern learning ; and, with that partiality so natural and so graceful in an old man, whose state engagements had left him little leisure to look into modern productions, while his retirement gave him occasion to look back upon the classic studies of his youth—decided in favour of the latter. "Certain it is," he says, "that, whether the fierceness of the Gothic humours, or noise of their perpetual wars, frighted it away, or that the unequal mixture of the modern languages would not bear it—the great heights and excellency both of poetry and music fell with the Roman learning and empire, and have never since recovered the admiration and applauses that before attended them. Yet, such as they are amongst us, they must be confessed to be the softest and sweetest, the most general and most innocent amusements of common time and life. They still find room in the courts of princes, and the cottages of shepherds. They serve to revive and animate the dead calm of poor and idle lives, and to allay or divert the violent passions and perturbations of the greatest and the busiest men. And both these effects are of equal use to human life; for the mind of man is like the sea, which is neither agreeable to the beholder nor the voyager, in a calm or in a storm, but is so to both when a little agitated by gentle gales; and so the mind, when moved by soft and easy passions or affections. I know very well that many who pretend to be wise by the forms of being grave, are apt to despise both poetry and music, as toys and trifles too light for the use or entertainment of serious men. But whoever find themselves wholly insensible to their charms, would, I think, do well to keep their own counsel, for fear of reproaching their own temper, and bringing the goodness of their natures, if not of their understandings, into question. While this world lasts, I doubt not but the pleasure and request of these two entertainments will do so too; and happy those that content themselves with these, or any other so easy and so innocent, and do not trouble the world or other men, because they cannot be quiet themselves, though nobody hurts them." "When all is done (he concludes), human life is at the greatest and the best but like a froward child, that must be played with, and humoured a little, to keep it quiet, till it falls asleep, and then the care is over."

BARBARA S——

ON the noon of the 14th of November, 1743 or 4, I forget which it was, just as the clock had struck one, Barbara S——, with her accustomed punctuality ascended the long ramb-

ling staircase, with awkward interposed landing-places, which led to
the office, or rather a sort of box with a desk in it, whereat sat the
then Treasurer of (what few of our readers may remember) the Old
Bath Theatre. All over the island it was the custom, and remains
so I believe to this day, for the players to receive their weekly
stipend on the Saturday. It was not much that Barbara had
to claim.

This little maid had just entered her eleventh year ; but her
important station at the theatre, as it seemed to her, with the
benefits which she felt to accrue from her pious application of her
small earnings, had given an air of womanhood to her steps and to
her behaviour. You would have taken her to have been at least
five years older.

Till latterly she had merely been employed in choruses, or where
children were wanted to fill up the scene. But the manager, observing a diligence and adroitness in her above her age, had for
some few months past intrusted to her the performance of whole
parts. You may guess the self-consequence of the promoted
Barbara. She had already drawn tears in young Arthur ; had
rallied Richard with infantine petulance in the Duke of York ;
and in her turn had rebuked that petulance when she was Prince of
Wales. She would have done the elder child in Morton's pathetic
after-piece to the life ; but as yet the " Children in the Wood "
was not.

Long after this little girl was grown an aged woman, I have seen
some of these small parts, each making two or three pages at most,
copied out in the rudest hand of the then prompter, who doubtless
transcribed a little more carefully and fairly for the grown-up
tragedy ladies of the establishment. But such as they were,
blotted and scrawled, as for a child's use, she kept them all ; and
in the zenith of her after reputation it was a delightful sight to
behold them bound up in costliest Morocco, each single—each
small part making a *book*—with fine clasps, gilt-splashed, &c.
She had conscientiously kept them as they had been delivered to
her ; not a blot had been effaced or tampered with. They were
precious to her for their affecting remembrancings. They were her
principia, her rudiments; the elementary atoms; the little steps by
which she pressed forward to perfection. " What," she would
say, " could Indian rubber, or a pumice stone, have done for
these darlings ? "

I am in no hurry to begin my story—indeed I have little or none
to tell—so I will just mention an observation of hers connected with
that interesting time.

Not long before she died I had been discoursing with her on the
quantity of real present emotion which a great tragic performer ex-

periences during acting. I ventured to think, that though in the first instance such players must have possessed the feelings which they so powerfully called up in others, yet by frequent repetition those feelings must become deadened in great measure, and the performer trust to the memory of past emotion, rather than express a present one. She indignantly repelled the notion, that with a truly great tragedian the operation,' by which such effects were produced upon an audience, could ever degrade itself into what was purely mechanical. With much delicacy, avoiding to instance in her *self*-experience, she told me, that so long ago as when she used to play the part of the Little Son to Mrs. Porter's Isabella, (I think it was) when that impressive actress has been bending over her in some heart-rending colloquy, she has felt real hot tears come trickling from her, which (to use her powerful expression) have perfectly scalded her back.

I am not quite so sure that it was Mrs. Porter; but it was some great actress of that day. The name is indifferent; but the fact of the scalding tears I most distinctly remember.

I was always fond of the society of players, and am not sure that an impediment in my speech (which certainly kept me out of the pulpit) even more than certain personal disqualifications, which are often got over in that profession, did not prevent me at one time of life from adopting it. I have had the honour (I must ever call it) once to have been admitted to the tea-table of Miss Kelly. I have played at serious whist with Mr. Liston. I have chatted with ever good-humoured Mrs. Charles Kemble. I have conversed as friend to friend with her accomplished husband. I have been indulged with a classical conference with Macready; and with a sight of the Player-picture gallery, at Mr. Matthews's, when the kind owner, to remunerate me for my love of the old actors (whom he loves so much) went over it with me, supplying to his capital collection, what alone the artist could not give them—voice; and their living motion. Old tones, half-faded, of Dodd and Parsons, and Baddeley, have lived again for me at his bidding. Only Edwin he could not restore to me. I have supped with——; but I am growing a coxcomb.

As I was about to say—at the desk of the then treasurer of the old Bath theatre—not Diamond's—presented herself the little Barbara S——.

The parents of Barbara had been in reputable circumstances. The father had practised, I believe, as an apothecary in the town. But his practice from causes which I feel my own infirmity too sensibly that way to arraign—or perhaps from that pure infelicity which accompanies some people in their walk through life, and which it is impossible to lay at the door of imprudence—was now reduced to nothing. They were in fact in the very teeth of starvation, when the manager, who knew and respected them in better days, took the little Barbara into his company.

At the period I commenced with, her slender earnings were the sole support of the family, including two younger sisters. I must throw a veil over some mortifying circumstances. Enough to say, that her Saturday's pittance was the only chance of a Sunday's (generally their only) meal of meat.

One thing I will only mention, that in some child's part, where in her theatrical character she was to sup off a roast fowl (O joy to Barbara!) some comic actor, who was for the night caterer for this dainty—in the misguided humour of his part, threw over the dish such a quantity of salt (O grief and pain of heart to Barbara!) that when he crammed a portion of it into her mouth, she was obliged sputteringly to reject it; and what with shame of her ill-acted part, and pain of real appetite at missing such a dainty, her little heart sobbed almost to breaking, till a flood of tears, which the well-fed spectators were totally unable to comprehend, mercifully relieved her.

This was the little starved, meritorious maid, who stood before old Ravenscroft, the treasurer, for her Saturday's payment.

Ravenscroft was a man, I have heard many old theatrical people besides herself say, of all men least calculated for a treasurer. He had no head for accounts, paid away at random, kept scarce any books, and summing up at the week's end, if he found himself a pound or so deficient, blest himself that it was no worse.

Now Barbara's weekly stipend was a bare half guinea.—By mistake he popped into her hand a—whole one.

Barbara tripped away.

She was entirely unconscious at first of the mistake : God knows, Ravenscroft would never have discovered it.

But when she had got down to the first of those uncouth landing-places, she became sensible of an unusual weight of metal pressing her little hand.

Now mark the dilemma.

She was by nature a good child. From her parents and those about her she had imbibed no contrary influence. But then they had taught her nothing. Poor men's smoky cabins are not always porticoes of moral philosophy. This little maid had no instinct to evil, but then she might be said to have no fixed principle. She had heard honesty commended, but never dreamed of its application to herself. She thought of it as something which concerned grown-up people—men and women. She had never known temptation, or thought of preparing resistance against it.

Her first impulse was to go back to the old treasurer, and explain

to him his blunder.   He was already so confused with age, besides
a natural want of punctuality, that she would have had some
difficulty in making him understand it.   She saw *that* in an instant.
And then it was such a bit of money! and then the image of a
larger allowance of butcher's meat on their table next day came
across her, till her little eyes glistened, and her mouth moistened.
But then Mr. Ravenscroft had always been so good-natured, had
stood her friend behind the scenes, and even recommended her promotion to some of her little parts.   But again the old man was
reputed to be worth a world of money.   He was supposed to have
fifty pounds a year clear of the theatre.   And then came staring
upon her the figures of her little stockingless and shoeless sisters.
And when she looked at her own neat white cotton stockings, which
her situation at the theatre had made it indispensable for her
mother to provide for her, with hard straining and pinching from
the family stock, and thought how glad she should be to cover their
poor feet with the same—and how then they could accompany her
to rehearsals, which they had hitherto been precluded from doing,
by reason of their unfashionable attire—in these thoughts she
reached the second landing-place—the second, I mean from the top
—for there was still another left to traverse.

Now virtue support Barbara!

And that never-failing friend did step in—for at that moment a
strength not her own, I have heard her say, was revealed to her—a
reason above reasoning—and without her own agency, as it seemed
(for she never felt her feet to move) she found herself transported
back to the individual desk she had just quitted, and her hand in the
old hand of Ravenscroft, who in silence took back the refunded
treasure, and who had been sitting (good man) insensible to the
lapse of minutes, which to her were anxious ages; and from that
moment a deep peace fell upon her heart, and she knew the quality
of honesty.

A year or two's unrepining application to her profession
brightened up the feet, and the prospects, of her little sisters, set
the whole family upon their legs again, and released her from the
difficulty of discussing moral dogmas upon a landing-place.

I have heard her say, that it was a surprise, not much short of
mortification to her, to see the coolness with which the old man
pocketed the difference, which had caused her such mortal throes.

This anecdote of herself I had in the year 1800, from the mouth
of the late Mrs. Crawford,[1] then sixty-seven years of age (she died
soon after); and to her struggles upon this childish occasion I have

---

[1] The maiden name of this lady was Street, which she changed, by successive
marriages, for those of Dancer, Barry, and Crawford.   She was Mrs. Crawford,
and a third time a widow, when I knew her.

sometimes ventured to think her indebted for that power of rending the heart in the representation of conflicting emotions, for which in after years she was considered as little inferior (if at all so in the part of Lady Randolph) even to Mrs. Siddons.

THE TOMBS IN THE ABBEY

IN A LETTER TO R——— S———, ESQ.

THOUGH in some points of doctrine, and perhaps of discipline I am diffident of lending a perfect assent to that church which you have so worthily *historified*, yet may the ill time never come to me, when with a chilled heart, or a portion of irreverent sentiment, I shall enter her beautiful and time-hallowed Edifices. Judge then of my mortification when, after attending the choral anthems of last Wednesday at Westminster, and being desirous of renewing my acquaintance, after lapsed years, with the tombs and antiquities there, I found myself excluded; turned out like a dog, or some profane person, into the common street, with feelings not very congenial to the place, or to the solemn service which I had been listening to. It was a jar after that music.

You had your education at Westminster; and doubtless among those dim aisles and cloisters, you must have gathered much of that devotional feeling in those young years, on which your purest mind feeds still—and may it feed! The antiquarian spirit, strong in you, and gracefully blending ever with the religious, may have been sown in you among those wrecks of splendid mortality. You owe it to the place of your education; you owe it to your learned fondness for the architecture of your ancestors; you owe it to the venerableness of your ecclesiastical establishment, which is daily lessened and called in question through these practices—to speak aloud your sense of them; never to desist raising your voice against them, till they be totally done away with and abolished; till the doors of Westminster Abbey be no longer closed against the decent, though low-in-purse, enthusiast, or blameless devotee, who must commit an injury against his family economy, if he would be indulged with a bare admission within its walls. You owe it to the decencies, which you wish to see maintained in its impressive services, that our Cathedral be no longer an object of inspection to the poor at those times only, in which they must rob from their attendance on the worship every minute which they can bestow upon the fabric. In vain the public prints have taken up this subject, in vain such poor nameless writers as myself express their indignation. A word from you, Sir—a hint in your Journal— would be sufficient to fling open the doors of the Beautiful Temple again, as we can remember them when we were boys. At that time of life, what would the imaginative faculty (such as it is) in both of us, have suffered, if the entrance to so much reflection had been obstructed by the demand of so much silver!—If we had scraped it up to gain an occasional admission (as we certainly should have done) would the sight of those old tombs have been as impressive to us (while we had been weighing anxiously prudence against sentiment) as when the gates stood open, as those of the adjacent Park; when we could walk in at any time, as the mood brought us, for a shorter or longer time, as that lasted? Is the being shown over a place the same as silently for ourselves detecting the genius of it? In no part of our beloved Abbey now can a person find entrance (out of service time) under the sum of *two shillings*. The rich and the great will smile at the anticlimax, presumed to lie in these two short words. But you can tell them, Sir, how much quiet worth, how much capacity for enlarged feeling, how much taste and genius, may coexist, especially in youth, with a purse incompetent to this demand.—A respected friend of ours, during his late visit to the metropolis, presented himself for admission to Saint Paul's. At the same time a decently clothed man, with as decent a wife, and child, were bargaining for the same indulgence. The price was only two-pence each person. The poor but decent man hesitated, desirous to go in; but there were three of them, and he turned away reluctantly. Perhaps he wished to have seen the tomb of Nelson. Perhaps the Interior of the Cathedral was his object. But in the state of his finances, even sixpence might reasonably seem too much. Tell the Aristocracy of the country (no man can do it more impressively); instruct them of what value these insignificant pieces of money, these minims to their sight, may be to their humbler brethren. Shame these Sellers out of the Temple. Stifle not the suggestions of your better nature with the pretext, that an indiscriminate admission would expose the Tombs to violation. Remember your boy-days. Did you ever see, or hear, of a mob in the Abbey, while it was free to all? Do the rabble come there, or trouble their heads about such speculations? It is all that you can do to drive them into your churches; they do not voluntarily offer themselves. They have, alas! no passion for antiquities; for tomb of king or prelate, sage or poet. If they had, they would be no longer the rabble.

For forty years that I have known the Fabric, the only well-attested charge of violation adduced, has been—a ridiculous dismemberment committed upon the effigy of that amiable spy, Major André. And is it for this—the wanton mischief of some schoolboy, fired perhaps with raw notions of Transatlantic Freedom—or the remote possibility of such a mischief occurring again, so easily to be prevented by stationing a constable within the walls, if the vergers are incompetent to the duty—is it upon such wretched pretences, that the people of England are made to pay a new Peter's Pence, so long abrogated; or must content themselves with contemplating the ragged Exterior of their Cathedral? The mischief was done about the time that you were a scholar there. Do you know any thing about the unfortunate relic?—

AMICUS REDIVIVUS

Where were ye, Nymphs, when the remorseless deep
Clos'd o'er the head of your loved Lycidas?

I DO not know when I have experienced a stranger sensation, than on seeing my old friend G. D., who had been paying me a morning visit a few Sundays back, at my cottage at Islington, upon taking leave, instead of turning down the right hand path by which he had entered—with staff in hand, and at noon day, deliberately march right forwards into the midst of the stream that runs by us, and totally disappear.

A spectacle like this at dusk would have been appalling enough; but, in the broad open daylight, to witness such an unreserved motion towards self-destruction in a valued friend, took from me all power of speculation.

How I found my feet, I know not. Consciousness was quite gone. Some spirit, not my own, whirled me to the spot. I remember nothing but the silvery apparition of a good white head emerging; nigh which a staff (the hand unseen that wielded it) pointed upwards, as feeling for the skies. In a moment (if time was in that time) he was on my shoulders, and I—freighted with a load more precious than his who bore Anchises.

And here I cannot but do justice to the officious zeal of sundry passers by, who, albeit arriving a little too late to participate in the honours of the rescue, in philanthropic shoals came thronging to communicate their advice as to the recovery; prescribing variously the application, or non-application, of salt, &c., to the person of the patient. Life meantime was ebbing fast away, amidst the stifle of conflicting judgments, when one, more sagacious than the rest, by a bright thought, proposed sending for the Doctor. Trite as the counsel was, and impossible, as one should think, to be missed on,—shall I confess ?—in this emergency, it was to me as if an Angel had spoken. Great previous exertions—and mine had not been inconsiderable—are commonly followed by a debility of purpose. This was a moment of irresolution.

MONOCULUS—for so, in default of catching his true name, I choose to designate the medical gentleman who now appeared—is a grave, middle-aged person, who, without having studied at the college, or truckled to the pedantry of a diploma, hath employed a great portion of his valuable time in experimental processes upon the bodies of unfortunate fellow-creatures, in whom the vital spark, to mere vulgar thinking, would seem extinct, and lost for ever. He omitteth no occasion of obtruding his services, from a case of common surfeit-suffocation to the ignobler obstructions, sometimes induced by a too wilful application of the plant *Cannabis* outwardly. But though he declineth not altogether these drier extinctions, his occupation tendeth for the most part to water-practice; for the convenience of which, he hath judiciously fixed his quarters near the grand repository of the stream mentioned, where, day and night, from his little watch-tower, at the Middleton's-Head, he listeneth to detect the wrecks of drowned mortality—partly, as he saith, to be upon the spot—and partly, because the liquids which he useth to prescribe to himself and his patients, on these distressing occasions, are ordinarily more conveniently to be found at these common hostelries, than in the shops and phials of the apothecaries. His ear hath arrived to such finesse by practice, that it is reported, he can distinguish a plunge at a half furlong distance; and can tell, if it be casual or deliberate. He weareth a medal, suspended over a suit, originally of a sad brown, but which, by time, and frequency of nightly divings, has been dinged into a true professional sable. He passeth by the name of Doctor, and is remarkable for wanting his left eye. His remedy—after a sufficient application of warm blankets, friction, &c., is a simple tumbler, or more, of the purest Cognac, with water, made as hot as the convalescent can bear it. Where he findeth, as in the case of my friend, a squeamish subject, he condescendeth to be the taster; and showeth, by his own example, the innocuous nature of the prescription. Nothing can be more kind or encouraging than this procedure. It addeth confidence to the patient, to see his medical adviser go hand in hand with himself in the remedy. When the doctor swalloweth his own draught, what peevish invalid can refuse to pledge him in the potion ? In fine, MONOCULUS is a humane, sensible man, who, for a slender pittance, scarce enough to sustain life, is content to wear it out in the endeavour to save the lives of others—his pretensions so moderate, that with difficulty I could press a crown upon him, for the price of restoring the existence of such an invaluable creature to society as G. D.

It was pleasant to observe the effect of the subsiding alarm upon the nerves of the dear absentee. It seemed to have given a shake to memory, calling up notice after notice, of all the providential deliverances he had experienced in the course of his long and innocent life. Sitting up in my couch—my couch which, naked and void of furniture hitherto, for the salutary repose which it administered, shall be honoured with costly valance, at some price, and henceforth be a state-bed at Colebrooke,—he discoursed of marvellous escapes—by carelessness of nurses—by pails of gelid, and kettles of the boiling element, in infancy—by orchard pranks, and snapping twigs, in schoolboy frolics—by descent of tiles at Trumpington, and of heavier tomes at Pembroke—by studious watchings, inducing frightful vigilance—by want, and the fear of want, and all the sore throbbings of the learned head.—Anon, he would burst out into little fragments of chaunting—of songs long ago—ends of deliverance-hymns, not remembered before since childhood, but coming up now, when his heart was made tender as a child's—for the *tremor cordis*, in the retrospect of a recent deliverance, as in a case of impending danger, acting upon an innocent heart, will produce a self-tenderness, which we should do ill to christen cowardice ; and Shakspeare, in the latter crisis, has made his good Sir Hugh to remember the sitting by Babylon, and to mutter of shallow rivers.

Waters of Sir Hugh Middleton—what a spark you were like to have extinguished for ever ! Your salubrious streams to this City, for now near two centuries, would hardly have atoned for what you were in a moment washing away. Mockery of a river—liquid artifice—wretched conduit ! henceforth rank with canals, and sluggish aqueducts. Was it for this, that, smit in boyhood with the explorations of that Abyssinian traveller, I paced the vales of Amwell to explore your tributary springs, to trace your salutary waters sparkling through green Hertfordshire, and cultured Enfield parks ?—Ye have no swans—no Naiads—no river God—or did the benevolent hoary aspect of my friend tempt ye to suck him in, that ye also might have the tutelary genius of your waters ?

Had he been drowned in Cam there would have been some consonancy in it ; but what willows had ye to wave and rustle over his moist sepulture ?—or, having no *name*, besides that un-meaning assumption of *eternal novity*, did ye think to get one by the noble prize, and henceforth to be termed the STREAM DYERIAN?

And could such spacious virtue find a grave
Beneath the imposthumed bubble of a wave?

I protest, George, you shall not venture out again—no, not by daylight—without a sufficient pair of spectacles—in your musing moods especially. Your absence of mind we have borne, till your presence of body came to be called in question by it. You shall not go wandering into Euripus with Aristotle, if we can help it. Fie, man, to turn dipper at your years, after your many tracts in favour of sprinkling only!

I have nothing but water in my head o' nights since this frightful accident. Sometimes I am with Clarence in his dream. At others, I behold Christian beginning to sink, and crying out to his good brother Hopeful (that is to me), "I sink in deep waters; the billows go over my head, all the waves go over me. Selah." Then I have before me Palinurus, just letting go the steerage. I cry out too late to save. Next follow—a mournful procession— *suicidal faces*, saved against their wills from drowning; dolefully trailing a length of reluctant gratefulness, with ropy weeds pendant from locks of watchet hue—constrained Lazari—Pluto's half-subjects—stolen fees from the grave—bilking Charon of his fare. At their head Arion—or is it G. D.?—in his singing garments marcheth singly, with harp in hand, and votive garland, which Machaon (or Dr. Hawes) snatcheth straight, intending to suspend it to the stern God of Sea. Then follow dismal streams of Lethe, in which the half-drenched on earth are constrained to drown downright, by wharfs where Ophelia twice acts her muddy death.

And, doubtless, there is some notice in that invisible world, when one of us approacheth (as my friend did so lately) to their inexorable precincts. When a soul knocks once, twice, at death's door, the sensation aroused within the palace must be considerable; and the grim Feature, by modern science so often dispossessed of his prey, must have learned by this time to pity Tantalus.

A pulse assuredly was felt along the line of the Elysian shades, when the near arrival of G. D. was announced by no equivocal indications. From their seats of Asphodel arose the gentler and the graver ghosts—poet, or historian—of Grecian or of Roman lore— to crown with unfading chaplets the half-finished love-labours of their unwearied scholiast. Him Markland expected—him Tyrwhitt hoped to encounter—him the sweet lyrist of Peter House, whom he had barely seen upon earth,[1] with newest airs prepared

---

[1] GRAIUM *tantum vidit.*

to greet ——; and, patron of the gentle Christ's boy,—who should have been his patron through life—the mild Askew, with longing aspirations, leaned foremost from his venerable Æsculapian chair, to welcome into that happy company the matured virtues of the man, whose tender scions in the boy he himself upon earth had so prophetically fed and watered.

———

SOME SONNETS OF SIR PHILIP SYDNEY

SYDNEY'S Sonnets—I speak of the best of them—are among the very best of their sort.   They fall below the plain moral dignity, the sanctity, and high yet modest spirit of self-approval, of Milton, in his compositions of a similar structure.   They are in truth what Milton, censuring the Arcadia, says of that work (to which they are a sort of after-tune or application), " vain and amatorious " enough, yet the things in their kind (as he confesses to be true of the romance) may be " full of worth and wit."   They savour of the Courtier, it must be allowed, and not of the Common-wealthsman.   But Milton was a Courtier when he wrote the Masque at Ludlow Castle, and still more a Courtier when he composed the Arcades.   When the national struggle was to begin, he becomingly cast these vanities behind him ; and if the order of time had thrown Sir Philip upon the crisis which preceded the Revolution, there is no reason why he should not have acted the same part in that emergency, which has glorified the name of a later Sydney.   He did not want for plainness or boldness of spirit.   His letter on the French match may testify, he could speak his mind freely to Princes.   The times did not call him to the scaffold.

The Sonnets which we oftenest call to mind of Milton were the compositions of his maturest years.   Those of Sydney, which I am about to produce, were written in the very hey-day of his blood.   They are stuck full of amorous fancies—far-fetched conceits, befitting his occupation ; for True Love thinks no labour to send out Thoughts upon the vast, and more than Indian voyages, to bring home rich pearls, outlandish wealth, gums, jewels, spicery, to sacrifice in self-depreciating similitudes, as shadows of true amiabilities in the Beloved.   We must be Lovers—or at least the cooling touch of time, the *circum præcordia frigus*, must not have so damped our faculties, as to take away our recollection that we were once so—before we can duly appreciate the glorious vanities, and graceful hyperboles, of the passion. The images which lie before our feet (though by some accounted the only natural) are least natural for the high Sydnean love to express its fancies by. They may serve for the loves of Tibullus, or the dear Author of the Schoolmistress; for passions that creep and whine in Elegies and Pastoral Ballads. I am sure Milton never loved at this rate. I am afraid some of his addresses (*ad Leonoram* I mean) have rather erred on the farther side; and that the poet came not much short of a religious indecorum, when he could thus apostrophise a singing-girl :—

> Angelus unicuique suus (sic credite gentes)
> Obtigit ætheriis ales ab ordinibus.
> Quid mirum, Leonora, tibi si gloria major,
> Nam tua præsentem vox sonat ipsa Deum?
> Aut Deus, aut vacui certè mens tertia cœli,
> Per tua secretò guttura serpit agens;
> Serpit agens, facilisque docet mortalia corda
> Sensim immortali assuescere posse sono.
> QUOD SI CUNCTA QUIDEM DEUS EST, PER CUNCTAQUE FUSUS,
> IN TE UNÂ LOQUITUR, CÆTERA MUTUS HABET.

This is loving in a strange fashion; and it requires some candour of construction (besides the slight darkening of a dead language) to cast a veil over the ugly appearance of something very like blasphemy in the last two verses. I think the Lover would have been staggered, if he had gone about to express the same thought in English. I am sure, Sydney has no flights like this. His extravaganzas do not strike at the sky, though he takes leave to adopt the pale Dian into a fellowship with his mortal passions.

I

> With how sad steps, O Moon, thou climb'st the skies;
> How silently; and with how wan a face!
> What! may it be, that even in heavenly place
> That busy Archer his sharp arrows tries?
> Sure, if that long-with-love-acquainted eyes
> Can judge of love, thou feel'st a lover's case;
> I read it in thy looks; thy languisht grace
> To me, that feel the like, thy state descries.
> Then, even of fellowship, O Moon, tell me,
> Is constant love deem'd there but want of wit?
> Are beauties there as proud as here they be?
> Do they above love to be loved, and yet
> Those lovers scorn, whom that love doth possess?
> Do they call *virtue* there—*ungratefulness?*

The last line of this poem is a little obscured by transposition. He means, Do they call ungratefulness there a virtue?

II

Come, Sleep, O Sleep, the certain knot of peace,
The baiting place of wit, the balm of woe,
The poor man's wealth, the prisoner's release,
The indifferent judge between the high and low ;
With shield of proof shield me from out the prease [1]
Of those fierce darts despair at me doth throw ;
O make in me those civil wars to cease :
I will good tribute pay, if thou do so.
Take thou of me sweet pillows, sweetest bed ;
A chamber deaf to noise, and blind to light ;
A rosy garland, and a weary head.
And if these things, as being thine by right,
Move not thy heavy grace, thou shalt in me,
Livelier than elsewhere, STELLA's image see.

III

The curious wits, seeing dull pensiveness
Bewray itself in my long-settled eyes,
Whence those same fumes of melancholy rise,
With idle pains, and missing aim, do guess.
Some, that know how my spring I did address,
Deem that my Muse some fruit of knowledge plies ;
Others, because the Prince my service tries,
Think, that I think state errors to redress ;
But harder judges judge, ambition's rage,
Scourge of itself, still climbing slippery place,
Holds my young brain captiv'd in golden cage.
O fools, or over-wise ! alas, the race
Of all my thoughts hath neither stop nor start,
But only STELLA's eyes, and STELLA's heart.

IV

Because I oft in dark abstracted guise
Seem most alone in greatest company,
With dearth of words, or answers quite awry,
To them that would make speech of speech arise ;
They deem, and of their doom the rumour flies,
That poison foul of bubbling *Pride* doth lie
So in my swelling breast, that only I
Fawn on myself, and others do despise ;
Yet *Pride*, I think, doth not my Soul possess,
Which looks too oft in his unflattering glass :
But one worse fault—*Ambition*—I confess,
That makes me oft my best friends overpass,
Unseen, unheard—while Thought to highest place
Bends all his powers, even unto STELLA's grace.

V

Having this day, my horse, my hand, my lance,
Guided so well that I obtained the prize,
Both by the judgment of the English eyes,
And of some sent from that *sweet enemy*,—France ;
Horsemen my skill in horsemanship advance ;
Townsfolk my strength ; a daintier judge applies

---

[1] Press.

His praise to sleight, which from good use doth rise ;
Some lucky wits impute it but to chance ;
Others, because of both sides I do take
My blood from them, who did excel in this,
Think Nature me a man of arms did make.
How far they shot awry ! the true cause is,
STELLA look'd on, and from her heavenly face
Sent forth the beams which made so fair my race.

VI

In martial sports I had my cunning tried,
And yet to break more staves did me address,
While with the people's shouts (I must confess)
Youth, luck, and praise, even fill'd my veins with pride—
When Cupid, having me (his slave) descried
In Mars's livery, prancing in the press,
" What now, Sir Fool ! " said he ; " I would no less :
Look here, I say." I look'd, and STELLA spied,
Who hard by made a window send forth light.
My heart then quak'd, then dazzled were mine eyes ;
One hand forgot to rule, th'other to fight ;
Nor trumpet's sound I heard, nor friendly cries.
My foe came on, and beat the air for me—
Till that her blush made me my shame to see.

VII

No more, my dear, no more these counsels try ;
O give my passions leave to run their race ;
Let Fortune lay on me her worst disgrace ;
Let folk o'er-charged with brain against me cry ;
Let clouds bedim my face, break in mine eye ;
Let me no steps, but of lost labour, trace ;
Let all the earth with scorn recount my case—
But do not will me from my love to fly.
I do not envy Aristotle's wit,
Nor do aspire to Cæsar's bleeding fame ;
Nor aught do care, though some above me sit ;
Nor hope, nor wish, another course to frame,
But that which once may win thy cruel heart :
Thou art my wit, and thou my virtue art.

VIII

LOVE still a boy, and oft a wanton, is,
School'd only by his mother's tender eye ;
What wonder then, if he his lesson miss,
When for so soft a rod dear play he try ?
And yet my STAR, because a sugar'd kiss
In sport I suck'd, while she asleep did lie,
Doth lour, nay chide, nay threat, for only this.
Sweet, it was saucy LOVE, not humble I.
But no 'scuse serves ; she makes her wrath appear
In beauty's throne—see now, who dares come near
Those scarlet judges, threat'ning bloody pain ?
O heav'nly Fool, thy most kiss-worthy face
Anger invests with such a lovely grace,
That anger's self I needs must kiss again.

IX

I never drank of Aganippe well,
Nor ever did in shade of Tempe sit,
And Muses scorn with vulgar brains to dwell ;
Poor lay-man I, for sacred rites unfit.
Some do I hear of Poets' fury tell,
But (God wot) wot not what they mean by it ;
And this I swear by blackest brook of hell,
I am no|pick-purse of another's wit.
How falls it then, that with so smooth an ease
My thoughts I speak, and what I speak doth flow
In verse, and that my verse best wits doth please ?
Guess me the cause—what is it thus ?—fye, no.
Or so ?—much less. How then ? sure thus it is,
My lips are sweet, inspired with Stella's kiss.

X

Of all the kings that ever here did reign,
Edward, named Fourth, as first in praise I name,
Not for his fair outside, nor well-lined brain—
Although less gifts imp feathers oft on Fame.
Nor that he could, young-wise, wise-valiant, frame
His sire's revenge, join'd with a kingdom's gain ;
And, gain'd by Mars could yet mad Mars so tame,
That Balance weigh'd what Sword did late obtain.
Nor that he made the Floure-de-luce so 'fraid,
Though strongly hedged of bloody Lions' paws
That witty Lewis to him a tribute paid.
Nor this, nor that, nor any such small cause—
But only, for this worthy knight durst prove
To lose his crown rather than fail his love.

XI

O happy Thames, that didst my Stella bear,
I saw thyself, with many a smiling line
Upon thy cheerful face, Joy's livery wear,
While those fair planets on thy streams did shine ;
The boat for joy could not to dance forbear,
While wanton winds, with beauty so divine
Ravish'd, stay'd not, till in her golden hair
They did themselves (O sweetest prison) twine.
And fain those Æol's youth there would their stay
Have made ; but, forced by nature still to fly,
First did with puffing kiss those locks display.
She, so dishevell'd, blush'd ; from window I
With sight thereof cried out, O fair disgrace,
Let honour's self to thee grant highest place !

XII

Highway, since you my chief Parnassus be ;
And that my Muse, to some ears not unsweet,
Tempers her words to trampling horses' feet,
More soft than to a chamber melody,—
Now blessed You bear onward blessed Me
To Her, where I my heart safe left shall meet,
My Muse and I must you of duty greet
With thanks and wishes, wishing thankfully.

> Be you still fair, honour'd by public heed,
> By no encroachment wrong'd, nor time forgot ;
> Nor blam'd for blood, nor shamed for sinful deed.
> And that you know, I envy you no lot
> Of highest wish, I wish you so much bliss,
> Hundreds of years you STELLA's feet may kiss.

Of the foregoing, the first, the second, and the last sonnet, are my favourites. But the general beauty of them all is, that they are so perfectly characteristical. The spirit of "learning and of chivalry,"—of which union, Spenser has entitled Sydney to have been the "president,"—shines through them. I confess I can see nothing of the "jejune" or "frigid" in them ; much less of the "stiff" and "cumbrous"—which I have sometimes heard objected to the Arcadia. The verse runs off swiftly and gallantly. It might have been tuned to the trumpet ; or tempered (as himself expresses it) to "trampling horses' feet." They abound in felicitous phrases—

> O heav'nly Fool, thy most kiss-worthy face—
>
> *8th Sonnet.*
>
> ———Sweet pillows, sweetest bed ;
> A chamber deaf to noise, and blind to light ;
> A rosy garland, and a weary head.
>
> *2nd Sonnet.*
>
> ———That sweet enemy,—France—
>
> *5th Sonnet.*

But they are not rich in words only, in vague and unlocalised feelings—the failing too much of some poetry of the present day—they are full, material, and circumstantiated. Time and place appropriates every one of them. It is not a fever of passion wasting itself upon a thin diet of dainty words, but a transcendent passion pervading and illuminating action, pursuits, studies, feats of arms, the opinions of contemporaries and his judgment of them. An historical thread runs through them, which almost affixes a date to them ; marks the *when* and *where* they were written.

I have dwelt the longer upon what I conceive the merit of these poems, because I have been hurt by the wantonness (I wish I could treat it by a gentler name) with which W. H. takes every occasion of insulting the memory of Sir Philip Sydney. But the decisions of the Author of Table Talk, &c., (most profound and subtle where they are, as for the most part, just) are more safely to be relied upon, on subjects and authors he has a partiality for, than on such as he has conceived an accidental prejudice against. Milton wrote Sonnets, and was a king-hater ; and it was congenial perhaps to sacrifice a courtier to a patriot. But I was unwilling to lose a *fine idea* from my mind. The noble images, passions, sentiments, and poetical delicacies of character, scattered all over the Arcadia (spite

of some stiffness and encumberment), justify to me the character
which his contemporaries have left us of the writer. I cannot
think with the Critic, that Sir Philip Sydney was that *opprobrious
thing* which a foolish nobleman in his insolent hostility chose to
term him. I call to mind the epitaph made on him, to guide me
to juster thoughts of him ; and I repose upon the beautiful lines in
the " Friend's Passion for his Astrophel," printed with the Elegies
of Spenser and others.

> You knew—who knew not Astrophel ?
> (That I should live to say I knew,
> And have not in possession still !)—
> Things known permit me to renew—
>   Of him you know his merit such,
>   I cannot say—you hear—too much.
>
> Within these woods of Arcady
> He chief delight and pleasure took ;
> And on the mountain Partheny,
> Upon the crystal liquid brook,
>   The Muses met him every day,
>   That taught him sing, to write, and say.
>
> When he descended down the mount,
> His personage seemed most divine :
> A thousand graces one might count
> Upon his lovely chearful eyne.
>   To hear him speak, and sweetly smile,
>   You were in Paradise the while,
>
> *A sweet attractive kind of grace ;*
> *A full assurance given by looks ;*
> *Continual comfort in a face,*
> *The lineaments of Gospel books—*
>   I trow that count'nance cannot lye,
>   Whose thoughts are legible in the eye.
>
>   *   *   *   *   *
>
> Above all others this is he,
> Which erst approved in his song,
> That love and honour might agree,
> And that pure love will do no wrong.
>   Sweet saints, it is no sin or blame
>   To love a man of virtuous name.
>
> Did never Love so sweetly breathe
> In any mortal breast before :
> Did never Muse inspire beneath
> A Poet's brain with finer store.
>   He wrote of Love with high conceit,
>   And beauty rear'd above her height.

Or let any one read the deeper sorrows (grief running into rage)
in the Poem,—the last in the collection accompanying the above,
—which from internal testimony I believe to be Lord Brooke's,—
beginning with " Silence augmenteth grief,"—and then seriously ask

himself, whether the subject of such absorbing and confounding regrets could have been *that thing* which Lord Oxford termed him.

NEWSPAPERS THIRTY-FIVE YEARS AGO

DAN STUART once told us, that he did not remember that he ever deliberately walked into the Exhibition at Somerset House in his life. He might occasionally have escorted a party of ladies across the way that were going in ; but he never went in of his own head. Yet the office of the Morning Post newspaper stood then just where it does now—we are carrying you back, Reader, some thirty years or more—with its gilt-globe-topt front facing that emporium of our artists' grand Annual Exposure. We sometimes wish, that we had observed the same abstinence with Daniel.

A word or two of D. S. He ever appeared to us one of the finest tempered of Editors. Perry, of the Morning Chronicle, was equally pleasant, with a dash, no slight one either, of the courtier. S. was frank, plain, and English all over. We have worked for both these gentlemen.

It is soothing to contemplate the head of the Ganges ; to trace the first little bubblings of a mighty river ;

> With holy reverence to approach the rocks,
> Whence glide the streams renowned in ancient song.

Fired with a perusal of the Abyssinian Pilgrim's exploratory ramblings after the cradle of the infant Nilus, we well remember on one fine summer holyday (a " whole day's leave " we called it at Christ's Hospital) sallying forth at rise of sun, not very well provisioned either for such an undertaking, to trace the current of the New River—Middletonian stream !—to its scaturient source, as we had read, in meadows by fair Amwell. Gallantly did we commence our solitary quest—for it was essential to the dignity of a DISCOVERY, that no eye of schoolboy, save our own, should beam on the detection. By flowery spots, and verdant lanes, skirting Hornsey, Hope trained us on in many a baffling turn ; endless, hopeless meanders, as it seemed ; or as if the jealous waters had *dodged* us, reluctant to have the humble spot of their nativity revealed ; till spent, and nigh famished, before set of the same sun, we sate down somewhere by Bowes Farm, near Tottenham, with a tithe of our proposed labours only yet accomplished ; sorely convinced in spirit, that that Brucian enterprise was as yet too arduous for our young shoulders.

Not more refreshing to the thirsty curiosity of the traveller is the tracing of some mighty waters up to their shallow fontlet, than it is to a pleased and candid reader to go back to the inexperienced essays, the first callow flights in authorship, of some established name in literature ; from the Gnat which preluded to the Æneid, to the Duck which Samuel Johnson trod on.

In those days every Morning Paper, as an essential retainer to its establishment, kept an author, who was bound to furnish daily a quantum of witty paragraphs. Sixpence a joke—and it was thought pretty high too—was Dan Stuart's settled remuneration in these cases. The chat of the day, scandal, but, above all, *dress*, furnished the material. The length of no paragraph was to exceed seven lines. Shorter they might be, but they must be poignant.

A fashion of *flesh*, or rather *pink*-coloured hose for the ladies, luckily coming up at the juncture, when we were on our probation for the place of Chief Jester to S.'s Paper, established our reputation in that line. We were pronounced a "capital hand." O the conceits which we varied upon *red* in all its prismatic differences ! from the trite and obvious flower of Cytherea, to the flaming costume of the lady that has her sitting upon "many waters." Then there was the collateral topic of ancles. What an occasion to a truly chaste writer, like ourself, of touching that nice brink, and yet never tumbling over it, of a seemingly ever approximating something "not quite proper ; " while, like a skilful posture-master, balancing betwixt decorums and their opposites, he keeps the line, from which a hair's-breadth deviation is destruction ; hovering in the confines of light and darkness, or where "both seem either; " a hazy uncertain delicacy ; Autolycus-like in the Play, still putting off his expectant auditory with "Whoop, do me no harm, good man ! " But, above all, that conceit arrided us most at that time, and still tickles our midriff to remember, where, allusively to the flight of Astræa—*ultima Cœlestûm terras reliquit*—we pronounced—in reference to the stockings still—that MODESTY TAKING HER FINAL LEAVE OF MORTALS, HER LAST BLUSH WAS VISIBLE IN HER ASCENT TO THE HEAVENS BY THE TRACT OF THE GLOWING INSTEP. This might be called the crowning conceit ; and was esteemed tolerable writing in those days.

But the fashion of jokes, with all other things, passes away ; as did the transient mode which had so favoured us. The ancles of our fair friends in a few weeks began to reassume their whiteness, and left us scarce a leg to stand upon. Other female whims followed, but none, methought, so pregnant, so invitatory of shrewd conceits, and more than single meanings.

Somebody has said, that to swallow six cross-buns daily consecutively for a fortnight would surfeit the stoutest digestion. But to have to furnish as many jokes daily, and that not for a fortnight, but for a long twelvemonth, as we were constrained to do, was a little harder execution. " Man goeth forth to his work until the evening "—from a reasonable hour in the morning, we presume it was meant. Now as our main occupation took us up from eight till five every day in the City ; and as our evening hours, at that time of life, had generally to do with any thing rather than business, it follows, that the only time we could spare for this manufactory of jokes—our supplementary livelihood, that supplied us in every want beyond mere bread and cheese—was exactly that part of the day which (as we have heard of No Man's Land) may be fitly denominated No Man's Time ; that is, no time in which a man ought to be up, and awake, in. To speak more plainly, it is that time, of an hour, or an hour and a half's duration, in which a man, whose occasions call him up so preposterously, has to wait for his breakfast.

O those headaches at dawn of day, when at five, or half-past-five in summer, and not much later in the dark seasons, we were compelled to rise, having been perhaps not above four hours in bed— (for we were no go-to-beds with the lamb, though we anticipated the lark ofttimes in her rising—we liked a parting cup at midnight, as all young men did before these effeminate times, and to have our friends about us—we were not constellated under Aquarius, that watery sign, and therefore incapable of Bacchus, cold, washy, bloodless—we were none of your Basilian water-sponges, nor had taken our degrees at Mount Ague—we were right toping Capulets, jolly companions, we and they)—but to have to get up, as we said before, curtailed of half our fair sleep, fasting, with only a dim vista of refreshing Bohea in the distance—to be necessitated to rouse ourselves at the destestable rap of an old hag of a domestic, who seemed to take a diabolical pleasure in her announcement that it was " time to rise ; " and whose chappy knuckles we have often yearned to amputate, and string them up at our chamber door, to be a terror to all such unseasonable rest-breakers in future—

" Facil " and sweet, as Virgil sings, had been the " descending " of the over-night, balmy the first sinking of the heavy head upon the pillow ; but to get up, as he goes on to say,

—revocare gradus, superasque evadere ad auras—

and to get up moreover to make jokes with malice prepended— there was the " labour," there the " work."

No Egyptian taskmaster ever devised a slavery like to that, our slavery. No fractious operants ever turned out for half the tyranny, which this necessity exercised upon us. Half a dozen jests in a day (bating Sundays too), why, it seems nothing! We make twice the number every day in our lives as a matter of course, and claim no Sabbatical exemptions. But then they come into our head. But when the head has to go out to them—when the mountain must go to Mahomet—

Reader, try it for once, only for one short twelvemonth.

It was not every week that a fashion of pink stockings came up ; but mostly, instead of it, some rugged, untractable subject ; some topic impossible to be contorted into the risible ; some feature, upon which no smile could play ; some flint, from which no process of ingenuity could procure a distillation. There they lay ; there your appointed tale of brick-making was set before you, which you must finish, with or without straw, as it happened. The craving Dragon—*the Public*—like him in Bel's temple—must be fed ; it expected its daily rations ; and Daniel, and ourselves, to do us justice, did the best we could on this side bursting him.

While we were wringing our coy sprightlinesses for the Post, and writhing under the toil of what is called " easy writing," Bob Allen, our *quondam* schoolfellow, was tapping his impracticable brains in a like service for the " Oracle." Not that Robert troubled himself much about wit. If his paragraphs had a sprightly air about them, it was sufficient. He carried this nonchalance so far at last, that a matter of intelligence, and that no very important one, was not seldom palmed upon his employers for a good jest ; for example sake—" *Walking yesterday morning casually down Snow Hill, who should we meet but Mr. Deputy Humphreys ! we rejoice to add, that the worthy Deputy appeared to enjoy a good state of health. We do not remember ever to have seen him look better.*" This gentleman, so surprisingly met upon Snow Hill, from some peculiarities in gait or gesture, was a constant butt for mirth to the small paragraph-mongers of the day ; and our friend thought that he might have his fling at him with the rest. We met A. in Holborn shortly after this extraordinary rencounter, which he told with tears of satisfaction in his eyes, and chuckling at the anticipated effects of its announcement next day in the paper. We did not quite comprehend where the wit of it lay at the time ; nor was it easy to be detected, when the thing came out, advantaged by type and letter-press. He had better have met any thing that morning than a Common Council Man. His services were shortly after dispensed with, on the plea that his paragraphs of late had been deficient in point. The one in question, it must be owned, had an air, in the opening especially, proper to awaken curiosity ; and the sentiment, or moral, wears the aspect of humanity, and good neighbourly feeling. But somehow the conclusion was not judged altogether to answer to the magnificent promise of the premises. We traced our friend's pen afterwards in the "True Briton," the "Star," the "Traveller,"—from all which he was successively dismissed, the Proprietors having "no further occasion for his services." Nothing was easier than to detect him. When wit failed, or topics ran low, there constantly appeared the following—"*It is not generally known that the three Blue Balls at the Pawnbrokers' shops are the ancient arms of Lombardy. The Lombards were the first money-brokers in Europe.*" Bob has done more to set the public right on this important point of blazonry, than the whole College of Heralds.

The appointment of a regular wit has long ceased to be a part of the economy of a Morning Paper. Editors find their own jokes, or do as well without them. Parson Este, and Topham, brought up the set custom of "witty paragraphs," first in the "World." Boaden was a reigning paragraphist in his day, and succeeded poor Allen in the Oracle. But, as we said, the fashion of jokes passes away; and it would be difficult to discover in the Biographer of Mrs. Siddons, any traces of that vivacity and fancy which charmed the whole town at the commencement of the present century. Even the prelusive delicacies of the present writer—the curt "Astræan allusion"—would be thought pedantic, and out of date, in these days.

From the office of the Morning Post (for we may as well exhaust our Newspaper Reminiscences at once) by change of property in the paper, we were transferred, mortifying exchange! to the office of the Albion Newspaper, late Rackstrow's Museum, in Fleet-street. What a transition—from a handsome apartment, from rose-wood desks, and silver-inkstands, to an office — no office, but a *den* rather, but just redeemed from the occupation of dead monsters, of which it seemed redolent—from the centre of loyalty and fashion, to a focus of vulgarity and sedition! Here in murky closet, inadequate from its square contents to the receipt of the two bodies of Editor, and humble paragraph-maker, together at one time, sat in the discharge of his new Editorial functions (the "Bigod" of Elia) the redoubted John Fenwick.

F., without a guinea in his pocket, and having left not many in the pockets of his friends whom he might command, had purchased (on tick doubtless) the whole and sole Editorship, Proprietorship, with all the rights and titles (such as they were worth) of the Albion, from one Lovell; of whom we know nothing, save that he had stood in the pillory for a libel on the Prince of Wales. With this hopeless concern—for it had been sinking ever since its commencement, and could now reckon upon not more than a hundred subscribers—F. resolutely determined upon pulling down the Government in the first instance, and making both our fortunes by way of corollary.   For seven weeks and more did this infatuated Democrat go about borrowing seven shilling pieces, and lesser coin, to meet the daily demands of the Stamp Office, which allowed no credit to publications of that side in politics.   An outcast from politer bread, we attached our small talents to the forlorn fortunes of our friend.   Our occupation now was to write treason.

Recollections of feelings—which were all that now remained from our first boyish heats kindled by the French Revolution, when if we were misled, we erred in the company of some, who are accounted very good men now—rather than any tendency at this time to Republican doctrines—assisted us in assuming a style of writing, while the paper lasted, consonant in no very under-tone to the right earnest fanaticism of F.   Our cue was now to insinuate, rather than recommend, possible abdications.   Blocks, axes, White-hall tribunals, were covered with flowers of so cunning a periphrasis —as Mr. Bayes says, never naming the *thing* directly—that the keen eye of an Attorney General was insufficient to detect the lurking snake among them.   There were times, indeed, when we sighed for our more gentleman-like occupation under Stuart.   But with change of masters it is ever change of service.   Already one paragraph, and another, as we learned afterwards from a gentleman at the Treasury, had begun to be marked at that office, with a view of its being submitted at least to the attention of the proper Law Officers—when an unlucky, or rather lucky epigram from our pen, aimed at Sir J——s M——h, who was on the eve of departing for India to reap the fruits of his apostacy, as F. pronounced it, (it is hardly worth particularising), happening to offend the nice sense of Lord, or, as he then delighted to be called, Citizen Stanhope, deprived F. at once of the last hopes of a guinea from the last patron that had stuck by us; and breaking up our establishment, left us to the safe, but somewhat mortifying, neglect of the Crown Lawyers.—It was about this time, or a little earlier, that Dan. Stuart made that curious confession to us, that he had "never deliberately walked into an Exhibition at Somerset House in his life."

BARRENNESS OF THE IMAGINATIVE FACULTY IN
THE PRODUCTIONS OF MODERN ART

HOGARTH excepted, can we produce any one painter within the last fifty years, or since the humour of exhibiting began, that has treated a story *imaginatively* ? By this we mean, upon whom his subject has so acted, that it has seemed to direct *him*— not to be arranged by him ? Any upon whom its leading or collateral points have impressed themselves so tyrannically, that he dared not treat it otherwise, lest he should falsify a revelation ? Any that has imparted to his compositions, not merely so much truth as is enough to convey a story with clearness, but that individualising property, which should keep the subject so treated distinct in feature from every other subject, however similar, and to common apprehensions almost identical; so as that we might say, this and this part could have found an appropriate place in no other picture in the world but this ? Is there anything in modern art—we will not demand that it should be equal—but in any way analogous to what Titian has effected, in that wonderful bringing together of two times in the " Ariadne," in the National Gallery ? Precipitous, with his reeling Satyr rout about him, re-peopling and re-illuming suddenly the waste places, drunk with a new fury beyond the grape, Bacchus, born in fire, fire-like flings himself at the Cretan. This is the time present. With this telling of the story an artist, and no ordinary one, might remain richly proud. Guido, in his harmonious version of it, saw no further. But from the depths of the imaginative spirit Titian has recalled past time, and laid it contributory with the present to one simultaneous effect. With the desert all ringing with the mad cymbals of his followers, made lucid with the presence and new offers of a god,— as if unconscious of Bacchus, or but idly casting her eyes as upon some unconcerning pageant—her soul undistracted from Theseus— Ariadne is still pacing the solitary shore, in as much heart-silence, and in almost the same local solitude, with which she awoke at day-break to catch the forlorn last glances of the sail that bore away the Athenian.

Here are two points miraculously co-uniting ; fierce society, with the feeling of solitude still absolute ; noon-day revelations, with the accidents of the dull grey dawn unquenched and lingering; the *present* Bacchus, with the *past* Ariadne ; two stories, with double Time ; separate, and harmonising. Had the artist made the woman one shade less indifferent to the God; still more, had she expressed a rapture at his advent, where would have been the story of the mighty desolation of the heart previous ? merged in

the insipid accident of a flattering offer met with a welcome acceptance. The broken heart for Theseus was not lightly to be pieced
up by a God.

We have before us a fine rough print, from a picture by Raphael
in the Vatican. It is the Presentation of the new-born Eve to
Adam by the Almighty. A fairer mother of mankind we might
imagine, and a goodlier sire perhaps of men since born. But
these are matters subordinate to the conception of the *situation*, displayed in this extraordinary production. A tolerably
modern artist would have been satisfied with tempering certain
raptures of connubial anticipation, with a suitable acknowledgment
to the Giver of the blessing, in the countenance of the first bridegroom ; something like the divided attention of the child (Adam
was here a child man) between the given toy, and the mother who
had just blest it with the bauble. This is the obvious, the first-
sight view, the superficial. An artist of a higher grade, considering
the awful presence they were in, would have taken care to subtract
something from the expression of the more human passion, and to
heighten the more spiritual one. This would be as much as an
exhibition-goer, from the opening of Somerset House to last
year's show, has been encouraged to look for. It is obvious to
hint at a lower expression, yet in a picture, that for respects of
drawing and colouring, might be deemed not wholly inadmissible
within these art-fostering walls, in which the raptures should be as
ninety-nine, the gratitude as one, or perhaps Zero ! By neither the
one passion nor the other has Raphael expounded the situation of
Adam. Singly upon his brow sits the absorbing sense of wonder
at the created miracle. The *moment* is seized by the intuitive
artist, perhaps not self-conscious of his art, in which neither of
the conflicting emotions—a moment how abstracted—have had
time to spring up, or to battle for indecorous mastery.—We have
seen a landscape of a justly admired neoteric, in which he aimed at
delineating a fiction, one of the most severely beautiful in antiquity
—the gardens of the Hesperides. To do Mr. —— justice, he had
painted a laudable orchard, with fitting seclusion, and a veritable
dragon (of which a Polypheme by Poussin is somehow a fac-simile
for the situation), looking over into the world shut out backwards,
so that none but a " still-climbing Hercules " could hope to catch
a peep at the admired Ternary of Recluses. No conventional porter
could keep his keys better than this custos with the " lidless eyes."
He not only sees that none *do* intrude into that privacy, but, as
clear as daylight, that none but *Hercules aut Diabolus* by any
manner of means *can*. So far all is well. We have absolute
solitude here or nowhere. *Ab extra* the damsels are snug enough.
But here the artist's courage seems to have failed him. He began

to pity his pretty charge, and, to comfort the irksomeness, has
peopled their solitude with a bevy of fair attendants, maids of
honour, or ladies of the bed-chamber, according to the approved
etiquette at a court of the nineteenth century; giving to the whole
scene the air of a *fête champêtre*, if we will but excuse the absence
of the gentlemen. This is well, and Watteauish. But what is become of the solitary mystery—the

> Daughters three,
> That sing around the golden tree?

This is not the way in which Poussin would have treated this
subject.

The paintings, or rather the stupendous architectural designs, of
a modern artist, have been urged as objections to the theory of our
motto. They are of a character, we confess, to stagger it. His
towered structures are of the highest order of the material sublime. Whether they were dreams, or transcripts of some elder
workmanship—Assyrian ruins old—restored by this mighty artist, they satisfy our most stretched and craving conceptions of
the glories of the antique world. It is a pity that they were
ever peopled. On that side, the imagination of the artist halts,
and appears defective. Let us examine the point of the story
in the "Belshazzar's Feast." We will introduce it by an apposite
anecdote.

The court historians of the day record, that at the first dinner
given by the late King (then Prince Regent) at the Pavilion, the
following characteristic frolic was played off. The guests were
select and admiring; the banquet profuse and admirable; the
lights lustrous and oriental; the eye was perfectly dazzled with
the display of plate, among which the great gold salt-cellar,
brought from the regalia in the Tower for this especial purpose,
itself a tower! stood conspicuous for its magnitude. And now
the Rev. * * * * the then admired court Chaplain, was proceeding with the grace, when, at a signal given, the lights were suddenly
overcast, and a huge transparency was discovered, in which glittered
in golden letters—

> " BRIGHTON—EARTHQUAKE—SWALLOW-UP-ALIVE!"

Imagine the confusion of the guests; the Georges and garters,
jewels, bracelets, moulted upon the occasion! The fans dropt, and
picked up the next morning by the sly court pages! Mrs. Fitz-
what's-her-name fainting, and the Countess of * * * * holding the
smelling bottle, till the good-humoured Prince caused harmony to
be restored by calling in fresh candles, and declaring that the
whole was nothing but a pantomime *hoax*, got up by the ingenious

Mr. Farley, of Covent Garden, from hints which his Royal High-ness himself had furnished! Then imagine the infinite applause that followed, the mutual rallyings, the declarations that "they were not much frightened," of the assembled galaxy.

The point of time in the picture exactly answers to the appear-ance of the transparency in the anecdote. The huddle, the flutter, the bustle, the escape, the alarm, and the mock alarm; the pretti-nesses heightened by consternation; the courtier's fear which was flattery, and the lady's which was affectation; all that we may conceive to have taken place in a mob of Brighton courtiers, sympathising with the well-acted surprise of their sovereign; all this, and no more, is exhibited by the well-dressed lords and ladies in the Hall of Belus. Just this sort of consternation we have seen among a flock of disquieted wild geese at the report only of a gun having gone off!

But is this vulgar fright, this mere animal anxiety for the pre-servation of their persons,—such as we have witnessed at a theatre, when a slight alarm of fire has been given—an adequate exponent of a supernatural terror? the way in which the finger of God, writing judgments, would have been met by the withered con-science? There is a human fear, and a divine fear. The one is disturbed, restless, and bent upon escape. The other is bowed down, effortless, passive. When the spirit appeared before Eliphaz in the visions of the night, and the hair of his flesh stood up, was it in the thoughts of the Temanite to ring the bell of his chamber, or to call up the servants? But let us see in the text what there is to justify all this huddle of vulgar consternation.

From the words of Daniel it appears that Belshazzar had made a great feast to a thousand of his lords, and drank wine before the thousand. The golden and silver vessels are gorgeously enumerated, with the princes, the king's concubines, and his wives. Then follows—

"In the same hour came forth fingers of a man's hand, and wrote over against the candlestick upon the plaster of the wall of the king's palace; and the *king* saw the part of the hand that wrote. Then the *king's* countenance was changed, and his thoughts troubled him, so that the joints of his loins were loosened, and his knees smote one against another."

This is the plain text. By no hint can it be otherwise inferred, but that the appearance was solely confined to the fancy of Bel-shazzar, that his single brain was troubled. Not a word is spoken of its being seen by any else there present, not even by the queen herself, who merely undertakes for the interpretation of the phe-nomenon, as related to her, doubtless, by her husband. The lords are simply said to be astonished; *i.e.* at the trouble and the

change of countenance in their sovereign. Even the prophet does
not appear to have seen the scroll, which the king saw. He recals
it only, as Joseph did the Dream to the King of Egypt. "Then
was the part of the hand sent from him [the Lord], and this
writing was written." He speaks of the phantasm as past.

Then what becomes of this needless multiplication of the miracle?
this message to a royal conscience, singly expressed—for it was
said, "thy kingdom is divided,"—simultaneously impressed upon
the fancies of a thousand courtiers, who were implied in it neither
directly nor grammatically?

But admitting the artist's own version of the story, and that the
sight was seen also by the thousand courtiers—let it have been
visible to all Babylon—as the knees of Belshazzar were shaken, and
his countenance troubled, even so would the knees of every man in
Babylon, and their countenances, as of an individual man, been
troubled; bowed, bent down, so would they have remained, stupor-
fixed, with no thought of struggling with that inevitable judgment.

Not all that is optically possible to be seen, is to be shown in
every picture. The eye delightedly dwells upon the brilliant
individualities in a " Marriage at Cana," by Veronese, or Titian, to
the very texture and colour of the wedding garments, the ring
glittering upon the bride's fingers, the metal and fashion of the
wine pots; for at such seasons there is leisure and luxury to be
curious. But in a "day of judgment," or in a "day of lesser
horrors, yet divine," as at the impious feast of Belshazzar, the
eye should see, as the actual eye of an agent or patient in the
immediate scene would see, only in masses and indistinction. Not
only the female attire and jewelry exposed to the critical eye of
the fashion, as minutely as the dresses in a lady's magazine, in the
criticised picture,—but perhaps the curiosities of anatomical science,
and studied diversities of posture in the falling angels and sinners
of Michael Angelo,—have no business in their great subjects.
There was no leisure of them.

By a wise falsification, the great masters of painting got at their
true conclusions ; by not showing the actual appearances, that is,
all that was to be seen at any given moment by an indifferent eye,
but only what the eye might be supposed to see in the doing or
suffering of some portentous action. Suppose the moment of the
swallowing up of Pompeii. There they were to be seen—houses,
columns, architectural proportions, differences of public and private
buildings, men and women at their standing occupations, the diver-
sified thousand postures, attitudes, dresses, in some confusion truly,
but physically they were visible. But what eye saw them at that
eclipsing moment, which reduces confusion to a kind of unity, and
when the senses are upturned from their proprieties, when sight

and hearing are a feeling only ? A thousand years have passed, and we are at leisure to contemplate the weaver fixed standing at his shuttle, the baker at his oven, and to turn over with antiquarian coolness the pots and pans of Pompeii.

" Sun, stand thou still upon Gibeah, and thou, Moon, in the valley of Ajalon." Who, in reading this magnificent Hebraism, in his conception, sees aught but the heroic son of Nun, with the out-stretched arm, and the greater and lesser light obsequious ? Doubtless there were to be seen hill and dale, and chariots and horsemen, on open plain, or winding by secret defiles, and all the circumstances and stratagems of war. But whose eyes would have been conscious of this array at the interposition of the synchronic miracle ? Yet in the picture of this subject by the artist of the "Belshazzar's Feast"—no ignoble work either—the marshalling and landscape of the war is everything, the miracle sinks into an anecdote of the day ; and the eye may " dart through rank and file traverse " for some minutes, before it shall discover, among his armed followers, *which is Joshua !* Not modern art alone, but ancient, where only it is to be found if anywhere, can be detected erring, from defect of this imaginative faculty. The world has nothing to show of the preternatural in painting, transcending the figure of Lazarus bursting his grave-clothes, in the great picture at Angerstein's. It seems a thing between two beings. A ghastly horror at itself struggles with newly-apprehending gratitude at second life bestowed. It cannot forget that it was a ghost. It has hardly felt that it is a body. It has to tell of the world of spirits.—Was it from a feeling, that the crowd of half-impassioned by-standers, and the still more irrelevant herd of passers-by at a distance, who have not heard or but faintly have been told of the passing miracle, admirable as they are in design and hue—for it is a glorified work—do not respond adequately to the action—that the single figure of the Lazarus has been attributed to Michael Angelo, and the mighty Sebastian unfairly robbed of the fame of the greater half of the interest ? Now that there were not indifferent passers-by within actual scope of the eyes of those present at the miracle, to whom the sound of it had but faintly, or not at all, reached, it would be hardihood to deny ; but would they see them ? or can the mind in the conception of it admit of such unconcerning objects ? can it think of them at all ? or what associating league to the imagination can there be between the seers, and the seers not, of a presential miracle ?

Were an artist to paint upon demand a picture of a Dryad, we will ask whether, in the present low state of expectation, the patron would not, or ought not to be fully satisfied with a beautiful naked figure recumbent under wide-stretched oaks? Disseat those woods, and place the same figure among fountains, and falls of pellucid water, and you have a—Naiad! Not so in a rough print we have seen after Julio Romano, we think—for it is long since—*there*, by no process, with mere change of scene, could the figure have reciprocated characters. Long, grotesque, fantastic, yet with a grace of her own, beautiful in convolution and distortion, linked to her connatural tree, co-twisting with its limbs her own, till both seemed either—these, animated branches; those, disanimated members—yet the animal and vegetable lives sufficiently kept distinct—*his* Dryad lay—an approximation of two natures, which to conceive, it must be seen; analogous to, not the same with, the delicacies of Ovidian transformations.

To the lowest subjects, and, to a superficial comprehension, the most barren, the Great Masters gave loftiness and fruitfulness. The large eye of genius saw in the meanness of present objects their capabilities of treatment from their relations to some grand Past or Future. How has Raphael—we must still linger about the Vatican—treated the humble craft of the ship-builder, in *his* " Building of the Ark? " It is in that scriptural series, to which we have referred, and which, judging from some fine rough old graphic sketches of them which we possess, seem to be of a higher and more poetic grade than even the Cartoons. The dim of sight are the timid and the shrinking. There is a cowardice in modern art. As the Frenchmen, of whom Coleridge's friend made the prophetic guess at Rome, from the beard and horns of the Moses of Michael Angelo collected no inferences beyond that of a He Goat and a Cornuto; so from this subject, of mere mechanic promise, it would instinctively turn away, as from one incapable of investiture with any grandeur. The dock-yards at Woolwich would object derogatory associations. The depôt at Chatham would be the mote and the beam in its intellectual eye. But not to the nautical preparations in the ship-yards of Civita Vecchia did Raphael look for instructions, when he imagined the Building of the Vessel that was to be conservatory of the wrecks of the species of drowned mankind. In the intensity of the action, he keeps ever out of sight the meanness of the operation. There is the Patriarch, in calm forethought, and with holy prescience, giving directions. And there are his agents—the solitary but sufficient Three— hewing, sawing, every one with the might and earnestness of a Demiurgus; under some instinctive rather than technical guidance; giant-muscled; every one a Hercules, or liker to those Vulcanian Three, that in sounding caverns under Mongibello wrought in fire—Brontes, and black Steropes, and Pyracmon. So work the workmen that should repair a world!

Artists again err in the confounding of *poetic* with *pictorial subjects*. In the latter, the exterior accidents are nearly everything, the unseen qualities as nothing. Othello's colour—the infirmities and corpulence of a Sir John Falstaff—do they haunt us perpetually in the reading? or are they obtruded upon our conceptions one time for ninety-nine that we are lost in admiration at the respective moral or intellectual attributes of the character? But in a picture Othello is *always* a Blackamoor; and the other only Plump Jack. Deeply corporealised, and enchained hopelessly in the grovelling fetters of externality, must be the mind, to which, in its better moments, the image of the high-souled, high-intelligenced Quixote—the errant Star of Knighthood, made more tender by eclipse—has never presented itself, divested from the unhallowed accompaniment of a Sancho, or a rabblement at the heels of Rosinante. That man has read his book by halves; he has laughed, mistaking his author's purport, which was—tears. The artist that pictures Quixote (and it is in this degrading point that he is every season held up at our Exhibitions) in the shallow hope of exciting mirth, would have joined the rabble at the heels of his starved steed. We wish not to see *that* counterfeited, which we would not have wished to see in the reality. Conscious of the heroic inside of the noble Quixote, who, on hearing that his withered person was passing, would have stepped over his threshold to gaze upon his forlorn habiliments, and the " strange bed-fellows which misery brings a man acquainted with?" Shade of Cervantes! who in thy Second Part could put into the mouth of thy Quixote those high aspirations of a super-chivalrous gallantry, where he replies to one of the shepherdesses, apprehensive that he would spoil their pretty net-works, and inviting him to be a guest with them, in accents like these: " Truly, fairest Lady, Actæon was not more astonished when he saw Diana bathing herself at the fountain, than I have been in beholding your beauty: I commend the manner of your pastime, and thank you for your kind offers; and, if I may serve you, so I may be sure you will be obeyed, you may command me: for my profession is this, To shew myself thankful, and a doer of good to all sorts of people, especially of the rank that your person shows you to be; and if those nets, as they take up but a little piece of ground, should take up the whole world, I would seek out new worlds to pass through, rather than break them: and (he adds,) that you may give credit to this my exaggeration, behold at least he that promiseth you this, is Don Quixote de la Mancha, if haply this name hath come to your hearing." Illustrious Romancer! were the " fine frenzies," which possessed the brain of thy own Quixote, a fit subject, as in this Second Part, to be exposed to the jeers of Duennas and Serving

Men ? to be monstered, and shown up at the heartless banquets of great men ? Was that pitiable infirmity, which in thy First Part misleads him, *always from within*, into half-ludicrous, but more than half-compassionable and admirable errors, not infliction enough from heaven, that men by studied artifices must devise and practise upon the humour, to inflame where they should soothe it ? Why, Goneril would have blushed to practise upon the abdicated king at this rate, and the she-wolf Regan not have endured to play the pranks upon his fled wits, which thou hast made thy Quixote suffer in Duchesses' halls, and at the hands of that unworthy noble-man.[1]

In the First Adventures, even, it needed all the art of the most consummate artist in the Book way that the world hath yet seen, to keep up in the mind of the reader the heroic attributes of the character without relaxing ; so as absolutely that they shall suffer no alloy from the debasing fellowship of the clown. If it ever obtrudes itself as a disharmony, are we inclined to laugh ; or not, rather, to indulge a contrary emotion ?—Cervantes, stung, per-chance, by the relish with which *his* Reading Public had received the fooleries of the man, more to their palates than the generosities of the master, in the sequel let his pen run riot, lost the harmony and the balance, and sacrificed a great idea to the taste of his contemporaries. We know that in the present day the Knight has fewer admirers than the Squire. Anticipating, what did actually happen to him—as afterwards it did to his scarce inferior follower, the Author of " Guzman de Alfarache "—that some less knowing hand would prevent him by a spurious Second Part : and judging, that it would be easier for his competitor to out-bid him in the comicalities, than in the *romance*, of his work, he abandoned his Knight, and has fairly set up the Squire for his Hero. For what else has he unsealed the eyes of Sancho ; and instead of that twilight state of semi-insanity—the madness at second-hand—the contagion, caught from a stronger mind infected—that war between native cunning, and hereditary deference, with which he has hitherto accompanied his master—two for a pair almost—does he substitute a downright Knave, with open eyes, for his own ends only following a confessed Madman ; and offering at one time to lay, if not actually laying, hands upon him ! From the moment that Sancho loses his reverence, Don Quixote is become a—treatable lunatic. Our artists handle him accordingly.

[1] Yet from this Second Part, our cried-up pictures are mostly selected ; the waiting-women with beards, &c.

REJOICINGS UPON THE NEW YEAR'S COMING
OF AGE

THE *Old Year* being dead, and the *New Year* coming of age,
which he does, by Calendar Law, as soon as the breath is
out of the old gentleman's body, nothing would serve the young
spark but he must give a dinner upon the occasion, to which all the
Days in the year were invited.   The *Festivals*, whom he deputed
as his stewards, were mightily taken with the notion.   They had
been engaged time out of mind, they said, in providing mirth and
good cheer for mortals below ; and it was time they should have a
taste of their own bounty.   It was stiffly debated among them,
whether the *Fasts* should be admitted.   Some said, the appearance of such lean, starved guests, with their mortified faces, would
pervert the ends of the meeting.   But the objection was over-
ruled by *Christmas Day*, who had a design upon *Ash Wednesday*
(as you shall hear), and a mighty desire to see how the old Domine
would behave himself in his cups.   Only the *Vigils* were requested
to come with their lanterns, to light the gentlefolks home at night.
    All the *Days* came to their day.   Covers were provided for
three hundred and sixty-five guests at the principal table ; with an
occasional knife and fork at the side-board for the *Twenty-Ninth
of February*.
    I should have told you, that cards of invitation had been issued.
The carriers were the *Hours* ; twelve little, merry, whirligig foot-
pages, as you should desire to see, that went all round, and found out
the persons invited well enough, with the exception of *Easter Day*,
Shrove Tuesday, and a few such *Moveables*, who had lately
shifted their quarters.
    Well, they all met at last, foul *Days*, fine *Days*, all sorts of
Days, and a rare din they made of it.   There was nothing but,
Hail ! fellow *Day*,—well met—brother *Day*—sister *Day*,—only
Lady Day kept a little on the aloof, and seemed somewhat scornful.   Yet some said, *Twelfth Day* cut her out and out, for she
came in a tiffany suit, white and gold, like a queen on a frost-cake,
all royal, glittering, and *Epiphanous*.   The rest came, some in
green, some in white—but old *Lent and his family* were not yet
out of mourning.   Rainy *Days* came in, dripping ; and sun-shiny
Days helped them to change their stockings.   *Wedding Day* was
there in his marriage finery, a little the worse for wear.   *Pay Day*
came late, as he always does ; and *Doomsday* sent word—he
might be expected.
    April Fool (as my young lord's jester) took upon himself to
marshal the guests, and wild work he made with it.   It would

have posed old Erra Pater to have found out any given *Day* in
the year, to erect a scheme upon—good *Days*, bad *Days*, were so
shuffled together, to the confounding of all sober horoscopy.

He had stuck the *Twenty First of June* next to the *Twenty
Second of December*, and the former looked like a Maypole siding
a marrow-bone. *Ash Wednesday* got wedged in (as was con-
certed) betwixt *Christmas* and *Lord Mayor's Days*. Lord!
how he laid about him! Nothing but barons of beef and turkeys
would go down with him—to the great greasing and detriment
of his new sackcloth bib and tucker. And still *Christmas Day*
was at his elbow, plying him the wassail-bowl, till he roared, and
hiccup'd, and protested there was no faith in dried ling, but commended it to the devil for a sour, windy, acrimonious, censorious,
hy-po-crit-crit-cri-tical mess, and no dish for a gentleman. Then
he dipt his fist into the middle of the great custard that stood
before his *left-hand neighbour*, and daubed his hungry beard all
over with it, till you would have taken him for the *Last Day in
December*, it so hung in icicles.

At another part of the table, *Shrove Tuesday* was helping the
Second of September to some cock broth,—which courtesy the
latter returned with the delicate thigh of a hen pheasant—so there
was no love lost for that matter. The *Last of Lent* was spunging
upon *Shrovetide's* pancakes ; which *April Fool* perceiving, told
him he did well, for pancakes were proper to a *good fry-day*.

In another part, a hubbub arose about the *Thirtieth of January*,
who, it seems, being a sour puritanic character, that thought
nobody's meat good or sanctified enough for him, had smuggled
into the room a calf's head, which he had had cooked at home for
that purpose, thinking to feast thereon incontinently ; but as it
lay in the dish, *March manyweathers*, who is a very fine lady, and
subject to the megrims, screamed out there was a " human head in
the platter," and raved about Herodias' daughter to that degree,
that the obnoxious viand was obliged to be removed ; nor did she
recover her stomach till she had gulped down a *Restorative*, con-
fected of *Oak Apple*, which the merry *Twenty Ninth of May*
always carries about with him for that purpose.

The King's health [1] being called for after this, a notable dispute arose between the *Twelfth of August* (a zealous old Whig
gentlewoman,) and the *Twenty Third of April* (a new-fangled
lady of the Tory stamp,) as to which of them should have the
honour to propose it. *August* grew hot upon the matter, affirming time out of mind the prescriptive right to have lain with her,
till her rival had basely supplanted her ; whom she represented as

---

[1] The late King.

little better than a *kept* mistress, who went about in *fine clothes*, while she (the legitimate BIRTHDAY) had scarcely a rag, &c.

April Fool, being made mediator, confirmed the right in the strongest form of words to the appellant, but decided for peace' sake that the exercise of it should remain with the present possessor. At the same time, he slily rounded the first lady in the ear, that an action might lie against the Crown for *bi-geny*.

It beginning to grow a little duskish, *Candlemas* lustily bawled out for lights, which was opposed by all the *Days*, who protested against burning daylight. Then fair water was handed round in silver ewers, and the *same lady* was observed to take an unusual time in *Washing* herself.

May Day, with that sweetness which is peculiar to her, in a neat speech proposing the health of the founder, crowned her goblet (and by her example the rest of the company) with garlands. This being done, the lordly *New Year* from the upper end of the table, in a cordial but somewhat lofty tone, returned thanks. He felt proud on an occasion of meeting so many of his worthy father's late tenants, promised to improve their farms, and at the same time to abate (if any thing was found unreasonable) in their rents.

At the mention of this, the four *Quarter Days* involuntarily looked at each other, and smiled ; *April Fool* whistled to an old tune of " New Brooms ; " and a surly old rebel at the farther end of the table (who was discovered to be no other than the *Fifth of November*,) muttered out, distinctly enough to be heard by the whole company, words to this effect, that, " when the old one is gone, he is a fool that looks for a better." Which rudeness of his, the guests resenting, unanimously voted his expulsion ; and the male-content was thrust out neck and heels into the cellar, as the properest place for such a *boutefeu* and firebrand as he had shown himself to be.

Order being restored—the young lord (who to say truth, had been a little ruffled, and put beside his oratory) in as few, and yet as obliging words as possible, assured them of entire welcome ; and, with a graceful turn, singling out poor *Twenty Ninth of February*, that had sate all this while mumchance at the side-board, begged to couple his health with that of the good company, before him— which he drank accordingly ; observing, that he had not seen his honest face any time these four years, with a number of endearing expressions besides. At the same time, removing the solitary *Day* from the forlorn seat which had been assigned him, he stationed him at his own board, somewhere between the *Greek Calends* and *Latter Lammas*.

Ash Wednesday, being now called upon for a song, with his eyes fast stuck in his head, and as well as the Canary he had swallowed would give him leave, struck up a Carol, which *Christmas Day* had taught him for the nonce; and was followed by the latter, who gave " Miserere " in fine style, hitting off the mumping notes and lengthened drawl of *Old Mortification* with infinite humour. *April Fool* swore they had exchanged conditions : but *Good Friday* was observed to look extremely grave; and *Sunday* held her fan before her face, that she might not be seen to smile.

Shrove-tide, Lord Mayor's Day, and *April Fool*, next joined in a glee—

Which is the properest day to drink ?

in which all the *Days* chiming in, made a merry burden.

They next fell to quibbles and conundrums. The question being proposed, who had the greatest number of followers—the *Quarter Days* said, there could be no question as to that ; for they had all the creditors in the world dogging their heels. But *April Fool* gave it in favour of the *Forty Days before Easter ;* because the debtors in all cases outnumbered the creditors, and they kept *lent* all the year.

All this while, *Valentine's Day* kept courting pretty *May*, who sate next him, slipping amorous *billets-doux* under the table, till the *Dog Days* (who are naturally of a warm constitution) began to be jealous, and to bark and rage exceedingly. *April Fool*, who likes a bit of sport above measure, and had some pretensions to the lady besides, as being but a cousin once removed,—clapped and halloo'd them on ; and as fast as their indignation cooled, those mad wags, the *Ember Days*, were at it with their bellows, to blow it into a flame ; and all was in a ferment : till old Madam *Septuagesima* (who boasts herself the *Mother of the Days*) wisely diverted the conversation with a tedious tale of the lovers which she could reckon when she was young ; and of one Master *Rogation Day* in particular, who was for ever putting the *question* to her ; but she kept him at a distance, as the chronicle would tell—by which I apprehend she meant the Almanack. Then she rambled on to the *Days that were gone*, the *good old Days*, and so to the *Days before the Flood*—which plainly showed her old head to be little better than crazed and doited.

Day being ended, the *Days* called for their cloaks and great coats, and took their leaves. *Lord Mayor's Day* went off in a Mist, as usual ; *Shortest Day* in a deep black Fog, that wrapt the little gentleman all round like a hedge-hog. Two *Vigils*—so watchmen are called in heaven—saw *Christmas Day* safe home— they had been used to the business before. Another *Vigil*—a stout, sturdy patrole, called the *Eve of St. Christopher*—seeing *Ash Wednesday* in a condition little better than he should be—

e'en whipt him over his shoulders, pick-a-back fashion, and *Old Mortification* went floating home, singing—

On the bat's back do I fly,

and a number of old snatches besides, between drunk and sober, but very few Aves or Penitentiaries (you may believe me) were among them. *Longest Day* set off westward in beautiful crimson and gold—the rest, some in one fashion, some in another; but *Valentine* and pretty *May* took their departure together in one of the prettiest silvery twilights a Lover's Day could wish to set in.

THE WEDDING

I DO not know when I have been better pleased than at being invited last week to be present at the wedding of a friend's daughter. I like to make one at these ceremonies, which to us old people give back our youth in a manner, and restore our gayest season, in the remembrance of our own success, or the regrets, scarcely less tender, of our own youthful disappointments, in this point of a settlement. On these occasions I am sure to be in good-humour for a week or two after, and enjoy a reflected honey-moon. Being without a family, I am flattered with these temporary adoptions into a friend's family; I feel a sort of cousin-hood, or uncleship, for the season; I am inducted into degrees of affinity; and, in the participated socialities of the little community, I lay down for a brief while my solitary bachelorship. I carry this humour so far, that I take it unkindly to be left out, even when a funeral is going on in the house of a dear friend. But to my subject.——

The union itself had been long settled, but its celebration had been hitherto deferred, to an almost unreasonable state of suspense in the lovers, by some invincible prejudices which the bride's father had unhappily contracted upon the subject of the too early marriages of females. He has been lecturing any time these five years —for to that length the courtship has been protracted—upon the propriety of putting off the solemnity, till the lady should have completed her five and twentieth year. We all began to be afraid that a suit, which as yet had abated of none of its ardours, might at last be lingered on, till passion had time to cool, and love go out in the experiment. But a little wheedling on the part of his wife, who was by no means a party to these overstrained notions, joined to some serious expostulations on that of his friends, who, from the growing infirmities of the old gentleman, could not promise ourselves many years enjoyment of his company, and were anxious to bring matters to a conclusion during his life-time, at length prevailed; and on Monday last the daughter of my old friend, Admiral —— having attained the *womanly* age of nine-teen, was conducted to the church by her pleasant cousin J——, who told some few years older.

Before the youthful part of my female readers express their indignation at the abominable loss of time occasioned to the lovers by the preposterous notions of my old friend, they will do well to consider the reluctance which a fond parent naturally feels at parting with his child.   To this unwillingness, I believe, in most cases may be traced the difference of opinion on this point between child and parent, whatever pretences of interest or prudence may be held out to cover it.   The hard-heartedness of fathers is a fine theme for romance writers, a sure and moving topic; but is there not something untender, to say no more of it, in the hurry which a beloved child is sometimes in to tear herself from the parental stock, and commit herself to strange graftings?   The case is heightened where the lady, as in the present instance, happens to be an only child.   I do not understand these matters experi-mentally, but I can make a shrewd guess at the wounded pride of a parent upon these occasions.   It is no new observation, I believe, that a lover in most cases has no rival so much to be feared as the father.   Certainly there is a jealousy in *unparallel subjects*, which is little less heart-rending than the passion which we more strictly christen by that name.   Mothers' scruples are more easily got over; for this reason, I suppose, that the protection transferred to a husband is less a derogation and a loss to their authority than to the paternal.   Mothers, besides, have a trembling fore-sight, which paints the inconveniences (impossible to be conceived in the same degree by the other parent) of a life of forlorn celibacy, which the refusal of a tolerable match may entail upon their child.   Mothers' instinct is a surer guide here, than the cold reasonings of a father on such a topic.   To this instinct may be imputed, and by it alone may be excused, the unbeseeming artifices, by which some wives push on the matrimonial projects of their daughters, which the husband, however approving, shall entertain with comparative indifference.   A little shamelessness on this head is pardonable. With this explanation, forwardness becomes a grace, and mater-nal importunity receives the name of a virtue.—But the parson stays, while I preposterously assume his office; I am preaching, while the bride is on the threshold.

Nor let any of my female readers suppose that the sage reflections which have just escaped me have the obliquest tendency of application to the young lady, who, it will be seen, is about to venture upon a change in her condition, at a *mature and competent age*, and not without the fullest approbation of all parties. I only deprecate *very hasty marriages*.

It had been fixed that the ceremony should be gone through at an early hour, to give time for a little *déjeuné* afterwards, to which a select party of friends had been invited. We were in church a little before the clock struck eight.

Nothing could be more judicious or graceful than the dress of the bride-maids—the three charming Miss Foresters—on this morning. To give the bride an opportunity of shining singly, they had come habited all in green. I am ill at describing female apparel ; but, while *she* stood at the altar in vestments white and candid as her thoughts, a sacrificial whiteness, *they* assisted in robes, such as might become Diana's nymphs—Foresters indeed —as such who had not yet come to the resolution of putting off cold virginity. These young maids, not being so blest as to have a mother living, I am told, keep single for their father's sake, and live altogether so happy with their remaining parent, that the hearts of their lovers are ever broken with the prospect (so inauspicious to their hopes) of such uninterrupted and provoking home-comfort. Gallant girls! each a victim worthy of Iphigenia!

I do not know what business I have to be present in solemn places. I cannot divest me of an unseasonable disposition to levity upon the most awful occasions. I was never cut out for a public functionary. Ceremony and I have long shaken hands ; but I could not resist the importunities of the young lady's father, whose gout unhappily confined him at home, to act as parent on this occasion, and *give away the bride*. Something ludicrous occurred to me at this most serious of all moments—a sense of my unfitness to have the disposal, even in imagination, of the sweet young creature beside me. I fear I was betrayed to some lightness, for the awful eye of the parson—and the rector's eye of Saint Mildred's in the Poultry is no trifle of a rebuke—was upon me in an instant, souring my incipient jest to the tristful severities of a funeral.

This was the only misbehaviour which I can plead to upon this solemn occasion, unless what was objected to me after the ceremony by one of the handsome Miss T——s, be accounted a solecism. She was pleased to say that she had never seen a gentleman before me give away a bride in black. Now black has been my ordinary apparel so long—indeed I take it to be the proper costume of an author—the stage sanctions it—that to have appeared in some lighter colour would have raised more mirth at my expense, than the anomaly had created censure. But I could perceive that the bride's mother, and some elderly ladies present (God bless them!) would have been well content, if I had come in any other colour than that. But I got over the omen by a lucky apologue, which I remembered out of Pilpay, or some Indian author, of all the birds being invited to the linnets' wedding, at which, when all the rest came in their gayest feathers, the raven alone apologised for his cloak because " he had no other." This tolerably reconciled the elders. But with the young people all was merriment, and shakings of hands, and congratulations, and kissing away the bride's tears, and kissings from her in return, till a young lady, who assumed some experience in these matters, having worn the nuptial bands some four or five weeks longer than her friend, rescued her, archly observing, with half an eye upon the bridegroom, that at this rate she would have " none left."

My friend the admiral was in fine wig and buckle on this occasion —a striking contrast to his usual neglect of personal appearance. He did not once shove up his borrowed locks (his custom ever at his morning studies) to betray the few grey stragglers of his own beneath them. He wore an aspect of thoughtful satisfaction. I trembled for the hour, which at length approached, when after a protracted *breakfast* of three hours—if stores of cold fowls, tongues, hams, botargoes, dried fruits, wines, cordials, &c., can deserve so meagre an appellation—the coach was announced, which was come to carry off the bride and bridegroom for a season, as custom has sensibly ordained, into the country ; upon which design, wishing them a felicitous journey, let us return to the assembled guests.

> As when a well-graced actor leaves the stage,
> The eyes of men
> Are idly bent on him that enters next,

so idly did we bend our eyes upon one another, when the chief performers in the morning's pageant had vanished. None told his tale. None sipt her glass. The poor Admiral made an effort— it was not much. I had anticipated so far. Even the infinity of full satisfaction, that had betrayed itself through the prim looks and quiet deportment of his lady, began to wane into something of misgiving. No one knew whether to take their leaves or stay. We seemed assembled upon a silly occasion. In this crisis, betwixt tarrying and departure, I must do justice to a foolish talent of mine, which had otherwise like to have brought me into disgrace in the fore-part of the day ; I mean a power, in any emergency, of thinking and giving vent to all manner of strange nonsense. In this awkward dilemma I found it sovereign. I rattled off some of my most excellent absurdities. All were willing to be relieved, at any expense of reason, from the pressure of the intolerable vacuum which had succeeded to the morning bustle. By this means I was fortunate in keeping together the better part of the company to a late hour : and a rubber of whist (the Admiral's favourite game) with some rare strokes of chance as well as skill, which came opportunely on his side—lengthened out till midnight—dismissed the old gentleman at last to his bed with comparatively easy spirits.

I have been at my old friend's various times since. I do not know a visiting place where every guest is so perfectly at his ease ; nowhere, where harmony is so strangely the result of confusion. Every body is at cross purposes, yet the effect is so much better than uniformity. Contradictory orders; servants pulling one way ; master and mistress driving some other, yet both diverse ; visitors huddled up in corners ; chairs unsymmetrised : candles disposed by chance ; meals at odd hours, tea and supper at once, or the latter preceding the former ; the host and the guest conferring, yet each upon a different topic, each understanding himself, neither trying to understand or hear the other ; draughts and politics, chess and political economy, cards and conversation on nautical matters, going on at once, without the hope, or indeed the wish, of distinguishing them, make it altogether the most perfect *concordia discors* you shall meet with. Yet somehow the old house is not quite what it should be. The Admiral still enjoys his pipe, but he has no Miss Emily to fill it for him. The instrument stands where it stood, but she is gone, whose delicate touch could sometimes for a short minute appease the warring elements. He has learnt, as Marvel expresses it, to "make his destiny his choice." He bears bravely up, but he does not come out with his flashes of wild wit so thick as formerly. His sea songs seldomer escape him. His wife, too, looks as if she wanted some younger body to scold and set to rights. We all miss a junior presence. It is wonderful how one young maiden freshens up, and keeps green, the paternal roof. Old and young seem to have an interest in her, so long as she is not absolutely disposed of. The youthfulness of the house is flown. Emily is married.

THE CHILD ANGEL

A DREAM

I CHANCED upon the prettiest, oddest, fantastical thing of a dream the other night, that you shall hear of. I had been reading the " Loves of the Angels," and went to bed with my head full of speculations, suggested by that extraordinary legend. It had given birth to innumerable conjectures ; and, I remember, the last waking thought, which I gave expression to on my pillow, was a sort of wonder, " what could come of it."

I was suddenly transported, how or whither I could scarcely make out—but to some celestial region. It was not the real heavens neither—not the downright Bible heaven—but a kind of fairyland heaven, about which a poor human fancy may have leave to sport and air itself, I will hope, without presumption.

Methought—what wild things dreams are !—I was present—at what would you imagine ?—at an angel's gossiping.

Whence it came, or how it came, or who bid it come, or whether it came purely of its own head, neither you nor I know—but there lay, sure enough, wrapped in its little cloudy swaddling bands—a Child Angel.

Sun-threads—filmy beams—ran through the celestial napery of what seemed its princely cradle. All the winged orders hovered round, watching when the new-born should open its yet closed eyes ; which, when it did, first one, and then the other—with a solicitude and apprehension, yet not such as, stained with fear, dims the expanding eye-lids of mortal infants, but as if to explore its path in those its unhereditary palaces—what an inextinguishable titter that time spared not celestial visages ! Nor wanted there to my seeming—O the inexplicable simpleness of dreams !— bowls of that cheering nectar,

—which mortals *caudle* call below—

Nor were wanting faces of female ministrants,—stricken in years, as it might seem,—so dexterous were those heavenly attendants to counterfeit kindly similitudes of earth, to greet, with terrestrial child-rites the young *present*, which earth had made to heaven.

Then were celestial harpings heard, not in full symphony as those by which the spheres are tutored ; but, as loudest instruments on earth speak oftentimes, muffled ; so to accommodate their sound the better to the weak ears of the imperfect-born. And, with the noise of those subdued soundings, the Angelet sprang forth, fluttering its rudiments of pinions—but forthwith flagged and was recovered into the arms of those full-winged angels. And a wonder it was to see how, as years went round in heaven—a year in dreams is as a day—continually its white shoulders put forth buds of wings, but, wanting the perfect angelic nutriment, anon was shorn of its aspiring, and fell fluttering—still caught by angel hands—for ever to put forth shoots, and to fall fluttering, because its birth was not of the unmixed vigour of heaven.

And a name was given to the Babe Angel, and it was to be called *Ge-Urania*, because its production was of earth and heaven.

And it could not taste of death, by reason of its adoption into immortal palaces : but it was to know weakness, and reliance, and the shadow of human imbecility ; and it went with a lame gait ; but in its goings it exceeded all mortal children in grace and swiftness. Then pity first sprang up in angelic bosoms ; and yearnings (like the human) touched them at the sight of the immortal lame one.

And with pain did then first those Intuitive Essences, with pain and strife to their natures (not grief), put back their bright intelligences, and reduce their ethereal minds, schooling them to degrees and slower processes, so to adapt their lessons to the gradual illumination (as must needs be) of the half-earth-born ; and what intuitive notices they could not repel (by reason that their nature is, to know all things at once), the half-heavenly novice, by the better part of its nature, aspired to receive into its understanding ; so that Humility and Aspiration went on even-paced in the instruction of the glorious Amphibium.

But, by reason that Mature Humanity is too gross to breathe the air of that super-subtile region, its portion was, and is, to be a child for ever.

And because the human part of it might not press into the heart and inwards of the palace of its adoption, those full-natured angels tended it by turns in the purlieus of the palace, where were shady groves and rivulets, like this green earth from which it came : so Love, with Voluntary Humility, waited upon the entertainment of the new-adopted.

And myriads of years rolled round (in dreams Time is nothing), and still it kept, and is to keep, perpetual childhood, and is the Tutelar Genius of Childhood upon earth, and still goes lame and lovely.

By the banks of the river Pison is seen, lone-sitting by the grave of the terrestrial Adah, whom the angel Nadir loved, a Child ; but not the same which I saw in heaven. A mournful hue overcasts its lineaments ; nevertheless, a correspondency is between the child by the grave, and that celestial orphan, whom I saw above ; and the dimness of the grief upon the heavenly, is as a shadow or emblem of that which stains the beauty of the terrestrial. And this correspondency is not to be understood but by dreams.

And in the archives of heaven I had grace to read, how that once the angel Nadir, being exiled from his place for mortal passion, upspringing on the wings of parental love (such power had parental love for a moment to suspend the else-irrevocable law) appeared for a brief instant in his station; and, depositing a wondrous Birth, straightway disappeared, and the palaces knew him no more. And this charge was the self-same Babe, who goeth lame and lovely—but Adah sleepeth by the river Pison.

————

A DEATH-BED

In a Letter to R. H. Esq. of B——

I CALLED upon you this morning, and found that you were gone to visit a dying friend. I had been upon a like errand. Poor N. R. has lain dying now for almost a week; such is the penalty we pay for having enjoyed through life a strong constitution. Whether he knew me or not, I know not, or whether he saw me through his poor glazed eyes; but the group I saw about him I shall not forget. Upon the bed, or about it, were assembled his Wife, their two Daughters, and poor deaf Robert, looking doubly stupified. There they were, and seemed to have been sitting all the week. I could only reach out a hand to Mrs. R. Speaking was impossible in that mute chamber. By this time it must be all over with him. In him I have a loss the world cannot make up. He was my friend, and my father's friend, for all the life that I can remember. I seem to have made foolish friendships since. Those are the friendships, which outlast a second generation. Old as I am getting, in his eyes I was still the child he knew me. To the last he called me Jemmy. I have none to call me Jemmy now. He was the last link that bound me to B——. You are but of yesterday. In him I seem to have lost the old plainness of manners and singleness of heart. Lettered he was not; his reading scarcely exceeded the Obituary of the old Gentleman's Magazine, to which he has never failed of having recourse for these last fifty years. Yet there was the pride of literature about him from that slender perusal; and more-

over from his office of archive-keeper to your ancient city, in which
he must needs pick up some equivocal Latin ; which, among his
less literary friends, assumed the air of a very pleasant pedantry.
Can I forget the erudite look with which, having tried to puzzle
out the text of a Black lettered Chaucer in your Corporation
Library, to which he was a sort of Librarian, he gave it up with
this consolatary reflection—" Jemmy," said he, " I do not know
what you find in these very old books, but I observe, there is a
deal of very indifferent spelling in them." His jokes (for he had
some) are ended ; but they were old Perennials, staple, and always
as good as new. He had one Song, that spake of the " flat
bottoms of our foes coming over in darkness," and alluded to a
threatened Invasion, many years since blown over ; this he reserved
to be sung on Christmas Night, which we always passed with him,
and he sang it with the freshness of an impending event. How
his eyes would sparkle when he came to the passage :—

> We'll still make 'em run, and we'll still make 'em sweat,
> In spite of the devil and Brussels' Gazette !

What is the Brussels' Gazette now ? I cry, while I endite these
trifles. His poor girls who are, I believe, compact of solid goodness, will have to receive their afflicted mother at an unsuccessful
home in a petty village in ——shire, where for years they have
been struggling to raise a Girls' School with no effect. Poor deaf
Robert (and the less hopeful for being so) is thrown upon a deaf
world, without the comfort to his father on his death-bed of knowing him provided for. They are left almost provisionless. Some
life assurance there is ; but, I fear, not exceeding ——. Their
hopes must be from your Corporation, which their father has
served for fifty years. Who or what are your Leading Members
now, I know not. Is there any, to whom without impertinence,
you can represent the true circumstances of the family ? You cannot say good enough of poor R., and his poor wife. Oblige me
and the dead, if you can.

———

OLD CHINA

I HAVE an almost feminine partiality for old china. When I
go to see any great house, I inquire for the china-closet, and
next for the picture gallery. I cannot defend the order of pre-

ference, but by saying, that we have all some taste or other, of too
ancient a date to admit of our remembering distinctly that it was
an acquired one.   I can call to mind the first play, and the first
exhibition, that I was taken to ; but I am not conscious of a time
when china jars and saucers were introduced into my imagination.

I had no repugnance then—why should I now have ?—to those
little, lawless, azure-tinctured grotesques, that under the notion
of men and women, float about, uncircumscribed by any element,
in that world before perspective—a china tea-cup.

I like to see my old friends—whom distance cannot diminish—
figuring up in the air (so they appear to our optics), yet on *terra
firma* still—for so we must in courtesy interpret that speck of
deeper blue, which the decorous artist, to prevent absurdity, has
made to spring up beneath their sandals.

I love the men with women's faces, and the women, if possible,
with still more womanish expressions.

Here is a young and courtly Mandarin, handing tea to a lady
from a salver—two miles off.   See how distance seems to set off
respect !   And here the same lady, or another—for likeness is
identity on tea-cups—is stepping into a little fairy boat, moored
on the hither side of this calm garden river, with a dainty mincing
foot, which in a right angle of incidence (as angles go in our world)
must infallibly land her in the midst of a flowery mead—a furlong
off on the other side of the same strange stream !

Farther on—if far or near can be predicated of their world—see
horses, trees, pagodas, dancing the hays.

Here—a cow and rabbit couchant, and co-extensive—so objects
show, seen through the lucid atmosphere of fine Cathay.

I was pointing out to my cousin last evening, over our Hyson
(which we are old fashioned enough to drink unmixed still of an
afternoon) some of these *speciosa miracula* upon a set of extraordinary old blue china (a recent purchase) which we were now for
the first time using ; and could not help remarking, how favourable circumstances had been to us of late years, that we could
afford to please the eye sometimes with trifles of this sort—when a
passing sentiment seemed to over-shade the brows of my companion.   I am quick at detecting these summer clouds in Bridget.

" I wish the good old times would come again," she said, " when
we were not quite so rich.   I do not mean, that I want to be poor ;
but there was a middle state ; "—so she was pleased to ramble on,
—" in which I am sure we were a great deal happier.   A purchase
is but a purchase, now that you have money enough and to spare.
Formerly it used to be a triumph.   When we coveted a cheap
luxury (and, O ! how much ado I had to get you to consent in
those times !) we were used to have a debate two or three days

before, and to weigh the *for* and *against*, and think what we might spare it out of, and what saving we could hit upon, that should be an equivalent. A thing was worth buying then, when we felt the money that we paid for it.

"Do you remember the brown suit, which you made to hang upon you, till all your friends cried shame upon you, it grew so thread-bare—and all because of that folio Beaumont and Fletcher, which you dragged home late at night from Barker's in Covent-garden? Do you remember how we eyed it for weeks before we could make up our minds to the purchase, and had not come to a determination till it was near ten o'clock of the Saturday night, when you set off from Islington, fearing you should be too late—and when the old bookseller with some grumbling opened his shop, and by the twinkling taper (for he was setting bedwards) lighted out the relic from his dusty treasures—and when you lugged it home, wishing it were twice as cumbersome— and when you presented it to me—and when we were exploring the perfectness of it (*collating* you called it)—and while I was repairing some of the loose leaves with paste, which your impatience would not suffer to be left till day-break—was there no pleasure in being a poor man? or can those neat black clothes which you wear now, and are so careful to keep brushed, since we have become rich and finical, give you half the honest vanity, with which you flaunted it about in that over-worn suit—your old corbeau—for four or five weeks longer than you should have done, to pacify your conscience for the mighty sum of fifteen—or sixteen shillings was it?—a great affair we thought it then—which you had lavished on the old folio. Now you can afford to buy any book that pleases you, but I do not see that you ever bring me home any nice old purchases now.

"When you come home with twenty apologies for laying out a less number of shillings upon that print after Lionardo, which we christened the 'Lady Blanch;' when you looked at the purchase, and thought of the money—and thought of the money, and looked again at the picture—was there no pleasure in being a poor man? Now, you have nothing to do but to walk into Colnaghi's, and buy a wilderness of Lionardos. Yet do you?

"Then, do you remember our pleasant walks to Enfield, and Potter's Bar, and Waltham, when we had a holyday—holydays, and all other fun, are gone, now we are rich—and the little hand-basket in which I used to deposit our day's fare of savory cold lamb and salad—and how you would pry about at noon-tide for some decent house, where we might go in, and produce our store— only paying for the ale that you must call for—and speculate upon the looks of the landlady, and whether she was likely to allow us a table-cloth—and wish for such another honest hostess, as Izaak Walton has described many a one on the pleasant banks of the Lea, when he went a fishing—and sometimes they would prove obliging enough, and sometimes they would look grudgingly upon us—but we had cheerful looks still for one another, and would eat our plain food savorily, scarcely grudging Piscator his Trout Hall ?   Now, when we go out a day's pleasuring, which is seldom moreover, we *ride* part of the way—and go into a fine inn, and order the best of dinners, never debating the expense—which, after all, never has half the relish of those chance country snaps, when we were at the mercy of uncertain usage, and a precarious welcome.

" You are too proud to see a play anywhere now but in the pit. Do you remember where it was we used to sit, when we saw the battle of Hexham, and the surrender of Calais, and Bannister and Mrs. Bland in the Children in the Wood—when we squeezed out our shillings a-piece to sit three or four times in a season in the one-shilling gallery—where you felt all the time that you ought not to have brought me—and more strongly I felt obligation to you for having brought me—and the pleasure was the better for a little shame—and when the curtain drew up, what cared we for our place in the house, or what mattered it where we were sitting, when our thoughts were with Rosalind in Arden, or with Viola at the Court of Illyria ?   You used to say, that the gallery was the best place of all for enjoying a play socially—that the relish of such exhibitions must be in proportion to the infrequency of going—that the company we met there, not being in general readers of plays, were obliged to attend the more, and did attend, to what was going on, on the stage—because a word lost would have been a chasm, which it was impossible for them to fill up. With such reflections we consoled our pride then—and I appeal to you, whether, as a woman, I met generally with less attention and accommodation, than I have done since in more expensive situations in the house ?   The getting in indeed, and the crowding up those inconvenient staircases, was bad enough,—but there was still a law of civility to women recognised to quite as great an extent as we ever found in the other passages—and how a little difficulty overcome heightened the snug seat, and the play, afterwards ! Now we can only pay our money, and walk in.   You cannot see, you say, in the galleries now.   I am sure we saw, and heard too, well enough then—but sight, and all, I think, is gone with our poverty.

" There was pleasure in eating strawberries, before they became quite common—in the first dish of peas, while they were yet dear —to have them for a nice supper, a treat.   What treat can we have now ?   If we were to treat ourselves now—that is, to have dainties a little above our means, it would be selfish and wicked. It is the very little more that we allow ourselves beyond what the actual poor can get at, that makes what I call a treat—when two people living together, as we have done, now and then indulge themselves in a cheap luxury, which both like; while each apologises, and is willing to take both halves of the blame to his single share. I see no harm in people making much of themselves in that sense of the word. It may give them a hint how to make much of others. But now—what I mean by the word—we never do make much of ourselves. None but the poor can do it. I do not mean the veriest poor of all, but persons as we were, just above poverty.

" I know what you were going to say, that it is mighty pleasant at the end of the year to make all meet—and much ado we used to have every Thirty-first Night of December to account for our exceedings—many a long face did you make over your puzzled accounts, and in contriving to make it out how we had spent so much—or that we had not spent so much—or that it was impossible we should spend so much next year—and still we found our slender capital decreasing — but then, betwixt ways, and projects, and compromises of one sort or another, and talk of curtailing this charge, and doing without that for the future — and the hope that youth brings, and laughing spirits (in which you were never poor till now,) we pocketed up our loss, and in conclusion, with ' lusty brimmers ' (as you used to quote it out of *hearty cheerful Mr. Cotton*, as you called him), we used to welcome in the ' coming guest.' Now we have no reckoning at all at the end of the old year—no flattering promises about the new year doing better for us."

Bridget is so sparing of her speech on most occasions, that when she gets into a rhetorical vein, I am careful how I interrupt it. I could not help, however, smiling at the phantom of wealth which her dear imagination had conjured up out of a clear income of poor — hundred pounds a year. " It is true we were happier when we were poorer, but we were also younger, my cousin. I am afraid we must put up with the excess, for if we were to shake the superflux into the sea, we should not much mend ourselves. That we had much to struggle with, as we grew up together, we have reason to be most thankful. It strengthened, and knit our compact closer. We could never have been what we have been to each other, if we had always had the sufficiency which you now complain of. The resisting power—those natural dilations of the youthful spirit, which circumstances cannot straiten — with us are long since passed away. Competence to age is supplementary youth ; a sorry supplement indeed, but I fear the best that is to be had. We must ride, where we formerly walked : live better, and lie softer—and shall be wise to do so—than we had means to do in those good old days you speak of. Yet could those days return— could you and I once more walk our thirty miles a-day—could Bannister and Mrs. Bland again be young, and you and I be young to see them—could the good old one shilling gallery days return— they are dreams, my cousin, now—but could you and I at this moment, instead of this quiet argument, by our well-carpeted fire-side, sitting on this luxurious sofa—be once more struggling up those inconvenient stair-cases, pushed about, and squeezed, and elbowed by the poorest rabble of poor gallery scramblers—could I once more hear those anxious shrieks of yours—and the delicious *Thank God, we are safe*, which always followed when the topmost stair, conquered, let in the first light of the whole cheerful theatre down beneath us—I know not the fathom line that ever touched a descent so deep as I would be willing to bury more wealth in than Crœsus had, or the great Jew R—— is supposed to have, to purchase it. And now do just look at that merry little Chinese waiter holding an umbrella, big enough for a bed-tester, over the head of that pretty insipid half-Madona-ish chit of a lady in that very blue summer-house."

POPULAR FALLACIES

I.—THAT A BULLY IS ALWAYS A COWARD

THIS axiom contains a principle of compensation, which disposes us to admit the truth of it. But there is no safe trusting to dictionaries and definitions. We should more willingly fall in with this popular language, if we did not find *brutality* sometimes awkwardly coupled with *valour* in the same vocabulary. The comic writers, with their poetical justice, have contributed not a little to mislead us upon this point. To see a hectoring fellow exposed and beaten upon the stage, has something in it wonderfully diverting. Some people's share of animal spirits is notoriously low and defective. It has not strength to raise a vapour, or furnish out the wind of a tolerable bluster. These love to be told that huffing is no part of valour. The truest courage with them is that which is the least noisy and obtrusive. But confront one of these silent heroes with the swaggerer of real life, and his confidence in the theory quickly vanishes. Pretensions do not uniformly bespeak non-performance. A modest inoffensive deportment does not necessarily imply valour; neither does the absence of it justify us in denying that quality. Hickman wanted modesty—we do not mean *him* of Clarissa—but who ever doubted his courage? Even the poets—upon whom this equitable distribution of qualities should be most binding—have thought it agreeable to nature to depart from the rule upon occasion. Harapha, in the "Agonistes," is indeed a bully upon the received notions. Milton has made him at once a blusterer, a giant, and a dastard. But Almanzor, in Dryden, talks of driving armies singly before him—and does it. Tom Brown had a shrewder insight into this kind of character than either of his predecessors. He divides the palm more equably, and allows his hero a sort of dimidiate pre-eminence:—" Bully Dawson kicked by half the town, and half the town kicked by Bully Dawson." This was true distributive justice.

II.—THAT ILL-GOTTEN GAIN NEVER PROSPERS

The weakest part of mankind have this saying commonest in their mouth. It is the trite consolation administered to the easy dupe, when he has been tricked out of his money or estate, that the acquisition of it will do the owner *no good*. But the rogues of this world—the prudenter part of them, at least—know better; and, if the observation had been as true as it is old, would not have failed by this time to have discovered it. They have pretty sharp distinctions of the fluctuating and the permanent. " Lightly come, lightly go," is a proverb, which they can very well afford to leave, when they leave little else, to the losers. They do not always find manors, got by rapine or chicanery, insensibly to melt away, as the poets will have it; or that all gold glides, like thawing snow, from the thief's hand that grasps it. Church land, alienated to lay uses, was formerly denounced to have this slippery quality. But some portions of it somehow always stuck so fast, that the denunciators have been vain to postpone the prophecy of refundment to a late posterity.

III.—THAT A MAN MUST NOT LAUGH AT HIS OWN JEST

The severest exaction surely ever invented upon the self-denial of poor human nature! This is to expect a gentleman to give a treat without partaking of it; to sit esurient at his own table, and commend the flavour of his venison upon the absurd strength of his never touching it himself. On the contrary, we love to see a wag *taste* his own joke to his party; to watch a quirk, or a merry conceit, flickering upon the lips some seconds before the tongue is delivered of it. If it be good, fresh, and racy

—begotten of the occasion ; if he that utters it never thought it before, he is naturally the first to be tickled with it; and any suppression of such complacence we hold to be churlish and insulting. What does it seem to imply, but that your company is weak or foolish enough to be moved by an image or a fancy, that shall stir you not at all, or but faintly? This is exactly the humour of the fine gentleman in Mandeville, who, while he dazzles his guests with the display of some costly toy, affects himself to "see nothing considerable in it."

IV.—THAT SUCH A ONE SHOWS HIS BREEDING.—THAT IT IS EASY TO PERCEIVE HE IS NO GENTLEMAN

A speech from the poorer sort of people, which always indicates that the party vituperated is a gentleman. The very fact which they deny, is that which galls and exasperates them to use this language. The forbearance with which it is usually received, is a proof what interpretation the bystander sets upon it. Of a kin to this, and still less politic, are the phrases with which, in their street rhetoric, they ply one another more grossly:—*He is a poor creature.—He has not a rag to cover——&c.;* though this last, we confess, is more frequently applied by females to females. They do not perceive that the satire glances upon themselves. A poor man, of all things in the world, should not upbraid an antagonist with poverty. Are there no other topics—as, to tell him his father was hanged—his sister, &c.——, without exposing a secret, which should be kept snug between them ; and doing an affront to the order to which they have the honour equally to belong? All this while they do not see how the wealthier man stands by and laughs in his sleeve at both.

V.—THAT THE POOR COPY THE VICES OF THE RICH

A smooth text to the latter; and, preached from the pulpit, is sure of a docile audience from the pews lined with satin. It is twice sitting upon velvet to a foolish squire to be told, that *he*— and not *perverse nature*, as the homilies would make us imagine, is the true cause of all the irregularities in his parish. This is striking at the root of free-will indeed, and denying the originality of sin in any sense. But men are not such implicit sheep as this comes to. If the abstinence from evil on the part of the upper classes is to derive itself from no higher principle, than the apprehension of setting ill patterns to the lower, we beg leave to discharge them from all squeamishness on that score : they may even take their fill of pleasures, where they can find them. The Genius of Poverty, hampered and straitened as it is, is not so barren of invention but it can trade upon the staple of its own vice, without drawing upon their capital. The poor are not quite such servile imitators as they take them for. Some of them are very clever artists in their way. Here and there we find an original. Who taught the poor to steal, to pilfer? They did not go to the great for schoolmasters in these faculties surely. It is well if in some vices they allow us to be—no copyists. In no other sense is it true that the poor copy them, than as servants may be said to *take after* their masters and mistresses, when they succeed to their reversionary cold meats. If the master, from indisposition or some other cause, neglect his food, the servant dines notwithstanding.

"O, but (some will say) the force of example is great." We knew a lady who was so scrupulous on this head, that she would put up with the calls of the most impertinent visitor, rather than let her servant say she was not at home, for fear of teaching her maid to tell an untruth; and this in the very face of the fact, which she knew well enough, that the wench was one of the greatest liars upon the earth without teaching; so much so, that her mistress possibly never heard two words of consecutive truth from her in her life. But nature must go for nothing: example must be every thing. This liar in grain, who never opened her mouth without a lie, must be guarded against a remote inference, which she (pretty casuist!) might possibly draw from a form of words—literally false, but essentially deceiving no one—that under some circumstances a fib might not be so exceedingly sinful—a fiction, too, not at all in her own way, or one that she could be suspected of adopting, for few servant-wenches care to be denied to visitors.

This word *example* reminds us of another fine word which is in use upon these occasions—*encouragement*. "People in our sphere must not be thought to give encouragement to such proceedings." To such a frantic height is this principle capable of being carried, that we have known individuals who have thought it within the scope of their influence to sanction despair, and give *éclat* to—suicide. A domestic in the family of a county member lately deceased, for love, or some unknown cause, cut his throat, but not successfully. The poor fellow was otherwise much loved and respected; and great interest was used in his behalf, upon his recovery, that he might be permitted to retain his place; his word being first pledged, not without some substantial sponsors to promise for him, that the like should never happen again. His master was inclinable to keep him, but his mistress thought otherwise; and John in the end was dismissed, her ladyship declaring that she "could not think of encouraging any such doings in the county."

VI.—THAT ENOUGH IS AS GOOD AS A FEAST

Not a man, woman, or child in ten miles round Guildhall, who really believes this saying. The inventor of it did not believe it himself. It was made in revenge by somebody, who was disappointed of a regale. It is a vile cold-scrag-of-mutton sophism; a lie palmed upon the palate, which knows better things. If nothing else could be said for a feast, this is sufficient, that from the superflux there is usually something left for the next day. Morally interpreted, it belongs to a class of proverbs, which have a tendency to make us undervalue *money*. Of this cast are those notable observations, that money is not health; riches cannot purchase every thing: the metaphor which makes gold to be mere muck, with the morality which traces fine clothing to the sheep's back, and denounces pearl as the unhandsome excretion of an oyster. Hence, too, the phrase which imputes dirt to acres—a sophistry so barefaced, that even the literal sense of it is true only in a wet season. This, and abundance of similar sage saws assuming to inculcate *content*, we verily believe to have been the invention of some cunning borrower, who had designs upon the purse of his wealthier neighbour, which he could only hope to carry by force of these verbal jugglings. Translate any one of these sayings out of the artful metonyme which envelops it, and the trick is apparent. Goodly legs and shoulders of mutton, exhilarating cordials, books, pictures, the opportunities of seeing foreign countries, independence, heart's ease, a man's own time to himself, are not *muck*—however we may be pleased to scandalise with that appellation the faithful metal that provides them for us.

VII.—OF TWO DISPUTANTS, THE WARMEST IS GENERALLY IN THE WRONG

Our experience would lead us to quite an opposite conclusion. Temper, indeed, is no test of truth; but warmth and earnestness are a proof at least of a man's own conviction of the rectitude of that which he maintains. Coolness is as often the result of an unprincipled indifference to truth or falsehood, as of a sober confidence in a man's own side in a dispute. Nothing is more insulting sometimes than the appearance of this philosophic temper. There is little Titubus, the stammering law-stationer in Lincoln's Inn— we have seldom known this shrewd little fellow engaged in an argument where we were not convinced he had the best of it, if his tongue would but fairly have seconded him. When he has been spluttering excellent broken sense for an hour together, writhing and labouring to be delivered of the point of dispute—the very gist of the controversy knocking at his teeth, which like some obstinate iron-grating still obstructed its deliverance—his puny frame convulsed, and face reddening all over at an unfairness in the logic which he wanted articulation to expose, it has moved our gall to see a smooth portly fellow of an adversary, that cared not a button for the merits of the question, by merely laying his hand upon the head of the stationer, and desiring him to be *calm* (your tall disputants have always the advantage), with a provoking sneer carry the argument clean from him in the opinion of all the by-standers, who have gone away clearly convinced that Titubus must have been in the wrong, because he was in a passion ; and that Mr. ——, meaning his opponent, is one of the fairest, and at the same time one of the most dispassionate arguers breathing.

VIII.—THAT VERBAL ALLUSIONS ARE NOT WIT, BECAUSE THEY WILL NOT BEAR A TRANSLATION

The same might be said of the wittiest local allusions. A custom is sometimes as difficult to explain to a foreigner as a pun. What would become of a great part of the wit of the last age, if it were tried by this test? How would certain topics, as aldermanity, cuckoldry, have sounded to a Terentian auditory, though Terence himself had been alive to translate them ? *Senator urbanus*, with *Curruca* to boot for a synonime, would but faintly have done the business. Words, involving notions, are hard enough to render ; it is too much to expect us to translate a sound, and give an elegant version to a jingle. The Virgilian harmony is not translatable, but by substituting harmonious sounds in another language for it. To Latinise a pun, we must seek a pun in Latin, that will answer to it ; as, to give an idea of the double endings in Hudibras, we must have recourse to a similar practice in the old monkish doggrel. Dennis, the fiercest oppugner of puns in ancient or modern times, professes himself highly tickled with the "a stick" chiming to "ecclesiastic." Yet what is this but a species of pun, a verbal consonance ?

IX.—THAT THE WORST PUNS ARE THE BEST

If by worst be only meant the most far-fetched and startling, we agree to it. A pun is not bound by the laws which limit nicer wit. It is a pistol let off at the ear ; not a feather to tickle the intellect. It is an antic which does not stand upon manners, but comes bounding into the presence, and does not show the less comic for being dragged in sometimes by the head and shoulders. What though it limp a little, or prove defective in one leg—all the better. A pun may easily be too curious and artificial. Who has not at one time or other been at a party of professors (himself perhaps an old offender in that line), where, after ringing a round of the most ingenious conceits, every man contributing his shot, and some there the most expert shooters of the day; after making a poor *word* run the gauntlet till it is ready to drop; after hunting and winding it through all the possible ambages of similar sounds; after squeezing, and hauling, and tugging at it, till the very milk of it will not yield a drop further,—suddenly some obscure, un-thought-of fellow in a corner, who was never 'prentice to the trade, whom the company for very pity passed over, as we do by a known poor man when a money-subscription is going round, no one calling upon him for his quota—has all at once come out with something so whimsical, yet so pertinent; so brazen in its pretensions, yet so impossible to be denied; so exquisitely good, and so deplorably bad, at the same time,—that it has proved a Robin Hood's shot; any thing ulterior to that is despaired of; and the party breaks up, unanimously voting it to be the very worst (that is, best) pun of the evening. This species of wit is the better for not being perfect in all its parts. What it gains in completeness, it loses in naturalness. The more exactly it satisfies the critical, the less hold it has upon some other faculties. The puns which are most entertaining are those which will least bear an analysis. Of this kind is the following, recorded, with a sort of stigma, in one of Swift's Miscellanies.

An Oxford scholar, meeting a porter who was carrying a hare through the streets, accosts him with this extraordinary question: "Prithee, friend, is that thy own hare, or a wig?"

There is no excusing this, and no resisting it. A man might blur ten sides of paper in attempting a defence of it against a critic who should be laughter-proof. The quibble in itself is not considerable. It is only a new turn given, by a little false pro-nunciation, to a very common, though not very courteous inquiry. Put by one gentleman to another at a dinner-party, it would have been vapid; to the mistress of the house, it would have shown much less wit than rudeness. We must take in the totality of time, place, and person; the pert look of the inquiring scholar, the desponding looks of the puzzled porter; the one stopping at leisure, the other hurrying on with his burthen; the innocent though rather abrupt tendency of the first member of the question, with the utter and inextricable irrelevancy of the second; the place —a public street, not favourable to frivolous investigations; the affrontive quality of the primitive inquiry (the common question) invidiously transferred to the derivative (the new turn given to it) in the implied satire; namely, that few of that tribe are expected to eat of the good things which they carry, they being in most countries considered rather as the temporary trustees than owners of such dainties,—which the fellow was beginning to understand; but then the *wig* again comes in, and he can make nothing of it: all put together constitute a picture: Hogarth could have made it intelligible on canvass.

Yet nine out of ten critics will pronounce this a very bad pun, because of the defectiveness in the concluding member, which is its very beauty, and constitutes the surprise. The same persons shall cry up for admirable the cold quibble from Virgil about the broken Cremona;[1] because it is made out in all its parts, and leaves nothing to the imagination. We venture to call it cold; because of thousands who have admired it, it would be difficult to find one who has heartily chuckled at it. As appealing to the judgment merely (setting the risible faculty aside,) we must pronounce it a monument of curious felicity. But as some stories are said to be too good to be true, it may with equal truth be asserted of this bi-verbal allusion, that it is too good to be natural. One cannot help suspecting that the incident was invented to fit the line. It would have been better had it been less perfect. Like some Virgilian hemistichs, it has suffered by filling up. The *nimium Vicina* was enough in conscience; the *Cremonæ* afterwards loads it. It is in fact a double pun; and we have always observed that a superfœtation in this sort of wit is dangerous. When a man has said a good thing, it is seldom politic to follow it up. We do not care to be cheated a second time; or, perhaps, the mind of man (with reverence be it spoken) is not capacious enough to lodge two puns at a time. The impression, to be forcible, must be simultaneous and undivided.

X.—THAT HANDSOME IS THAT HANDSOME DOES

Those who use this proverb can never have seen Mrs. Conrady.

The soul, if we may believe Plotinus, is a ray from the celestial beauty. As she partakes more or less of this heavenly light, she informs, with corresponding characters, the fleshly tenement which she chooses, and frames to herself a suitable mansion.

All which only proves that the soul of Mrs. Conrady, in her pre-existent state, was no great judge of architecture.

To the same effect, in a Hymn in honour of Beauty, divine Spenser, *platonizing*, sings :—

——" Every spirit as it is more pure,
And hath in it the more of heavenly light,

[1] Swift.

> So it the fairer body doth procure
> To habit in, and it more fairly dight
> With cheerful grace and amiable sight.
> For of the soul the body form doth take :
> For soul is form, and doth the body make."

But Spenser, it is clear, never saw Mrs. Conrady.

These poets, we find, are no safe guides in philosophy ; for here, in his very next stanza but one, is a saving clause, which throws us all out again, and leaves us as much to seek as ever :—

> " Yet oft it falls, that many a gentle mind
> Dwells in deformed tabernacle drown'd,
> Either by chance, against the course of kind,
> Or through unaptness in the substance found,
> Which it assumed of some stubborn ground,
> That will not yield unto her form's direction,
> But is perform'd with some foul imperfection."

From which it would follow, that Spenser had seen somebody like Mrs. Conrady.

The spirit of this good lady—her previous *anima*—must have stumbled upon one of these untoward tabernacles which he speaks of. A more rebellious commodity of clay for a ground, as the poet calls it, no gentle mind—and sure her's is one of the gentlest—ever had to deal with.

Pondering upon her inexplicable visage—inexplicable, we mean, but by this modification of the theory—we have come to a conclusion that, if one must be plain, it is better to be plain all over, than, amidst a tolerable residue of features, to hang out one that shall be exceptionable. No one can say of Mrs. Conrady's countenance, that it would be better if she had but a nose. It is impossible to pull her to pieces in this manner. We have seen the most malicious beauties of her own sex baffled in the attempt at a selection. The *tout ensemble* defies particularising. It is too complete—too consistent, as we may say—to admit of these invidious reservations. It is not as if some Apelles had picked out here a lip—and there a chin—out of the collected ugliness of Greece, to frame a model by. It is a symmetrical whole. We challenge the minutest connoisseur to cavil at any part or parcel of the countenance in question ; to say that this, or that, is improperly placed. We are convinced that true ugliness, no less than is affirmed of true beauty, is the result of harmony. Like that too it reigns without a competitor. No one ever saw Mrs. Conrady, without pronouncing her to be the plainest woman that he ever met with in the course of his life. The first time that you are indulged with a sight of her face, is an era in your existence ever after. You are glad to have seen it—like Stonehenge. No one can pretend to forget it. No one ever apologised to her for meeting her in the street on such a day and not knowing her : the pretext would be too bare. Nobody can mistake her for another. Nobody can say of her, " I think I have seen that face somewhere, but I cannot call to mind where." You must remember that in such a parlour it first struck you—like a bust. You wondered where the owner of the house had picked it up. You wondered more when it began to move its lips—so mildly too ! No one ever thought of asking her to sit for her picture. Lockets are for remembrance ; and it would be clearly superfluous to hang an image at your heart, which, once seen, can never be out of it. It is not a mean face either ; its entire originality precludes that. Neither is it of that order of plain faces which improve upon acquaintance. Some very good but ordinary people, by an unwearied perseverance in good offices, put a cheat upon our eyes : juggle our senses out of their natural impressions ; and set us upon discovering good indications in a countenance, which at first sight promised nothing less. We detect gentleness, which had escaped us, lurking about an under lip. But when Mrs. Conrady has done you a service, her face remains the same ; when she has done you a thousand, and you know that she is ready to double the number, still it is that individual face. Neither can you say of it, that it would be a good face if it was not marked by the small pox—a compliment which is always more admissive than excusatory—for either Mrs. Conrady never had the small pox ; or, as we say, took it kindly. No, it stands upon its own merits fairly. There it is. It is her mark, her token ; that which she is known by.

XI.—THAT WE MUST NOT LOOK A GIFT-HORSE IN THE MOUTH

Nor a lady's age in the parish register. We hope we have more delicacy than to do either : but some faces spare us the trouble of these *dental* inquiries. And what if the beast, which my friend would force upon my acceptance, prove, upon the face of it, a sorry Rozinante, a lean, ill-favoured jade, whom no gentleman could think of setting up in his stables ? Must I, rather than not be obliged to my friend, make her a companion to Eclipse or Lightfoot ? A horse-giver, no more than a horse-seller, has a right to palm his spavined article upon us for good ware. An equivalent is expected in either case ; and, with my own good will, I would no more be cheated out of my thanks, than out of my money. Some people have a knack of putting upon you gifts of no real value, to engage you to substantial gratitude. We thank them for nothing. Our friend Mitis carries this humour of never refusing a present, to the very point of absurdity—if it were possible to couple the ridiculous with so much mistaken delicacy, and real good-nature.

Not an apartment in his fine house (and he has a true taste in household decorations), but is stuffed up with some preposterous print or mirror—the worst adapted to his pannels that may be —the presents of his friends that know his weakness; while his noble Vandykes are displaced, to make room for a set of daubs, the work of some wretched artist of his acquaintance, who, having had them returned upon his hands for bad likenesses, finds his account in bestowing them here gratis. The good creature has not the heart to mortify the painter at the expense of an honest refusal. It is pleasant (if it did not vex one at the same time) to see him sitting in his dining parlour, surrounded with obscure aunts and cousins to God knows whom, while the true Lady Marys and Lady Bettys of his own honourable family, in favour to these adopted frights, are consigned to the staircase and the lumber-room. In like manner his goodly shelves are one by one stript of his favourite old authors, to give place to a collection of presentation copies— the flower and bran of modern poetry. A presentation copy, reader—if haply you are yet innocent of such favours—is a copy of a book which does not sell, sent you by the author, with his foolish autograph at the beginning of it; for which, if a stranger, he only demands your friendship; if a brother author, he expects from you a book of yours which does sell, in return. We can speak to experience, having by us a tolerable assortment of these gift-horses. Not to ride a metaphor to death—we are willing to acknowledge, that in some gifts there is sense. A duplicate out of a friend's library (where he has more than one copy of a rare author) is intelligible. There are favours, short of the pecuniary—a thing not fit to be hinted at among gentlemen—which confer as much grace upon the acceptor as the offerer: the kind, we confess, which is most to our palate, is of those little conciliatory missives, which for their vehicle generally choose a hamper—little odd presents of game, fruit, perhaps wine—though it is essential to the delicacy of the latter that it be home-made. We love to have our friend in the country sitting thus at our table by proxy; to apprehend his presence (though a hundred miles may be between us) by a turkey, whose goodly aspect reflects to us his " plump corpusculum ; " to taste him in grouse or woodcock; to feel him gliding down in the toast peculiar to the latter; to concorporate him in a slice of Canterbury brawn. This is indeed to have him within ourselves ; to know him intimately : such participation is methinks unitive, as the old theologians phrase it. For these considerations we should be sorry if certain restrictive regulations, which are thought to bear hard upon the peasantry of this country, were entirely done away with. A hare, as the law now stands, makes many friends. Caius conciliates Titius (knowing his *goût*) with a leash of par-

tridges. Titius (suspecting his partiality for them) passes them to
Lucius ; who in his turn, preferring his friend's relish to his own,
makes them over to Marcius ; till in their ever widening progress,
and round of unconscious circum-migration, they distribute the
seeds of harmony over half a parish.   We are well disposed to this
kind of sensible remembrances ; and are the less apt to be taken by
those little airy tokens—inpalpable to the palate—which, under
the names of rings, lockets, keep-sakes, amuse some people's fancy
mightily.   We could never away with these indigestible trifles.
They are the very kickshaws and foppery of friendship.

XII.—THAT HOME IS HOME THOUGH IT IS NEVER SO HOMELY

Homes there are, we are sure, that are no homes : the home of
the very poor man, and another which we shall speak to presently.
Crowded places of cheap entertainment, and the benches of ale-
houses, if they could speak, might bear mournful testimony to the
first.   To them the very poor man resorts for an image of the
home, which he cannot find at home.   For a starved grate, and a
scanty firing, that is not enough to keep alive the natural heat
in the fingers of so many shivering children with their mother,
he finds in the depth of winter always a blazing hearth, and a
hob to warm his pittance of beer by.   Instead of the clamours
of a wife, made gaunt by famishing, he meets with a cheerful
attendance beyond the merits of the trifle which he can afford
to spend.   He has companions which his home denies him, for
the very poor man has no visiters.   He can look into the goings
on of the world, and speak a little to politics.   At home there
are no politics stirring, but the domestic.   All interests, real or
imaginary, all topics that should expand the mind of man, and
connect him to a sympathy with general existence, are crushed
in the absorbing consideration of food to be obtained for the
family.   Beyond the price of bread, news is senseless and impertinent.   At home there is no larder.   Here there is at least
a show of plenty ; and while he cooks his lean scrap of butcher's
meat before the common bars, or munches his humbler cold viands,
his relishing bread and cheese with an onion, in a corner, where
no one reflects upon his poverty, he has sight of the substantial joint providing for the landlord and his family.   He takes
an interest in the dressing of it ; and while he assists in removing
the trivet from the fire, he feels that there is such a thing as beef
and cabbage, which he was beginning to forget at home.   All
this while he deserts his wife and children.   But what wife, and
what children ?   Prosperous men, who object to this desertion,
image to themselves some clean contented family like that which

they go home to. But look at the countenance of the poor wives who follow and persecute their good man to the door of the public house, which he is about to enter, when something like shame would restrain him, if stronger misery did not induce him to pass the threshold. That face, ground by want, in which every cheerful, every conversable lineament has been long effaced by misery,—is that a face to stay at home with? is it more a woman, or a wild cat? alas! it is the face of the wife of his youth, that once smiled upon him. It can smile no longer. What comforts can it share? what burthens can it lighten? Oh, 'tis a fine thing to talk of the humble meal shared together! But what if there be no bread in the cupboard? The innocent prattle of his children takes out the sting of a man's poverty. But the children of the very poor do not prattle. It is none of the least frightful features in that condition, that there is no childishness in its dwellings. Poor people, said a sensible old nurse to us once, do not bring up their children; they drag them up. The little careless darling of the wealthier nursery, in their hovel is transformed betimes into a premature reflecting person. No one has time to dandle it, no one thinks it worth while to coax it, to soothe it, to toss it up and down, to humour it. There is none to kiss away its tears. If it cries, it can only be beaten. It has been prettily said that "a babe is fed with milk and praise." But the aliment of this poor babe was thin, unnourishing; the return to its little baby-tricks, and efforts to engage attention, bitter ceaseless objurgation. It never had a toy, or knew what a coral meant. It grew up without the lullaby of nurses, it was a stranger to the patient fondle, the hushing caress, the attracting novelty, the costlier plaything, or the cheaper off-hand contrivance to divert the child; the prattled nonsense (best sense to it), the wise impertinences, the wholesome lies, the apt story interposed, that puts a stop to present sufferings, and awakens the passion of young wonder. It was never sung to—no one ever told to it a tale of the nursery. It was dragged up, to live or to die as it happened. It had no young dreams. It broke at once into the iron realities of life. A child exists not for the very poor as any object of dalliance; it is only another mouth to be fed, a pair of little hands to be betimes inured to labour. It is the rival, till it can be the co-operator, for food with the parent. It is never his mirth, his diversion, his solace; it never makes him young again, with recalling his young times. The children of the very poor have no young times. It makes the very heart to bleed to overhear the casual street-talk between a poor woman and her little girl, a woman of the better sort of poor, in a condition rather above the squalid beings which we have been contemplating. It is not of toys, of nursery books, of summer holidays (fitting that age); of the promised sight, or play; of praised sufficiency at school. It is of mangling and clear-starching, of the price of coals, or of potatoes. The questions of the child, that should be the very outpourings of curiosity in idleness, are marked with forecast and melancholy providence. It has come to be a woman, before it was a child. It has learned to go to market; it chaffers, it haggles, it envies, it murmurs; it is knowing, acute, sharpened; it never prattles. Had we not reason to say, that the home of the very poor is no home?

There is yet another home, which we are constrained to deny to be one. It has a larder, which the home of the poor man wants; its fireside conveniences, of which the poor dream not. But with all this, it is no home. It is—the house of the man that is infested with many visiters. May we be branded for the veriest churl, if we deny our heart to the many noble-hearted friends that at times exchange their dwelling for our poor roof! It is not of guests that we complain, but of endless, purposeless visitants; droppers in, as they are called. We sometimes wonder from what sky they fall. It is the very error of the position of our lodging; its horoscopy was ill calculated, being just situate in a medium—a plaguy suburban mid-space—fitted to catch idlers from town or country. We are older than we were, and age is easily put out of its way. We have fewer sands in our glass to reckon upon, and we cannot brook to see them drop in endlessly succeeding impertinences. At our time of life, to be alone sometimes is as needful as sleep. It is the refreshing sleep of the day. The growing infirmities of age manifest themselves in nothing more strongly, than in an inveterate dislike of interruption. The thing which we are doing, we wish to be permitted to do. We have neither much knowledge nor devices; but there are fewer in the place to which we hasten. We are not willingly put out of our way, even at a game of nine-pins. While youth was, we had vast reversions in time future; we are reduced to a present pittance, and obliged to economise in that article. We bleed away our moments now as hardly as our ducats. We cannot bear to have our thin wardrobe eaten and fretted into by moths. We are willing to barter our good time with a friend, who gives us in exchange his own. Herein is the distinction between the genuine guest and the visitant. This latter takes your good time, and gives you his bad in exchange. The guest is domestic to you as your good cat, or household bird; the visitant is your fly, that flaps in at your window, and out again, leaving nothing but a sense of disturbance, and victuals spoiled. The inferior functions of life begin to move heavily. We cannot concoct our food with interruptions. Our chief meal, to be nutritive, must be solitary. With difficulty

we can eat before a guest ; and never understood what the relish of
public feasting meant. Meats have no sapor, nor digestion fair
play, in a crowd. The unexpected coming in of a visitant stops
the machine. There is a punctual generation who time their
calls to the precise commencement of your dining-hour—not to
eat—but to see you eat. Our knife and fork drop instinctively,
and we feel that we have swallowed our latest morsel. Others
again show their genius, as we have said, in knocking the moment
you have just sat down to a book. They have a peculiar com-
passionating sneer, with which they " hope that they do not interrupt
your studies." Though they flutter off the next moment, to carry
their impertinences to the nearest student that they can call their
friend, the tone of the book is spoiled ; we shut the leaves, and,
with Dante's lovers, read no more that day. It were well if the
effect of intrusion were simply co-extensive with its presence ; but
it mars all the good hours afterwards. These scratches in appearance leave an orifice that closes not hastily. " It is a prostitution
of the bravery of friendship," says worthy Bishop Taylor, " to
spend it upon impertinent people, who are, it may be, loads to
their families, but can never ease my loads." This is the secret
of their gaddings, their visits, and morning calls. They too have
homes, which are—no homes.

XIII.—THAT YOU MUST LOVE ME, AND LOVE MY DOG

" Good sir, or madam, as it may be—we most willingly embrace
the offer of your friendship. We long have known your excellent
qualities. We have wished to have you nearer to us ; to hold you
within the very innermost fold of our heart. We can have no
reserve towards a person of your open and noble nature. The
frankness of your humour suits us exactly. We have been long
looking for such a friend. Quick—let us disburthen our troubles
into each other's bosom—let us make our single joys shine by
reduplication—But yap, yap, yap !—what is this confounded cur ?
he has fastened his tooth, which is none of the bluntest, just in the
fleshy part of my leg."

" It is my dog, sir. You must love him for my sake. Here,
Test—Test—Test ! "

" But he has bitten me."

" Ay, that he is apt to do, till you are better acquainted with
him. I have had him three years. He never bites me."

Yap, yap, yap !—" He is at it again."

" Oh, sir, you must not kick him. He does not like to be
kicked. I expect my dog to be treated with all the respect due to
myself."

"But do you always take him out with you, when you go a friendship-hunting?"

"Invariably. 'Tis the sweetest, prettiest, best-conditioned animal. I call him my *test*—the touchstone by which I try a friend. No one can properly be said to love me, who does not love him."

"Excuse us, dear sir—or madam aforesaid—if upon further consideration we are obliged to decline the otherwise invaluable offer of your friendship. We do not like dogs."

"Mighty well, sir—you know the conditions—you may have worse offers. Come along, Test."

The above dialogue is not so imaginary, but that, in the intercourse of life, we have had frequent occasions of breaking off an agreeable intimacy by reason of these canine appendages. They do not always come in the shape of dogs; they sometimes wear the more plausible and human character of kinsfolk, near acquaintances, my friend's friend, his partner, his wife, or his children. We could never yet form a friendship—not to speak of more delicate correspondences—however much to our taste, without the intervention of some third anomaly, some impertinent clog affixed to the relation—the understood *dog* in the proverb. The good things of life are not to be had singly, but come to us with a mixture; like a schoolboy's holiday, with a task affixed to the tail of it. What a delightful companion is * * * *, if he did not always bring his tall cousin with him! He seems to grow with him; like some of those double births, which we remember to have read of with such wonder and delight in the old "Athenian Oracle," where Swift commenced author by writing Pindaric Odes (what a beginning for him!) upon Sir William Temple. There is the picture of the brother, with the little brother peeping out at his shoulder; a species of fraternity, which we have no name of kin close enough to comprehend. When * * * * comes, poking in his head and shoulders into your room, as if to feel his entry, you think, surely you have now got him to yourself—what a three hours' chat we shall have! —but, ever in the haunch of him, and before his diffident body is well disclosed in your apartment, appears the haunting shadow of the cousin, over-peering his modest kinsman, and sure to over-lay the expected good talk with his insufferable procerity of stature, and uncorresponding dwarfishness of observation. Misfortunes seldom come alone. 'Tis hard when a blessing comes accompanied. Cannot we like Sempronia, without sitting down to chess with her eternal brother? or know Sulpicia, without knowing all the round of her card-playing relations? must my friend's brethren of necessity be mine also? must we be hand and glove with Dick Selby the parson, or Jack Selby the calico printer, because W. S., who is neither, but a ripe wit and a critic, has the misfortune to claim a common parentage with them? Let him lay down his brothers; and 'tis odds but we will cast him in a pair of our's (we have a superflux) to balance the concession. Let F. H. lay down his garrulous uncle; and Honorius dismiss his vapid wife, and super-fluous establishment of six boys—things between boy and manhood—too ripe for play, too raw for conversation—that come in, im-pudently staring their father's old friend out of countenance; and will neither aid, nor let alone, the conference: that we may once more meet upon equal terms, as we were wont to do in the dis-engaged state of bachelorhood.

It is well if your friend, or mistress, be content with these canicular probations. Few young ladies but in this sense keep a dog. But when Rutilia hounds at you her tiger aunt; or Ruspina expects you to cherish and fondle her viper sister, whom she has preposterously taken into her bosom, to try stinging con-clusions upon your constancy; they must not complain if the house be rather thin of suitors. Scylla must have broken off many excellent matches in her time, if she insisted upon all, that loved her, loving her dogs also.

An excellent story to this moral is told of Merry, of Della Cruscan memory. In tender youth, he loved and courted a modest appanage to the Opera, in truth a dancer, who had won him by the artless contrast between her manners and situation. She seemed to him a native violet, that had been transplanted by some rude accident into that exotic and artificial hotbed. Nor, in truth, was she less genuine and sincere than she appeared to him. He wooed and won this flower. Only for appearance' sake, and for due honour to the bride's relations, she craved that she might have the attendance of her friends and kindred at the approaching solemnity. The request was too amiable not to be conceded; and in this solicitude for conciliating the good will of mere relations, he found a presage of her superior attentions to himself, when the golden shaft should have "killed the flock of all affections else." The morning came; and at the Star and Garter, Richmond—the place appointed for the breakfasting—accompanied with one English friend, he impatiently awaited what reinforcements the bride should bring to grace the ceremony. A rich muster she had made. They came in six coaches—the whole corps du ballet—French, Italian, men and women. Monsieur de B., the famous *pirouetter* of the day, led his fair spouse, but craggy, from the banks of the Seine. The Prima Donna had sent her excuse. But the first and second Buffa were there; and Signor Sc—, and Signora Ch—, and Madame V—, with a countless cavalcade besides of chorusers, figurantes, at the sight of whom Merry afterwards

declared, that "then for the first time it struck him seriously, that
he was about to marry—a dancer." But there was no help for it.
Besides, it was her day ; these were, in fact, her friends and kinsfolk.
The assemblage, though whimsical, was all very natural. But
when the bride—handing out of the last coach a still more extraordinary figure than the rest—presented to him as her *father*—
the gentleman that was to *give her away*—no less a person than
Signor Delpini himself—with a sort of pride, as much as to say,
See what I have brought to do us honour !—the thought of so
extraordinary a paternity quite overcame him ; and slipping away
under some pretence from the bride and her motley adherents, poor
Merry took horse from the back yard to the nearest sea-coast, from
which, shipping himself to America, he shortly after consoled himself with a more congenial match in the person of Miss Brunton ;
relieved from his intended clown father, and a bevy of painted
Buffas for bridemaids.

XIV.—THAT WE SHOULD RISE WITH THE LARK

At what precise minute that little airy musician doffs his night
gear, and prepares to tune up his unseasonable matins, we are
not naturalists enough to determine. But for a mere human
gentleman—that has no orchestra business to call him from his
warm bed to such preposterous exercises—we take ten, or half
after ten (eleven, of course, during this Christmas solstice), to be
the very earliest hour, at which he can begin to think of abandoning his pillow. To think of it, we say ; for to do it in earnest,
requires another half hour's good consideration. Not but there
are pretty sun-risings, as we are told, and such like gawds, abroad
in the world, in summer time especially, some hours before what we
have assigned ; which a gentleman may see, as they say, only for
getting up. But, having been tempted once or twice, in earlier
life, to assist at those ceremonies, we confess our curiosity abated.
We are no longer ambitious of being the sun's courtiers, to attend
at his morning levees. We hold the good hours of the dawn too
sacred to waste them upon such observances ; which have in them,
besides, something Pagan and Persic. To say truth, we never
anticipated our usual hour, or got up with the sun (as 'tis called),
to go a journey, or upon a foolish whole day's pleasuring, but
we suffered for it all the long hours after in listlessness and head-
achs ; Nature herself sufficiently declaring her sense of our presumption, in aspiring to regulate our frail waking courses by the
measures of that celestial and sleepless traveller. We deny not
that there is something sprightly and vigorous, at the outset especially, in these break-of-day excursions. It is flattering to get

the start of a lazy world ; to conquer death by proxy in his image. But the seeds of sleep and mortality are in us ; and we pay usually in strange qualms, before night falls, the penalty of the unnatural inversion.   Therefore, while the busy part of mankind are fast huddling on their clothes, are already up and about their occupations, content to have swallowed their sleep by wholesale ; we chose to linger a-bed, and digest our dreams.   It is the very time to recombine the wandering images, which night in a confused mass presented ; to snatch them from forgetfulness ; to shape, and mould them.   Some people have no good of their dreams.   Like fast feeders, they gulp them too grossly, to taste them curiously.   We love to chew the cud of a foregone vision : to collect the scattered rays of a brighter phantasm, or act over again, with firmer nerves, the sadder nocturnal tragedies ; to drag into day-light a struggling and half-vanishing night-mare ;   to handle and examine the terrors, or the airy solaces.   We have too much respect for these spiritual communications, to let them go so lightly.   We are not so stupid, or so careless, as that Imperial forgetter of his dreams, that we should need a seer to remind us of the form of them.   They seem to us to have as much significance as our waking concerns ;   or rather to import us more nearly, as more nearly we approach by years to the shadowy world, whither we are hastening.   We have shaken hands with the world's business ; we have done with it ; we have discharged ourself of it.   Why should we get up ? we have neither suit to solicit, nor affairs to manage.   The drama has shut in upon us at the fourth act.   We have nothing here to expect, but in a short time a sick bed, and a dismissal.   We delight to anticipate death by such shadows as night affords.   We are already half acquainted with ghosts.   We were never much in the world.   Disappointment early struck a dark veil between us and its dazzling illusions.   Our spirits showed grey before our hairs.   The mighty changes of the world already appear as but the vain stuff out of which dramas are composed.   We have asked no more of life than what the mimic images in play-houses present us with.   Even those types have waxed fainter.   Our clock appears to have struck.   We are SUPERANNUATED.   In this dearth of mundane satisfaction, we contract politic alliances with shadows.   It is good to have friends at court.   The abstracted media of dreams seem no ill introduction to that spiritual presence, upon which, in no long time, we expect to be thrown.   We are trying to know a little of the usages of that colony ; to learn the language, and the faces we shall meet with there, that we may be the less awkward at our first coming among them.   We willingly call a phantom our fellow, as knowing we shall soon be of their dark companion-

ship.   Therefore, we cherish dreams.   We try to spell in them
the alphabet of the invisible world ; and think we know already,
how it shall be with us.   Those uncouth shapes, which, while we
clung to flesh and blood, affrighted us, have become familiar.   We
feel attenuated into their meagre essences, and have given the hand
of half-way approach to incorporeal being.   We once thought life
to be something ; but it has unaccountably fallen from us before
its time.   Therefore we choose to dally with visions.   The sun has
no purposes of ours to light us to.   Why should we get up ?

XV.—THAT WE SHOULD LIE DOWN WITH THE LAMB

We could never quite understand the philosophy of this arrangement, or the wisdom of our ancestors in sending us for
instruction to these woolly bedfellows.   A sheep, when it is
dark, has nothing to do but to shut his silly eyes, and sleep if
he can.   Man found out long sixes.—Hail candle-light ! without
disparagement to sun or moon, the kindliest luminary of the three
—-if we may not rather style thee their radiant deputy, mild vice-
roy of the moon !—We love to read, talk, sit silent, eat, drink,
sleep, by candle-light.   They are every body's sun and moon.   This
is our peculiar and household planet.   Wanting it, what savage
unsocial nights must our ancestors have spent, wintering in caves
and unillumined fastnesses !   They must have lain about and
grumbled at one another in the dark.   What repartees could have
passed, when you must have felt about for a smile, and handled a
neighbour's cheek to be sure that he understood it ?   This accounts
for the seriousness of the elder poetry.   It has a sombre cast (try
Hesiod or Ossian), derived from the tradition of those unlantern'd
nights.   Jokes came in with candles.   We wonder how they saw
to pick up a pin, if they had any.   How did they sup ? what a
melange of chance carving they must have made of it !—here one
had got a leg of a goat, when he wanted a horse's shoulder—there
another had dipt his scooped palm in a kid-skin of wild honey,
when he meditated right mare's milk.   There is neither good
eating nor drinking in fresco.   Who, even in these civilised times,
has never experienced this, when at some economic table he has
commenced dining after dusk, and waited for the flavour till the
lights came ?   The senses absolutely give and take reciprocally.
Can you tell pork from veal in the dark ? or distinguish Sherris
from pure Malaga ?   Take away the candle from the smoking
man ; by the glimmering of the left ashes, he knows that he is still
smoking, but he knows it only by an inference ; till the restored
light, coming in aid of the olfactories, reveals to both senses the
full aroma.   Then how he redoubles his puffs ! how he burnishes !

—There is absolutely no such thing as reading, but by a candle. We have tried the affectation of a book at noon-day in gardens, and in sultry arbours; but it was labour thrown away. Those gay motes in the beam come about you, hovering and teazing, like so many coquets, that will have you all to their self, and are jealous of your abstractions. By the midnight taper, the writer digests his meditations. By the same light, we must approach to their perusal, if we would catch the flame, the odour. It is a mockery, all that is reported of the influential Phœbus. No true poem ever owed its birth to the sun's light. They are abstracted works—

> " Things that were born, when none but the still night,
> And his dumb candle, saw his pinching throes."

Marry, daylight—daylight might furnish the images, the crude material; but for the fine shapings, the true turning and filing (as mine author hath it), they must be content to hold their inspiration of the candle. The mild internal light, that reveals them, like fires on the domestic hearth, goes out in the sunshine. Night and silence call out the starry fancies. Milton's Morning Hymn on Paradise, we would hold a good wager, was penned at midnight; and Taylor's richer description of a sun-rise smells decidedly of the taper. Even ourself, in these our humbler lucubrations, tune our best measured cadences (Prose has her cadences) not unfrequently to the charm of the drowsier watchman, " blessing the doors;" or the wild sweep of winds at midnight. Even now a loftier speculation than we have yet attempted, courts our endeavours. We would indite something about the Solar System. —*Betty, bring the candles.*

XVI.—THAT A SULKY TEMPER IS A MISFORTUNE

We grant that it is, and a very serious one—to a man's friends, and to all that have to do with him; but whether the condition of the man himself is so much to be deplored, may admit of a question. We can speak a little to it, being ourself but lately recovered—we whisper it in confidence, reader—out of a long and desperate fit of the sullens. Was the cure a blessing? The conviction which wrought it, came too clearly to leave a scruple of the fanciful injuries—for they were mere fancies—which had provoked the humour. But the humour itself was too self-pleasing, while it lasted —we know how bare we lay ourself in the confession—to be abandoned all at once with the grounds of it. We still brood over wrongs which we know to have been imaginary; and for our old acquaintance, N——, whom we find to have been a truer friend than we took him for, we substitute some phantom—a Caius or a Titius—as like him as we dare to form it, to wreak our yet unsatisfied resentments on. It is mortifying to fall at once from the pinnacle of neglect; to forego the idea of having been ill-used and contumaciously treated by an old friend. The first thing to aggrandise a man in his own conceit, is to conceive of himself as neglected. There let him fix if he can. To undeceive him is to deprive him of the most tickling morsel within the range of self-complacency. No flattery can come near it. Happy is he who suspects his friend of an injustice; but supremely blest, who thinks all his friends in a conspiracy to depress and undervalue him. There is a pleasure (we sing not to the profane) far beyond the reach of all that the world counts joy—a deep, enduring satisfaction in the depths, where the superficial seek it not, of discontent. Were we to recite one half of this mystery, which we were let into by our late dissatisfaction, all the world would be in love with disrespect; we should wear a slight for a bracelet, and neglects and contumacies would be the only matter for courtship. Unlike to that mysterious book in the Apocalypse, the study of this mystery is unpalatable only in the commencement. The first sting of a suspicion is grievous; but wait—out of that wound, which to flesh and blood seemed so difficult, there is balm and honey to be extracted. Your friend passed you on such or such a day,—having in his company one that you conceived worse than ambiguously disposed towards you, —passed you in the street without notice. To be sure he is something shortsighted; and it was in your power to have accosted *him.* But facts and sane inferences are trifles to a true adept in the science of dissatisfaction. He must have seen you; and S——, who was with him, must have been the cause of the contempt. It galls you, and well it may. But have patience. Go home, and make the worst of it, and you are a made man from this time. Shut yourself up, and—rejecting, as an enemy to your peace, every whispering suggestion that but insinuates there may be a mistake—reflect seriously upon the many lesser instances which you had begun to perceive, in proof of your friend's disaffection towards you. None of them singly was much to the purpose, but the aggregate weight is positive; and you have this last affront to clench them. Thus far the process is any thing but agreeable. But now to your relief comes in the comparative faculty. You conjure up all the kind feelings you have had for your friend; what you have been to him, and what you would have been to him, if he would have suffered you; how you defended him in this or that place; and his good name—his literary reputation, and so forth, was always dearer to you than your own! Your heart, spite of itself, yearns towards him.   You could weep tears of blood but for a restraining pride.   How say you? do you not yet begin to apprehend a comfort? some allay of sweetness in the bitter waters?   Stop not here, nor penuriously cheat yourself of your reversions.   You are on vantage ground.   Enlarge your speculations, and take in the rest of your friends, as a spark kindles more sparks.   Was there one among them, who has not to you proved hollow, false, slippery as water?   Begin to think that the relation itself is inconsistent with mortality.   That the very idea of friendship, with its component parts, as honour, fidelity, steadiness, exists but in your single bosom.   Image yourself to yourself, as the only possible friend in a world incapable of that communion.   Now the gloom thickens.   The little star of self-love twinkles, that is to encourage you through deeper glooms than this.   You are not yet at the half point of your elevation.   You are not yet, believe me, half sulky enough.   Adverting to the world in general, (as these circles in the mind will spread to infinity) reflect with what strange injustice you have been treated in quarters where, (setting gratitude and the expectation of friendly returns aside as chimeras,) you pretended no claim beyond justice, the naked due of all men. Think the very idea of right and fit fled from the earth, or your breast the solitary receptacle of it, till you have swelled yourself into at least one hemisphere; the other being the vast Arabia Stony of your friends and the world aforesaid.   To grow bigger every moment in your own conceit, and the world to lessen: to deify yourself at the expense of your species; to judge the world—this is the acme and supreme point of your mystery—these the true PLEASURES of SULKINESS.   We profess no more of this grand secret than what ourself experimented on one rainy afternoon in the last week, sulking in our study.   We had proceeded to the penultimate point, at which the true adept seldom stops, where the consideration of benefit forgot is about to merge in the meditation of general injustice—when a knock at the door was followed by the entrance of the very friend, whose not seeing of us in the morning, (for we will now confess the case our own), an accidental oversight, had given rise to so much agreeable generalization!   To mortify us still more, and take down the whole flattering superstructure which pride had piled upon neglect, he had brought in his hand the identical S——, in whose favour we had suspected him of the contumacy.   Asseverations were needless, where the frank manner of them both was convictive of the injurious nature of the suspicion. We fancied that they perceived our embarrassment; but were too proud, or something else, to confess to the secret of it.   We had been but too lately in the condition of the noble patient in Argos:

Qui se credebat miros audire tragœdos,
In vacuo lætus sessor plausorque theatro—

and could have exclaimed with equal reason against the friendly
hands that cured us—

Pol me occidistis, amici,
Non servâstis, ait ; cui sic extorta voluptas,
Et demptus per vim mentis gratissimus error.

APPENDIX

CONSISTING OF LAMB'S ESSAYS ON "THE OLD ACTORS"
AS ORIGINALLY PRINTED IN THE *LONDON MAGA-*
ZINE. SEE NOTE ON PAGE 461

ON SOME OF THE OLD ACTORS

(*London Magazine*, Feb., 1822)

OF all the actors who flourished in my time—a melancholy phrase if taken aright, reader—Bensley had most of the swell of soul, was greatest in the delivery of heroic conceptions, the emotions consequent upon the presentment of a great idea to the fancy. He had the true poetical enthusiasm—the rarest faculty among players. None that I remember possessed even a portion of that fine madness which he threw out in Hotspur's famous rant about glory, or the transports of the Venetian incendiary at the vision of the fired city.[1] His voice had the dissonance, and at times the inspiriting effect of the trumpet. His gait was uncouth and stiff, but no way embarrassed by affectation; and the thorough-bred gentleman was uppermost in every movement. He seized the moment of passion with the greatest truth; like a faithful clock never striking before the time; never anticipating or leading you to anticipate. He was totally destitute of trick and artifice. He seemed come upon the stage to do the poet's message simply, and he did it with as genuine fidelity as the nuncios in Homer deliver the errands of the gods. He let the passion or the sentiment do its own work without prop or bolstering. He would have scorned to mountebank it; and betrayed none of that *cleverness* which is the bane of serious acting. For this reason, his Iago was the only endurable one which I remember to have seen. No spectator from his action could divine more of his artifice than Othello was supposed to do. His confessions in soliloquy alone put you in possession of the mystery. There were no bye-intimations to make the audience fancy their own discernment so much greater than that of the Moor—who commonly stands like a great helpless mark set up for mine Ancient, and a quantity of barren spectators, to shoot their bolts at. The Iago of Bensley did not go to work so grossly. There was a triumphant tone about the character, natural to a general consciousness of power; but none of that petty vanity which chuckles and cannot contain itself upon any little success-

---

[1] How lovelily the Adriatic whore
Dress'd in her flames will shine—devouring flames—
Such as will burn her to her wat'ry bottom,
And hiss in her foundation.

Pierre, in Venice Preserved.

ful stroke of its knavery—which is common with your small villains, and green probationers in mischief. It did not clap or crow before its time. It was not a man setting his wits at a child, and winking all the while at other children who are mightily pleased at being let into the secret; but a consummate villain entrapping a noble nature into toils, against which no discernment was available, where the manner was as fathomless as the purpose seemed dark, and without motive. The part of Malvolio, in the Twelfth Night, was performed by Bensley, with a richness and a dignity of which (to judge from some recent castings of that character) the very tradition must be worn out from the stage. No manager in those days would have dreamed of giving it to Mr. Baddeley, or Mr. Parsons: when Bensley was occasionally absent from the theatre, John Kemble thought it no derogation to succeed to the part. Malvolio is not essentially ludicrous. He becomes comic but by accident. He is cold, austere, repelling; but dignified, consistent, and, for what appears, rather of an over-stretched morality. Maria describes him as a sort of Puritan; and he might have worn his gold chain with honour in one of our old round-head families, in the service of a Lambert, or a Lady Fairfax. But his morality and his manners are misplaced in Illyria. He is opposed to the proper *levities* of the piece, and falls in the unequal contest. Still his pride, or his gravity, (call it which you will) is inherent, and native to the man, not mock or affected, which latter only are the fit objects to excite laughter. His quality is at the best unlovely, but neither buffoon nor contemptible. His bearing is lofty, a little above his station, but probably not much above his deserts. We see no reason why he should not have been brave, honourable, accomplished. His careless committal of the ring to the ground (which he was commissioned to restore to Cesario), bespeaks a generosity of birth and feeling.[1] His dialect on all occasions is that of a gentleman, and a man of education. We must not confound him with the eternal low steward of comedy. He is master of the household to a great Princess, a dignity probably conferred upon him for other respects than age or length of service.[2] Olivia, at the first indication of his supposed madness, declares that she "would not have him miscarry for half of her dowry." Does this look as if the character was meant to appear little or insignificant? Once, indeed, she accuses him to his face—of what?—of being "sick of self-love,"—but with a gentleness

---

[1] *Viola.* She took the ring from me; I'll none of it.

Mal. Come, Sir, you peevishly threw it to her; and her will is, it should be so returned. If it be worth stooping for, there it lies in your eye; if not, be it his that finds it.

[2] Mrs. Inchbald seems to have fallen into the common mistake of the character in some sensible observations, otherwise, upon this Comedy. "It might be asked," she says, "whether this credulous steward was much deceived in imputing a degraded taste, in the sentiments of love, to his fair lady Olivia, as she actually did fall in love with a domestic; and one, who from his extreme youth, was perhaps a greater reproach to her discretion, than had she cast a tender regard upon her old and faithful servant." But where does she gather the fact of his age? Neither Maria nor Fabian ever cast that reproach upon him.

and considerateness which could not have been, if she had not thought that this particular infirmity shaded some virtues. His rebuke to the knight, and his sottish revellers, is sensible and spirited ; and when we take into consideration the unprotected condition of his mistress, and the strict regard with which her state of real or dissembled mourning would draw the eyes of the world upon her house-affairs, Malvolio might feel the honour of the family in some sort in his keeping, as it appears not that Olivia had any more brothers, or kinsmen, to look to it—for Sir Toby had dropped all such nice respects at the buttery hatch. That Malvolio was meant to be represented as possessing some estimable qualities, the expression of the Duke in his anxiety to have him reconciled, almost infers : " Pursue him, and intreat him to a peace." Even in his abused state of chains and darkness, a sort of greatness seems never to desert him. He argues highly and well with the supposed Sir Topas,[1] and philosophizes gallantly upon his straw. There must have been some shadow of worth about the man ; he must have been something more than a mere vapour—a thing of straw, or Jack in office—before Fabian and Maria could have ventured sending him upon a courting errand to Olivia. There was some consonancy (as he would say) in the undertaking, or the jest would have been too bold even for that house of misrule. There was " example for it," said Malvolio ; " the lady of the Strachy married the yeoman of the wardrobe." Possibly too he might remember—for it must have happened about his time—an instance of a Duchess of Malfy (a countrywoman of Olivia's, and her equal at least) descending from her state to court her steward—

> The misery of them that are born great !
> They are forced to woo, because none dare woo them.

To be sure the lady was not very tenderly handled for it by her brothers in the sequel, but their vengeance appears to have been whetted rather by her presumption in re-marrying at all, (when they had meditated the keeping of her fortune in their family) than by her choice of an inferior, of Antonio's noble merits especially, for her husband ; and, besides, Olivia's brother was just dead. Malvolio was a man of reading, and possibly reflected upon these lines, or something like them in his own country poetry—

> ——Ceremony has made many fools.
> It is as easy way unto a duchess
> As to a hatted dame, if her love answer :
> But that by timorous honours, pale respects,
> Idle degrees of fear, men make their ways
> Hard of themselves.

" 'Tis but fortune, all is fortune. Maria once told me, she did affect me ; and I have heard herself come thus near, that, should she fancy,

---

[1] *Clown.* What is the opinion of Pythagoras concerning wild fowl ?
Mal. That the soul of our grandam might haply inhabit a bird.
Clown. What thinkest thou of his opinion ?
Mal. I think nobly of the soul, and no way approve of his opinion.

it should be one of my complexion." If here was no encourage-nent, the devil is in it. I wish we could get at the private history of all this. Between the Countess herself, serious or dissembling—for one hardly knows how to apprehend this fantastical great lady—and the practices of that delicious little piece of mischief, Maria—

> The lime twigs laid
> By Machiavel the waiting maid—

the man might well be rapt into a fool's paradise.

Bensley threw over the part an air of Spanish loftiness. He looked, spake, and moved like an old Castilian. He was starch, spruce, opinionated, but his superstructure of pride seemed bottomed upon a sense of worth. There was something in it beyond the coxcomb. It was big and swelling, but you could not be sure that it was hollow. You might wish to see it taken down, but you felt that it was upon an elevation. He was magnificent from the outset ; but when the decent sobrieties of the character began to give way, and the poison of self-love in his conceit of the Countess's affection gradually to work, you would have thought that the hero of La Mancha in person stood before you. How he went smiling to himself! with what ineffable carelessness would he twirl his gold chain! what a dream it was! you were infected with the illusion, and did not wish that it should be removed! you had no room for laughter ! if an unseasonable reflection of morality obtruded itself, it was a deep sense of the pitiable infirmity of man's nature, that can lay him open to such frenzies—but in truth you rather admired than pitied the lunacy while it lasted—you felt that an hour of such mistake was worth an age with the eyes open. Who would not wish to live but for a day in the conceit of such a lady's love as Olivia ? Why, the Duke would have given his principality but for a quarter of a minute, sleeping or waking, to have been so deluded. The man seemed to tread upon air, to taste manna, to walk with his head in the clouds, to mate Hyperion. O ! shake not the castles of his pride—endure yet for a season, bright moments of confidence—" stand still ye watches of the element," that Malvolio may be still in fancy fair Olivia's lord—but fate and retribution say no—I hear the mischievous titter of Maria—the witty taunts of Sir Toby—the still more insupportable triumph of the foolish knight—the counterfeit Sir Topas is unmasked—and " thus the whirligig of time," as the true clown hath it, " brings in his revenges." I confess that I never saw the catastrophe of this character while Bensley played it without a kind of tragic interest. There was good foolery too. Few now remember Dodd. What an Aguecheek the stage lost in him! Lovegrove, who came nearest to the old actors, revived the character some few seasons ago, and made it sufficiently grotesque ; but Dodd was *it*, as it came out of nature's hands. It might be said to remain *in puris naturalibus*. In expressing slowness of apprehension this actor surpassed all others. You could see the first dawn of an idea stealing slowly over his countenance, climbing up by little and little, with a painful process, till it cleared up at last to the fulness of a twilight conception—its highest meridian. He seemed to keep back his intellect, as some have had the power to retard their pulsation. The balloon takes less time in filling, than it took to cover the expansion of his broad moony face over all its quarters with expression. A glimmer of understanding would appear in a corner of his eye, and for lack of fuel go out again. A part of his forehead would catch a little intelligence, and be a long time in communicating it to the remainder.

I am ill at dates, but I think it is now better than five and twenty years ago that walking in the gardens of Gray's Inn—they were then far finer than they are now—the accursed Verulam Buildings had not encroached upon all the east side of them, cutting out delicate green crankles, and shouldering away one of two of the stately alcoves of the terrace—the survivor stands gaping and relationless as if it remembered its brother—they are still the best gardens of any of the Inns of Court, my beloved Temple not forgotten—have the gravest character, their aspect being altogether reverend and law-breathing—Bacon has left the impress of his foot upon their gravel walks——taking my afternoon solace on a summer day upon the aforesaid terrace, a comely sad personage came towards me, whom from his grave air and deportment I judged to be one of the old Benchers of the Inn. He had a serious thoughtful forehead, and seemed to be in meditations of mortality. As I have an instinctive awe of old Benchers, I was passing him with that sort of subindicative token of respect which one is apt to demonstrate towards a venerable stranger, and which rather denotes an inclination to greet him than any positive motion of the body to that effect—a species of humility and will-worship which I observe nine times out of ten rather puzzles than pleases the person it is offered to—when the face turning full upon me strangely identified itself with that of Dodd. Upon close inspection I was not mistaken. But could this sad thoughtful countenance be the same vacant face of folly which I had hailed so often under circumstances of gaiety ; which I had never seen without a smile, or recognized but as the usher of mirth ; that looked out so formally flat in Foppington, so frothily pert in Tattle, so impotently busy in Backbite ; so blankly divested of all meaning, or resolutely expressive of none, in Acres, in Fribble, and a thousand agreeable impertinences ? Was this the face—full of thought and carefulness—that had so often divested itself at will of every trace of either to give me diversion, to clear my cloudy face for two or three hours at least of its furrows ? Was this the face—manly, sober, intelligent,—which I had so often despised, made mocks at, made merry with ? The remembrance of the freedoms which I had taken with it came upon me with a reproach of insult. I could have asked it pardon. I thought it looked upon me with a sense of injury. There is something strange as well as sad in seeing actors—your pleasant fellows particularly—subjected to and suffering the common lot—their fortunes, their casualties, their deaths, seem to belong to the scene, their actions to be amenable to poetic justice only. We can hardly connect them with more awful responsibilities. The death of this fine actor took place shortly after this meeting. He had quitted the stage some months; and, as I learned afterwards, had been in the habit of resorting daily to these gardens almost to the day of his decease. In these serious walks probably he was divesting himself of many scenic and some real vanities—weaning himself from the frivolities of the lesser and the greater theatre—doing gentle penance for a life of no very reprehensible fooleries,—taking off by degrees the buffoon mask which he might feel he had worn too long —and rehearsing for a more solemn cast of part. Dying he "put on the weeds of Dominic." [1]

The elder Palmer (of stage-treading celebrity) commonly played Sir Toby in those days; but there is a solidity of wit in the jests of that half-Falstaff which he did not quite fill out. He was as much too showy as Moody (who sometimes took the part) was dry and sottish. In sock or buskin there was an air of swaggering gentility about Jack Palmer. He was a *gentleman* with a slight infusion of *the footman*. His brother Bob (of recenter memory) who was his shadow in every thing while he lived, and dwindled into less than a shadow afterwards —was a *gentleman* with a little stronger infusion of the *latter ingredient;* that was all. It is amazing how a little of the more or less makes a difference in these things. When you saw Bobby in the Duke's Servant,[2] you said, what a pity such a pretty fellow was only a servant. When you saw Jack figuring in Captain Absolute, you thought you could trace his promotion to some lady of quality who fancied the handsome fellow in his top-knot, and had bought him a commission. Therefore Jack in Dick Amlet was insuperable.

Jack had two voices,—both plausible, hypocritical, and insinuating; but his secondary or supplemental voice still more decisively histrionic than his common one. It was reserved for the spectator; and the dramatis personæ were supposed to know nothing at all about it. The *lies* of young Wilding, and the *sentiments* in Joseph Surface, were thus marked out in a sort of italics to the audience. This secret correspondence with the company before the curtain (which is the bane and death of tragedy) has an extremely happy effect in some kinds of comedy, in the more highly artificial comedy of Congreve or of Sheridan especially, where the absolute sense of reality (so indispensable to scenes of interest) is not required, or would rather interfere to diminish your pleasure. The fact is, you do not believe in such characters as Surface —the villain of artificial comedy—even while you read or see them.

---

[1] Dodd was a man of reading, and left at his death a choice collection of old English literature. I should judge him to have been a man of wit. I know one instance of an impromptu which no length of study could have bettered. My merry friend, Jem White, had seen him one evening in Aguecheek, and recognizing Dodd the next day in Fleet Street, was irresistibly impelled to take off his hat and salute him as the identical Knight of the preceding evening with a " Save you, *Sir Andrew.*" Dodd, not at all disconcerted at this unusual address from a stranger, with a courteous half-rebuking wave of the hand, put him off with an " Away, *Fool.*"

[2] High Life Below Stairs.

If you did, they would shock and not divert you. When Ben, in Love for Love, returns from sea, the following exquisite dialogue occurs at his first meeting with his father—

Sir Sampson. Thou hast been many a weary league, Ben, since I saw thee.
Ben. Ey, ey, been! Been far enough, an that be all—Well father, and how do all at home? how does brother Dick, and brother Val?
Sir Sampson. Dick! body o' me, Dick has been dead these two years. I writ you word when you were at Leghorn.
Ben. Mess, that's true; Marry, I had forgot. Dick's dead, as you say—Well, and how?—I have a many questions to ask you—

Here is an instance of insensibility which in real life would be revolting, or rather in real life could not have co-existed with the warm-hearted temperament of the character. But when you read it in the spirit with which such playful selections and specious combinations rather than strict *metaphrases* of nature should be taken, or when you saw Bannister play it, it neither did, nor does wound the moral sense at all. For what is Ben—the pleasant sailor which Bannister gave us —but a piece of a satire—a creation of Congreve's fancy—a dreamy combination of all the accidents of a sailor's character—his contempt of money—his credulity to women—with that necessary estrangement from home which it is just within the verge of credibility to suppose *might* produce such an hallucination as is here described. We never think the worse of Ben for it, or feel it as a stain upon his character. But when an actor comes, and instead of the delightful phantom—the creature dear to half-belief—which Bannister exhibited—displays before our eyes a downright concretion of a Wapping sailor—a jolly warm-hearted Jack Tar—and nothing else—when instead of investing it with a delicious confusedness of the head, and a veering undirected goodness of purpose—he gives to it a downright daylight understanding, and a full consciousness of its actions; thrusting forward the sensibilities of the character with a pretence as if it stood upon nothing else, and was to be judged by them alone—we feel the discord of the thing; the scene is disturbed; a real man has got in among the dramatis personæ, and puts them out. We want the sailor turned out. We feel that his true place is not behind the curtain, but in the first or second gallery.

(*To be resumed occasionally.*)

Elia.

THE OLD ACTORS

(*London Magazine*, April, 1822)

THE artificial Comedy, or Comedy of manners, is quite extinct on our stage. Congreve and Farquhar show their heads once in seven years only to be exploded and put down instantly. The times cannot bear them. Is it for a few wild speeches, an occasional licence of dialogue? I think not altogether. The business of their dramatic characters will not stand the moral test. We screw every thing up to that. Idle gallantry in a fiction, a dream, the passing pageant of an evening, startles us in the same way as the alarming indications of profligacy in a son or ward in real life should startle a parent or guardian. We have no such middle emotions as dramatic interests left. We see a stage libertine playing his loose pranks of two hours' duration, and of no after consequence, with the severe eyes which inspect real vices with their bearings upon two worlds. We are spectators to a plot or intrigue (not reducible in life to the point of strict morality) and take it all for truth. We substitute a real for a dramatic person, and judge him accordingly. We try him in our courts, from which there is no appeal to the *dramatis personæ*, his peers. We have been spoiled with—not sentimental comedy—but a tyrant far more pernicious to our pleasures which has succeeded to it, the exclusive and all-devouring drama of common life ; where the moral point is every thing ; where, instead of the fictitious half-believed personages of the stage (the phantoms of old comedy) we recognise ourselves, our brothers, aunts, kinsfolk, allies, patrons, enemies,—the same as in life,—with an interest in what is going on so hearty and substantial, that we cannot afford our moral judgment, in its deepest and most vital results, to compromise or slumber for a moment. What is *there* transacting, by no modification is made to affect us in any other manner than the same events or characters would do in our relationships of life. We carry our fire-side concerns to the theatre with us. We do not go thither, like our ancestors, to escape from the pressure of reality, so much as to confirm our experience of it ; to make assurance double, and take a bond of fate. We must live our toilsome lives twice over, as it was the mournful privilege of Ulysses to descend twice to the shades. All that neutral ground of character which stood between vice and virtue ; or which, in fact, was indifferent to neither, where neither properly was called in question—that happy breathing-place from the burden of a perpetual moral questioning—the sanctuary and quiet Alsatia of hunted casuistry—is broken up and disfranchised as injurious to the interests of society. The privileges of the place are taken away by law. We dare not dally with images or names of wrong. We bark like foolish dogs at shadows. We dread infection from the scenic representation of disorder ; and fear a painted pustule. In our anxiety that our morality should not take cold, we wrap it up in a great blanket surtout of precaution against the breeze and sunshine.

I confess for myself that (with no great delinquencies to answer for) I am glad for a season to take an airing beyond the diocese of the strict conscience,—not to live always in the precincts of the law courts, —but now and then, for a dream-while or so, to imagine a world with no meddling restrictions—to get into recesses, whither the hunter cannot follow me—

————————Secret shades
Of woody Ida's inmost grove,
While yet there was no fear of Jove—

I come back to my cage and my restraint the fresher and more healthy
for it. I wear my shackles more contentedly for having respired the
breath of an imaginary freedom. I do not know how it is with others,
but I feel the better always for the perusal of one of Congreve's—nay,
why should I not add even of Wycherley's—comedies. I am the gayer
at least for it ; and I could never connect those sports of a witty fancy
in any shape with any result to be drawn from them to imitation in
real life. They are a world of themselves almost as much as a fairy-
land. Take one of their characters, male or female (with few exceptions they are alike), and place it in a modern play, and my virtuous
indignation shall rise against the profligate wretch as warmly as the
Catos of the pit could desire ; because in a modern play I am to judge
of right and wrong, and the standard of *police* is the measure of
poetical justice. The atmosphere will blight it. It cannot thrive here.
It is got into a moral world where it has no business ; from which it
must needs fall head-long ; as dizzy and incapable of keeping its stand,
as a Swedenborgian bad spirit that has wandered unawares within the
sphere of one of his good men or angels. But in its own world do we
feel the creature is so very bad ?
   The Fainalls and the Mirabels, the Dorimants, and Lady Touchwoods, in their own sphere do not offend my moral sense—or, in fact,
appeal to it at all. They seem engaged in their proper element.
They break through no laws, or conscientious restraints. They know
of none. They have got out of Christendom into the land—what shall
I call it ?—of cuckoldry—the Utopia of gallantry, where pleasure is
duty, and the manners perfect freedom. It is altogether a speculative
scene of things, which has no reference whatever to the world that is.
No good person can be justly offended as a spectator, because no good
person suffers on the stage. Judged morally, every character in these
plays—the few exceptions only are *mistakes*—is alike essentially vain
and worthless. The great art of Congreve is especially shown in this,
that he has entirely excluded from his scenes,—some little generosities
in the part of Angelica perhaps excepted,—not only any thing like a
faultless character, but any pretensions to goodness or good feelings whatsoever. Whether he did this designedly, or instinctively,
the effect is as happy, as the design (if design) was bold. I used to
wonder at the strange power which his Way of the World in particular
possesses of interesting you all along in the pursuits of characters, for
whom you absolutely care nothing—for you neither hate nor love his
personages—and I think it is owing to this very indifference for any,
that you endure the whole. He has spread a privation of moral light,
I will call it, rather than by the ugly name of palpable darkness, over
his creations ; and his shadows flit before you without distinction or
preference. Had he introduced a good character, a single gush of
moral feeling, a revulsion of the judgment to actual life and actual

duties, the impertinent Goshen would have only lighted to the discovery of deformities, which now are none, because we think them none.

Translated into real life, the characters of his, and his friend Wycherley's dramas, are profligates and strumpets,—the business of their brief existence, the undivided pursuit of lawless gallantry. No other spring of action, or possible motive of conduct, is recognised; principles which universally acted upon must reduce this frame of things to a chaos. But we do them wrong in so translating them. No such effects are produced in *their* world. When we are among them, we are amongst a chaotic people. We are not to judge them by our usages. No reverend institutions are insulted by their proceedings,—for they have none among them. No peace of families is violated,—for no family ties exist among them. No purity of the marriage bed is stained,—for none is supposed to have a being. No deep affections are disquieted,—no holy wedlock bands are snapped asunder,—for affection's depth and wedded faith are not of the growth of that soil. There is neither right nor wrong,—gratitude or its opposite,—claim or duty,—paternity or sonship. Of what consequence is it to virtue, or how is she at all concerned about it, whether Sir Simon, or Dapperwit, steal away Miss Martha ; or who is the father of Lord Froth's, or Sir Paul Pliant's children?

The whole is a passing pageant, where we should sit as unconcerned at the issues, for life or death, as at a battle of the frogs and mice. But like Don Quixote, we take part against the puppets, and quite as impertinently. We dare not contemplate an Atlantis, a scheme, out of which our coxcombical moral sense is for a little transitory ease excluded. We have not the courage to imagine a state of things for which there is neither reward nor punishment. We cling to the painful necessities of shame and blame. We would indict our very dreams.

Amidst the mortifying circumstances attendant upon growing old, it is something to have seen the School for Scandal in its glory. This comedy grew out of Congreve and Wycherley, but gathered some allays of the sentimental comedy which followed theirs. It is impossible that it should be now acted, though it continues, at long intervals, to be announced in the bills. Its hero, when Palmer played it at least, was Joseph Surface. When I remember the gay boldness, the graceful solemn plausibility, the measured step, the insinuating voice—to express it in a word—the downright *acted* villany of the part, so different from the pressure of conscious actual wickedness,—the hypocritical assumption of hypocrisy,—which made Jack so deservedly a favourite in that character, I must needs conclude the present generation of playgoers more virtuous than myself, or more dense. I freely confess that he divided the palm with me with his better brother ; that, in fact, I liked him quite as well. Not but there are passages,—like that, for instance, where Joseph is made to refuse a pittance to a poor relation, —incongruities which Sheridan was forced upon by the attempt to join the artificial with the sentimental comedy, either of which must destroy the other—but over these obstructions Jack's manner floated him so lightly, that a refusal from him no more shocked you, than the easy compliance of Charles gave you in reality any pleasure ; you got over the paltry question as quickly as you could, to get back into the regions of pure comedy, where no cold moral reigns. The highly artificial manner of Palmer in this character counteracted every disagreeable impression which you might have received from the contrast, supposing them real, between the two brothers. You did not believe in Joseph with the same faith with which you believed in Charles. The latter was a pleasant reality, the former a no less pleasant poetical foil to it. The comedy, I have said, is incongruous ; a mixture of Congreve with sentimental incompatibilities ; the gaiety upon the whole is buoyant ; but it required the consummate art of Palmer to reconcile the discordant elements.

A player with Jack's talents, if we had one now, would not dare to do the part in the same manner. He would instinctively avoid every turn which might tend to unrealize, and so to make the character fascinating. He must take his cue from his spectators, who would expect a bad man and a good man as rigidly opposed to each other, as the death-beds of those geniuses are contrasted in the prints, which I am sorry to see have disappeared from the windows of my old friend Carrington Bowles, of St. Paul's Church-yard memory—(an exhibition as venerable as the adjacent cathedral, and almost coeval) of the bad and good man at the hour of death ; where the ghastly apprehensions of the former,—and truly the grim phantom with his reality of a toasting fork is not to be despised,—so finely contrast with the meek complacent kissing of the rod,—taking it in like honey and butter,—with which the latter submits to the scythe of the gentle bleeder, Time, who wields his lancet with the apprehensive finger of a popular young ladies' surgeon. What flesh, like loving grass, would not covet to meet half-way the stroke of such a delicate mower ?—John Palmer was twice an actor in this exquisite part. He was playing to you all the while that he was playing upon Sir Peter and his lady. You had the first intimation of a sentiment before it was on his lips. His altered voice was meant to you, and you were to suppose that his fictitious co-flutterers on the stage perceived nothing at all of it. What was it to you if that half-reality, the husband, was over-reached by the puppetry—or the thin thing (Lady Teazle's reputation) was persuaded it was dying of a plethory ? The fortunes of Othello and Desdemona were not concerned in it. Poor Jack has passed from the stage—in good time, that he did not live to this our age of seriousness. The fidgety pleasant old Teazle *King* too is gone in good time. His manner would scarce have passed current in our day. We must love or hate—acquit or condemn—censure or pity—exert our detestable coxcombry of moral judgment upon every thing. Joseph Surface, to go down now, must be a downright revolting villain—no compromise—his first appearance must shock and give horror—his specious plausibilities, which the pleasurable faculties of our fathers welcomed with such hearty greetings, knowing that no harm (dramatic harm even) could come, or was meant to come of them, must inspire a cold and killing aversion. Charles (the real canting person of the scene—for the hypocrisy of Joseph has its ulterior legitimate ends, but his brother's professions of a good heart centre in down-right self-satisfaction) must be *loved*, and Joseph *hated*. To balance one disagreeable reality with another, Sir Peter Teazle must be no longer the comic idea of a fretful old bachelor bridegroom, whose teazings (while King acted it) were evidently as much played off at you, as they were meant to concern any body on the stage,—he must be a real person, capable in law of sustaining an injury—a person towards whom duties are to be acknowledged—the genuine crim-con antagonist of the villainous seducer, Joseph. To realize him more, his sufferings under his unfortunate match must have the downright pungency of life—must (or should) make you not mirthful but uncomfortable, just as the same predicament would move you in a neighbour or old friend. The delicious scenes which give the play its name and zest, must affect you in the same serious manner as if you heard the reputation of a dear female friend attacked in your real presence. Crabtree, and Sir Benjamin—those poor snakes that lived but in the sunshine of your mirth—must be ripened by this hot-bed process of realization into asps or amphisbænas; and Mrs. Candour—O! frightful! become a hooded serpent. Oh who that remembers Parsons and Dodd—the wasp and butterfly of the School for Scandal—in those two characters; and charming natural Miss Pope, the perfect gentlewoman as distinguished from the fine lady of comedy, in this latter part—would forego the true scenic delight—the escape from life—the oblivion of consequences—the holiday barring out of the pedant Reflection—those Saturnalia of two or three brief hours, well won from the world—to sit instead at one of our modern plays—to have his coward conscience (that forsooth must not be left for a moment) stimulated with perpetual appeals—dulled rather, and blunted, as a faculty without repose must be—and his moral vanity pampered with images of notional justice, notional beneficence, lives saved without the spectators' risk, and fortunes given away that cost the author nothing?

No piece was, perhaps, ever so completely cast in all its parts as this *manager's comedy*. Miss Farren had succeeded to Mrs. Abingdon in Lady Teazle; and Smith, the original Charles, had retired, when I first saw it. The rest of the characters, with very slight exceptions, remained. I remember it was then the fashion to cry down John Kemble, who took the part of Charles after Smith; but, I thought, very unjustly. Smith, I fancy, was more airy, and took the eye with a certain gaiety of person. He brought with him no sombre recollections of tragedy. He had not to expiate the fault of having pleased beforehand in lofty declamation. He had no sins of Hamlet or of Richard to atone for. His failure in these parts was a passport to success in one of so opposite a tendency. But as far as I could judge, the weighty sense of Kemble made up for more personal incapacity than he had to

answer for.   His harshest tones in this part came steeped and dulcified
in good humour.   He made his defects a grace.   His exact declamatory
manner, as he managed it, only served to convey the points of his dialogue with more precision.   It seemed to head the shafts to carry them
deeper.   Not one of his sparkling sentences was lost.   I remember
minutely how he delivered each in succession, and cannot by any effort
imagine how any of them could be altered for the better.   No man
could deliver brilliant dialogue—the dialogue of Congreve or of
Wycherley—because none understood it—half so well as John Kemble.
His Valentine, in Love for Love, was, to my recollection, faultless.
He flagged sometimes in the intervals of tragic passion.   He would
slumber over the level parts of an heroic character.   His Macbeth has
been known to nod.   But he always seemed to me to be particularly
alive to pointed and witty dialogue.   The relaxing levities of tragedy
have not been touched by any since him—the playful court-bred spirit
in which he condescended to the players in Hamlet—the sportive relief
which he threw into the darker shades of Richard—disappeared with
him.   Tragedy is become a uniform dead weight.   They have fastened
lead to her buskins.   She never pulls them off for the ease of a moment.
To invert a commonplace from Niobe, she never forgets herself to
liquefaction.   John had his sluggish moods, his torpors—but they were
the halting stones and resting places of his tragedy—politic savings, and
fetches of the breath—husbandry of the lungs, where nature pointed
him to be an economist—rather, I think, than errors of the judgment.
They were, at worst, less painful than the eternal tormenting unappeasable vigilance, the "lidless dragon eyes," of present fashionable
tragedy.   The story of his swallowing opium pills to keep him lively
upon the first night of a certain tragedy, we may presume to be a piece
of retaliatory pleasantry on the part of the suffering author.   But,
indeed, John had the art of diffusing a complacent equable dulness
(which you knew not where to quarrel with) over a piece which he did
not like, beyond any of his contemporaries.   John Kemble had made
up his mind early, that all the good tragedies, which could be written,
had been written; and he resented any new attempt.   His shelves
were full.   The old standards were scope enough for his ambition.   He
ranged in them absolute—and " fair in Otway, full in Shakspeare
shone."   He succeeded to the old lawful thrones, and did not care to
adventure bottomry with a Sir Edward Mortimer, or any casual specu-
lator that offered.   I remember, too acutely for my peace, the deadly
extinguisher which he put upon my friend G.'s " Antonio."   G., satiate
with visions of political justice (possibly not to be realized in our
time), or willing to let the sceptical worldlings see, that his anticipations
of the future did not preclude a warm sympathy for men as they are and
have been—wrote a tragedy.   He chose a story, affecting, romantic,
Spanish—the plot simple, without being naked—the incidents uncommon, without being overstrained.   Antonio, who gives the name to the
piece, is a sensitive young Castilian, who, in a fit of his country honour,
immolates his sister——

But I must not anticipate the catastrophe—the play, reader, is extant in choice English—and you will employ a spare half crown not injudiciously in the quest of it.

The conception was bold, and the dénouement—the time and place in which the hero of it existed, considered—not much out of keeping ; yet it must be confessed, that it required a delicacy of handling both from the author and the performer, so as not much to shock the prejudices of a modern English audience. G., in my opinion, had done his part.

John, who was in familiar habits with the philosopher, had undertaken to play Antonio. Great expectations were formed. A philosopher's first play was a new era. The night arrived. I was favoured with a seat in an advantageous box, between the author and his friend M——. G. sate cheerful and confident. In his friend M.'s looks, who had perused the manuscript, I read some terror. Antonio in the person of John Philip Kemble at length appeared, starched out in a ruff which no one could dispute, and in most irreproachable mustachios. John always dressed most provokingly correct on these occasions. The first act swept by, solemn and silent. It went off, as G. assured M., exactly as the opening act of a piece—the protasis—should do. The cue of the spectators was to be mute. The characters were but in their introduction. The passions and the incidents would be developed hereafter. Applause hitherto would be impertinent. Silent attention was the effect all-desirable. Poor M. acquiesced—but in his honest friendly face I could discern a working which told how much more acceptable the plaudit of a single hand (however misplaced) would have been than all this reasoning. The second act (as in duty bound) rose a little in interest ; but still John kept his forces under—in policy, as G. would have it—and the audience were most complacently attentive. The protasis, in fact, was scarcely unfolded. The interest would warm in the next act, against which a special incident was provided. M. wiped his cheek, flushed with a friendly perspiration—'tis M.'s way of showing his zeal—"from every pore of him a perfume falls—." I honour it above Alexander's. He had once or twice during this act joined his palms in a feeble endeavour to elicit a sound—they emitted a solitary noise without an echo—there was no deep to answer to his deep. G. repeatedly begged him to be quiet. The third act at length brought on the scene which was to warm the piece progressively to the final flaming forth of the catastrophe. A philosophic calm settled upon the clear brow of G. as it approached. The lips of M. quivered. A challenge was held forth upon the stage, and there was promise of a fight. The pit roused themselves on this extraordinary occasion, and, as their manner is, seemed disposed to make a ring,—when suddenly Antonio, who was the challenged, turning the tables upon the hot challenger, Don Gusman (who by the way should have had his sister) baulks his humour, and the pit's reasonable expectation at the same time, with some speeches out of the new philosophy against duelling. The audience were here fairly caught—their courage was up, and on the alert—a few blows, *ding dong*, as R——s the dramatist afterwards expressed it to me, might have done the business—when their most exquisite moral sense was suddenly called in to assist in the mortifying negation of their own pleasure. They could not applaud, for disappointment; they would not condemn, for morality's sake. The interest stood stone still; and John's manner was not at all calculated to unpetrify it. It was Christmas time, and the atmosphere furnished some pretext for asthmatic affections. One began to cough—his neighbour sympathised with him—till a cough became epidemical. But when, from being half-artificial in the pit, the cough got frightfully naturalised among the fictitious persons of the drama; and Antonio himself (albeit it was not set down in the stage directions) seemed more intent upon relieving his own lungs than the distresses of the author and his friends,—then G. "first knew fear;" and mildly turning to M., intimated that he had not been aware that Mr. K. laboured under a cold; and that the performance might possibly have been postponed with advantage for some nights further—still keeping the same serene countenance, while M. sweat like a bull. It would be invidious to pursue the fates of this ill-starred evening. In vain did the plot thicken in the scenes that followed, in vain the dialogue wax more passionate and stirring, and the progress of the sentiment point more and more clearly to the arduous developement which impended. In vain the action was accelerated, while the acting stood still. From the beginning, John had taken his stand; had wound himself up to an even tenor of stately declamation, from which no exigence of dialogue or person could make him swerve for an instant. To dream of his rising with the scene (the common trick of tragedians) was preposterous; for from the onset he had planted himself, as upon a terrace, on an eminence vastly above the audience, and he kept that sublime level to the end. He looked from his throne of elevated sentiment upon the under-world of spectators with a most sovran and becoming contempt. There was excellent pathos delivered out to them : an they would receive it, so; an they would not receive it, so. There was no offence against decorum in all this; nothing to condemn, to damn. Not an irreverent symptom of a sound was to be heard. The procession of verbiage stalked on through four and five acts, no one venturing to predict what would come of it, when towards the winding up of the latter, Antonio, with an irrelevancy that seemed to stagger Elvira herself—for she had been coolly arguing the point of honour with him—suddenly whips out a poniard, and stabs his sister to the heart. The effect was, as if a murder had been committed in cold blood. The whole house rose up in clamorous indignation demanding justice. The feeling rose far above hisses. I believe at that instant, if they could have got him, they would have torn the unfortunate author to pieces. Not that the act itself was so exorbitant, or of a complexion different from what they themselves would have applauded upon another occasion in a Brutus, or an Appius—but for want of attending to Antonio's *words*, which palpably led to the expectation of no less

dire an event, instead of being seduced by his *manner*, which seemed
to promise a sleep of a less alarming nature than it was his cue to
inflict upon Elvira, they found themselves betrayed into an accomplice-
ship of murder, a perfect misprision of parricide, while they dreamed of
nothing less. M., I believe, was the only person who suffered acutely
from the failure ; for G. thenceforward, with a serenity unattainable but
by the true philosophy, abandoning a precarious popularity, retired
into his fast hold of speculation,—the drama in which the world was to
be his tiring room, and remote posterity his applauding spectators at
once, and actors.   Elia.

THE OLD ACTORS

(London Magazine, October, 1822)

I DO not know a more mortifying thing than to be conscious of a
    foregone delight, with a total oblivion of the person and manner
which conveyed it. In dreams I often stretch and strain after the
countenance of Edwin, whom I once saw in Peeping Tom. I cannot catch a feature of him. He is no more to me than Nokes or
Pinkethman. Parsons, and still more Dodd, were near being lost to
me, till I was refreshed with their portraits (fine treat) the other day
at Mr. Mathews's gallery at Highgate ; which, with the exception of the
Hogarth pictures, a few years since exhibited in Pall Mall, was the
most delightful collection I ever gained admission to. There hang the
players, in their single persons, and in grouped scenes, from the Restoration——Bettertons, Booths, Garricks, justifying the prejudices
which we entertain for them—the Bracegirdles, the Mountforts, and
the Oldfields, fresh as Cibber has described them—the Woffington (a
true Hogarth) upon a couch, dallying and dangerous—the Screen Scene
in Brinsley's famous comedy, with Smith and Mrs. Abingdon, whom I
have not seen, and the rest, whom having seen, I see still there.
There is Henderson, unrivalled in Comus, whom I saw at second hand
in the elder Harley—Harley, the rival of Holman, in Horatio—Holman, with the bright glittering teeth in Lothario, and the deep paviour's
sighs in Romeo—the jolliest person ("our son is fat") of any Hamlet
I have yet seen, with the most laudable attempts (for a personable
man) at looking melancholy—and Pope, the abdicated monarch of
tragedy and comedy, in Harry the Eighth and Lord Townley. There
hang the two Aickins, brethren in mediocrity—Wroughton, who in
Kitely seemed to have forgotten that in prouder days he had personated
Alexander—the specious form of John Palmer, with the special effront-
ery of Bobby—Bensley, with the trumpet-tongue, and little Quick (the
retired Dioclesian of Islington) with his squeak like a Bart'lemew

fiddle. There are fixed, cold as in life, the immovable features of Moody, who, afraid of o'erstepping nature, sometimes stopped short of her—and the restless fidgetiness of Lewis, who, with no such fears, not seldom leaped o' the other side. There hang Farren and Whit-field, and Burton and Phillimore, names of small account in those times, but which, remembered now, or casually recalled by the sight of an old play-bill, with their associated recordations, can "drown an eye unused to flow." There too hangs (not far removed from them in death) the graceful plainness of the first Mrs. Pope, with a voice unstrung by age, but which, in her better days, must have competed with the silver tones of Barry himself, so enchanting in decay do I remember it—of all her lady parts exceeding herself in the Lady Quakeress (there earth touched heaven !) of O'Keefe, when she played it to the "merry cousin" of Lewis—and Mrs. Mattocks, the sensiblest of viragos—and Miss Pope, a gentlewoman ever, to the verge of ungentility, with Churchill's compli-ment still burnishing upon her gay Honeycomb lips. There are the two Bannisters, and Sedgwick, and Kelly, and Dignum (Diggy), and the bygone features of Mrs. Ward, matchless in Lady Loverule ; and the collective majesty of the whole Kemble family, and (Shakspeare's woman) Dora Jordan ; and, by her, *two Antics*, who in former and in latter days have chiefly beguiled us of our griefs ; whose portraits we shall strive to recall, for the sympathy of those who may not have had the benefit of viewing the matchless Highgate Collection.

MR. SUETT

O for a "slip-shod muse," to celebrate in numbers, loose and shambling as himself, the merits and the person of Mr. Richard Suett, comedian !

Richard, or rather Dicky Suett—for so in his lifetime he was best pleased to be called, and time hath ratified the appellation—lieth buried on the north side of the cemetery of Holy Paul, to whose service his nonage and tender years were set apart and dedicated. There are who do yet remember him at that period—his pipe clear and harmonious. He would often speak of his chorister days, when he was "cherub Dicky."

What clipped his wings, or made it expedient that he should ex-change the holy for the profane state ; whether he had lost his good voice (his best recommendation to that office), like Sir John, "with hallooing and singing of anthems ;" or whether he was adjudged to lack something, even in those early years, of the gravity indispensable to an occupation which professeth to "commerce with the skies"—I could never rightly learn ; but we find him, after the probation of a twelve-month or so, reverting to a secular condition, and become one of us.

I think he was not altogether of that timber, out of which cathedral seats and sounding boards are hewed. But if a glad heart—kind and therefore glad—be any part of sanctity, then might the robe of Motley, with which he invested himself with so much humility after his depri-vation, and which he wore so long with so much blameless satisfaction to himself and to the public, be accepted for a surplice—his white stole, and *albe*.

The first fruits of his secularization was an engagement upon the boards of Old Drury, at which theatre he commenced, as I have been told, with adopting the manner of Parsons in old men's characters. At the period in which most of us knew him, he was no more an imitator than he was in any true sense himself imitable.

He was the Robin Good-Fellow of the stage. He came in to trouble all things with a welcome perplexity, himself no whit troubled for the matter. He was known, like Puck, by his note—*Ha! Ha! Ha!*—sometimes deepening to *Ho! Ho! Ho!* with an irresistible accession, derived perhaps remotely from his ecclesiastical education, foreign to his prototype, of—*O La!* Thousands of hearts yet respond to the chuckling *O La!* of Dicky Suett, brought back to their remembrance by the faithful transcript of his friend Mathews's mimicry. The "force of nature could no further go." He drolled upon the stock of these two syllables richer than the cuckoo.

Care, that troubles all the world, was forgotten in his composition. Had he had but two grains (nay, half a grain) of it, he could never have supported himself upon those two spider's strings, which served him (in the latter part of his unmixed existence) as legs. A doubt or a scruple must have made him totter, a sigh have puffed him down; the weight of a frown had staggered him, a wrinkle made him lose his balance. But on he went, scrambling upon those airy stilts of his, with Robin Good-Fellow, "thorough brake, thorough briar," reckless of a scratched face or a torn doublet.

Shakspeare foresaw him, when he framed his fools and jesters. They have all the true Suett stamp, a loose gait, a slippery tongue, this last the ready midwife to a without-pain-delivered jest; in words light as air, venting truths deep as the centre; with idlest rhymes tagging conceit when busiest, singing with Lear in the tempest, or Sir Toby at the buttery hatch.

Jack Bannister and he had the fortune to be more of personal favourites with the town than any actors before or after. The difference, I take it, was this:—Jack was more *beloved* for his sweet, good-natured, moral, pretensions. Dicky was more *liked* for his sweet, good-natured, no pretensions at all. Your whole conscience stirred with Bannister's performance of Walter in the Children in the Wood—how dearly beautiful it was!—but Dicky seemed like a thing, as Shakspeare says of Love, too young to know what conscience is. He put us into Vesta's days. Evil fled before him—not as from Jack, as from an antagonist,—but because it could not touch him, any more than a cannon-ball a fly. He was delivered from the burthen of that death; and, when Death came himself, not in metaphor, to fetch Dicky, it is recorded of him by Robert Palmer, who kindly watched his exit, that he received the last stroke, neither varying his accustomed tranquillity, nor tune, with the simple exclamation, worthy to have been recorded in his epitaph—*O La!—O La! Bobby!*

MR. MUNDEN

NOT many nights ago we had come home from seeing this extraordinary performer in Cockletop; and when we retired to our pillow, his whimsical image still stuck by us, in a manner as to threaten sleep. In vain we tried to divest ourselves of it by conjuring up the most opposite associations. We resolved to be serious. We raised up the gravest topics of life; private misery, public calamity. All would not do.

> —————There the antic sate
> Mocking our state——

his queer visnomy—his bewildering costume—all the strange things which he had raked together—his serpentine rod swagging about in his pocket—Cleopatra's tear, and the rest of his relics—O'Keefe's wild farce, and *his* wilder commentary—till the passion of laughter, like grief in excess, relieved itself by its own weight, inviting the sleep which in the first instance it had driven away.

But we were not to escape so easily. No sooner did we fall into slumbers, than the same image, only more perplexing, assailed us in the shape of dreams. Not one Munden, but five hundred, were dancing before us, like the faces which, whether you will or no, come when you have been taking opium—all the strange combinations, which this strangest of all strange mortals ever shot his proper countenance into, from the day he came commissioned to dry up the tears of the town for the loss of the now almost forgotten Edwin. O for the power of the pencil to have fixed them when we awoke! A season or two since there was exhibited a Hogarth gallery. We do not see why there should not be a Munden gallery. In richness and variety the latter would not fall far short of the former.

There is one face of Farley, one face of Knight, one face (but what a one it is!) of Liston; but Munden has none that you can properly pin down, and call *his*. When you think he has exhausted his battery of looks, in unaccountable warfare with your gravity, suddenly he sprouts out an entirely new set of features, like Hydra. He is not one, but legion. Not so much a comedian, as a company. If his name could be multiplied like his countenance, it might fill a play-bill. He, and he alone, literally *makes faces*: applied to any other person, the phrase is a mere figure, denoting certain modifications of the human countenance. Out of some invisible wardrobe he dips for faces, as his friend Suett used for wigs, and fetches them out as easily. We should not be surprised to see him some day put out the head of a river horse; or come forth a pewit, or lapwing, some feathered metamorphosis.

We have seen this gifted actor in Sir Christopher Curry—in Old Dornton—diffuse a glow of sentiment which has made the pulse of a crowded theatre beat like that of one man; when he has come in aid of the pulpit, doing good to the moral heart of a people. We have seen some faint approaches to this sort of excellence in other players.

But in what has been truly denominated "the sublime of farce," Munden stands out as single and unaccompanied as Hogarth. Hogarth, strange to tell, had no followers. The school of Munden began, and must end, with himself.

Can any man *wonder*, like him? can any man *see ghosts*, like him? or *fight with his own shadow*—sessa—as he does in that strangely-neglected thing, the Cobler of Preston—where his alternations from the Cobler to the Magnifico, and from the Magnifico to the Cobler, keep the brain of the spectator in as wild a ferment, as if some Arabian Night were being acted before him, or as if Thalaba were no tale! Who like him can throw, or ever attempted to throw, a supernatural interest over the commonest daily-life objects? A table, or a joint stool, in his conception, rises into a dignity equivalent to Cassiopeia's chair. It is invested with constellatory importance. You could not speak of it with more deference, if it were mounted into the firmament. A beggar in the hands of Michael Angelo, says Fuseli, rose the Patriarch of Poverty. So the gusto of Munden antiquates and ennobles what it touches. His pots and his ladles are as grand and primal as the seething-pots and hooks seen in old prophetic vision. A tub of butter, contemplated by him, amounts to a Platonic idea. He understands a leg of mutton in its quiddity. He stands wondering, amid the commonplace materials of life, like primæval man, with the sun and stars about him.

ELIA

NOTES

ELIA

Lᴀᴍʙ took the name of Elia, which should, he said, be pronounced Ellia (William Hone rhymed it to "desire"), from an old clerk, an Italian, at the South-Sea House in Lamb's time, that is, in 1791-1792. Writing to John Taylor in July, 1821, just after he had taken over the magazine (see below), Lamb says, referring to the South-Sea House essay, "having a brother now there, and doubting how he might relish certain descriptions in it, I clapt down the name of Elia to it, which passed off pretty well, for Elia himself added the function of an author to that of a scrivener, like myself." No literary work by the original Elia has, however, come to light.

Continuing Lamb says:—

"I went the other day (not having seen him [Elia] for a year) to laugh over with him at my usurpation of his name, and found him, alas! no more than a name, for he died of consumption eleven months ago, and I knew not of it. So the name has fairly devolved to me, I think; and 'tis all he has left me."

Elia. Essays which have appeared under that signature in the London Magazine, was published early in 1823. Lamb's original intention was to furnish the book with a whimsical preface, as we learn from the following letter to John Taylor, dated December 7, 1822:—

"Dᴇᴀʀ Sɪʀ,—I should like the enclosed Dedication to be printed, unless you dislike it. I like it. It is in the olden style. But if you object to it, put forth the book as it is; only pray don't let the printer mistake the word *curt* for *curst.*

"C. L.

"DEDICATION.

"Tᴏ ᴛʜᴇ Fʀɪᴇɴᴅʟʏ ᴀɴᴅ Jᴜᴅɪᴄɪᴏᴜs Rᴇᴀᴅᴇʀ,

who will take these Papers, as they were meant; not understanding every thing perversely in its absolute and literal sense, but giving fair construction, as to an after-dinner conversation; allowing for the rashness and necessary incompleteness of first thoughts; and not remembering, for the purpose of an after taunt, words spoken peradventure after the fourth glass, the Author wishes (what he would will for himself) plenty of good friends to stand by him, good books to solace him,

prosperous events to all his honest undertakings, and a candid interpretation to his most hasty words and actions. The other sort (and he
hopes many of them will purchase his book too) he greets with the
curt invitation of Timon, 'Uncover, dogs, and lap:' or he dismisses
them with the confident security of the philosopher,—'you beat but on
the case of Elia.'

"On better consideration, pray omit that Dedication. The Essays
want no Preface: they are *all Preface*. A Preface is nothing but
a talk with the reader; and they do nothing else. Pray omit it.

"There will be a sort of Preface in the next Magazine, which may act
as an advertisement, but not proper for the volume.

"Let ELIA come forth bare as he was born.

"C. L.

"N.B.—*No Preface.*"

The "sort of Preface in the next number" was the "Character of
the Late Elia" (see page 151).

Elia did not reach a second edition in Lamb's lifetime, that is to
say, just twelve years, although the editions into which it has passed
between his death and the present day are practically uncountable.
Why, considering the popularity of the essays as they appeared in the
London Magazine, the book should have found so few purchasers is a
problem difficult of solution. Lamb himself seems to have attributed
some of the cause to Southey's objection, in the *Quarterly Review*,
that *Elia* "wanted a sounder religious feeling" (see Vol. I., page 226);
but that probably made no serious difference. Possibly the book was
too dear: it was published at 9s. 6d.

Ordinary reviewers do not seem to have perceived at all that a rare
humorist, humanist and master of prose had arisen, although among
the finer intellects who had any inclination to search for excellence
for excellence' sake Lamb made his way. William Hazlitt, for example, drew attention to the rich quality of *Elia*; as also did
Leigh Hunt; and William Hone, who cannot, however, as a critic
be mentioned with these, was tireless in advocating the book. Among
strangers to Lamb who from the first extolled his genius was Miss
Mitford. But *Elia* did not sell.

Ten years passed before Lamb collected his essays again, and then
in 1833 was published *The Last Essays of Elia*, with Edward Moxon's
imprint. The mass of minor essays in the *London Magazine* and elsewhere, which Lamb disregarded when he compiled his two collections,
will be found in Vol. I. of the present edition. *The Last Essays of
Elia* had little, if any, better reception than the first; and Lamb had
the mortification of being asked by the Norris family to suppress the
exquisite and kindly little memoir of Randal Norris, entitled "A Death-
Bed" (see page 246), which was held to be too personal. When, in
1835, after Lamb's death, a new edition of *Elia* and *The Last Essays
of Elia* was issued, the "Confessions of a Drunkard" took its place
(see Vol. I., page 133).

E L I A.

ESSAYS WHICH HAVE APPEARED UNDER THAT SIGNATURE

IN THE

LONDON MAGAZINE.

––––––––

LONDON:

PRINTED FOR TAYLOR AND HESSEY,

93, FLEET STREET,

AND 13, WATERLOO PLACE.

1823.

Meanwhile a Philadelphian firm had been beforehand with Lamb, and had issued in 1828 a second series of *Elia*. The American edition of *Elia* had been the same as the English except for a slightly different arrangement of the essays. But when in 1828 the American second series was issued, it was found to contain three pieces not by Lamb at all. A trick of writing superficially like Lamb had been growing in the *London Magazine* ever since the beginning; hence the confusion of the American editor. The three articles not by Lamb, as he pointed out to N. P. Willis (see *Pencillings by the Way*), are "Twelfth Night," "The Nuns and Ale of Caverswell," and "Valentine's Day." Of these Allan Cunningham wrote the second, and B. W. Procter (Barry Cornwall) the other two. The volume contained only eleven essays which Lamb himself selected for *The Last Essays of Elia*: it was eked out with the three spurious pieces above referred to, with several pieces never collected by Lamb, and with four of the humorous articles in the *Works*, 1818. Bernard Barton's sonnet "To Elia" stood as introduction. Altogether it was a very interesting book, as books lacking authority often are.

In the notes that follow reference is often made to Lamb's Key. This is a paper explaining certain initials and blanks in *Elia*, which Lamb drew up for R. B. Pitman, a fellow clerk at the East India House, and which passed into the hands of the late Alexander Ireland. The MS. is now in the possession of the author of *With Elia and His Friends*, who suggests that it would perhaps be wise not to place too much faith in all Lamb's attributions. I give it here in full, merely remarking that the first numerals refer to the pages of the original edition of *Elia* and those in brackets to the present volume :—

M. .	.	.	. Page	13 [6]	Maynard, hang'd himself.
G. D.	.	.	,,	21 [10]	George Dyer, Poet.
H. .	.	.	,,	32 [14]	Hodges.
W.	.	.	,,	45 [20]	
Dr. T——e	.	.	,,	46 [20]	Dr. Trollope.
Th.	.	.	,,	47 [21]	Thornton.
S. .	.	.	,,	47 [21]	Scott, died in Bedlam.
M. .	.	.	,,	47 [21]	Maunde, dismiss'd school.
C. V. le G.	.	.	,,	48 [21]	Chs. Valentine le Grice.
F. .	.	.	,,	49 [22]	Favell; left Cambrg because he was asham'd of his father, who was a house-painter there.
Fr. .	.	.	,,	50 [22]	Franklin, Gramr Mast., Hertford.
T. .	.	.	,,	50 [22]	Marmaduke Thompson.
K. .	.	.	,,	59 [26]	Kenney, Dramatist. Author of *Raising Wind*, &c.
S. T. C. .		.	,,	60 [26]	Samuel Taylor Coleridge. [Not in Lamb's autograph.]
Alice W——n.		.	,,	63 [28]	Feigned (Winterton).
***	.	.	,,	64 [28]	
****	.	.	,,	64 [28]	}No meaning.
***	.	.	,,	64 [28]	
	.	.	,,	64 [28]	
Mrs. S. .	.	.	,,	87 [38]	Mrs. Spinkes.
R. .	.	.	,,	98 [43]	Ramsay, London Library, Ludg. St.; now extinct.
Granville S.	.	.	,,	98 [43]	Granville Sharp. [Not in Lamb's autograph.]
E. B.	.	.	,,	130 [57]	Edward Burney, half-brother of Miss Burney.
B. .	.	.	,,	141 [62]	Braham, now a Xtian.
*** *** ****	.	.	,,	170 [74]	Distrest Sailors.

The " London Magazine "

The *London Magazine*, with John Scott (1783-1821) as its editor, was founded in 1820 by Baldwin, Cradock & Joy. Its first number was dated January, 1820, and Lamb's first contribution was in the number for August, 1820. Lamb had known Scott when editor of *The Champion* in 1814 (see Vol. I., page 449), but, according to Talfourd, it was Hazlitt who introduced Lamb to the *London Magazine*.

John Scott, who was the author of two interesting books of travel, *A Visit to Paris in 1814* and *Paris Revisited in 1815*, was an admirable editor, and all was going exceedingly well until he plunged into a feud with *Blackwood's Magazine* in general, and John Gibson Lockhart in particular, the story of which in full may be read in Mr. Lang's *Life and Letters of Lockhart*, 1896. This is no place for the narration. Let it suffice that Scott resented *Blackwood's* attitude to the Cockney school of literature ; that he replied furiously and indiscreetly ; that Lockhart had no course but to challenge him ; that Scott did not meet the challenge with the alacrity which one could wish ; that finally he accepted the challenge of Lockhart's friend and second J. H. Christie, and a duel with pistols was fought at Chalk Farm on February 16, 1821. Peter George Patmore, father of Coventry Patmore, assistant editor of the *London Magazine*, and afterwards a friend of Lamb, stood as second to Scott, who was shot above the hip. The wound was at first thought lightly of, but Scott died on February 27, 1821—an able man much regretted.

The magazine did not at first show signs of Scott's loss ; it continued to bear the imprint of its original publishers and its quality remained very high. With Lamb and Hazlitt writing regularly this could hardly be otherwise. But four months after the death of Scott and eighteen months after its establishment the *London Magazine* passed into the hands of the publishers Taylor & Hessey, the first number with their imprint being dated August, 1821. Although for a while no diminution of merit was perceptible and rather an access of gaiety—for Taylor brought Hood with him and John Hamilton Reynolds—yet the high editorial standards of Scott ceased to be applied. Thenceforward the decline of the magazine was steady.

John Taylor (1781-1864), senior partner in the firm of Taylor & Hessey, was known as the identifier of Sir Philip Francis with the author of "Junius," on which subject he had issued three books.

ELIA.

ESSAYS

WHICH HAVE APPEARED UNDER THAT SIGNATURE

IN THE

LONDON MAGAZINE.

———

SECOND SERIES.

———

PHILADELPHIA:

CAREY, LEA AND CAREY—CHESNUT STREET.

J. R. A. SKERRETT, PRINTER.

————

1828.

Although unfitted for the post, he acted as editor of the *London Magazine* until it was again sold in 1825. Previously the office of Taylor's firm had been at 93 Fleet Street, but he now moved to 13 Waterloo Place, where the *London Magazine* dinners (at one of which Lamb probably first met Bernard Barton) were held.

With the beginning of 1825 Taylor made a change in the magazine. He started a new series, and increased the size and the price. But the experiment did not answer; the spirit had evaporated; and in the autumn he sold it to Henry Southern (1799-1853), who had founded the *Retrospective Review* in 1820. The last number of the *London Magazine* to bear Taylor & Hessey's name, and (in my opinion) to contain anything by Lamb, was August, 1825. The September number was published by Hunt & Clarke. Its subsequent history has little interest.

Lamb wrote more or less steadily for the *London Magazine* from August, 1820, until the end of 1823, but from January to August, 1824, he contributed nothing. We have no definite information on the matter, but there is every indication in Lamb's *Letters* that Taylor was penurious and not clever in his relations with contributors. Scott Lamb seems to have admired and liked; but even in Scott's day payment does not seem to have been prompt. Lamb was paid, according to Barry Cornwall, two or three times the amount of other writers, who received for prose a pound a page. Lamb himself says that the rate for him was twenty guineas a sheet, a sheet being sixteen pages; and he told Moore that he had received £170 for two years' Elia. In a letter to Barton in January, 1823, Lamb remarks: "B—— [Baldwin] who first engaged me as 'Elia' has not paid me up yet (nor any of us without repeated mortifying appeals)."

The following references to the *London* in Lamb's letters to Barton tell the story of its decadence quite clearly enough. In May, 1823 :—

"I cannot but think *the London* drags heavily. I miss Janus [Wainewright]. And O how it misses Hazlitt — Procter, too, is affronted (as Janus has been) with their abominable curtailment of his things."

Again, a little later, in September :—

"The 'London' I fear falls off.—I linger among its creaking rafters, like the last rat. It will topple down, if they don't get some Buttresses. They have pulled down three, W. Hazlitt, Procter, and their best stay, kind light-hearted Wainwright, their Janus."

In January, 1824, at the beginning of his eight months' silence :—

"The London must do without me for a time, a time, and half a time, for I have lost all interest about it."

Again, in December, 1824 :—

"Taylor & Hessey finding their magazine goes off very heavily at 2s. 6d., are prudently going to raise their price another shilling; and having already more authors than they want, intend to increase the number of them. If they set up against the New Monthly, they must change their present hands. It is not tying the dead carcase of a Review to a half-dead Magazine will do their business."

In January, 1825 (to Sarah Hutchinson) :—

" You ask about the editor of the Lond. I know of none. This first specimen [of a new series] is flat and pert enough to justify subscribers, who grudge at t'other shilling."

In this number, January, 1825, Lamb was represented by the " Letter to an Old Gentleman whose Education has been Neglected," the " Vision of Horns," and the " Biographical Memoir of Mr. Liston."

Next month Lamb writes, again to Barton :—

" Our second Number [of the new series] is all trash. What are T. & H. about ? It is whip syllabub, ' thin sown with aught of profit or delight '. Thin sown ! not a germ of fruit or corn. Why did poor Scott die ! There was comfort in writing with such associates as were his little band of scribblers, some gone away, some affronted away, and I am left as the solitary widow [in one of Barton's poems] looking for watercresses."

Finally, in August, 1825 :—

" Taylor has dropt the ' London '. It was indeed a dead weight. It was Job in the Slough of Despond. I shuffle off my part of the pack, and stand like Christian with light and merry shoulders."

In addition to Lamb and Hazlitt the *London Magazine* had more or less regular contributions, in its best days, from De Quincey, Allan Cunningham (Nalla), T. G. Wainewright, afterwards the poisoner, but in those days an amusing weaver of gay artificial prose, John Clare, Bernard Barton, H. F. Cary, Richard Ayton, George Darley, Thomas Hood, John Hamilton Reynolds, Sir John Bowring, John Poole, B. W. Procter ; while among occasional writers for it were Thomas Carlyle, Landor and Julius Hare.

The essay, " Stage Illusion," in the number for August, 1825, was, I believe, the last that Lamb contributed. (In this connection see Mr. Bertram Dobell's *Sidelights on Charles Lamb*, 1903.) He then passed over to Colburn's *New Monthly Magazine*, where the " Popular Fallacies " appeared, together with certain other of his later essays. His last contribution to that magazine was dated September, 1826. In 1827 he was chiefly occupied in selecting Garrick play extracts for Hone's *Table Book*, at the British Museum, and for a while after that he seems to have been more interested in writing acrostics and album verses than prose. In 1831, however, Moxon's *Englishman's Magazine* offered harbourage for anything Lamb cared to give it, and a brief revival of Elia (under the name of Peter) resulted. With its death in October, 1831, Lamb's writing career practically ceased.

In the notes that follow I have enumerated only the principal differences between the text of the essays in *Elia* and *The Last Essays of Elia* and the text as they first appeared in the *London Magazine* and other places.

Page 1. THE SOUTH-SEA HOUSE.
London Magazine, August, 1820.

Although the "Bachelor's Complaint of the Behaviour of Married People," "Valentine's Day," and "On the Acting of Munden," were all written before this essay, it is none the less the first of the essays of Elia. I have remarked, in the notes to a small edition of *Elia*, that it is probably unique in literature for an author to find himself, as Lamb did, in his forty-fourth year, by recording impressions gathered in his seventeenth ; but I think now that Lamb probably visited his brother at the South-Sea House from time to time in later years, and gathered other impressions then. I am led to this conclusion partly by the fact that Thomas Tame (see below) was not appointed Deputy-Accountant until four or five years after Lamb had left.

We do not know exactly what Lamb's duties were at the South-Sea House or how long he was there : probably only for the twenty-three weeks—from September, 1791—mentioned in the receipt below, discovered by Mr. J. A. Rutter in a little exhibition of documents illustrative of the South Sea Bubble in the Albert Museum at Exeter :—

Rec^d 8th feb^y 1792 of the Honble South Sea Company by the hands of their Secretary Twelve pounds 1s. 6d. for 23 weeks attendance in the Examiners Office.

£12 1 6.   CHAS. LAMB ;

which shows that Lamb's salary was half a guinea weekly, paid half-yearly. His brother John was already in the service of the company, where he remained till his death, rising to Accountant. It has been conjectured that it was through his influence that Charles was admitted, with the view of picking up book-keeping ; but the real patron and introducer was Joseph Paice, one of the directors, whom we meet on pages 80 and 361. Whether Lamb had ideas of remaining, or whether he merely filled a temporary gap in the Examiners' Office, we cannot tell. He passed to the East India House in the spring of 1792.

In the September number of the *London Magazine*, an interesting little eulogy of this essay was dropped into a review of Keats' *Poems*, probably from the pen of Scott the editor, with the purpose of instructing the poet in the difference between true sentiment and false. Thus :—

. . . That most beautiful Paper, (by a correspondent of course) in our last number, on the "ledger-men" of the South Sea House, is an elegant reproof of such short-sighted views of character ; such idle hostilities against the realities of life. How free from intolerance of every sort must the spirit be, that conceived that paper,—or took off so fair and clear an impression from facts ! It would not be prone to find suggestion of invective in the sound of Sabbath bells, as Mr. Keats has done in a former work. The author of Endymion and Hyperion must delight in that Paper ;—and, to give another example of what we mean, he must surely feel the gentle poetical beauty which is infused into the starlight tale of Rosamund Gray, through its vein of "natural piety." What would that tale be without the Grandmother's Bible ? How eclipsed would be the gleaming light of such a character as Rosamund's, in a re-modelled state of society, where it should be the fashion for wives to be considered as dainties at a pic-nic party, each man bringing his own with him—but ready to give and take with those about him ! Creeds here are out of the question altogether ;—we only speak with reference to the wants and instincts of the human soul. We mention these things, not because we desire to see Mr. Keats playing the hypocrite, or enlisted as a florid declaimer on the profitable side of things ; but because, with our admiration of his powers, we are loath to see him irrecoverably committed to a flippant and false system of reasoning on human nature ;—because to his picturesque imagination, we wish that he would add a more pliable, and, at the same time, a more magnanimous sensibility.

The South Sea Company was incorporated in 1710. The year of the Bubble was 1720. The South-Sea House, remodelled, is now a congeries of offices.

Page 1, line 6. *The Flower Pot.* An inn in Bishopsgate Street where coaches and carriers started for the north of London. Lamb became an annuitant—of the East India Company—in 1825, when he retired on a pension.

Page 1, line 13. *Like Balclutha's.* Lamb gives the quotation from Ossian (*Couthon*) in the footnote ; but the true reading is, " I have seen the walls of Balclutha, and they were desolate."

Page 1, last line. *" Unsunned heap."* From Milton's *Comus,* 398. Probably Lamb was thinking also of Mammon in the *Faerie Queen,* II., Canto VII., Stanzas 3, 4, 5 and 20.

Page 2, line 3. *Forty years ago.* To be accurate, twenty-eight to thirty.

Page 2, line 14. *Inquisitive.* In the *London Magazine,* "that wished." " Seeking," in line 16, was " sought."

Page 2, line 20. *Vaux.* Guy Fawkes.

Page 2, line 34. *Accounts . . . puzzle me.* Here Elia begins his " matter-of-lie " career. Lamb was at this time in the Accountants' Office of the India House, living among figures all day.

Page 2, line 8 from foot. *Columniations.* The *New English Dictionary* gives Lamb's word in this connection as its sole reference.

Page 3, line 2. *Pounce-boxes.* For drying ink, with powder, before blotting-paper was used.

Page 3, line 22. *Evans.* William Evans. The Directories of those days printed lists of the chief officials in some of the public offices, and it is possible to trace the careers of the clerks whom Lamb names. All are genuine. Evans, whose name is given one year as Evan Evans, was appointed cashier (or deputy-cashier) in 1792.

Page 3, line 24. *Visage.* In the *London Magazine* " visnomy."

Page 3, line 27. *Maccaronies.* This word for dandies came in in the seventeen-seventies.

Page 3, line 28. *Melancholy as a gib-cat.* Falstaff's phrase in " 1. Henry IV.," Act I., Scene 2, line 83.

Page 3, line 31. *Ready to imagine himself one.* Lamb was fond of this conceit. See his little essay " The Last Peach " (Vol. I., page 283), and the mischievous letter to Bernard Barton, after Fauntleroy's trial, warning him against peculation.

Page 3, line 34. *Anderton's.* Either the coffee-shop in Fleet Street, now Anderton's Hotel, or a city offshoot of it. The portrait, if it ever was in existence, is no longer known there.

Page 3, last line but one. *Pennant.* Thomas Pennant (1726-1798), the Welsh antiquary, and the author of *Of London,* 1790.

Page 4, line 1. *Rosomond's pond, etc.* Rosamond's Pond, filled up in 1770, was at the south-west corner of St. James's Park, across the end of the present Bird Cage Walk ; the Mulberry Garden occupied the site of Buckingham Palace and Gardens. It was a pleasure resort in the seventeenth century. The mulberry trees were planted by James I., who wished to introduce them to England and rear silkworms. The Great Conduit in Cheapside stood in the middle of the street, near the Poultry; and the Little Conduit, in the middle of the street, facing Foster Lane. Water was brought thither underground from Paddington. In times of public rejoicing they ran wine.

Page 4, line 4. *Those grotesque figures.* Referring to the Huguenot refugees from France after Louis XIV. revoked the Edict of Nantes in 1685. The scene of Hogarth's picture "Noon" is laid in Hog Lane (now a portion of Charing Cross Road), where a French church (now St. Mary's) used to stand.

Page 4, line 15. *Strained to the height.* These words were in quotation marks in the *London Magazine*. From *Paradise Lost*, VIII., 454.

Page 4, line 28. *House of Derwentwater.* James Radcliffe (1689-1716), third Earl of Derwentwater, was beheaded for his share in the Jacobite rising of 1715.

Page 4, line 36. *Decus et solamen.* From Virgil (*Æneid*, X., 859)—"glory and consolation."

Page 4, line 37. *John Tipp.* John Lamb succeeded Tipp as Accountant somewhen about 1806.

Page 4, line 39. *He " thought an accountant. . ."* An adaptation of Parson Adams' remarks on schoolmasters in Fielding's *Joseph Andrews*, Chapter III.: Book III., Chapter V.: "Indeed if this good man had an enthusiasm, or what the vulgar call a blind side, it was this: he thought a schoolmaster the greatest character in the world, and himself the greatest of all schoolmasters: neither of which points he would have given up to Alexander the Great at the head of an army."

Page 4, line 42. *With other notes.* In quotation marks in the *London Magazine*. From *Paradise Lost*, III., 17.

Page 5, line 2. *I know not, etc.* This parenthesis was not in the *London Magazine*, but the following footnote was appended to the sentence:—

"I have since been informed, that the present tenant of them is a Mr. Lamb, a gentleman who is happy in the possession of some choice pictures, and among them a rare portrait of Milton, which I mean to do myself the pleasure of going to see, and at the same time to refresh my memory with the sight of old scenes. Mr. Lamb has the character of a right courteous and communicative collector."

Mr. Lamb was, of course, John Lamb, or James Elia (see the essay "My Relations," page 70), then (in 1820) Accountant of the South-Sea House. He left the Milton to his brother. It is now in America.

Page 5, line 3. *"Sweet breasts."* Middleton in "More Dissemblers besides Women" has the phrase: "Well, go thy ways for as sweet-breasted a page as ever lay at his master's feet in a truckle-bed."

Page 5, line 7. *Like Lord Midas.* The ears of Midas, the wealthy King of Phrygia, were changed to those of an ass for saying that Pan played better than Apollo.

Page 5, fifth line from foot. *With Fortinbras.* See "Hamlet," Act IV., Scene 4, line 55.

Page 6, line 5. *Henry Man.* This was Henry Man (1747-1799), deputy-secretary of the South Sea-House from 1776, and an author of light trifles in the papers, and of one or two books. The *Miscellaneous Works in Verse and Prose of the late Henry Man* was published in 1802, among the subscribers being three of the officials named in this essay—John Evans, R. Plumer, and Mr. Tipp, and also Thomas Maynard, who, though assigned to the Stock Exchange, is probably the "childlike, pastoral M——" of a later paragraph. Small politics are for the most part kept out of Man's volumes, which are high-spirited rather than witty, but this punning epigram (of which Lamb was an admirer) on Lord Spencer and Lord Sandwich may be quoted :—

> Two Lords whose names if I should quote,
> Some folks might call me sinner :
> The one invented *half a coat,*
> The other *half a dinner.*
>
> Such lords as these are useful men,
> Heaven sends them to console one ;
> Because there's now not one in ten,
> That can procure a *whole one.*

Page 6, line 14. "*New-born gauds.*" From "Troilus and Cressida," Act III., Scene 3, line 176.

Page 6, line 15. *Public Ledgers and Chronicles.* Man contributed a series of letters on education to Woodfall's *Morning Chronicle.* He also wrote for the *London Gazette.*

Page 6, line 15. *Chatham, etc.* The topics referred to are the American War of Independence and John Wilkes' struggle with Parliament. Chatham, Shelburne, Rockingham and Richmond were statesmen, and Howe, Keppel, Burgoyne and Clinton soldiers, connected with the American War. Bull was Lord Mayor of London in 1773, Wilkes in 1774, and Sawbridge in 1775. Dunning defended Wilkes before Pratt.

Page 6, line 21. *Plumer.* Richard Plumer (spelled Plomer in the directories), deputy-secretary after Man. Lamb was peculiarly interested in the Plumers from the fact that his grandmother, Mrs. Field, had been housekeeper of their mansion at Blakesware, near Ware (see notes to "Dream Children" and "Blakesmoor in H——shire," pages 377 and 405). The fine old Whig was William Plumer, who had been her employer, and was now living at Gilston. He died in 1821.

The following passage from the memoir of Edward Cave (1691-1754), which Dr. Johnson wrote for the *Gentleman's Magazine* (which Cave established) in 1754, shows that Lamb was mistaken about Plumer :—

He [Cave] was afterwards raised to the office of clerk of the franks, in which he acted with great spirit and firmness ; and often stopped franks which were given by members of parliament to their friends ; because he thought such extension of a peculiar right illegal. This raised many complaints, and having stopped, among others, a frank given to the old dutchess of *Marlborough* by Mr. *Walter Plumer*, he was cited before the house, as for breach of privilege, and accused, I suppose very unjustly, of opening letters to detect them. He was treated with great harshness and severity, but declining their questions by pleading his oath of secrecy, was at last dismissed. And it must be recorded to his honour, that when he was ejected from his office, he did not think himself discharged from his trust, but continued to refuse to his nearest friends any information about the management of the office.

I borrow from Canon Ainger an interesting note on Walter Plumer, written in the eighteen-eighties, showing that Lamb was mistaken on other matters too :—

The present Mr. Plumer, of Allerton, Totness, a grandson of Richard Plumer of the South-Sea House, by no means acquiesces in the tradition here recorded as to his grandfather's origin. He believes that though the links are missing, Richard Plumer was descended in regular line from the Baronet, Sir Walter Plumer, who died at the end of the seventeenth century. Lamb's memory has failed him here in one respect. The " Bachelor Uncle," Walter Plumer, uncle of William Plumer of Blakesware, was most certainly not a bachelor (see the pedigree of the family in Cussans' *Hertfordshire*).

Page 6, line 39. *M——*. According to the Key to the initials and blanks in some of the essays, which Lamb filled in for a curious correspondent (see page 301), M—— stood for one Maynard. " Maynard, hang'd himself" is Lamb's entry. He was chief clerk in the Old Annuities and Three Per Cents, 1788-1793.

Page 6, line 41. *Song sung by Amiens.* See " As You Like It," Act II., Scene 5.

Page 7, lines 5, 7. *Woollett . . . Hepworth.* I know nothing of these. Newton is of course Sir Isaac.

Page 7, line 12. *Solemn mockery.* In Ireland's " Vortigern," the would-be Shakespeare drama, is the line :—

> And when this solemn mockery is o'er.

Kemble gave the line with peculiar emphasis on the first (and last) night, and the house taking the cue, the play was damned.

Page 7, line 16. *John Naps.* In the Induction to " The Taming of the Shrew " one of the servants says to Christopher Sly :—

> Why, sir, you know no house nor no such maid,
> Nor no such men as you have reckon'd up,
> As Stephen Sly and old John Naps of Greece
> And Peter Turph and Henry Pimpernell
> And twenty more such names and men as these
> Which never were nor no man ever saw.
>
> Induction, Scene 2, lines 93-98.

Lamb may suddenly have felt the misgiving that he had told too much, and therefore invented this sudden cross-trail. Mr. Sidney Lee, by the way, says in his *Life of Shakespeare* that John Naps of Greece should be John Naps of Greet, a village near Winchmere, in Gloucestershire.

Page 7. Oxford in the Vacation.
London Magazine, October, 1820, where it is dated at the end, " August 5, 1820. From my rooms facing the Bodleian." My own impression is that Lamb wrote the essay at Cambridge, under the influence of Cambridge, where he spent a few weeks in the summer of 1820, and transferred the scene to Oxford by way of mystification. He knew Oxford, of course, but he had not been there for some years and it was at Cambridge that he met Dyer and that he saw the Milton MSS,

Concerning a visit to Oxford (in 1810), Hazlitt had written, in his *Table Talk* essay "On the Conversation of Authors," in the preceding (the September) number of the *London Magazine* :—

L—— [that is, Lamb] once came down into the country to see us. He was "like the most capricious poet Ovid among the Goths." The country people thought him an oddity, and did not understand his jokes. It would be strange if they had ; for he did not make any while he staid. But when we crossed the country to Oxford, then he spoke a little. He and the old colleges were hail-fellow well-met ; and in the quadrangles, he "walked gowned."

The quotation is a reference to Lamb's sonnet, "I was not Trained in Academic Bowers" (see page 311) :—

Yet can I fancy, wandering 'mid thy towers,
Myself a nursling, Granta, of thy lap ;
My brow seems tightening with the Doctor's cap,
And I walk *gownèd*.

Page 7, line 24. *Vivares . . . Woollet.* François Vivares (1709-1780), a French engraver of landscapes, who settled in England, and worked for Alderman Boydell (see page 416). His engravings of Claude were peculiarly fine. His son Thomas also engraved. William Woollet (1735-1785), one of the first of English line engravers, especially of landscape.

Page 7, line 32. *Agnize.* Lamb was fond of this word. I have seen it stated ingeniously that it was of his own coinage—from *agnus,* a lamb—but the derivation is *ad gnoscere,* to acknowledge, to recognise, and the word is to be found in other places—in "Othello," for example (Act I., Scene 3, line 232) :—

I do agnise
A natural and prompt alacrity.

Page 8, line 15. *Joseph's vest.* See Genesis xxxvii.
Page 8, line 18. *Red-letter days.* See note on page 317. The holidays at the India House, which are given in the London directories of Lamb's early time there, make a considerable list. But in 1820 the Accountants' Office, where Lamb was, kept only five days in the year.
Page 8, line 21. *"Andrew and John."* Probably an adaptation of Milton's line :—

Andrew and Simon, famous after known.
Paradise Regained, II., line 7.

Page 8, line 24. *Baskett Prayer Book.* John Baskett, succeeded by his sons Thomas and Robert Baskett, was the King's printer for some years until his death in 1742.
Page 8, line 33. *"Far off their coming shone."*

Attended with ten thousand thousand saints,
He onward came, far off his coming shone.
Paradise Lost, VI., lines 767-768.

Page 8, line 35. *The Epiphany.* Twelfth Day. Lamb's reference to himself as little better than one of the profane is probably a recollection of Falstaff's confession to Prince Hal ("1. Henry IV.,"

Act I., Scene 2, line 105), "Now am I, if a man should speak truly, little better than one of the wicked."

Page 8, at the foot. *Selden . . . Archbishop Usher.* John Selden (1584-1654) and his friend James Ussher (1581-1656), Archbishop of Armagh, both great ecclesiastical critics. The greater part of Selden's library is in the Bodleian; Usher's books went to Trinity College, Dublin; but Lamb is referring, I imagine, to copies of their writings. The Bodleian was founded by Sir Thomas Bodley (1545-1613).

Page 9, line 3. *I can here . . . enact the student.* Lamb had distilled the matter of this paragraph into his sonnet, "I was not Trained in Academic Bowers," written at Cambridge in August of the preceding year (see above and Vol. V., page 55).

Page 9, line 25. *Beadsman.* A man employed to pray for others, dropping a bead with each prayer.

Page 9, line 29. *Chaucer.* There is no absolute evidence that Chaucer was at either University.

Page 9, line 31. *Cook . . . Manciple.* There was a cook and a manciple among the Canterbury Pilgrims. A manciple is chief of a college commissariat.

Page 9. *Footnote.* "Persons of short times may know what 'tis to live, but not the life of Man, who, having little behind them, are but Januses of one Face" (*Christian Morals*, Part III., Section 22). In Roman mythology Janus is re-.esented with two faces because he knew both the past and ... ...ture.

Page 10, line 3. *Arride.* To gratify laughingly. One of Lamb's favourite old words. Ben Jonson uses it in "Every Man Out of His Humour."

Page 10, line 15. "*Variæ lectiones.*" "Different readings."

Page 10, line 16. *Unsettle my faith.* At this point, in the *London Magazine*, Lamb appended the footnote :—

"There is something to me repugnant, at any time, in written hand. The text never seems determinate. Print settles it. I had thought of the Lycidas as of a full-grown beauty—as springing up with all its parts absolute—till, in evil hour, I was shown the original written copy of it, together with the other minor poems of its author, in the Library of Trinity, kept like some treasure to be proud of. I wish they had thrown them in the Cam, or sent them, after the latter cantos of Spenser, into the Irish Channel. How it staggered me to see the fine things in their ore! interlined, corrected! as if their words were mortal, alterable, displaceable at pleasure! as if they might have been otherwise, and just as good! as if inspirations were made up of parts, and those fluctuating, successive, indifferent! I will never go into the work-shop of any great artist again, nor desire a sight of his picture, till it is fairly off the easel; no, not if Raphael were to be alive again, and painting another Galatea."

In the Appendix to Vol. I., page 376, I have printed a passage from the original MS. of *Comus*, which there is reason to believe was contributed to the *London Magazine* by Lamb. These original MSS. of Milton recently have been facsimiled for subscribers. The latter cantos of Spenser were probably never written. The assumption that they were lost at sea is, I believe, Lamb's.

Raphael's "Galatea" is in the Farnesina.

Page 10, line 16. *No Herculanean raker.* No disturber of the ashes under which Herculaneum, at the foot of Vesuvius, was buried.

Page 10, line 17. *The three witnesses.* See the First Epistle of John v. 7 and onwards. Gibbon, and others before him, had stated these verses to be an interpolation. Archdeacon Travis defended their genuineness; but it was left for Porson to prove them spurious, which he did in the *Letters to Travis*, 1790. The verses are omitted from the Revised Version.

Page 10, line 18. *Porson.* Richard Porson (1759-1808), the famous Greek scholar.

Page 10, line 19. *G. D.* George Dyer (1755-1841), Lamb's friend for many years. This is the first mention of him in the essays; but we shall meet him again, particularly in "Amicus Redivivus" (page 209). George Dyer was educated at Christ's Hospital long before Lamb's time there, and, becoming a Grecian, had entered Emmanuel College, Cambridge. He became at first an usher in Essex, then a private tutor to the children of Robert Robinson, the Unitarian, whose life he afterwards excellently wrote, then an usher again, at Northampton, one of his colleagues being John Clarke, father of Lamb's friend, Charles Cowden Clarke. In 1792 he settled in Clifford's Inn as a hack; wrote poems, made indexes, examined libraries for a great bibliographical work (never published), and contributed "all that was original" to Valpy's classics in 141 volumes. Under this work his sight gave way; and he once showed Hazlitt two fingers the use of which he had lost in copying out MSS. of Procrus and Plotinus in a fine Greek hand. Fortunately a good woman took him under her wing; they were married in 1825; and Dyer's last days were happy. His best books were his *Life of Robert Robinson* and his *History of the University and Colleges of Cambridge*. Lamb and his friends laughed at him and loved him. In addition to the stories told by Lamb in his letters and essays, there are amusing characteristics of Dyer in Crabb Robinson's diary, in Leigh Hunt, in Hazlitt, in Talfourd, and in other places. All bear upon his gentleness, his untidiness and his want of humour. One of the most famous stories tells of Dyer's criticism of Williams, the terrible Ratcliffe Highway murderer. Dyer, who would never say an ill word of any one, was asked his opinion of this cold-blooded assassin of two families. "He must," he replied after due thought, "be rather an eccentric character."

Page 10, line 24. *A tall Scapula.* That is, a tall copy of Johann Scapula's *Greek Lexicon*.

Page 10, line 31. "*In calm and sinless peace.*" Milton says of Christ that He sat among the Tempter's hellish furies

Unappall'd in calm and sinless peace.
Paradise Regained, IV., line 425.

Page 10, line 34. *Injustice to him.* In the *London Magazine* the
following footnote came here, almost certainly by Lamb:—

"Violence or injustice certainly none, Mr. Elia. But you will
acknowledge that the charming unsuspectingness of our friend has
sometimes laid him open to attacks, which, though savouring (we
hope) more of waggery than malice—such is our unfeigned respect for
G. D.—might, we think, much better have been omitted. Such was
that silly joke of L[amb], who, at the time the question of the Scotch
Novels was first agitated, gravely assured our friend—who as gravely
went about repeating it in all companies—that Lord Castlereagh had
acknowledged himself to be the author of Waverly! *Note—not by
Elia.*"

Page 10, line 35. *"Strike an abstract idea."* I do not find this
quotation—if it be one; but when John Lamb once knocked Hazlitt
down, during an argument on pigments, Hazlitt refrained from striking
back, remarking that he was a metaphysician, who dealt not in blows
but in ideas. Lamb may be slyly remembering this.

Page 10, line 39. *C——.* Cambridge. Dyer added a work on
Privileges of the University of Cambridge to his *History.*

Page 11, line 12. *Our friend M.'s.* Basil Montagu, Q.C. (1770-
1851), legal writer, philanthropist; and the friend of Wordsworth and
Coleridge. The Mrs. M. here referred to was Montagu's third wife, a
Mrs. Skepper. It was she who was called by Edward Irving "the noble
lady," and to whom Carlyle addressed some early letters. A. S. was
Anne Skepper, afterwards Mrs. Bryan Waller Procter, a fascinating lady
who lived to a great age and died as recently as 1888. The Montagus
then lived at 25 Bedford Square.

Page 11, line 21. *Queen Lar.* The Lares and Penates were the household gods of the Romans. Queen Lar is Lamb's deduction from Lares.

Page 11, line 27. *Sosia.* The two Sosias—the real and the false—
lead to complications in Plautus' comedy of errors, the "Amphitruo,"
from which Shakespeare borrowed a scene for his "Comedy of Errors"
(which for the most part was based upon Plautus' "Menœchmi").

Page 11, line 31. *For with G. D.—to be absent.* See 2 Corinthians v. 8. This paragraph refers to Dyer's pamphlets on public
questions—his *Complaints of the Poor People of England*, for example.
Harrington was James Harrington (1611-1677), author of *Oceana*, a
work (like Plato's *Republic*) on a model state. Baxter replied to it in
the *Holy Commonwealth.*

Page 11, line 34. *Starts like a thing surprised.* Here we have
an interesting example of Lamb's gift of fused quotation. Wordsworth's line in the "Ode on Intimations of Mortality,"

Tremble like a guilty thing surprised,

and Shakespeare's phrase in "Hamlet" (Act I., Scene 1, line 148),

Started like a guilty thing,

were probably both in his mind as he wrote.

Page 11, line 41. *Obtruded personal presence.* In the *London Magazine* the following passage came here :—

" D. commenced life, after a course of hard study in the 'House of pure Emanuel,' as usher to a knavish fanatic schoolmaster at * * *, at a salary of eight pounds per annum, with board and lodging. Of this poor stipend, he never received above half in all the laborious years he served this man. He tells a pleasant anecdote, that when poverty, staring out at his ragged knees, has sometimes compelled him, against the modesty of his nature, to hint at arrears, Dr. * * * would take no immediate notice, but, after supper, when the school was called together to even-song, he would never fail to introduce some instructive homily against riches, and the corruption of the heart occasioned through the desire of them—ending with 'Lord, keep thy servants, above all things from the heinous sin of avarice. Having food and raiment, let us therewithal be content. Give me Agar's wish,'—and the like ;— which to the little auditory, sounded like a doctrine full of Christian prudence and simplicity,—but to poor D. was a receipt in full for that quarter's demands at least.

" And D. has been under-working for himself ever since ;—drudging at low rates for unappreciating booksellers,—wasting his fine erudition in silent corrections of the classics, and in those unostentatious but solid services to learning, which commonly fall to the lot of laborious scholars, who have not the art to sell themselves to the best advantage. He has published poems, which do not sell, because their character is inobtrusive like his own,—and because he has been too much absorbed in ancient literature, to know what the popular mark in poetry is, even if he could have hit it. And, therefore, his verses are properly, what he terms them, *crotchets ;* voluntaries; odes to Liberty, and Spring; effusions; little tributes, and offerings, left behind him, upon tables and window-seats, at parting from friends' houses; and from all the inns of hospitality, where he has been courteously (or but tolerably) received in his pilgrimage. If his muse of kindness halt a little behind the strong lines, in fashion in this excitement-craving age, his prose is the best of the sort in the world, and exhibits a faithful transcript of his own healthy natural mind, and cheerful innocent tone of conversation."

Agar's wish, *i.e.,* Agur's wish : " Give me neither poverty nor riches" (Prov. xxx. 8). Lamb's slip, Agar for Agur, may be due, Mr. W. J. Craig suggests to me, to a similar error in Defoe's *Memoirs of Colonel Jacques*, where we read of "Solomon or Agar's prayer."— Dyer's poetry is to be found chiefly in his *Poetics*, 1812.

The foregoing passage called forth a protest from one W. K. necessitating the following reply from Lamb, which was printed in the *London Magazine*, under the "Lion's Head," for December, 1820 :—

"Elia requests the Editor to inform W. K. that in his article on Oxford, under the initials G. D., it is his ambition to make more familiar to the public, a character, which, for integrity and single-heartedness, he has long been accustomed to rank among the best patterns of his species. That, if he has failed in the end which he proposed, it was an error of judgment merely. That, if in pursuance of his purpose, he has drawn forth some personal peculiarities of his friend into notice, it was only from the conviction that the public, in living subjects especially, do not endure pure panegyric. That the anecdotes, which he produced, were no more than he conceived necessary to awaken attention to character, and were meant solely to illustrate it. That it is an entire mistake to suppose, that he undertook the character to set off his own wit or ingenuity. That, he conceives, a candid interpreter might find something intended, beyond a heartless jest. That G. D., however, having thought it necessary to disclaim the anecdote respecting Dr. ——, it becomes him, who never for a moment can doubt the veracity of his friend, to account for it from an imperfect remembrance of some story he heard long ago, and which, happening to tally with his argument, he set down too hastily to the account of G. D. That, from G. D.'s strong affirmations and proofs to the contrary, he is bound to believe it belongs to no part of G. D.'s biography. That the transaction, supposing it true, must have taken place more than forty years ago. That, in consequence, it is not likely to 'meet the eye of many who might be justly offended.'

"Finally, that what he has said of the Booksellers, referred to a period of many years, in which he has had the happiness of G. D.'s acquaintance ; and can have nothing to do with any present or prospective engagements of G. D., with those gentlemen, to the nature of which he professes himself an entire stranger."

The result of the protest was that Lamb omitted the passage objected to when he collected *Elia* in 1823. It might well be restored now ; but I have preferred to print everything in the body of this edition as Lamb arranged it for press.

Page 11, last line. "*Better than all the waters* . . ." "Are ¦not

Abana and Pharpar, rivers of Damascus, better than all the waters of Israel?" (2 Kings v. 12).

Page 12, line 1. *Delectable Mountains . . . House Beautiful.* In the *Pilgrim's Progress.*

———

Page 12. CHRIST'S HOSPITAL FIVE AND THIRTY YEARS AGO. *London Magazine,* November, 1820.

This essay, which is based upon the "Recollections of Christ's Hospital" on page 139 of Vol. I., is a curious blend of Lamb's own experiences at school with those of Coleridge. Both boys entered at the same time—on July 17, 1782 : Coleridge was then nearly ten, Lamb was seven and a half. Coleridge was "clothed" on July 18 and went to Hertford for a while ; Lamb was clothed on October 9. Lamb left the school in November, 1789, Coleridge in September, 1791.

Compare notes on pages 434-439 of Vol. I. The most complete and interesting book on the school that exists is Mr. E. H. Pearce's *Annals of Christ's Hospital,* 1901.

The school which Lamb knew is now no more. The house-breakers have been busy in Newgate these many months (1903) and the boys are all in new buildings in the midst of green fields near Horsham, many miles from Lamb's city and its roar.

Page 12, line 19. *The worthy sub-treasurer.* Randal Norris (see note on page 453). I have not been able to discover the cause of his influence.

Page 12, lines 21, 22. *Crug . . . piggins.* Crug is still current slang. In the school museum one of these piggins is preserved.

Page 12, line 28. *Three banyan days.* Three vegetarian days. Coleridge complains (in a letter to Poole) that he was never sufficiently fed except on Wednesdays. He gives the following table of food :—

Our diet was very scanty. Every morning a bit of dry bread and some bad small beer. Every evening a larger piece of bread, and cheese or butter, whichever we liked. For dinner,—on Sunday, boiled beef and broth ; Monday, bread and butter, and milk and water ; Tuesday, roast mutton ; Wednesday, bread and butter, and rice milk ; Thursday, boiled beef and broth ; Friday, boiled mutton and broth ; Saturday, bread and butter, and pease-porridge. Our food was portioned ; and, excepting on Wednesdays, I never had a bellyfull. Our appetites were damped, never satisfied ; and we had no vegetables.

Page 12, line 29. *Double-refined.* Sugar.

Page 12, line 32. *Caro equina.* Horseflesh. Mr. Pearce's chapter on food at the school is very interesting, and records great changes. Rotten-roasted or rare, *i.e.,* over-roasted or under-done.

Page 13, line 4. *The good old relative.* Aunt Hetty, or more properly, Sarah Lamb. See page 70 and note on page 355. Compare the "Lines written on the Day of my Aunt's Funeral," Vol. V., page 19 :—

I have not forgot
How thou didst love thy Charles, when he was yet
A prating schoolboy : I have not forgot
The busy joy on that important day,
When, childlike, the poor wanderer was content

To leave the bosom of parental love,
His childhood's play-place, and his early home,
For the rude fosterings of a stranger's hand,
Hard, uncouth tasks, and schoolboys' scanty fare.
How did thine eyes peruse him round and round
And hardly knew him in his yellow coats,
Red leathern belt, and gown of russet blue.

Page 13, line 7. *The Tishbite.* See 1 Kings xvii. ; but Lamb may have been thinking of the passage in *Paradise Regained*, II., lines 266-270, to which he refers in "Grace Before Meat" (page 94).

Page 13, line 14. *I was a poor friendless boy.* Here Lamb speaks as Coleridge, who came all the way from Ottery St. Mary, in Devonshire (not Calne, in Wiltshire), and had no London friends. In *John Woodvil* Lamb borrowed St. Mary Ottery again (see Vol. V., page 174). Coleridge has recorded how unhappy he was in his early days at school.

Page 13, line 31. *Whole-day-leaves.* In this connection the following passage from Trollope's *History of Christ's Hospital*, 1834, is interesting :—

Those days, on which *leave* is given to be absent from the Hospital during the whole day, are called *whole-day leaves*. . . . A *ticket* is a small oval medal attached to the button-hole, without which, except on leaves, no boy is allowed to pass the gates. Subjoined is a list of the holidays, which have been hitherto kept at Christ's Hospital ; but it is in contemplation to abridge them materially. Of the policy of such a measure great doubts may fairly be entertained, inasmuch as the vacations are so short as to give sufficient respite neither to master nor scholar ; and these occasional breaks, in the arduous duties of the former more especially, enable him to repair the exhausted energies of body and mind by necessary relaxation. If those days, which are marked with an asterisk, fall on a Sunday, they are kept on the Monday following ; and likewise the state holidays.

HOLIDAYS KEPT AT CHRIST'S HOSPITAL

Jan.	25. St Paul's conversion.	July	25. St. James.
	*30. King Charles's martyrdom.		Thursday after St. James
Feb.	2. Candlemas Day.		(Nurses' Holiday.)
	24. St. Matthias.	Aug.	24. St. Bartholomew.
	Shrove Tuesday.	Sept.	*2. London burnt.
	Ash Wednesday.		*21. St. Matthew.
March	25. Lady Day.		29. St. Michael.
April	23. St. George.	Oct.	18. St. Luke.
	25. St. Mark.		*23. King Edward VI. born.
May	1. St. Philip and St. James.		28. St. Simon and St. Jude.
	*29. Restoration of King Charles II.	Nov.	1. All Saints.
	Ascension Day.		*5. Gunpowder Plot.
	Whit Monday.		*9. Lord Mayor's Day.
	Whit Tuesday.		*17. Queen Elizabeth's birth-day.
June	11. St. Barnabas.		30. St. Andrew.
	24. St. John Baptist.	Dec.	21. St. Thomas.
	29. St. Peter.		

Also the birthdays of the King and Queen, and the Prince and Princess of Wales : and the King's accession, proclamation, and coronation.

In addition to the generous allowance of holidays above given the boys had every alternate Wednesday for a whole day ; eleven days at Easter, four weeks in the summer, and fifteen days at Christmas. In 1837 the holiday system was remodelled. Compare Lamb's other remarks on his whole-day rambles in "Recollections of Christ's Hospital" (Vol. I., page 148) and in the essays in the present volume entitled "Amicus Redivivus" (page 211) and "Newspapers" (page 220).

Page 14, line 8. *The Tower.* Blue-coat boys still have this right of free entrance to the Tower; but the lions are no more. They were transferred to the Zoological Gardens in 1831.

Page 14, line 10. *L.'s governor.* Meaning Samuel Salt, M.P. (see note on page 365); but it was actually his friend Mr. Timothy Yeats who signed Lamb's paper. More accurately, Lamb's father lived under Salt's roof.

Page 14, line 20. *Callow overseer.* In the *London Magazine* the word was printed "callous."

Page 14, line 29. *H——.* According to Lamb's Key this was Hodges; but in the British Museum copy of *Elia*, first edition, some one has written Huggins. It is immaterial. Nevis and St. Kitt's (St. Christopher's) are islands in the British West Indies. Tobin would be James Webbe Tobin, of Nevis, who died in 1814, the brother of the playwright John Tobin, author of "The Honeymoon."

Page 14, line 37. *A young ass.* The general opinion at Christ's Hospital is that Lamb invented this incident; and yet it has the air of being true.

Page 14, line 42. *Caligula's minion.* The Emperor Caligula raised a horse to the post of chief consul.

Page 14, line 44. *Waxing fat.* Like Jeshurun (Deut. xxxii. 15).

Page 15, line 2. *Jericho.* See Joshua vi.

Page 15, line 6. *L.'s admired Perry.* John Perry, steward from 1761 to 1785, mentioned in Lamb's earlier essay.

Page 15, line 13. *Verrio.* Rowlandson and Pugin's drawing of Verrio's great picture is reproduced in Vol. I., opposite page 438.

Page 15, line 18. *Harpies.* Lamb makes the same allusion (to the *Æneid*, III., 247-257) in "Grace before Meat," page 93, again close to a reference to Jeshurun waxing fat.

Page 15, line 18. *In the hall of Dido.* See the *Æneid*, I., where Æneas studies the pictures in the temple which Dido was raising to Juno and is comforted by them: "*Animum pictura pascit inani*"— "he feeds his soul on the 'bodiless presentment'"—line 464.

Page 15, line 21. *Gags.* Still current slang.

Page 15, line 26. *——.* No name in the Key. The quotation is an adaptation of:—

It is reported thou didst eat strange flesh
Which some did die to look on.
"Antony and Cleopatra," Act I., Scene 4, lines 67-68.

It is perhaps worth remarking that in *David Copperfield* Dickens has a school incident of a similar character.

Page 15, line 39. *The accursed thing.* See Joshua vii. 13.

Page 16, line 13. *Mr. Hathaway.* Matthias Hathaway, steward from 1790 to 1813.

Page 16, line 32. *I was a hypochondriac lad.* Here Lamb drops the Coleridge mask and speaks as himself. The footnote to this paragraph refers to John Howard, the philanthropist, for whom Lamb seems to have had only dislike (see the reference to his features in the essay on "The Old Benchers," page 88). In the *London Magazine* it ended, " Methinks I could willingly 'spit upon his stony gaberdine' "—an adaptation from "The Merchant of Venice," Act I., Scene 3, line 113. Howard's statue is in St. Paul's Cathedral.

Page 17, line 10. *Auto da fe.* Act of faith. An execution of heretics under the Spanish Inquisition.

Page 17, line 11. "*Watchet weeds.*" Watchet—blue.

> Him whom Seine's blue nymphs deplore
> In watchet weeds on Gallia's shore.
> > Collins' "Ode to the Manners."

Page 17, line 16. *Disfigurements in Dante.* See *The Inferno,* Cantos 28 to 30.

Page 17, line 25. *Ultima Supplicia.* "Extreme penalties."

Page 17, line 27. *Bamber Gascoigne, and Peter Aubert.* Bamber Gascoigne, M.P. (1725-1791), of Bifrons, in Essex. Of Peter Aubert I can find nothing, except that the assistant secretary of the East India Company at the time Lamb wrote this essay was Peter Auber, afterwards full secretary. His name here may be a joke.

Page 17, line 36. *San Benito.* The yellow robe worn by victims at an *auto da fé.*

Page 18, line 8. *Matthew Field.* The Rev. Matthew Feilde, also vicar of Ugley and curate of Berden. For the Rev. James Boyer see below.

Page 18, line 18. "*Like a dancer.*" In "Antony and Cleopatra," Act III., Scene 11, lines 35-36, of Octavius :—

> he at Philippi, kept
> His sword e'en like a dancer.

Lamb was fond of this phrase. Mrs. Battle, he said, "held not her good sword (her cards) 'like a dancer.' "

Page 18, line 27. "*Insolent Greece . . .*" Ben Jonson's phrase in his elegy on Shakespeare.

Page 18, line 28. "*Peter Wilkins,*" etc. *The Adventures of Peter Wilkins,* by Robert Paltock, 1751, is still read ; but *The Voyages and Adventures of Captain Robert Boyle,* 1726, has had its day. It was a blend of unconvincing travel and some rather free narrative : a piece of sheer hackwork to meet a certain market. See Lamb's sonnet to Stothard, Vol. V., page 75. *The Fortunate Blue-Coat Boy* I have not seen. Canon Ainger describes it as a rather foolish romance, showing how a Blue-coat boy marries a rich lady of rank. The sub-title is " Memoirs of the Life and Happy Adventures of Mr. Benjamin Templeman ; formerly a Scholar in Christ's Hospital. By an Orphanotropian," 1770.

Page 18, line 34. "*French and English.*" Boys still play " French and English." A piece of paper is covered with dots, and the players —one French and one English—in turn close their eyes and slash a pencil across it. The dots through which the line has passed are counted after each stroke, and that nation wins whose pencil annihilates most.

Page 18, line 37. *Rousseau and Locke,* whose systems of education agreed in the desirability of combining the practical with the theoretical (see Rousseau's *Emilia,* 1762, and Locke's *Thoughts Concerning the Education of Children,* 1693).

Page 19, line 8. *Helots . . . Spartans.* Referring to the practice of Spartan parents of exhibiting to their sons, as a warning, a drunken Helot or slave.

Page 19, line 13. *The Samite.* Pythagoras of Samos, who forbade his pupils to speak until they had listened through five years of his lectures.

Page 19, line 14. *Our little Goshen.* See Exodus viii. 22. Lamb was fond of this allusion.

Page 19, line 17. *Gideon's miracle.* See Judges vi. 37, 38 ; but in verses 39 and 40 the converse happened. Lamb here remembers Cowley's lines in "The Complaint," Stanza 7 :—

> For ev'ry tree, and ev'ry land around,
> With pearly dew was crown'd,
> And upon all the quicken'd ground
> The fruitful seed of Heav'n did brooding lie,
> And nothing but the Muse's fleece was dry.

Page 19, line 24. *"Playing holiday."*

> If all the year were playing holidays,
> To sport would be as weary as to work.
>
> "I. Henry IV.," Act I., Scene 2, lines 227-228.

Page 19, line 27. *The Ululantes.* "The howling sufferers." "Hence [Tartarus] are clearly heard groanings and the sound of the cruel scourge" (*Æneid,* VI., 557).

Page 19, line 29. *Easter anthems.* These were written also sometimes by the boys.

Page 19, line 30. *Scrannel pipes.* "Grate on their scrannel pipes" (Milton's *Lycidas,* 124).

Page 19, line 31. *Flaccus's quibble.* In the *Satires,* Book I., VII., 34-5, where *Rex* has the double meaning of King, a private surname, and king, a monarch. The thin jests in Terence are in "Andrea," Act V., Scene 2—*tristis severitas in vultu*—"puritanic rigour in his countenance," says one of the comic characters of a palpable liar ; and in the "Adelphi," Act III., Scene 3, where, after a father has counselled his son to look into the lives of men as in a mirror, the slave counsels the scullions to look into stew-pans as in a mirror.

Page 19. *Footnote.* I have not discovered a copy of Matthew Feilde's play.

Page 20, line 14. *Rabidus furor.* "Rabid rage." From Catullus probably—*Attis,* 38.

Page 20, line 22. *Squinting W——.* Not identifiable.

Page 20, line 31. *Coleridge, in his literary life.* Coleridge speaks in the *Biographia Literaria* of having had the "inestimable advantage of a very sensible, though at the same time a very severe master, the Reverend James Bowyer [Boyer]," and goes on to attribute to that

THE COLERIDGE MEMORIAL AT CHRIST'S HOSPITAL

A bronze statuette of Lamb, Coleridge and Middleton
Designed by Barkentin

NOTES

master's discrimination and thoroughness much of his own classical knowledge and early interest in poetry and criticism. Coleridge gives this example of Boyer's impatient humour:—

> In our own English compositions (at least for the last three years of our school education), he showed no mercy to phrase, metaphor, or image, unsupported by a sound sense, or where the same sense might have been conveyed with equal force and dignity in plainer words. *Lute, harp* and *lyre, Muse, Muses* and *inspirations, Pegasus, Parnassus* and *Hippocrene*, were all an abomination to him. In fancy I can almost hear him now exclaiming, "Harp? Harp? Lyre? Pen and ink, boy, you mean! Muse, boy, muse? Your nurse's daughter, you mean! Pierian spring? Oh, aye! the cloister pump, I suppose!"

Touching Boyer's cruelty, Coleridge adds that his "severities, even now, not seldom furnish the dreams by which the blind fancy would fain interpret to the mind the painful sensations of distempered sleep."

In *Table Talk* Coleridge tells another story of Boyer. "The discipline at Christ's Hospital in my time," he says, "was ultra-Spartan; all domestic ties were to be put aside. 'Boy!' I remember Bowyer saying to me once when I was crying the first day of my return after the holidays, 'Boy! the school is your father! Boy! the school is your mother! Boy! the school is your brother! the school is your sister! the school is your first cousin, and your second cousin, and all the rest of your relations! Let's have no more crying!'"

Leigh Hunt in his autobiography also has reminiscences of Boyer and Feilde.

James Boyer or Bowyer was born in 1736, was admitted to the school in 1744, and passed to Balliol. He resigned his Upper Grammar Mastership in 1799, and probably retired to the rectory of Gainscolne to which he had been appointed by the school committee six years earlier. They also gave him £500 and a staff.

Page 20, line 32. *Author of the Country Spectator.* Thomas Fanshaw Middleton (1769-1822), afterwards Bishop of Calcutta, who was at school with Lamb and Coleridge. In the little statuette group which is called the Coleridge Memorial, subscribed for in 1872, on the centenary of Coleridge's birth, and held in rotation by the ward in which most prizes have been gained in the year (see plate opposite page 320), Middleton is the tallest figure. The story which it celebrates is to the effect that Middleton found Coleridge reading Virgil in the playground and asked him if he were learning a lesson. Coleridge replied that he was "reading for pleasure," an answer which Middleton reported to Boyer, and which led to Boyer taking special notice of him. The *Country Spectator* was a magazine conducted by Middleton in 1792-1793.

Page 20, line 35. *C——.* Coleridge again.

Page 20, line 40. *Lancelot Pepys Stevens.* Rightly spelled Stephens, afterwards Under Grammar Master at the school.

Page 20, line 42. *Dr. T——e.* Arthur William Trollope (1768-1827), who succeeded Boyer as Upper Grammar Master. He resigned in 1826.

Page 21, line 5. *The fasces.* Here, the birch rod. The fasces were the bundles of rods, with an axe in the centre, carried by lictors before Roman magistrates.

Page 21, line 7. *Cicero De Amicitia.* Cicero's essay on Friendship.

Page 21, line 9. *Th—.* Sir Edward Thornton (1766-1852), diplomatist, who was sent as Envoy Extraordinary and Minister Plenipotentiary to Lower Saxony, to Sweden, to Denmark and other courts, afterwards becoming minister to Portugal.

Page 21, line 12, etc. *Middleton.* See note above. The treatise was *The Doctrine of the Greek Article as applied to the Criticism and the Illustration of the New Testament*, 1808. It was directed chiefly against Granville Sharpe. Middleton was the first Bishop of Calcutta —hence the phrase "*regni novitas*" (from the *Æneid*, I., 562), an infant realm.—Bishop Jewel, of Salisbury (1522-1571), author of the *Apologia pro Ecclesia Anglicana*, and the judicious Richard Hooker (about 1533 to 1600), author of *A Treatise on the Laws of Ecclesiastical Polity.*

Page 21, line 22. *Richards.* This was George Richards (1767-1837). His poem on "Aboriginal Britons," which won a prize given in 1791 by Earl Harcourt, is mentioned favourably in Byron's *English Bards and Scotch Reviewers.* Richards became vicar of St. Martin's-in-the-Fields and a Governor of Christ's Hospital. He founded a gold medal for Latin hexameters.

Page 21, lines 24, 25. *S—— . . . M——.* According to the Key "Scott, died in Bedlam," and "Maunde, dismiss'd school."

Page 21, line 26. "*Finding some of Edward's race.*" From Prior's *Carmen Seculare* for 1700 :—

> Finding some of Stuart's race
> Unhappy, pass their annals by.

Lamb alters Stuart to Edward because Edward VI. founded Christ's Hospital.

Page 21, line 34. *Mirandula.* Giovanni Pico della Mirandola (1463-1494), a young Italian of extraordinary attainments, the friend of Lorenzo de Medici.

Page 21, line 35. *Jamblichus, or Plotinus.* Two of the Neo-Platonic philosophers. Lamb is thinking of Horace, Ep. I., 3, 10.

Page 21, line 39. *The words of old Fuller.* Adapting a passage in Fuller's *Worthies*, describing the wit combats between Shakespeare and Ben Jonson (under "Warwickshire ").

Page 21, line 40. *C. V. Le G——.* Charles Valentine Le Grice (1773-1858), whom we meet also in the essay on "Grace Before Meat" (page 96). Le Grice, in his description of Lamb as a schoolboy in Talfourd's *Memorials*, remarked: "I never heard his name mentioned without the addition of Charles, although, as there was no other boy of the name of Lamb, the addition was unnecessary ; but there was an implied kindness in it, and it was a proof that his gentle manners excited that kindness."

Page 22, line 3. *Allen.* Robert Allen, whom we meet again in the essay on "Newspapers" (page 223). After a varied and not fortunate career he died of apoplexy in 1805.

Page 22, line 9. *Nireus formosus.* See the *Iliad*, II., 673. Chapman says : "Nireus was the fairest man that to fair Ilius came."

Page 22, line 16. *The junior Le G——.* Samuel Le Grice became a soldier and died in the West Indies. Lamb wrote of him to Coleridge in 1796, after the tragedy at his home, at a time when friends were badly needed, "Sam Le Grice who was then in town was with me the first 3 or 4 days, and was as a brother to me, gave up every hour of his time to the very hurting of his health and spirits, in constant attendance and humouring my poor father."

Page 22, line 16. *F——.* Joseph Favell, afterwards Captain, who had a commission from the Duke of York—as had Sam Le Grice— and was killed in the Peninsula, at Salamanca, 1812. Lamb states in the essay on "Poor Relations," where Favell figures as "W.," that he met his death at St. Sebastian. Other particulars concerning him will be found there (see page 160). Both Sam Le Grice and Favell were to have accompanied Coleridge and Southey to the Susquehanna as Pantisocrats.

Page 22, line 24. *Fr——.* Frederick William Franklin, master of the Hertford branch of the school from 1801 to 1827. He died in 1836.

Page 22, line 25. *Marmaduke T——.* Marmaduke Thompson, to whom Lamb dedicated *Rosamund Gray* in 1798.

Page 22, line 26. *Catalogue of Grecians.* Lamb was at Christ's Hospital from 1782 to 1789, and his list is not quite complete. He himself never was a Grecian ; that is to say, one of the picked scholars on the grammar side of the school, two of whom were sent up to Cambridge with a hospital exhibition every year, on the understanding that they should take orders. Lamb was one of the Deputy-Grecians from whom the Grecians were chosen, but his stammer standing in his way and a church career being out of the question, he never became a full Grecian. Writing to George Dyer, who had been a Grecian, in 1831, Lamb says : "I don't know how it is, but I keep my rank in fancy still since school-days. I can never forget I was a deputy Grecian ! . . . Alas ! what am I now ? What is a Leadenhall clerk, or India pensioner, to a deputy Grecian ? How art thou fallen, O Lucifer ! "

Blackwood's Magazine, in its feud with the *London*, fell on this particular essay in November, 1820, when was printed a letter from "Olinthus Petre, D.D." (a pseudonym of Maginn's), mentioning the "impertinences of a Cockney Scribbler, who signs himself Elia, full of all kinds of personal, and often abusive allusions, to every individual who had the misfortune of being educated at the same school with himself." Later, in May, 1821, "Dr. Petre" apologised to some extent, on the grounds of admiring Mr. Lamb and finding that Elia and he were one ; but he still, while eulogising *John Woodvil*, disapproved strongly of his ribald treatment of George Dyer and his sneer at

Middleton, Bishop of Calcutta—which were put down to the contamination of his evil Cockney associates.

Lamb's memory is preserved at Christ's Hospital by a medal (see opposite page) which is given for the best English essays. It was first struck in 1875, the centenary of his birth.

Page 22. THE TWO RACES OF MEN.
London Magazine, December, 1820.

Writing to Wordsworth in April of 1816, Lamb says :—

" I have not bound the poems yet. I wait till people have done borrowing them. I think I shall get a chain and chain them to my shelves, *more Bodleiano*, and people may come and read them at chain's length. For of those who borrow, some read slow ; some mean to read but don't read ; and some neither read nor meant to read, but borrow to leave you an opinion of their sagacity. I must do my money-borrowing friends the justice to say that there is nothing of this caprice or wantonness of alienation in them. When they borrow my money they never fail to make use of it."

Probably the germ of the essay is to be found in this passage, as Lamb never forgot his thoughts.

Page 22, line 33. *"Parthians, and Medes . . ."* See Acts ii. 9.

Page 22, last lines. *" He shall serve his brethren."* Possibly a recollection of Genesis ix. 25, " And he said, Cursed be Canaan ; a servant of servants shall he be unto his brethren."

Page 23, line 5. *Brinsley.* Richard Brinsley Sheridan, the dramatist and a great spendthrift. He died in 1816. Lamb knew him slightly.

Page 23, line 12. *Beyond Tooke.* That is, beyond the philological theories of *The Diversions of Purley* by John Horne Tooke (1736-1812).

Page 23, line 14. *The primitive community.* See Acts ii. 44.

Page 23, line 16. *" Calleth all the world up . . ."* " And it came to pass in those days, that there went out a decree from Cæsar Augustus, that all the world should be taxed " (Luke ii. 1).

Page 23, line 24. *Candlemas . . . Holy Michael.* Candlemas, February 2, a Scotch quarter-day ; Michaelmas, September 29, an English quarter-day. Messrs. Hallward and Hill suggest that Lamb had in mind Sir Thomas Browne's sentence in *Christian Morals* (Part 1, Section VI.) : " The Almighty rewarder, who observes no ides, but every day for his payments."

Page 23, line 25. *Lene tormentum.* Horace's phrase, *Odes*, III., 21, line 13,—" the gentle stimulus."

Page 23, line 27. *The cloak of the traveller.* One of Æsop's fables.

Page 23, line 28. *True Propontic.* The Propontic or Propontes —the Sea of Marmora. Lamb was probably thinking of Othello's simile (Act III., Scene 3, lines 453-456) :—

> Like to the Pontic sea,
> Whose icy current and compulsive course
> Ne'er feels retiring ebb, but keeps due on
> To the Propontic and the Hellespont.

The Pontic was the Euxine.

THE LAMB MEDAL AT CHRIST'S HOSPITAL

Page 23, line 32. *The reversion promised.* "He that hath pity upon the poor lendeth unto the Lord; and that which he hath given will he pay him again" (Prov. xix. 17).

Page 23, line 39. *Ralph Bigod.* John Fenwick, an unlucky friend of the Lambs, an anticipatory Micawber, of whom we know too little, and seem likely to find out little more. Lamb mentions him again in the essay on "Chimney Sweepers" (page 113), and in that on "Newspapers" (page 224), in his capacity as editor of *The Albion*, for which Lamb wrote its extinguishing epigram in the summer of 1801. There are references to the Fenwicks in Mary Lamb's letters to Sarah Stoddart and in Lamb's letters; but nothing very informing. After financial embarrassments in England they emigrated to America. The Bigods, whose name Lamb himself borrowed for his friend, were Earls of Norfolk in old time.

Page 24, line 7. "*To slacken virtue . . .*" *Paradise Regained*, II., lines 455-456.

Page 24, line 10. "*Borrowing and to borrow.*" A perversion (making the original refer to Alexander the Great) of "conquering and to conquer" in Revelation vi. 2.

Page 24, line 23. "*Stocked with so fair a herd.*"

> *Comus.*   I shall ere long
> Be well stock't with as fair a herd as graz'd
> About my mother Circe.
>
> *Comus*, lines 151-153.

Page 24, line 36. *Hagar's offspring.* See Genesis xxi.

Page 24, line 42. "*Cana fides.*" Virgil's phrase in the *Æneid*, I., 292, signifying there "ancient honour," and here "grey hair," the badge of ancient honour.

Page 25, line 18. *Comberbatch.* Coleridge, who had enlisted as a young man in the 15th Light Dragoons as Silas Titus Comberback.

Page 25, line 22. *Bloomsbury.* Lamb was then in rooms at 20 Great Russell Street (now Russell Street), Covent Garden, which is not in Bloomsbury.

Page 25, line 22. *Switzer-like.* Enormous; referring to the Swiss Guards, who are of great stature.

Page 25, line 23. *Guildhall giants.* The Guildhall giants early in the last century were moved from their station by the door and placed upon octagon stone columns by the west window. "In their present situation," Hone wrote in 1825, "they are as much out of place as a church weathercock would be if it were removed from the steeple, and put on the sounding board of the pulpit" (*Every-Day Book*, Vol. I.).

Page 25, lines 24 to 27. *Opera Bonaventuræ, Bellarmine, Holy Thomas.* St. Bonaventure, called the Seraphic Doctor, was Bishop of Albano in the thirteenth century, and the author of theological works. Cardinal Bellarmine was another Italian divine, in the sixteenth century. Thomas Aquinas, the author principally of *A Summary of Theology*, was an Italian divine of the thirteenth century. Lamb bought another *Thomas Aquinas* in 1829 from a stall in the Barbican. He tells Barton about it in the letter of March 25, 1829.

Page 25, line 27. *Ascapart.* Ascapart was the giant slain by Bevis, of Southampton. See Drayton's *Polyolbion* (Song II.), which was among the books in Lamb's library (a folio, 1748).

Page 25, line 31. *The claimant's.* In the *London Magazine,* "a person's."

Page 25, line 32. *Should he go on acting.* The *Letters* contain references to this habit of Coleridge's. Writing to him in 1809 Lamb says, referring among other loans to the volume of Dodsley with Vittoria Corombona ("The White Devil," by John Webster) in it :—

"While I think on it, Coleridge, I fetch'd away my books which you had at the *Courier* Office, and found all but a third volume of the old plays, containing the 'White Devil,' Green's 'Tu Quoque,' and the 'Honest Whore,' perhaps the most valuable volume of them all— *that* I could not find. Pray, if you can, remember what you did with it, or where you took it out with you a walking perhaps; send me word, for, to use the old plea, it spoils a set. I found two other volumes (you had three), the *Arcadia* and *Daniel*, enriched with manuscript notes. I wish every book I have were so noted. They have thoroughly converted me to relish *Daniel*, or to say I relish him, for after all, I believe I did relish him."

And several years later (probably in 1820) we find him addressing Coleridge with reference to Luther's *Table Talk* :—

"Why will you make your visits, which should give pleasure, matter of regret to your friends ? You never come but you take away some folio, that is part of my existence. With a great deal of difficulty I was made to comprehend the extent of my loss. My maid, Becky, brought me a dirty bit of paper, which contained her description of some book which Mr. Coleridge had taken away. It was *Luster's Tables*, which, for some time, I could not make out. 'What! has he carried away any of the *tables*, Becky ?' 'No, it wasn't any tables, but it was a book that he called *Luster's Tables*.' I was obliged to search personally among my shelves, and a huge fissure suddenly disclosed to me the true nature of the damage I had sustained."

I fancy that writing this letter gave Lamb the idea of the present essay.

Allsop tells us that Lamb once said of Coleridge: " He sets his mark upon whatever he reads; it is henceforth sacred. His spirit seems to have breathed upon it; and, if not for its author, yet for his sake, we admire it."

Page 25, line 43. *Priam's refuse sons.* The reference is to the *Iliad*, XXIV., 486, &c., where Priam begs from Achilles the body of Hector, the best beloved son of the fifty born to him, nine of whom were still living.

Page 26, line 1. *John Buncle.* Most of Lamb's books, to the eternal regret of English collectors, are in America; Lamb's copy of *John Buncle*, with an introductory note written in by Coleridge, was sold, with other books from his library, in New York in 1848. *The Life of John Buncle, Esq.*, a book highly praised by Hazlitt, was by Thomas Amory (1691 ?-1788), published, Part I. in 1756 and Part II. in 1766. A condensed reprint was issued in 1823 entitled *The Spirit of Buncle*, in which, Mr. W. C. Hazlitt suggests, Lamb may have had a hand with William Hazlitt.

Page 26, line 2. *"Eyes closed."* I cannot trace this quotation; but the phrase "mourns his ravished mate" is in Cuthbert Shaw's "Evening Address to a Nightingale" :—

> Say dost thou mourn thy ravish'd mate?

Page 26, line 9. *Proselytes of the gate . . . true Hebrews.* A proselyte of the gate, *i.e.*, a stranger converted to Judaism, was not bound by such severe religious laws as the Hebrew born.

Page 26, line 12. *Deodands.* The word is not strictly used here. A deodand is, in law parlance, a personal article which, having occasioned the death of some one, is forfeit to the Crown for pious uses, *i.e.*, given to God.

Page 26, line 18. *Spiteful K.* James Kenney (1780-1849), the dramatist, then resident at Versailles, where Lamb and his sister visited him in 1822. He married Louisa Mercier, daughter of Louis Sebastian Mercier, the French critic, and widow of Lamb's earlier friend, Thomas Holcroft. One of their two sons was named Charles Lamb Kenney (1821-1881). Lamb recovered Margaret of Newcastle's *Letters* (folio, 1664), which is among the books in America, as is also the Fulke Greville (small folio, 1633).

Page 26, line 26. *" Unworthy land . . ."* It is usually conjectured that Lamb invented these beautiful lines. Messrs. Hallward and Hill point out that the phrase " thy sex's wonder" occurs in Cyril Tourneur. I find something of the kind twice. " The Atheist's Tragedy," Act III., Scene 4, has this :—

> *Castabella.* Believe me, sir, it never troubles me.
> I am as much respectlesse to enjoy
> Such pleasure, as ignorant what it is.
> *Charlemont.* Thy sexe's wonder. Unhappy Charlemont !
> *D'Arnville.* Come, let's to supper.

In " The Revenger's Tragedy " (Act II.) Lusurioso says :—

> I never thought their sex had been a wonder
> Until this minute.

Lamb knew both plays intimately, and quoted from them in the *Dramatic Specimens*.

Page 26, at foot. *S. T. C. . . . annotations.* Lamb's copy of Daniel's *Poetical Works*, two volumes, 1718, and of Browne's *Enquiries into Vulgar and Common Errors*, folio, 1658, both with marginalia by himself and Coleridge, are in existence, but I cannot say where: probably in America. Lamb's copy of Beaumont and Fletcher, with Coleridge's notes (see " Old China," page 174), is, however, safe in the British

Museum. His Fulke Greville, as I have said, is in America, but I fancy it has nothing of Coleridge in it, nor has his Burton—quarto, 1621—which still exists.

Coleridge's notes in the Beaumont and Fletcher folio are not numerous, but usually ample and seriously critical. At the foot of a page of the "Siege of Corinth," on which he had written two notes (one, "O flat! flat! flat! Sole! Flounder! Place! all stinking! stinkingly flat!"), he added:—

N.B.—I shall not be long here, Charles!—I gone, you will not mind my having spoiled a book in order to leave a Relic.
S. T. C.　　　　　Oct^r, 1811.

Underneath the initials S. T. C. are the initials W. W. which suggest that Wordsworth was present.

The Museum also has Lamb's Milton, with annotations by himself and Coleridge. There is, by the way, a Museum legend of one reader who in the interests of a fair page went carefully over certain of Coleridge's marginalia with india-rubber, and removed every mark.

In the *Descriptive Catalogue of the Library of Charles Lamb*, privately issued by the New York Dibdin Club in 1897, is a list of five of Lamb's books now in America containing valuable and unpublished marginalia by Coleridge : *The Life of John Buncle*, Donne's *Poems* (" I shall die soon, my dear Charles Lamb, and then you will not be vexed that I have scribbled your book. S. T. C., 2^d May, 1811 "), Reynolds' *God's Revenge against . . . Murder*, 1651 ("O what a beautiful *concordia discordantium* is an unthinking good man's soul !"), *The History of Philip de Commines* in English, and Petwin's *Letters Concerning the Mind*.

***

Page 27. NEW YEAR'S EVE.
London Magazine, January, 1821.

The melancholy pessimism of this essay led to some remonstrance from robuster readers of the *London Magazine*. In addition to the letter from "A Father" referred to below, the essay produced, seven months later, in the August number of the *London Magazine*, a long poetical "Epistle to Elia," signed "Olen," in which very simply and touchingly Lamb was reminded that the grave is not the end, was asked to consider the promises of the Christian faith, and finally was offered a glimpse of some of the friends he would meet in heaven— among them Ulysses, Shakespeare and Alice W——n. Taylor, the publisher and editor of the magazine, sent Lamb a copy. He replied, acknowledging the kindness of the author, and adding :—

"Poor Elia . . . does not pretend to so very clear revelations of a future state of being as 'Olen' seems gifted with. He stumbles about dark mountains at best; but he knows at least how to be thankful for this life, and is too thankful, indeed, for certain relationships lent him here, not to tremble for a possible resumption of the gift. He is too apt to express himself lightly, and cannot be sorry for the present occasion, as it has called forth a reproof so Christian-like."

Lamb thought the poet to be James Montgomery, but it was in reality Charles Abraham Elton. The poem was reprinted in a volume entitled *Boyhood and other Poems*, in 1835.

"New Year's Eve" also produced a commentary from Horace Smith, of the *Rejected Addresses*, in the shape of perhaps his best exercise in prose —" Death—Posthumous Memorials—Children "—printed anonymously in the *London Magazine* for March, 1821. It begins :—

How I could expatiate upon the quaint lugubrious pleasantry, the social yet deep philosophy of your friend ELIA, as particularly illustrated in his delightful paper upon New Year's Eve!—but the bandying of praises among Correspondents has too *Magazinish* a look :—I have learnt his essay by heart. Is it possible, said I to myself, when I first devoured it, that such a man can really feel such horrors at the thought of death, which he describes with so much humorous solemnity ? But when I came to his conclusion, wherein he talks of the fears, "just now expressed, or *affected*," I had presently a clue to his design.—Ha ! I exclaimed, thou art the very Janus who hast always delighted in antithetical presentments ; who lovest to exhibit thy tragic face in its most doleful gloom, that thou mayst incontinently turn upon us the sunshine of thy comic smile. Thou wouldst not paint the miseries endured by a friendless boy at Christ's, without a companion piece, pourtraying the enjoyments of a more fortunate youngster. Thou wouldst not pour forth the phials of thy wrath upon the plant tobacco, without the redemption of an eulogy upon its virtues, more eloquent than Sir Walter Raleigh's : nor hast thou now, as I trust, pronounced thy anathema against the "foul ugly phantom," without being prepared, in the same happy strain, to chant a palinode.

It is conceivable that Lamb was reasoned with privately upon the sentiments expressed in this essay ; and perhaps we may take the following sonnet which he contributed over his own name to the *London Magazine* for April, 1821, as a kind of defiant postscript thereto, a further challenge to those who reproached him for his remarks concerning death, and who suggested that he did not really mean them :—

> They talk of time, and of time's galling yoke,
> That like a millstone on man's mind doth press,
> Which only works and business can redress :
> Of divine Leisure such foul lies are spoke,
> Wounding her fair gifts with calumnious stroke.
> But might I, fed with silent meditation,
> Assoiled live from that fiend Occupation—
> *Improbus labor*, which my spirits hath broke—
> I'd drink of time's rich cup, and never surfeit—
> Fling in more days than went to make the gem
> That crowned the white top of Methusalem—
> Yea on my weak neck take, and never forfeit,
> Like Atlas bearing up the dainty sky,
> The heaven-sweet burthen of eternity.

When, in his *Album Verses* (1830), Lamb reprinted this sonnet, under the title "Leisure," he added the phrase

DEUS NOBIS HÆC OTIA FECIT.

"A God provided for me this repose,"—citing the words of Virgil's shepherd boy (Eclogues, I., 6) who was rescued from eviction by Augustus. See Vol. V., page 56. See also page 428 of this volume for a reference of Lamb's to this poem.

It was also probably the present essay which led to Lamb's difference with Southey and the famous letter of remonstrance. Southey accused *Elia* of wanting "a sounder religious feeling," and Lamb suggests in his reply that "New Year's Eve" was the chief offender. See Vol. I., page 227, for Lamb's amplification of one of its passages.

It may be interesting here to quote Coleridge's description of Lamb as "one hovering between heaven and earth, neither hoping much nor fearing anything."

The present essay caused still another difficulty. In Mr. W. C. Hazlitt's *Four Generations of a Literary Family* is a letter from Hazlitt to Scott, the editor of the *London Magazine*, dated by Mr. W. C. Hazlitt April 12, 1820, where we read: "Do you keep the Past and Future? You see Lamb argues the same view of the subject. That 'young master' will anticipate all my discoveries, if I don't mind." "New Year's Eve" did not appear until January, 1821, and yet it is pretty certain, as Mr. Bertram Dobell has pointed out, that Hazlitt had that essay in mind. We find the phrase "young master" in it (page 28, line 29), and Hazlitt's essay "On the Past and Future" is to a large extent written on similar lines of thought. How to account for the disparity in the date of the letter and the date of publication of Lamb's essay I do not know, except by the supposition that the letter is undated or indistinctly dated, and Mr. W. C. Hazlitt has conjectured an earlier date than is proper. It is unlikely that Hazlitt would have seen Lamb's essay in manuscript, for he was not on good terms with Lamb at the time. The essay "On the Past and Future" appeared in *Table Talk*, 1821. Even closer resemblances to passages in "New Year's Eve" may be found in Hazlitt's essay "On the Fear of Death," published in *Table Talk*, Vol. II., 1822.

Hazlitt, according to Coleridge, was more indebted to Lamb for ideas than ever Lamb was to Hazlitt. Hazlitt was a professional writer; Lamb never can be considered so; and from time immemorial professional writers have taken ideas where they found them. Many of Lamb's ideas came and went in conversation. Hazlitt must have needed all or most of his for his work, and others too.

Hazlitt was, however, before Lamb with a subject on more than one occasion. See for example his remarks on the character of Quakers in his essay on the "Tendency of Sects" in *The Examiner*, September 10, 1815. But neither man needed the brains of the other.

Page 27, line 18. *Bells*. The music of bells seems always to have exerted fascination over Lamb. See the reference in the story of the "First Going to Church," in *Mrs. Leicester's School*, Vol. III.; in his poem "Sabbath Bells," Vol. V., page 9; and his "John Woodvil," Vol. V., page 174.

Page 27, line 26. *"I saw the skirts of the departing Year."* From Coleridge's "Ode to the Departing Year," as printed in 1796 and 1797. Lamb was greatly taken by this line. He wrote to Coleridge on January 2, 1797, in a letter of which only a small portion has been printed:—

"The opening [of the Ode] is in the spirit of the sublimest allegory. The idea of the 'skirts of the departing year, seen far onwards, waving

in the wind,' is one of those noble Hints at which the Reader's imagination is apt to kindle into grand conceptions."
Afterwards Coleridge altered "skirts" to "train."

Page 27, line 33. *"Welcome the coming . . ."* Pope's *Odyssey*, XV., 84, and Second Sat. of Horace, Book II., line 160.

Page 28, line 9. *Seven . . . years.* See note to "Dream Children," page 377. Alice W——n is identified with Ann Simmons, who lived near Blakesware when Lamb was a youth, and of whom he wrote his love sonnets. According to the Key the name is "feigned."

Page 28, line 13. *Old Dorrell.* See the poem "Going or Gone," Vol. V., page 70, and note. There seems really to have been such an enemy of the Lamb fortunes. He was one of the witnesses to the will of John Lamb, the father,—William Dorrell.

Page 28, line 28. *"Other me."* I cannot trace the quotation, if such it be, unless Lamb is thus translating *alter ego.* Possibly by his inverted commas he meant only to emphasise the age of the old idea of dual personality.

Page 28, line 32. *Small-pox at five.* There is no other evidence than this casual mention that Lamb ever suffered from this complaint. Possibly he did not. He went to Christ's Hospital at the age of seven.

Page 28, line 36. *God help thee, Elia . . .* This is a memory of Bottom's "Bless thee Bottom, thou art translated" ("Midsummer-Night's Dream," Act III., Scene 1, lines 121, 122).

Page 28, line 39. *From what have I not fallen.* Lamb had had this idea many years before. In 1796 he wrote this sonnet (text of 1818):—

> We were two pretty babes, the youngest she,
>   The youngest, and the loveliest far, I ween,
>   And Innocence her name. The time has been
> We two did love each other's company;
>   Time was, we two had wept to have been apart:
>   But when by show of seeming good beguil'd,
>   I left the garb and manners of a child,
> And my first love for man's society,
>   Defiling with the world my virgin heart—
> My loved companion dropp'd a tear, and fled,
> And hid in deepest shades her awful head.
>   Beloved, who shall tell me where thou art—
> In what delicious Eden to be found—
> That I may seek thee the wide world around?

Page 29, line 7. *Phantom cloud of Elia.* The speculations in the paragraph that ends with these words were fantastical at any rate to one reader, who, under the signature "A Father," contributed to the February number of the *London Magazine* a eulogy of paternity, in which Elia was reasoned with and rebuked. "Ah! Elia! hadst thou possessed 'offspring of thine own to dally with,' thou wouldst never have made the melancholy avowal that thou hast 'almost ceased to hope!'" Lamb did not reply.

Page 29, line 15. *Not childhood alone . . .* The passage between these words and "freezing days of December" was taken by Charles Lloyd, Lamb's early friend, as the motto of a poem, in his *Poems*, 1823, entitled "Stanzas on the Difficulty with which, in Youth, we Bring Home to our Habitual Consciousness the Idea of Death."

Page 29, line 26. " *Like a weaver's shuttle.*" " My days are swifter than a weaver's shuttle, and are spent without hope " (Job vii. 6).

Page 29, line 29. *Reluct.* Resist, struggle against. From *reluctare.*

Page 29, line 39. *Lavinian shores.* Referring to Æneas, at the beginning of the *Æneid*, I., 2, who after the sack of Troy had settled in Italy, the Lavinian land.

Page 30, line 3. *Midnight darlings.* Leigh Hunt records, in his essay " My Books " (see note on page 415), that he once saw Lamb kiss an old folio—Chapman's *Homer.*

Page 30, line 9. " *Sweet assurance of a look.*" A favourite quotation of Lamb's (here adapted) from Matthew Roydon's elegy on Sir Philip Sidney :—

> A sweet attractive kind of grace,
> A full assurance given by looks.

A portion of the poem is quoted in the essay on "Some Sonnets of Sir Philip Sidney," page 219. It is printed in all editions of Spenser.

Page 30, line 21. *That innutritious one . . . in the Canticles.* Lamb must have had in mind the verse, " We have a little sister, and she hath no breasts " (Song of Solomon viii. 8).

Page 30, line 22. *I hold with the Persian.* The sun-worshipper. The phrase "minions of the moon" is to be found in " 1 Henry IV.," Act I., Scene 2, line 30.

Page 30, line 31. *With Friar John.* In *Rabelais.* Friar John when fighting would give his fallen foe " to all the devils in hell ! "

Page 30, line 34. *Privation.* Milton speaks of night as

> Privation mere of light and absent day.
> *Paradise Regained*, IV., line 400.

Page 30, line 38. " *Lie down with kings and emperors . . .*" This seems to be one of Lamb's ingeniously compounded quotations—from Job iii. 13 and 14 : " I should have slept : then had I been at rest with kings and counsellors of the earth," and Sir Thomas Browne's *Urn Burial*, V. : " what time the persons of these ossuaries entered the famous nations of the dead and slept with princes and counsellors." I borrow this suggestion from Messrs. Hallward and Hill.

Page 30, line 40. " *So shall the fairest face appear.*" A quotation from "William and Margaret," by David Mallet.

Page 30, last line. " *Such as he now is . . .*" A common sentiment on tombstones.

Page 31, line 8. *Cheerful Mr. Cotton.* Charles Cotton (1630-1687), who helped with *The Complete Angler.*

Page 32, line 17. *A wave of . . . Helicon.* When, once before, Lamb had used Helicon as though it were a stream (Hippocrene) and not a mountain—an old confusion—he altered it (see note on page 288 of Vol. V. to his early lines "To Sara and S. T. C.").

Page 32.   MRS. BATTLE'S OPINIONS ON WHIST.
London Magazine, February, 1821.

Mrs. Battle was probably, in real life, to a large extent Sarah Burney, the wife of Rear-Admiral James Burney, Lamb's friend, and the centre of the whist-playing set to which he belonged.   The theory that Lamb's grandmother, Mrs. Field, was the original Mrs. Battle, does not, I think, commend itself, although that lady may have lent a trait or two.   It has possibly arisen from the relation of the passage in the essay on Blakesware (see page 155), where Mrs. Battle is said to have died in the haunted room, to that in "Dream Children," where Lamb says that Mrs. Field occupied this room.

The fact that Mrs. Battle and Mrs. Burney were both Sarahs is a small piece of evidence towards their fusion, but there is something more conclusive in the correspondence.   Writing in March, 1830, concerning the old whist days, to William Ayrton, one of the old whist-playing company, and the neighbour of the Burneys in Little James Street, Pimlico, Lamb makes use of an elision which, I think, may be taken as more than support of the theory that Mrs. Battle and Mrs. Burney were largely the same—practically proof.   "Your letter, which was only not so pleasant as your appearance would have been, has revived some old images; Phillips (not the Colonel), with his few hairs bristling up at the charge of a revoke, which he declares impossible; the old Captain's significant nod over the right shoulder (was it not ?); Mrs. B——'s determined questioning of the score, after the game was absolutely gone to the d——l." Lamb, I think, would have written out Mrs. Burney in full had he not wished to suggest Mrs. Battle too.

This conjecture is borne out by the testimony of the late Mrs. Lefroy, in her youth a friend of the Burneys and the Lambs, who told Canon Ainger that though Mrs. Battle had many differing points she was undoubtedly Mrs. Burney.   But of course there are the usual cross-trails—the reference to the pictures at Sandham ; to Walter Plumer ; to the legacy to Lamb ; and so forth.   Perhaps among the Blakesware portraits was one which Lamb chose as Mrs. Battle's presentment ; perhaps Mrs. Field had told him of an ancient dame who had certain of Mrs. Battle's characteristics, and he superimposed Mrs. Burney upon this foundation.

For further particulars concerning the Burney whist parties see the notes to the "Letter to Southey," Vol. I., page 482.

Admiral Burney (1750-1821), a son of Dr. Burney, the historian of music, and friend of Johnson and Reynolds, was the brother of Fanny Burney, afterwards Madame d'Arblay.   See also "The Wedding," page 239 of this volume, for another glimpse of Lamb's old friend.   Admiral Burney wrote *An Essay on the Game of Whist,* which was published in 1821.   As he lived until November, 1821, he probably read the present essay.   Writing to Wordsworth, March 20, 1822, Lamb says: "There's Capt. Burney gone !—what fun has whist now ; what matters it what you lead, if you can no longer fancy him looking over you ?"

Page 32, line 21. · *"A clean hearth."* To this, in the *London Magazine*, Lamb put the footnote :—

"This was before the introduction of rugs, reader. You must remember the intolerable crash of the unswept cinder, betwixt your foot and the marble."

Page 32, line 27. *Win one game, and lose another.* To this, in the *London Magazine*, Lamb put the note :—

"As if a sportsman should tell you he liked to kill a fox one day, and lose him the next."

Page 33, line 27. *Mr. Bowles.* The Rev. William Lisle Bowles (1762-1850), whose sonnets had so influenced Coleridge's early poetical career. His edition of Pope was published in 1806. I have tried in vain to discover if Mr. Bowles' MS. and notes for this edition are still in existence. If so they might contain Lamb's contribution. But it is rather more likely, I fear, that Lamb invented the story. The game of ombre is in Canto III. of *The Rape of the Lock.*

Page 33, line 34. *Spadille.* The ace of spades.

Page 33, line 38. *" Sans Prendre Vole."* This, perhaps, needs a note. Quadrille is ombre as played by four. It is primarily all against all, but he who thinks he can make the best game may improve his chances by demanding a partner, which is done by "calling a king," namely, the king of the suit he leads ; the player who plays the king in it becomes thereby his partner for the hand, his " friend." Hence partners change with every hand. But if one's hand is very good one can play *sans prendre* or *sans appeler, i.e.,* without calling or taking a king and partner. The highest achievement in any case is to make a *vole, i.e.,* a " grand slam," *i.e.,* to take all the tricks. A *sans prendre vole* is, therefore, a " grand slam without a partner," when single-handed you take every card in the pack.

Page 34, fourth line from foot. *" Hoary majesty of spades."* Pope's phrase in *The Rape of the Lock,* III., 56. " Pam in all his glory." Pam, the knave of clubs. See Pope again.

Page 35, line 8. *Ephesian journeyman.* See Acts of the Apostles xix.

Page 35, line 15. *Old Walter Plumer.* See the essay on "The South Sea-House," page 6.

Page 37, line 1. *Bad passions.* Here came in the *London Magazine,* in parenthesis, " (dropping for a while the speaking mask of old Sarah Battle)."

Page 37, line 18. *Bridget Elia.* This is Lamb's first reference in the essays to Mary Lamb under this name. See " Mackery End " (page 75) and " Old China " (page 247).

Page 37, line 30. *I capotted her.* To capot, at piquet, is to win all the cards.

Page 38.   A CHAPTER ON EARS.
London Magazine, March, 1821.
Lamb was not so utterly without ear as he states.   Crabb Robinson
in his diary records more than once that Lamb hummed tunes, and
Barron Field, in the memoir of Lamb contributed by him to the
Annual Biography and Obituary for 1836, mentions his love for
certain beautiful airs, among them Kent's "O that I had wings like a
dove" (mentioned in this essay), and Handel's "From mighty kings."
Lamb says (see note on page 351) that it was Braham who awakened a
love of music in him.   Compare Lamb's lines to Clara Novello, Vol.
V., page 90, and also Mary Lamb's postscript to his "Free Thoughts
on Eminent Composers," Vol. V., page 322.
    Page 38, line 11.   *Defoe.*   Defoe had his ears cropped and was
placed in the pillory :—

> Earless on high, stood, unabashed, Defoe.
>
> Pope's *Dunciad*, Book II., line 147.

Lamb supplied the reference in a note in the *London Magazine.*
    Page 38, line 14.   *I was never . . . in the pillory.*   This sentence
led to an amusing article in the *London Magazine* for the next month,
April, 1821, entitled "The Confessions of H. F. V. H. Delamore, Esq.,"
unmistakably, I think, by Lamb, which will be found in Vol. I. of this
edition, wherein Lamb confesses to a brief sojourn in the stocks at
Barnet for brawling on Sunday, an incident for the broad truth of
which we have the testimony of his friend Brook Pulham.
    Page 38, line 18.   *Melted at the concourse of sweet sounds.*   A
reference to the lines in "The Merchant of Venice" on the same
subject (Act V., Scene 1, lines 83-85) :—

> The man that hath no music in himself,
> Nor is not moved with concord of sweet sounds,
> Is fit for treasons, stratagems, and spoils.

    Page 38, lines 19, 21.   "*Water parted from the sea,*" "*In Infancy.*"
Songs by Arne in "Artaxerxes," Lamb's "First Play" (see page 97).
    Page 38, line 24.   *Mrs. S*——.   The Key gives "Mrs. Spinkes."
We meet a Will Weatherall in "Distant Correspondents," page 105 ;
but I have not been able to discover more concerning either.
    Page 38, line 30.   *Alice W*——*n.*   See note to "Dream Children,"
page 377.
    Page 38, line 38.   *My friend A.*   Probably William Ayrton (1777-
1818), the musical critic, one of the Burneys' whist-playing set, and a
friend and correspondent of Lamb's.   See the musical rhyming letter
to him from Lamb, May 17, 1817.
    Page 39, line 16.   *Baralipton.*   A term given in the *Memoria
Technica* to the first mode of the first figure of the syllogism.
    Page 39, line 20.   *Jubal.*   See Genesis iv. 21.
    Page 39, line 40.   *The Enraged Musician.*   A reference to
Hogarth's picture with that title, where street noises are driving the
performer mad.   See Vol. I., opposite page 420.

Page 40, line 5. *"Party in a parlour . . ."* From a stanza in Wordsworth's *Peter Bell,* first edition. Wordsworth afterwards expunged it, but Shelley's satire, *Peter Bell the Third,* extended it mercilessly.

Page 40, line 22. *Disappointing book in Patmos.* See Revelation x. 10.

Page 40, line 23. *Described by Burton.* See *Anatomy of Melancholy,* Part I., Section 2, Mem. 2, Subsection 6, not quite correctly copied by Lamb.

Page 40, line 28. *Amabilis insania.* "Delightful ecstasy." From Horace, *Odes,* III., 4, 5. *Mentis gratissimus error.* "Pleasing hallucinations." From Horace, *Epistles,* II., 2, 140.

Page 40, line 40. *Subrusticus pudor.* "Awkward bashfulness." From Cicero's *Letters,* "Ad Fam.," V., 12, 1.

Page 41, line 4. *My friend, Nov——.* Vincent Novello (1781-1861), the organist, the father of Mrs. Cowden Clarke, and a great friend of Lamb.

Page 41, lines 12, 14. *That . . . or that other.* See Psalms lv. 6, and xix. 9. Converted into anthems by Benjamin Cook and William Boyce respectively.

Page 41, line 17. *"Rapt above earth . . ."* An adaptation from *The Complete Angler,* Part I., Chapter IV. :—

> I was for that time lifted above earth ;
> And possest joys not promis'd in my birth.

Page 41, line 21. *Her "earthly" with his "heavenly."* See 1 Corinthians xv. 48.

Page 41, line 25. *Those Arions.* Arion was a lyric poet of Lesbos, who, on a voyage, when threatened with death by sailors that coveted his riches, begged to be allowed to play one more melody. They granted leave ; he played ; and, drawing a shoal of dolphins to the vessel's side by his harmony, he leapt on the back of one and was carried safely away. The Tritons were sea gods, half dolphin and half man.

Page 41, line 34. *Malleus hereticorum*—the heretics' hammer——the title of a work by Johann Faber (1478-1541), the opponent of the heretics Luther and Zwinglius. The grand heresiarch, the chief of heretics.

Page 41, line 36. *I am Marcion, Ebion and Cerinthus.* Three early sectarians. Marcion dispensed with the Old Testament and adhered to the teaching of Paul ; Ebion, a Nazarene, founded the Ebionites, some of whom believed in Christ and others denied Him ; Cerinthus combined Judaism, pagan philosophy and Christianity. The existence of Ebion is, however, doubtful ; the Ebionites probably took their name from the Hebrew word "Ebyjon," meaning a poor or humble man. Gibbon says in Chapter XLVII. of the *Decline and Fall:* "Cerinthus of Asia . . . laboured to reconcile the Gnostic with the Ebionite, by confessing in the same Messiah the supernatural union of a man and a God, and this mystic doctrine was adopted with many fanciful improvements by Carpocrates, Basilides and Valentine, the heretics of the Egyptian school." For Gog and Magog in this connection see Revelation xx. 7-9, where they personate all unbelievers.

Page 41, line 38. *Lutheran beer.* Edmund Ollier, the son of Charles Ollier, the publisher of Lamb's *Works*, 1818, in his reminis-. cences of Lamb, prefixed to one edition of *Elia*, tells this story : " Once at a musical party at Leigh Hunt's, being oppressed with what to him was nothing better than a prolonged noise . . . he said—'If one only had a pot of porter, one might get through this.' It was procured for him and he weathered the Mozartian storm."

Page 41. *Footnote.* Another friend of Vincent Novello's uses the same couplet (from Watt's *Divine Songs for Children*, Song XXVIII., " For the Lord's Day, Evening ") in the description of glees by the old cricketers at the Bat and Ball on Broad Halfpenny Down, near Hambledon—I refer to John Nyren, author of *The Young Cricketer's Tutor*, 1833. There is no evidence that Lamb and Nyren ever met, but one feels that they ought to have done so, in Novello's hospitable rooms.

In the *London Magazine* this essay had the following postscript :—

" P.S.—A writer, whose real name, it seems, is *Boldero*, but who has been entertaining the town for the last twelve months, with some very pleasant lucubrations, under the assumed signature of *Leigh Hunt*,[1] in his Indicator, of the 31st January last, has thought fit to insinuate, that I *Elia* do not write the little sketches which bear my signature, in this Magazine ; but that the true author of them is a Mr. L——b. Observe the critical period at which he has chosen to impute the calumny !—on the very eve of the publication of our last number— affording no scope for explanation for a full month—during which time, I must needs lie writhing and tossing, under the cruel imputation of nonentity.—Good heavens ! that a plain man must not be allowed *to be*——

" They call this an age of personality : but surely this spirit of antipersonality (if I may so express it) is something worse.

"Take away my moral reputation : I may live to discredit that calumny.

Injure my literary fame,—I may write that up again—

But when a gentleman is robbed of his identity, where is he ?

" Other murderers stab but at our existence, a frail and perishing trifle at the best. But here is an assassin who aims at our very essence ; who not only forbids us *to be* any longer, but *to have been* at all. Let our ancestors look to it——

" Is the parish register nothing ? Is the house in Princes-street,

---

" [1] Clearly a fictitious appellation ; for if we admit the latter of these names to be in a manner English, what is *Leigh ?* Christian nomenclature knows no such."

Cavendish-square, where we saw the light six-and-forty years ago, nothing? Were our progenitors from stately Genoa, where we flourished four centuries back, before the barbarous name of Boldero [1] was known to a European mouth, nothing? Was the goodly scion of our name, transplanted into England, in the reign of the seventh Henry, nothing? Are the archives of the steel yard, in succeeding reigns (if haply they survive the fury of our envious enemies) showing that we flourished in prime repute, as merchants, down to the period of the commonwealth, nothing?

" Why then the world, and all that's in't is nothing—
The covering sky is nothing, Bohemia is nothing.—

"I am ashamed that this trifling writer should have power to move me so."

"[1] It is clearly of transatlantic origin."

Leigh Hunt, in *The Indicator*, January 31 and February 7, 1821, had reprinted from *The Examiner* a review of Lamb's *Works*, with a few prefatory remarks in which it was stated: "We believe we are taking no greater liberty with him [Charles Lamb] than our motives will warrant, when we add that he sometimes writes in the *London Magazine* under the signature of Elia."

In Lamb's reply, printed above, he may have invented the Genoese ancestry or it may have truly belonged to the old Italian clerk of the South Sea-House, whose name Elia he had borrowed (see page 299). The quotation, "Why, then the world," &c., is from a speech of Leontes in "The Winter's Tale," Act I., Scene 2, lines 293, 294. The reason for calling Hunt Boldero is not now clear.

In *The Indicator* of March 7, 1821, Leigh Hunt replied to Elia. Leigh Hunt was no match for Lamb in this kind of raillery, and the first portion of the reply is rather cumbersome. At the end, however, he says: "There *was*, by the bye, a family of the name of Elia who came from Italy,—Jews; which may account for this boast about Genoa. See also in his last article in the London Magazine [the essay on "Ears"] some remarkable fancies of conscience in reference to the Papal religion. They further corroborate what we have heard; *viz.* that the family were obliged to fly from Genoa for saying that the Pope was the author of Rabelais; and that Elia is not an anagram, as some have thought it, but the Judaico-Christian name of the writer before us, whose surname, we find, is not Lamb, but Lomb;—Elia Lomb! What a name! He told a friend of ours so in company, and would have palmed himself upon him for a Scotchman, but that his countenance betrayed him."

It is amusing to note that Maginn, writing the text to accompany the Maclise portrait of Lamb in *Fraser's Magazine* in 1835, gravely states that Lamb's name was really Lomb, and that he was of Jewish extraction.

The subject of Lamb's birth reopened a little while later. In the "Lion's Head," which was the title of the pages given to correspondence in the *London Magazine*, in the number for November, 1821, was the following short article from Lamb's pen :—

"ELIA TO HIS CORRESPONDENTS.—A Correspondent, who writes himself Peter Ball, or Bell,—for his hand-writing is as ragged as his manners—admonishes me of the old saying, that some people (under a courteous periphrasis I slur his less ceremonious epithet) had need have good memories. In my 'Old Benchers of the Inner Temple,' I have delivered myself, and truly, a Templar born. Bell clamours upon this, and thinketh that he hath caught a fox. It seems that in a former paper, retorting upon a weekly scribbler who had called my good identity in question, (see P.S. to my 'Chapter on Ears,') I profess myself a native of some spot near Cavendish Square, deducing my remoter origin from Italy. But who does not see, except this tinkling cymbal, that in that idle fiction of Genoese ancestry I was answering a fool according to his folly—that Elia there expresseth himself ironically, as to an approved slanderer, who hath no right to the truth, and can be no fit recipient of it ? Such a one it is usual to leave to his delusions ; or, leading him from error still to contradictory error, to plunge him (as we say) deeper in the mire, and give him line till he suspend himself. No understanding reader could be imposed upon by such obvious rhodomontade to suspect me for an alien, or believe me other than English. —To a second Correspondent, who signs himself ' a Wiltshire man,' and claims me for a countryman upon the strength of an equivocal phrase in my ' Christ's Hospital,' a more mannerly reply is due. Passing over the Genoese fable, which Bell makes such a ring about, he nicely detects a more subtle discrepancy, which Bell was too obtuse to strike upon. Referring to the passage (in page 484 of our second volume [1]), I must confess, that the term ' native town,' applied to Calne, *primâ facie* seems to bear out the construction which my friendly Correspondent is willing to put upon it. The context too, I am afraid, a little favours it. But where the words of an author, taken literally, compared with some other passage in his writings, admitted to be authentic, involve a palpable contradiction, it hath been the custom of the ingenuous commentator to smooth the difficulty by the supposition, that in the one case an allegorical or tropical sense was chiefly intended. So by the word ' native,' I may be supposed to mean a town where I might have been born ; or where it might be

[1] See page 13 of this volume.

desirable that I should have been born, as being situate in wholesome
air, upon a dry chalky soil, in which I delight ; or a town, with the
inhabitants of which I passed some weeks, a summer or two ago, so
agreeably, that they and it became in a manner native to me. Without
some such latitude of interpretation in the present case, I see not how
we can avoid falling into a gross error in physics, as to conceive that a
gentleman may be born in two places, from which all modern and
ancient testimony is alike abhorrent. Bacchus cometh the nearest to
it, whom I remember Ovid to have honoured with the epithet 'Twice
born.'[1] But not to mention that he is so called (we conceive) in
reference to the places *whence* rather than the places *where* he was
delivered,—for by either birth he may probably be challenged for a
Theban—in a strict way of speaking, he was a *filius femoris* by no
means in the same sense as he had been before a *filius alvi,* for that
latter was but a secondary and tralatitious way of being born, and he
but a denizen of the second house of his geniture. Thus much by
way of explanation was thought due to the courteous 'Wiltshire
man.'—To 'Indagator,' 'Investigator,' 'Incertus,' and the rest of
the pack, that are so importunate about the true localities of his birth
—as if, forsooth, Elia were presently about to be passed to his parish—
to all such churchwarden critics he answereth, that, any explanation
here given notwithstanding, he hath not so fixed his nativity (like a
rusty vane) to one dull spot, but that, if he seeth occasion, or the
argument shall demand it, he will be born again, in future papers, in
whatever place, and at whatever period, shall seem good unto him.

> " Modò me Thebis—modò Athenis.

> " ELIA."

> "[1] Imperfectus adhuc infans genetricis ab alvo
> Eripitur, patrioque tener (si credere dignum est)
> Insuitur femori——
> Tutaque bis geniti sunt incunabula Bacchi.
> " *Metamorph.* lib. iii., 310."

Concerning the quotation with which Lamb closes : The true
dramatic poet, says Horace, is he

> Meum qui pectus inaniter angit,
> Irritat, mulcet, falsis terroribus implet,
> Ut magus, et modo me Thebis, modo ponit Athenis.
> *Epist.* II., i., lines 211-213.

(Who racks my heart with shadows, fires, allays, fills with imaginary terrors, and sets
me now at Thebes and now at Athens.)

The passage from Ovid runs, in English : "The child, an embryo yet,
is snatched from his mother's womb, and (if we may believe it) sewn

up, a soft lump, in his father's thigh. And assured is the nativity of twice-born Bacchus."

Page 42. ALL FOOLS' DAY.
London Magazine, April, 1821.
Page 42, line 12. *Stultus sum.* " I am a fool."
Page 42, line 16. *Sparkling gooseberry.* In relation to gooseberry fools.
Page 42, line 18. *Amiens.* From Jaques' third verse to Amiens' song, "As You Like It," Act II., Scene 5: "What's that ducdame?" asks Amiens. "'Tis a Greek invocation to call fools into a circle."
Page 42, line 28. *" The crazy old church clock . . ."* From "The Fountain"—Wordsworth—last stanza.
Page 42, line 30. *Empedocles.* Lamb appended this footnote in the *London Magazine* :—

> He who, to be deem'd
> A god, leap'd fondly into Etna's flames.
> *Paradise Lost,* III., lines 470-471.

Page 42, line 31. *Samphire-picking.* A reference to " King Lear," Act IV., Scene 6, lines 14, 15 :—

> *Edgar.* Half way down
> Hangs one that gathers samphire, dreadful trade !

Page 42, line 34. *Cleombrotus.* Lamb's *London Magazine* footnote :—

> He who, to enjoy
> Plato's Elysium, leap'd into the sea.
> *Paradise Lost,* III., lines 471-472.

Page 42, line 36. *Calenturists.* A Calenturist is one who, bemused at sea, under the influence of the calenture, a hot fever, believing himself to see a fair island of green fields, leaps overboard. Wordsworth describes the Calenture in "The Brothers."
Page 42, line 37. *Gebir.* Messrs. Hallward and Hill, in their edition of the *Essays of Elia,* have the following note, which I take the liberty of borrowing :—

The connection of the name of Gebir with the building of the tower of Babel (Genesis, XI. 1-10) is curious. Gebir is Jabir ibn Haijan, an Arabian alchemist of the eighth century A.D., said to have been born in Mesopotamia. But Landor has a poem entitled *Gebir,* which he took from Clara Reeve's *Progress of Romance,* where the story of Gebir is said to have been derived from the ancient history of Egypt. Moreover, Landor's prince, Gebir, tries to build a city, but finds his labours destroyed "not by mortal hand". These two data appear to have been sufficient warrant, in Lamb's mind, for turning the historic Jabir into Gebir, builder of the tower of Babel, and founder of the world-wide society of freemasons. The freemasons have a tradition that their society originated at the building of the tower of Babel.

Page 42, line 37. *Plasterers at Babel.* Lamb's *London Magazine* note :—

> The builders next of Babel on the plain
> Of Sennaar.
> *Paradise Lost,* III., lines 466-467.

Page 42, line 39. *My right hand.* Lamb, it is probably unnecessary to remind the reader, stammered too.

Page 42, line 40. *Herodotus.* Lamb invented this reference. Herodotus says nothing of the Tower of Babel. A toise is about six feet and a half.

Page 43, line 4. *Our Monument.* The monument, in Fish Street Hill, is 202 feet high.

Page 43, line 6. *Alexander in tears.* Alexander the Great wept because there were no more worlds to conquer. "Cry, baby, cry," is a memory of an old nursery rhyme.

Page 43, line 9. *Mister Adams.* In Chapter III. of Fielding's *Joseph Andrews* we learn that Parson Adams and Mrs. Slipsop had theological discussions; but there were no sermons in the Parson's portmanteau, however much Mrs. Slipsop may have needed them: they had been left behind.

Page 43, line 14. *Raymund Lully.* An alchemist and philosopher (1235-1315), who sought the philosopher's stone. Known as Doctor Illuminatus. In the *London Magazine* Raymund Lully was not mentioned; the remark was addressed to "Mr.——".

Page 43, line 16. *Duns.* Duns Scotus (1265?-1308?), metaphysician, author of *De modis significandi sive Grammatica Speculativa* and other philosophic works. Known as Doctor Subtilis. There was nothing of Duns in the *London Magazine;* the sentence ran: "Mr. Hazlitt, I cannot indulge you in your definitions." This was at a time (see note to "New Year's Eve") when Lamb and Hazlitt were not on good terms.

Page 43, line 20. *Master Stephen . . . Cokes.* Master Stephen, the simpleton in Ben Jonson's "Every Man in His Humour." Cokes, a foolish gentleman in his "Bartholomew Fair."

Page 43, lines 20, 22, 23. *Aguecheek . . . Shallow . . . Silence . . . Slender.* Aguecheek in "Twelfth Night;" Slender in "Merry Wives of Windsor;" Shallow in "Merry Wives" and "2 Henry IV.;" and Silence in "2 Henry IV."

Page 43, line 26. *Honest R——.* Lamb's Key gives "Ramsay, London Library, Ludgate Street; now extinct." I have tried in vain to find out more about Ramsay. The London Library was established at 5 Ludgate Street in 1785. Later, the books were lodged at Charles Taylor's house in Hatton Garden, and were finally removed to the present London Institute in Finsbury Circus.

Page 43, line 31. *Good Granville S——.* Lamb's Key gives Granville Sharp. This was the eccentric Granville Sharp, the Quaker abolitionist (1735-1813).

Page 43, line 33. *"King Pandion . . ."* From Richard Barnfield's lyric "As it Fell upon a Day."

Page 43, line 36. *Armado and Quisada.* Armado in "Love's Labour's Lost." Quisada, Don Quixote.

Page 43, line 41. *The song of Macheath.* In Gay's "Beggar's Opera";—

How happy could I be with either,
Were t'other dear charmer away.

Page 44, line 1. *That Malvolian smile.* See "Twelfth Night," Act III., Scene 4, where Malvolio, gulled by Maria's letter, comes smiling into his mistress's presence.

Page 44, line 11. *Those Parables.* See Matthew vii. 24-28; Matthew xxv. 14-30 and Luke xix. 12-27; Matthew xxv. 1-13.

Page 44, line 29. *It is observed.* I have not discovered where Sir Thomas Browne makes the observation.

Page 44, line 34. *White boys.* Dr. Busby, the famous headmaster of Westminster, used to call his favourite scholars his white boys. The phrase is a common term of endearment in the old dramatists.

Page 45. A QUAKER'S MEETING.
London Magazine, April, 1821.

Lamb's connection with Quakers was somewhat intimate throughout his life. In early days he was friendly with the Birmingham Lloyds— Charles, Robert and Priscilla, of the younger generation, and their father, Charles Lloyd, the banker and translator of Horace and Homer (see *Charles Lamb and the Lloyds,* 1898); and later with Bernard Barton, the Quaker poet of Woodbridge. Also he had loved from afar Hester Savory, the subject of his poem "Hester" (see Vol. V., page 30). A passage from a letter written in February 1797 to Coleridge bears upon this essay :—

"Tell Lloyd I have had thoughts of turning Quaker, and have been reading, or am rather just beginning to read, a most capital book, good thoughts in good language, William Penn's 'No Cross, No Crown,' I like it immensely. Unluckily I went to one of his meetings, tell him, in St. John Street [Clerkenwell] yesterday, and saw a man under all the agitations and workings of a fanatic, who believed himself under the influence of some 'inevitable presence.' This cured me of Quakerism ; I love it in the books of Penn and Woolman, but I detest the vanity of a man thinking he speaks by the Spirit. . . ."

Hood said that Lamb in outward appearance resembled a Quaker.

Page 45. *Motto.* Richard Flecknoe (*fl.* 1640-1670), one of the chief objects of Dryden's satirical contempt, and the hero of *MacFlecknoe.* The second couplet of the passage here quoted was parodied by Lamb in his "Farewell to Tobacco" :—

Stinking'st of the stinking kind,
Filth of the mouth and fog of the mind.

Lamb included this quotation from Flecknoe's "Love's Dominion" in his Garrick extracts (see Vol. IV.).

Page 45, line 23. *"Before the winds were made."* I cannot find this quotation. Messrs. Hallward and Hill suggest that Lamb was

remembering Proverbs viii. 23-25 and Davenant's couplet in his poem
"To the Queen":—

> Smooth on the face of waters first appear'd,
> Ere tides began to flow or winds were heard.

Page 45, line 26. *With . . . Ulysses.* "The ship stood still.
Ulysses guessed that the island of the Sirens was not far off, and that
they had charmed the air so with their magic singing. Therefore he
made him cakes of wax, as Circe had instructed him, and stopped
the ears of his men with them" (Lamb's *Adventures of Ulysses*,
Chapter III.).

Page 45, line 31. *The uncommunicating muteness of fishes.*
Lamb had in mind this thought on the silence of fishes when he was
at work on *John Woodvil* Simon remarks, in the exquisite passage
(Vol. V., page 152) in reply to the question, "What is it you love?"

> The fish in th' other element
> That knows no touch of eloquence.

Page 45, line 32. *"Boreas . . ." Paradise Lost,* X., line 699.

Page 45, line 34. *The blown Baltic.* The phrase is Collins', in
the "Ode to Liberty," line 70.

Page 45, line 37. *Her deeps.* See Psalms xlii. 7.

Page 46, line 3. *The Carthusian.* One of the rules of this order
of monks is continual silence.

Page 46, line 10. *Zimmerman.* Referring to Zimmerman *On
Solitude.*

Page 46, line 14. *" Or under hanging mountains . . ."*

> Now under hanging mountains,
> Beside the fall of fountains.
>   Pope, "Ode on St. Cecilia's Day."

Page 46, line 18. *" To be felt."* See Exodus x. 21.

Page 46, line 22. *" Sands, ignoble things . . ."* From Francis
Beaumont's lines " On the Tombs in Westminster Abbey."

Page 46, line 29. *" How reverend . . ."* An adaptation of Congreve's
description of York Minster in "The Mourning Bride" (Mary Lamb's
"first play"), Act I., Scene 1 :—

> How reverend is the face of this tall pile . . .
> Looking tranquillity !

Page 46, line 38, etc. *Fox and Dewesbury.* George Fox (1624-
1691) founded the Society of Friends. William Dewesbury was one
of Fox's first colleagues, and a famous preacher. William Penn (1644-
1718), the founder of Pennsylvania, was the most illustrious of the early
converts to Quakerism. Lamb refers to him again, before his judges,
in the essay on " Imperfect Sympathies," page 64. George Fox's
Journal was lent to Lamb by a friend of Bernard Barton's in 1823.
On returning it, Lamb remarked (February, 17, 1823) :—

" I have quoted G. F. in my ' Quaker's Meeting ' as having said he was 'lifted up in spirit' (which I felt at the time to be not a Quaker phrase), 'and the Judge and Jury were as dead men under his feet.' I find no such words in his Journal, and I did not get them from Sewell, and the latter sentence I am sure I did not mean to invent. I must have put some other Quaker's words into his mouth."

Sewel was a Dutchman—William Sewel (1654-1720). His title runs : *History of the Rise, Increase and Progress of the Christian People called Quakers, written originally in Low Dutch by W. Sewel, and by himself translated into English*, 1722. James Naylor (1617-1660) was one of the early Quaker martyrs—"my favourite" Lamb calls him in a letter. John Woolman (1720-1772) was an American Friend. His principal writings are to be found in *A Journal of the Life, Gospel Labours, and Christian Experiences of that faithful minister of Jesus Christ, John Woolman, late of Mount Holly in the Province of Jersey, North America*, 1795. A modern edition, with a preface by Whittier, the Quaker poet, is obtainable.

Page 48, line 5. *As Wordsworth phrases it.*

> The Man who makes this feverish complaint
> Is one of giant stature, who could dance
> Equipped from head to foot in iron mail.
> From " 'Tis said that some have died for love."

Page 48, line 11. *To set off against Paul.* Probably referring to Raphael's cartoon in the Vatican.

Page 48, line 21. *Jocos Risus-que.* The Levities—the spirits of humour and laughter. *Faster than the Loves*—Proserpine when carried off to Hades by Pluto (or Dis) was gathering flowers at Enna attended by Cupid.

> Not that fair field
> Of Enna, where Proserpin gathering flow'rs
> Herself a fairer flow'r by gloomy Dis
> Was gather'd . . .
> *Paradise Lost*, IV., lines 268-271.

Page 48, line 26. *Not made with hands.* See 2 Corinthians v. 1.

Page 48, line 27. *Trophonius.* The cave of Trophonius was one of the chief oracles of Greece. Its replies being almost always dreadful, the applicants returned silent and austere.

Page 48, line 28. *That unruly member.* See James iii.

Page 48, line 35. *" Forty feeding like one."*

> The cattle are grazing,
> Their heads never raising ;
> There are forty feeding like one.
> From Wordsworth's lines " Written in March."

Page 48, at the end. *Whitsun-conferences.* The Whitsun Conference—Yearly Meeting as it is called—is still held at the Society's headquarters in Bishopsgate Street ; but distinctive Quaker attire is practically extinct, and white has vanished. Silence also is not encouraged as of old. Women preachers are no longer in the majority, if ever they were. The phrase " Shining Ones " is Bunyan's.

Page 49. THE OLD AND THE NEW SCHOOLMASTER.
London Magazine, May, 1821.

Page 49, line 9. *Ortelius . . . Arrowsmith.* Abraham Ortellius (1527-1598), the Dutch geographer and the author of *Theatrum Orbis Terræ*, 1570. Aaron Arrowsmith (1750-1823) was a well-known cartographer at the beginning of the nineteenth century. Lamb would perhaps have known something of his *Atlas of Southern India*, a very useful work at the East India House.

Page 49, line 13. *A very dear friend.* Barron Field (see the essay on "Distant Correspondents," page 104).

Page 49, line 24. *The four great monarchies.* Assyrian, Persian, Roman, Grecian.

Page 49, line 27. *Egypt, and her shepherd kings.* The Arabian tribe of Hyksos, the shepherd kings, who are said to have ruled Egypt from B.C. 2080 for 260 years.

Page 49, line 27. *My friend M.* Thomas Manning (1772-1840), the mathematician and traveller, and Lamb's correspondent.

Page 49, line 30. *A better man than myself.* Shakespeare, according to Ben Jonson's elegy, "To the memory of my beloved Master, William Shakespeare, and what he hath left us " :—

> And though thou hadst small Latin and less Greek.

Page 49, line 35. *" On Devon's leafy shores."* From Wordsworth's *Excursion*, III.

Page 50, line 6. *Daily jaunts.* Though Lamb was then (1821) living at 20 Great Russell Street, Covent Garden, he rented rooms at 14 Kingsland Row, Dalston, in which to take holidays and do his literary work undisturbed. At that time Dalston was the country and Kingsland Green an open space opposite Lamb's lodging.

Page 50. *Footnote. A "wide solution."* The passage is in Sir Thomas Browne's *Urn Burial*, Chapter V. :—

> What song the Syrens sang, or what name Achilles assumed when he hid himself among women, though puzzling questions,[1] are not beyond all conjecture. What time the persons of these ossuaries entered the famous nations of the dead, and slept with princes and counsellors, might admit a wide solution.
>
> [1] The puzzling questions of Tiberius unto grammarians. *Marcel. Donatus, in Suet.*

Page 51, line 8. *The North Pole Expedition.* This would probably be Sir John Franklin's expedition which set out in 1819 and ended in disaster, the subject of Franklin's book, *Narrative of a Journey to the Shores of the Polar Sea in the years 1819, 20, 21, 22* (1823). Sir John Ross made an expedition in 1818, and Sir William Edward Parry in 1819, and again in 1821-1823 with Lyon. The panorama was possibly at Burford's Panorama in the Strand, afterwards moved to Leicester Square.

Page 51, line 30. *Lilys . . . Linacres.* William Lily (1468 ?-1522) and Thomas Linacre (1460?-1524), the friends of More, Erasmus and Colet, were the fathers of English scholarship. Shakespeare quotes from Lily's *English Grammar.*

Page 51, line 40. *Flori . . . Spici-legia.* Their anthologies and gleanings; that is to say, beauties of the Latin authors to be translated by the young.

Page 51, lines 42-45. *Basileus . . . Pamela . . .* King Basileus, Pamela, Philoclea, Mopsa and Damætas are to be found in Sidney's *Arcadia.*

Page 52, line 1. *Colet's . . . Accidence.* John Colet (1467 ?-1519) was Dean of St. Paul's and the founder of St. Paul's School, of which Lily was the first headmaster. Linacre was engaged to write a Latin grammar, but, being dissatisfied with it, Colet himself wrote in 1509 the work from which Lamb quotes—Colet's *Latin Accidence.*

Page 52, line 32. *Cum multis aliis.* "With many others."

Page 52, line 33. *Tractate on Education.* Milton's *Tractate on Education,* addressed to his friend, Samuel Hartlib, was published in 1644. The quotation above is from that work. This paragraph of Lamb's essay was afterwards humorously expanded in his "Letter to an Old Gentleman whose Education has been Neglected" (see Vol. I., page 213). Here is a passage from Milton's *Tractate* :—

> After evening repast, till bedtime, their thoughts would be best taken up in the easy grounds of religion, and the story of scripture. The next step would be to the authors of agriculture, Cato, Varro, and Columella, for the matter is most easy ; and if the language be difficult, so much the better, it is not a difficulty above their years. And here will be an occasion of inciting, and enabling them hereafter to improve the tillage of their country, to recover the bad soil, and to remedy the waste that is made of good ; for this was one of Hercules's praises. Ere half these authors be read, (which will soon be with plying hard and daily) they cannot choose but be masters of any ordinary prose. So that it will be then seasonable for them to learn in any modern author the use of the globes, and all the maps ; first with the old names, and then with the new ; or they might be then capable to read any compendious method of natural philosophy. And at the same time might be entering into the Greek tongue, after the same manner as was before prescribed in the Latin ; whereby the difficulties of grammar being soon overcome, all the historical physiology of Aristotle and Theophrastus are open before them, and, as I may say, under contribution. The like access will be to Vitruvius, to Seneca's natural questions, to Mela, Celsus, Pliny, or Solinus. And having thus passed the principles of arithmetic, geometry, astronomy, and geography, with a general compact of physics, they may descend in mathematics to the instrumental science of trigonometry, and from thence to fortification, architecture, enginery, or navigation.

Page 52, line 40. *Mollia tempora fandi.* Adapted from Virgil's *Æneid,* IV., 293, 294, signifying the most favourable times.

Page 53, line 4. *That Great Book.* Several writers had used the phrase : Wordsworth probably most recently—in " The Brothers," " the great book of the world."

Page 53, line 12. *Mr. Bartley's Orrery.* George Bartley (1782 ?-1858), the comedian, lectured on astronomy and poetry at the Lyceum during Lent at this time. An orrery is a working model of the solar system. The Panopticon was, I assume, a forerunner of the famous Panopticon in Leicester Square.

Page 53, line 20. *"Plaything for an hour."* A quotation from Charles and Mary Lamb's *Poetry for Children*—*"* Parental Recollections " :—

A child's a plaything for an hour.

Page 53, line 24. *By distance made* [*more*] *sweet.* A phrase from Collins' " Ode to the Passions." But Lamb may have quoted from Wordsworth's adaptation of it in " Personal Talk ".

Page 55, end of essay. *" Can I reproach her for it."* After these words, in the *London Magazine,* came :—

"These kind of complaints are not often drawn from me. I am aware that I am a fortunate, I mean a prosperous man. My feelings prevent me from transcribing any further."

————

Page 55. VALENTINE'S DAY.

This essay first appeared in *The Examiner,* February 14 and 15, 1819, and again in *The Indicator,* February 14, 1821. Signed * * *

Page 55, beginning. *Bishop Valentine.* Saint, not Bishop, Valentine was an early Roman Christian, who for befriending martyrs was put to death in the reign of Claudius II., February 14, 270. When raised to the Calendar he was given the day preceding that formerly kept during the Lupercalia as the festival of Februta-Juno, goddess of fruitfulness, on which day, February 15, the Roman youths had the custom of drawing the names of girls. Hence his association with Love.

Page 55, last line. *Jerome . . . Whitgift.* St. Jerome, who died in 420, and translated the Vulgate from the Hebrew ; St. Ambrose, Bishop of Milan, who died in 397, and humbled Theodosius and converted St. Augustine ; St. Cyril, Patriarch of Alexandria, who died in 444, debated with and confuted Nestorius and encouraged the tumult which led to the death of Hypatia ; St. Augustine, Bishop of Hippo, who died in 430, the author of the *Confessions* and of the contention that unbaptised infants were lost ; Origen, who died in 254 and whose zeal led him to take very extreme views as to the duty of the religious teachers ; George Bull, Bishop of St. David's (1634-1710) ; Matthew Parker, Archbishop of Canterbury (1504-1575) ; and John Whitgift, Archbishop of Canterbury (1530 ?-1604).

Page 56, line 5. *" Brush'd with the hiss . . ."* From *Paradise Lost,* I., line 768.

Page 56, line 10. *Twopenny postman.* Hone computed, in his *Every-Day Book,* Vol. I., 1825, that " two hundred thousand letters beyond the usual daily average annually pass through the twopenny post-office in London on Valentine's Day." The Bishop's vogue is now (1903) almost over.

Page 56, line 31. *It " gives a very echo . . ."*

Viola. It gives a very echo to the seat
Where Love is throned.
" Twelfth Night," Act II., Scene 4, lines 21, 22.

Page 56, line 37. *Duncan.*

> *Lady Macbeth.* The raven himself is hoarse
> That croaks the fatal entrance of Duncan.
> " Macbeth," Act I., Scene 5, lines 39, 40.

Page 56, line 42. *" Having been will always be."*

> In the primal sympathy
> Which having been must ever be.
> Wordsworth's " Ode on the Intimations of Immortality."

Page 57, line 11. *E. B.* Lamb's Key gives "Edward Burney, half brother of Miss Burney." This was Edward Francis Burney (1760-1848), who illustrated many old authors, among them Richardson.

Page 57, line 32. *Cayster.* A river abounding in swans. See the *Iliad*, II., 461. This is Chapman's rendering :—

> and as about the flood,
> Cayster, in an Asian mead, flocks of the aery brood,
> Cranes, geese, or long-neck'd swans, here, there, proud of their pinions fly,
> And in their falls lay out such throats, that with their sprightful cry
> The meadow shrieks again.

Page 57, line 33. *Iris dipt the woof.*

> Iris had dipt the woof.
> *Paradise Lost*, XI., line 244.

Page 58, line 4. *Sings poor Ophelia.*

> To-morrow is Saint Valentine's day,
> All in the morning betime,
> And I a maid at your window
> To be your Valentine.
> " Hamlet," Act IV., Scene 5.

Page 58. IMPERFECT SYMPATHIES.
London Magazine, August, 1821, where the title ran: "Jews, Quakers, Scotchmen, and other Imperfect Sympathies."
Page 58. *Motto.* Sir Thomas Browne's *Religio Medici*, Part II., Section 1.
Page 58, second quotation. *" Standing on earth . . ."*

> Standing on earth, not rapt above the pole.
> *Paradise Lost*, VII., line 23.

Page 58, line 7 below second quotation. *Apathies.* In the *London Magazine* Lamb had written "dispathies."
Page 59, line 29. *Minerva.* Minerva, goddess of wisdom, sprang, fully grown and armed, from the head of Jupiter.
Page 59. *Footnote.* " *Hierarchie of Blessed Angels.*" The passage is in Book IV., "The Dominations."
Page 60, line 4. *Order and completeness.* Lamb rearranged this essay in this part. Here in the *London Magazine* came the sentence below, line 12, beginning, " He has no falterings," which then had,

after "embryo conceptions," "and every stage that stops short of
absolute certainty and conviction." "Dim instincts" was in quotation
marks.

Page 60, line 28. *John Buncle.* See note on page 327.

Page 60, line 34. *A print . . . after Leonardo.* The Virgin of the
Rocks. See Vol. V., page 39, for Lamb's and his sister's verses on
this picture. Crabb Robinson's MS. diary tells us that the Scotchman
was one Smith, a friend of Godwin. His exact reply to Lamb's remark
about "my beauty" was: "Why, sir, from all I have heard of you, as
well as from what I have myself seen, I certainly entertain a very high
opinion of your abilities, but I confess that I have not formed any
opinion concerning your personal pretensions."

Page 61, line 12. *Provoking.* In the *London Magazine* Lamb
wrote "proverbial."

Page 61, line 14. *The poetry of Burns.* "Burns was the god of
my idolatry," Lamb wrote to Coleridge in 1796. Coleridge's lines
on Burns, "To a Friend who had declared his intention of writing
no more poetry," were addressed to Lamb. Barry Cornwall records
seeing Lamb kiss his copy of the poet.

Page 61, line 20. *You can admire him.* In the *London Magazine*
Lamb added:—

"I have a great mind to give up Burns. There is certainly a brag-
ging spirit of generosity, a swaggering assertion of independence, and
all that, in his writings."

Page 61, line 20. *Thomson.* James Thomson (1700-1748), author
of *The Seasons*, was born at Ednam, in Roxburghshire. His life has
lately been included in the "Famous Scots" series.

Page 61, line 21. *Smollett.* Tobias George Smollett (1721-1771),
the novelist, came of a Dumbartonshire family. Rory was Roderick
Random's schoolboy name. His companion was Strap. See *Roderick
Random*, Chapter XIII., for the passage in question. Smollett con-
tinued the *History of England* of David Hume (1711-1776), also a
Scotchman, and one of the authors whom Lamb could not read (see
"Detached Thoughts on Books and Reading," page 172).

Lamb's criticism of Scotchmen did not pass without comment. The
pleasantest remark made upon it was that of Christopher North (John
Wilson) some dozen years later (after he had met Lamb), in a *Blackwood* paper entitled "Twaddle on Tweedside" (May, 1833), wherein
he wrote:—

Charles Lamb ought really not to abuse Scotland in the pleasant way he so often does
in the sylvan shades of Enfield ; for Scotland loves Charles Lamb ; but he is wayward and
wilful in his wisdom, and conceits that many a Cockney is a better man even than
Christopher North. But what will not Christopher forgive to Genius and Goodness?
Even Lamb bleating libels on his native land. Nay, he learns lessons of humanity,
even from the mild malice of Elia, and breathes a blessing on him and his household in
their Bower of Rest.

Coleridge was much pleased by this little reference to his friend.

He described it as "very sweet indeed" (see his *Table Talk*, May 14, 1833).

Page 61, line 33. *Hugh of Lincoln.* Hugh was a small Lincoln boy who, tradition states, was tortured to death by the Jews. His dead body being touched by a blind woman, she received sight.

Many years earlier Lamb had spoken of the Jew in English society with equal frankness (see his note to the "Jew of Malta" in the *Specimens*, Vol. IV. of this edition).

Page 62, line 1. *So deadly a disunion.* In the *London Magazine*, "such a mighty antipathy."

Page 62, line 15. *B——.* John Braham, *née* Abraham (1774 ?-1856), the great tenor. Writing to Manning in 1808, Lamb says :—

"Do you like Braham's singing ? The little Jew has bewitched me. I follow him like as the boys followed Tom the Piper. He cures me of melancholy as David cured Saul. . . . I was insensible to music till he gave me a new sense. . . . Braham's singing, when it is impassioned, is finer than Mrs. Siddons's or Mr. Kemble's acting ! and when it is not impassioned it is as good as hearing a person of fine sense talking. The brave little Jew ! "

Two years later Lamb tells Manning of Braham's absence from London, adding : " He was a rare composition of the Jew, the gentleman, and the angel ; yet all these elements mixed up so kindly in him that you could not tell which preponderated." In this essay Lamb refers to Braham's singing in Handel's oratorio " Israel in Egypt." Concerning Braham's abandonment of the Jewish faith see Lamb's sarcastic essay "The Religion of Actors," Vol. I., page 287, and notes.

Page 62, line 32. *Jael.* See Judges iv.

Page 62, line 37. *Fuller.* Lamb quotes this simile in his "Specimens from Fuller's Writings" (Vol. I., page 112). It is to be found in the *Holy State*, II., Chapter XX., "The Good Sea Captain."

Page 62, line 41. *I love Quaker ways.* See notes to " A Quaker's Meeting," above.

Page 63, line 1. *Desdemona.*

> *Desdemona.* That I did love the Moor to live with him,
> My downright violence and storm of fortunes
> May trumpet to the world.
> "Othello," Act I., Scene 3, lines 249-251.

Page 63, line 7. *According to Evelyn.* John Evelyn, the diarist (1620-1706). See his *Acetaria : a Discourse of Sallets,* referred to by Lamb again in his sonnet to Dora Wordsworth (see Vol. V., page 73).

Page 63, line 9. *" To sit a guest . . ."*

> Sometimes that with Elijah he partook,
> Or as a guest with Daniel at his pulse.
> *Paradise Regained*, II., lines 277-278.

Page 63, third line from foot. *A more sacred example.* A reference probably to Luke xi. 53, 54. *To be adduced.* In the *London Magazine* Lamb wrote : " perhaps to be more than hinted at."

Page 64, line 7. *Penn.* This was on the occasion of the trial of

William Penn and William Mead in 1670, at the Old Bailey, for creating a tumult by preaching in the street. In Sewel's *History of the People called Quakers*, the dialogue runs: "'Well,' said the recorder, 'if I should suffer you to ask questions till to-morrow morning, you would be never the wiser.' 'That is,' said W. Penn, 'according as the answers are.'"

Page 64, line 10. *I was travelling.* Lamb did not really take part in this story. It was told him by Sir Anthony Carlisle (1768-1840), the surgeon, as he confessed to his Quaker friend, Bernard Barton (March 11, 1823), who seemed to miss its point. Lamb described Carlisle as "the best story-teller I ever heard."

Page 65. WITCHES, AND OTHER NIGHT-FEARS.
London Magazine, October, 1821.
Compare with this essay Maria Howe's story of "The Witch Aunt," in *Mrs. Leicester's School* (see Vol. III.), which Lamb had written thirteen years earlier.

Page 65, seventh line from foot. *Silly Headborough.* The chief of the district. See "The Taming of the Shrew" (Induction, lines 11-14) :—

> *Hostess.* I know my remedy, I must go fetch the head borough.
> *Sly.* Third, or fourth, or fifth borough, I'll answer him by law.

Some editors (in the Globe edition, for example), to lend more point to Sly's answer, make the Hostess threaten to fetch the "third borough."

Page 65, next line. *Prospero.* See "The Tempest," Act I., Scene 2, lines 144-148.

Page 65, at foot. *In Spenser.* See *The Faerie Queen*, II., Canto VII., Stanza 64.

Page 66, line 8. *History of the Bible, by Stackhouse.* Thomas Stackhouse (1677-1752) was rector of Boldon, in Durham ; his *New History of the Holy Bible from the Beginning of the World to the Establishment of Christianity*—the work in question—was published in 1737.

Page 66, line 9. *The pictures . . . —one of the ark.* See the plate in the Notes to Vol. III. of this edition.

Page 66, line 30. *Slain monster in Spenser.* See *The Faerie Queen*, I., Canto XII., Stanza 10—the dragon slain by St. George, the Red Cross Knight.

Page 67, line 22. *The Witch raising up Samuel.* See the plate on the opposite page.

This paragraph was the third place in which Lamb recorded his terror of this picture of the Witch of Endor in Stackhouse's *Bible*, but the first occasion in which he took it to himself. In one draft of *John Woodvil*—not that which was printed (see Vol. V., page 364)—the hero says :—

> I can remember when a child the maids
> Would place me on their lap, as they undrest me,
> As silly women use, and tell me stories
> Of Witches—make me read "Glanvil on Witchcraft,
> And in conclusion show me in the Bible,

SAUL CONSULTING A WITCH AT ENDOR

From Stackhouse's "New History of the Holy Bible"

> The old Family Bible, with the pictures in it,
> The 'graving of the Witch raising up Samuel,
> Which so possest my fancy, being a child,
> That nightly in my dreams an old Hag came
> And sat upon my pillow.

Then again, in *Mrs. Leicester's School*, in the story of Maria Howe, called "The Witch Aunt," one of the three stories in that book which Lamb wrote, Stackhouse's *Bible* is found once more.

Page 67, at foot. "*Headless bear . . .*"

> Methinks I hear, methinks I see
> Ghosts, goblins, fiends; my fantasy
> Presents a thousand ugly shapes,
> Headless bears, black men, and apes.
> From "The Abstract of Melancholy," prefixed to Burton's *Anatomy.*

Page 68, line 3. *Dear little T. H.* This was the unlucky passage which gave Southey his chief text in his criticism of *Elia* as a book wanting "a sounder religious feeling," and which led to Lamb's expostulatory "Letter" (see page 329 and Vol. I., page 226). Southey commented thus :—

> This poor child, instead of being trained up in the way in which he should go, had beer bred in the ways of modern philosophy; he had systematically been prevented from know ing anything of that Saviour who said, "Suffer little children to come unto Me, and forbid them not; for of such is the Kingdom of Heaven;" care had been taken that he should not pray to God, nor lie down at night in reliance upon His good Providence!

T. H. was Thornton Hunt, Leigh Hunt's eldest son and Lamb's "favourite child" (see Vol. V., pages 35 and 300).

Page 68, line 9. "*Thick-coming fancies.*"

Doctor (of Lady Macbeth).   Not so sick, my lord,
As she is troubled with thick-coming fancies.
"Macbeth," Act V., Scene 3, lines 37, 38.

Page 68, line 13. *Gorgons, and Hydras . . .* See *Paradise Lost*, II., line 628. *Celæno and the Harpies.* See Virgil's *Æneid*, III.

Page 68, line 19. "*Names, whose sense . . .*" From Spenser's *Epithalamium*, lines 343-344.

Page 68, line 29. "*Like one that on a lonesome road . . .*" From *The Ancient Mariner*, Part VI.

Page 69, line 14. *Inner eye.* The words were placed within quotation marks in the *London Magazine*—possibly as a delicate association of the passage with Wordsworth—"the inward eye which is the bliss of solitude"—and the Lambs' visit to his Westmoreland Fells (though he was absent) in 1802.

Page 69, line 20. "*Where Alph, the sacred river, runs.*" From Coleridge's "Kubla Khan; or, A Vision in a Dream."

Page 69, line 21. *Barry Cornwall.* Bryan Waller Procter (1787-1874), Lamb's friend. The reference is to "A Dream," a poem in Barry Cornwall's *Dramatic Scenes*, 1819, which Lamb greatly admired. See his sonnet to the poet in Vol. V., page 57, where it is mentioned again. "A Dream" began thus :—

VOL. II.—23

The night was gloomy. Through the skies of June
Rolled the eternal moon,
'Midst dark and heavy clouds that bore
A shadowy likeness to those fabled things
That sprung of old from man's imaginings.
Each seem'd a fierce reality : some wore
The forms of sphinx and hippogriff, or seemed
Nourished among the wonders of the deep,
And wilder than the poet ever dreamed :
And there were cars—steeds with their proud necks bent—
Tower,—and temple,—and broken continent :
And all, as upon a sea,
In the blue ether floated silently.

This was the close :—

And then I heard the sullen waters roar,
And saw them cast their surf upon the strand,
And then, rebounding toward some far-seen land,
They washed and washed its melancholy shore,
And the terrific spirits, bred
In the sea-caverns, moved by those fierce jars,
Rose up like giants from their watery bed,
And shook their silver hair against the stars.
Then, bursts like thunder—joyous outcries wild—
Sounds as from trumpets, and from drums,
And music, like the lulling noise that comes
From nurses when they hush their charge to sleep,
Came in confusion from the deep.
Methought one told me that a child
Was that night unto the great Neptune born ;
And then old Triton blew his curled horn,
And the Leviathan lashed the foaming seas,
And the wanton Nereides
Came up like phantoms from their coral halls,
And laughed and sung like tipsy Bacchanals,
Till all the fury of the ocean broke
Upon my ear.——I trembled and awoke.

Page 69, line 33. *Ino Leucothea.* Ino, daughter of Cadmus and Harmonia, fleeing from her husband, leaped into the sea and was transformed into a sea goddess by Neptune, under the name Leucothoe. She is called the "white goddess." In Chapter V. of Lamb's *Adventures of Ulysses* is a beautiful passage describing her rescue of Ulysses.

Page 69. *Last paragraph.* In the original MS. of this essay (now in the Dyce and Forster collection at South Kensington) the last paragraph ran thus :—

"When I awoke I came to a determination to write prose all the rest of my life ; and with submission to some of our young writers, who are yet diffident of their powers, and balancing perhaps between verse and prose, they might not do unwisely to decide the preference by the texture of their natural dreams. If these are prosaic, they may depend upon it they have not much to expect in a creative way from their artificial ones. What dreams must not Spenser have had ! "

———

Page 70. My RELATIONS.
London Magazine, June, 1821.

Page 70, beginning. *At that point of life.* Lamb was forty-six on February 10, 1821.

Page 70, line 10. *Browne's Christian Morals.* *Christian Morals* was published posthumously in 1716, thirty-four years after Sir Thomas Browne's death. The passage is in Section XXII. of the third part. Browne is referring to the man who has lived sixty years :—

> He may have a close apprehension what it is to be forgotten, while he hath lived to find none who could remember his Father, or scarce the friends of his youth, and may sensibly see with what a face in no long time oblivion will look upon himself.

By an error Wilkin's edition of Browne's *Works*, 1846 (Vol. IV., page 108), omits "it" before "is to be forgotten."

Page 70, line 17. *I had an aunt.* Aunt Hetty, who died in 1797 (see the essay on "Christ's Hospital," page 13, and note on page 316).

Page 70, line 23. *Thomas à Kempis, in Stanhope's Translation.* George Stanhope (1660-1728), Dean of Canterbury. His translation of à Kempis's *Imitatio Christi* was published in 1698 under the title *The Christian's Pattern ; or, A Treatise of the Imitation of Christ.*

Page 70, line 31. *The Adventures of an Unfortunate Young Nobleman.* The full title of this work is : *The Unfortunate Young Nobleman ; a Tale of Sympathy, Founded on Fact. In which are depicted the Unprecedented Sufferings of an Affectionate Husband, and the Forlorn State of an amiable Mother and her Infant Child.* The story tells how the unfortunate Mons. du F——, eldest son of the Baron du F——, married against his father's will, and suffered in consequence many privations, including imprisonment in a convent, from which he escaped by a jump of fifty feet.

Page 70, line 32. *The chapel in Essex-street.* The headquarters of "that heresy," Unitarianism. Lamb was at first a Unitarian, but afterwards dropped away from all sects.

Page 71, line 10. *Brother, or sister, I never had any—to know them.* Lamb is writing strictly as the imagined Elia, Elia being Lamb in mind rather than Lamb in fact. It amused him to present his brother John and his sister Mary as his cousins James and Bridget Elia. We have here an excellent example of his whimsical blending of truth and invention : brothers and sisters he denies, yet admits one sister, Elizabeth, who died in both their infancies. Lamb had in reality two sisters named Elizabeth, the former of whom he never knew. She was born in 1762. The second Elizabeth, his parents' fifth child, was born in 1768, seven years before Charles. Altogether the Lambs had seven children, of whom only John (born 1763), Mary Anne (born 1764) and Charles (born 1775) grew up. Again Lamb confesses to several cousins in Hertfordshire, and to two others. The two others were fictitious, but it was true that he had Hertfordshire relations (see the essay "Mackery End, in Hertfordshire," page 75).

John Lamb's character is perhaps sufficiently described in this essay and in "Dream Children," page 102. He was a well-to-do official in the South-Sea House, succeeding John Tipp as accountant. Crabb Robinson found him too bluff and noisy to be bearable; and he once knocked Hazlitt down in a dispute about painting. He died on October 26, 1821, to his brother's great grief, leaving Charles everything. He married late in life a Mrs. Dowden. Probably she had her own money and needed none of her second husband's. Hence the peculiarity of the will. Mrs. John Lamb died in 1826.

John Lamb's sympathy with animals led him to write in 1810 a pamphlet entitled *A Letter to the Right Hon. William Windham, on his opposition to Lord Erskine's Bill for the Prevention of Cruelty to Animals*—Mr. Windham having expressed it as his opinion that the subject was not one for legislation. Lamb sent the pamphlet to Crabb Robinson on February 7, 1810, saying :—

"My Brother whom you have met at my rooms (a plump good looking man of seven and forty!) has written a book about humanity, which I transmit to you herewith. Wilson the Publisher has put it in his head that you can get it Reviewed for him. I dare say it is not in the scope of your Review—but if you could put it into any likely train, he would rejoyce. For alas! our boasted Humanity partakes of Vanity. As it is, he teazes me to death with chusing to suppose that I could get it into all the Reviews at a moment's notice.—I !! who have been set up as a mark for them to throw at and would willingly consign them all to Hell flames and Megæra's snaky locks.

But here's the Book—and don't shew it Mrs. Collier, for I remember she makes excellent Eel soup, and the leading points of the Book are directed against that very process."

Crabb Robinson's review would be probably *The London Review*, founded by Richard Cumberland, in February, 1809, and ending in November of the same year. Either Lamb was unaware of its cessation or his letter should be dated not 1810 but 1809.

The pamphlet in question was identified by Mr. Luther S. Livingston, who found it in a volume of odds and ends from Lamb's library. This is the passage—one red-hot sentence—concerning eels :—

"If an eel had the wisdom of Solomon, he could not help himself in the ill-usage that befalls him; but if he had, and were told, that it was necessary for our subsistence that he should be eaten, that he must be skinned first, and then broiled; if ignorant of man's usual practice, he would conclude that the cook would so far use her reason as to cut off his head first, which is not fit for food, as then he might be skinned and broiled without harm; for however the other parts of his body might be convulsed during the culinary operations, there could be no feeling of consciousness therein, the communication with the brain being cut off; but if the woman were immediately to stick a fork into his eye, skin him alive, coil him up in a skewer, head and all, so that in the extremest agony he could not move, and forthwith broil him to death : then were the same Almighty Power that formed man from the dust, and breathed into his nostrils the breath of life, to call the eel into a new existence, with a knowledge of the treatment he had undergone, and he found that the instinctive disposition which man has in common with other carnivorous animals, which inclines him to cruelty, was not the sole cause of his torments; but that men did not attend to consider whether the sufferings of such insignificant creatures could be lessened: that eels were not the only sufferers; that lobsters and other shell fish were put into cold water and boiled to death by slow degrees in many parts of the sea coast; that these, and many other such wanton atrocities, were the consequence of carelessness occasioned by the pride of mankind despising their low estate, and of the general opinion that there is no punishable sin in the illtreatment of animals designed for our use; that, therefore, the woman did not bestow so much thought on him as to cut his head off first, and that she would have laughed at any considerate person who should have desired such a thing; with what fearful indignation might he inveigh against the unfeeling metaphysician that, like a cruel spirit alarmed at the appearance of a dawning of mercy upon animals, could not rest satisfied with opposing the Cruelty Prevention Bill by the plea of possible inconvenience to mankind, highly magnified and emblazoned, but had set forth to the vulgar and unthinking of all ranks, in the jargon of proud learning, that man's obligations of morality towards the creatures subjected to his use are imperfect obligations!"

The poem "The Beggar-Man," in *Poetry for Children,* 1809 (see Vol. III., page 395), was also from John Lamb's pen.

Page 71, line 25. *Yorick.* Laurence Sterne, author of *Tristram Shandy.*

Page 72, line 25. *John Murray's street.* Albemarle Street, Piccadilly.

Page 72, line 29. *"Thus sitting, thus consulting."* See *Paradise Lost,* II., line 164.

Page 73, line 35. *"Cynthia of the minute."* Pope's phrase in the third "Moral Essay," the "Epistle to Martha Blount," lines 17-20 :—

> Come then, the colours and the ground prepare,
> Dip in the rainbow, trick her off in air ;
> Choose a firm cloud, before it fall, and in it
> Catch, ere she change, the Cynthia of this minute.

Page 74, line 1. *"Set forth in pomp . . ."* "Richard II.," Act V., Scene 1, lines 78-80.

Page 74, line 25. *That "all for pity he could die."* Like the poet in *The Faerie Queen,* Book I., Canto III., Stanza 1.

Page 74, line 28. *Thomas Clarkson.* Thomas Clarkson (1760-1846), the anti-slavery agitator, a friend of Lamb's. The quotation, "true yoke-fellow with Time," is from Wordsworth's sonnet to Clarkson.

Page 74, line 38. *Society for the Relief of*—Distrest Sailors, says Lamb's Key.

Page 75, line 10. *"Through the green plains of pleasant Hertfordshire."* This line occurs in a sonnet of Lamb's written many years before the essay (see Vol. V., page 14). Probably, however, Lamb did not invent it, for (Mr. W. J. Craig points out) in Leland's *Itinerary*, which Lamb must have known, if only on account of the antiquary's remarks on Hertfordshire, is quoted a poem by William Vallans (*fl.* 1578-1590), "The Tale of the Two Swans," containing the line—

The fruitful fields of pleasant Hertfordshire—

which one can easily understand would have lingered in Lamb's mind very graciously.

In the *London Magazine* the essay ended with the words, "Till then, Farewell."

Page 75. MACKERY END, IN HERTFORDSHIRE.
London Magazine, July, 1821. Reprinted in *Elia*, 1823, as written, save for the omission of italics from many passages.

Bridget Elia, who is met also in "Mrs. Battle" (page 37), in "My Relations" (page 71) and in "Old China" (page 247), was, of course, Mary Lamb.

Page 75, line 19. "*With a difference.*" Lamb may have been thinking of Ophelia's words to Hamlet—"O you must wear your rue with a difference" ("Hamlet," Act IV., Scene 5, line 183).

Page 75, line 29. *She must have a story.* Thomas Westwood, in his reminiscences of the Lambs in later years, printed in *Notes and Queries*, speaks of Mary Lamb's passion for novel-reading in the Enfield days, when he was a boy.

Page 75, last line. *She "holds Nature more clever."* From Gay's "Epitaph of Byewords," line 4.

Page 76, line 6. *Margaret Newcastle.* Lamb's devotion to this lady is expressed again in the essay on "The Two Races of Men," page 26, in the essay on Beggars on page 115 and again in "Detached Thoughts on Books and Reading," page 174.

Page 76, line 9. *Free-thinkers . . .* William Godwin, perhaps alone among Lamb's friends, quite answers to the description of leader of novel philosophies and systems; but there had been also Thomas Holcroft and John Thelwall among the Lambs' acquaintance (see the list of Lamb's friends in his "Letter to Southey," Vol. I., page 229). And Hazlitt and Leigh Hunt would come within this description.

Page 76, line 32. *Stuff of the conscience.* From "Othello," Act I., Scene 2, line 2.

Page 76, line 37. *Good old English reading.* The reference is to Samuel Salt's library in the Temple (see note on page 265, 3 of "The Old Benchers of the Inner Temple").

Page 77, line 9. *Mackery End.* The position of Mackery End is indicated in the accompanying chart, kindly prepared for me by Miss M. C. G. Jackson.

The farmhouse still stands, although new front rooms have been added. At the end of the present hall, one passes through what was in Lamb's time the front door, and thereafter the house is exactly as it used to be save that its south windows have been filled in. By kind invita-

MACKERY END. FRONT VIEW (RESTORED)

MACKERY END. BACK VIEW (AS IN LAMB'S DAY)

tion of Mr. Dolphin Smith, the present farmer, who has been there over forty years, I spent some time in the same parlour in which the Lambs had been entertained. Harpenden, on the north-west, has grown immensely since Lamb's day, and the houses at the Folly, between Wheathampstead and the Cherry Trees, are new ; but Mackery End, or Mackrye End as the farmer's waggons have it, remains un-encroached upon. The views on the opposite page are from photographs of the present front, and of the back of the house, which is practically untouched since Lamb's day. Near by is the fine old mansion which is Mackery End house proper ; Lamb's Mackery End was the farm.

Lamb's first visit there must have been when he was a very little boy—somewhere about 1780. Probably we may see recollections of it in Mary Lamb's story "The Farmhouse" in *Mrs. Leicester's School* (see Vol. III. of this edition).

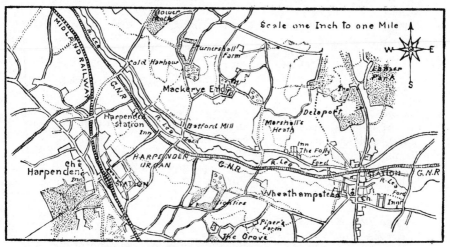

MAP OF MACKERY END

Page 77, line 13. *A great-aunt.* Mary Field, Lamb's grandmother, was Mary Bruton, whose sister married, as he says, a Gladman, and was the great-aunt mentioned. The present occupier of the farm is neither Gladman nor Bruton ; but both names are still to be found in the county. A Miss Sarah Bruton, a direct descendant of Lamb's great-aunt, is now living at Wheathampstead. She has on her walls two charming oval portraits of ancestresses, possibly—for she is uncertain as to their identity—two of the handsome sisters whom Lamb extols.

Writing to Manning, May 28, 1819, Lamb says :—

"How are my cousins, the Gladmans of Wheathampstead, and farmer Bruton ? Mrs. Bruton is a glorious woman.

" Hail, Mackery End !

This is a fragment of a blank verse poem which I once meditated, but got no further."

Page 77, line 15. *I wish that I could throw into a heap.* In the *London Magazine* these words were in italics.

Page 77, line 38. *The "heart of June."* From Ben Jonson's Epithalamion on the nuptials of Mr. Hierome Weston and Lady Francis Stuart :—

> When look'd the Year, at best,
> So like a Feast ?
> Or were Affairs in tune,
> By all the Sphears' consent, so in the Heart of *June ?*

Page 77, next line. *"But thou, that didst appear so fair . . ."* From Wordsworth's "Yarrow Visited," Stanza 6. Writing to Wordsworth in 1815, Lamb said of this stanza that he thought "no lovelier" could be found in "the wide world of poetry." From a letter to Taylor, of the *London Magazine,* belonging to the summer of 1821, we gather that the proof-reader had altered the last word of the third line to "air" to make it rhyme to "fair." Lamb says : "*Day* is the right reading, and *I implore you to restore it.*"

Page 77, line 2 from foot. *Waking bliss.* From *Comus,* lines 263, 264 :—

> Such sober certainty of waking bliss
> I never heard till now.

Page 78, line 29. *The two scriptural cousins.* See Luke i. 39 and 40.

Page 78, line 34. *B. F.* Barron Field (see note to "Distant Correspondents," page 379), then living in Sydney, where he composed, and had printed for private circulation in 1819, a volume of poems reviewed by Lamb (see Vol. I., page 197), in 1819, one of which was entitled "The Kangaroo." It was the first book printed in Australia. Field edited Heywood for the old Shakespeare Society.

Page 79. MODERN GALLANTRY.

London Magazine, November, 1822.

De Quincey writes in "London Reminiscences" concerning the present essay :—

Among the prominent characteristics of Lamb, I know not how it is that I have omitted to notice the peculiar emphasis and depth of his courtesy. This quality was in him a really chivalrous feeling, springing from his heart, and cherished with the sanctity of a duty. He says somewhere in speaking of himself [?] under the mask of a third person, whose character he is describing, that, in passing a servant girl, even at a street-crossing, he used to take off his hat. Now, the *spirit* of Lamb's gallantry would have prompted some such expression of homage, though the customs of the country would not allow it to be *literally* fulfilled, for the very reason that would prompt it—*viz.,* in order to pay respect—since the girl would, in such a case, suppose a man laughing at her. But the instinct of his heart was to think highly of female nature, and to pay a real homage (not the hollow demonstration of outward honour which a Frenchman calls his "homage," and which is really a mask for contempt) to the sacred *idea* of pure and virtuous womanhood.

Barry Cornwall has the following story in his Memoir of Lamb :—

Lamb, one day, encountered a small urchin loaded with a too heavy package of grocery. It caused him to tremble and stop. Charles inquired where he was going, took (although weak) the load upon his own shoulder, and managed to carry it to Islington, the place of destination. Finding that the purchaser of the grocery was a female, he went with the urchin before her, and expressed a hope that she would intercede with the poor boy's master, in order to prevent his being over-weighted in future. "Sir," said the dame, after the manner of Tisiphone, frowning upon him, "I buy my sugar and have nothing to do with the man's manner of sending it." Lamb at once perceived the character of the purchaser, and taking off his hat, said, humbly, "Then I hope, ma'am, you'll give me a drink of small beer." This was of course refused. He afterwards called upon the grocer, on the boy's behalf. With what effect I do not know.

Page 79, line 13. *Upon the point of gallantry.* Here, in the *London Magazine*, came the words :—

"as upon a thing altogether unknown to the old classic ages. This has been defined to consist in a certain obsequiousness, or deferential respect, paid to females, as females."

Page 79, line 25. *Dorimant.* Dorimant is an exquisite in Etheredge's comedy "The Man of Mode."

Page 80, line 22. *"Antiquated virginity."* The phrase occurs in *The Rambler*, No. 39, but was possibly a common periphrasis in conversation. The phrase "overstood the market" refers to goods kept too long in the vain hope of realising a higher figure.

Page 80, line 26. *Joseph Paice.* Joseph Paice was, as Lamb pointed out to Barton in a letter in January, 1830, a real person, and all that Lamb records. According to Miss Anne Manning's *Family Pictures*, 1860, Joseph Paice, who was a friend of Thomas Coventry (see page 365), took Lamb into his office at 27 Bread Street Hill somewhere in 1789 or 1790 to learn book-keeping and business habits. He passed thence to the South Sea-House and thence to the East India House. Miss Manning (who was the author of *Flemish Interiors*) helps to fill out Lamb's sketch into a full-length portrait. She tells us that Mr. Paice's life was one long series of gentle altruisms and the truest Christianities.

Charles Lamb speaks of his holding an umbrella over a market-woman's fruit-basket, lest her store should be spoilt by a sudden shower ; and his uncovering his head to a servant-girl who was requesting him to direct her on her way. These traits are quite in keeping with many that can still be authenticated :—his carrying presents of game *himself,* for instance, to humble friends, who might ill have spared a shilling to a servant ; and his offering a seat in his hackney-coach to some poor, forlorn, draggled beings, who were picking their way along on a rainy day. Sometimes these chance guests have proved such uncongenial companions, that the kind old man has himself faced the bad weather rather than prolong the acquaintance, paying the hackney-coachman for setting down the stranger at the end of his fare. At lottery times, he used to be troubled with begging visits from certain improvident hangers-on, who had risked their all in buying shares of an unlucky number. About the time the numbers were being drawn, there would be a ring at the gate-bell, perhaps at dinner time. His spectacles would be elevated, an anxious expression would steal over his face, as he half raised himself from his seat, to obtain a glance at the intruder—"Ah, I thought so, I expected as much," he would gently say. "I expected I should soon have a visit from poor Mrs.—— or Mrs. ——. Will you excuse me, my dear madam," (to my grandmother) "for a moment, while I just tell her it is quite out of my power to help her?" counting silver into his hand all the time. Then, a parley would ensue at the hall-door—complainant telling her tale in a doleful voice : "My good woman, I really cannot," etc. ; and at last the hall-door would be shut. "Well, sir," my grandmother used to say, as Mr. Paice returned to his seat, "I do not think you have sent Mrs. —— away quite penniless." "Merely enough for a joint of meat, my good madam—just a trifle to buy her a joint of meat."

Family Pictures should be consulted by any one who would know more of this gentleman and of Susan Winstanly.

Page 80, line 27. *Edwards.* Thomas Edwards (1699-1757), author of *Canons of Criticism,* 1748. The sonnet in question, which was modelled on that addressed by Milton to Cyriack Skinner, was addressed to Paice, as the author's nephew, bidding him carry on the family line. Paice, however, as Lamb tells us, did not marry.

Page 81, line 7. *Calidore . . . Tristan.* Sir Calidore, the pattern of courtesy, modelled upon Sir Philip Sidney, is the hero of Book VI. of *The Faerie Queen.* Tristan, or Tristram, the sorrowful knight of Arthur's Round Table (see Malory, Part II.).

———

Page 82. THE OLD BENCHERS OF THE INNER TEMPLE.
London Magazine, September, 1821.
Lamb's connection with the Temple was fairly continuous until 1817, when he was thirty-eight. He was born at No. 2 Crown Office Row in

Nº 2 CROWN OFFICE ROW

1775, and he did not leave it, except for visits to Hertfordshire, until 1782, when he entered Christ's Hospital. There he remained, save for holidays, until 1789, returning then to Crown Office Row for the brief period between leaving school and the death of Samuel Salt, under whose roof the Lambs dwelt, in February, 1792. The 7 Little Queen Street, the 45 and 36 Chapel Street, Pentonville, and the first 34

Southampton Buildings (with Gutch) periods, followed; but in 1801 Lamb and his sister were back in the Temple again, at 16 Mitre Court Buildings, since rebuilt. They moved from there, after a brief return to 34 Southampton Buildings, to 4 Inner Temple Lane (since rebuilt and now called Johnson's Buildings) in 1809, where they remained until the move to 20 Great Russell Street in 1817. With each change after that (except for another and briefer sojourn in Southampton Buildings in 1830), Lamb's home became less urban. His last link with the Temple may be said to have snapped with the death of Randal Norris, sub-treasurer of the Inner Temple, in 1827 (see "A Death-Bed," page 246), although now and then he slept at Crabb Robinson's chambers.

The Worshipful Masters of the Bench of the Hon. Society of the Inner Temple—to give the Benchers their full title—have the government of the Inner Temple in their hands.

A map of the Temple, made for me by Miss M. C. G. Jackson, will be found on page 364.

Page 82, at foot. *Spenser.* In the *Prothalamion*, Stanza 8.

Page 83, line 8. *"Of building strong . . ."* A reference to Paper Buildings in the Temple. Probably Lamb improvised this "quotation." The situation of these and other buildings mentioned by Lamb, together with the Temple's intricate ways, may be seen at once in the accompanying map.

Page 83, line 15. *Elizabethan hall . . . fountain.* The hall in Fountain Court. A fountain is still there, but the old mysterious mechanism has gone.

Page 83, line 21. *Moral inscriptions.* Among the mottoes now to be seen are "Disciti justiciam moniti" ("Learn justice of this lesson"), opposite the Hall in Fountain Court, and "Pereunt et imputantur" ("They slip away and are reckoned against us"), in Middle Temple Lane. The sundial in the great garden opposite Crown Office Row is of "simple altar-like structure."

Page 83, line 27. *"Ah! yet doth beauty . . ."* From Shakespeare's 104th sonnet.

Page 83, line 41. *"Carved it out quaintly . . ."*

> *King.* O God! methinks it were a happy life,
> To be no better than a homely swain;
> To sit upon a hill, as I do now,
> To carve out dials quaintly, point by point.
> "3 Henry VI.," Act II., Scene 5, lines 21-24.

Page 84, line 1. *Marvell.* Andrew Marvell (1621-1678), one of Lamb's favourite poets. The punctuation of Grosart's edition, 1872, differs slightly.

Page 84, eleventh line from foot. *Little green nook behind the South Sea House.* This little nook has gone.

Page 85, line 11. *The winged horse.* Concerning the winged horse, the badge of the Inner Temple, Mrs. E. T. Cook in her *Highways and Byways of London*, 1902, has this interesting passage:—

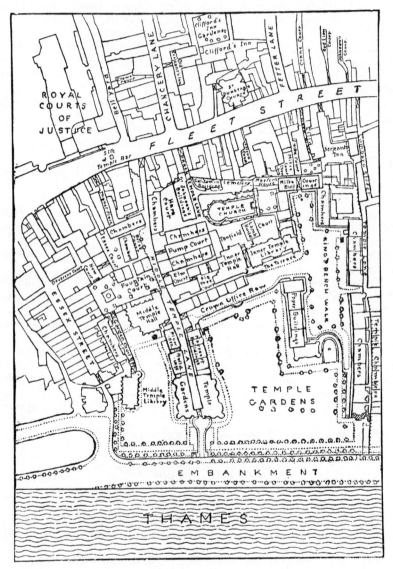

MAP OF THE TEMPLE

This winged horse has a curious history; for, when the horse was originally chosen as an emblem, he had no wings, but was ridden by two men at once to indicate the self-chosen poverty of the brotherhood; in lapse of years the figures of the men became worn and abraded, and when restored were mistaken for wings.

Page 85, line 22. *J——ll*. Joseph Jekyll, great-nephew of Joseph Jekyll, Master of the Rolls, well known as a wit and diner-out. He became a Bencher in 1795, and was made a Master in Chancery in 1815, through the influence of the Prince Regent. Under his direction the hall of the Inner Temple and the Temple Church were restored, and he compiled a little book entitled *Facts and Observations relating to the Temple Church and the Monuments contained in it*, 1811. He became a Bencher in 1805, and died in 1837, aged eighty-five. Jekyll was a friend of George Dyer, and was interested in Lamb's other friends, the Norrises. A letter from him, thanking Lamb for a copy of the *Last Essays of Elia*, is printed in Mr. W. C. Hazlitt's *The Lambs*. He had another link of a kind with Lamb in being M.P. for "sweet Calne in Wiltshire" (see page 13). Jekyll's chambers were at 6 King's Bench Walk. On the same staircase lived for a while George Colman the Younger.

Page 85, line 24. *Thomas Coventry*. Thomas Coventry became a Bencher in 1766. He was the nephew of William, fifth Earl of Coventry, and resided at North Cray Place, near Bexley, in Kent, and in Serjeant's Inn, where he died in 1797, in his eighty-fifth year. He is buried in the Temple Church. Coventry was a sub-governor of the South Sea-House, and it was he who presented Lamb's friend, James White (see page 112), to Christ's Hospital. He was M.P. for Bridport from 1754 to 1780. As an illustration of Coventry's larger benefactions it may be remarked that he presented £10,000 worth of South Sea stock to Christ's Hospital in 1782.

Page 85, at foot. *Samuel Salt*. Samuel Salt was the son of the Rev. John Salt, of Audley, in Staffordshire; and he married a daughter of Lord Coventry, thus being connected with Thomas Coventry by marriage. He was M.P. for Liskeard for some years, and a governor of the South-Sea House.

Samuel Salt, who became a Bencher in 1782, rented at No. 2 Crown Office Row two sets of chambers, in one of which the Lamb family dwelt. John Lamb, Lamb's father, who is described as a scrivener in Charles's Christ's Hospital application form, was Salt's right-hand man, not only in business, but privately, while Mrs. Lamb acted as housekeeper and possibly as cook. Samuel Salt played the part of tutelary genius to John Lamb's two sons. It was he who arranged for Charles to be nominated for Christ's Hospital (by Timothy Yeats); probably he was instrumental also in getting him into the East India House; and in all likelihood it was he who paved the way for the younger John Lamb's position in the South-Sea House. It was also Samuel Salt who gave to Charles and Mary the freedom of his library (see the reference in the essay on "Mackery End," page 76): a privilege which, to ourselves, is the most important of all. Salt died in February, 1792, and is buried in the vault of the Temple Church. He left to John Lamb £500 in South Sea stock and a small annual sum, and to Elizabeth Lamb £200 in money; but with his death the prosperity of the family ceased.

Canon Ainger states that he possesses a medallion portrait of Samuel Salt modelled by John Lamb, which he will, I hope, some day reproduce.

Page 86, line 8. *Lovel.* See next page.

Page 86, line 20. *Miss Blandy.* Mary Blandy was the daughter of Francis Blandy, a lawyer at Henley-on-Thames. The statement that she was to inherit £10,000 induced an officer in the marines, named Cranstoun, a son of Lord Cranstoun, to woo her, although he already had a wife living. Her father proving hostile, Cranstoun supplied her with arsenic to bring about his removal. Mr. Blandy died on August 14, 1751. Mary Blandy was arrested, and hanged on April 6 in the next year, after a trial which caused immense excitement. The defence was that Miss Blandy was ignorant of the nature of the powder, and thought it a means of persuading her father to her point of view. In this belief the father, who knew he was being tampered with, also shared. Cranstoun avoided the law, but died in the same year. Lamb had made use of Salt's *faux pas*, many years earlier, in " Mr. H." (see Vol. V. page 200).

Page 86, line 40. *His eye lacked lustre.* At these words, in the *London Magazine*, came this passage :—

" Lady Mary Wortley Montague was an exception to her sex : she says, in one of her letters, ' I wonder what the women see in S. I do not think him by any means handsome. To me he appears an extraordinary dull fellow, and to want common sense. Yet the fools are all sighing for him.' "

I have not found the passage.

Page 86, line 41. *Susan P——.* This is Susannah Peirson, sister of the Peter Peirson to whom we shall come directly. Samuel Salt left her a choice of books in his library, together with a money legacy and a silver inkstand, hoping that reading and reflection would make her life "more comfortable." B——d Row would be Bedford Row.

Page 87, line 11. *J., the counsel.* I cannot be sure who this was. The Law Directory of that day does not help.

Page 87, line 18. *Hic currus et arma fuêre.* Adapted from Virgil's *Æneid*, I., line 17.

Page 87, line 21. *Elwes.* John Elwes, the miser (1714-1789), whose *Life* was published in 1790 after running through *The World*— the work of Topham, that paper's editor, who is mentioned in Lamb's essay on "Newspapers," page 224.

Page 87, line 37. *"Flapper."* This is probably an allusion to the flappers in *Gulliver's Travels*—the servants who, in Laputa, carried bladders with which every now and then they flapped the mouths and ears of their employers, to recall them to themselves and disperse their meditations.

Page 87, at foot. *Lovel.* Lovel was the name by which Lamb refers to his father, John Lamb. We know nothing of him in his prime beyond what is told in this essay, but after Mrs. Lamb's death, there are in the *Letters* glimpses of him as a broken, querulous old man. He seems to have crumbled very rapidly after Samuel Salt's death in 1792. He died in 1799. Of John Lamb's early days all our information is contained in this essay, in his own *Poetical Pieces*, where he describes his life as a footman, and in the essay on " Poor Relations " (page 162), where his boyish memories of Lincoln are mentioned. The accompanying portrait, opposite page 368, speaks to his likeness to Garrick. Of his verses it was perhaps too much (though prettily filial) to say they were " next to Swift and Prior ; " but they have much good humour and spirit. John Lamb's poems were printed in a thin quarto under the title *Poetical Pieces on Several Occasions*. The dedication was to " The Forty-Nine Members of the Friendly Society for the Benefit of their Widows, of whom I have the honour of making the Number Fifty," and in the dedicatory epistle it is stated that the Society was in some degree the cause of Number Fifty's commencing author, on account of its approving and printing certain lines which were spoken by him at an annual meeting at the Devil Tavern. The first two poetical pieces are apologues on marriage and the happiness that it should bring, the characters being drawn from bird life (see note on page 451). Then follow verses written for the meetings of the Society, and miscellaneous compositions. Of these the description of a lady's footman's daily life, from within, has a good deal of sprightliness, and displays quite a little mastery of the mock-heroic couplet. The last poem is a long rhymed version of the story of Joseph. With this exception, for which Lamb's character-sketch does not quite prepare us, it is very natural to think of the author as Lovel. One of the pieces, a familiar letter to a doctor, begins thus :—

> My good friend,
> For favours to my son and wife,
> I shall love you whilst I've life,
> Your clysters, potions, help'd to save,
> Our infant lambkin from the grave.

The infant lambkin was probably John Lamb, but of course it might have been Charles. The expression, however, proves that punning ran in the family. Lamb's library contained his father's copy of *Hudibras*.

I quote two other pieces from the volume, a copy of which is now in the British Museum :—

A LETTER FROM A CHILD TO HIS GRANDMOTHER

> Dear Grandmam,
>   Pray to God to bless
> Your Grandson dear with happiness ;
> Pray that I may be a good Boy,
> Be Grandmam's, Dad's, and Mother's joy ;
> That as I do advance each Year,
> I may be taught my God to fear,
> My little frame, from passion free,
> To Man's Estate, from Infancy ;

From vice that leads a youth aside,
And to have wisdom for my guide,
That I may neither lie, nor swear,
But in the path of Virtue steer,
My actions gen'rous, fair, and just,
Be always true unto my Trust,
    And then the Lord will ever bless
      Your Grandson dear,
        John L——b the Less.

The Following Prologue was spoke by the author, at the tragedy of " Macbeth," and a Pantomime Entertainment, performed at Bath, by 'Prentice boys :—

Ladies, to keep you warm, (for 'tis cold weather,)
We've laid the Pit and Boxes all together,
Therefore sit close, that ev'ry he and she
May have a peep at our comic tragedy.
The Actors here behind are ready dress'd,
Forgive their faults, they'll really do their best.
Perhaps you think they'll rant and make a noise,
You must excuse, they are but 'prentice boys,
Just left their work, young striplings under age,
Whose great ambition is to tread the stage :
Their wardrobe's thin the actors but a few,
And not one female 'mongst the spouting crew,
To tell the truth th' whole acting apparatis
Is very small so very hard their fate is.
They want not hands the painted scenes to change,
They have but one and that you'll say is strange,
'Tis both a comic and a tragic scene,
It serves for farces and for harlequin.
When ghosts and witches down below shou'd sink,
For want of traps behind the scene they slink,
They've but three swords to push, to slash and hew,
A motley coat and an old wig that's blue,
A bowl for poison (sometimes to make punch in),
Two masks, a drum, and Mackbeth's wooden Truncheon.
I'll leave the audience to find out the rest,
And pass my word the boys will do their best.

Lamb's phrase, descriptive of his father's decline, is taken with a variation from his own poems—from the " Lines written on the Day of my Aunt's Funeral" (*Blank Verse*, 1798) :—

One parent yet is left,—a wretched thing,
A sad survivor of his buried wife,
A palsy-smitten, childish, old, old man,
A semblance most forlorn of what he was—
A merry cheerful man.

See Vol. V., page 19.
Page 87, last line. " *Would strike.*" Lear says of Caius :—

He's a good fellow, I can tell you that ;
He'll strike, and quickly too.
      " King Lear," Act V., Scene 3, lines 283, 284.

Page 88, line 8. *Better was not concerned.* At these words, in the *London Magazine*, came :—

" He pleaded the cause of a delinquent in the treasury of the Temple so effectually with S. the then treasurer—that the man was allowed to

JOHN LAMB

THE FATHER OF CHARLES LAMB

keep his place. L. had the offer to succeed him. It had been a lucrative promotion. But L. chose to forego the advantage, because the man had a wife and family."

Page 88, line 25. *Bayes.* Mr. Bayes is the author and stage manager in Buckingham's "Rehearsal." This phrase is not in the play and must have been John Lamb's own, in reference to Garrick.

Page 88, line 37. *Peter Pierson.* Peter Peirson (as his name was rightly spelled) was the son of Peter Peirson of the parish of St. Andrew's, Holborn, who lived probably in Bedford Row. He became a Bencher in 1800, died in 1808, and is buried in the Temple Church. When Charles Lamb entered the East India House in April, 1792, Peter Peirson and his brother, John Lamb, were his sureties.

Page 88, next line. "*As now our stout triumvirs . . .*" I cannot find this quotation.

Page 88, last line. *Our great philanthropist.* Probably John Howard, whom, as we have seen in the essay on "Christ's Hospital" (page 17), Lamb did not love. He was of singular sallowness.

Page 89, line 3. *Daines Barrington.* Daines Barrington (1727-1800), the correspondent of Gilbert White, many of whose letters in *The Natural History of Selborne* are addressed to him. Indeed it was Barrington who inspired that work—a circumstance which must atone for his exterminatory raid on the Temple sparrows. His chambers were at 5 King's Bench Walk. Barrington became a Bencher in 1777 and died in 1800. He is buried in the Temple Church. His Episcopal brother was Shute Barrington (1734-1826), Bishop successively of Llandaff, Salisbury and Durham.

Page 89, line 11. *Old Barton.* Thomas Barton, who became a Bencher in 1775 and died in 1791. His chambers were in King's Bench Walk. He is buried in the vault of the Temple Church.

Page 89, line 15. *Read.* John Reade, who became a Bencher in 1792 and died in 1804. His rooms were in Mitre Court Buildings.

Page 89, line 15. *Twopenny.* Canon Ainger, the present Master of the Temple (1903), states that Richard Twopenny, whom Lamb describes, was not a Bencher, but merely a resident in the Temple. He was strikingly thin. Twopenny was stockbroker to the Bank of England, and died in 1809.

Page 89, line 17. *Wharry.* John Wharry, who became a Bencher in 1801, died in 1812, and was buried in the Temple Church.

Page 89, line 30. *Jackson.* This was Richard Jackson, some time M.P. for New Romney, to whom Johnson, Boswell tells us, refused the epithet "Omniscient" as blasphemous, changing it to "all knowing." He was made a Bencher in 1770 and died in 1787.

Page 89, line 42. *Mingay.* James Mingay, who was made a Bencher in 1785, died in 1812. He was M.P. for Thetford and senior King's Counsel. He was also Recorder of Aldborough, Crabbe's town. He lived at 4 King's Bench Walk.

Page 90, line 4. *Michael Angelo's Moses.* In the Sistine Chapel. Lamb refers to this conception more than once in his writings.

Page 90, line 5. *Baron Maseres.* This was Francis Maseres (1731-1824), mathematician, reformer and Cursiter Baron of the Exchequer. He lived at 5 King's Bench Walk, and at Reigate, and wore a three-cornered hat and ruffles to the end. In April, 1801, Lamb wrote to Manning :—

"I live at No. 16 Mitre-court Buildings, a pistol-shot off Baron Maseres'. You must introduce me to the Baron. I think we should suit one another mainly. He lives on the ground floor, for convenience of the gout; I prefer the attic story, for the air. He keeps three footmen and two maids ; I have neither maid nor laundress, not caring to be troubled with them! His forte, I understand, is the higher mathematics; my turn, I confess, is more to poetry and the belles lettres. The very antithesis of our characters would make up a harmony. You must bring the Baron and me together."

Baron Maseres, who was made a Bencher in 1774, died in 1824.

Page 90, line 14. *"Old men covered with a mantle."* "And he [Saul] said unto her [the witch of Endor], What form is he of? And she said, An old man cometh up; and he is covered with a mantle" (1 Sam. xxviii. 14). It was the illustration to this verse which so terrified Lamb's childish mind (see "Witches, and other Night-Fears," page 67).

Page 90, line 20. *That little Goshen.* See note on page 320.

Page 90, line 28. *R. N.* Randal Norris, sub-treasurer of the Inner Temple (see the essay "A Death-Bed," page 246, and note, page 452).

Page 90, at foot. *Plain-speaking.* In the *London Magazine* Lamb wrote "personal."

Page 91, line 3. *Urban's obituary.* Sylvanus Urban, the dynastic title of the editor of *The Gentleman's Magazine*, a periodical from which the ancient glory has departed.

Page 91, line 9. *"Ye yourselves are old."*

> *Lear.* If you do love old men, if your sweet sway
> Allow obedience, if yourselves are old,
> Make it your cause.
> "King Lear," Act II., Scene 4, lines 193-195.

Page 91, line 11. *Hookers and Seldens.* Richard Hooker (1554 ?-1600), the "judicious," was Master of the Temple. John Selden (1584-1654), the jurist, who lived in Paper Buildings and practised law in the Temple, was buried in the Temple Church with much pomp.

Page 91. GRACE BEFORE MEAT.

London Magazine, November, 1821.

This was one essay, Lamb suggested, which Southey may have had in mind when in an article in the *Quarterly Review* he condemned *Elia* as wanting "a sounder religious feeling" (see also notes on pages 329 and 353). In his "Letter to Southey" (Vol. I., page 226), which contained Lamb's protest against Southey's strictures, he wrote:—

"I am at a loss what particular essay you had in view (if my poor ramblings amount to that appellation) when you were in such a hurry to thrust in your objection, like bad news, foremost.—Perhaps the Paper on 'Saying Graces' was the obnoxious feature. I have endeavoured there to rescue a voluntary duty—good in place, but never, as I remember, literally commanded—from the charge of an undecent formality. Rightly taken, sir, that paper was not against graces, but want of grace ; not against the ceremony, but the carelessness and slovenliness so often observed in the performance of it."

Page 92, line 7. *Homo Humanus.* A glance at the abbey of Theleme founded by Gargantua for persons of sweet reasonableness (see *Rabelais*, Book I., Chapters LII.-LVII.).

Page 92, line 28. *A "rarus hospes."* "An uncommon guest."

Page 92, line 40. *To praise the Gods amiss.* Lamb does not use quotation marks, but he was probably thinking of the passage in *Comus* (lines 175-177):—

> When for their teeming flocks, and granges full,
> In wanton dance they praise the bounteous Pan,
> And thank the gods amiss.

Page 93, line 17. *Jeshurun.* See Deuteronomy xxxii. 15.

Page 93, line 18. *Virgil knew.* See the *Æneid,* III., lines 247-257, where Celæno shouts and curses after Æneas and the Trojans.

Page 93, line 33. *The banquet . . . in the Paradise Regained.* See Book II., lines 340-347, describing the luxuries laid before Christ by Satan.

Page 94, line 1. *A gaudy day.* A feast day.

Page 94, line 2. *Heliogabalus.* The most luxuriously licentious of the Roman Emperors. Died 222 A.D.

Page 94, line 10. *"As appetite is wont to dream . . ."* *Paradise Regained,* II., lines 264-278.

Page 95, line 7. *C——.* Coleridge ; but Lamb may really have said it.

Page 95, line 17. *The author of the Rambler.* Dr. Johnson. Veal pie with prunes in it was perhaps his favourite dish.

Page 95, line 27. *Dagon.* The fish god worshipped by the Philistines. See Judges xvi. 23 and 1 Samuel v. for the full significance of Lamb's reference.

Page 95, line 30. *The Chartreuse.* The monastery of the Carthusians (see note on page 344) at Grenoble, in France.

Page 95, line 35. *Hog's Norton.* An old proverb runs : "I think thou wast born at Hoggs-Norton, where piggs play upon the organs." Hog's Norton is on the borders of Oxfordshire and Warwickshire. One account of the origin of the legend is the organ-playing of a villager named Pigg. In Witt's *Recreations* there is this epigram on pigs devouring a bed of penny-royal, commonly called organs :—

A goodwife once, a bed of organs set,
The pigs came in, and eat up every whit ;
The goodman said, Wife, you your garden may
Hog's Norton call, here pigs on organs play.

Page 96, line 17. *Lucian.* Lucian's *Dialogues,* written in the second century, treat religious matters with delicate raillery. A flamen was a priest in the service of a particular god.

Page 96, line 22. *To want reverence.* In the *London Magazine,* " to be unreverend."

Page 96, line 25. *C. V. L.* Charles Valentine le Grice (see note on page 322). Later in life, in 1798, Le Grice himself became a clergyman.

Page 96, line 28. *Our old form at school.* The Christ's Hospital graces in Lamb's day were worded thus :—

GRACE BEFORE MEAT

Give us thankful hearts, O Lord God, for the Table which thou hast spread for us. Bless thy good Creatures to our use, and us to thy service, for Jesus Christ his sake. *Amen.*

GRACE AFTER MEAT

Blessed Lord, we yield thee hearty praise and thanksgiving for our Founders and Benefactors, by whose Charitable Benevolence thou hast refreshed our Bodies at this time. So season and refresh our Souls with thy Heavenly Spirit, that we may live to thy Honour and Glory. Protect thy Church, the King, and all the Royal Family. And preserve us in peace and truth through Christ our Saviour. *Amen.*

Page 96, line 32. *" Non tunc illis erat locus."* From Horace's *Ars Poetica,* line 19, " Sed nunc non erat his locus." " But that was not the occasion for such things."

Page 96, last line. *Trowsers instead of mutton.* Leigh Hunt's *Autobiography* refers also to this exchange. " Horresco referens " is Virgil's phrase in the *Æneid,* II., line 204—" I tremble at the recollection."

Page 97. MY FIRST PLAY.

London Magazine, December, 1821.

Lamb had already sketched out this essay in the " Table Talk " in Leigh Hunt's *Examiner,* December 9, 1813, under the title " Playhouse Memoranda " (see Vol. I., page 158, and note). Leigh Hunt reprinted it in *The Indicator,* December 13, 1820.

Page 97, line 2. *Cross Court.* Lamb had written " Russell Court " in the *London Magazine.* Cross Court has lately been destroyed.

Page 97, line 4. *Printing-office.* Lamb had written " wine vault " in the *London Magazine.*

Page 97, line 6. *Garrick's Drury.* Garrick's Drury Lane was condemned in 1791, and superseded in 1794 by the new theatre, the burning of which in 1809 led to the *Rejected Addresses.* The present Drury Lane Theatre dates from 1812.

Page 97, line 15. *My godfather F.* Lamb's godfather was Francis Fielde. *The British Directory* for 1793 gives him as Francis

Field, oilman, 62 High Holborn. Whether or no he played the part in Sheridan's matrimonial comedy that is attributed to him I do not know (Moore makes the friend a Mr. Ewart); but it does not sound like an invented story. Richard Brinsley Sheridan carried Miss Linley, the oratorio singer, from Bath and the persecutions of Major Mathews, in March, 1772, and placed her in France. They were married near Calais, and married again in England in April, 1773. Sheridan became manager of Drury Lane, in succession to Garrick, in 1776, the first performance under his control being on September 21. Lamb is supposed to have had some personal acquaintance with Sheridan. Mary Lamb speaks of him as helping the Sheridans, father and son, with a pantomime; but of the work we know nothing definite. I do not consider the play printed in part in the late Charles Kent's edition of Lamb, on the authority of P. G. Patmore, either to be by Lamb or to correspond to Mary Lamb's description.

Page 97, line 19. *John Palmer.* See the note on page 394.

Page 97, at foot. *Seneca or Varro.* Seneca, the Roman philosopher, flourished in the first century A.D.; Varro, a famous Roman author, died 28 B.C.

Page 98, line 3. *Honours which St. Andrew's has to bestow.* "St. Andrew's" in the *London Magazine*, meaning the parish of St. Andrew's, Holborn. The records do not mention Field.

Page 98, line 7. *His testamentary beneficence.* Lamb was not joking. Writing to *The Athenæum*, January 5, 1901, Mr. Thomas Greg says:—

Three-quarters of a century after it passed out of Lamb's possession I am happy to tell the world—or that small portion of it to whom any fact about his life is precious—exactly where and what this landed property is. By indentures of lease and release dated March 23 and 24, 1779, George Merchant and Thomas Wyman, two yeomen of Braughing in the county of Hertford, conveyed to Francis Fielde, of the parish of St. Andrew's, Holborn, in the county of Middlesex, oilman, for the consideration of £20., all that messuage or tenement, with the orchard, gardens, yards, barns, edifices, and buildings, and all and singular the appurtenances therewithal used or occupied, situate, lying, and being at West Mill Green in the parish of Buntingford West Mill in the said county of Hertford, etc. On March 5, 1804, Francis Fielde, of New Cavendish Street, Esq., made his will, and, with the exception of two annuities to female relatives, left all his residuary estate, real and personal, to his wife Sarah Fielde.

This will was proved on November 5, 1809. By indentures of lease and release dated August 20 and 21, 1812, Sarah Fielde conveyed the said property to Charles Lamb, of Inner Temple Lane, gentleman. By an indenture of feoffment dated February 15, 1815, made between the said Charles Lamb of the first part, the said Sarah Fielde of the second part, and Thomas Greg the younger, of Broad Street Buildings, London, Esq., the said property was conveyed to the said Thomas Greg the younger for £50.

The said Thomas Greg the younger died in 1839, and left the said property to his nephew, Robert Philips Greg, now of Coles Park, West Mill, in the same county; and the said Robert Philips Greg in 1884 conveyed it to his nephew, Thomas Tylston Greg, of 15 Clifford's Inn, London, in whose possession it now is in substantially the same condition as it was in 1815.

The evidence that the Charles Lamb who conveyed the property in 1815 is Elia himself is overwhelming.

1. The essay itself gives the locality correctly: it is about two and a half miles from Puckeridge.

2. The plot of land contains as near as possible three-quarters of an acre, with an old thatched cottage and small barn standing upon it. The barn, specially mentioned in all the deeds, is a most unusual adjunct of so small a cottage. The property, the deeds of which go back to 1708, appears to have been isolated and held by small men, and consists

of a long narrow tongue of land jutting into the property now of the Savile family (Earls of Mexborough), but formerly of the Earls of Hardwicke.

3. The witness to Charles Lamb's signature on the deed of 1815 is William Hazlitt, of 19, York Street, Westminster.

4. Lamb was living in Inner Temple Lane in 1815, and did not leave the Temple till 1817.

5. The essay was printed in the *London Magazine* for December, 1821, six years after "the estate has passed into more prudent hands."

6. And lastly, the following letter in Charles Lamb's own handwriting, found with the deeds which are in my possession, clinches the matter :—

"MR. SARGUS,—This is to give you notice that I have parted with the Cottage to Mr. Grig Junr. to whom you will pay rent from Michaelmas last. The rent that was due at Michaelmas I do not wish you to pay me. I forgive it you as you may have been at some expences in repairs.

"Yours

"CH. LAMB.

"Inner Temple Lane, London,
"23 *Feb.*, 1815."

LAMB'S COTTAGE, "BUTTON SNAP," NEAR PUCKERIDGE

It is certainly not the fact that Lamb acquired the property, as he states, by the will of his godfather, for it was conveyed to him some three years after the latter's death by Mrs. Fielde. But strict accuracy of fact in Lamb's ' *Essays* ' we neither look for nor desire. In all probability Mrs. Fielde conveyed him the property in accordance with an expressed wish of her husband in his lifetime. Reading also between the lines of the essay, it is interesting to notice that Francis Fielde, the Holborn oilman of 1779, in 1809 has become Francis Fielde, Esq., of New Cavendish Street. In the letter quoted above Lamb speaks of his purchaser as " Mr. Grig Junr.," more, I am inclined to think, from his desire to have his little joke than from mere inaccuracy, for he must have known the correct name of his purchaser. But Mr. Greg, Jun., was only just twenty-one when he bought the property, and the expression "as merry as a grig" running in Lamb's mind might have proved irresistible to him. Lastly, the property is now called, and has been so far back as I can trace, "Button Snap." No such name is found in any of the title-deeds, and it was impossible before to understand whence it arose. Now it is not : Lamb must have so christened his little property in jest, and the name has stuck.

THOMAS GREG.

I give a picture of Lamb's cottage from a photograph which I took in the summer of 1901. It has never before been portrayed. The cottage now bears a tablet associating it with Lamb.

Page 98, line 29. *Troilus and Cressida.* The plate in question from Rowe's Shakespeare is reproduced opposite page 378. See Act V., Scene 2 of that play for the scene in question.

Page 98, line 38. "*Fair Auroras.*" The first song in "Artaxerxes" (see below) contains this phrase. It begins :—

Fair Aurora, prithee stay.

Page 98, line 41. *The maternal lap.* With the exception of a brief mention on page 28—"the gentle posture of maternal tenderness"—this is Lamb's only reference to his mother in all the essays—probably from the wish not to wound his sister, who would naturally read all he wrote ; although we are told by Talfourd that she spoke of her mother with composure. But it is possible to be more sensitive for others than they are for themselves.

Page 98, line 42. *The play was Artaxerxes.* The opera, by Thomas Augustine Arne (1710-1778), produced in 1762, founded on Metastasio's "Artaserse." The date of the performance was in all probability December 1, 1780, although Lamb suggests that it was later ; for that was the only occasion in 1780-81-82 on which "Artaxerxes" was followed by "Harlequin's Invasion," a pantomime dating from 1759, the work of Garrick. It shows Harlequin invading the territory of Shakespeare ; Harlequin is defeated and Shakespeare restored. I give, opposite page 376, a reproduction of this epoch-making playbill.

Page 99, line 3. *Daniel.* The Book of Daniel.

Page 99, line 6. *Burning idol.* The fourth scene of Act III. of "Artaxerxes," according to Messrs. Hallward and Hill, is "Temple and Throne, the Image of the Sun with a lighted Altar."

Page 99, line 14. *St. Denys.* St. Denys, patron saint of France, who after his decapitation on Montmartre rose up and carried his head in his hands for two miles.

Page 99, line 15. *The Lady of the Manor.* Here Lamb's memory, I fancy, betrayed him. This play (a comic opera by William Kenrick) was not performed at Drury Lane or Covent Garden in the period mentioned. Lamb's pen probably meant to write "The Lord of the Manor," General Burgoyne's opera, with music by William Jackson, of Exeter, which was produced in 1780. It was frequently followed in the bill by "Robinson Crusoe," but never by "Lun's Ghost," whereas Wycherley's "Way of the World" was followed by "Lun's Ghost" at Drury Lane on January 9, 1782. We may therefore assume that Lamb's second visit to the theatre was to see "The Lord of the Manor," followed by " Robinson Crusoe," some time in 1781, and his third to see "The Way of the World," followed by " Lun's Ghost" on January 9, 1782. "Lun's Ghost" was produced on January 3, 1782. Lun was the name under which John Rich (1682?-1761), the pantomimist and theatrical manager, had played in pantomime.

Page 99, line 20. *Lud.* King Lud, who is accredited by legend with the founding of London.

Page 99, line 36. *Round Church . . . of the Templars.* This allusion to the Temple Church and its Gothic heads was used before by Lamb in his story " First Going to Church" in *Mrs. Leicester's School* (see Vol. III.). In that volume Mary Lamb had told the story of what we may take to be her first play (see "Visit to the Cousins"), the piece being Congreve's " Mourning Bride."

Page 99, line 38. *The season* 1781-2. Lamb was six on February 10, 1781. He says, in his " Play-house Memoranda," of the same occasion, "Oh when shall I forget first seeing a play, at the age of five or six ? "

Page 99, line 40. *At school.* Lamb was at Christ's Hospital from 1782 to 1789.

Page 100, line 3. *"Was nourished, I could not tell how."* This is not a line of poetry, as suggested, but probably a recollection of Walton's statement in *The Complete Angler*, that "it is reported by good authors that grasshoppers and some fish have no mouths, but are nourished and take breath by porousness of their gills man knows not how."

Page 100, line 8. *"Royal ghost."* This may be a reference to "Hamlet," Act I., Scene 4.

Page 100, line 14. *A phantom of a voice.* Possibly a recollection of Wordsworth's lyric "To the Cuckoo" :—

> O cuckoo, shall I call thee bird,
> Or but a wandering voice?

Page 100, line 22. *Mrs. Siddons in " Isabella."* Mrs. Siddons first played this part at Drury Lane on October 10, 1782. The play was " Isabella," a version by Garrick of Southerne's " Fatal Marriage." Mrs. Siddons also appeared frequently as Isabella in " Measure for Measure;" but Lamb clearly says "in" Isabella, meaning the play. Lamb's sonnet, in which he collaborated with Coleridge, on Mrs. Siddons, which was printed in the *Morning Chronicle* in December, 1794 (see Vol. V., page 3), was written when he was nineteen. It runs (text of 1797) :—

> As when a child on some long winter's night
> Affrighted clinging to its Grandam's knees
> With eager wond'ring and perturb'd delight
> Listens strange tales of fearful dark decrees
> Mutter'd to wretch by necromantic spell ;
> Or of those hags, who at the witching time
> Of murky midnight ride the air sublime,
> And mingle foul embrace with fiends of Hell :
> Cold Horror drinks its blood ! Anon the tear
> More gentle starts, to hear the Beldame tell

THE SIXTH TIME.

By His MAJESTY's COMPANY,

At the Theatre Royal in Drury-Lane,

This present FRIDAY, December 1, 1780,

Will be presented the ENGLISH OPERA of

ARTAXERXES.

Arbaces by Mifs PRUDOM,
Artaxerxes by Mrs. BADDELEY,
Rimenes by Mr. DU BELLAMY,
And Artabanes by Mr. VERNON.
Semira by Mifs WRIGHT,
And Mandane by a Young LADY,

With NEW DRESSES and Decorations.

To which will be added the Pantomime Entertainment of

HARLEQUIN's INVASION.

Harlequin by Mr. WRIGHT,
Snip by Mr. PARSONS,
Simon by Mr. MOODY,
Gafconade by Mr. BADDELEY,
Mercury by Mr. FAWCETT,
Corporal bounce Mr. CHAPLIN, Abram Mr. HOLCROFT,
Juftice by Mr. WRIGHTEN, Forge by Mr. BURTON,
Bogg by Mr PHILLIMORE, Taffy by Mr. R. PALMER,
Old Woman by Mr. SUETT,
Mrs. Snip by Mrs. LOVE,
Sukey Chitterlin by Mifs COLLETT,
And Dolly Snip by Mifs POPE.

Places for the Boxes to be taken of Mr. FOSBROOK, at the Stage-Door.
The Doors will be opened at a QUARTER after FIVE o'Clock,
To begin at a QUARTER after SIX.   Vivant Rex & Regina.

To-morrow, (the Fourth Night) The New Comedy of
The GENEROUS IMPOSTOR.

THE PLAYBILL OF LAMB'S FIRST PLAY

Of pretty babes, that lov'd each other dear,
Murder'd by cruel Uncle's mandate fell :
Ev'n such the shiv'ring joys thy tones impart,
Ev'n so thou, SIDDONS! meltest my sad heart !

In the *London Magazine* the sentence referring to Mrs. Siddons in
"Isabella" ran: "as it might have interfered with the genuine
emotions with which (with unmixed perception)," &c.

Page 100. DREAM-CHILDREN.
London Magazine, January, 1822.

John Lamb died on October 26, 1821, leaving all his property to his
brother. Charles was greatly upset by his loss. Writing to Wordsworth in March, 1822, he said: "We are pretty well save colds and
rheumatics, and a certain deadness to every thing, which I think I may
date from poor John's Loss. . . . Deaths over-set one, and put one out
long after the recent grief." (His friend Captain Burney died in the
same month.) Lamb probably began "Dream-Children,"—in some
ways, I think, his most perfect prose work—almost immediately upon
his brother's death. The essay "My Relations" (page 70) may be
taken in connection with this as completing the picture of John Lamb.
His lameness was caused by the fall of a stone in 1796, but I doubt if
the leg were really amputated.

The description in this essay of Blakesware, the seat of the Plumers,
is supplemented by the essay on page 153, entitled "Blakesmoor in
H——shire" (see notes). Except that Lamb substitutes Norfolk for
the nearer county, the description is accurate ; it is even true that
there is a legend in the Plumer family concerning the mysterious death
of two children and the loss of the baronetcy thereby—Sir Walter
Plumer, who died in the seventeenth century, being the last to hold
the title. In his poem "The Grandame" (see Vol. V., page 5),
Lamb refers to Mrs. Field's garrulous tongue and her joy in recount-
ing the oft-told tale ; and it may be to his early associations with the
old story that his great affection for Morton's play, "The Children in
the Wood," which he so often commended—particularly with Miss
Kelly in the caste—was due. The actual legend of the children in
the wood belongs, however, to Norfolk.

William Plumer's newer and more fashionable mansion was at
Gilston, which is not in the adjoining county, but also in Hertfordshire,
near Harlow, only a few miles distant from Blakesware. Mrs. Field
died of cancer in the breast in August, 1792, and was buried in Widford
churchyard, hard by Blakesware.

According to Lamb's Key the name Alice W——n was "feigned."
If by Alice W——n Lamb, as has been suggested, means Ann
Simmons, of Blenheims, near Blakesware, he was romancing when
he said that he had courted her for seven long years, although the
same statement is made in the essay on "New Year's Eve" (see page
28). We know that in 1796 he abandoned all ideas of marriage.
Writing to Coleridge in November of that year, in reference to his

love sonnets, he says : "It is a passion of which I retain nothing. . . . Thank God, the folly has left me for ever. Not even a review of my love verses renews one wayward wish in me." This was 1796. Therefore, as he was born in 1775, he must have begun the wooing of Alice W——n when he was fourteen in order to complete the seven long years of courtship. My own feeling, as I have stated in the notes to the love sonnets in Vol. V., is that Lamb was never a very serious wooer, and that Alice W——n was more an abstraction around which now and then to group tender imaginings of what might have been than any tangible figure.

A proof that Ann Simmons and Alice W——n are one has been found in the circumstance that Miss Simmons did marry a Mr. Bartrum, or Bartram, mentioned by Lamb in this essay as being the father of Alice's real children. Bartrum was a pawnbroker in Princes Street, Coventry Street. Mr. W. C. Hazlitt says that Hazlitt had seen Lamb wandering up and down before the shop trying to get a glimpse of his old friend.

The August, 1822, number of the *London Magazine* contained the following unsigned sonnet, inspired by "Dream-Children" :—

TO ELIA

Elia, thy reveries and vision'd themes
To Care's lorn heart a luscious pleasure prove ;
Wild as the mystery of delightful dreams,
Soft as the anguish of remember'd love :
Like records of past days their memory dances
Mid the cool feelings Manhood's reason brings,
As the unearthly visions of romances
Peopled with sweet and uncreated things ;—
And yet thy themes thy gentle worth enhances !
Then wake again thy wild harp's tenderest strings,
Sing on, sweet Bard, let fairy loves again
Smile in thy dreams, with angel ecstasies ;
Bright o'er our souls will break the heavenly strain
Through the dull gloom of earth's realities.

"Dream-Children" has lately been made the theme of a very graceful and charming *suite* by Dr. Edward Elgar.

Page 103, line 6 from foot. *Tedious shores of Lethe.* The passage in Lamb's mind was almost certainly, Canon Ainger remarks, that in the *Æneid*, VI., lines 748-751, where Anchises expounds to Æneas the doctrine of the Soul of the Universe. Speaking of those who have passed through their period of probation he says :—

Has omnes, ubi mille rotam volvere per annos,
Lethæum ad fluvium deus evocat agmine magno ;
Scilicet immemores supera ut convexa revisant
Rursus, et incipiant in corpora velle reverti.

(All these when they have travelled round the circle of a thousand years, God summons in mighty throngs to the river of Lethe, that so, forgetful of the past, they may go back to visit again the vault of the sky, and begin without reluctance to return to the body. Lonsdale and Lee's translation.)

PLATE FROM "TROILUS AND CRESSIDA" IN ROWE'S SHAKSPEARE

Page 104. DISTANT CORRESPONDENTS.
London Magazine, March, 1822.

The germ of this essay will be found in a letter to Barron Field, to whom the essay is addressed, of August 31, 1817. Barron Field (1786-1846) was a son of Henry Field, apothecary to Christ's Hospital. His brother, Francis John Field, through whom Lamb probably came to know Barron, was a clerk in the India House.

Barron Field was associated with Lamb on Leigh Hunt's *Reflector* in 1810-1812. He also was dramatic critic for *The Times* for a while. In 1816 he was appointed judge of the Supreme Court of New South Wales, where he remained until 1824. For other information see the note, in Vol. I., page 469, to his *First-Fruits of Australian Poetry,* reviewed by Lamb. In the same number of the *London Magazine* which included the present essay was Field's account of his outward voyage to New South Wales.

Page 104, line 12. *Mrs. Rowe.* Elizabeth Rowe (1674-1737), author of *Friendship in Death, in Twenty Letters from the Dead to the Living.*

Page 104, line 13. *Cowley's Post-Angel.*

> Let a Post-Angel start with thee,
> And then the goal of earth shall reach as soon as he.
> > Cowley's " Hymn to Light," Stanza 6.

Page 104, line 23. *Plato's man.* Here we see some of the curious lore in Lamb's mind. He probably had his knowledge of Plato's man from Milton's Latin poem, " On the Platonic Idea as it was understood by Aristotle," which may be read in Cowper's translation. The italicised words in the following lines explain Lamb's allusion to the man in the moon :—

> Inform us who is he,
> That great original by nature chos'n
> To be the archetype of human kind,
> Unchangeable, immortal, with the poles
> Themselves coeval, one, yet ev'ry where,
> An image of the god, who gave him being.
>
> .   .   .   .
>
> He dwells not in his father's mind, but, though
> Of common nature with ourselves, exists
> Apart, and occupies a local home.
> Whether, companion of the stars, he spend
> Eternal ages, roaming at his will
> From sphere to sphere the tenfold heav'ns ; or *dwell*
> *On the moon's side that nearest neighbours earth. . . .*

I borrow this suggestion from Messrs. Hallward and Hill.

Page 104, line 31. *Our mutual friend P.* Not identifiable. The Bench would be the King's Bench Prison. A little later one of Lamb's friends, William Hone, was confined there for three years.

Page 104, line 38. *A laugh with Munden.* Written " Joey Munden " in the *London Magazine* (see note on page 397).

Page 105, line 15. *Will Weatherall.* Not identifiable. Lamb alludes to a Fanny Weatheral on page 38.

Page 106, line 8. *The late Lord C.* This was Thomas Pitt, second Baron Camelford (1775-1804), who after a quarrelsome life, first in the navy and afterwards as a man about town, was killed in a duel at Kensington, just where Melbury Road now is. The spot chosen by him for his grave was on the borders of the Lake of Lampierre, near three trees; but there is a doubt if his body ever rested there, for it lay for years in the crypt of St. Anne's, Soho. Its ultimate fate was the subject of a story by Charles Reade.

Page 106, line 31. *Spirit of Saint Gothard.* St. Gothard, Bishop of Hildesheim, patron saint of those in peril at sea.

Page 106, last line. *Your puns.* Compare the "Popular Fallacies" on punning, page 257.

Page 107, lines 6, 7. *Melior lutus . . . sol pater.* Lamb refers directly to Juvenal, Sat. XIV., 34 :—

> Juvenes, quibus arte benigna
> Et meliore luto finxit præcordia Titan.

(Youths whose breast the Titan moulded with genial art and of a finer clay.)

Juvenal probably refers to the belief expressed by Shakespeare in lines in "Antony and Cleopatra," which Lamb seems to have had in mind. First,

> The fire
> That quickens Nilus' slime.

(Act I., Scene 3, lines 68, 69), and then, "Your serpent of Egypt is bred now of your mud by the operation of your sun" (Act II., Scene 7, line 29).

Page 107, line 25. *Peter Wilkins's island.* See note on page 319.

Page 107, line 26. *Diogenes.* Diogenes, the cynic, carried through Corinth a lighted lantern by day, seeking an honest man.

Page 107, last line. *Bleach.* Illegitimacy, according to some old authors, wears out in the third generation, enabling a natural son's descendant to resume the ancient coat-of-arms. Lamb refers to this sanction.

Page 108, line 1. *Delphic voyages.* That is, the voyages to Delphos to consult the oracle.

Page 108, line 8. *Hare-court.* The Lambs lived at 4 Inner Temple Lane (now rebuilt as Johnson's Buildings) from 1809 to 1817. Writing to Coleridge in June, 1809, Lamb says :—

"The rooms are delicious, and the best look backwards into Hare Court, where there is a pump always going. Hare Court trees come in at the window, so that it's like living in a garden."

Barron Field was entered on the books of the Inner Temple in 1809 and was called to the Bar in 1814.

Page 108, line 17. *"Aye me ! while thee the seas . . ."*

> Let our frail thoughts dally with false surmise.
> Ay me ! whilst thee the shores, and sounding seas
> Wash far away.
>
> *Lycidas*, lines 153-155.

Page 108, line 23. *Sally W——r.* Lamb's Key gives "Sally Winter;" but as to who she was we have no knowledge.

Page 108, line 26. *J. W.* James White. See next essay.

Page 108, line 28. *To greet you, of me, or mine.* In the *London Magazine* was added :—

"Something of home matters I could add ; but *that,* with certain remembrances, never to be omitted, I reserve for the grave postscript to this light epistle ; which postscript, for weighty reasons, justificatory in any court of feeling, I think better omitted in the first edition.

"Elia.

"London, *March* 1, 1822."

———

Page 108. The Praise of Chimney-Sweepers.

London Magazine, May, 1822, where it has a sub-title, "A May-Day Effusion."

This was not Lamb's only literary association with chimney-sweepers. In Vol. I. of this edition, page 154, will be found a sweep in the country that there is good reason to believe is Lamb's work, which appeared in *The Examiner* in 1813. Again, in 1824, James Montgomery, the poet, edited a book—*The Chimney-Sweepers' Friend and Climbing Boys' Album*—with the benevolent purpose of interesting people in the hardships of the climbing boys' life and producing legislation to alleviate it. The first half of the book is practical : reports of committees, and so forth ; the second is sentimental : verses by Bernard Barton, William Lisle Bowles, and many others ; short stories of kidnapped children forced to the horrid business ; and kindred themes. Among the "favourite poets of the day" to whom Montgomery applied were Scott, Wordsworth, Rogers, Moore, Joanna Baillie and Lamb. Lamb replied by copying out (with the alteration of Toddy for Dacre) "The Chimney-Sweeper" from Blake's *Songs of Innocence,* described by Montgomery as "a very rare and curious little work." In that poem it will be remembered the little sweep cries "weep, weep, weep." Lamb compares the cry more prettily to the "peep, peep" of the sparrow.

Page 109, line 9. *Fauces Averni.* "The jaws of hell." From the *Æneid,* VI., 201.

Page 109, line 19. *Stage direction in Macbeth.* See Act IV., Scene 1.

Page 109, line 25. *Kibed.* Chapped or chilblained.

Page 109, line 34. *Shop* . . . Mr. Thomas Read's Saloop Coffee House was at No. 102 Fleet Street.

Page 110, line 13. *Inculcate.* In the *London Magazine* Lamb had written "explicate."

Page 111, line 15. *The March to Finchley.* I have extracted the detail from Hogarth's plate (see opposite page 382).

Page 111, line 25. *To "air" them.*

Iachimo. I beg but leave to air this jewel.
"Cymbeline," Act II., Scene 4, line 96.

Page 111, line 31. *"A sable cloud . . ."*

> Was I deceiv'd, or did a sable cloud
> Turn forth her silver lining on the night?
>
> *Comus*, lines 221-222.

Page 111, line 42. *Rachels.* See Jeremiah xxxi. 15.

Page 111, last line. *The young Montagu.* Edward Wortley Montagu (1713-1776), the traveller, ran away from Westminster School more than once, becoming, among other things, a chimney-sweeper.

Page 112, line 3. *Arundel Castle.* The Sussex seat of the Dukes of Norfolk. The late duke was Charles Howard, eleventh duke, who died in 1815, and who spent enormous sums of money on curiosities. I can find no record of the story of the sweep. Perhaps Lamb invented it, or applied it to Arundel.

Page 112, line 8. *Venus . . . Ascanius.* See the *Æneid*, I., line 696.

Page 112, line 39. *Jem White.* James White (1775-1820), who was at Christ's Hospital with Lamb, and who wrote *Falstaff's Letters*, 1796, in his company (see Vol. I., page 191, and note). "There never was his like," Lamb told another old schoolfellow, Valentine Le Grice, in 1833 ; "we shall never see such days as those in which he flourished." See the essay "On Some of the Old Actors," page 138, for an anecdote of White.

Page 112, at foot. *The fair of St. Bartholomew.* Held on September 3 at Smithfield, until 1855. George Daniel, in his recollections of Lamb, records a visit they paid together to the Fair. Lamb took Wordsworth through its noisy mazes in 1802.

Page 113, line 19. *Bigod.* John Fenwick (see note to "The Two Races of Men," page 325).

Page 113, line 21. *Rochester.* John Wilmot, 2nd Earl of Rochester (1647-1680), Charles II.'s boon companion.

Page 113, line 28. *Whereat the universal host . . .* Lamb here paraphrases three lines of Milton : —

> At which the universal host up sent
> A shout that tore Hell's concave, and beyond
> Frighted the reign of Chaos and old Night.
>
> *Paradise Lost*, I., lines 541-543.

Page 114, line 9. *"Golden lads and lasses . . ."* From the song in "Cymbeline," Act IV., Scene 2, lines 262, 263 :—

> Golden lads and girls all must,
> As chimney-sweepers, come to dust.

Page 114, line 15. *And the glory of Smithfield . . .* It is pointed out by Messrs. Hallward and Hill that in Tom Brown's Letter to George Melnoth is the sentence : "The glory of Smithfield is departed for ever, and love and intrigues have left the cloister; in short, Bartholomew Fair is over."

THE CHIMNEY SWEEPER

Detail of Hogarth's "March to Finchley," from the engraving by T. Cook

Page 114. A COMPLAINT OF THE DECAY OF BEGGARS IN THE METROPOLIS.

London Magazine, June, 1822.

The origin of this essay was the activity at that time of the Society for the Suppression of Mendicity, founded in 1818, of which a Mr. W. H. Bodkin was the Hon. Secretary. The Society's motto was " Benefacta male collocata, malefacta existima;" and it attempted much the same work now performed by the Charity Organisation Society. Perhaps the delight expressed in its annual reports in the exposure of impostors was a shade too hearty—at any rate one can see therein cause sufficient for Lamb's counterblast. Lamb was not the only critic of Mr. Bodkin's zeal. Hood, in the *Odes and Addresses*, published in 1825, included the following remonstrance to Mr. Bodkin. Possibly the Witherington in the sixth stanza is the same man that Lamb describes on page 118 :—

ODE TO H. BODKIN, ESQ., SECRETARY TO THE SOCIETY FOR THE SUPPRESSION OF MENDICITY.

" This is your charge—you shall comprehend all vagrom men."
" Much Ado About Nothing."

* * * *

Oh, when I take my walks abroad,
　How many Poor I *miss!*
Had Doctor Watts walk'd now a days
　He would have written this !

So well thy Vagrant catchers prowl,
　So clear thy caution keeps
The path—O, Bodkin, sure thou hast
　The eye that never sleeps !

No Belisarius pleads for alms,
　No Benbow, lacking legs ;
The pious man in black is now
　The only man that begs !

Street-Handels are disorganiz'd,
　Disbanded every band !—
The silent *scraper* at the door
　Is scarce allow'd to stand !

The Sweeper brushes with his broom,
　The Carstairs with his chalk
Retires,—the Cripple leaves his stand,
　But cannot sell his walk.

The old Wall-blind resigns the wall,
　The Camels hide their humps,
The Witherington without a leg
　Mayn't beg upon his stumps !

Poor Jack is gone, that used to doff
　His batter'd tatter'd hat,
And show his dangling sleeve, alas !
　There seem'd no arm in that !

* * * *

The Society's activity led to a special commission of the House of Commons in 1821 to inquire into the laws relating to vagrants, concerning which Lamb speaks on page 119, the clergyman alluded to being Dr. Henry Butts Owen, of Highgate. The result of the commission was an additional stringency, brought about by Mr. George Chetwynd's bill.

It was this essay, says Hood, which led to his acquaintance with Charles Lamb. After its appearance in the *London Magazine*, of which Hood was then sub-editor, he wrote Lamb a letter on coarse paper purporting to come from a grateful beggar; Lamb did not admit the discovery of the perpetrator of the joke, but soon afterwards Lamb called on Hood when he was ill, and a friendship followed to which we owe Hood's charming recollections of Lamb—among the best that were written of him by any one.

Page 114, line 19. *Alcides.* Hercules.

Page 114, line 23. *Eleventh persecution.* There had been ten historic persecutions of the Christians, under Roman emperors, from Nero to Diocletian.

Page 114, line 26. *" With sighing sent."*

> From haunted spring, and dale
> Edg'd with poplar pale,
> The parting genius is with sighing sent.
> Milton's Hymn " On the Morning of Christ's Nativity," Stanza 20.

Page 114, line 28. *Bellum ad exterminationem.* "War to extermination."

Page 115, line 4. *Dionysius.* This was the second Dionysius, or Dionysius the Younger, tyrant of Sicily, and for a while the pupil of Plato. On losing Syracuse he fled to Corinth and kept a school—in order, said Cicero, to be still a tyrant.

Page 115, line 8. *Belisarius.* A general under Justinian, who after a career of triumph died in neglect, and, it is said, in beggary, passing among the people with the cry, " Date obolum Belisario," " Give Belisarius a coin." Vandyck's picture of Belisarius represents him uttering this appeal.

Page 115, line 11. *The Blind Beggar.* The reference is to the ballad of " The Beggar's Daughter of Bednall Green." The version in the *Percy Reliques* relates the adventures of Henry, Earl of Leicester, the son of Simon de Montfort, who was blinded at the battle of Evesham and left for dead, and thereafter begged his way with his pretty Bessee. In the *London Magazine* Lamb had written " Earl of Flanders," which he altered to " Earl of Cornwall" in *Elia.* The ballad says Earl of Leicester.

Page 115, line 23. *Dear Margaret Newcastle.* One of Lamb's recurring themes of praise (see " The Two Races of Men," page 26, " Mackery End in Hertfordshire," page 76, and " Detached Thoughts on Books and Reading," page 174). " Romancical," according to the *New English Dictionary,* is Lamb's own word. This is the only reference given for it.

Page 115, line 29. *Lear.* See " King Lear," Act III., Scene 4, line 104.

Page 115, line 30. *Answer " mere nature."* It is Timon who uses this phrase :—

> Call the creatures
> Whose naked natures live in all the spite
> Of wreakful heaven, whose bare unhoused trunks,
> To the conflicting elements exposed,
> Answer mere nature.
> " Timon of Athens," Act IV., Scene 3, lines 227-231.

Page 115, line 30. *Cresseid . . . clap-dish.* Chaucer's poem does not refer to Cressida's beggary. In *The Testament of Cresseid* by the Scottish poet Robert Henryson (1430 ?-1506 ?) she goes a-begging with a clapper. In " Twelfth Night " the clown says: "Cressida was a beggar" (Act III., Scene 1, line 62). A clapdish, says Halliwell's

Dictionary of Archaic and Provincial Words, was "a dish or rather box
with a movable lid, carried by beggars in former times to attract notice
by the noise it made and to bring people to their doors." Cresseid's
"other whiteness than beauty" is a reference to her leprosy, mentioned
in Chaucer's *Testament of Cresside*.

Page 115, line 34. *The Lucian wits.* Lamb was probably thinking of
Rabelais. In Book II., Chapter XXX., Epistemon describes Alexander
the Great as occupied in hell mending stockings and Semiramis killing
lice for beggars.

Page 115, line 40. *"True ballad."* "King Cophetua and the
Beggar Maid" is in the *Percy Reliques.* Autolycus in "The Winter's
Tale" (Act IV., Scene 4, line 286) describes his ballad of the mermaid
as "very pitiful and as true."

Page 115, last line. *"Neighbour grice."* A grice, a slip. In the
London Magazine, in a footnote, Lamb gave Timon as the reference :—

> *Timon.*   For every grise of fortune
> Is smooth'd by that below.
> "Timon of Athens," Act IV., Scene 3, lines 16, 17.

Page 115, last line. *Poor rents and comings-in.* Lamb omits
quotation marks, but his mind evidently was upon Henry V.'s question,
"What are thy rents, what are thy comings in?" ("Henry V.," Act
IV., Scene 1, line 260).

Page 116, line 6. *No rascally comparative.* Another Shakespearian
echo :—

> *King.* To laugh at gibing boys and stand the push
> Of every beardless vain comparative.
> "1 Henry IV.," Act III., Scene 2, lines 66, 67.

Page 116, line 23. *Less change than the Quaker's.* In the
London Magazine this sentence then followed : "His coat is coeval
with Adam's."

Page 116, line 26. *In one stay.* In one place. See Spenser's
Faerie Queen, Book VII., Canto 7, stanza 47 :—

> So nothing here long standeth in one stay.

Page 116, line 37. *Spital sermons.* On Monday of Easter week
it was the custom for the Christ's Hospital boys to walk in procession
to the Royal Exchange, and on Tuesday to the Mansion House ; on
each occasion returning with the Lord Mayor to hear a special sermon
—a spital sermon, as it was called—and an anthem. The sermon is
now preached only on Easter Tuesday.

Page 116, line 40. *"Look upon that poor and broken bankrupt
there."* The first Lord, in "As You Like It," quoting Jaques (see
Act II., Scene 1, lines 56, 57).

Page 116, line 42. *Blind Tobits.* See the Book of Tobit, in the
Apocrypha.

Page 117, line 9. *Overseers of St. L——.* Lamb's Key states
that both the overseers and the mild rector were inventions. In the
London Magazine the rector's parish is "P——."

Page 117, line 12. *Vincent Bourne.* See Lamb's essay on Vincent Bourne, Vol. I., page 337, and note. This poem was translated by Lamb himself, and was first published in *The Indicator* for May 3, 1820. See Vol. V. for Lamb's other translations from Bourne.

Page 118, line 27. *A well-known figure.* This beggar I take to be Samuel Horsey, whose portrait, from Kirby's *Wonderful and Scientific Museum*, Vol. I., 1803, will be found on the opposite page. He is there stated to have been known as the King of the Beggars, and a very prominent figure in London. His mutilation is ascribed to the falling of a piece of timber in Bow Lane, Cheapside, some nineteen years before ; but it may have been, as Lamb says, in the Gordon Riots of 1780.

There is the figure of Horsey on his little carriage, with several other of the more notable beggars of the day plying their calling, in an etching of old houses at the corner of Chancery Lane and Fleet Street, made by J. T. Smith in 1789 for his *Ancient Topography of London,* 1815. Smith also gives in his *Vagabondia,* 1817, a back view of Horsey, and says :—

> Of this man there are various opinions ; and it is much to be doubted if the truth can be obtained even from his own mouth. He states that Mr. Abernethy cut off his legs in St. Bartholomew's Hospital, but he does not declare from what cause ; so that being deprived of the power of gaining a subsistence by labour, he was forced to become a beggar. By some persons he is styled the King of Beggars, but certainly without the least foundation. He says that no one has been less acquainted with beggars than himself ; and as for his having the command of a district, that he utterly denies. His walks, or rather movements, are not always confined ; on some days he slides to Charing-Cross, but is oftener to be seen at the door of Mr. Coutts's banking-house, perhaps with an idea that persons, just after they have received money, are more likely to bestow charity.

Smith ends with the following account of one of Horsey's unique accomplishments :—

> Of all other men, Horsey has the most dexterous mode of turning, or rather swinging himself into a gin-shop. He dashes the door open by forcibly striking the front of his sledge and himself against it.

In his *Book for a Rainy Day* John Thomas Smith claims to be a friend of Lamb's, but I do not find him mentioned by Lamb.

Page 118, line 39. *Antæus.* The giant, son of Neptune and Terra, who was renewed in strength every time he touched his mother Earth.

Page 118, line 41. *An Elgin marble.* Lord Elgin's collection of sculpture from the Parthenon and other Athenian temples, brought to England in 1802, was, after being on view in his own house and at Burlington House, bought for the nation in 1816.

Page 118, line 45. *This mandrake.* According to old legend the mandrake, a vegetable which more or less resembles the human figure, shrieks when uprooted.

Page 118, line 49. *Lapithan controversy.* The Lapithæ and the Centaurs fell out at the marriage feast of Pirithous, and after a fierce battle the Lapithæ were victorious.

Page 118, last line. *The os sublime.* See Ovid's remark in the *Metamorphoses,* I., 84-86 :—

SAMUEL HORSEY,
Aged 55.
A Singular Beggar in the Streets of London

Publishd Aug 30. 1803. by. R. S. Kirby. London House Yard & I. Scott. 447. Strand.

From Kirby's "Wonderful and Eccentric Museum"

Pronaque cum spectent animalia cœtera terram,
Os homini sublime dedit, cœlumque videre
Jussit.

(And while the other animals face downwards to the ground, he gave to man an upward-looking visage, and bade him behold the heaven.)

Page 119, line 13. *Lusus . . . Accidentium.* A *lusus naturæ* is a freak of nature, a *lusus accidentium* a freak of chance.

Page 119, line 30. *There was a Yorick.* See note on page 357. See also the quotations on page 399.

Page 119, line 33. *"Age, thou hast lost thy breed."* Possibly an adaptation of Casca's speech:—

Rome, thou hast lost the breed of noble bloods.
"Julius Cæsar," Act I., Scene 2, line 151.

Page 119, line 42. *Blind Bartimeus.* See Mark x. 46.

Page 120, line 26. *Feigned or not.* In the *London Magazine* the essay did not end here. It continued thus:—

"'Pray God your honour relieve me,' said a poor beadswoman to my friend L—— one day; 'I have seen better days.' 'So have I, my good woman,' retorted he, looking up at the welkin which was just then threatening a storm—and the jest (he will have it) was as good to the beggar as a tester.

"It was at all events kinder than consigning her to the stocks, or the parish beadle—

"But L. has a way of viewing things in rather a paradoxical light on some occasions.

"Elia.

"P.S.—My friend Hume (not MP.) has a curious manuscript in his possession, the original draught of the celebrated 'Beggars' Petition' (who cannot say by heart the 'Beggar's Petition?') as it was written by some school usher (as I remember) with corrections interlined from the pen of Oliver Goldsmith. As a specimen of the doctor's improvement, I recollect one most judicious alteration—

"*A pamper'd menial drove me from the door.*

"It stood originally—

"*A livery servant drove me, &c.*

"Here is an instance of poetical or artificial language properly substituted for the phrase of common conversation; against Wordsworth.

"I think I must get H. to send it to the LONDON, as a corollary to the foregoing."

The foregoing passage needs some commentary. Lamb's friend L—— was Lamb himself. He tells the story to Manning in the letter of January 2, 1810.—Lamb's friend Hume was Joseph Hume of the victualling office, Somerset House, to whom letters from Lamb will be found in Mr. W. C. Hazlitt's *Lamb and Hazlitt*, 1900. Hume translated *The Inferno* of Dante into blank verse, 1812.—The "Beggar's Petition," a stock piece for infant recitation a hundred years ago, was a poem beginning thus :—

> Pity the sorrows of a poor old man
> Whose trembling limbs have borne him to your door,
> Whose days are dwindled to the shortest span ;
> Oh give relief, and Heaven will bless your store.

It was written by the Rev. Thomas Moss, of Trentham, in Staffordshire, and was first printed in his *Poems* in 1769. The version there given has "pamper'd menial."

In the reference to Wordsworth Lamb pokes fun at the statement, in his friend's preface to the second edition of *Lyrical Ballads*, that the purpose of that book was to relate or describe incidents and situations from common life as far as possible in a selection of language really used by men.

Lamb's *P.S.* concerning the "Beggar's Petition" was followed in the *London Magazine* by this *N.B. :—*

"N.B. I am glad to see JANUS veering about to the old quarter. I feared he had been rust-bound.

"C. being asked why he did not like Gold's ' London ' as well as ours —it was in poor S.'s time—replied—

> " *—Because there is no* WEATHERCOCK
> *And that's the reason why."*

The explanation of this note is that "Janus Weathercock "—one of the pseudonyms of Thomas Griffiths Wainewright—after a long absence from its pages, had sent to the previous month's *London Magazine*, May, 1822, an amusing letter of criticism of that periodical, commenting on some of its regular contributors. Therein he said: "Clap Elia on the back for such a series of good behaviour."—Who C. is cannot be said ; possibly Lamb, as a joke, intends Coleridge to be indicated ; but poor S. would be John Scott, the first editor of the *London Magazine*, who was killed in a duel. C.'s reply consisted of the last lines of Wordsworth's "Anecdote for Fathers ; or, Falsehood Corrected." Accurately they run :—

> At Kelve there was no weather-cock
> And that's the reason why.

The hero of this poem was a son of Lamb's friend Basil Montagu.

Gold's *London Magazine* was a contemporary of the better known London magazine of the same name. In Vol. III. appeared an article entitled "The Literary Ovation," describing an imaginary dinner-party given by Messrs. Baldwin, Cradock & Joy in February, 1821, at which Lamb was supposed to be present and to sing a song by Webster, one of his old dramatists. Mr. Bertram Dobell conjectures that Wainewright may have written this squib.

The same number of the *London Magazine*—June, 1822—that con-

tained this essay printed also, under the " Lion's Head," the following
notice :—

" Elia assures his pleasant Remembrancer * * * * * that he has
not lost sight of the topic he recommends so warmly. He has only
put it off for a Number or two."

Neither the correspondent nor the topic can now be identified.

Page 120. A DISSERTATION UPON ROAST PIG.
London Magazine, September, 1822.

There has been some discussion as to the origin of the central idea
of this essay. A resemblance is found in a passage in *The Turkish
Spy*, where, after describing the annual burnt-offering of a bull by the
Athenians, *The Spy* continues :—

> In process of time a certain priest, in the midst of his bloody sacrifice, taking up a piece
> of the broiled flesh which had fallen from the altar on the ground, and burning his fingers
> therewith, suddenly clapt them to his mouth to mitigate the pain. But, when he had once
> tasted the sweetness of the fat, not only longed for more of it, but gave a piece to his
> assistant ; and he to others ; who, all pleased with the new-found dainties, fell to eating of
> flesh greedily. And hence this species of gluttony was taught to other mortals.

" Este," a contributor to *Notes and Queries*, June 21, 1884, wrote :—

> A quarto volume of forty-six pages, once in " Charles Lamb's library " (according to a
> pencilled note in the volume) is before me, entitled : *Gli Elogi del Porco, Capitoli Berneschi
> di Tigrinto Bistonio P. A., E. Accademico Ducale de' Dissonanti di Modena. In Modena
> per gli Eredi di Bartolomeo Soliani Stampatori Ducali MDCCLXI. Con Licenza de'
> Superiori*, [wherein] some former owner of the volume has copied out Lamb's prose with
> many exact verbal resemblances from the poem.

It has also been suggested that Porphyry's tract on *Abstinence
from Animal Food*, translated by William Taylor, bears a likeness to
the passage. Taylor's translation, however, was not published till 1823,
some time after Lamb's essay.

These parallels merely go to show that the idea was a commonplace ;
at the same time it is not Lamb, but Manning, who told him the story,
that must declare its origin. Not only in the essay, but in a letter
to Barton in March, 1823, does Lamb express his indebtedness to his
traveller friend. Allsop, indeed, in his *Letters of Coleridge*, claims to
give the Chinese story which Manning lent to Lamb and which produced the " Dissertation." It runs thus :—

> A child, in the early ages, was left alone by its mother in a house in which was a pig. A
> fire took place; the child escaped, the pig was burned. The child scratched and pottered
> amongst the ashes for its pig, which at last it found. All the provisions being burnt, the
> child was very hungry, and not yet having any artificial aids, such as golden ewers and
> damask napkins, began to lick or suck its fingers to free them from the ashes. A piece of
> fat adhered to one of his thumbs, which, being very savoury alike in taste and odour, he
> rightly judged to belong to the pig. Liking it much, he took it to his mother, just then
> appearing, who also tasted it, and both agreed that it was better than fruit or vegetables.
> They rebuilt the house, and the woman, after the fashion of good wives, who, says the
> chronicle, are now very scarce, put a pig into it, and was about to set it on fire, when an old
> man, one whom observation and reflection had made a philosopher, suggested that a pile of
> wood would do as well. (This must have been the father of economists.) The next pig
> was killed before it was roasted, and thus
>
> " From low beginnings,
> We date our winnings."

Manning, by the way, contributed articles on Chinese jests to the *New Monthly Magazine* in 1826.

A preliminary sketch of the second portion of this essay will be found in the letter to Coleridge dated March 9, 1822. See also the letters of Mr. and Mrs. Bruton, January 6, 1823, to Mrs. Collier, November 2, 1824, and to H. Dodwell, October 7, 1827, both in acknowledgment of pigs sent to Lamb probably from an impulse found in this essay.

Later, Lamb abandoned the extreme position here taken. In the little essay entitled "Thoughts on Presents of Game," 1833 (see Vol. I., page 343), he says: "Time was, when Elia . . . preferred to all a roasted pig. But he disclaims all such green-sickness appetites in future." The late Charles Kent, in his centenary edition of Lamb's works, printed these "Thoughts" next the "Dissertation," under the title "A Recantation."

Page 120, ninth line from foot. *Seventy thousand.* An examination of the original MS. of this essay, which has been facsimiled in more than one edition of Lamb, inclines one to think that Lamb wrote "twenty." It is now in America.

Page 120, seventh line from foot. *Confucius.* Here Lamb was inventing.

Page 121, line 29. *He tasted—crackling!* At these words, in the *London Magazine*, came the sentence: "He stood in a posture of idiot wonder."

Page 123, line 15. *Like our Locke.* John Locke, the philosopher (1632-1704), author of the *Essay Concerning the Human Understanding*.

Page 123, lines 29, 30. *Mundus edibilis . . . princeps obsoniorum.* "Of all the delicacies in the whole world of things to eat, I will maintain it to be the most delicate, the chief of tidbits."

Page 123, line 34. *Amor immunditiæ.* "Love of dirt"—an allusion to original sin in the porcine Adam and Eve.

Page 124, line 11. *Radiant jellies—shooting stars.* Messrs. Hallward and Hill have this interesting note: "In Donne's *Eclogues* there is a reference to the superstition that shooting stars left jellies behind them where they fell:—

> " As he that sees a star fall runs apace,
> And finds a jelly in the place."

Mr. W. J. Craig tells me that in Philemon Holland's translation of Pliny, Book XI., Chapter XII., is the suggestion that honey on the leaves at daybreak is "Either a certaine sweat of the skies, or some unctuous jelly proceeding from the stars." The belief is still popular in Ireland that the jelly-like fungoid growth on damp hillsides is caused by shooting stars.

Page 124, line 18. *" Ere sin could blight . . ."* From Coleridge's "Epitaph on an Infant":—

> Ere Sin could blight or Sorrow fade,
> Death came with friendly care;
> The opening bud to Heaven conveyed,
> And bade it blossom there.

Page 124, line 23. *For such a tomb* . . . Lamb probably had in mind the final couplet from Milton's epitaph on Shakespeare :—

> And so sepulchred in such pomp dost lie,
> That kings for such a tomb would wish to die.

Page 124, line 25. *He is the best of Sapors.* This sentence was printed as a quotation of verse in the *London Magazine.* The word sapor is probably from Sir Thomas Browne's vocabulary.

Page 125, line 5. *" Tame villatic fowl."* A phrase from Milton's *Samson Agonistes*, line 1695.

Page 125, line 9. *Like Lear.*

> *Lear (to Regan).* I gave you all.
> "King Lear," Act II., Scene 4, line 253.

Page 125, line 16. *My good old aunt.* Probably Aunt Hetty. See the essay on "Christ's Hospital," page 13, for another story of her. The phrase, "Over London Bridge," unless an invention, suggests that before this aunt went to live with the Lambs—probably not until they left the Temple in 1792—she was living on the Surrey side. But it was possibly an Elian mystification. Lamb had another aunt, but of her we know nothing.

Page 126, line 7. *St. Omer's.* The French Jesuit College. Lamb, it is unnecessary to say, was never there.

Page 126. A BACHELOR'S COMPLAINT OF THE BEHAVIOUR OF MARRIED PEOPLE.

This paper is, by many years, the earliest of the *Elia* essays. It was printed first in *The Reflector*, No. IV., in 1811 or 1812. When Lamb brought his *Works* together, in 1818, he omitted it. In September, 1822, it appeared in the *London Magazine* as one of the reprints of Lamb's earlier writings, of which the "Confessions of a Drunkard" (see Vol. I., page 133, and note) was the first. In that number also appeared the "Dissertation upon Roast Pig" (see page 120), thereby offering the reader an opportunity of comparing Lamb's style in 1811 with his riper and richer style of 1822. The germ of the essay must have been long in Lamb's mind, for we find him writing to Hazlitt in 1805 concerning Mrs. Rickman : "A good-natured woman though, which is as much as you can expect from a friend's wife, whom you got acquainted with as a bachelor."

The essay in *The Reflector* began thus : "Mr. Reflector, I am a single man not quite turned of forty, who have spent . . ." and so forth. There were other slight changes. In *The Reflector* "joke" (page 128, line 4) was "jest." To "Morellas" (page 131, line 40) was this footnote : "I don't know how to spell this word ; I mean Morella cherries." The signature was "Innuptus." When reprinted in the *London Magazine* the letter ended with "Your humble servant, Elia." There are several other small differences.

Page 128, line 27. *" Like as the arrows* . . ." See Psalms cxxvii.

4, 5. They are slightly altered to the words as Lamb gives them, in the Prayer-book.

Page 129, line 5. "*Love me, love my dog.*" See "Popular Fallacies," page 266, for an expansion of this paragraph.

Page 129, line 24. *One daisy differs* . . . A recollection probably of 1 Corinthians xv. 41 : "One star differeth from another star in glory."

Page 130, line 30. "*Decent affection and complacent kindness.*"

> Decent affection and complacent kindness
> Were all I wished for.
>
> Home's "Douglas," Act I., Scene i.

Page 131, line 26. *Oysters.* The *Reflector* added : "which she had opened out of compliment to me."

Page 132. ON SOME OF THE OLD ACTORS.

In February, 1822, Lamb began a series of three articles in the *London Magazine* on "The Old Actors." The second was printed in April and the third in October of the same year. Afterwards, in reprinting them in *Elia*, he rearranged them into the essays, "On Some of the Old Actors," "On the Artificial Comedy of the Last Century," and "On the Acting of Munden," omitting a considerable portion altogether. The essay in its original tripart form will be found in the Appendix to this volume.

In one of his theatrical notices in *The Examiner* (see Vol. I., page 186) Lamb remarks, "Defunct merit comes out upon us strangely," and certain critics believe that he praised some of the old actors beyond their deserts. But no one can regret any such excesses.

Page 132, line 9. *Twelfth Night.* When recalling early playgoing days in "Old China" (page 250), Lamb refers again to this play —Viola in Illyria.

Page 132, lines 15 to 19. *Whitfield, Packer, Benson, Burton, Phillimore* and *Barrymore.* Whitfield, who made his London début as Trueman in "George Barnwell" about 1776, was a useful man at Covent Garden and Drury Lane.—John Hayman Packer (1730-1806), known in Lamb's time for his old men. He acted at Drury Lane until 1805.—Benson, who married a sister of Mrs. Stephen Kemble, wrote one or two plays, and was a good substitute in emergencies. He committed suicide during brain fever in 1796.—Burton was a creditable utility actor at Covent Garden and Drury Lane.—Phillimore filled small parts at Drury Lane.—Barrymore was of higher quality, a favourite character actor both at Drury Lane and the Haymarket.

Page 132, line 22. *Mrs. Jordan.* Mrs. Jordan, born in 1762, ceased to act in England in 1814 and died in 1816. Nell was her famous part, in Coffey's "The Devil to Pay." Miss Hoyden is in Vanbrugh's "Relapse." Lamb is referring to Viola in Act I., Scene 5, and Act II., Scene 4, of "Twelfth Night."

Page 133, line 10. *Mrs. Powel.* Mrs. Powel, previously known

as Mrs. Farmer, and afterwards Mrs. Renaud, was at Drury Lane from
1788 to 1811. She ended her London career in 1816 and died in 1829.

Page 133, line 24. *Of all the actors.* The *London Magazine*
article began at this point (see page 279). Robert Bensley (1738 ?-
1817 ?) was at Drury Lane from 1775 to 1796, when he retired (alter-
nating it with the Haymarket). G. H. Boaden and George Colman
both bear out Lamb's eulogy of Bensley as Malvolio; but otherwise he
is not the subject of much praise.

Page 133, line 30. *Fine madness.* Lamb was perhaps thinking of
Drayton's lines on Marlowe in his poem "To my Friend Henry
Reynolds, of Poets and Poesy" :—

> Of Marlowe, bathed in the Thespian springs,
> Had in him those brave translunary things
> That the first poets had . . .
> For that fine madness still he did retain
> Which rightly should possess a poet's brain.

Page 133, line 30. *Hotspur's . . . rant.* See " 1 Henry IV.,"
Act I., Scene 3, line 201, etc. :—

> By heaven, methinks it were an easy leap
> To pluck bright honour from the pale-faced moon,
> Or dive into the bottom of the deep,
> Where fathom-line could never touch the ground,
> And pluck up drowned honour by the locks.

Page 133, line 31. *Venetian incendiary.* Pierre in Otway's "Venice
Preserved." Lamb appended the passage in a footnote in the *London
Magazine* (see page 279).

Page 134, line 7. *Mine Ancient.* Iago.

Page 134, line 7. *Barren spectators.* See Hamlet's speech to the
players, Act III., Scene 2, line 45.

Page 134, line 23. *Baddeley . . . Parsons . . . John Kemble.*
Robert Baddeley (1733-1794), the husband of Mrs. Baddeley, and the
original Moses in the "School for Scandal." William Parsons (1736-
1795), the original Crabtree in the "School for Scandal," and a favourite
actor of Lamb's. John Philip Kemble (1757-1823), who managed
Drury Lane from 1788 to 1801.

Page 134, line 42. *Of birth and feeling.* In the *London Magazine* a footnote came here (see page 280).

Page 135, line 1. *Length of service.* In the *London Magazine* a
footnote came here (see page 280).

Page 135, line 26. *Consonancy.* Malvolio says of the letter:
"There is no consonancy in the sequel" ("Twelfth Night," Act II.,
Scene 5, line 141).

Page 135, line 28. *House of misrule.* A long passage came here
in the *London Magazine* (see page 281).

Page 135, line 39. *Hero of La Mancha.* Compare a similar
analysis of Don Quixote's character on page 233.

Page 135. *Footnote.* See "Twelfth Night," Act IV., Scene 2,
lines 54-60.

Page 136, line 12. *Hyperion.* The sun.

Page 136, line 14. *" Stand still, ye watches . . ."*

> Stand still, you watches of the element;
> All times and seasons, rest you at a stay,
> That Edward may be still fair England's king!
> Marlowe's " Edward II.," Act V., Scene 1, lines 66, 68.

Page 136, line 22. *Dodd.* James William Dodd (1740 ?-1796).

Page 136, line 23. *Lovegrove.* William Lovegrove (1778-1816), famous in old comedy parts and as Peter Fidget in " The Boarding-House."

Page 136, line 26. *In puris naturalibus.* "Naked."

Page 136, at foot. *The gardens of Gray's Inn.* These gardens are said to have been laid out under the supervision of Bacon, who retained his chambers in the Inn until his death. As Dodd died in 1796 and Lamb wrote in 1822, it would be fully twenty-six years and perhaps more since Lamb met him.

Page 137, lines 21-23. *Foppington, etc.* Foppington in Vanbrugh's " Relapse," Tattle in Congreve's " Love for Love," Backbite in Sheridan's " School for Scandal," Acres in " The Rivals " by the same author, and Fribble in Garrick's " Miss in her Teens."

Page 138, line 1. *" The weeds of Dominic."*

> And they who to be sure of Paradise
> Dying put on the weeds of Dominic.
> *Paradise Lost*, III., lines 478, 479.

Page 138, line 3. *If few can remember.* The praise of Suett that follows is interpolated here from the third part of Lamb's original essay (see page 295). Richard Suett, who had been a Westminster chorister (not St. Paul's), left the stage in June, 1805, and died in July.

Page 138, line 14. *Like Sir John*—Falstaff (see " 1 Henry IV.," Act I., Scene 2, line 213).

Page 138, line 17. *" Commerce with the skies."*

> And looks commercing with the skies.
> Milton, *Il Penseroso*, line 39.

Page 138. *Footnote. Jem White.* See note on page 382.

Page 139, line 2. *His friend Mathews.* Charles Mathews (1776-1835), whom Lamb knew (see note on page 462).

Page 139, line 3. *" Force of nature . . ."* From Dryden's lines on Milton, " Under Mr. Milton's Picture before his ' Paradise Lost.' "

Page 139, line 13. *" Thorough brake . . ."* Robin Goodfellow in the " Midsummer-Night's Dream," Act II., Scene 1.

Page 139, line 21. *Jack Bannister.* John Bannister retired from the stage in 1815. He died in 1836.

Page 139, line 26. *Children in the Wood.* Morton's play, of which Lamb was so fond. It is mentioned again in " Barbara S——" and "Old China."

Page 139, line 27. *As Shakspeare says.*

> Love is too young to know what conscience is.
> Sonnet 151.

Page 139, line 29. *Vesta's days.* Vesta, goddess of fire, who gave her name to the vestal virgins.

Page 139, line 38. *The elder Palmer.* The first part of the essay is here resumed again. The elder Palmer was John Palmer, who died on the stage, in 1798, when playing in "The Stranger." Lamb's remarks tend to confuse him with Gentleman Palmer, who died before Lamb was born. Robert Palmer, John's brother, died about 1805.

Page 139, line 41. *Moody.* John Moody (1727 ?-1812), famous as Teague in "The Committee."

Page 140, lines 4 to 9. *The Duke's Servant, etc.* The Duke's servant in Garrick's "High Life below Stairs," Captain Absolute in Sheridan's "Rivals," Dick Amlet in Vanbrugh's "Confederacy."

Page 140, lines 14, 15. *Young Wilding . . . Joseph Surface.* In Foote's "Liar" and Sheridan's "School for Scandal."

Page 140, line 24. *Ben, in Love for Love.* See Act IV., Scene 6.

Page 141. ON THE ARTIFICIAL COMEDY OF THE LAST CENTURY.

See note to the essay "On Some of the Old Actors," page 392.

See also "A Vision of Horns" (Vol. I., page 254) for, as it seems to me, a whimsical extension to the point of absurdity of the theory expressed in this essay—a theory which Lord Macaulay, in his review of Leigh Hunt's edition of the Dramatic Works of Wycherley, Congreve, etc., in 1840, opposed with characteristic vigour. His comments run thus :—

In the name of art, as well as in the name of virtue, we protest against the principle that the world of pure comedy is one into which no moral enters. If comedy be an imitation, under whatever conventions, of real life, how is it possible that it can have no reference to the great rule which directs life, and to feelings which are called forth by every incident of life? If what Mr. Charles Lamb says were correct, the inference would be that these dramatists did not in the least understand the very first principles of their craft. Pure landscape-painting into which no light or shade enters, pure portrait-painting into which no expression enters, are phrases less at variance with sound criticism than pure comedy into which no moral enters.

But it is not the fact that the world of these dramatists is a world into which no moral enters. Morality constantly enters into that world, a sound morality, and an unsound morality ; the sound morality to be insulted, derided, associated with every thing mean and hateful ; the unsound morality to be set off to every advantage, and inculcated by all methods, direct and indirect. It is not the fact that none of the inhabitants of this conventional world feel reverence for sacred institutions and family ties. Fondlewife, Pinchwife, every person in short of narrow understanding and disgusting manners, expresses that reverence strongly. The heroes and heroines, too, have a moral code of their own, an exceedingly bad one, but not, as Mr. Charles Lamb seems to think, a code existing only in the imagination of dramatists. It is, on the contrary, a code actually received and obeyed by great numbers of people. We need not go to Utopia or Fairyland to find them. They are near at hand. Every night some of them cheat at the hells in the Quadrant, and others pace the Piazza in Covent Garden. Without flying to Nephelococcygia or to the Court of Queen Mab, we can meet with sharpers, bullies, hard-hearted impudent debauchees, and women worthy of such paramours. The morality of the Country Wife and the Old Bachelor is the morality, not, as Mr. Charles Lamb maintains, of an unreal world, but of a world which is a great deal too real. It is the morality, not of a chaotic people, but of low town-rakes, and of those ladies whom the newspapers call "dashing Cyprians." And the question is simply this, whether a man of genius who constantly and systematically endeavours to make this sort of character attractive, by uniting it with beauty, grace, dignity, spirit, a high social position, popularity, literature, wit, taste, knowledge of the world, brilliant success in every undertaking, does or does not make an ill use of his powers. We own that we are unable to understand how this question can be answered in any way but one.

Hartley Coleridge, in a letter to Edward Moxon concerning Leigh Hunt's edition of Wycherley and Congreve, happily remarked, as Canon Ainger points out: "Nothing more or better can be said in defence of these writers than what Lamb has said in his delightful essay . . . which is, after all, rather an apology for the audiences who applauded and himself who delighted in their plays, than for the plays themselves. . . . But Lamb always took things by the better handle."

Page 142, line 14. *Make assurance double.*

> But yet I'll make assurance double sure,
> And take a bond of fate.
> "Macbeth," Act IV., Scene 1, lines 83, 84.

Page 142, line 21. *Alsatia.* A certain district, forming a sanctuary for debtors, in the precinct of Whitefriars, was called Alsatia. It took its name probably from Alsace. In Scott's *Fortunes of Nigel* it is described. The right of sanctuary was withdrawn in 1697. Shadwell wrote a play on the subject, "The Squire of Alsatia."

Page 142, line 24. *We bark like foolish dogs.* Mr. W. J. Craig traces the phrase to George Chapman's "Eugenia," Induction to Vigil II. :—

> Country dogs that mock men's daily cark,
> And after then all night at shadows bark.

Page 142, line 35. *"Secret shades . . ."* From *Il Penseroso*, lines 28-30.

Page 143, line 5. *Catos of the pit.* From Cato, the Roman Censor.

Page 143, line 10. *A Swedenborgian bad spirit.* According to the system of Emmanuel Swedenborg there are three heavens and three hells, these peopled by good spirits, those by evil.

Page 143, line 13. *The Fainalls, etc.* Fainall in Congreve's "Way of the World," Mirabel in Farquhar's "Inconstant," Dorimant in Etheredge's "Man of Mode," and Lady Touchstone in Congreve's "Double Dealer."

Page 143, line 28. *Angelica.* In "Love for Love."

Page 143, line 42. *The impertinent Goshen.* See note on page 320.

Page 144, lines 18, 19. *Sir Simon, etc.* All these characters are in Wycherley's "Love in a Wood."

Page 144, line 24. *An Atlantis.* Bacon's *Atlantis* was the account of an island in the Atlantic inhabited by a people who lived strictly according to moral laws.

Page 145, line 25. *Carrington Bowles.* Carington Bowles, the print publisher of 69 St. Paul's Churchyard (see note on page 528 of Vol. I. ; see also Vol. V., page 309).

Page 146, line 2. *King.* Thomas King (1730-1805), at one time manager of Drury Lane, the original Sir Peter Teazle, on May 8, 1777, the first night of the "School for Scandal," and the most famous actor in the part until he retired in 1802.

Page 146, line 31. *Asps or amphisbænas.* A recollection of Milton's line :—

Scorpion and Asp, and Amphisbæna dire.
Paradise Lost, X., line 524.

Page 146, line 34. *Miss Pope.* Jane Pope (1742-1818), the original Mrs. Candour, left the stage in 1808.

Page 147, line 2. *Manager's comedy.* Sheridan was manager of Drury Lane when the "School for Scandal" was produced.

Page 147, lines 2, 3. *Miss Farren . . . Mrs. Abingdon.* Elizabeth Farren, afterwards Countess of Derby, played Lady Teazle for the last time in 1797. Mrs. Abingdon had retired from Drury Lane in 1782.

Page 147, line 6. *Smith.* "Gentleman" Smith took his farewell of the stage, as Charles Surface, in 1788.

Page 147, last line. "*Lidless dragon eyes.*" From Coleridge's "Ode on the Departing Year," Stanza VIII.

Page 147, same line. *Fashionable tragedy.* See page 291 for the continuation of this essay in the *London Magazine*.

———

Page 148. ON THE ACTING OF MUNDEN.

See note to the essay "On Some of the Old Actors," page 392. Lamb lifted this essay into the *London Magazine* from *The Examiner*, where it had appeared on November 7 and 8, 1819, with slight changes. At the end Lamb wrote, in reference to Talfourd (see Vol. I., page 532, where a portion of Talfourd's article is printed) :—

"This faint sketch we beg to be taken as a mere corollary to some admirable strictures on the character of this great performer, in a paper signed T. N. T. which appeared some months back in the *Champion*. *Non tam certandi cupidus quam te imitari aveo.*" [My desire is not to rival ; I am eager to take example by you.]

Other original readings, worthy of note, were Emery for Farley at the beginning of the third paragraph, and, in the last, after "as if some Arabian Night were being acted before him" the words "or as if *Thalaba* were no tale."

Page 148. *Title. Munden.* Joseph Shepherd Munden (1758-1832) acted at Covent Garden practically continuously from 1790 to 1811. He moved to Drury Lane in 1813, and remained there till the end. His farewell performance was on May 31, 1824. See Vol. I., page 378, for a description of it, by Lamb or another. See also Vol. I., pages 268 and 341, for other Munden papers. We know Lamb to have met Munden from Raymond's *Memoirs of Elliston* (see note on page 413).

Page 148, line 3. *Cockletop.* In O'Keeffe's farce "Modern Antiques." This farce is no longer played, although a skilful hand might, I think, make it attractive to our audiences. Barry Cornwall in his memoir of Lamb has a passage concerning Munden as Cockletop, which helps to support Lamb's praise. Support is not necessary, but useful; it is one of the misfortunes of the actor's calling that he can live only in the praise of his critics.

In the Drama of "Modern Antiques," especially, space was allowed him for his movements. The words were nothing. The prosperity of the piece depended exclusively on the genius of the actor. Munden enacted the part of an old man credulous beyond ordinary credulity; and when he came upon the stage there was in him an almost sublime look of wonder, passing over the scene and people around him, and settling apparently somewhere beyond the moon. What he believed in, improbable as it was to mere terrestrial visions, you at once conceived to be quite possible,—to be true. The sceptical idiots of the play pretend to give him a phial nearly full of water. He is assured that this contains Cleopatra's tear. Well; who can disprove it? Munden evidently recognised it. "What a large tear!" he exclaimed. Then they place in his hands a druidical harp, which to vulgar eyes might resemble a modern gridiron. He touches the chords gently: "pipes to the spirit ditties of no tone;" and you imagine Æolian strains. At last, William Tell's cap is produced. The people who affect to cheat him, apparently cut the rim from a modern hat, and place the scull-cap in his hands; and then begins the almost finest piece of acting that I ever witnessed. Munden accepts the accredited cap of Tell, with confusion and reverence. He places it slowly and solemnly on his head, growing taller in the act of crowning himself. Soon he swells into the heroic size; a great archer; and enters upon his dreadful task. He weighs the arrow carefully; he tries the tension of the bow, the elasticity of the string; and finally, after a most deliberate aim, he permits the arrow to fly, and looks forward at the same time with intense anxiety. You hear the twang, you see the hero's knitted forehead, his eagerness; you tremble;—at last you mark his calmer brow, his relaxing smile, and are satisfied that the son is saved!—It is difficult to paint in words this extraordinary performance, which I have several times seen; but you feel that it is transcendent. You think of Sagittarius, in the broad circle of the Zodiac; you recollect that archery is as old as Genesis; you are reminded that Ishmael, the son of Hagar, wandered about the Judæan deserts and became an archer.

Page 148, line 9. *" There the antic sate . . ."*

There the antic sits
Scoffing his state and grinning at his pomp.
"Richard II.," Act III., Scene 2, lines 162, 163.

Page 148, line 24. *Edwin.* This would probably be John Edwin the Elder (1749-1790). But John Edwin the Younger (1768-1805) might have been meant. He was well known in Nipperkin, one of Munden's parts.

Page 148, line 29. *Farley . . . Knight . . . Liston.* Charles Farley (1771-1859), mainly known as the deviser of Covent Garden pantomimes (see page 448); Edward Knight (1774-1826), an eccentric little comedian; John Liston (1776 ?-1846), whose mock biography Lamb wrote (see Vol. I., page 248). In his paper (if it be his) on Munden's farewell Lamb speaks of his "bouquet of faces."

Page 148, line 39. *Suett.* See note on page 394.

Page 149, line 1. *Sir Christopher Curry . . . Old Dornton.* Sir Christopher in "Inkle and Yarico," by the younger Colman; Old Dornton in Holcroft's "Road to Ruin."

Page 149, line 11. *Fight with his own shadow—"SESSA".* Probably a recollection of "King Lear" where Edgar speaks of coursing his own shadow (Act III., Scene 4, line 58), and again cries, "Dolphin, my boy, my boy, sessa! let him trot by"—line 104. Sessa is an interjection. In "The Taming of the Shrew" we have, "Let the world slide, sessa!"

Page 149, line 12. *The Cobbler of Preston.* A play, founded on "The Taming of the Shrew," by Charles Johnson, written in 1716.

To John Forster Esqr
A Legacy from Elia ,

THE LAST ESSAYS

OF

ELIA.

BEING

A SEQUEL TO ESSAYS PUBLISHED UNDER THAT NAME

———◆———

LONDON :
EDWARD MOXON, DOVER STREET.
1833.

Page 149, line 21. *Fuseli.* Henry Fuseli, the painter (1741-1825).

THE LAST ESSAYS OF ELIA.

Page 151. PREFACE.

London Magazine, January, 1823, where it was entitled "A Character of the late Elia. By a Friend." Signed Phil-Elia. Lamb did not reprint it for ten years, and then with certain omissions.

In the *London Magazine* the "Character" began thus :—

"A CHARACTER OF THE LATE ELIA

" BY A FRIEND

"This gentleman, who for some months past had been in a declining way, hath at length paid his final tribute to nature. He just lived long enough (it was what he wished) to see his papers collected into a volume. The pages of the LONDON MAGAZINE will henceforth know him no more.

"Exactly at twelve last night his queer spirit departed, and the bells of Saint Bride's rang him out with the old year. The mournful vibrations were caught in the dining-room of his friends T. and H. ; and the company, assembled there to welcome in another First of January, checked their carousals in mid-mirth and were silent. Janus wept. The gentle P——r, in a whisper, signified his intention of devoting an Elegy ; and Allan C——, nobly forgetful of his countrymen's wrongs, vowed a Memoir to his *manes,* full and friendly as a Tale of Lyddal-cross."

Elia had just been published when this paper appeared, and it was probably Lamb's serious intention to stop the series. He was, however, prevailed to continue. T. and H. were Taylor & Hessey (see page 302), the owners of the *London Magazine.* Janus was Janus Weathercock, Thomas Griffiths Wainewright ; P——r was Bryan Waller Procter, or Barry Cornwall, who afterwards wrote Lamb's life, and Allan C—— was Allan Cunningham, who called himself "Nalla" in the *London Magazine.* "The Twelve Tales of Lyddal Cross" ran serially in the magazine in 1822.

Page 151, line 21. *A former Essay.* In the *London Magazine* "his third essay," referring to "Christ's Hospital Five and Thirty Years Ago" (page 12).

Page 152, line 1. *My late friend.* The opening sentences of this paragraph seem to have been deliberately modelled, as indeed is the whole essay, upon Sterne's character of Yorick in *Tristram Shandy,* Vol. I., Chapter XI. Compare the following description of Yorick :—

But, in plain truth, he was a man unhackneyed and unpractised in the world, and was altogether as indiscreet and foolish on every other subject of discourse where policy is wont to impress restraint. Yorick had no impression but one, and that was what arose from the nature of the deed spoken of ; which impression he would usually translate into plain English, without any periphrasis ;—and too oft without much distinction or either person, time, or place ; so that when mention was made of a pitiful or an ungenerous proceeding—he never gave himself a moment's time to reflect who was the hero of the piece,—what his station,—or how far he had power to hurt him hereafter ;—but if it was a dirty action,—without more ado,—The man was a dirty fellow,—and so on. And as his comments had usually the ill fate to be terminated either in a *bon mot*, or to be enlivened throughout with some drollery or humour of expression, it gave wings to Yorick's indiscretion. In a word, though he never sought, yet, at the same time, as he seldom shunned, occasions of saying what came uppermost, and without much ceremony—he had but too many temptations in life of scattering his wit and his humour, his gibes and his jests, about him.—They were not lost for want of gathering.

Mr. Percy Fitzgerald first drew attention to this parallel.

Page 152, line 23. *It was hit or miss with him.* Canon Ainger has pointed out that Lamb's description of himself in company is corroborated by Hazlitt in his essay " On Coffee-House Politicians " :—

> I will, however, admit that the said Elia is the worst company in the world in bad company, if it be granted me that in good company he is nearly the best that can be. He is one of those of whom it may be said, *Tell me your company, and I'll tell you your manners.* He is the creature of sympathy, and makes good whatever opinion you seem to entertain of him. He cannot outgo the apprehensions of the circle ; and invariably acts up or down to the point of refinement or vulgarity at which they pitch him. He appears to take a pleasure in exaggerating the prejudices of strangers against him ; a pride in confirming the prepossessions of friends. In whatever scale of intellect he is placed, he is as lively or as stupid as the rest can be for their lives. If you think him odd and ridiculous, he becomes more and more so every minute, *à la folie*, till he is a wonder gazed at by all—set him against a good wit and a ready apprehension, and he brightens more and more . . .

P. G. Patmore's testimony is also corroborative :—

> To those who did not know him, or, knowing, did not or could not appreciate him, Lamb often passed for something between an imbecile, a brute, and a buffoon ; and the first impression he made on ordinary people was always unfavourable—sometimes to a violent and repulsive degree.

Page 152, line 29. *His companions.* See the " Letter to Southey," Vol. I., page 229, for a list of many of Lamb's friends.

Page 153, line 27. *Toga virilis.* " Garb of manhood."

Page 153, line 30. *Some of his writings.* In the *London Magazine* the essay did not end here. It continued :—

" He left little property behind him. Of course, the little that is left (chiefly in India bonds) devolves upon his cousin Bridget. A few critical dissertations were found in his escritoire, which have been handed over to the Editor of this Magazine, in which it is to be hoped they will shortly appear, retaining his accustomed signature.

" He has himself not obscurely hinted that his employment lay in a public office. The gentlemen in the Export department of the East India House will forgive me, if I acknowledge the readiness with which they assisted me in the retrieval of his few manuscripts. They pointed out in a most obliging manner the desk, at which he had been planted for forty years ; showed me ponderous tomes of figures, in his own remarkably neat hand, which, more properly than his few printed tracts, might be called his ' Works.' They seemed affectionate to his memory, and universally commended his expertness in book-keeping. It seems he was the inventor of some ledger, which should combine the precision and certainty of the Italian double entry (I think they called it) with the brevity and facility of some newer German system— but I am not able to appreciate the worth of the discovery. I have often heard him express a warm regard for his associates in office, and how fortunate he considered himself in having his lot thrown in amongst them. There is more sense, more discourse, more shrewd- ness, and even talent, among these clerks (he would say) than in twice the number of authors by profession that I have conversed with. He would brighten up sometimes upon the 'old days of the India House,' when he consorted with Woodroffe, and Wissett, and Peter Corbet (a descendant and worthy representative, bating the point of sanctity, of old facetious Bishop Corbet), and Hoole who translated Tasso, and Bartlemy Brown whose father (God assoil him therefore) modernised Walton—and sly warm-hearted old Jack Cole (King Cole they called him in those days), and Campe, and Fombelle—and a world of choice spirits, more than I can remember to name, who associated in those days with Jack Burrell (the *bon vivant* of the South Sea House), and little Eyton (said to be a *facsimile* of Pope—he was a miniature of a gentleman) that was cashier under him, and Dan Voight of the Custom House that left the famous library.

"Well, Elia is gone—for aught I know, to be reunited with them— and these poor traces of his pen are all we have to show for it. How little survives of the wordiest authors! Of all they said or did in their lifetime, a few glittering words only! His Essays found some favourers, as they appeared separately; they shuffled their way in the crowd well enough singly; how they will *read*, now they are brought together, is a question for the publishers, who have thus ventured to draw out into one piece his 'weaved-up follies.'

"PHIL-ELIA."

This passage calls for some remark. Cousin Bridget was, of course, Mary Lamb.—Lamb repeated the joke about his *Works* in his "Auto-biography " (see Vol. I., page 320) and in "The Superannuated Man " (see page 197).—Some record of certain of the old clerks mentioned by Lamb still remains; but I can find nothing of the others. Whether or not Peter Corbet really derived from the Bishop we do not know, but the facetious Bishop Corbet was Richard Corbet (1582-1635), Bishop of Oxford and Norwich, whose conviviality was famous and who wrote the "Fairies' Farewell." John Hoole (1727-1803), who translated Tasso and wrote the life of Scott of Amwell and a number of other works, was principal auditor at the end of his time at the India House. He retired about 1785, when Lamb was ten years old. Writing to Coleridge on January 5, 1797, Lamb speaks of Hoole as "the great boast and ornament of the India House," and says that he found Tasso, in Hoole's translation, "more vapid than smallest small beer sun-vinegared." The moderniser of Walton would be Moses Browne (1704-1787), whose edition of *The Complete Angler*, 1750, was undertaken at the suggestion of Dr. Johnson. The phrase "weaved-up follies" is Shakespeare's :—

> *King.*   Must I ravel out
> My weaved-up folly?
>   "Richard II.," Act IV., Scene 1, lines 228, 229.

Under the title of "The Lion's Head" in the *London Magazine* for the same month, January, 1823, the editor wrote :—

Elia is dead !—at least so a *Friend* says ; but if he be dead, we have seen him in one of those hours "when he is wont to walk;" and his *ghostship* has promised us very *material* assistance in our future Numbers. We were greatly tempted to put the Irish question to him of "Why did you die?"—But as we know how very unusual a thing it is for a gentleman to give his reasons for such a step, we resisted the temptation. Mercy on us !—we hope we are wrong,—but we have our shadowy suspicions, that Elia, poor gentleman ! has not been honestly dealt by. Mercutio was killed by one Will Shakespeare, a poacher, though his death was laid to other hands ;—and Sir Roger De Coverley (a gentleman more near our own time) perished under very mysterious circumstances. We could lay our finger upon the very man we suspect as being guilty of Elia's death ! Elia's ghost, however, cannot sleep in its grave, for it has been constantly with us since his death, and vows it must still write for its peace of mind. Indeed, the first paper in our present Number is one of its *grave* consolations.

We may safely assume Hood to have written this. The paper referred to was "Rejoicings on the New Year's Coming of Age" (see page 235).

Elia's death was in fact a joke with the *London Magazine* staff for some little while. In addition to the editor's note and Lamb's own obituary notice, the January number had a farewell article from Janus Weathercock containing these passages :—

And first, then, for JOHN CLARE ; for *first* doth he stand in the sixth volume. "Princely Clare," as Elia would call thee, some three hours after the cloth was drawn.—Alas ! good Clare, never again shall thou and he engage in those high combats, those wit-fights ! Never shall his companionable draught cause thee an after-look of anxiety into the tankard ! —no more shall he, pleasantly malicious, make thy ears tingle, and thy cheeks glow, with the sound of that perplexing constrainment ! that conventional gagging-bill !—that Grammar ! ! till in the bitterness of thy heart thou cursedst Lindley Murray by all the stars. —Not once again shall thy sweetly-simple Doric phrase and accent beget the odious *pun*. Thou mayest imbibe thy ale in peace, and defy Priscian unducked,—For Priscian's champion is gone—Elia is gone !—Little didst thou think that evening would be the last, when thou and I, and two or three more, Messer Brunetto, Dugdale Redivivus, T——, that anthery Cicero, parted with the humanity-loving Elia beneath the chaste beams of the watery moon, warmed with his hearty cheer—the fragrant steam of his "*great plant*,"—his savoury conversation, and the genuine good nature of his cousin Bridget gilding all. There was something solemn in the manner of our clasping palms,—it was first "hands round," then "hands across."—That same party shall never meet again !—But pardon, gracious Spirit ! that I thus, but parenthetically, memorize thee—yet a few more lines shall flow to thy most embalmed remembrance. Rest then awhile ! . . .

But ELIA's ghost is impatient.

Yet what can I say of thee more than all know? that thou hadst the gaiety of a boy, with the knowledge of a man ;—as gentle a heart as ever sent tears to the eyes.— Marry ! the great bile would sometimes slip over his tongue's tip ; then would he spit it out, and look more sweetly for the riddance.—How wittily would he mistake your meaning, and put in a conceit most seasonably out of season!—His talk without affectation was compressed, like his beloved Elizabethans, even unto obscurity;—like grains of fine gold, his sentences would beat out into whole sheets. I say, "without affectation," for he was not the blind-brained man to censure in others his own vice.—Truly "without affectation," for nothing rubbed him the wrong way so much as *pretence ;*—then the sparks flew about!—Yet, though he would strip and whip soundly such beggars in velvet rags, the thong never flew in the face of a wise moderation to do her any hurt.[1] He had small mercy on spurious fame; and a caustic observation on *the fashion for men of genius* (vulgarly so termed) was a standing dish :—he contended that several of our minor talents, who now emulate Byron, Coleridge, and the old Dramatists, had, fifty years ago, rested contented satellites to old Sylvanus Urban—tranquil imitators of Johnson and Goldsmith. One of these flaunting, arrogant ephemera was particularly odious to him—(in one species of his scribbling he resembleth a gilt chimney-sweeper—in another a blow-fly;—this is my remark). Sometimes would he defame, "after a sort," his printed (not painted) mistresses.

> " As perplexed lovers use
> At a need, when in despair,
> To paint forth their fairest fair ;
> Or in part but to express
> That exceeding comeliness
> Which their fancies doth so strike,
> They borrow language of dislike.
>
> .   .   .   .
>
> " No other way they know
> A contentment to express,
> Borders so upon excess,
> That they do not rightly wot
> Whether it be pain or not.   " *Farewell to Tobacco.*"

Sir Thomas Brown was a "bosom cronie" of his—so was Burton, and old Fuller. In his amorous vein he dallied with that peerless Duchess of many-folio odour ;—and with the hey-day comedies of Beaumont and Fletcher he induced light dreams. He would deliver critical touches on these like one inspired; but it was good to let him choose his own game :—if another began, even on the acknowledged pets, he was liable to interrupt —or rather append, in a mode difficult to define, whether as misapprehensive or mischievous. One night, at C——'s, the above dramatic partners were the temporary subject of chat. Mr. * * * commended the passion and haughty style of a tragedy (I don't know which of them), but was instantly taken up by Elia; who told him, " *That* was nothing,—the lyrics were the high things—the lyrics!"—and so having stricken * * * with some amaze—he concluded with a brief intense eulogy on the "Little Thief!" [Beaumont and Fletcher's "Night Walker"].

He had likewise two perversities—a dislike to all German literature,—by which language he was, I *believe*, scrupulously intact ;—the other was a most vehement assertion of equality between Harrington and Fairfax, as translators.—Venial aberrations! I know of no others.

His death was somewhat sudden; yet he was not without wormy forebodings. Some of these he expressed, as you may recollect, Dear Proprietor! at your hospitable table, the —— of last ——. I accompanied him home at rather an early hour in the morning, and being benignantly invited to enter, I entered. His smoking materials were ready on the table,— I cannot smoke, and therefore, during the exhaustion of a pipe, I soothed my nerves with a single tumbler of * * * and water. He recurred several times to his sensation of approaching death—not gloomily—but as a retirement from business,—a pleasant journey to a sunnier climate. The serene solemnity of his voice overcame me ;—the tears poured thick from their well-heads—I tried to rally myself and him—but my throat swelled—and stopped my words.

His pipe had gone out—he held it to the flame of the candle—but in vain.

It was empty!—his mind had been wandering. He smiled placidly and knocked out the ashes—"even so silently," said he, "may my fiery spark steal from its vehicle of ashes and clay!"

I felt oppressed—many things had contributed lately to break and daunt my once elastic spirit.—I rose to go—he shook me by the hand ;—neither of us spoke—with that I went my way—*and I saw him no more!*—

How much is lost to this miserable world—which knew him not while it possessed him ! —I knew him—I, who am left to weep.—Eheu! Elian! Vale!

[1] Somewhere in Fuller.

It should perhaps be explained that John Clare was the poet (1793-1864), a rustic by birth, who came to London and, exploited by Octavius Gilchrist, was taken up by the *London Magazine* and made rather too much of, for he contracted an unfortunate liking for genial company. His wood notes are very sweet, but he wrote too copiously and with too little anxiety for an immortal. Among his poems is a pleasant sonnet to Charles Lamb. In a poetical epistle by Charles Abraham Elton to John Clare in the *London Magazine* for August, 1824, is this couplet, referring to Lamb :—

> Does Agnus fling his crotchets wild,
> In wit a man, in heart a child?

Messer Brunetto was H. F. Cary (1772-1844), the translator of Dante, afterwards a closer friend of Lamb's. Dugdale Redivivus and T——, the Anthery Cicero, I do not identify with certainty.

In February's *London Magazine* the joke cropped up again. Under the title, "The Literary Police Office, Bow Street," appeared an amusing skit on the leading authors of the day, each of whom was supposed to be brought before the magistrates for some offence : William Wordsworth for stealing a pony from a Mrs. Foy of Westmoreland ; Samuel Taylor Coleridge for idling and sleeping at Highgate in the daytime and being unable to give a satisfactory account of himself; Lord Byron, "a young person, apparently of ferocious habits," for having assaulted several literary gentlemen ; and so forth. Among them was Charles Lamb. The report ran thus :—

CHARLES LAMB was brought up, charged with the barbarous murder of the late Mr. Elia. He was taken late in the evening, at a house of resort for characters of his description, in Fleet-street—and he had with him at the time of his caption a crape mask—a phosphorus (or hock) bottle—a dark lanthorn—a *skeleton* key—a centre bit (out of the haunch)—and a large clasp knife (and fork). The evidence was indisputable—and Mr. Lamb was committed. There appears to have been no apparent motive for this horrible murder, unless the prisoner had an eye to poor Mr. Elia's situation in the LONDON MAGAZINE. The prisoner is a large gaunt-looking fellow, with a queer eye, and a broad overhanging brow. If no witnesses had come forward—his looks would *have appeared against him !*

The writer of this pasquinade was John Hamilton Reynolds (1796-1852), Hood's brother-in-law, and, later, his collaborator in the *Odes and Addresses,* who wrote in the *London Magazine* over the signature Edward Herbert.

The same number of the *London Magazine* contained Bernard Barton's sonnet to Elia :—

> Delightful Author !—unto whom I owe
>   Moments and moods of fancy and of feeling
> Afresh to grateful Memory now appealing,
> Fain would I " bless thee—ere I let thee go! "
> From month to month has the exhaustless flow
>   Of thy original mind, its wealth revealing,
>   With quaintest humour, and deep pathos healing
> The world's rude wounds, revived Life's early glow :
> And, mixt with this, at times, to earnest thought
>   Glimpses of truth, most simple and sublime,

By thy imagination have been brought
Over my spirit.   From the olden time
Of Authorship thy Patent should be dated,
And thou with Marvell, Browne, and Burton, mated.

In the number for March, 1823, under "The Lion's Head," was this further announcement :—

Elia is *not* dead !—We thought as much—and even hinted our thought in the number for January. The following letter declaring Elia's existence is in his own handwriting, and was left by his own hand.   We never saw a man so extremely alive, as he was, to the injury done him :—

"Elia returns his thanks to the facetious Janus Weathercock, who, during his late unavoidable excursion to the Isles of Sark, Guernsey and Jersey, took advantage of his absence to plot a sham account of his death ; and to impose upon the town a posthumous Essay, signed by his Ghost—which, how like it is to any of the undoubted Essays of the author, may be seen by comparing it with his volume just published.   One or two former papers, with his signature, which are not re-printed in the volume, he has reason to believe were pleasant forgeries by the same ingenious hand."

This was, of course, a joke of Lamb's, for Wainewright had nothing to do with the essay named—"Rejoicings on the New Year's Coming of Age."   Nor did Lamb visit the Channel Islands.

The list of "Books lately published" in the January number of the magazine contained an announcement of *Elia*, in one volume, post 8vo, 9s. 6d.

———

Page 153.   BLAKESMOOR IN H——SHIRE.
London Magazine, September, 1824.

With this essay Lamb made his reappearance in the magazine, after eight months' absence.

By Blakesmoor Lamb meant Blakesware, the manor-house near Widford, in Hertfordshire, where his grandmother, Mary Field, had been housekeeper for many years.   Compare the essay "Dream-Children," page 100.

Blakesware, which was built by Sir Francis Leventhorpe about 1640, became the property of the Plumers in 1683, being then purchased by John Plumer, of New Windsor, who died in 1718.   It descended to William Plumer, M.P. for Yarmouth, in the Isle of Wight, and afterwards for Hertfordshire, who died in 1767, and was presumably Mrs. Field's first employer.   His widow and the younger children remained at Blakesware until Mrs. Plumer's death in 1778, but the eldest son, William Plumer, moved at once to Gilston, a few miles east of Blakesware, a mansion which for a long time was confused with Blakesware by commentators on Lamb.   This William Plumer, who was M.P. for Lewes, for Hertfordshire, and finally for Higham Ferrers, and a governor of Christ's Hospital, kept up Blakesware after his mother's death in 1778 (when Lamb was three) exactly as before, but it remained empty save for Mrs. Field and the servants under her. Mrs. Field became thus practically mistress of it, as Lamb says in "Dream-Children." Hence the increased happiness of her grandchildren when they visited her. Mrs. Field died in 1792, when Lamb was seventeen.

William Plumer died in 1822, aged eighty-six, having apparently arranged with his widow, who continued at Gilston, that Blakesware should be pulled down—a work of demolition which at once was begun. This lady, *née* Jane Hamilton, afterwards married a Mr. Lewin, and then, in 1828, Robert Ward (1765-1846), author of *Tremaine* and other novels, who took the name of Plumer-Ward, and may be read of, together with curious details of Gilston House, in P. G. Patmore's *My Friends and Acquaintances.*

Nothing now remains of Lamb's Blakesware, of which a picture is given on the opposite page, but a few mounds, beneath which are bricks and rubble. The present house, the seat of Sir Martin Gosselin, is a

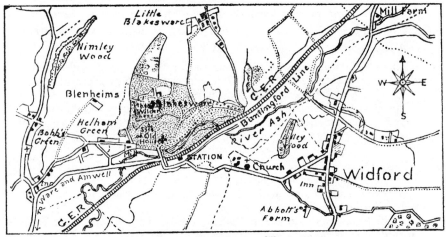

MAP OF BLAKESWARE AND WIDFORD

quarter of a mile behind the old one, high on the hill. In Lamb's day this hillside was known as the Wilderness, and where now is turf were formal walks with clipped yew hedges and here and there a statue. The stream of which he speaks is the Ashe, running close by the walls of the old house. Standing there now, among the trees which mark its site, it is easy to reconstruct the past as described in the essay. The above map of Blakesware and Widford has been prepared for me by Miss M. C. G. Jackson.

The Twelve Cæsars, the tapestry and other more notable possessions of Blakesware, although moved to Gilston on the demolition of Blakesware, are there no longer, and their present destination is a mystery. Gilston was pulled down in 1853, following upon a sale by auction, when all its treasures were dispersed. Some, I have discovered, were bought by the enterprising tenant of the old Rye House Inn at Broxbourne, but absolute identification of anything now seems impossible.

BLAKEWARE ABOUT 1795

From a drawing in the possession of Mrs. Geo. Nunn of Hertford

Blakesware is again described in *Mrs. Leicester's School*, in Mary Lamb's story of "The Young Mahometan" (see Vol. III.). There the Twelve Cæsars are spoken of as hanging on the wall, as if they were medallions; but Mr. E. S. Bowlby tells me that he perfectly remembers the Twelve Cæsars at Gilston, about 1850, as busts, just as Lamb says. In "Rosamund Gray" (see Vol. I., page 25) Lamb describes the Blakesware wilderness. See also notes to "The Last Peach," Vol. I., page 501, to "Dream-Children" in this volume, page 377, and to "Going or Gone," Vol. V., page 319.

Lamb has other references to Blakesware and the irrevocability of his happiness there as a child, in his letters. Writing to Southey on October 31, 1799, he says :—

"Dear Southey,—I have but just got your letter, being returned from Herts, where I have passed a few red-letter days with much pleasure. I would describe the county to you, as you have done by Devonshire; but alas! I am a poor pen at that same. I could tell you of an old house with a tapestry bedroom, the 'Judgment of Solomon' composing one pannel, and 'Actæon spying Diana naked' the other. I could tell of an old marble hall, with Hogarth's prints, and the Roman Cæsars in marble hung round. I could tell of a *wilderness*, and of a village church, and where the bones of my honoured grandam lie; but there are feelings which refuse to be translated, sulky aborigines, which will not be naturalised in another soil. Of this nature are old family faces, and scenes of infancy."

And again, to Bernard Barton, in August, 1827 :—

"You have well described your old-fashioned grand paternall Hall. Is it not odd that every one's earliest recollections are of some such place. I had my Blakesware (Blakesmoor in the 'London'). Nothing fills a child's mind like a large old Mansion . . . better if un- or partially-occupied; peopled with the spirits of deceased members of the County and Justices of the Quorum. Would I were buried in the peopled solitude of one, with my feelings at 7 years old!

"Those marble busts of the Emperors, they seem'd as if they were to stand for ever, as they had stood from the living days of Rome, in that old Marble Hall, and I to partake of their permanency; Eternity was, while I thought not of Time. But he thought of me, and they are toppled down, and corn covers the spot of the noble old Dwelling and its princely gardens. I feel like a grasshopper that chirping about the grounds escaped his scythe only by my littleness. Ev'n now he is whetting one of his smallest razors to clean wipe me out, perhaps. Well!"

Writing to Barton in August, 1824, concerning the present essay, Lamb describes it as a "futile effort . . . 'wrung from me with slow pain'."

Page 155, lines 2-6. *Ovid.* The *Metamorphoses* relate (Book III.) how Actæon, for daring to behold Diana and her attendants bathing, was changed to a stag and hunted to death. In Book VI. we have the story of Marsyas, who challenged Apollo to a contest of musical skill, the winner to flay the loser, and Apollo won.

Page 155, line 7. *Mrs. Battle.* There was a haunted room at Blakesware, but the suggestion that the famous Mrs. Battle (see page 333) died in it was probably due to a sudden whimsical impulse. Lamb states in "Dream-Children" that Mrs. Field occupied this room.

Page 155, line 34. *Garden-loving poet.* Andrew Marvell again. From the poem "Upon Appleton House." The punctuation in Grosart's edition, 1872, differs considerably.

Page 156, line 22. "*Resurgam.*" This was not the motto of the Plumers.

Page 156, line 32. *Damœtas . . . Ægon.* In a letter to Coleridge in 1796 Lamb supplies the meaning of Damœtas: a modern shepherd, one that keeps other people's sheep. Ægon is the name for a shepherd in Virgil's *Eclogues* and in Theocritus.

Page 156, line 33. *The hills of Lincoln.* See Lamb's sonnet "On the Family Name," Vol. V., page 41. Lamb's father came from Lincoln.

Page 156, at foot. *Those old W——s.* Lamb thus disguised the name of Plumer. He could not have meant Wards, for Robert Ward did not marry William Plumer's widow till four years after this essay was printed.

Page 157, line 1. *Gone over.* In the *London Magazine* Lamb had written "traversed."

Page 157, line 7. *Yellow H——shire hair.* Hertfordshire. I cannot find that yellow hair is common in this county. It is in Norfolk—a Scandinavian legacy—but Lamb is not here, as in "Dream-Children" (see page 377), endeavouring to confuse these counties.

Page 157, line 8. *My Alice.* See note on page 377.

Page 157, line 9. *Mildred Elia, I take it.* After these words, in the *London Magazine*, came this passage :—

"From her, and from my passion for her—for I first learned love from a picture—Bridget took the hint of those pretty whimsical lines, which thou mayst see, if haply thou hast never seen them, Reader, in the margin.[1] But my Mildred grew not old, like the imaginary Helen."

[1] "High-born Helen, round your dwelling,
  These twenty years I've paced in vain :
Haughty beauty, thy lover's duty
  Hath been to glory in his pain.

"High-born Helen, proudly telling
  Stories of thy cold disdain ;
I starve, I die, now you comply,
  And I no longer can complain.

"These twenty years I've lived on tears,
  Dwelling for ever on a frown ;

On sighs I've fed, your scorn my bread;
I perish now you kind are grown.

" Can I, who loved my beloved
  But for the scorn ' was in her eye,'
Can I be moved for my beloved,
  When she returns me sigh for sigh?

" In stately pride, by my bedside,
  High-born Helen's portrait hung;
Deaf to my praise, my mournful lays
  Are nightly to the portrait sung.

" To that I weep, nor ever sleep,
  Complaining all night long to her.—
Helen, grown old, no longer cold,
  Said—' you to all men I prefer.' "

This ballad, written in gentle ridicule of Lamb's affection for the Blakesware portrait, and Mary Lamb's first known poem, was printed in the *John Woodvil* volume, 1802, and in the *Works*, 1818.

———

Page 157. POOR RELATIONS.
London Magazine, May, 1823.
Page 158, line 5. *A death's head at your banquet.* Referring to the Egyptian custom of carrying a skeleton through the room at a feast to remind the feasters of their necessary end.
Page 158, line 6. *Agathocles' pot.* The father of Agathocles, tyrant of Syracuse, was a potter.
Page 158, line 6. *Mordecai . . . Lazarus.* See Esther iii. 2 and Luke xvi. 20.
Page 158, line 7. *A lion . . . a frog . . . a fly.* See 1 Kings xiii. 24; Exodus viii. 3, 6; Ecclesiastes x. 1.
Page 158, line 8. *A mote . . .* See Matthew vii. 3.
Page 158, line 9. *The one thing not needful.* See Luke x. 42.
Page 158, line 10. *The hail in harvest.* Possibly a reference to Proverbs xxvi. 1.
Page 158, line 10. *A pound of sweet.* After these words, in the *London Magazine*, came one more descriptive clause—"the bore *par excellence.*"
Page 158, line 30. *Tide-waiter.* A custom-house officer who boards vessels as the tide brings them into port.
Page 159, line 28. *Aliquando sufflaminandus erat.* "It was necessary to put the drag on sometimes." "Tanta illi erat velocitas orationis ut vitium fieret. Itaque D. Augustus optime dixit *Aterius noster sufflaminandus est*" (Seneca). "Such was his rapidity of speech that it passed into a defect. And so Augustus of blessed memory well observed, ' *Our friend Aterius needs the drag.*'"
Page 159, line 37. *Richard Amlet, Esq.* In "The Confederacy" by Sir John Vanbrugh—a favourite part of John Palmer's (see the essay "On Some of the Old Actors," page 140).
Page 160, line 2. *Poor W——.* In the Key Lamb identifies

W—— with Favell, who "left Cambridge because he was asham'd of his father, who was a house-painter there." Favell has already been mentioned in the essay on "Christ's Hospital" (see page 22 and note).

Page 160, line 12. *Our tallness.* Lamb was diminutive.

Page 160, line 21. *Nessian venom.* Hercules was killed by wearing a shirt, or tunic, soaked in the poisonous blood of the Centaur Nessus.

Page 160, line 22. *Latimer . . . Hooker.* Latimer was a servitor at Christ's College, Cambridge ; Hooker at Corpus Christi College, Oxford.

Page 161, line 17. *"Knew his mounted sign . . ."* Adapted from Milton. In *Paradise Lost*, Book IV., a battle between Satan and the angelic squadron is averted by the display in the heavens of the golden scales, with Satan in the lighter one. Gabriel bids Satan look up and read his lot in the celestial sign :—

> The Fiend lookt up and knew
> His mounted scale aloft : nor more ; but fled
> Murmuring.
>
> Lines 1013-1015.

Page 161, line 40. *At Lincoln.* The Lambs, as we have seen, came from Lincolnshire. The old feud between the Above and Below Boys seems now to have abated, but a social gulf between the two divisions of the city remains.

Page 162, line 12. *Young Grotiuses.* Among the works of Hugo Grotius (1583-1645) was *De Jure Belli et Pacis.*

Page 162, line 30. *My aunt.* See note on page 355.

Page 162, line 39. *John Billet.* Probably not the real name. Lamb gives the innkeeper at Widford, in "Rosamund Gray," the name of Billet, when it was really Clemitson.

Page 163. STAGE ILLUSION.

London Magazine, August, 1825, where it was entitled "Imperfect Dramatic Illusion."

This was, I think, Lamb's last contribution to the *London*, which had been growing steadily heavier and less hospitable to gaiety. Some one, however, contributed to it from time to time papers more or less in the Elian manner. There had been one in July, 1825, on the Widow Fairlop, a lady akin to "The Gentle Giantess." In September, 1825, was an essay entitled "The Sorrows of ** *** " (an ass), which might, both from style and sympathy, be almost Lamb's ; but was, I think, by another hand. And in January, 1826, there was an article on whist, with quotations from Mrs. Battle, deliberately derived from her creator. These and other essays are printed in Mr. Bertram Dobell's *Sidelights on Charles Lamb*, 1903, with interesting comments.

The present essay to some extent continues the subject treated of in "The Artificial Comedy," page 141, but it may be taken also as containing some of the matter of the promised continuation of the essay "On the Tragedies of Shakspeare," which was to deal with the comic characters of that dramatist (see Vol. I., page 414).

Page 163, line 28. *Jack Bannister.* See note on page 394. His greatest parts were not those of cowards ; but his Bob Acres was justly famous. Sir Anthony Absolute and Tony Lumpkin were perhaps his chief triumphs. He left the stage in 1815.

Page 164, line 25. *Gatty.* Henry Gattie (1774-1844), famous for old-man parts, notably Monsieur Morbleu in Moncrieff's "Monsieur Tonson." He was also the best Dr. Caius, in "The Merry Wives of Windsor," of his time. He left the stage in 1833, and settled down as a tobacconist and raconteur at Oxford.

Page 164, line 30. *Mr. Emery.* John Emery (1777-1822), the best impersonator of countrymen in his day. Zekiel Homespun in Colman's "Heir at Law" was one of his great parts. Tyke was in Morton's "School of Reform," produced in 1805, and no one has ever played it so well. He also played Caliban with success.

Page 165, line 11. *Osric.* In "Hamlet."

Page 165, line 31. *A very judicious actor.* This actor I have not identified. Benjamin Wrench (1778-1843) was a dashing comedian, a Wyndham of his day. In "Free and Easy" he played Sir John Freeman.

Page 166. To THE SHADE OF ELLISTON.

Englishman's Magazine, August, 1831, where it formed, with the following essay, one article, under the title "Reminiscences of Elliston."

Robert William Elliston (1774-1831), actor and manager, famous for his stage lovers, both in comedy and tragedy. His Charles Surface was said to be unequalled, and both in Hotspur and Hamlet he was great. His last performance was in June, 1831, a very short time before his death.

Page 166, line 5. WILD OATS. A reference to O'Keeffe's comedy of that name, in which Elliston played Rover.

Page 166, line 15. *Palace of Dainty Devices.* There is an Elizabethan poetical miscellany entitled *The Paradise of Dainty Devices*, 1576.

Page 166, line 25. "*Up thither . . .*" Milton's lines (*Paradise Lost*, III., 445-458) run :—

> Up hither like aerial vapours flew
> Of all things transitory and vain, when sin
> With vanity had fill'd the works of men :
> Both all things vain, and all who on vain things
> Built their fond hopes of glory or lasting fame,
> Or happiness in this or th' other life ;
> All who have their reward on earth, the fruits
> Of painful superstition and blind zeal,
> Nought seeking but the praise of men, here find
> Fit retribution, empty as their deeds ;
> All th' unaccomplished works of Nature's hand,
> Abortive, monstrous, or unkindly mixt,
> Dissolv'd on Earth, fleet hither, and in vain,
> Till final dissolution, wander here.

Something of the same idea was expressed by Lamb eighteen years earlier in the prologue to Coleridge's *Remorse* (Vol. V., page 125).

Page 166, line 33. *Thy Regent Planet.* Alluding to Elliston's eccentricities and follies.

Page 166, line 38. *Thin ghosts.* In the *London Magazine* the passage ran :—

"Thin ghosts of Figurantes (never plump on earth) admire, while with uplifted toe retributive you inflict vengeance incorporeal upon the shadowy rear of obnoxious author, just arrived :—

> 'what *seem'd* his tail
> The likeness of a kingly kick had on.
>
> . . .
>
> Yet soon he heals : for spirits, that live throughout
> Vital in every part, not as frail man
> In entrails, head, or heart, liver or veins,
> Can in the liquid texture mortal wound
> Receive no more, than can the liquid air,
> All heart they live, all head, all eye.'"

The first quotation is an adaptation of *Paradise Lost*, II., lines 672-673 :—

> what seem'd his head
> The likeness of a kingly crown had on.

The second is from *Paradise Lost*, VI., lines 344-350.

Page 166, line 38. *Fye on sinful Phantasy.* See this song in "The Merry Wives of Windsor," Act V., Scene 5.

Page 167, line 18. *À la Foppington.* In Vanbrugh's "Relapse."

Page 167, line 20. *Old Thracian Harper.* Orpheus, who charmed Charon to sleep by the music of his lyre.

Page 167, line 22. *Pura et puta anima.* "A pure and clear soul."

Page 167, line 30. *Rhadamanthus.* One of the judges of hell. His brothers were Minos and Farpeda.

Page 167, line 39. *Medusean ringlets.* Medusa's locks were changed by Minerva into serpents.

Page 167, line 39. "*Whip the offending Adam . . .*"

> Consideration, like an angel, came
> And whipp'd the offending Adam out of him.
> "Henry V.," Act I., Scene 1, lines 28, 29.

In the *Englishman's Magazine* the article ended, after "Plaudito, et Valeto" ("I praise and say farewell"), with : "Thy friend upon Earth, though thou did'st connive at his d———n."

The article was signed Mr. H., the point being that Elliston had played Mr. H. at Drury Lane in Lamb's unlucky farce of that name in 1806.

———

Page 168. ELLISTONIANA.
See note at the head of "To the Shade of Elliston" above.

Page 168, line 4. *My first introduction.* This paragraph was a footnote in the *Englishman's Magazine.* Elliston, according to the *Memoirs* of him by George Raymond, which have Lamb's phrase, "Joyousest of once embodied spirits" for motto, opened a circulating library at Leamington in the name of his sons William and Henry, and served there himself at times.

Possibly Lamb was visiting Charles Chambers at Leamington when he saw Elliston. That he did see him there we know from Raymond's book, where an amusing occurrence is described, illustrating Munden's frugality. It seems that Lamb, Elliston and Munden drove together to Warwick Castle. On returning Munden stopped the carriage just outside Leamington, on the pretext that he had to make a call on an old friend—a regular device, as Elliston explained, to avoid being present at the inn when the hire of the carriage was paid.

Page 168, line 18. *Lovelace.* See Richardson's *Clarissa Harlowe*, Letter CXXIII. Lovelace also sold sixpennyworth of snuff.

Page 168, line 24. *To descant upon his merits.* Before these words, in the *Englishman's Magazine*, came this sentence :—

"The anecdotes which I have to tell of him are trivial, save in as much as they may elucidate character."

Page 168, line 29. *Wrench.* See note on page 411. Wrench succeeded Elliston at Bath, and played in the same parts, and with something of the same manner.

Page 169, line 5. *Appelles . . . G. D.* Apelles, painter to Alexander the Great, was said to let no day pass without experimenting with his pencil. G. D. was George Dyer, whom we first met in "Oxford in the Vacation."

Page 169, line 20. *Ranger.* In Hoadley's "Suspicious Husband," one of Elliston's great parts.

Page 169, line 39. *Cibber.* Colley Cibber (1671-1757), the actor, who was a very vain man, created the part of Foppington in 1697— his first great success.

Page 169, line 41. *Ben Jonson.* In "Timber; or, Discoveries Made upon Men and Matter." Lamb does not quote verbatim.

Page 170, line 9. *St. Dunstan's . . . punctual giants.* Old St. Dunstan Church, in Fleet Street, had huge figures which struck the hours, and which disappeared with the church, pulled down to make room for the present one some time before 1831. They are mentioned in Emily Barton's story in *Mrs. Leicester's School* (see Vol. III.). Moxon records that Lamb shed tears when the figures were taken away.

Page 170, line 14. *Drury Lane.* Drury Lane opened, under Elliston's management, on October 4, 1819, with "Wild Oats," in which he played Rover. He left the theatre, a bankrupt, in 1826.

Page 170, line 20. *The consular exile.* Marius, in B.C. 88. See Plutarch's Life of him.

Page 170, line 21. *A more illustrious exile.* Napoleon.

Page 170, line 26. *The . . . Olympic.* Lamb is wrong in his dates. Elliston's tenancy of the Olympic preceded his reign at Drury Lane. It was to the Surrey that he retired after the Drury Lane period, producing there Jerrold's "Black-Eyed Susan" in 1829.

Page 170, line 38. *Sir A—— C——.* Sir Anthony Carlisle (see note on page 352).

Page 170, at foot. *"Highest heaven."*

> So Jove usurping reign'd : these first in Crete
> And Ida known, thence on the snowy top
> Of cold Olympus rul'd the middle air
> Their highest heaven.
>
> *Paradise Lost*, I., lines 514-517.

Page 171, line 9. *A Vestris.* Madame Vestris (1797-1856), the great comédienne, who was one of Elliston's stars at Drury Lane.

Page 171, line 21. *The son of Peleus.* Achilles (see the beginning of Book XXI. of the *Iliad*).

Page 172, line 3. *Latinity.* Elliston was buried in St. John's Church, Waterloo Road, and a marble slab with a Latin inscription by Nicholas Torre, his son-in-law, is on thé wall. Elliston was the nephew of Dr. Elliston, Master of Sidney College, Cambridge, who sent him to St. Paul's School—not, however, that founded by Colet—but to St. Paul's School, Covent Garden. He was intended for the church.

Page 172. DETACHED THOUGHTS ON BOOKS AND READING.

London Magazine, July, 1822, where, at the end, were the words, "To be continued;" but Lamb did not return to the topic.

For some curious reason Lamb passed over this essay when collecting *Elia* for the press. It was not republished till 1833, in the *Last Essays*.

Page 172. *Motto. The Relapse.* The comedy by Sir John Vanbrugh. Lamb liked this quotation. He uses it in his letter about William Wordsworth, junior, to Dorothy Wordsworth, November 25, 1819 ; and again in his "Reminiscence of Sir Jeffery Dunstan" (see Vol. I., page 313).

Page 172, line 25. *Shaftesbury.* The 3rd Earl of Shaftesbury (1671-1713), author of the *Characteristics* (see the essay on "The Genteel Style in Writing," page 199).

Page 172, line 26. *Jonathan Wild. The Life of Jonathan Wild the Great* by Fielding.

Page 172, line 26. *I can read any thing which I call a book.* Writing to Wordsworth in August, 1815, Lamb says : "What any man can write, surely I may read."

Page 172, line 30. *Pocket Books.* In the *London Magazine* Lamb added in parenthesis "the literary excepted," the reference being to the *Literary Pocket Book* which Leigh Hunt brought out annually from 1819 to 1822.

Page 172, lines 32, 33. *Hume . . . Jenyns.* Hume would be David Hume (1711-1776), the philosopher and historian of England ; Edward Gibbon (1737-1794), historian of Rome ; William Robertson, D.D., (1721-1793), historian of America, Charles V., Scotland and India ; James Beattie (1735-1803), author of "The Minstrel" and a number of essays, who had, however, one recommendation to Lamb, of which Lamb may have been unaware—he loved Vincent Bourne's poems and was one of the first to praise them ; and Soame Jenyns (1704-1787), author of *The Art of Dancing,* and the *Inquiry into Evil* which Johnson reviewed so mercilessly. It is stated in Moore's *Diary,* according to Procter, that Lamb "excluded from his library Robertson, Gibbon and Hume, and made instead a collection of the works of the heroes of *The Dunciad.*"

Page 172, line 35. *Josephus.* Author of *Jewish Antiquities* and *The History of the Jewish War.*

Page 172, line 35. *Paley.* William Paley (1743-1805), the author of *Moral Philosophy, Horæ Paulinæ* and *Christian Evidences.*

Page 173, line 5. "*Seem its leaves.*" Possibly an adaptation of the description of "that other shape" in *Paradise Lost,* II., 672-673, quoted on page 412.

Page 173, line 5. *Population Essay.* That was the day of population essays. Malthus' *Essay on Population,* 1798, had led to a number of replies.

Page 173, line 6. *A Steele, or a Farquhar.* Sir Richard Steele (1672-1729), of *The Tatler* and *Spectator,* and author of "The Funeral," a comedy which Lamb mentions in his early essay on "Burial Societies" (Vol. I., page 92), and George Farquhar (1678-1707), the author of "The Beaux' Stratagem" and other merry plays.

Page 173, line 6. *Adam Smith.* Adam Smith (1723-1790), the Political Economist—author of *The Wealth of Nations.*

Page 173, line 7. *Encyclopædias.* The *Encyclopædia Anglicana* and *The Encyclopædia Metropolitana* were great authorities at the beginning of the nineteenth century.

Page 173, lines 10, 11. *Paracelsus . . . Raymund Lully.* As nothing by either of these alchemists and philosophers was in the sale of Lamb's books, I cannot say what editions of their many works he possessed. For Raymond Lully see note on page 342. Paracelsus was a German doctor (1493-1541), a Professor at Basle, who wrote of medicine, the elixir of life and mysticism. His real name was Theophrastus Bombast von Hohenheim. Lamb added after "Lully," in the *London Magazine,* "I have them both, reader."

Page 173, line 13. *My ragged veterans.* Crabb Robinson recorded in his diary that Lamb had the "finest collection of shabby books" he ever saw ; "such a number of first-rate works in very bad condition is, I think, nowhere to be found." Leigh Hunt stated in his essay on "My Books" in *The Literary Examiner,* July 5, 1823, that Lamb's library had

an handsome contempt for appearance. It looks like what it is, a selection made at precious intervals from the book-stalls ;—now a Chaucer at nine and twopence ; now a Montaigne or a Sir Thomas Browne at two shillings ; now a Jeremy Taylor, a Spinoza ; an old English Dramatist, Prior, and Sir Philip Sidney ; and the books are "neat as imported." The very perusal of the backs is a "discipline of humanity." There Mr. Southey takes his place again with an old Radical friend : there Jeremy Collier is at peace with Dryden : there the lion, Martin Luther, lies down with the Quaker lamb, Sewel : there Guzman d'Alfarache thinks himself fit company for Sir Charles Grandison, and has his claims admitted. Even the "high fantastical" Duchess of Newcastle, with her laurel on her head, is received with grave honours, and not the less for declining to trouble herself with the constitutions of her maids.

It is in the same essay that Leigh Hunt mentions that he once saw Lamb kiss an old folio—Chapman's Homer—the work he paraphrased for children under the title *The Adventures of Ulysses.*

Page 173, line 34. *Lethean cup.* Lethe, one of the rivers of hell whose waters conferred forgetfulness.

Page 173, line 41. *"Eterne."*

> *Lady Macbeth.* But in them nature's copy's not eterne.
>> "Macbeth," Act III., Scene 2, line 38.

Page 173, at foot. *"We know not where . . ."*

> *Othello.* I know not where is that Promethean heat
> That can thy light relume.
>> "Othello," Act V., Scene 2, lines 12, 13.

Page 174, line 1. *Life of the Duke of Newcastle.* Lamb's copy, a folio containing also the "Philosophical Letters," is in America (see note on page 327).

Page 174, line 6. *Sydney, Bishop Taylor, Milton . . .* I cannot say where are Lamb's copies of Sydney and Fuller; but the British Museum has his Milton, rich in MS. notes, a two-volume edition, 1751. The Taylor, which Lamb acquired in 1798, is the 1678 folio *Sermons.* I cannot say where it now is.

Page 174, line 11. *Shakspeare.* Lamb's Shakespeare was not sold at the sale of his library; only a copy of the *Poems,* 12mo, 1714. His annotated copy of the *Poems,* 1640, is in America. There is a reference to one of Rowe's plates in the essay "My First Play" (see page 98 and plate opposite page 378). The Shakespeare gallery engravings were the costly series of illustrations to Shakespeare commissioned by John Boydell (1719-1804), Lord Mayor of London in 1790. The pictures were exhibited in the Shakespeare Gallery in Pall Mall, and the engravings were published in 1802.

After the word "Shakespeare," in the *London Magazine,* came the sentence : "You cannot make a *pet* book of an author whom everybody reads."

In an unpublished letter to Wordsworth, February 1, 1806, Lamb says : "Shakespear is one of the last books one should like to give up, perhaps the one just before the Dying Service in a large Prayer book." In the same letter he says of binding : "The Law Robe I have ever thought as comely and gentlemanly a garb as a Book would wish to wear."

Page 174, line 19. *Beaumont and Fletcher.* See note on page 328 for an account of Lamb's copy, now in the British Museum.

Page 174, line 21. *No sympathy with them.* After these words, in the *London Magazine,* came, "nor with Mr. Gifford's Ben Jonson." This edition by Lamb's old enemy, William Gifford, editor of the *Quarterly,* was published in 1816. Lamb's copy of Ben Jonson was dated 1692, folio. It is now in America, I believe.

Page 174, line 24. *The reprint of the Anatomy of Melancholy.* This reprint was, I think, published in 1800, in two volumes, marked ninth edition. Lamb's copy was dated 1621, quarto. I do not know where it now is.

Page 174, line 28. *Malone.* This was Edmund Malone (1741-1812), the critic and editor of Shakespeare, who in 1793 persuaded the Vicar of Stratford-on-Avon to whitewash the coloured bust of the poet in the chancel. A *Gentleman's Magazine* epigrammatist, sharing Lamb's view, wrote :—

> Stranger, to whom this monument is shown,
> Invoke the poet's curse upon Malone;
> Whose meddling zeal his barbarous taste betrays,
> And daubs his tombstone, as he mars his plays.

Lamb has been less than fair to Malone. To defend his action in the matter of the bust of Shakespeare is impossible, except by saying that he acted in good faith and according to the fashion of his time. But he did great service to the fame of Shakespeare and thus to English literature, and was fearless and shrewd in his denunciation of the impostor Ireland.

Page 175, line 3. *The Fairy Queen.* Lamb's copy was a folio, 1617, 12, 17, 13. Against Canto XI., Stanza 32, he has written : " Dear Venom, this is the stave I wot of. I will maintain it against any in the book."

Page 175, line 4. *Bishop Andrewes.* Lancelot Andrewes, Bishop of Winchester (1555-1626).

Page 175, line 31. *Nando's.* A coffee-house in Fleet Street, at the east corner of Inner Temple Lane, and thus at one time close to Lamb's rooms.

Page 175, line 33. *" The Chronicle is in hand, Sir."* In the *London Magazine* the following paragraph was here inserted :—

" As in these little Diurnals I generally skip the Foreign News, the Debates—and the Politics—I find the Morning Herald by far the most entertaining of them. It is an agreeable miscellany, rather than a newspaper."

The *Morning Herald,* under Alexander Chalmers, had given more attention to social gossip than to affairs of State ; but under Thomas Wright it suddenly, about the time of Lamb's essay, became politically serious and left aristocratic matters to the *Morning Post.*

Page 175, line 37. *Town and Country Magazine.* This magazine flourished between 1769 and 1792.

Page 175, line 42. *Poor Tobin.* Possibly John Tobin (1770-1804), the playwright, though I think not. More probably the Tobin mentioned in Lamb's letter to Wordsworth about " Mr. H." in June, 1806 (two years after John Tobin's death), to whom Lamb read the manager's letter concerning the farce. This would be James, John Tobin's brother (see note on page 318).

Page 176, line 2. *Candide.* Voltaire's satire.

Page 176, line 5. *Her Cythera.* Cythera was a Grecian island sacred to Venus.

Page 176, line 5. *Pamela.* Richardson's novel—*Pamela; or, Virtue Rewarded,* 1740.

Page 176, line 17. *Skinner's-street.* Skinner's Street, projected by Alderman Skinner, was built in 1802. It ran from Newgate to Holborn Bridge, occupying (except for its gradient) the site of that part of Holborn Viaduct which now lies between Newgate Street and the viaduct proper over Farringdon Street. At No. 41 Mrs. William Godwin had established her Juvenile Library, which put forth the Lambs' books for children. Skinner Street wholly disappeared in 1867, when the Holborn Viaduct was begun.

Page 176, line 19. *Lardner.* Nathaniel Lardner (1684-1768), the Unitarian theologian, whose great work was *On the Credibility of Gospel History.*

Page 176, line 23. *The five points.* The five points of doctrine of the Calvinists, namely, Original Sin, Predestination, Irresistible Grace, Particular Redemption and the Final Perseverance of the Saints. After these words came, in the *London Magazine*, the following paragraph :—

" I was once amused—there is a pleasure in *affecting* affectation—at the indignation of a crowd that was justling in with me at the pit-door of Covent Garden theatre, to have a sight of Master Betty—then at once in his dawn and his meridian—in Hamlet. I had been invited quite unexpectedly to join a party, whom I met near the door of the playhouse, and I happened to have in my hand a large octavo of Johnson and Steevens's Shakspeare, which, the time not admitting of my carrying it home, of course went with me to the theatre. Just in the very heat and pressure of the doors opening—the *rush*, as they term it—I deliberately held the volume over my head, open at the scene in which the young Roscius had been most cried up, and quietly read by the lamp-light. The clamour became universal. ' The affectation of the fellow,' cried one. ' Look at that gentleman *reading*, papa,' squeaked a young lady, who in her admiration of the novelty almost forgot her fears. I read on. ' He ought to have his book knocked out of his hand,' exclaimed a pursy cit, whose arms were too fast pinioned to his side to suffer him to execute his kind intention. Still I read on—and, till the time came to pay my money, kept as unmoved, as Saint Antony at his Holy Offices, with the satyrs, apes, and hobgoblins, mopping, and making mouths at him, in the picture, while the good man sits undisturbed at the sight, as if he were sole tenant of the desart.—The individual rabble (I recognised more than one of their ugly faces), had damned a slight piece of mine but a few nights before, and I was determined the culprits should not a second time put me out of countenance."

Master Betty was William Henry West Betty (1791-1874), known as the "Young Roscius," whose Hamlet and Douglas sent playgoers wild in 1804-5-6. Pitt, indeed, once adjourned the House in order that his Hamlet might be witnessed. His most cried-up scenes in "Hamlet" were the "To be or not to be" soliloquy, and the fencing scene before the king and his mother. The piece of Lamb's own which had been hissed was, of course, "Mr. H.," produced on December 10, 1806; but very likely he added this reference as a symmetrical afterthought, for he would probably have visited Master Betty much earlier in his career, that phenomenon's first appearance at Covent Garden being two years before the advent of Hogsflesh.

Page 176, line 32. *"Snatch a fearful joy."* From Gray's "Ode on a Distant Prospect of Eton College."

Page 176, line 32. *Martin B——.* Martin Charles Burney, son of Admiral Burney, and a lifelong friend of the Lambs—to whom Lamb dedicated the prose part of his *Works* in 1818 (see Vol. V., page 42, and note).

Page 176, at foot. *A quaint poetess.* Mary Lamb. The poem is in *Poetry for Children*, 1809 (see Vol. III. of this edition). In line 17 the word "then" has been inserted by Lamb. The punctuation also differs from that of the *Poetry for Children*.

Page 177. THE OLD MARGATE HOY.

London Magazine, July, 1823. This, like others of Lamb's essays, was translated into French and published in the *Revue Britannique* in 1833. It was prefaced by the remark: "L'auteur de cette délicieuse esquisse est Charles Lamb, connu sous le nom d'Eliah."

Page 177, line 15. *I have said so before.* See "Oxford in the Vacation," page 8.

Page 177, line 18. *My beloved Thames.* Lamb describes a riparian holiday at and about Richmond in a letter to Robert Lloyd in 1804.

Page 177, line 22. *Worthing . . .* There is no record of the Lambs' sojourn at Worthing or Eastbourne. They were at Brighton in 1817, and Mary Lamb at any rate enjoyed walking on the Downs there; in a letter to Miss Wordsworth of November 21, 1817, she described them as little mountains, *almost as good as* Westmoreland scenery. They were at Hastings—at 13 Standgate Street—in 1823 (see Lamb's letters to Bernard Barton, July 10, 1823, to Hood, August 10, 1824, and to Dibdin, June, 1826). The only evidence that we have of Lamb knowing Worthing is his "Mr. H." That play turns upon the name Hogsflesh, afterwards changed to Bacon. The two chief innkeepers at Worthing at the end of the eighteenth century and the beginning of its prosperity were named Hogsflesh and Bacon, and there was a rhyme concerning them which was well known (see notes to "Mr. H." in Vol. V.).

Page 177, line 24. *Many years ago.* A little later Lamb says he was then fifteen. This would make the year 1790. It was probably on this visit to Margate that Lamb conceived the idea of his sonnet, "O, I could laugh," which Coleridge admired so much (see Vol. V., page 4).

Page 177, line 29. *Thou old Margate Hoy.* This old sailing-boat gave way to a steam-boat, the *Thames*, some time after 1815. The *Thames*, launched in 1815, was the first true steam-boat the river had seen. The old hoy, or lighter, was probably sloop-rigged.

Page 177, at foot. *That fire-god.* Vulcan (see the *Iliad*, XX.-XXI.), which tells how the Trojan river rose to destroy Achilles, but Vulcan was sent by Jove to beat back water with fire.

Page 178, line 14. *Like another Ariel.*

> *Ariel.* Now on the beak,
> Now in the waist, the deck, in every cabin,
> I flamed amazement.
>> "The Tempest," Act I., Scene 2, lines 196-198.

Page 178, fourth line from foot. *Our enemies.* Lamb refers here to the attacks of *Blackwood's Magazine* on the Cockneys, among whom he himself had been included (see note on page 323). In the *London Magazine* he had written "unfledged" for "unseasoned."

Page 178, next line. *Aldermanbury, or Watling-street.* In the *London Magazine* Lamb had written "Thames, or Tooley Street."

Page 179, line 18. *Princess—Elizabeth.* This would be Elizabeth, Landgravine of Hesse Homburg (1770-1840), daughter of George III., who from her gift of drawing was known as "The Muse."

Page 179, line 29. *"Ignorant present."*

> *Lady Macbeth.* Thy letters have transported me beyond
> This ignorant present.
>> "Macbeth," Act I., Scene 5, lines 57, 58.

Page 179, last line. *The Reculvers.* The western towers of the old parish church of Reculver, on the Kentish shore of the mouth of the Thames, bear this name among navigators.

Page 180, line 16. *Margate . . . Infirmary.* The Royal Sea Bathing Infirmary, opened in 1796.

Page 180, line 24. *Pent up in populous cities.* Almost certainly a recollection of Milton's

> As one who long in populous city pent.
>> *Paradise Lost*, IX., line 445.

Page 181, line 12. *Plata . . . Orellana.* Plata, the River Plate. The Orellana is the Amazon. In Thomson's *Seasons* we read of "the mighty Orellana." The quotation that follows, "For many a day . . ." is from that poem—"Summer," line 1004, &c.

Page 181, line 16. *"Still-vexed Bermoothes."* From "The Tempest," Act I., Scene 2, line 229. Another recollection of Shakespeare occurs in the next lines, where Lamb remembers the Archbishop of Canterbury's simile in "Henry V.," Act I., Scene 2, lines 164, 165 :—

> As is the ooze and bottom of the sea,
> With sunken wreck and sumless treasuries.

Page 181, line 20. *"Be but as buggs . . ."* From Spenser's

Faerie Queen, II., Canto XII., Stanza 25. "Frighten" should be "fearen."

Page 181, line 36. *Gebir.* *Gebir,* by Walter Savage Landor (1775-1864), who was a fortnight older than Lamb, and who afterwards came to know him personally, was published in 1798.

Page 181, line 38. *This detestable Cinque Port.* A letter from Mary Lamb to Randal Norris, concerning this, or another, visit to Hastings, says: "We eat turbot, and we drink smuggled Hollands, and we walk up hill and down hill all day long." Lamb, in a letter to Barton, admitted a benefit: "I abused Hastings, but learned its value."

Page 181, last line. *Fresh streams, and inland murmurs.* There is little doubt that Lamb was recalling Wordsworth's lines "Composed a few Miles above Tintern Abbey":—

> Again I hear
> Those waters rolling from their mountain springs
> With a soft inland murmur.

He remembered also Psalm xlii. 1.

Page 182, line 9. *Amphitrites.* Amphitrite was the wife of Neptune.

Page 182, line 15. *Meschek.* "Woe is me that I sojourn in Mesech" (Ps. cxx. 5).

Page 182, line 32. *Foolish dace.* A recollection probably of Isaac Walton's characterisation of this fish, in *The Complete Angler,* where the dace and roach are grouped together in opposition to the cleverness of the carp.

Page 182, line 38. "*To read strange matter in.*"

> *Lady Macbeth.* Your face, my thane, is as a book where men
> May read strange matters.
> "Macbeth," Act I., Scene 5, lines 63, 64.

Page 183, line 19. "*The daughters of Cheapside . . .*" From Thomas Randolph's "Ode to Master Anthony Stafford":—

> The beauties of the Cheap and wives of Lombard Street.

The reference to Lothbury is probably in recollection of Wordsworth's "Reverie of Poor Susan," which Lamb greatly liked.

Page 183. THE CONVALESCENT.

London Magazine, July, 1825.

We learn from the *Letters* that Lamb had a severe nervous breakdown in the early summer of 1825 after liberation from the India House. Indeed, his health was never sound for long together when he became a free man.

Page 184, line 11. *Mare Clausum.* A closed sea, as opposed to *Mare Apertum.* John Selden wrote a book with this title.

Page 186, line 16. *Lernean pangs . . . Philoctetes.* Hercules dipped his arrows in the bite of the Lernæan hydra and their wound was incurable. They were bequeathed to Philoctetes, who on the voyage to Troy wounded himself by chance in the foot with one, and the sore grew so noisome that the Greeks marooned him on Lemnos. But he had to be fetched thence by Diomed and Ulysses before Troy could be taken : and in the play by Sophocles which represents this fetching, there is a strong presentment of his pains.

Page 186, line 31. *"What a speck . . ."* I do not find this. Lamb may have been thinking of Falstaff (in " 1 Henry IV." III., 3.) " Bardolph, am I not fallen away vilely since this last action ? do I not bate ? do I not dwindle ? "

Page 186, line 34. *In Articulo Mortis.* "At the moment of death."

Page 187, line 1. *Tityus.* Tityus, the giant, covered nine acres when he lay on the ground.

Page 187, line 4. *Insignificant Essayist.* In the *London Magazine* " essayist " was " monthly contributor."

Page 187. SANITY OF TRUE GENIUS.

New Monthly Magazine, May, 1826, where it appeared as one of the Popular Fallacies (see page 252) under the title, " That great Wit is allied to Madness ; " beginning : " So far from this being true, the greatest wits will ever be found to be the sanest writers . . ." and so forth. Compare the essay " On the Tragedies of Shakespeare," Vol. I., page 97. Lamb's thesis is borrowed from Dryden's couplet (in *Absalom and Achitophel*, Part I., lines 163, 164) :—

> Great wits are sure to madness near allied,
> And thin partitions do their bounds divide.

Page 187, line 14. *Cowley.* The lines are from Abraham Cowley's " Ode on the Death of Mr. William Hervey," Stanza 13.

Page 187, line 19. *Mistake.* In the *New Monthly Magazine* " fallacy."

Page 187, line 26. *Burning marl.*

> To support uneasy steps
> Over the burning marle.
>
> *Paradise Lost*, I., lines 295-296.

Page 187, line 28. *" And old night."*

> The universal host upsent
> A shout that tore Hell's concave, and beyond
> Frighted the reign of Chaos and Old Night.
>
> *Paradise Lost*, I., lines 541-543.

Page 187, line 29. *" Human mind untuned."*

> *Cordelia.* The untuned and jarring senses, O, wind up
> Of this child-changed father.
>
> " King Lear," Act IV., Scene 7, lines 16, 17.

Page 187, lines 34, 35. *Kent . . . Flavius.* Lamb was always greatly impressed by the character of Kent (see his essay on " Hogarth," Vol. I., page 72 ; his " Table Talk," Vol. I., page 346 ; and his versions, in the *Tales from Shakespear*, of " King Lear " and " Timon ").

Page 188, line 5. *Proteus.* An ocean deity, Neptune's son and the tender of the monsters of the sea.

Page 188, line 25. *" Maddest fits."* From Wither's "Shepherds' Hunting," Eclogue 4, the Praise of Poesy by Philarete—a favourite poem of Lamb's (see Vol. I., page 181) :—

> Though our wise ones call thee madness,
> Let me never taste of gladness,
> If I love not thy maddest fits
> More than all their greatest wits.

Page 188, line 27. *Lane's novels.* The publications of William Lane, of the Minerva Press, in Leadenhall Street, near the East India House, which approximated to the stories which we now know as of the Bow Bells type.

Page 188, line 29. *A happier genius.* Probably Sir Walter Scott was meant.

Page 188, line 31. *" Betossed."*

> *Romeo.* . . . My betossed soul.
> " Romeo and Juliet," Act V., Scene 3, line 76.

Page 188, last line. *Prate not of their " whereabout."*

> *Macbeth.* The very stones prate of my whereabout.
> " Macbeth," Act II., Scene 1, line 58.

Page 189, line 5. *That wonderful episode.* See *The Faerie Queen,* Book II., Canto 7.

Page 189. CAPTAIN JACKSON.
London Magazine, November, 1824.
No one has yet been able to identify Captain Jackson. The suggestion has been made that Randal Norris sat for the picture ; but the circumstance that Lamb, in the first edition of the *Last Essays,* included " A Death-Bed " (see page 246), with a differing portrait of Randal Norris therein, is, I think, good evidence against this theory. Perhaps the captain was one of the imaginary characters which Lamb sent out every now and then, as he told Bernard Barton (in the letter of March 20, 1826), " to exercise the ingenuity of his friends ; " although his reality seems overpowering.

Apart from his own interest, the captain is noteworthy in constituting, with Ralph Bigod (see page 23), a sketch (possibly unknown to Dickens) for Wilkins Micawber.

Page 190, line 10. *Althea's horn.* Amalthea's horn—Amalthea, the daughter of the King of Crete, who fed the infant Jupiter, and was rewarded with a horn of plenty.

Page 190, line 17. *The " mind, the mind . . . "* Possibly an inexact recollection of Davy's speech to Justice Shallow in " 2 Henry IV.," Act V., Scene 3, lines 31, 32 : " What you want in meat, we'll have in drink : but you must bear ; the heart's all."

Page 190, line 20. *The widow's cruse—the loaves and fishes.*
See 1 Kings xvii. 16; Matthew xv. 32 and onwards.

Page 190, line 34. *Verè hospitibus sacra.* "Truly sacred to guests."

Page 190, line 36. *Remainder crust.* Jaques, in "As You Like It," Act II., Scene 7, lines 39, 40, says of Touchstone's brain that it is as "dry as the remainder biscuit after a voyage."

Page 191, line 4. "*Why, Soldiers, Why.*" This old song, first found in a ballad opera, "The Patron," 1729, is called variously "The Duke of Berwick's March," "Why, Soldiers, Why," and "How stands the Glass around?"

> How stands the glass around?
> For shame, ye take no care, my boys!
> How stands the glass around?
> Let mirth and wine abound,
> The trumpets sound,
> The colours they are flying, boys,
> To fight, kill or wound,
> May we still be found
> Content with our hard fare, my boys,
> On the cold, cold ground.

The chorus begins :—

> Why, soldiers, why
> Should we be melancholy boys?

It is sometimes called General Wolfe's song.

Page 191, line 24. *Glover . . . Leonidas.* Richard Glover (1712-1785), the poet, author of *Leonidas*, 1737. I cannot find that he ever lived at Westbourne Green.

Page 192, line 29. *The old ballad.* The old ballad "Waly, Waly." This was among the poems copied by Lamb into Miss Isola's Extract Book.

Page 192, line 40. "*Equipage etern.*" I have not been able to trace this quotation.

Page 192, last line. *Tibbs, and Bobadil.* Beau Tibbs in Goldsmith's "Citizen of the World," and Bobadil in Ben Jonson's "Every Man in His Humour."

Page 193. THE SUPERANNUATED MAN.
London Magazine, May, 1825.

Except that Lamb has disguised his real employment, this essay is practically a record of fact. After thirty-three years of service at the East India House he went home "for ever" on Tuesday, March 29, 1825, with a pension of £441, or two-thirds of his regular salary, less a small annual deduction as a provision for his sister. At a Court of Directors held on that day this minute was drawn up: "Resolved that the resignation of Mr. Charles Lamb, of the Accountant General's office, on account of certified ill health, be accepted, and it appearing that he has served the Company faithfully for 33 years, and is now in receipt of an income of £730 per annum, he be allowed a pension of £450 . . .

to commence from this day." Lamb's letters to Wordsworth, April 6, 1825, to Barton, the same date, and to Miss Hutchinson, a little later, all tell the story. This is how Lamb put it to Barton :—

"DEAR B. B.—My spirits are so tumultuary with the novelty of my recent emancipation, that I have scarce steadiness of hand, much more mind, to compose a letter.

I am free, B. B.—free as air

> The little bird that wings the sky
> Knows no such Liberty!

I was set free on Tuesday in last week at 4 o'clock.

I came home for ever! . . .

I went and sat among 'em all at my old 33 years desk yester morning ; and deuce take me if I had not yearnings at leaving all my old pen-and-ink fellows, merry sociable lads, at leaving them in the Lurch, fag, fag, fag.

I would not serve another 7 years for seven hundred thousand pound."

To Miss Hutchinson Lamb said : "I would not go back to my prison for seven years longer for £10000 a year."

In the *London Magazine* the essay was divided into two parts, with the two quotations now at the head apportioned each to one part. Part II. began at "A fortnight has passed," on page 197. The essay was signed "J. D.," whose address was given as "Beaufort-terrace, Regent-street ; late of Ironmonger-court, Fenchurch-street."

Page 193. *First motto.* "*Sera tamen . . .*" From Virgil, *Eclogues*, I., 27 :—

> *Melibœus.* Et quæ tanta fuit Romani tibi causa videndi?
> *Tityus.* Libertas ; quæ sera tamen respexit inertem
> Candidior postquam tondenti barba cadetat.
> *Melibœus.* And what urgent reason bid you visit Rome?
> *Tityus.* Freedom ; which, though belated, yet thought on helpless me after my beard began to show white on the razor.

Page 193. *Second motto.* "*A Clerk I was . . .*" Lamb attributes this to John O'Keeffe (1747-1833), the author of countless farces and comic operas ; but in Buckstone's edition of George Colman, 1871, it is said to be Colman's. It was sung by Edwin as Drudge in "Inkle and Yarico," 1787, a farce in which Lamb greatly admired Miss Kelly.

Page 193, eighth line from foot. *Recreation.* At "recreation," in the *London Magazine*, came the footnote :—

"Our ancestors, the noble old Puritans of Cromwell's day, could distinguish between a day of religious rest and a day of recreation ; and while they exacted a rigorous abstinence from all amusements (even to the walking out of nursery maids with their little charges in the fields) upon the Sabbath ; in the lieu of the superstitious observance of the Saints days, which they abrogated, they humanely gave to the apprentices, and poorer sort of people, every alternate Thursday for a day of entire sport and recreation. A strain of piety and policy to be commended above the profane mockery of the Stuarts and their Book of Sports."

Lamb had said the same thing to Barton in a letter in the spring, 1824, referring there to "Southey's book" as his authority—this being *The Book of the Church*, 1824.

Page 194, line 13. *Native . . . Hertfordshire.* This was a slight exaggeration. Lamb was London born and bred. But Hertfordshire was his mother and grandmother's county, and all his love of the open air was centred there (see the essay on "Mackery End," page 75).

Page 194, line 30. *My health.* Lamb had really been seriously unwell for some time, as the *Letters* tell us.

Page 194, line 34. *I was fifty.* Lamb was fifty on February 10, 1825.

Page 194, line 35. *I had grown to my desk.* In his first letter to Barton (September 11, 1822) Lamb wrote : "I am like you a prisoner to the desk. I have been chained to that galley thirty years, a long shot. I have almost grown to the wood." Again, to Wordsworth : "I sit like Philomel all day (but not singing) with my breast against this thorn of a Desk."

Page 195, line 29. *Boldero, Merryweather . . .* Feigned names of course. It was Boldero that Lamb pretended was Leigh Hunt's true name (see page 337). And in his fictitious biography of Liston (Vol. I., page 248) Liston's mother was said to have been a Miss Merryweather. In Lamb's early city days there was a banking firm in Cornhill, called Boldero, Adey, Lushington & Boldero.

Page 195, line 30. *Esto perpetua !* "Be thou continual."

Page 196, line 6. *I could walk it away.* Writing to Wordsworth in March 1822, concerning the possibility of being pensioned off, Lamb had said :—

"I had thought in a green old age (O green thought!) to have retired to Ponder's End—emblematic name—how beautiful ! in the Ware road, there to have made up my accounts with heaven and the Company, toddling about between it and Cheshunt, anon stretching on some fine Izaac Walton morning, to Hoddsdon or Amwell, careless as a Beggar, but walking walking ever till I fairly walkd myself off my legs, dying walking."

And again, writing to Southey after the emancipation, he says (August, 1825) : "Mary walks her twelve miles a day some days, and I twenty on others. 'Tis all holiday with me now, you know."

Page 196, line 15. *"That's born . . ."*

> I know no more the way to temporal rule,
> Than he that's born and has his years come to him
> In a rough desart.
> Middleton's " Mayor of Queenborough," Act I., Scene i, lines 101-103.

Page 196, line 36. *A Tragedy by Sir Robert Howard.* From "The Vestal Virgin ; or, The Roman Ladies," by Sir Robert Howard (1626-1698). Lamb included this passage in the "Serious Fragments" at the end of the Garrick plays (see Vol. IV.).

Page 197, line 18. *Ch——*. John Chambers, son of the Rev.
Thomas Chambers, Vicar of Radway-Edgehill, Warwickshire, and an
old Christ's Hospitaller, to whom Lamb wrote the famous letter on
India House society, printed in the *Letters*, Canon Ainger's edition,
under December, 1818. John Chambers lived until 1872, and had
many stories of Lamb.

Page 197, line 18. *Do——*. Probably Henry Dodwell, to whom
Lamb wrote the letters of July, 1816, from Calne, and that of October,
7, 1827, thanking him for a gift of a sucking pig. But there seems
(see the letter to Chambers above referred to) to have been also a
clerk named Dowley. It was Dodwell who annoyed Lamb by reading
The Times till twelve o'clock every morning.

Page 197, line 19. *Pl——*. According to the late H. G. Bohn's
notes on Chambers' letter, this was W. D. Plumley.

Page 197, line 26. *My "works."* See note on page 401. The
old India House ledgers of Lamb's day are no longer in existence, but
a copy of Booth's *Tables of Interest* is preserved, with some mock
notices from the press on the fly leaves in Lamb's hand. Lamb's
portrait by Meyer was bought for the India Office in 1902.

Page 197, line 28. *Aquinas.* The first complete edition of the
works of St. Thomas Aquinas, 1570, filled seventeen folios.

Page 197, line 38. *My own master.* As a matter of fact Lamb
found the time rather heavy on his hands now and then ; and he took
to searching for beauties in the Garrick plays in the British Museum
(see Vol. IV. of this edition) as a refuge. The Elgin marbles were
moved there in 1816.

Page 198, line 3. *Everlasting flints.*

Friar Laurence.   O so light a foot
         Will ne'er wear out the everlasting flint.
              "Romeo and Juliet," Act II., Scene 6, lines 16, 17.

Page 198, line 26. *Lucretian pleasure.* A reference to the
beginning of Lucretius' *De Rerum Natura*, Book II. :—

          Suave, mari magno turbantibus aequora ventis,
          E terra magnum alterius spectare laborem,

which Munro translates : "It is sweet, when on the great sea the
winds trouble its waters, to behold from land another's deep distress."

Page 198, line 29. *And what is it all for ?* At these words, in the
London Magazine, came the passage :—

"I recite those verses of Cowley, which so mightily agree with my
constitution.

          "Business ! the frivolous pretence
          Of human lusts to shake off innocence :
          Business ! the grave impertinence :
          Business ! the thing which I of all things hate :
          Business ! the contradiction of my fate.

Or I repeat my own lines, written in my Clerk state :—

> " Who first invented work—and bound the free
> And holyday-rejoicing spirit down
> To the ever-haunting importunity
> Of business, in the green fields, and the town—
> To plough, loom, anvil, spade—and oh ! most sad,
> To this dry drudgery of the desk's dead wood?
> Who but the Being unblest, alien from good,
> Sabbathless Satan ! he who his unglad
> Task ever plies 'mid rotatory burnings,
> That round and round incalculably reel—
> For wrath divine hath made him like a wheel—
> In that red realm from whence are no returnings ;
> Where toiling, and turmoiling, ever and aye
> He, and his thoughts, keep pensive worky-day !

"O this divine Leisure !—Reader, if thou art furnished with the Old Series of the London, turn incontinently to the third volume (page 367), and you will see my present condition there touched in a 'Wish' by a daintier pen than I can pretend to. I subscribe to that Sonnet *toto corde*."

The sonnet referred to, beginning—

> They talk of time and of time's galling yoke,

will be found quoted on page 329. It was, of course, by Lamb himself. To the other sonnet he gave the title "Work" (see Vol. V., page 55). Cowley's lines are from "The Complaint."

Page 198, line 31. NOTHING-TO-DO. Lamb wrote to Barton in 1827 : " Positively, the best thing a man can have to do, is nothing, and next to that perhaps—good works."

Page 198, line 36. "*As low as to the fiends.*"

> *First Player.* Break all the spokes and fellies from her wheel,
> And bowl the round nave down the hill of heaven,
> As low as to the fiends !
> " Hamlet," Act II., Scene 2, lines 517-519.

Page 198, line 37. *I am no longer.* In the *London Magazine* "I am no longer J——s D——n."

Page 198, line 37. *I am Retired Leisure.*

> And add to these retired Leisure,
> That in trim gardens takes his pleasure.
> Milton, *Il Penseroso*, lines 49-50.

Page 198, line 41. *Cum dignitate.* From the phrase "Otium cum dignitate"—"Ease with dignity."

Page 199, line 1. *Opus operatum est.* "The ceremony has been performed."

Page 199. THE GENTEEL STYLE IN WRITING.

New Monthly Magazine, March, 1826, where it was one of the Popular Fallacies, under the title, "That my Lord Shaftesbury and Sir William Temple are models of the Genteel Style in Writing.—

We should prefer saying—of the Lordly and the Gentlemanly. Nothing," &c.

Page 199, line 5. *My Lord Shaftesbury.* Anthony Ashley Cooper, third Earl of Shaftesbury (1671-1713), the grandson of the great statesman, and the author of the *Characteristicks of Men, Manners, Opinions and Times,* 1711, and other less known works. In the essay "Detached Thoughts on Books and Reading" (page 172) Lamb says, "Shaftesbury is not too genteel for me."

Page 199, line 5. *Sir William Temple.* Sir William Temple (1628-1699), diplomatist and man of letters, the patron of Swift, and the husband of the letter-writing Dorothy Osborne. His first diplomatic mission was in 1665, to Christopher Bernard von Glialen, the prince-bishop of Munster, who grew the northern cherries (see page 200). Afterwards he was accredited to Brussels and the Hague, and sub-sequently became English ambassador at the Hague. He was recalled in 1670, and spent the time between then and 1674, when he returned, in adding to his garden at Sheen, near Richmond, and in literary pursuits. He re-entered active political life in 1674, but retired again in 1680, and moved to an estate near Farnham; which he named Moor Park, laid out in the Dutch style, and made famous for its wall fruit. Hither Swift came, as amanuensis, in 1689, and he was there, with intervals of absence, in 1699, when Temple died, "and with him," Swift wrote in his *Diary,* "all that was good and amiable among men." He was buried in Westminster Abbey, but his heart, by his special wish, was placed in a silver casket under the sun-dial at Moor Park, near his favourite window seat.

Temple's essays, under the title *Miscellanea,* were published in 1680 and 1692; his works, in several volumes, between 1700 and 1709. The best-known essay is that on "Ancient and Modern Learning," but Lamb refers also to those "On Health and Long Life," "Of the Cure of the Gout," "Of Gardening." The quotation on pages 200 and 201 does not exactly end Temple's garden essay, as Lamb says. Lamb has slightly altered Temple's punctuation.

Abraham Cowley's *Essays,* including one on "The Garden," had been published in his *Works* in 1668.

Page 201, line 21. *Say with Horace.* The *Epistles,* I., xviii., lines 104-112.

Page 202. BARBARA S——.
London Magazine, April, 1825.

This little story exhibits, perhaps better than anything that Lamb wrote, his curious gift of blending fact and fancy, of building upon a foundation of reality a structure of whimsicality and invention. In the late Charles Kent's edition of Lamb's works is printed a letter from Miss Kelly, the actress, and a friend of the Lambs, in which the true story is told; for it was she, as indeed Lamb admitted to Wordsworth in a letter in 1825, who told him the incident—"beautifully," he says elsewhere.

By Mr. Kent's kind permission I am able to quote passages from Miss Kelly's letter, which was written in 1875 :—

I perfectly remember relating an incident of my childhood to Charles Lamb and his dear sister, and I have not the least doubt that the intense interest he seemed to take in the recital, induced him to adopt it as the principal feature in his beautiful story of "Barbara S——." Much, however, as I venerate the wonderful powers of Charles Lamb as a writer—grateful as I ever must feel to have enjoyed for so many years the friendship of himself and his dear sister, and proudly honoured as I am by the two exquisite sonnets he has given to the world as tributary to my humble talent, I have never been able thoroughly to appreciate the extraordinary skill with which he has, in the construction of his story, desired and contrived so to mystify and characterize the events, as to keep me out of sight, and render it utterly impossible for any one to guess at me as the original heroine. . . .

In the year 1799, Miss Jackson, one of my mother's daughters, by her first husband, was placed under the special care of dear old Tate Wilkinson, proprietor of the York Theatre, there to practice, as in due progression, what she had learned of Dramatic Art, while a Chorus Singer at the Theatre Royal, Drury Lane, coming back, as she did after a few years, as the wife of the late celebrated, inimitable Charles Mathews, to the Haymarket Theatre. In 1799, through the influence of my uncle, Michael Kelly, the celebrated singer and composer of that day, I was allowed to become a miniature chorister in her place.

One Saturday, during the limited season of nine months in the year, Mr. Peake (dear, good old gentleman!) looking, as I remember he always did—anxiously perplexed—doubtless as to how he could best dole out the too frequently insufficient amount provided for the ill-paid company, silently looked me in the face, while he carefully folded a very *dirty*, *ragged* bank note—put it into my hand, patted my cheek, and with a slight pressure on my shoulder, hinting there was no time for our usual gossip—as good as said, "go, my dear," and I hurried down the long gallery, lined down each side with performers of all degrees, more than one of whom whispered as I passed—"Is it full pay, dear?" I nodded "Yes," and proceeded to my seat on the window of the landing-place.

It was a great comfort in those days, to have a bank-note to look at; but not always easy to open one. Mine had been cut and repaired with a line of gum paper, about twenty times as thick as the note itself, threatening the total destruction of the thin part.

Now observe in what small matters Fanny and Barbara, were in a marked degree different characters. Barbara, at 11 years of age, was some time before she felt the different size of a guinea to a half guinea, *held tight in her hand.* I, at nine years old, was not so untaught, or innocent. I was a woman of the world. I took *nothing* for granted. I had a deep respect for Mr. Peake, but the join might have disfigured the note—destroyed its currency; and it was my business to see all safe. So, I carefully opened it. A two pound-note instead of one! The blood rushed into my face, the tears into my eyes, and for a moment, something like an ecstasy of joy passed through my mind. "Oh! what a blessing to my dear mother!"—"To whom?"—in an instant said my violently beating heart,—"My mother?" Why she would spurn me for the wish. How shall I ever own to her my guilty thought? I trembled violently—I staggered back on my way to the Treasury, but no one would let me pass, until I said, "But Mr. Peake has given me too much." "Too much, has he?" said one, and was followed by a coarse, cold, derisive, general laugh. Oh! how it went to my heart; but on I went.

"If you please, Mr. Peake, you have given me a two——."

"A what?"

"A two, Sir!"

"A two!—God bless my soul!—tut-tut-tut-tut—dear, dear, dear!—God bless my soul! There, dear," and without another word, he, in exchange, laid a one pound note on the desk; a new one, quite clean,—a bright, honest looking note,—mine, the one I had a right to,—my own,—within the limit of my poor deservings.

Thus, my dear sir, I give (as you say you wish to have the *facts* as accurately stated as possible) the simple, absolute truth.

As a matter of fact Miss Kelly did afterwards play in Morton's "Children in the Wood," to Lamb's great satisfaction. The incident of the roast fowl is in that play.

In Vol. I., page 184 and onwards, will be found more than one eulogy of Miss Kelly's acting. See also notes in that volume, where Lamb's two sonnets upon her will be found.

Page 204, line 14. *Real hot tears.* In Crabb Robinson's diary Miss Kelly relates that when, as Constance, in " King John," Mrs. Siddons (not Mrs. Porter) wept over her, her collar was wet with Mrs. Siddons' tears. Miss Kelly, of course, was playing Arthur.

Page 204, line 20. *Impediment . . . pulpit.* This is more true than the casual reader may suppose. Had Lamb not had an impediment in his speech, he would have become, at Christ's Hospital, a Grecian, and have gone to one of the universities ; and the ordinary fate of a Grecian was to take orders.

Page 204, line 25. *Mr. Liston.* Mrs. Cowden Clarke says that Liston, the comedian, and his wife were among the visitors to the Lambs' rooms at Great Russell Street.

Page 204, line 26. *Mrs. Charles Kemble, née* Maria Theresa De Camp, mother of Fanny Kemble.

Page 204, line 28. *Macready.* The only record of any conference between Macready and Lamb is Macready's remark in his *Diary* that he met Lamb at Talfourd's, and Lamb said that he wished to draw his last breath through a pipe, and exhale it in a pun. But this was long after the present essay was written.

Page 204, line 29. *Picture Gallery . . . Mr. Matthews.* See note on page 462.

Page 204, line 38. *Not Diamond's.* Dimond was the proprietor of the old Bath Theatre.

Page 206, at foot. *Mrs. Crawford.* Anne Crawford (1734-1801), *née* Street, who was born at Bath, married successively a Mr. Dancer, Spranger Barry the actor, and a Mr. Crawford. Her great part was Lady Randolph in Home's " Douglas."

Page 207. THE TOMBS IN THE ABBEY.

London Magazine, October, 1823, where, with slight differences, it formed the concluding portion of the " Letter of Elia to Robert Southey, Esquire," which will be found in Vol. I., page 226. In the notes in that volume all points are accounted for ; but a little may be said here. This, the less personal portion of the " Letter to Southey," seems to have been all that Lamb cared to retain. He admitted afterwards, when his anger against Southey had cooled, that his " guardian angel " had been " absent " at the time he wrote it.

The Dean of Westminster at the time was Ireland, the friend of Gifford—dean from 1815 to 1842. Lamb's protest against the two-shilling fee was supported a year or so later than its first appearance by Reynolds, in *Odes and Addresses,* 1825, in a sarcastic appeal to the Dean and Chapter of Westminster to reduce that sum. The passage in Lamb's essay being reprinted in 1833, suggests that the reform still tarried. The evidence, however, of J. T. Smith, in his *Book for a Rainy Day,* is that it was possible in 1822 to enter Poet's Corner for sixpence. Dean Stanley, in his *Historical Memorials of Westminster Abbey,* writes : " Free admission was given to the larger

part of the Abbey under Dean Ireland. Authorised guides were first
appointed in 1826, and the nave and transepts opened, and the fees
lowered in 1841. . . ."

Lamb's reference to Southey and to André's monument is character-
istically mischievous. He is reminding Southey of his early sympathy
with rebels—his "Wat Tyler" and pantisocratic days. Major John
André, Sir Henry Clinton's adjutant-general, was caught returning from
an interview with an American traitor—a perfectly honourable proceeding in warfare—and was hanged by Washington as a spy in 1780.
No blame attached either to judge or victim. André's remains were
reburied in the Abbey in 1821. Lamb speaks of injury to André's
figure in the monument, but the usual thing was for the figure of
Washington to be attacked. Its head has had to be renewed more
than once. Minor thefts have also been committed. According to
Mrs. Gordon's *Life of Dean Buckland,* one piece of vandalism at any
rate was the work of an American, who returned to the dean two
heads which he had appropriated as relics.

Page 209. AMICUS REDIVIVUS.
London Magazine, December, 1823.
A preliminary sketch of the first portion of this essay will be found in
the letter from Lamb to Sarah Hazlitt, written probably in November,
1823. In Barry Cornwall's *Memoir* of Lamb, Chapter VI., there is also
an account of the accident to Dyer—Procter (Barry Cornwall) having
chanced to visit the Lambs just after the event. For an account of
George Dyer see notes to the essay on "Oxford in the Vacation,"
pages 312-315. In 1823 he was sixty-eight; later he became quite
blind. In his *Poetics,* 1812, is "An Ode on the Close of Autumn, after
an Excursion through Hertfordshire and Essex," in which the New River
is thus mentioned :—

> Now bear me to the distant wood,[1]
> And bear me to the silent stream,
> Where oft I strayed in serious mood,
>   Lost in some youthful dream.
> To me, O Hornsey, what retreat so fair?
>   What shade to me so consecrate as thine?
> And on thy banks, poor streamlet,[2] did I care
>   For all the spring-haunts of the tuneful Nine?
> Ah! pleasures, how ye lengthen as ye fade,
> As spreads the sun's faint orb at twilight's dubious shade!
>
> [1] Hornsey Wood.   [2] The New River.

We have another glimpse of G. D. on that fatal day, in the reminiscences of Mr. Ogilvie, an India House clerk with Lamb, as communicated to the Rev. Joseph H. Twichell (see *Scribner's Magazine,* March,
1876) :—

At the time George Dyer was fished out of New River in front of Lamb's house at
Islington, after he was resuscitated, Mary brought him a suit of Charles's clothes to put on
while his own were drying. Inasmuch as he was a giant of a man, and Lamb undersized;

inasmuch, moreover, as Lamb's wardrobe afforded only knee breeches for the nether limbs (Dyer's were colossal), the spectacle he presented when the clothes were on—or as much on as they could be—was vastly ludicrous.

Allsop, in a letter to Mr. Percy Fitzgerald, remarked, of Dyer's immersion, that Lamb had said to him: "If he had been drowned it would have made me famous. Think of having a Crowner's quest, and all the questions and dark suspicions of murder. People would haunt the spot and say, 'Here died the poet of Grongar Hill.'" The poet of "Grongar Hill" was, of course, John Dyer—another of Lamb's instances of the ambiguities arising from proper names.

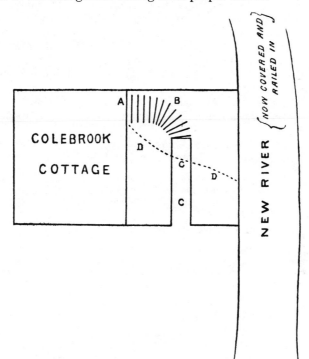

PLAN OF COLEBROOK COTTAGE AND THE NEW RIVER.

Page 209. *Motto.* "*Where were ye, Nymphs?* . . ." From *Lycidas,* lines 50, 51.

Page 209, fifth line from foot. *Anchises.* Anchises, the father of Æneas, was carried by his son out of Troy, after it was taken, through the flames of the city.

Page 209, at foot. *The rescue.* At these words, in the *London Magazine,* Lamb put this footnote:—

"The topography of my cottage, and its relation to the river, will explain this; as I have been at some cost to have the whole engraved (in time, I hope, for our next number), as well for the satisfaction of the reader, as to commemorate so signal a deliverance."

Since Lamb's project was not carried out, I offer a rough map of my own. The cottage at Colebrooke Row, it should be said, stands to this day (1903) ; but the New River has been covered in. There is, however, no difficulty in reproducing the situation. One descends from the front door (A) by a curved flight of steps (B), a little path from which (C, C), parallel with the New River, takes one out into Cole- brooke Row (or rather Duncan Terrace, as this part of the Row is now called). Under the front door-steps is another door from which Dyer may possibly have emerged ; if so it would be the simplest thing for him to walk straight ahead, along the dotted line D, D, disregarding the little footpath (C, C), crossing it in his direct progress from the lower door, and find himself in the river.

Page 210, line 19. *The plant Cannabis.* Hemp. Lamb means attempts at hanging.

Page 210, line 24. *The Middleton's-Head.* The inn, named after Sir Hugh Myddelton, the engineer of the New River, situated close to Sadlers Wells.

Page 211, line 21. *Of songs long ago.* Lamb may have had Wordsworth's "Solitary Reaper" in mind :—

> Will no one tell me what she sings?
> Perhaps the plaintive numbers flow
> For old, unhappy, far-off things,
> And battles long ago.

Page 211, line 28. *Good Sir Hugh.*

Sir Hugh Evans. 'Pless my soul, how full of chollors I am, and trempling of mind ! . . . Pless my soul !

> To shallow rivers, to whose falls
> Melodious birds sings madrigals ;
> There will we make our peds of roses,
> And a thousand fragrant posies.
> To shallow—

Mercy on me ! I have a great dispositions to cry.
" The Merry Wives of Windsor," Act III., Scene I, lines 11-22.

Shakespeare also shows Leontes under the *tremor cordis* ("The Winter's Tale," Act I., Scene 2, line 110).

Page 211, line 36. *That Abyssinian traveller.* James Bruce (1730-1794), the explorer of the sources of the Nile, was famous many years before his *Travels* appeared, in 1790, the year after which Lamb left school. The New River, made in 1609-1613, has its source in the Chadwell and Amwell springs. It was peculiarly Lamb's river : Amwell is close to Blakesware and Widford ; Lamb explored it as a boy ; at Islington he lived opposite it, and rescued George Dyer from its depths ; and he retained its company both at Enfield and Edmonton.

In the essay on "Newspapers," page 220, is a passage very similar to this.

Page 211, last line. *Eternal novity.* Writing to Hood in 1824

Lamb speaks of the New River as "rather elderly by this time." Dyer, it should be remembered, was of Emmanuel College, and the historian of Cambridge University.

Page 212, line 3. *"And could such spacious virtue . . . ?"* From John Cleveland's poem on the death of Edward King (*"Lycidas"*), in *Obsequies to the Memorie of Mr. Edward King*, 1638:—

> But can his spatious Virtue find a Grave
> Within the imposthum'd bubble of a Wave?

Page 212, line 9. *Euripus.* Aristotle is said to have drowned himself in this strait—between Euboea and Boeotia—because he could not discover the mystery of its irregular tides.

Page 212, line 10. *To turn dipper.* Dipper, slang for Baptist. Dyer had written *An Inquiry into the Nature of Subscription to the Thirty-Nine Articles*, which had led to some discussion, particularly with regard to baptism.

Page 212, line 13. *With Clarence.* See "Richard III.," Act I., Scene 4.

Page 212, line 14. *Christian.* See *The Pilgrim's Progress*, Part I., almost the end.

Page 212, line 17. *Palinurus,* Æneas' pilot, who slept and fell into the sea.

Page 212, line 23. *Arion.* See note on page 336.

Page 212, line 25. *Machaon . . . Dr. Hawes.* Machaon, the physician to the Greeks, who healed the wounds inflicted by the Trojans. Dr. William Hawes (1736-1808), founder of the Royal Humane Society, and a pioneer in the art of resuscitating the nearly-drowned.

Page 212, line 34. *Grim Feature.* Milton's phrase for Death (*Paradise Lost*, X., line 279).

Page 212, line 36. *Tantalus*, who, in Hell, is eternally baulked of his desire.

Page 212, last paragraph. George Dyer contributed "all that was original" to Valpy's edition of the classics—141 volumes. He also wrote the *History of the University and Colleges of Cambridge, including notices relating to the Founders and Eminent Men*. Among the eminent men of Cambridge are Jeremiah Markland (1693-1776), of Christ's Hospital and St. Peter's, the classical commentator; and Thomas Gray, the poet, the sweet lyrist of Peterhouse, who died in 1771, when Dyer was sixteen. Tyrwhitt would probably be Thomas Tyrwhitt (1730-1786), of Queen's College, Oxford, the editor of Chaucer; but Robert Tyrwhitt (1735-1817), his brother, the Unitarian, might be expected to take interest in Dyer also, for G. D. was, in Lamb's phrase, a "One-Goddite" too. The mild Askew was Anthony Askew (1722-1772), doctor and classical scholar, who, being physician to Christ's Hospital when Dyer was there, lent the boy books, and was very kind to him.

Page 212, footnote. *Graium tantum vidit.* Adapted from Ovid's account of his own youth (*Trist.*, IV., 10, 51):—

> Virgilium vidi tantum ; nec amara Tibullo
> Tempus amicitiæ fata dedere meæ.

(Virgil I saw and no more ; nor did harsh fate grant Tibullus time to be my friend.)

Page 213. SOME SONNETS OF SIR PHILIP SYDNEY.
London Magazine, September, 1823, where it was entitled "Nugæ Criticæ. By the Author of Elia. No. 1. Defence of the Sonnets of Sir Philip Sidney." Signed "L." The second and last of the "Nugæ Criticæ" series was the note on "The Tempest" (see Vol. I., page 243).

It may be interesting here to relate that Henry Francis Cary, the translator of Dante, and Lamb's friend, had, says his son in his memoir, lent Lamb Edward Phillips's *Theatrum Poetarum Anglicanorum*, which was returned after Lamb's death by Edward Moxon, with the leaf folded down at the account of Sir Philip Sidney. Mr. Cary thereupon wrote his "Lines to the memory of Charles Lamb," which begin :—

> So should it be, my gentle friend ;
> Thy leaf last closed at Sidney's end.
> Thou, too, like Sidney, wouldst have given
> The water, thirsting and near heaven.

Lamb has some interesting references to Sidney in the note to Beaumont and Fletcher's "Maid's Tragedy" in the *Dramatic Specimens*.

Page 213, line 12. *Milton, censuring the Arcadia.* In Milton's *Eikonoklastes*, replying to the *Eikon Basilike*, wherein Charles I. was said to have used a prayer from the *Arcadia*. Milton's passage runs :—

Who would have imagined so little fear in him of the true all-seeing deity, so little reverence of the Holy Ghost, whose office is to dictate and present our Christian prayers, so little care of truth in his last words, or honour to himself, or to his friends, or sense of his afflictions, or of that sad hour which was upon him, as immediately before his death to pop into the hand of that grave bishop who attended him, for a special relique of his saintly exercises, a prayer stolen word for word from the mouth of a heathen woman praying to a heathen god ; and that in no serious book, but the vain amatorious poem of sir Philip Sidney's Arcadia ; a book in that kind full of worth and wit, but among religious thoughts and duties not worthy to be named ; nor to be read at any time without good caution, much less in time of trouble and affliction to be a Christian's prayerbook ? They who are yet incredulous of what I tell them for a truth, that this philippic prayer is no part of the king's goods, may satisfy their own eyes at leisure, in the 3d book of sir Philip's Arcadia, p. 248, comparing Pamela's prayer with the first prayer of his majesty, delivered to Dr. Juxton immediately before his death, and entitled a Prayer in time of Captivity, printed in all the best editions of his book.

Page 213, line 18. *The Masque at Ludlow Castle . . . the Arcades.* The masque was *Comus*, 1634. *Arcades*, another masque, written a year earlier (see Lamb on Milton, Vol. I., page 376, and note to same, page 541).

Page 213, line 19. *The national struggle.* The Civil War, culminating in the execution of Charles I. Milton's first contribution to the struggle was his *Tenure of Kings and Magistrates*, 1648-1649, published just after the execution. Then he became Latin Secretary to the Council. He replied to the *Eikon Basilike* of Dr. John Gauden with *Eikonoklastes* in the same year. But between *Comus* and these works, in addition to *Lycidas*, 1638, he had been occupied in writing his tracts on divorce, the "Areopagitica," the "Tractate on Education," "Reasons of Church Government," etc. The "later Sydney" was Sir Algernon Sidney (1622-1682), great-nephew of Sir Philip Sidney. Though a Republican, and an officer of the Parliamentary army, when appointed a commissioner for the trial of Charles I. he refused to serve, saying to Cromwell, "I will keep myself clean from having my hand in this business." He was beheaded on a series of political charges in 1682.

Sir Philip Sidney was born in 1554 and fell at Zutphen in 1586—a time of no great stress. His letter on the French match was a treatise prepared in 1580 and sent to Queen Elizabeth as a protest against her proposed marriage with the Duke of Anjou, a remonstrance so hot in its zeal as to lead to Sidney's banishment from court for some months— during which he wrote the *Arcadia*.

Page 213, line 30. *Hey-day of his blood.*

> For at your age
> The hey-day in the blood is tame, it's humble,
> And waits upon the judgment.
>> "Hamlet," Act III., Scene 4, lines 68-70.

Page 213, at foot. *Circum præcordia frigus.* "Chill at the midriff."

Page 214, line 5. *Tibullus, or the . . . Author of the Schoolmistress.* In the *London Magazine* Lamb wrote "Catullus." Tibullus was one of the tenderest of Latin poets. William Shenstone (1714-1763) wrote "The Schoolmistress," a favourite poem with Lamb. The "prettiest of poems" he called it in a letter to John Clare.

Page 214, line 8. *Ad Leonoram.* The following translation of Milton's sonnet was made by Leigh Hunt :—

TO LEONORA SINGING AT ROME

> To every one (so have ye faith) is given
> A winged guardian from the ranks of heaven.
> A greater, Leonora, visits thee :
> Thy voice proclaims the present deity.
> Either the present deity we hear,
> Or he of the third heaven hath left his sphere,
> And through the bosom's pure and warbling wells,
> Breathes tenderly his smoothed oracles ;
> Breathes tenderly, and so with easy rounds
> Teaches our mortal hearts to bear immortal sounds.
>
> If God is all, and in all nature dwells,
> In thee alone he speaks, mute ruler in all else.

The Latin in Masson's edition of Milton differs here and there from Lamb's version.

Page 214. *Sonnet I.* Lamb cites the sonnets from *Astrophel and Stella* in his own order. That which he calls I. is XXXI.; II., XXXIX.; III., XXIII.; IV., XXVII.; V., XLI.; VI., LIII.; VII., LXIV.; VIII., LXXIII.; IX., LXXIV.; X., LXXV.; XI., CIII.;

XII., LXXXIV. I have left the sonnets as Lamb copied them, but there are certain differences. For example (page 215), Sonnet II., line 9, "sweet" should be "smooth;" line 10, "to" and "to" should be "of" and "of;" line 12, "by" should be "in." Sonnet III., line 7, "my" should be "of." Sonnet IV., line 11, "worse" should be "worst." Page 217, Sonnet IX., line 12, "me" should be "we." Sonnet XI., line 2, should run:—

> I saw thee with full many a smiling line;

line 6, "beauty" should be "beauties."

Page 218, line 9. *"Learning and of chivalry."* Misquoted from Spenser's dedication of the *Shepheards' Calendar* to Sidney:—

> Go, little booke : thy selfe present,
> As child whose parent is unkent,
> To him that is the president,
> Of Noblesse and of chivalrie.

Page 218, line 13. *Which I have . . . heard objected.* A criticism of Hazlitt's, in his sixth lecture on Elizabethan literature, delivered in 1820 at the Surrey Institution, is here criticised. Hazlitt's remarks on Sidney were uniformly slighting. "His sonnets inlaid in the Arcadia are jejune, far-fetch'd and frigid. . . . [The *Arcadia*] is to me one of the greatest monuments of the abuse of intellectual power upon record. . . . [Sidney is] a complete intellectual coxcomb, or nearly so;" and so forth. The lectures were published in 1821. Elsewhere, however, Hazlitt found in Sidney much to praise.

Page 218, line 16. *"Trampling horses' feet."* See line 3 of the 12th Sonnet, on page 217.

Page 218, line 30. *Thin diet of dainty words.* To this sentence, in the *London Magazine*, Lamb put the following footnote:—

"A profusion of verbal dainties, with a disproportionate lack of matter and circumstance, is I think one reason of the coldness with which the public has received the poetry of a nobleman now living; which, upon the score of exquisite diction alone, is entitled to something better than neglect. I will venture to copy one of his Sonnets in this place, which for quiet sweetness, and unaffected morality, has scarcely its parallel in our language.

"TO A BIRD THAT HAUNTED THE WATERS OF LACKEN IN THE WINTER

"By Lord Thurlow

> "O melancholy Bird, a winter's day,
> Thou standest by the margin of the pool,
> And, taught by God, dost thy whole being school
> To Patience, which all evil can allay.
> God has appointed thee the Fish thy prey ;
> And given thyself a lesson to the Fool
> Unthrifty, to submit to moral rule,
> And his unthinking course by thee to weigh.
> There need not schools, nor the Professor's chair,
> Though these be good, true wisdom to impart.

> He who has not enough, for these, to spare
> Of time, or gold, may yet amend his heart,
> And teach his soul, by brooks, and rivers fair :
> Nature is always wise in every part."

This sonnet, by Edward Hovell-Thurlow, second Baron Thurlow (1781-1829), an intense devotee of Sir Philip Sidney's muse, was a special favourite with Lamb. He copied it into his Commonplace Book, and De Quincey has described, in his "London Reminiscences," how Lamb used to read it aloud.

Page 218, line 37. *W. H.* In the *London Magazine*, "a favourite critic of our day."

Page 219, line 3. *The Critic.* In the *London Magazine*, "Mr. Hazlitt."

Page 219, line 4. *A foolish nobleman.* Lamb refers to Sidney's quarrel in the tennis-court with the Earl of Oxford, who called him "a puppy."

Page 219, line 5. *Epitaph made on him.* After these words, in the *London Magazine*, came "by Lord Brooke." Fulke Greville, Lord Brooke, wrote Sidney's *Life*, published in 1652. After Sidney's death appeared many elegies upon him, eight of which were printed at the end of Spenser's *Colin Clout's Come Home Again*, in 1595. That which Lamb quotes is by Matthew Roydon, Stanzas 15 to 18 and 26 and 27. The poem beginning "Silence augmenteth grief" is attributed to Brooke, chiefly on Lamb's authority, in Ward's *English Poets*. This is one stanza :—

> He was (woe worth that word !) to each well-thinking mind
> A spotless friend, a matchless man, whose virtue ever shined,
> Declaring in his thoughts, his life and that he writ,
> Highest conceits, longest foresights, and deepest works of wit.

Sidney was only thirty-two at his death.

Page 220. NEWSPAPERS THIRTY-FIVE YEARS AGO.
Englishman's Magazine, October, 1831, being the second paper under the heading "Peter's Net," of which "Recollections of a Late Royal Academician" was the first (see note, Vol. I., page 331). The title ran thus :—

PETER'S NET

BY THE AUTHOR OF "ELIA"

No. II.—On the Total Defect of the faculty of Imagination observable in the works of modern British Artists.

For explanation of this title see note to the essay that follows, page 446. When reprinting the essay in the *Last Essays of Elia*, 1833, Lamb altered the title to the one it now bears : the period referred to thus seeming to be about 1798, but really 1801-1803.

Page 220, line 5. *Dan Stuart.* See next page.

Page 220, line 6. *The Exhibition at Somerset House.* Between the years 1780 and 1838 the Royal Academy held its exhibitions at Somerset House. It then moved, first to Trafalgar Square, next to the National Gallery, and to Burlington House, its present quarters, in 1869. The *Morning Post* office is still almost opposite Somerset House, at the corner of Wellington Street.

Page 220, line 14. *A word or two of D. S.* Daniel Stuart (1766-1846), one of the Perthshire Stuarts, whose father was out in the '45, and his grandfather in the '15, began, with his brother, to print the *Morning Post* in 1788. In 1795 they bought it for £600, Daniel assumed the editorship, and in two years' time the circulation had risen from 350 to 1,000. Mackintosh (afterwards Sir James), Stuart's brother-in-law, was on the staff; and in 1797 Coleridge began to contribute. Coleridge's "Devil's Walk" was the most popular thing printed in Stuart's time; his political articles also helped enormously to give the paper prestige. Stuart sold the *Morning Post* in 1803 for £25,000, and then turned his attention to the development of *The Courier,* an evening paper, in which he also had occasional assistance from Coleridge and more regular help from Mackintosh.

Lamb's memory served him badly in the essay. So far as I can discover, his connection with the *Morning Post,* instead of ending when Stuart sold the paper, can hardly be said to have existed until after that event. The paper changed hands in September, 1803 (two years after the failure of *The Albion*), and Lamb's hand almost immediately begins to be apparent. He had, we know, made earlier efforts to get a footing there, but had been only moderately successful. The first specimens prepared for Stuart, in 1800, were not accepted. In the late summer of 1801 he was writing for the *Morning Chronicle*—a few comic letters, as I imagine—under James Perry; but that lasted only a short time. At the end of 1801 Lamb tried the *Post* again. In January and February, 1802, Stuart printed some epigrams by him on public characters, two criticisms of G. F. Cooke, in Richard III. and Lear, and the essay "The Londoner" (see Vol. I., pages 36, 39 and 399). Possibly there were also some paragraphs. In a letter to Rickman in January, 1802, Lamb says that he is leaving the *Post,* partly on account of his difficulty in writing dramatic criticisms on the same night as the performance.

We know nothing of Lamb's journalistic adventures between February, 1802, and October, 1803, when the fashion of pink stockings came in, and when he was certainly back on the *Post* (Stuart having sold it to establish *The Courier*), and had become more of a journalist than he had ever been. I quote a number of the paragraphs which I take to be his on this rich topic; but the specimen given in the essay is not discoverable :—

"*Oct.* 8.—The fugitive and mercurial matter, of which a *Lady's blush* is made, after coursing from its natural position, the *cheek,* to the *tip* of the *elbow,* and thence diverging for a time to the *knee,* has finally settled in the *legs,* where, in the form of a pair of *red hose,* it combines with the posture and situation of *the times,* to put on a most *warlike* and *martial appearance."*

" *Nov.* 2.—BARTRAM, who, as a *traveller,* was possessed of a very *lively fancy,* describes vast plains in the interior of America, where his *horse's fetlocks* for miles were dyed a perfect *blood colour,* in the juice of the *wild strawberries.* A less ardent fancy than BARTRAM's may apply this beautiful phenomenon of summer, to solve the present *strawberry appearance* of the *female leg* this autumn in England."

" *Nov.* 3.—The *roseate tint,* so agreeably diffused through the silk stockings of our females, induces the belief that the *dye is cast* for their lovers."

" *Nov.* 8.—A popular superstition in the North of Germany is said to be the true original of the well-known sign of Mother REDCAP. Who knows but that *late posterity,* when, what is regarded by us now as *fashion,* shall have long been classed among the *superstitious observances* of an age gone by, may dignify their signs with the antiquated personification of a Mother RED LEGS ? "

" *Nov.* 9.—Curiosity is on tip-toe for the arrival of ELPHY BEY's fair *Circassian* Ladies. The attraction of their *naturally-placed, fine, proverbial bloom,* is only wanting to reduce the *wandering colour* in the ' elbows ' and ' ancles ' of our *belles,* back to its native *metropolis* and *palace,* the ' cheek.' "

" *Nov.* 22.—*Pink stockings* beneath *dark pelices* are emblems of *Sincerity* and *Discretion ;* signifying a *warm heart* beneath a *cool exterior."*

" *Nov.* 29.—The decline of red stockings is as fatal to the wits, as the going out of a fashion to an overstocked jeweller : some of these gentry have literally for some months past *fed* on *roses."*

" *Dec.* 21.—The fashion of red stockings, so much cried down, dispraised, and followed, is on the eve of departing, to be consigned to the family tomb of ' all the fashions,' where sleep in peace the *ruffs* and *hoops,* and *fardingales* of past centuries ; and

> " All its beauty, all its pomp, decays
> Like *Courts removing,* or like *ending plays."*

On February 7, 1804, was printed Lamb's " Epitaph on a young Lady who Lived Neglected and Died Obscure " (see Vol. V., page 80), and now and then we find a paragraph likely to be his ; but, as we know from a letter from Mary Lamb to Sarah Stoddart, he had left the *Post* in the early spring, 1804. I think this was the end of his journalism, until he began to write a little for *The Examiner* in 1812.

In 1838 Stuart was drawn into a correspondence with Henry Coleridge in the *Gentleman's Magazine* (May, June, July and August) concerning some statements about Coleridge's connection with the *Morning Post* and *The Courier* which were made in Gillman's *Life*. Stuart, in the course of straightening out his relations with Coleridge, referred thus to Lamb :—

> But as for good Charles Lamb, I never could make anything out of his writings. Coleridge often and repeatedly pressed me to settle him on a salary, and often and repeatedly did I try ; but it would not do. Of politics he knew nothing ; they were out of his line of reading and thought ; and his drollery was vapid, when given in short paragraphs fit for a newspaper ; yet he has produced some agreeable books, possessing a tone of humour and kind feeling, in a quaint style, which it is amusing to read, and cheering to remember.

For further remarks concerning Lamb's journalism see below when we come to *The Albion* and his connection with it.

Page 220, line 15. *Perry, of the Morning Chronicle.* James Perry (1756-1821), the editor of the *Morning Chronicle*—the leading Whig paper, for many years—from about 1789. Perry was a noted talker and the friend of many brilliant men, among them Porson. Southey's letters inform us that Lamb was contributing to the *Chronicle* in the summer of 1801, and I fancy I see his hand now and then ; but his identifiable contributions to the paper came much later than the period under notice. Coleridge contributed to it a series of sonnets to eminent persons in 1794, in one of which, addressed to Mrs. Siddons, he collaborated with Lamb (see Vol. V., page 3, and note).

Page 220, line 21. *"With holy reverence . . ."* Mr. W. J. Craig ran these lines to earth in the Scottish poet, William Armstrong's *The Art of Preserving Health*, 1744. The passage (Book II., lines 357-360) runs :—

> I hear the din
> Of waters thundering o'er the ruined cliffs,
> With holy rev'rence I approach the rocks
> Whence glide the streams renown'd in ancient song.

Page 220, line 23. *The Abyssinian Pilgrim.* For notes to this passage about the New River see page 434.

Page 221, line 7. *The Gnat.* Virgil is supposed to have written as quite a young man some small bucolic poems before the *Bucolica*, the earliest work known to be his. Among them was the " Culex " or Gnat. It was translated by Spenser.

Page 221, line 8. *The Duck . . . Samuel Johnson trod on.*

> There has been another story of his [Johnson's] infant precocity, generally circulated, and generally believed, the truth of which I am to refute upon his own authority. It is told [by Mrs. Piozzi and Sir John Hawkins] that, when a child of three years old, he chanced to tread upon a duckling, the eleventh of a brood, and killed it ; upon which, it is said, he dictated to his mother the following epitaph :—
>
> > " Here lies good master duck
> > Whom Samuel Johnson trod on ;
> > If it had lived it had been *good luck*,
> > For then we'd had an *odd one.*"
> > [Boswell's *Life of Johnson*, Chapter I.]

Page 221, line 9. *In those days* . . . This paragraph began, in the *Englishman's Magazine,* with the following sentence :—

"We ourself—PETER—in whose inevitable NET already Managers and R.A.s lie caught and floundering—and more peradventure shall flounder—were, in the humble times to which we have been recurring, small Fishermen indeed, essaying upon minnows ; angling for quirks, not *men.*"

The phrase "Managers and R.A.s" refers to the papers on Elliston and George Dawe which had preceded this essay, although the Elliston essay had not been ranged under the heading "Peter's Net." The George Dawe paper is in Vol. I. of this edition, page 331.

Page 221, line 21. *The . . . obvious flower of Cytherea.* The rose.

Page 221, line 22. *The lady . . . sitting upon "many waters."* Babylon, arrayed in purple and scarlet (see Rev. xvii.).

Page 221, line 30. *Autolycus-like in the Play.* See "The Winter's Tale," Act IV., Scene 4.

Page 221, line 34. *Astræa.* Astræa, chaste goddess of justice in the golden age, whom the impiety of man in the age of brass drove to heaven, where she now dwells as Virgo. The Latin, "The last of the Celestials has abandoned earth."

Page 222, line 5. *" Man goeth forth . . . "* "Man goeth forth unto his work and to his labour until the evening" (Ps. civ. 23).

Page 222, line 13. *No Man's Land.* All over the country are districts known as No Man's Land ; but it is perhaps worth recording that one is situated close to Mackery End, which Lamb must have known well.

Page 222, line 27. *Basilian water-sponges.* The Basilian order of monks were pledged to austerity ; but probably Lamb intended merely a joke upon his friend Basil Montagu's teetotalism (see note in Vol. I., page 431, to "Confessions of a Drunkard," a paper quoted in Montagu's *Some Enquiries into the Effects of Fermented Liquors).* In John Forster's copy of the *Last Essays of Elia,* in the South Kensington Museum, a legacy from Elia, there is written "Basil Montagu!" against this passage. Moreover the context runs, "we were right toping Capulets"—as opposed to the (Basil) Montagus.

Page 222, line 37. *"Facil" . . . as Virgil sings.*

> Tros Anchisiade, facilis descensus Averno ;
> Noctes atque dies patet atri janua Ditis :
> Sed revocare gradum, superasque evadere ad auras,
> Hoc opus, hic labor, est.
>
>   *Æneid*, VI., lines 126-129.

The translation is :—

Trojan son of Anchises, easy is the descent to hell ; night and day open stands the portal of gloomy Dis ; but to recall your feet, and escape to the upper air—that is the toil, the task !

Page 222, at foot. *No Egyptian taskmaster.* See Exodus v.

Page 223, line 15. *Like him in Bel's temple.* See "Bel and the

Dragon" in the Apocrypha. The reference to Daniel is double : to Daniel the prophet, in that story, and to Daniel Stuart. The dragon was never in Bel's temple. The sentence ended in the *Englishman's Magazine*, "taking pitch," &c.

Page 223, line 19. *Bob Allen.* See the essay on "Christ's Hospital" (page 22) and note.

Page 223, line 21. *The "Oracle."* This daily paper was started in the 1780's by Peter Stuart, Daniel Stuart's brother, as a rival to *The World* (see below).

Page 223, line 27. *Mr. Deputy Humphreys.* I am disappointed to have been able to find nothing more about this Common Council butt.

Page 224, line 3. *The "True Briton," the "Star," the "Traveller."* *The True Briton*, a government organ in the 1790's, which afterwards assimilated Cobbett's *Porcupine.* *The Star* was founded by Peter Stuart, Daniel Stuart's brother, in 1788. It was the first London evening paper to appear regularly. *The Traveller*, founded about 1803, still flourishes under the better-known title of *The Globe.*

Page 224, lines 14, 16. *Este . . . Topham . . . Boaden.* Edward Topham (1751-1820), author of the *Life of John Elwes*, the miser, founded *The World*, a daily paper, in 1787. Parson Este, the Rev. Charles Este, was one of his helpers. James Boaden (1762-1839), dramatist, biographer and journalist, and editor of *The Oracle* for some years, wrote the *Life of Mrs. Siddons*, 1827.

Page 224, line 27. *The Albion.* Lamb's memory of his connection with *The Albion* was at fault. His statement is that he joined it on the sale of the *Morning Post* by Stuart, which occurred in 1803 ; but as a matter of fact his association with it was in 1801. This we know from his letters to Manning in August of that year, quoting the epigram on Mackintosh (see below) and announcing the paper's death. Mackintosh, says Lamb, was on the eve of departing to India to reap the fruits of his apostasy—referring to his acceptance of the post of Recordership of Bombay offered to him by Addington. But this was a slip of memory. Mackintosh's name had been mentioned in connection with at least two posts before this—a judgeship in Trinidad and the office of Advocate-General in Bengal, and Lamb's epigram may have had reference to one or the other. In the absence of a file of *The Albion*, which I have been unable to find, it is impossible to give exact dates or to reproduce any of Lamb's other contributions.

Page 224, line 36. *John Fenwick.* See the essay "The Two Races of Men," page 23 and note. Writing to Manning on September 24, 1802, Lamb describes Fenwick as a ruined man hiding from his creditors. In January, 1806, he tells Stoddart that Fenwick is "coming to town on Monday (if no kind angel intervene) to surrender himself to prison." And we meet him again as late as 1817, in a letter to Barron Field, on August 31, where his editorship of *The Statesman* is mentioned. In Mary Lamb's letters to Sarah Stoddart (in Hazlitt's *Mary and Charles Lamb*) there are indications that Mrs. Fenwick and family were mindful of the Lambs' charitable impulses.

After "Fenwick," in the *Englishman's Magazine*, Lamb wrote: "Of him, under favour of the public, something may be told hereafter." It is sad that the sudden discontinuance of the magazine with this number for ever deprived us of further news of this man.

Page 224, line 41. *Lovell*. Daniel Lovell, subsequently owner and editor of *The Statesman*, which was founded by John Hunt, Leigh Hunt's brother, in 1806. He had a stormy career, much chequered by imprisonment and other punishment for freedom of speech. He died in 1818.

Page 225, line 4. *Daily demands of the Stamp Office*. The newspaper stamp in those days was threepence-halfpenny, raised in 1815 to fourpence. In 1836 it was reduced to a penny, and in 1855 abolished.

Page 225, line 11. *Accounted very good men now*. A hit, I imagine, particularly at Southey (see note on page 432). Also at Wordsworth and Mackintosh himself.

Page 225, line 17. *Mr. Bayes*. The chief character in "The Rehearsal," Buckingham's comedy.

Page 225, line 26. *Sir J——s M——h*. Sir James Mackintosh (1765-1832), the philosopher, whose apostasy consisted in his public recantation of the opinions in favour of the French Revolution expressed in his *Vindiciæ Gallicæ*, published in 1791. In 1803 he accepted the offer of the Recordership of Bombay. Lamb's epigram, which, as has been stated above, cannot have had reference to this particular appointment, runs thus in the version quoted in the letter to Manning of August, 1801 :—

> Though thou'rt like Judas, an apostate black,
> In the resemblance one thing thou dost lack :
> When he had gotten his ill-purchased pelf,
> He went away, and wisely hang'd himself :
> This thou may'st do at last ; yet much I doubt,
> If thou hast any bowels to gush out.

Page 225, line 29. *Lord . . . Stanhope*. This was Charles, third earl (1753-1816), whose sympathies were with the French Revolution. His motion in the House of Lords against interfering with France's internal affairs was supported by himself alone, which led to a medal being struck in his honour with the motto, "The Minority of One, 1795 ;" and he was thenceforward named "Minority," or "Citizen," Stanhope. George Dyer, who had acted as tutor to his children, was one of Stanhope's residuary legatees.

Page 225, line 33. *It was about this time . . .* With this sentence Lamb brought back his essay to its original title, and paved the way for the second part—now printed under that heading.

At the end of this paper, in the *Englishman's Magazine*, were the words, "To be continued." For the further history of the essay see the notes that follow.

Page 226. Barrenness of the Imaginative Faculty in the Productions of Modern Art.

Athenæum, January 12, 19, 26, and February 2, 1833, where it was
thus entitled: "On the Total Defects of the Quality of Imagination,
observable in the Works of Modern British Artists." By the Author
of the Essays signed "Elia."

The following editorial note was prefixed to the first instalment:—

"This Series of Papers was intended for a new periodical, which
has been suddenly discontinued. The distinguished writer having
kindly offered them to the Athenæum, we think it advisable to perfect
the Series by this reprint; and, from the limited sale of the work in
which it originally appeared, it is not likely to have been read by one
in a thousand of our subscribers."

The explanation of this passage has been made simple by the re-
searches of the late Mr. Dykes Campbell. Lamb intended the essay
originally for the *Englishman's Magazine*, November number, to follow
the excursus on newspapers. But that magazine came to an end with
the October number. In the letter from Lamb to Moxon dated
October 24, 1831, Lamb says, referring to Moxon's announcement that
the periodical would cease:—

"Will it please, or plague you, to say that when your Parcel came I
damned it, for my pen was warming in my hand at a ludicrous
description of a Landscape of an R.A., which I calculated upon sending
you to morrow, the last day you gave me."

That was the present essay. Subsequently—at the end of 1832—
Moxon started a weekly paper entitled *The Reflector*, edited by John
Forster, in which the printing of Lamb's essay was begun. It lasted
only a short time, and on its cessation Lamb sent the ill-fated manuscript to *The Athenæum*, where it at last saw publication completed.
Of *The Reflector* all trace seems to have vanished, and with it possibly
other writings of Lamb's.

In *The Athenæum* of December 22, 1832, the current *Reflector* (No.
2) is advertised as containing "An Essay on Painters and Painting by
Elia."

Page 226, line 3. *Hogarth.* Compare Lamb's criticism of Hogarth,
Vol. I., page 70.

Page 226, line 19. *Titian's "Ariadne."* This picture is now
No. 35 in the National Gallery. It is reproduced on the opposite
page. Writing to Wordsworth in May, 1833, it is amusing to note,
Lamb says: "Inter nos the Ariadne is not a darling with me, several
incongruous things are in it, but in the composition it served me as
illustrative." The legend of Ariadne tells that after being abandoned
by Theseus, whom she loved with intense passion, she was wooed by
Bacchus.

Page 226, line 25. *Guido's version.* A picture of the legend by
Guido Reni (1575-1642).

Page 227, line 4. *A picture by Raphael.* See the engraving reproduced opposite page 448.

TITIAN'S ARIADNE.

From the original in the National Gallery

Page 227, line 20. *Somerset House.* See note on page 440.

Page 227, line 32. *Neoteric . . . Mr.* ——. Probably J. M. W. Turner and his "Garden of the Hesperides," now in the National Gallery. It is true it was painted in 1806, but Lamb does not describe it as a picture of the year and Turner was certainly the most notable neoteric, or innovator, of that time.

Page 227, line 36. *Polypheme by Poussin.* Nicolas Poussin (1594-1665), the French painter.

Page 227, line 38. *"Still-climbing Hercules."*

> *Biron.* For valour, is not Love a Hercules,
> Still climbing trees in the Hesperides.
> "Love's Labour's Lost," Act IV., Scene 3, lines 340, 341.

Page 227, line 39. *Ternary of Recluses.* The three Hesperides, or daughters of Hesperus, who guarded the golden apple of Juno.

Page 227, line 40. *"Lidless eyes."* From Coleridge's "Ode on the Departing Year" (Stanza VIII.):—

> Yet as she lies
> By livid fount, or red volcanic stream,
> If ever to her lidless dragon-eyes,
> O Albion ! thy predestined ruins rise,
> The fiend-hag on her perilous couch doth leap,
> Muttering distempered triumph in her charmed sleep.

Page 228, line 6. *Watteauish.* Antoine Watteau (1684-1721), the painter of *fêtes champêtres.*

Page 228, line 8. *"Daughters three . . ."*

> There I suck the liquid air,
> All amidst the gardens fair
> Of Hesperus, and his daughters three
> That sing about the golden tree.
> *Comus*, lines 980-983.

Page 228, line 13. *Of a modern artist.* In *The Athenæum* this had been printed "of M——," meaning John Martin (1789-1854). His "Belshazzar's Feast," which Lamb analyses below, was painted in 1821, and made him famous. It was awarded a £200 premium, and was copied on glass and exhibited with great success as an illuminated transparency in the Strand. Lord Lytton said of Martin that "he was more original, more self-dependent, than Raphael or Michael Angelo." Lamb had previously expressed his opinion of Martin, in a letter to Bernard Barton, dated June 11, 1827, in a passage which contains the germ of this essay :—

"Martin's Belshazzar (the picture) I have seen. Its architectural effect is stupendous ; but the human figures, the squalling, contorted little antics that are playing at being frightened, like children at a sham ghost who half know it to be a mask are detestable. Then the *letters* are nothing more than a transparency lighted up, such as a Lord might order to be lit up on a sudden at a Christmas Gambol, to scare the ladies. The *type* is as plain as Baskervil—they should have been dim, full of mystery, letters to the mind rather than the eye." See the plate opposite page 450.

Page 228, line 25. *The late King.* George IV., who built, when Prince of Wales, the Brighton Pavilion. As I cannot find this incident in any memoirs of the Regency, I assume Lamb to have invented it, after his wont, when in need of a good parallel. "Mrs. Fitz-what's-her-name" stands of course for Mrs. Fitzherbert.

Page 229, line 1. *The ingenious Mr. Farley.* Charles Farley (1771-1859), who controlled the pantomimes at Covent Garden from 1806 to 1834, and invented a number of mechanical devices for them. He also acted, and had been the instructor of the great Grimaldi. Lamb alludes to him in the essay on "The Acting of Munden," page 148.

Page 229, line 13. *Belus.* Belshazzar.

Page 229, lines 23, 25. *Eliphaz . . . the Temanite.* See Job iv.

Page 229, line 28. *The words of Daniel.* See Daniel v.

Page 230, line 20. *Veronese.* Paolo Veronese (1528 ?-1588).

Page 230, line 24. "*Day of judgment.*" One of Martin's last pictures was a "Day of Judgment."

Page 230, line 24. *A "day of lesser horrors, yet divine."* I do not find this quotation.

Page 231, line 5. "*Sun, stand thou still . . .*" See Joshua x. 12. Martin's picture of "Joshua commanding the Sun to stand still" was painted in 1816. Writing to Barton, in the letter quoted from above, Lamb says: "Just such a confus'd piece is his Joshua, fritter'd into 1000 fragments, little armies here, little armies there—you should see only the *Sun* and *Joshua*. . . . for Joshua, I was ten minutes finding him out." See the plate opposite page 452.

Page 231, line 16. "*Dart through rank and file traverse.*"

> He through the armed files
> Darts his experienc't eye ; and soon traverse
> The whole battalion views.
>
> *Paradise Lost*, I., lines 567-569.

Page 231, line 22. *The great picture at Angerstein's.* This picture is "The Resurrection of Lazarus," by Fra Sebastiano del Piombo, with the assistance, it is conjectured, of Michael Angelo. The picture is now No. 1 in the National Gallery, the nucleus of which collection was once the property of John Julius Angerstein (1735-1823). Angerstein's art treasures were to be seen until his death in his house in Pall Mall, where the Reform Club now stands (see note on page 529 of Vol. I.).

Page 232, line 4. *Julio Romano.* Giulio Pippi, or Giulio Romana, who completed, with Gianfrancesco Penni, the Raphael frescoes in the Vatican. He died in 1546. I have not found this particular drawing.

Page 232, line 20. *Raphael's "Building of the Ark."* See the engraving reproduced opposite page 456.

Page 232, line 25. *The Frenchmen, of whom Coleridge's friend.* See the *Biographia Literaria*, 1847 ed., Vol. II., pp. 126-127.

R.V.I.

Adduxit eam ad Adam, dixitq, Adam, hoc nunc os ex osibus meii,
Et caro ex carne mea Gen. II

N.C.F

ADAM AND EVE

From Raphael's Bible

Page 232, line 41. *Demiurgus.* In Eastern mythology a subordinate deity engaged in the creation of the world.

Page 232, line 43. *Vulcanian three.* The vulcanian Cyclops were Brontes, Steropes and Pyracmon, whose workshops were beneath the volcanoes of Sicily, of which Mongibello is one.

Page 233, line 24. *" Strange bedfellows . . ."*

> *Trinculo.* Misery acquaints a man with strange bedfellows.
> "The Tempest," Act II., Scene 2, lines 41, 42.

Page 233, line 30. *" Truly, fairest Lady . . ."* The passage quoted by Lamb is from Skelton's translation of *Don Quixote*, Part II., Chapter LVIII. The first sentence runs: "Truly, fairest Lady, Actæon was not more astonished or in suspense when on the sodaine he saw Diana," and so forth.

Page 233, third line from foot. *" Fine frenzies."*

> *Theseus.* The poet's eye, in a fine frenzy rolling,
> Doth glance from heaven to earth, from earth to heaven.
> "A Midsummer-Night's Dream," Act V., Scene 1, lines 12, 13.

Page 234, lines 7, 8. *Goneril . . . Regan.* In " King Lear."

Page 234, line 26. *" Guzman de Alfarache."* The Picaresque romance by Mateo Aleman—*Vida y Lechos del picaro Guzman de Alfarache*, Part I., 1599; Part II., 1605. It was translated into English by James Mabbe in 1622 as *The Rogue; or, The Life of Guzman de Alfarache.* Lamb had a copy.

Page 235. Rejoicings upon the New Year's Coming of Age.
London Magazine, January, 1823.

This paper, being printed in the same number as that which announced Elia's death (see page 402), was signed " Elia's Ghost."

Lamb returned to this vein of fancy two years or so later when (in 1825) he contributed to his friend William Hone's *Every-Day Book* the petition of the Twenty-Ninth of February, a day of which Hone had taken no account, and of the Twelfth of August, which from being kept as the birthday of King George IV. during the time that he was Prince of Wales, was, on his accession to the throne, disregarded in favour of April 23, St. George's Day. For these letters see Vol. I. of this edition, pages 297 and 302.

Page 235, line 17. *The Vigils.* The Vigils are the days preceding festivals.

Page 235, line 34. *Tiffany suit.* Tiffany (from Theophany) a very thin silk or gauze. Twelfth Day or Epiphany.

Page 236, line 1. *Erra Pater.* An old term for an almanac or one who made it; an astrologer.

Page 236, line 4. *Twenty First of June . . . Twenty Second of December.* The longest and shortest days.

Page 236, line 12. *Dried ling.* Dried fish, food for fasting.

Page 236, line 19. *Shrove Tuesday . . . Second of September.*

It used to be a custom to throw sticks and stones at cocks on Shrove Tuesday. Lamb's pen seems to have slipped in the matter of September 2, for pheasants are not game until October 1, and September 1 is the date for partridges.

Page 236, line 25. *Thirtieth of January.* Charles I. was beheaded on January 30. Roundheads used to eat a calf's head on the anniversary of that day.

Page 236, line 32. *Herodias' daughter.* See Mark vi.

Page 236, line 35. *Twenty Ninth of May.* Oak Apple Day. The date of the Restoration, or Charles II.'s entry into London, 1660.

Page 236, line 37. *A notable dispute.* See note above for explanation of this quarrel.

Page 237, line 7. *Bi-geny.* A pun on bigamy, meaning two births.

Page 237, line 11. *The same lady . . . Washing.* I suspect Lamb to have confused Candlemas with Halloween. I can find no superstition connected with washing on Candlemas Day or Eve, whereas Halloween has several, not unconnected with one's future husband or wife.

Page 237, line 23. *"New Brooms."* A reference to new brooms sweeping clean.

Page 237, line 30. *Boutefeu.* Incendiary.

Page 237, line 42. *Greek Calends and Latter Lammas.* Two phrases signifying never. The Greeks had no calends. Romans who did not propose to liquefy a debt would postpone payment till the Greek calends.

Page 238, line 3. *"Miserere."* The fifty-first psalm.

Page 238, line 10. *"Which is the properest day . . . ?"* The old catch :—

> Which is the properest day to drink ?
> Saturday ? Sunday ? Monday ?
> Every day in the week I think,
> Why should I name but one day !

Page 238, line 16. *Forty Days before Easter.* Lent; referring to those who borrow.

Page 238, line 26. *Ember Days.* These are the Wednesdays, Fridays and Saturdays after the first Sunday in Lent, the Feast of Pentecost, Holy-rood Day (September 14) and St. Lucia's Day (December 15).

Page 238, line 27. *Old Madam Septuagesima.* So called from being the seventieth day from Easter, or thereabouts ; the third Sunday before Lent ; the ninth before Easter.

Page 238, line 30. *Rogation Day.* The Rogation Days are the Monday, Tuesday and Wednesday following Rogation Sunday, the fifth after Easter Day, which is the Day of Supplication.

Page 239, line 3. *"On the bat's back . . ."* From Ariel's song in "The Tempest." Lamb confesses, in at least two of his letters, to a precisely similar plight.

BELSHAZZAR'S FEAST

After the picture by John Martin

Page 239. THE WEDDING.

London Magazine, June, 1825.

The wedding was that of Sarah Burney, daughter of Lamb's old friends, Rear-Admiral James Burney and his wife Sarah Burney, to her cousin, John Payne, of Pall Mall, at St. Margaret's, Westminster, in April, 1821. The clergyman was the Rev. C. P. Burney, who was not, however, vicar of St. Mildred's in the Poultry, but of St. Paul's, Deptford, in Kent. Admiral Burney lived only six months longer, dying in November.

Canon Ainger has pointed out that when Lamb was revising this essay for its appearance in the *Last Essays of Elia,* he was, like the admiral, about to lose by marriage Emma Isola, who was to him and his sister what Miss Burney had been to her parents. She married Edward Moxon in July, 1833.

Page 241, line 17. *Foresters indeed.* " Let us be Diana's foresters," says Falstaff (" 1 Henry IV.," Act I., Scene 2, line 29).

Page 241, line 24. *Iphigenia.* Iphigenia, daughter of Agamemnon and Clytemnestra, was condemned by soothsayers to be sacrificed to Diana as an appeasement to that goddess for the death of her favourite stag, which Agamemnon had killed. She was, however, saved by Diana, who made her one of her priestesses.

Page 241, line 26. *An unseasonable disposition to levity.* Writing to P. G. Patmore in 1827 Lamb says : " I have been to a funeral, where I made a pun, to the consternation of the rest of the mourners." Again, writing to Southey : " I am going to stand godfather ; I don't like the business ; I cannot muster up decorum for these occasions ; I shall certainly disgrace the font ; I was at Hazlitt's marriage and was like to have been turned out several times during the ceremony. Anything awful makes me laugh. I misbehaved once at a funeral."

Page 241, line 41. *Miss T——s.* In the *London Magazine* " Miss Turner's."

Page 241, line 43. *Black . . . the costume of an author.* See note on page 453.

Page 242, line 1. *Lighter colour.* Here the *London Magazine* had : " a pea-green coat, for instance, like the bridegroom."

Page 242, line 5. *A lucky apologue.* I do not find this fable ; but Lamb's father, in his volume of poems, described in a note on page 367, has something in the same manner in his ballad " The Sparrow's Wedding " :—

> The chatt'ring Magpye undertook
> Their wedding breakfast for to cook,
> He being properly bedight
> In a cook's cloathing, black and white.

Page 242, line 30. " *As when a well-graced actor . . .*"

> *York.* As in a theatre, the eyes of men,
> After a well-graced actor leaves the stage,
> Are idly bent on him that enters next.
>> " Richard II.," Act V., Scene 2, lines 23-25.

Page 243, line 5. *The Admiral's favourite game.* Admiral Burney

wrote a treatise on whist (see notes to " Mrs. Battle's Opinions on
Whist," page 333).

Page 243, line 8. *Comparatively easy spirits.* After these words,
in the *London Magazine,* came a break.

Page 243, line 10. *Various times since.* There is a suggestion
here, since the admiral died in November, 1821, that Lamb wrote this
essay between July and November of that year, and had kept it by
him until the time of publication, four years later.

Page 243, line 23. *Concordia discors.* " Harmony out of un-
harmony." The phrase is Horace's (*Epistles,* I., xii., 19), and also Ovid's
(*Metamorphoses,* I., 433).

Page 243, line 29. To "*make his destiny his choice.*" From
Marvell's poem, quoted in " Blakesmoor in H——shire," " Upon
Appleton House," in reference to the coming wedding of Mary Fair-
fax :—

> Whence for some universal good,
> The priest shall cut the sacred bud ;
> While her glad parents most rejoice
> And make their destiny their choice.

Page 244. THE CHILD ANGEL.
London Magazine, June, 1823.

Thomas Moore's *Loves of the Angels* was published in 1823. Lamb
used it twice for his own literary purposes : on the present occasion,
with tenderness, and again, eight years later, with some ridicule, for
his comic ballad, " Satan in Search of a Wife," 1831, was ironically dedicated to the admirers of Moore's poem (see Vol. V., page 110).

Page 244, line 16. *Gossiping.* Christening.

Page 244, line 31. "*Which mortals . . .*" Lamb probably invented this quotation on a well-known model. Pope has (" Rape of
the Lock," I., 77, 78) :—

> 'Tis but their Sylph, the wise Celestials know,
> Tho' Honour is the word with Men below.

Page 246. A DEATH-BED.

Hone's *Table Book,* Vol. I., cols. 425-426, 1827. Signed " L.," and
dated London, February 10, 1827. The essay is very slightly altered
from a letter written by Lamb to Crabb Robinson, January 20, 1827,
describing the death of Randal Norris. It was printed in the first edition
only of the *Last Essays of Elia ;* its place being taken afterwards by
the " Confessions of a Drunkard," an odd exchange. The essay was
omitted, in deference, it is believed, to the objection of Mrs. Norris to
her reduced circumstances being more public. As the present edition
adheres to the text of the first edition, " The Death-Bed " is included
in its original place as decided by the author. The " Confessions of a
Drunkard " will be found on page 133 of Vol. I.

Randal Norris was for many years sub-treasurer of the Inner Temple
(see postscript to the essay on the " Old Benchers," page 90). Writ-

JOSHUA COMMANDING THE SUN TO STAND STILL.

After the picture by John Martin

ing to Wordsworth in 1830 Lamb spoke of him as "sixty years ours and our father's friend." An attempt has been made to identify him with the Mr. Norris of Christ's Hospital who was so kind to the Lambs after the tragedy of September, 1796. I cannot find any trace of Randal Norris having been connected with anything but the law and the Inner Temple ; but possibly the Mr. Norris of the school was a relative.

Mrs. Randal Norris was connected with Widford, the village adjoining Blakesware, where she had known Mary Field, Lamb's grandmother. It was thither that she and her son retired after Randal Norris's death, to join her daughters, Miss Betsy and Miss Jane, who had a school for girls known as Goddard House School. Lamb kept up his friendship with them to the end, and they corresponded with Mary Lamb after his death. Mrs. Norris died in 1843, aged seventy-eight, and was buried at Widford. The grave of Richard Norris, the son, is also there. He died in 1836. One of the daughters, Elizabeth, married Charles Tween, of Widford, and lived until 1894. The other daughter, Jane, married Arthur Tween, his brother, and lived until 1891.

Mary Lamb was a bridesmaid at the Norris's wedding and after the ceremony accompanied the bride and bridegroom to Richmond for the day. So one of their daughters told Canon Ainger.

Crabb Robinson seems to have exerted himself for the family, as Lamb wished. Mr. W. C. Hazlitt says that an annuity of £80 was settled upon Mrs. Norris.

Page 246, line 21. *Poor deaf Robert.* In the letter—"Richard."

Page 246, line 30. *To the last he called me Jemmy.* In the letter to Crabb Robinson—"To the last he called me Charley. I have none to call me Charley now."

Page 246, line 32. *That bound me to B——.* In the letter to Crabb Robinson—"that bound me to the Temple."

Page 247, line 5. *Your Corporation Library.* In the letter— "The Temple Library."

Page 247, line 11. *He had one Song.* I have not been able to find this song.

Page 247. OLD CHINA.

London Magazine, March, 1823.

This essay forms a pendant, or complement, to "Mackery End in Hertfordshire," page 75, completing the portrait of Mary Lamb begun there. It was, with "The Wedding" (page 239), Wordsworth's favourite among the *Last Essays.*

Page 248, line 26. *Dancing the hays.* An old English dance.

Page 248, line 31. *Speciosa miracula.* "Shining wonders." Horace, *Ars Poetica,* 144, uses the phrase in describing the wonders of the *Odyssey.*

Page 249, line 5. *The brown suit.* P. G. Patmore, in his recollections of Lamb in the *Court Journal,* 1835, afterwards reprinted, with some alterations, in his *My Friends and Acquaintances,* stated that Lamb laid aside his snuff-coloured suit in favour of black, after twenty years of the India House ; and he suggests that Wordsworth's stanzas in " A Poet's Epitaph" was the cause :—

> But who is he, with modest looks,
> And clad in homely russet brown ?
> He murmurs near the running brooks
> A music sweeter than their own.
>
> He is retired as noontide dew,
> Or fountain in a noon-day grove ;
> And you must love him, ere to you
> He will seem worthy of your love.

Whatever Patmore's theory may be worth, it is certain that Lamb adhered to black after the change.

Page 249, line 7. *Beaumont and Fletcher.* See note on page 328.

Page 249, line 8. *Barker's.* Barker's old book-shop was at No. 20 Great Russell Street, over which the Lambs went to live in 1817. It had then, however, become Mr. Owen's, a brazier's (Wheatley's *London Past and Present* gives Barker's as 19, but a contemporary directory says 20). Great Russell Street is now Russell Street.

Page 249, line 12. *From Islington.* This would be when Lamb and his sister lived at 36 Chapel Street, Pentonville, a stone's throw from the Islington boundary, in 1799-1800, after the death of their father.

Page 249, line 25. *Corbeau.* A draper's word—from corbeau, a raven.

Page 249, line 33. *The "Lady Blanch."* See Mary Lamb's poem on this picture, Vol. V., page 38, and note. The picture, which is there reproduced, is known as " Modesty and Vanity."

Page 249, line 36. *Colnaghi's.* Colnaghi, the printseller, then in Cockspur Street. After this word came in the *London Magazine* " (as W—— calls it)." The reference, Mr. Roger Rees tells me, is to Wainewright's article " C. van Vinkbooms, his Dogmas for Dilletanti," in the same magazine for December, 1821, where he wrote : " I advise Colnaghi and Molteno to import a few impressions immediately of those beautiful plates from Da Vinci. The . . . and Miss Lamb's favourite, ' Lady Blanche and the Abbess,' commonly called 'Vanitas et Modestia ' (Campanella, 10s. 6d.), for I foresee that this Dogma will occasion a considerable call for them—let them, therefore, be ready."

Page 250, line 6. *Piscator . . . Trout Hall.* See *The Complete Angler*, Cotton's continuation.

Page 250, line 12. *To see a play.* "The Battle of Hexham" and "The Surrender of Calais" were by George Colman the Younger ; "The Children in the Wood," a favourite play of Lamb's, especially with Miss Kelly in it, was by Thomas Morton. Mrs. Bland was Maria Theresa Bland, *née* Romanzini, 1769-1838, who married Mrs. Jordan's brother. Jack Bannister we have met, in " The Old Actors."

Page 251, line 24. *" Lusty brimmers."*

> Then let us welcome the new guest
> With lusty brimmers of the best.

THE RAISING OF LAZARUS

From the picture by Sebastian del Piombo in the National Gallery

From Charles Cotton's "The New Year," quoted in "New Year's Eve," page 31, with a hint of Pope's line—

> Welcome the coming, speed the parting guest—

also quoted in the same essay.

Page 252, line 16. *The great Jew R———.* This would be Nathan Meyer Rothschild (1777-1836), the founder of the English branch of the family and the greatest financier of modern times.

Page 252. POPULAR FALLACIES.

This series of little essays was printed in the *New Monthly Magazine* in 1826, beginning in January. The order of publication there was not the same as that in the *Last Essays of Elia*; one of the papers, "That a Deformed Person is a Lord," was not reprinted by Lamb at all (it will be found on page 290 of Vol. I. of this edition); and two others were converted into separate essays (see "The Sanity of True Genius" (page 187 of the present volume) and "The Genteel Style in Writing" (page 199)).

After Lamb's death a new series of Popular Fallacies was contributed to the *New Monthly Magazine* by L. B. (probably Laman Blanchard) in 1835, preceded by an invocation to the spirit of Charles Lamb.

Page 252. I.—THAT A BULLY IS ALWAYS A COWARD.
New Monthly Magazine, January, 1826.

Page 253, line 2. *Hickman.* This would be, I think, Tom Hickman, the pugilist. In Hazlitt's fine account of "The Fight," Hickman, or the Gas-Man, "vapoured and swaggered too much, as if he wanted to grin and bully his adversary out of the fight." And again, "'This is the *grave digger*' (would Tom Hickman exclaim in the moments of intoxication from gin and success, showing his tremendous right hand); 'this will send many of them to their long homes; I haven't done with them yet.'" But he went under to Neale, of Bristol, on the great day that Hazlitt describes.

Page 253, line 3. *Him of Clarissa.* Mr. Hickman, in Richardson's novel *Clarissa*, the lover of Miss Bayes.

Page 253, line 6. *Harapha.* In *Samson Agonistes*. The Giant of Gath.

Page 253, line 8. *Almanzor.* In Dryden's *Conquest of Granada*.

Page 253, line 10. *Tom Brown.* Tom Brown, of Shifnal (1663-1704), author of a number of satirical and broadly-comic writings. Among his *Letters from the Dead to the Living* is one from Bully Dawson to his successor in the taverns. In *The Spectator*, No. 1, Bully Dawson is mentioned. A footnote describes him as a sharper and debauchee well-known in London in that day (1710).

Page 253. II.—THAT ILL-GOTTEN GAIN NEVER PROSPERS.
New Monthly Magazine, January, 1826.

Page 253. III.—That a Man must not Laugh at His own Jest.
New Monthly Magazine, January, 1826.
Page 253, third line of essay. *Esurient.* Hungry.
Page 254, line 7. *In Mandeville.* In Bernard Mandeville's *Fable of the Bees,* a favourite book of Lamb's. See Vol. I., p. 423.

Page 254. IV.—That such a one Shows His Breeding, etc.
New Monthly Magazine, January, 1826. In that version the phrase " his sister, &c.," ran, " his sister made a —— "

Page 254. V.—That the Poor Copy the Vices of the Rich.
New Monthly Magazine, January, 1826.

Page 256. VI.—That Enough is as Good as a Feast.
New Monthly Magazine, January, 1826.

Page 256. VII.—Of Two Disputants, the Warmest is Generally in the Wrong.
New Monthly Magazine, January, 1826.
Page 256, sixth line from foot. *Little Titubus.* I do not know who this was, if any more than an abstraction ; but it should be remembered that Lamb himself stammered.

Page 257. VIII.—That Verbal Allusions are not Wit, etc.
New Monthly Magazine, January, 1826.
Page 257, fourteenth line of essay. *" Hudibras."* By Samuel Butler (1612-1680). The couplet admired by Dennis runs : –

> And pulpit, drum ecclesiastic,
> Was beat with fist instead of a stick.

John Dennis, the critic (1657-1734) and literary swashbuckler, oppugned puns in *Letters upon several occasions written by and between Mr. Dryden, Mr. Wycherly, Mr. ——, Mr. Congreve and Mr. Dennis.* In reply to a panegyric upon puns from Mr. Wycherley he abused the habit thoroughly : " If punning be a diversion, it is a very strange one. . . . The first approach to wit is a contempt of quibbling ; " and so forth.

Page 257. IX.—That the Worst Puns are the Best.
New Monthly Magazine, January, 1826.
Compare the reflections on puns in the essay on " Distant Correspondents" (page 107). Compare also the review of Hood's *Odes and Addresses* (Vol. I., page 285). Cary's account of a punning contest after Lamb's own heart makes the company vie with each in puns on the names of herbs. After anise, mint and other words had been ingeniously perverted Lamb's own turn, the last, was reached, and it seemed impossible that anything was left for him. He hesitated. " Now then, let us have it," cried the others, all expectant. " Patience," he replied ; " it's c-c-cumin."
Page 258, line 25. *One of Swift's Miscellanies.* This joke, often attributed to Lamb himself, will be found in *Ars Pun-ica, sive flos*

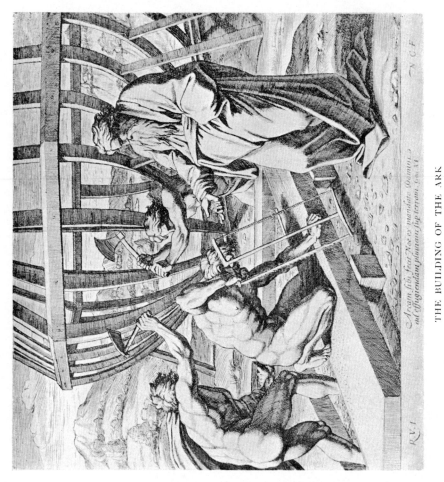

THE BUILDING OF THE ARK

From Raphael's Bible

Linguarum, The Art of Punning; or, The Flower of Languages, by Dr. Sheridan and Swift, which will be found in Vol. XIII. of Scott's edition of Swift. Among the directions to the punster is this :—

Rule 3. The Brazen Rule. He must have better assurance, like Brigadier C——, who said, " That, as he was passing through a street, he made to a country fellow who had a hare swinging on a stick over his shoulder, and, giving it a shake, asked him whether it was his own *hair* or a periwig ! " Whereas it is a notorious Oxford jest.

Page 259, line 10. *Virgil . . . broken Cremona.* Swift (as Lamb explained in the original essay in the *New Monthly Magazine*), seeing a lady's mantua overturning a violin (possibly a Cremona), quoted Virgil's line : " Mantua væ miseræ nimium vicina Cremonæ ! " (*Eclogues,* IX., 28), " Mantua, alas ! too near unhappy Cremona."

Page 259. X.—THAT HANDSOME IS THAT HANDSOME DOES.
New Monthly Magazine, March, 1826.
Whether a Mrs. Conrady existed, or was invented or adapted by Lamb to prove his point, I have not been able to discover. But the evidence of Lamb's "reverence for the sex," to use Procter's phrase, is against her existence. The *Athenæum* reviewer on February 16, 1833, says, however, quoting the fallacy : "Here is a portrait of Mrs. Conrady. We agree with the writer that 'no one that has looked on her can *pretend* to forget the lady.'"
Page 259, second line of essay. *If we may believe Plotinus.* Part of the theory of Plotinus (205-270), the Neo-Platonic philosopher. In this sentence, Mr. W. J. Craig conjectures, Lamb was paraphrasing Dryden's lines in *Absalom and Achitophel* (156-158) :—

> A fiery soul, which working out its way,
> Fretted the pigmy body to decay,
> And o'er-informed the tenement of clay.

Page 259, at foot. *Divine Spenser.* The lines are in Spenser's "Hymn in Honour of Beauty," Stanza 19 ; as also is the next quotation, Stanza 21. Not quite correctly quoted.

Page 261. XI.—THAT WE MUST NOT LOOK A GIFT-HORSE IN THE MOUTH.
New Monthly Magazine, April, 1826.
Page 261, fifth line of essay. *Rozinante.* Don Quixote's charger.
Page 261, seventh line of essay. *Eclipse or Lightfoot.* Famous race-horses. Eclipse was never beaten. He won 344 races and £158,000.
Page 261, third line from foot. *Our friend Mitis.* I do not identify Mitis among Lamb's many friends.
Page 262, line 16. *Presentation copies.* The late Mr. Thomas Westwood, the son of the Westwoods with whom the Lambs lived at Edmonton, writing to *Notes and Queries* some thirty years ago, gave an amusing account of Lamb pitching presentation copies out of the window into the garden—a Barry Cornwall, a Bernard Barton, a Leigh Hunt and so forth.
Page 262, line 31. *Odd presents of game.* Compare the little essay on " Presents of Game," Vol. I., page 343, and note.

Page 262, line 36. *"Plump corpusculum."* I have not traced this quotation.

Page 262, line 42. *Certain restrictive regulations.* The game-laws. "The hare . . . makes many friends," is an allusion to Gay's version of Æsop's fable, "The Hare and Many Friends."

Page 263. XII.—That Home is Home Though it is Never so Homely.

New Monthly Magazine, March, 1826. In that place the first sentence began with the word "Two ; " the second ended with "of our assertions ; " and (fourteenth line of essay) it was said of the very poor man that he "can ask" no visitors. Lamb, in a letter, wished Wordsworth particularly to like this fallacy and that on rising with the lark, page 269.

Page 264, line 22. *It has been prettily said.* By Lamb himself, or more probably by his sister, in *Poetry for Children,* 1809. See "The First Tooth," Vol. III., which ends upon the line

A child is fed with milk and praise.

Page 265, line 10. *There is yet another home.* Writing to Mrs. Wordsworth on February 18, 1818, Lamb gives a painful account, very similar in part to this essay, of the homeless home to which he was reduced by visitors. But by the time he wrote the essay, when all his day was his own, the trouble was not acute. He tells Bernard Barton on March 20, 1826, "My tirade against visitors was not meant *particularly* at you or A. K. I scarce know what I meant, for I do not just now feel the grievance. I wanted to make an *article."* Compare the first of the "Lepus" papers in Vol. I., page 270.

Page 265, line 26. *It is the refreshing sleep of the day.* After this sentence, in the magazine, came this passage :—

" O the comfort of sitting down heartily to an old folio, and thinking surely that the next hour or two will be your own—and the misery of being defeated by the useless call of somebody, who is come to tell you, that he is just come from hearing Mr. Irving ! What is that to you ? Let him go home, and digest what the good man said to him. You are at your chapel, in your oratory."

Mr. Irving was the Rev. Edward Irving (1792-1834), whom Lamb knew slightly and came greatly to admire.

Page 265, line 29. *We have neither much knowledge* . . . Compare Ecclesiastes ix. 10 : "Whatsoever thy hand findeth to do, do it with thy might ; for there is no work, nor device, nor knowledge, nor wisdom, in the grave, whither thou goest."

Page 266, line 14. *With Dante's lovers.* Paolo and Francesca, in the fifth canto of *The Inferno :* "Quel giorno più non vi leggemmo avante."

Page 266, line 18. *Says . . . Bishop Taylor.* The passage is in "A Discourse of the Nature, Offices, and Measures of Friendship." See Hebers' edition, 1822, Vol. XI., p. 309.

Page 266. XIII.—That you must Love Me, and Love My Dog.
New Monthly Magazine, February, 1826.
Compare "A Bachelor's Complaint," page 126. I cannot identify
the particular friend whom Lamb has hidden under asterisks ; although
his cousin would seem to have some likeness to one of the Bethams
mentioned in the essay "Many Friends" (Vol. I., page 270), and in
the letter to Landor of October, 1832 (usually dated April), after his
visit to the Lambs.

Page 267, line 27. *The old "Athenian Oracle."* This was a three-
volume selection of articles from *The Athenian Mercury* (originally
Athenian Gazette), a kind of *Notes and Queries,* conducted between
1689 and 1696 by John Dunton (1659-1733) the bookseller. Sir
William Temple contributed to it, and Swift's "Pindaric Ode, in the
Manner of Cowley," was printed there, which caused Dryden to say,
"Cousin Swift, you will never be a poet."

Page 267, line 38. *Procerity.* Height. From *proceritas.*

Page 267, fifth line from foot. *Sempronia, etc.* Probably Lamb
was inventing (see next note).

Page 268, line 5. *Honorius dismiss his vapid wife.* Writing to
Bernard Barton on March 20, 1826, Lamb says :—

"In another thing I talkd of somebody's *insipid wife,* without a
correspondent object in my head : and a good lady, a friend's wife,
whom I really *love* (don't startle, I mean in a licit way) has looked
shyly on me ever since. The blunders of personal application are
numerous. I send out a character every now and then, on purpose to
exercise the ingenuity of my friends."

Page 268, line 21. *Merry, of Della Cruscan memory.* Robert Merry
(1755-1798), an affected versifier who settled in Florence as a young
man, and contributed to the *Florence Miscellany.* He became a
member of the Della Cruscan Academy, and on returning to England
signed his verses, in *The World,* "Della Crusca." A reply to his first
effusion, "Adieu and Recall to Love," was written by Mrs. Hannah
Cowley, author of *The Belle's Stratagem,* and signed "Anna Matilda ; "
this correspondence continued ; a fashion of sentiment was thus
started ; and for a while Della Cruscan poetry was the rage. The
principal Della Cruscan poems were published in the *British Album*
in 1789, and the collection was popular until Gifford's *Baviad*
(followed by his *Mæviad*) appeared in 1791, and satirised its conceits
so mercilessly that the school collapsed. A meeting with Anna
Matilda in the flesh and the discovery that she was twelve years
his senior had, however, put an end to Merry's enthusiasm long before
Gifford's attack. Merry afterwards threw in his lot with the French
Revolution, and died in America. He married, as Lamb says, Elizabeth Brunton, an excellent tragic actress, in 1791. But that was in
England. The journey to America came later.

The story of Merry's avoidance of the lady of his first choice is probably true. Carlo Antonio Delpini was a famous pantomimist in his
day at Drury Lane, Covent Garden and the Haymarket. He also was

stage manager at the Opera for a while, and occasionally arranged
entertainments for George IV. at Brighton.   He died in 1828.

Page 268, line 34.   *The golden shaft.*

> *Duke.* How will she love, when the rich golden shaft
> Hath kill'd the flock of all affections else
> That live in her.
>> " Twelfth Night," Act I., Scene 1, lines 35-37.

Page 269.   XIV.—THAT WE SHOULD RISE WITH THE LARK.
New Monthly Magazine, February, 1826.

Compare "The Superannuated Man," page 193, to which this little
essay, which, with that following, is one of Lamb's most characteristic
and perfect works, serves as a kind of postscript.

Page 270, line 19.   *Imperial forgetter of his dreams.*   Nebuchad-
nezzar (see Daniel ii.).

Page 271.   XV.—THAT WE SHOULD LIE DOWN WITH THE LAMB.
New Monthly Magazine, February, 1826.

Page 271, last line.   *How he burnishes !*   Mr. W. J. Craig has pointed
out that Sussex folk have a phrase " You burnish nicely "—you look
well ; and suggests that the word here has kindred meaning.   But
might it not rather apply to the illuminating of the smoker's face by
the fire in the pipe stimulated by the redoubled puffs ?   Burnish—
to make bright ?

Page 272, line 12.   *" Things that were born . . ."*   These lines are
from the Apological Dialogue at the end of Ben Jonson's " Poetaster."

Page 272, line 16.   *As mine author hath it.*   Ben Jonson again.
In the verses " To the Memory of my Beloved, the Author, Mr. William
Shakespeare and what He hath Left us " :—

> Look how the father's face
> Lives in his issue ; even so the race
> Of Shakespeare's mind and manners, brightly shines
> In his well torned, and true filed lines.

Page 272, line 19.   *Milton's Morning Hymn.*   Beginning :—

> These are thy glorious works, Parent of good.
>> *Paradise Lost*, V., line 153, &c.

Page 272, line 21.   *Taylor's richer description of a sun-rise.*   This
is in Taylor's *Holy Dying*, Chapter I., Section III.   As it was an
especially favourite passage with Lamb I quote it here :—

> . . . the life of a man comes upon him slowly and insensibly.   But as when the sun
> approaches towards the gates of the morning, he first opens a little eye of heaven, and sends
> away the spirits of darkness, and gives light to a cock, and calls up the lark to matins, and by
> and by gilds the fringes of a cloud, and peeps over the eastern hills, thrusting out his golden
> horns, like those which decked the brow of roses when he was forced to wear a veil because him-
> self had seen the face of God ; and still while a man tells the story, the sun gets up higher, till
> he shows a fair face and a full light, and then he shines one whole day, under a cloud often,
> and sometimes weeping great and little showers, and sets quickly ; so is a man's reason and
> his life.

Page 272, line 24.   *" Blessing the doors."*

> Or the bell-man's drowsy charm
> To bless the door from nightly harm.
>> *Il Penseroso*, lines 83, 84.

Page 272.   XVI.—That a Sulky Temper is a Misfortune.
New Monthly Magazine, September, 1826.

This was the last of the series and Lamb's last contribution to the *New Monthly Magazine.*

Page 273, line 19.   *Mysterious book in the Apocalypse.*   See Revelation x.

Page 274, at foot.   *Noble patient in Argos.*   For "Argos" Lamb wrote "Horace" in the magazine.   The reference is to *Epistles,* II., 2, lines 129-140, which describe the Argive gentleman, "who imagined that he was at a performance by tragic actors, and quite contented would sit in the empty theatre and applaud."   He was cured with hellebore, whereupon he exclaimed : " By Pollux, my friend, you may have cured me, but you have killed me too ; for you have delivered me from a great joy and robbed my soul of its pleasantest illusion."

APPENDIX

Page 279.   On some of the Old Actors, etc.

See notes to the essays "On Some of the Old Actors," "The Artificial Comedy" and "The Acting of Munden," pages 392 to 399.   Two portions of these essays, not reprinted by Lamb, call for comment: the story of the first night of "Antonio," on pages 291-294, and the account of Charles Mathews' collection of pictures, on page 294.

Page 291, line 27.   *Opium pills.*   Referring to George Colman's attack on Kemble for failing to make a mark in Sir Edward Mortimer in "The Iron Chest," produced in 1796.

Page 291, line 36.   *"Fair in Otway . . ."*   From Pope's "Imitations of Horace," II., Epistle 1.

Page 291, line 40.   *My friend G.'s "Antonio."*   William Godwin's tragedy, produced on December 13, 1800, at Drury Lane.   Lamb had written the epilogue (see Vol. V., page 121).   Compare the letter to Manning of December 16, 1800.

Page 292, line 32.   *M. wiped his cheek.*   Writing to Godwin after the failure Lamb says : " The breast of Hecuba, where she did suckle Hector, looked not to be more lovely than Marshal's forehead when it spit forth sweat, at Critic-swords contending.   I remember two honest lines by Marvel . . .

> ' Where every Mower's wholesome heat
> Smells like an Alexander's sweat.' "

And again, to Manning : " His [Marshal's] face was lengthened, and all over perspiration ; I never saw such a care-fraught visage ; I could have hugged him, I loved him so intensely.   ' From every pore of him a perfume fell.' "   The first quotation is from " Coriolanus," Act I., Scene 3, lines 43-46 :—

> the breasts of Hecuba,
> When she did suckle Hector, look'd not lovelier

> Than Hector's forehead when it spit forth blood
> At Grecian sword, contemning.

Some editions have "contending." The second is from Lee's "Rival Queens," Act I., Scene 3, line 44.

Page 293, line 1. *R——s the dramatist.* I imagine this to be Frederic Reynolds (1764-1841), author of "The Dramatist" and many other plays. We know Lamb to have known him later, from a mention in a letter to J. B. Dibdin.

Page 293, line 14. *"First knew fear."*

> Then Satan first knew pain.
>
> *Paradise Lost*, VI., line 327.

Page 293, at foot. *Brutus . . . Appius.* Brutus in "Julius Cæsar," or possibly in the play called "Brutus," by John Howard Payne, Lamb's friend (produced December 3, 1818), in which Brutus kills his son—a closer parallel. Appius was probably a slip of the pen for Virginius, who in Sheridan Knowles' drama that bears his name kills his daughter to protect her from Appius.

Page 294, line 6. *G. thenceforward.* Godwin did, however, write another play, "Faulkener," for which Lamb wrote the prologue. It was moderately successful.

Page 294, line 13. *I do not know, etc.* The paragraph beginning with these words is often printed by editors of Lamb as a separate article entitled "The Old Actors." Charles Mathews' collection of theatrical portraits is now in the Garrick Club. In his lifetime it occupied the gallery at Ivy Lodge, Highgate (or more properly Kentish town). A year or so before Mathews' death in 1835, his pictures were exhibited at the Queen's Bazaar in Oxford Street, Lamb's remarks being printed in the catalogue *raisonné*.

In the notes that follow I have not given particulars of the old actors whom Lamb merely enumerates, but have explained only certain allusions.

Page 294, line 16. *Peeping Tom.* "Peeping Tom of Coventry," by John O'Keeffe.

Page 294, line 28. *Brinsley's famous comedy.* "The School for Scandal," by Richard Brinsley Sheridan.

Page 294, line 36. *Lord Townley.* In "The Provoked Husband," by Vanbrugh and Cibber.

Page 294, line 38. *Kitely.* In Ben Jonson's "Every Man in his Humour."

Page 294, last line. *Retired Dioclesian.* John Quick (1748-1831), the comedian, who had retired to Hornsey Row (afterwards Will's Row), Islington, where possibly, like the ex-Roman emperor, he cultivated his garden.

Page 295, line 7. *"Drown an eye . . ."* From Shakespeare, Sonnet XXX., line 5 :—

> Then can I drown an eye, unused to flow.

Page 295, line 12. *Lady Quakeress . . . of O'Keefe.* In "The Young Quakers," by O'Keeffe.

Page 295, line 15. *Churchill's compliment.* Charles Churchill (1731-1764), wrote in *The Rosciad* (1761), lines 695 to 702 :—

> With all the native vigour of sixteen,
> Among the merry troop conspicuous seen,
> See lively Pope advance in jig, and trip
> Corinna, Cherry, Honeycomb and Snip :
> Not without art, but yet to Nature true,
> She charms the town with humour just, yet new :
> Cheer'd by her promise, we the loss deplore
> The fatal time when Clive shall be no more.

Page 295, line 18. *Lady Loverule.* In "The Devil to Pay," by Charles Coffey. Also in "The Merry Cobler," the second part of the same play.

Page 295, line 20. *Two Antics.* These were Suett and Munden, eulogies of whom (see pages 138 and 148) followed this introduction in the *London Magazine.*

INDEX

A

Accountants, Lamb on, 2.
Actors and acting, Lamb's essays on, 132, 141, 148, 163, 166, 168, 202, 279, 285, 294.
Actors among Lamb's friends, 204.
Adams, Parson, 43, 342.
Agar's wish, 314.
Aguecheek, Lamb on, 136.
Ainger, Canon, his notes on Lamb, 309, 319, 333, 366, 369, 378, 396, 400, 451, 453.
Albion, The, and Lamb, 224, 440, 444.
Alice W——, 28, 38, 101, 102, 301, 335, 377.
ALL FOOLS' DAY, 42, 341.
Allen, Bob, 22, 223, 323, 444.
Allsop, Thomas, quoting Lamb, 326.
— — and " Roast Pig," 389.
— — quotes Lamb on G. H., 433.
Almsgiving, Lamb on, 120.
Alsatia, the debtors' sanctuary, 142, 396.
America, Lamb relics in, 307, 326, 327, 328, 390, 416.
AMICUS REDIVIVUS, 209, 432.
Anatomy and love, 56.
Anatomy of Melancholy quoted, 40.
André, Major, 209, 432.
Anna Matilda, 459.
Antiquity, Lamb on, 9.
" Antonio," by Godwin, 291, 461.
Arcadia, The, by Sidney, 213, 436.
Arrowsmith, Aaron, 346.
" Artaxerxes," 98, 375.
Artificial comedy, Lamb's essay on, 141, 395.
Artists, their want of imagination, 226.
Arundel Castle and the chimney-sweep legend, 112.
Athenæum, The, Lamb's contribution to, 446.
Athenian Oracle, The, 267, 459.
Australia, Lamb on, 107.
Ayrton, William, 333, 335.

VOL. II.—30

B

BACHELOR'S COMPLAINT OF THE BE-HAVIOUR OF MARRIED PEOPLE, 126, 391.
Baldwin, Cradock & Joy, 302.
Bannister, Jack, 139, 163, 394, 411.
BARBARA S., 202, 429.
Barker's book-shop, 249, 454.
BARRENNESS OF THE IMAGINATIVE FACULTY IN THE PRODUCTIONS OF MODERN ART, 226, 446.
Barrington, Daines, 89, 369.
Bartholomew Fair, 112, 382.
Barton, Bernard, Lamb's letters to, 303, 407, 425, 428, 447, 458, 459.
— — his sonnet to Elia, 404.
— Thomas, 89, 369.
Baskett prayer-book, 8.
Battle, Mrs., 32, 155, 408.
— — on whist, 32.
— — her identity, 333.
Beaumont and Fletcher, Lamb's copy, 327.
Beauty, Lamb on, 259.
" Beggars' Petition," 387.
Begging, Lamb's essay on, 114, 383.
Belisarius, 115, 384.
" Belshazzar's Feast," Martin's picture of, 229, 447.
Benchers, The Old, Lamb's essay on, 82.
Bensley, Robert, 133, 282, 393.
Betty, Master, 418.
Bigod, Ralph, Lamb's name for Fenwick, 23, 325.
Billet, John, 162.
Binding, Lamb on, 416.
Blackwood's Magazine on Lamb, 323.
— — and Scott, 302.
Blake, William, and Lamb, 381.
BLAKESMOOR IN H——SHIRE, 153, 405.
Blakesware near Widford, 100, 153, 377, 405.